Daniel Heinsius, *Auriacus, sive Libertas saucia (Orange, or Liberty Wounded),*
1602

Drama and Theatre in Early Modern Europe

The titles published in this series are listed at *brill.com/dtem*

Daniel Heinsius,
Auriacus, sive Libertas saucia
(*Orange, or Liberty Wounded*) 1602

Edited and Translated by

Jan Bloemendal

BRILL

LEIDEN | BOSTON

Cover illustration: Daniel Heinsius. Portrait by Willem van Swanenburg.

Library of Congress Cataloging-in-Publication Data

Names: Heinsius, Daniel, 1580-1655, author. | Bloemendal, Jan, editor. | Heinsius, Daniel, 1580-1655. Auriacus. 2020. | Heinsius, Daniel, 1580-1655. Auriacus. English. 2020.
Title: Daniel Heinsius, Auriacus, sive Libertas saucia = (Orange, or Liberty wounded), 1602 / edited and translated by Jan Bloemendal.
Other titles: Auriacus, sive Libertas saucia | Drama and theatre in early modern Europe ; 10.
Description: Boston : Brill, 2020. | Series: Drama and theatre in early modern Europe, 2211341X ; 10 | Includes bibliographical references and index.
Identifiers: LCCN 2019059227 (print) | LCCN 2019059228 (ebook) | ISBN 9789004410220 (hardback) | ISBN 9789004425361 (ebook)
Subjects: LCSH: Heinsius, Daniel, 1580-1655. Auriacus.
Classification: LCC PA8525 .A9713 2020 (print) | LCC PA8525 (ebook) | DDC 872/.4–dc23
LC record available at https://lccn.loc.gov/2019059227
LC ebook record available at https://lccn.loc.gov/2019059228

Typeface for the Latin, Greek, and Cyrillic scripts: "Brill". See and download: brill.com/brill-typeface.

ISSN 2211-341X
ISBN 978-90-04-41022-0 (hardback)
ISBN 978-90-04-42536-1 (e-book)

Contents

FIGURE 1   Daniel Heinsius
PORTRAIT BY WILLEM VAN SWANENBURG (1607) RIJKSMUSEUM AMSTERDAM

Foreword

In today's world the poet who is also a professor, or even primarily a professor, is familiar to us, and in the United States probably vital for the continued flourishing of the art. In the English-speaking world, we think for instance of Charles Bernstein, Paul Muldoon, Eavan Boland, Susan Stewart, Jeremy Prynne and Andrew Motion, and in earlier or slightly earlier generations A.E. Housman, A.R. Ammons, Seamus Heaney and John Hollander. Some of these were or are professors of creative writing, there to teach the art of writing poetry, and a few are esteemed scholars who also enjoy enviable reputations as poets: Hollander, Prynne, Stewart, John Fuller, Robert Crawford and even a few poets who are eminent in a non-literary academic field, such as the philosopher John Koethe. For the Netherlands, we could think of Leo Vroman, Rutger Kopland, Nachoem Wijnberg and Piet Gerbrandy, and in slightly earlier times of W.A.P. Smit and Willem Asselbergs, who was known as a poet by his pseudonym Anton van Duinkerken.

Daniel Heinsius (1580–1655) has a claim to be the original scholar poet in the modern world, a brilliant and highly original field-changing scholar in the humanist tradition, an international magnet for scholars and students alike at the illustrious and then new University of Leiden, who was also in his own lifetime revered as a poet in three languages, Latin, Dutch and Greek. Was he in fact the first poet superstar of academe? He was famous and influential as a poet and dramatist in his own country and lifetime, kick-started a major literary revival in the German-speaking world and was an internationally influential Latin poet and critical theorist. His understanding of tragedy was internationally and eventually globally influential.

Why do we not think of him as a household literary name? The two reasons are very simple. Dutch literature is not internationally well known, and few Dutch writers of any period are translated into other languages. More importantly, Latin no longer functions as an international literary language, and we have long lost the collective ability to appreciate its power and achievement in this sphere. Such knowledge is reserved today for experts among whom is Jan Bloemendal, the editor of this volume.

Bloemendal's edition of Heinsius' early foray into playwriting, with its extensive introduction, parallel English translation, and capacious, exhaustive commentary substantially helps set the record straight. Moreover it is the first edition of the play since the initial publication in 1602. The translation enables non-specialists to see the play's distinctive qualities of high early modern Latin

literature, its peculiar imaginative grasp and astonishing poetic power, its evo-
lution from earlier forms of Latin, and its contribution to the understanding of
a critical historical moment in Dutch and European history, the assassination
of William of Orange in July 1584, military leader of the Dutch Revolt. The tragic
event itself was formative in the forging of Netherlands national consciousness,
and Heinsius' drama plays a role in this. We see too how the *Auriacus* was key
to the rise of his reputation, and exemplary of his growing ability to shape the
classical and humanist tradition.

Heinsius owed much to William of Orange and like many Dutch people at
this time felt that they had an intertwined personal history. He was himself an
infant refugee, his parents arranging for him to be carried from his native Ghent
while it was under threat from the Spanish into the greater safety of Zeeland,
the southern borderland of the new Dutch Republic. English exile and time
in Rijswijk near The Hague ended in the relocation of the Heinsius family to
Flushing, safe among the English garrisons in Zeeland. Study of the law having failed to take with him, Heinsius pursued at university his early interest in
poetry and in 1598 joined the circle of the great classical scholar Julius Caesar Scaliger in Leiden, with its focus on classical philology, and classical and
Neo-Latin poetry. This put him under the sway of Justus Lipsius, Janus Dousa,
Joseph Justus Scaliger, Guilielmus Coddaeus and Petrus Scriverius, among others: much of the vital hub of the intellectual life of the Dutch Republic at this
time. He was made professor of poetics in 1603, of Greek two years later, and of
politics in 1612. *Auriacus* was the earliest product of an undergraduate project
intended to revive neo-Latin tragedy by imitating Seneca over and against the
allegorical and morality drama of the chambers of rhetoric, and in this goal
Heinsius was hand in glove with his friend and contemporary Hugo Grotius
(Hugo de Groot), the future eminent scholar, lawyer and statesman.

The distinctive fact to grasp is that Heinsius was functioning as a fully-
fledged classical scholar and editor before he had graduated, before he even
entered university as one of its teachers. The impact of the *Auriacus*, printed
and almost certainly first performed in early 1602, was such that it allowed
Heinsius to begin his long and influential teaching career at Leiden University.
It was considered by experts to be the equal of or to have exceeded its classical models and the best examples of Latin drama in his own time, such as
those of the Scottish humanist and tutor of King James VI and I and George
Buchanan. In his Scaligerian (as in the elder Scaliger, forenamed Julius Caesar)
and Senecan 'reforming' of two previous Latin treatments of the assassination, and in borrowing from a neo-Latin epic on William by Georgius Benedicti
Wertelo, Heinsius set the stage for Netherlandish tragedy in Latin and Dutch
during the next century, both as a direct model to be imitated and more gen-

erally for beginning a Senecan vogue. The play's approval by German men of letters also began his international reputation. The construction of a tragedy in *Auriacus* opened the door to Heinsius' single most influential work, *De tragica constitutione* (1611), a reflection on Aristotle's treatise on tragedy and attached to his edition of it, but the poetry of *Auriacus* also helped to shape Heinsius' powerful elegiac verse, a major component of his later works.

The present edition is not merely a monumental study of one hitherto overlooked crucial play by a major figure in European letters. Its aesthetic vitality and political acuity open the door to a full-scale reconsideration of early modern European drama in Latin and in the vernacular languages, and further reassessment of seventeenth-century neo-Latin verse. That comes next: bring it on.

Nigel Smith (Princeton University)

Acknowledgements

This edition of Daniel Heinsius' *Auriacus, sive Libertas saucia* (*Orange, or Liberty Wounded*, 1602) is a reworking of my doctoral thesis (Daniel Heinsius, *Auriacus, sive Libertas saucia (1602): Editie met vertaling, inleiding en commentaar/An Edition with Translation, Introduction and Commentary (and with a Summary in English)*, Voorthuizen: Florivallis, 1997). I would like to thank my supervisors Riet Schenkeveld-van der Dussen and Jan den Boeft, as well as Lia van Gemert. This dissertation was written in Dutch and published with a private press so that it was not widely available; moreover, since its publication much research has been carried out on Neo-Latin drama. Therefore, it seemed appropriate to prepare a new edition, now in English. I made it during my stay as a visiting professor at Princeton University (January–June, 2018), for which I am grateful to the Humanities Council and the English Department there. Will Kelly of Minerva PLS corrected the English of the translation and the commentary and Robin Buning kindly read the introduction and commented on it, as did Nigel Smith.

Jan Bloemendal

DANIELIS HEINSII

AVRIACVS,

Siue

LIBERTAS SAVCIA.

Accedunt eiusdem

IAMBI

Partim morales, partim ad amicos, partim
amicorum causâ scripti.

LVGDVNI BATAVORVM,

Apud Andream Cloucquium,

sub signo Angeli Coronati.

ANNO ∞ . IↃ. CIↃ.

FIGURE 2   Daniel Heinsius, *Auriacus sive Libertas saucia*
LEIDEN: ANDREAS CLOUCQUIUS, 1602, TITLE PAGE

Abbreviations

ADB   *Allgemeine deutsche Biographie* (Leipzig: Duncker and Humblot, 1875–1912); also https://www.deutsche-biographie.de/.

AGN   D.P. Blok (ed.), *Algemene Geschiedenis der Nederlanden* (Haarlem and Weesp: Fibula/Van Dishoeck, 1981–1983).

Alexiou, *Lament*   Margaret Alexiou, *The Ritual Lament in Greek Tradition* (Cambridge: Cambridge University Press, 1974).

Asmuth, 'Die niederländische Literatur'   Bernhard Asmuth, 'Die niederländische Literatur', in: Eckard Lefèvre (ed.), *Der Einfluss Senecas auf das europäische Drama* (Darmstadt: Wissenschaftliche Buchgesellschaft, 1978), pp. 235–275.

Austin   *P. Vergilii Maronis Aeneidos liber secundus*, ed. R.G. Austin (Oxford: Clarendon Press, 1964); *P. Vergilii Maronis Aeneidos liber quartus*, ed. R.G. Austin (Oxford: Clarendon Press, 1955); *P. Vergilii Maronis Aeneidos liber sextus*, ed. R.G. Austin (Oxford: Clarendon Press, 1977).

Bataafs Athene   Collegium Classicum c.n. M.F. (ed.), *Bataafs Athene: Een bloemlezing van klassiek Griekse poëzie van de hand van Leidse humanisten van de zestiende tot en met de twintigste eeuw* (Leiden: Dimensie, 1993).

Becker-Cantarino, *Daniel Heinsius*   Barbara Becker-Cantarino, *Daniel Heinsius* (New York: Twayne Publishers, 1978) Twayne's World Author Series, 477.

Bloemendal, 'Hercules'   Jan Bloemendal, 'Willem van Oranje: Een Hercules op Leidse planken', *De zeventiende eeuw* 10 (1994), pp. 159–167.

Bloemendal, 'Mon Dieu, mon Dieu ...'   Jan Bloemendal, 'Mon Dieu, mon Dieu ...: Aspecten van literatuur en werkelijkheid in Daniel Heinsius, *Auriacus sive Libertas saucia* (1602)', *Bulletin: Geschiedenis, Kunst en Cultuur* 5 (1996), pp. 91–107.

BNB   *Biographie nationale de Belgique* (Brussels: Thiry-Van Buggenhout; Bruylant: Académie Royale des Sciences, des Lettres et des Beaux-Arts de Belgique, 1866–1986), 44 vols.

Bömer, *Ovidius Fasti*   Franz Bömer, *P. Ovidius Naso, Die Fasten*, II, *Kommentar* (Heidelberg: Winter, 1958).

Bömer, *Ovidius Metamorphosen*   Franz Bömer, *P. Ovidius Naso, Metamorphosen: Kommentar* (Heidelberg: Winter, 1969–1986) 7 vols.

Bonner   Stanley F. Bonner, *Roman Declamation in the Late Republic and Early Empire* (Liverpool: University Press of Liverpool, 1949).

Briels, *Zuidnederlanders*   Johannes G.C.A. Briels, *Zuidnederlanders in de Republiek 1572–1630: Een demografische en cultuurhistorische studie* (Sint-Niklaas: Danthe, 1985).

Brink   Charles O. Brink, *Horace on Poetry 2: The 'Ars Poetica'* (Cambridge: Cambridge University Press, 1971).

Canter, *Rhetorical Elements*   Howard V. Canter, *Rhetorical Elements in the Tragedies of Seneca* (Urbana: University of Illinois, 1925).

Cats, *Sinne- en minnebeelden*, ed. Luijten   Jacob Cats, *Sinne- en minnebeelden*, ed. J.C.A. Luijten (The Hague: Constantijn Huygens Instituut, 1996).

CIG   August Boeckh (ed.), *Corpus Inscriptionum Graecarum* (Berlin: Reimer, 1828–1877) 4 vols.

Crusius-Rubenbauer, *Römische Metrik*   Friedrich Crusius and Hans Rubenbauer, *Römische Metrik: Eine Einführung* (Munich: Max Hüber, 1961).

Curtius, *European Literature and Latin Middle Ages*   Ernst Robert Curtius, *European Literature and the Latin Middle Ages* (London and Henley: Routledge and Kegan Paul,ʰ1979 [Bern: Franke, 1948[1]]).

DBF   J. Balteau a.o. (eds), *Dictionnaire de biographie française* (Paris: Letouzey, 1933–) 7 vols.

Drexler, *Römische Metrik*   Hans Drexler, *Einführung in die römische Metrik* (Darmstadt: Wissenschaftliche Buchgesellschaft, 1980).

Du Cange   Charles du Fresne, sieur Du Cange et al., *Glossarium mediae et infimae aetatis* (Niort: L. Favre, 1883–1887) 10 vols; also http://ducange .enc.sorbonne.fr/.

Duits, *Van Bartholomeusnacht tot Bataafse opstand*   Henk Duits, *Van Bartholomeusnacht tot Bataafse opstand: Studies over de relatie tussen politiek en toneel in het midden van de zeventiende eeuw* (Hilversum: Verloren, 1990) Doctoral thesis Amsterdam.

ENLW   Philip J. Ford, Jan Bloemendal and Charles Fantazzi (eds), *Brill's Encyclopaedia of the Neo-Latin World* (Leiden: Brill, 2014).

Eyffinger, *Grotius poeta*   Arthur C.G.M. Eyffinger, *Grotius poeta: Aspecten van Hugo Grotius' dichterschap* ([The Hague], s.n., 1981) Doctoral thesis Amsterdam.

Fantham, *Seneca's Troades*   Elaine Fantham, *Seneca's Troades: A Literary Introduction with Text, Translation and Commentary* (Princeton: Princeton University Press, 1982).

Fitch, *Seneca's Hercules Furens*   John G. Fitch, *Seneca's Hercules Furens: A Critical Text with Introduction and Commentary* (Ithaca, etc.: Cornell University Press, 1987) Cornell Studies in Classical Philology, 45.

Forcellini   Aegidius Forcellini, *Totius latinitatis lexicon*, ed. Jacobus Facciolati (Padua: Typis Seminarii apud Joannem Manfrè, 1771–1816) 5 vols.

Forster, *Janus Gruter's English Years*   Leonard W. Forster, *Janus Gruter's English Years: Studies in the Continuity of Dutch Literature in Exile in Elizabethan England* (Leiden: University Press; London: Oxford University Press, 1967).

Frank, *Seneca's Phoenissae*   Marica Frank, *Seneca's Phoenissae: Introduction and Commentary* (Leiden: Brill, 1995) Mnemosyne Supplementum, 138.

Frederiks, *De moord van 1584*   J.G. Frederiks, *De moord van 1584: Oorspronkelijke verhalen en gelijktijdige berichten van den moord gepleegd op Prins Willem van Oranje* (The Hague: Nijhoff, 1884).

Geurts, *Opstand in pamfletten*   Pieter A.M. Geurts, *De Nederlandse opstand in de pamfletten 1566–1584* (Utrecht: Dekker and Van de Vegt, 1983) Doctoral thesis Nijmegen, 1956.

Grafton, *Joseph Scaliger*   Anthony Grafton, *Joseph Scaliger: A Study in the History of Classical Scholarship, I: Textual Criticism and Exegesis; II: Historical Chronology* (Oxford: Clarendon Press, 1983–1993).

Groenveld, 'Natie en nationaal gevoel'   Simon Groenveld, 'Natie en nationaal gevoel in de zestiende-eeuwse Nederlanden', in: C. van der Kieft a.o. (eds), *Scrinium et Scripura: Opstellen aangeboden aan J.L. van der Gouw* (Groningen: Erven B. van der Kamp, 1980), pp. 372–387.

Grotius, *BW*   Hugo Grotius, *Briefwisseling*, ed. P.C. Molhuysen a.o. (The Hague: Nijhoff; Amsterdam: Royal Netherlands Academy of Arts and Sciences, 1928–2000) 17 vols.

Grotius, *Dichtwerken/Poetry*   Hugo Grotius, *De dichtwerken/The Poetry* I, 1A/B (*Sacra in quibus Adamus exul*), ed. B.L. Meulenbroek, in coll. with Gerdien Kuiper and L.Ph. Rank (Assen: Van Gorcum, 1970–1971); I, 2, 1A/B, ed. B.L. Meulenbroek (Assen: Van Gorcum, 1972–1973); I, 2, 2A/B, ed. B.L. Meulenbroek (Assen: Van Gorcum, 1977); I, 2, 3A/B (*Original Poetry 1602–1603*), ed. Arthur Eyffinger (Assen, etc.: Van Gorcum, 1988); I, 2, 4A/B (*Original Poetry 1604–1608*), ed. Edwin Rabbie (Assen, etc.: Van Gorcum, 1992); I, 2, 5A/B (*Christus patiens*), ed. B.L. Meulenbroek, in coll. with Arthur C. Eyffinger (Assen: Van Gorcum, 1978); I, 4 (*Sophompaneas*), ed. Arthur C. Eyffinger, in coll. with Pim Rietbroek (Assen, etc.: Van Gorcum, 1992).

Grotius, *Parallelon*, ed. Meerman   Hugo Grotius, *Parallelon rerumpublicarum liber tertius: De moribus ingenioque populorum Atheniensium, Romarorum, Batavorum*, ed. J. Meerman (Haarlem: A. Loosjes, 1801–1803), 4 vols.

Haitsma Mulier and Van der Lem, *Repertorium*   E.O.G. Haitsma Mulier and Anton van der Lem, in collab. with Paul Knevel, *Repertorium van geschiedschrijvers in Nederland* (Den Haag: Nederlands Historisch Genootschap, 1990).

Heesakkers and Reinders, *Genoeglijk bovenal zijn mij de Muzen*   Chris Heesakkers and Wilma Reinders, *Genoeglijk bovenal zijn mij de Muzen: De Leidse Neolatijnse dichter Janus Dousa (1545–1604)* (Leiden: Dimensie, 1993).

Heinsius, *Auriacus*, ed. Bloemendal   Jan Bloemendal, *Daniel Heinsius, Auriacus, sive*
            Libertas saucia (1602): Editie met vertaling, inleiding en commentaar
            (*with a summary in English*) (Voorthuizen: Florivallis, 1997) Doctoral
            thesis Utrecht.

Heinsius, *On Plot in Tragedy*   Daniel Heinsius, *On Plot in Tragedy*, trans. Paul R. Sellin
            and John MacManmon (Northridge, CA: San Fernando Valley State
            College, 1971).

Heitmann, *Fortuna und Virtus*   Klaus Heitmann, *Fortuna und Virtus: Eine Studie zu*
            Petrarcas Lebensweisheit (Cologne: Böhlau, 1958) Studi italiani, 1.

Hooft, *Neederlandsche historien*   P.C. Hooft, *Neederlandsche historien, sedert de*
            ooverdraght der heerschappye van kaizar Karel den Vyfden, op kooning
            Philips zynen zoon (Amsterdam: Louys Elzevier, 1642).

Hunink, *Lucanus Bellum Civile Book III*   Vincent J.C. Hunink, *M. Annaeus Lucanus Bel-*
            lum Civile Book III: A Commentary (Amsterdam: J.C. Gieben, 1992)
            Doctoral thesis Nijmegen.

ILE   Alois Gerlo a.o. (eds), *Iusti Lipsi Epistolae* (Brussels: Koninklijke
            Vlaamse Academie voor Wetenschappen, Letteren en Schone Kun-
            sten van België, 1878–2006) 14 vols.

Janson, *Latin Prose Prefaces*   Tore Janson, *Latin Prose Prefaces: Studies in Literary In-*
            ventions (Stockholm, etc.: Almqvist and Wicksel, 1964) Acta Univer-
            sitatis Stockholmiensis, I, 3.

Kambylis, *Die Dichterweihe*   Athanasios Kambylis, *Die Dichterweihe und ihre Symbolik:*
            Untersuchungen zu Hesiodos, Kallimachos, Properz und Ennius (Hei-
            delberg: Winter, 1965),

Keil   Heinrich Keil, *Grammatici Latini* (Leipzig: Teubner, 1855–1880), 7
            vols.

Kilianus, *Etymologicum*   Cornelius Kilianus, *Etymologicum Teutonicae linguae, sive*
            dictionarium Teutonico-Latinum [...], ed. Gerard Hasselt (Utrecht:
            Roeland de Meyere, 1777).

Kirchner, *Fortuna*   Gottfried Kirchner, *Fortuna in Dichtung und Emblematik des*
            Barock: Tradition und Bedeutungswandel eines Motivs (Stuttgart:
            Metzler, 1970).

Konst, *De hartstochten in de tragedie*   Jan W.H. Konst, *Woedende wraakghierigheidt en*
            vruchtelooze weeklachten: De hartstochten in de Nederlandse tragedie
            van de zeventiende eeuw (s.l.: s.n., 1993) Doctoral thesis Utrecht.

Kühner-Stegmann   Raphael Kühner, Friedricht Holzweissig and Carl Stegmann, *Aus-*
            führliche Grammatik der lateinischen Sprache (Darmstadt: Wissen-
            schaftliche Buchgesellschaft, 1982 [= Hannover 1912–1914]|), 2 vols.

LCL   Loeb Classical Library

Lewis and Short   Charlton T. Lewis and Charles Short, *A Latin Dictionary, Founded on*

Andrew's Edition of Freud's Latin Dictionary (Oxford: Clarendon Press, 1958).

Lewis, *The Discarded Image*   C.S. Lewis, *The Discarded Image: An Introduction to Medieval and Renaissance Literature* (Cambridge: Cambridge University Press, 1994 [1967[1]]),

Lexicon Latinitatis Nederlandicae Medii aevi   Johannes W. Fuchs, Olga Weyers, Marijke Gumbert (eds), *Lexicon Latinitatis Nederlandicae Medii aevi* (Leiden: Brill, 1971–2005).

LSJ   Henry G. Liddell, Robert Scott and Henry S. Jones, *A Greek-English Lexicon* (Oxford: Clarendon Press, 1996).

Lunsingh Scheurleer and Posthumus Meyjes, *Leiden University*   Th.H. Lunsingh Scheurleer and G.H.M. Posthumus Meyjes (eds), *Leiden University in the Seventeenth Century: An Exchange of Learning* (Leiden: Universitaire Pers Leiden, 1975).

Marquardt-Mau, *Privatleben*   Joachim Marquardt, *Das Privatleben der Römer*, ed. A. Mau (Darmstadt: Wissenschaftliche Buchgesellschaft, 1990 [= Leipzig: S. Hirzel, 1886]).

Meter, *The Literary Theories*   Jan H. Meter, *The Literary Theories of Daniel Heinsius: A Study of the Development and Background of his Views on Literary Theory and Criticism During the Period from 1602 to 1612* (Assen: Van Gorcum, 1984).

Molhuysen, *Bronnen*   Philipp C. Molhuysen (ed.), *Bronnen tot de geschiedenis der Leidsche universiteit: Eerste deel: 1574–7 febr. 1610* (The Hague: Martinus Nijhoff, 1913) RGP, 20.

Motley, *Dutch Republic*   John Lothrop Motley, *The Rise of the Dutch Republic: A History: A New Edition Complete in One Volume* (London: Routledge, 1869 [= New York: Harper, 1856[1], 3 vols]).

Motto, *Seneca Sourcebook*   Anna L. Motto, *Seneca Sourcebook: Guide to the Thought of Lucius Annaeus Seneca* (Amsterdam: Hakkert, 1970).

NDB   *Neue deutsche Biographie* (Berlin: Duncker and Humblot, 1953–).

Nellen, *Hugo Grotius*   Henk J. Nellen, *Hugo Grotius (1583–1645): A Lifelong Struggle for Peace in Church and State, 1583–1645*, trans. J.C. Grayson (Leiden and Boston: Brill, 2015).

Neue-Wagener   C. Friedrich Neue and Carl Wagener, *Formenlehre der lateinischen Sprache* (Leipzig: Reisland, 1892–1905) 4 vols.

Nisbet-Hubbard   Robin G.M. Nisbet and Margaret Hubbard, *A Commentary on Horace: Odes, Book I* (Oxford: Oxford University Press, 1970); *Book II* (Oxford: Oxford University Press, 1978).

NNBW   Philipp C. Molhuysen and Petrus J. Blok (eds), *Nieuw Nederlandsch biografisch woordenboek* (Leiden: Sijthoff, 1911–1937), 10 vols.

OLD   Peter G.W. Glare (ed.), *Oxford Latin Dictionary* (Oxford: Clarendon
                    Press, 2005).

Otto, *Sprichwörter*   August Otto, *Die Sprichwörter und sprichwörtlichen Redensarten
                    der Römer* (Hildesheim: Olms, 1962 [= Leipzig: Teubner, 1890]).

Parker, *Philip II*   Geoffrey Parker, *Philip II* (London: Hutchinson, 1979).

Pease   Arthur S. Pease (ed.), *M. Tulli Ciceronis De natura deorum* (Cam-
                    bridge, MA: Harvard University Press, 1955–1958), 2 vols.

Pohlenz, *Die Stoa*   Max Pohlenz, *Die Stoa: Geschichte einer geistigen Bewegung* (Göt-
                    tingen: Vandenhoeck and Rupprecht, 1948–1949), 2 vols.

RAC   Theodor Klauser a.o. (eds), *Reallexikon für Antike und Christentum*
                    (Stuttgart: Hiersemann; Leipzig, s.n., 1941–).

RE   Georg Wyssowa a.o., *Paulys Real-Encyclopädie der classischen Alter-
                    tumswissenschaft* (Stuttgart: Metzler; Munich: Druckenmüller, 1894–
                    1997).

Regenbogen, 'Schmerz und Tod'   Otto Regenbogen, 'Schmerz und Tod in den Tragö-
                    dien Senecas', in: *id.*, *Kleine Schriften*, ed. F. Dirlmeier (Munich:
                    Beck'sche Verlagsbuchhandlung, 1961), pp. 409–462 [= *Vorträge der
                    Bibliothek Warburg* 7 (1930), pp. 167–218].

Roscher   Wilhelm H. Roscher, *Ausführliches Lexikon der griechischen und rö-
                    mischen Mythologie* (Leipzig: Teubner, 1884–1937) 6 vols.

Rosenmeyer, *Senecan Drama and Stoic Cosmology*   Thomas G. Rosenmeyer, *Senecan
                    Drama and Stoic Cosmology* (Berkeley, etc.: University of California
                    Press, 1989).

Scal., *Poet.*   Julius Caesar Scaliger, *Poetices libri septem* (Lyon: Antonius Vincen-
                    tius, 1561).

Scaliger, *Poetica/Dichtkunst*   Julius Caesar Scaliger, *Poetices libri septem/Sieben Bücher
                    über der Dichtkunst*, ed. Luc Deitz, Gregor Vogt-Spira and Manfred
                    Fuhrmann (Stuttgart-Bad Canstatt: Frommann-Holzboog, 1994–
                    2011), 6 vols.

Schäfer and Lefèvre, *Ianus Dousa*   Eckart Schäfer and Eckard Lefèvre (eds), *Ianus
                    Dousa: Neulateinischer Dichter und Klassischer Philologe* (Tübingen:
                    Gunter Narr Verlag, 2009) Neolatina, 17.

Schumann   Otto Schumann, *Lateinisches Hexameter-Lexikon: Dichterisches For-
                    melgut von Ennius bis zum Archipoeta* (Munich: Monumenta Germa-
                    niae historica, 1979–1989), 7 vols.

Secundus, *Opera omnia*, ed. Bosscha   *Ioannis Nicolai Secundi Hagani Opera omnia,
                    emendatius et cum notís adhuc ineditis Petri Burmanni Secundi*, ed.
                    Petrus Bosscha (Leiden 1821).

Sellin, *Daniel Heinsius and Stuart England*   Paul R. Sellin, *Daniel Heinsius and Stuart
                    England: With a Short-Title Checklist of the Works of Daniel Heinsius*

(Leiden: University Press; London: Oxford University Press, 1968) Publications of the Sir Thomas Browne Institute Leiden, General Series 3.

Smits-Veldt, *Samuel Coster*   Mieke B. Smits-Veldt, *Samuel Coster, ethicus-didacticus: Een onderzoek naar dramatische opzet en morele instructie van Ithys, Polyxena en Iphigenia* (Groningen: Wolters-Noordhoff/Forsten, 1986)

Spanoghe   Emile Spanoghe, *Synonymia latino-teutonica* (*ex etymologico C. Kiliani deprompta*): *Latijnsch-Nederlandsch woordenboek der XVIIe eeuw* (Antwerp, etc.: Buschman, etc., 1889–1902) 3 vols, Uitgaven der Antwerpsche Biblophilen 16, 18, 22.

Stachel, *Seneca und das deutsche Renaissancedrama*   Paul Stachel, *Seneca und das deutsche Renaissancedrama: Studien zur Literatur- und Stilgeschichte des 16. und 17. Jahrhunderts* (Berlin: Mayer and Müller, 1907) Palaestra, 46.

Stephanus, *Dictionarium*   Carolus Stephanus (Charles Estienne), *Dictionarium historicum, geographicum, poeticum* [...] (Paris: Stephanus, 1596).

SVF   Johann von Arnim, *Stoicorum veterum fragmenta* (Leipzig: Teubner, 1921–1924).

Tarrant, *Seneca Agamemnon*   Richard J. Tarrant, *Seneca Agamemnon* (Cambridge: Cambridge University Press, 1976) Cambridge Classical Texts and Commentaries, 18.

Ter Horst, *Daniel Heinsius*   Dirk J.H. ter Horst, *Daniel Heinsius (1580–1655)* (Utrecht: Hooijenbos, 1934) Doctoral thesis Leiden.

TGL   H. Stephanus (H. Estienne), *Thesaurus Graecae Linguae* (Paris: Stephanus, 1572) 5 vols; (London: in aedibus Valpianis, 1816–1828) 9 vols; (Paris: Firmin Didot, 1831–1865) 8 vols.

Töchterle, *Seneca Oedipus*   Karl-Heinz Töchterle, *Lucius Annaeus Seneca Oedipus: Kommentar mit Einleitung, Text und Übersetzung* (Heidelberg: Winter, 1994).

TLL   *Thesaurus Linguae Latinae* (Leipzig: Teubner, 1900–).

Tupet, *La magie*   A.-M. Tupet, *La magie dans la poésie latine, I: Des origines à la fin du règne d'Auguste* (Paris: Les Belles Lettres, 1976).

Van Campen, *Lucani Bellum Civile Liber II*   Ferdinand H.M. van Campen, *M. Annaei Lucani, De bello civili liber II: Text, Introduction and Commentary* (Amsterdam: Gieben, 1992) Doctoral thesis Amsterdam.

Van Dam, *Statius Silvae, Book II*   Harm-Jan van Dam, *P. Papinius Statius Silvae, Book II: A Commentary* (Leiden: Brill, 1984) Mnemosyne Supplementum 82, Doctoral thesis Leiden.

Van de Bilt, *Lipsius en Seneca*   Tini M. van de Bilt, *Lipsius' De constantia en Seneca: De invloed van Seneca op Lipsius' geschrift over de standvastigheid van gemoed* (Nijmegen, etc.: Dekker and Van de Vegt, 1946) Doctoral thesis, Nijmegen.

Van der Aa   Abraham J. van der Aa, *Biographisch woordenboek der Nederlanden, bevattende levensbeschrijvingen van zoodanige personen, die zich op eenigerlei wijze in ons vaderland hebben vermaard gemaakt* (Haarlem: Brederode, 1852–1878) 20 vols.

Veenstra, 'Dromen zonder Freud'   Fokke Veenstra, 'Dromen zonder Freud', *Spektator* 4 (1974–1975), pp. 582–616.

Veenstra, *Ethiek en moraal*   Fokke Veenstra, *Ethiek en moraal bij P.C. Hooft: Twee studies in renaissancistische levensidealen* (Zwolle: Theenk Willink, 1968), Zwolse reeks van taal- en letterkundige studies, 18.

Von Moos, *Consolatio*   Peter von Moos, *Consolatio: Studien zur mittellateinischen Trostliteratur über den Tod und zum Problem der christlichen Trauer* (Munich: W. Fink, 1971–1972) 4 vols.

Williams, *Tradition and Originality*   Gordon Williams, *Tradition and Originality in Roman Poetry* (Oxford: Clarendon Press, 1968).

Witstein, *Funeraire poëzie*   Sonja F. Witstein, *Funeraire poëzie in de Nederlandse Renaissance: Enkele funeraire gedichten van Heinsius, Hooft, Huygens en Vondel bezien tegen de achtergrond van de theorie betreffende het genre* (Assen: Van Gorcum, 1969) Neerlandica Traiectina, 17, Doctoral thesis Utrecht.

WNT   Matthias de Vries, Lammert A. te Winkel a.o, *Woordenboek der Nederlandsche Taal* (The Hague: 1882–1998) 29 vols.

Introduction

At 2 o'clock in the afternoon of the 10th of July 1584, William of Orange, one of the main leaders of the Dutch Revolt against King Philip II of Spain, who was the sovereign ruler of the Netherlands, was killed by the Frenchman Balthasar Gérards. This has been characterized as 'the first assassination of a head of state with a hand-gun'.[1] One can doubt the status of William as a 'head of state', but the shocking event soon began to be used to construct a national identity in the Low Countries, especially in the Northern provinces. One of the building blocks in this construction was the Latin tragedy *Auriacus, sive Libertas saucia* (*[William of] Orange, or Liberty Wounded*, 1602), written seventeen years after Prince William's death by the student Daniel Heinsius (1580–1655).

1   Life and Work of Daniel Heinsius till 1602

'When, deprived of all my goods, house and land, I had withdrawn nothing from the tyranny of the Spaniards for the sake of the common faith than only my poor soul, and if I had any hope in my parents, it was still in them while they themselves were most unfortunate, you have taken me in, cherished and embraced me.'[2] This expresses Heinsius' gratefulness to the province of Holland for receiving him as one of the many refugees in the town of Leiden. As a three-year old boy, Daniel Heins or Heyns (9 June 1580–26 February 1655) was taken by his parents Nicolaes Heins or Heyns and Elisabeth Navegeer (or Navigheer) on their flight from Ghent.[3] His father Nicolaes had been a Registrar at the anti-Spanish Council of Flanders, where Daniel's uncle Daniel de Borchgrave—Daniel was named after him—was Attorney General. Nicolaes was more moderate than the group of fierce Calvinists who exerted a severe theocracy in the city in the years 1577–1583, but with whom De Borchgrave sympathized.[4]

---

1   Lisa Jardine, *The Awful End of Prince William the Silent: The First Assassination of a Head of State with a Hand-Gun* (New York: Harper Collins, 2005).

2   *Auriacus*, 'To the States of Holland and West-Friesland', below, p. 78, ll. 318–321.

3   On Heinsius' life, see Ter Horst, *Daniel Heinsius*; Becker-Cantarino, *Daniel Heinsius*; and on his works, among other publications, Eckard Lefèvre and Eckart Schäfer (eds), *Daniel Heinsius: Klassischer Philologe und Poet* (Tübingen: Gunter Narr, 2008) Neolatina, 13.

4   On the riots in Ghent, see Motley, *Dutch Republic*, pp. 731 and 774–777; on Nicolaes' role, see Meter, *The Literary Theories*, p. 6.

Since 1578 the Duke of Parma Alexander Farnese had been re-catholizing the Southern Netherlands, reimposing Spanish dominion on town after town. So in 1583, when the reconquest of Ghent by Farnese's troops seemed to be only a matter of time, the parents of Daniel Heinsius sent their child to a safer place. In 1583 or the beginning of 1584 a maid brought him to the Zeeland town of Veere where two nieces of his mother lived. Shortly after, his parents and his sister also left Ghent. Via Dover and London—there were many contacts between the Calvinists in the Netherlands and England—the family settled in the village of Rijswijk, near The Hague.

However, in Rijswijk the family experienced the consequences of the position taken by their relative De Borchgrave,[5] who had associated himself with Robert Dudley, the first Earl of Leicester and his politics. In January 1586, after the Fall of Antwerp in 1585, Leicester had become Governor-General of the Netherlands on behalf of Queen Elizabeth I of England. Because of this, he was hated by the Dutch 'regenten', leaders of Dutch cities and heads of organizations, who feared that his actions on behalf of the English queen would affect their own power and put the country's interests in jeopardy. De Borchgrave acted as a spy for the English governor in the discussions of the Council of State.[6] Although this attitude is explicable as a result of the hope that Southern Dutch Calvinist refugees set for a war policy to free the South, the annoyances that the regents experienced also had an impact on the Heinsius family. In addition, the great influx of Flemings in the Northern Netherlands led to social and demographic problems, which in turn produced a certain mistrust of immigrants.

The family consequently moved to Flushing, where they felt safe from possible repercussions, since, under the Treaty of Nonsuch (19 August 1585), English garrisons were stationed there. The presence of a large group of Flemings ensured that the Heinsius family quickly felt at home. Daniel Heinsius attended the Latin school, where he may well have read the *Disticha Catonis*, Terence and Cicero's letters, *De officiis* and orations, Virgil's *Bucolics* and *Aeneid*, Ovid's *Heroides*, Plautus, Horace, and other authors.[7] As he himself wrote, he was

---

5 Meter, *The Literary Theories*, pp. 9–10.

6 According to Meter, *The Literary Theories*, p. 9, this was the reason why Heinsius in his autobiography did not mention his uncle.

7 On the Latin school in Flushing, see Hendrik W. Fortgens, 'De Latijnse School te Vlissingen', *Archief* (1946–1947), pp. 40–65; on the usual curriculum at Latin schools in the Low Countries, see Petrus N.M. Bot, *Humanisme en onderwijs in Nederland* (Utrecht etc.: Spectrum, 1955), pp. 141–146, on the first years; 152–159 (esp. 156–158) on the students' reading to improve their style.

annoyed by the lessons on grammar and prosody, but loved Greek.[8] He developed a sense for poetry there, and his tutors therefore made him write verses as a punishment.[9] He shared this love of poetry with his fellow pupil and later fellow student in Leiden Petrus Hondius, also a son of immigrants. They preferred bucolic and georgic poetry, which enjoyed some fame in the Low Countries in those days.[10] Such poetry is also echoed in *Auriacus* and Heinsius' second play *Herodes infanticida* (*Herod the Murderer of Children*, 1632).[11]

8 Iohannes Meursius, *Athenae Batavae: sive de urbe Leidensi et Academia, virisque claris, qui utramque ingenio suo, atque scriptis illustrarunt, libri duo* (Leiden: Cloucquius, 1625), p. 212; see also Meter, *The Literary Theories*, p. 11.

9 Meursius, *Athenae Batavae*, p. 212: "Quae res cum non usquequaque praeceptoribus placeret, qui libenter tamen connivebant, quicquid delinquebat, versibus plerunque iussus expiabat, qui de facili proveniebant" (His teachers did not quite like his playfulness, but they gladly pardoned it, because he usually attoned for all his misbehavings with verses that easily came out of his pen). Some of the poems added to his 1600 Seneca edition may be products from this punishment.

10 See Pieter A.F. van Veen, *De soeticheyt des buyten-levens, vergheselschapt met de boucken: Het hofdicht als tak van de georgische literatuur* (Utrecht: Hes and De Graaf, 1985) Doctoral thesis Leiden, 1960, pp. 10–14, on the early specimens of countryside house poetry. On Hondius' *Moufe-schans*, see *ibid.*, pp. 19–23; on the life of this Zeeland preacher, see *NNBW* VIII, 812–813, and Pieter J. Meertens, *Letterkundig leven in Zeeland in de zestiende en de eerste helft der zeventiende eeuw* (Amsterdam: Noord-Hollandsche Uitgevers Maatschappij, 1943) Doctoral thesis Utrecht, pp. 341–354, and p. 406, n. 711; Willemien B. de Vries, *Wandeling en verhandeling: De ontwikkeling van het Nederlandse hofdicht in de zeventiende eeuw (1613–1710)* (Hilversum: Verloren, 1998), pp. 73–130. For that matter, Hondius also started writing a history of the Dutch revolt, so national history was also a common interest of Heinsius and Hondius. On their friendship, see Pieter J. Meertens, 'De Groot en Heinsius en hun Zeeuwse vrienden', *Archief* (1949–1950), pp. 53–99, esp. 82–84; on their exchange of poetry, see Barbara Becker-Cantarino, 'Die Stammbucheintragungen von Daniel Heinsius', in: Jörg-Ulrich Fechner (ed.), *Stammbücher als kulturhistorische Quellen* (Munich: Kraus, 1981) Wolfenbütteler Forschungen, 11, pp. 137–164, esp. 143–145.

11 Oliver Bach, 'Exkurs: Daniel Heinsius' *Herodes Infanticida* (1632)—Politische Theologie zwischen Tragödienform und stofflich gebotener Episierung', in: *id.*, *Zwischen Heilsgeschichte und säkularer Jurisprudenz: Politische Theologie in den Trauerspielen des Andreas Gryphius* (Berlin and Boston: De Gruyter, 2014) Frühe Neuzeit, 188, pp. 298–305; Ferdinand Stürner, 'Daniel Heinsius' Tragödie *Herodes Infanticida*', in: Eckard Lefèvre and Eckart Schäfer (eds), *Daniel Heinsius: Klassisicher Philologe und Poet* (Tübingen: Gunter Narr, 2008) Neolatina, 13, pp. 415–439; Jan Bloemendal, 'Daniel Heinsius's *Herodes Infanticida* (1632) as a Senecan Drama', in: John Hilton and Anne Gosling (eds), *Alma parens originalis? The Receptions of Classical Literature and Thought in Africa, Europe, the United States and Cuba* (Bern: Peter Lang, 2007), pp. 217–236; *id.*, 'Mythology on the Early Modern Humanists' and Rhetoricians' Stage in the Netherlands: The Case of Heinsius' *Herodes infanticida*', in: Carl Van de Velde (ed.), *Classical Mythology in the Netherlands in the Age of Renaissance and Baroque/La mythologie classique aux temps de la Renaissance et du Baroque dans les Pays-Bas: Proceedings of the International Conference, Antwerp, 19–*

In July 1596 Heinsius matriculated (with the comment: 'vir inter literatos princeps') at the orthodox Calvinist University of Franeker to study law.[12] However, he liked Greek literature more than his law studies. When it was clear that law was not his main interest, his father sent him to Leiden University, where he matriculated on 30 September 1598. He attended courses in law, but also took lessons from the Professor of Greek Bonaventura Vulcanius.[13] His *artes* study again flourished to the detriment of the study of law. His father took him back to Flushing, where Daniel went through a period of depression. His father gave in and on 11 October 1600 he was matriculated again. In Leiden Heinsius already had befriended the famous son of the famous father Julius Caesar Scaliger, the university professor Josephus Justus Scaliger.[14] From 1600 he also got acquainted with members of the Dutch regent families, such as the curator of Leiden University Janus Dousa, the student and later jurist and diplomat Hugo Grotius,[15] and the diplomat Cornelis van der Myle.[16] Thus, he got engaged in Scaliger's circle of people interested in classical philology, and classical and Neo-Latin poetry. He had found a 'safe haven'. Heinsius' gratitude as expressed in the letter of dedication to the States of Holland and West Friesland, although slightly exaggerated, is therefore not a matter of mere politeness.

Leiden University had been founded in 1575, as a reward for the constancy of the town during the long siege by the Spaniards in the years 1573–1574.[17] The University, which opened on 8 February, was in part meant to be an educational institution for Calvinist ministers.[18] One of Heinsius' fellow students and

21 May 2005/Actes du Colloque international, Anvers, 19–21 mai 2005 (Leuven: Peeters, 2009), pp. 333–350; Russ Leo, 'Herod and the Furies: Daniel Heinsius and the Representation of Affect in Tragedy', *Journal of Medieval and Early Modern Studies*, 49 (2019), pp. 137–167; Becker-Cantarino, *Daniel Heinsius*, pp. 131–142; Volker Janning, *Der Chor im neulateinischen Drama: Formen und Funktionen* (Münster: Rhema Verlag, 2005), pp. 167–168 and 345–346; Stachel, *Seneca und das deutsche Renaissancedrama*. I am preparing an edition.

12 Ter Horst, *Daniel Heinsius*, p. 14.
13 On him, see Hélène Cazes (ed.), *Bonaventura Vulcanius, Works and Networks: Bruges 1538-Leiden 1614* (Leiden and Boston: Brill, 2010).
14 On Scaliger, see Grafton, *Joseph Scaliger*.
15 On Grotius, see Nellen, *Hugo Grotius*.
16 On Van der Myle, see *NNBW* 8, 1192–1198, and Hendrik A.W. van der Vecht, *Cornelis van der Myle* (Sappemeer: D. Klein, 1907) Doctoral thesis Leiden.
17 This story already appears in an epic of 1584, Benedicti's *De rebus gestis* I, 681–682, see the comm. on *Aur.* 1805.
18 On the first years of Leiden University, see Jan A. van Dorsten, *Poets, Patrons, and Professors: Sir Philip Sidney, Daniel Rogers, and the Leiden Humanists* (Leiden: Leiden University Press; London: Oxford University Press, 1962) Doctoral thesis Leiden, pp. 1–8 and 33–47; J.J. Woltjer, 'Introduction', in: Th.H. Lunsingh Scheurleer and Guillaume H.M. Posthumus

friends was Hugo de Groot, or Hugo Grotius, with whom he shared an interest in classical literature and a poetic talent, and they found each other—and
rivalled!—in poetry.[19] In 1601 they collaborated in a project to revive Neo-Latin
tragedy in the Northern Netherlands, which resulted in Grotius' *Adamus exul*
(*Adam in Exile*, 1601) and Heinsius' *Auriacus*.[20] They did so by a creative imitation of Senecan tragedy and by opposing Neo-Latin school theatre and Dutch
rhetoricians' drama, including morality plays.[21] Although Heinsius seemingly
took the initiative, Grotius' play was published first.[22]

Auriacus was not Heinsius' first attempt in literature, and he discovered
and developed some of his literary techniques and themes when younger. In
Franeker, he had written and published *Apotheosis viri clariss. D. Georgii Paludani* [...], 1596, on the death of Joris van den Broeck.[23] In this collection of

---

Meyjes (eds), *Leiden University in the Seventeenth Century: An Exchange of Learning* (Leiden: Universitaire Pers Leiden, 1975), pp. 1–19; and Chris L. Heesakkers, 'Leids humanisme
in de vroege Gouden Eeuw', *Hermeneus* 66 (1994), pp. 186–196.

19   See Jan Hendrik Meter, 'Daniël Heinsius en Hugo Grotius: Van dichterlijke vriendschap
tot politieke vervreemding', *Acta Universitatis Vratislaviensis* 1299 (Wroclaw, 1991) Neerlandica Wratislaviensia, 5, pp. 79–123; and J.P. Heering, 'Kunstbroeders en rivalen: Heinsius en Grotius', in: H.J. Adriaanse (ed.), *Voorbeeldige vriendschap: Vrienden en vriendinnen
in theologie en cultuur: Aangeboden aan prof. dr. E.J. Kuiper* [...] (Groningen: Styx, 1993),
pp. 47–56.

20   Arthur C. Eyffinger in Grotius, *Dichtwerken/Poetry* I, 2, 5A/B: *Christus Patiens*, p. 21, opts
for collaboration in writing tragedy, or even a co-production; Gerdien C. Kuiper, 'Heinsius' *Auriacus*: Oranje of de Gewonde Vrijheid', *Hermeneus* 56 (1984), pp. 251–257, esp. 256,
and Meter, 'Heinsius en Grotius', p. 90, think of creative competition.

21   See also below, pp. 27–31; and Meter, *The Literary Theories*, pp. 37–38. On school drama,
see Anneke Fleurkens, 'Meer dan vrije expressie: Schooltoneel tijdens de renaissance', *Literatuur* 5 (1988), pp. 75–82; and Jan Bloemendal and Howard B. Norland (eds), *Neo-Latin
Drama and Theatre in Early Modern Europe* (Leiden and Boston: Brill, 2013), *passim*.

22   On Heinsius' primacy, see Grotius' poem 'Heinsi, vetustae ...', Hugo Grotius, *Poemata
omnia: Editio quinta* (Amsterdam: Joh. Ravesteyn, 1670), p. 231; and Grotius, *Dichtwerken/
Poetry* I, 1A: *Adamus exul*, p. 311: "Heinsi, vetustae restitutor Orchestrae, ornas cothurno
qui pedes Sophocleo, primusque Syrma vincis Euripideum [...]" (Heinsius, who revived
ancient theatre, who wore Sophocles' buskins and was the first to surpass Euripides' scenic
garb). Heinsius himself, too, in a poem on Grotius, 'Ingens cothumi splendor [...]' (Grotius,
Dichtwerken/Poetry I, 1A, p. 313), points at his own initiative: "Cogitur retro tuus pedem
referre cultor et suavibus regni prioris exulare finibus" (He who admires you [i.e. Heinsius
himself] is now forced to step back and leave the pleasant region of his former reign [i.e.
tragedy]).

23   *Apotheosis viri clariss. D. Georgii Paludani rerum per Zelandiam bellicarum legati, apud
Walachros, Vlissingae mortui, autore Daniele Heynsio Flandro* (Franeker: Aegidius Radaeus,
1596). The booklet (30 pp. 8°), printed by the official printer of the States of Frisia and
Franeker Academy Radaeus, contains a letter of dedication in prose to Heinsius' father
Nicolaes Heins and his teachers Olivarius and Belosius, a verse dedication to the two

poems, he already used motifs which would reoccur in *Auriacus*, such as a
Homeric comparison with the fight between a shepherd and a lion,[24] and a
raging goddess who could be a Fury or the Inquisition, accompanied by the
personifications of evil powers including Ambush, Hunger, and Poverty.[25]

This piece of poetry was followed by a philological enterprise: the edition
of five philosophical works by Seneca: *De providentia, De vita beata, De tranquillitate animi, De brevitate vitae,* and *An in sapientem cadat iniuria* (i.e. *De
constantia sapientis*), all published in Leiden in 1599 with the University printer
Raphelengius. It is an early example of Heinsius' interest in Seneca. In the letter of dedication he praises the philosopher's important subjects, manifold
aphorisms and gravity ("rerum gravitas", "sententiarum praegnans acumen"
and "pondus").[26] Heinsius defends his choice of Seneca by pointing at his con-
geniality with Christianity. To Seneca's works Heinsius added some poems of
his own hand with Stoic content, which he also included in the *Iambi* added to
Auriacus. Some of these poems contain lines that almost literally recur in the
tragedy.[27]

Around 1599–1600 Heinsius worked as a philologist on the Greek lexicog-
rapher Hesychius and the poet Nonnus, both from the fifth century. Traces of
Hesychius of Alexandria's dictionary *Synagoge* may be found in 'Amico lectori',
on the cases that the substantive *tabum* admits.[28] However, if Heinsius planned
an edition of the *Synagoge*, it was never published.[29] Nonnus' *Dionysiaca*, an
epic in Greek on Bacchus in fourty-eight books is an accumulation of mythological erudition and sensitive description. The *editio princeps* was delivered by
Gerard Falckenburg in 1569, which, however was severely criticized by Leiden

---

teachers, and poems with wordplays on their names, and a *Carmen de morte clarissimi
viri D. Georgii Paludani* [...], as well as two epitaphs, an Echo poem and a Sapphic ode
to honour the same Joris van den Broeck. The Dyce collection of the Victoria and Albert
Museum has a copy (sign. D 21 A 13 4586 S 8v), which Heinsius had given to Michael Man-
deville, with a hand written dedication: "Modestissimo eruditissimoque ado[les]centi
D. Michaeli Mandewyl domino et amico fraterna benevolent[ia] mihi coniuncto d.d.
autor."

24   *Apotheosis*, p. A[7r–v]; *Aur.* 144–160.
25   *Apotheosis*, p. [8r–v]; *Aur.* 405–412.
26   For this letter of dedication to Olivarius, one of Heinsius' teachers in Flushing, see Hein-
     sius, *Auriacus*, ed. Bloemendal, appendix 1.11a.
27   See the comm. *ad* 3, 6–13, 23–45, 69, 84–96, 112–123, 396, 415–429, 498 and 712–714.
28   See p. 120, ll. 16–21 and the comm. *ad loc.* to Vulcanius' edition of Philoxenus' Latin-Greek
     dictionary as another possible source.
29   However, annotations by Heinsius on Hesychius appeared in editions by Schrevelius
     (1668) and Alberti (1746–1766), see Sellin, *Daniel Heinsius and Stuart England*, p. 230,
     nos 234–235, and Meter, *The Literary Theories*, pp. 23–24.

philologists. A new edition was an intellectual challenge for Joseph Scaliger, who also roused Heinsius' interest. But whereas Scaliger criticized the poet's bombastic display of learnedness and the excessive length of the poem, Heinsius admired Nonnus' theme and style, as well as his concept of Bacchus as a comforter. Probably because of this criticism Heinsius for a long time ignored the poem and he would deliver a speech on it no earlier than 1610.[30]

In 1600 Heinsius edited Silius Italicus' *Punica*, an edition based on a Cologne manuscript that Scaliger had obtained, and published annotations to this epic as *Crepundia Siliana* in 1601.[31] He accounted for his restrained editorial method in his emendations. In fact, however, he showed more enthusiasm for changing the text. In the *Crepundia* he annotated the first books quite intensively, but in the course of the work the annotations became scarcer and briefer. In the commentary notes he testifies to his admiration for the poetry of Nonnus and Theocritus. The theme Heinsius discerns and praises in this epic is the struggle between moral power and fickle fortune, between *virtus* and *fortuna*, the same theme as in *Auriacus*.[32] However, only few instances of actual reception of this poem can be traced in the tragedy.[33]

In that same year, 1601, Heinsius made his debut as a poet in Dutch, when his emblem book *Quaeris quid sit amor?*—in spite of the Latin title, it is in the

---

30   For Heinsius' admiration of Nonnus' style, see Meter, *The Literary Theories*, pp. 20–21. The speech is *Dissertatio de Nonni Dionysiacis*, in Νόννου Πανοπολίτου Διονυσιακά (Hannover: Marnius and the heirs of Aubrius, 1610). Instances of reception of the *Dionysiaca* in *Auriacus.* can be found in II, 1 (see n.ll. 326–332), and IV, 1, where Ino and Athamas are mentioned, who are the subject of *Dionysiaca* book X.

31   See Meter, *The Literary Theories*, pp. 21–23.

32   "Bellum sine exemplo, et in quo virtus cum fortuna certasse [...] videtur", Silius Italicus, *De secundo bello Punico:* [...] *Notae* [...] *paulo uberiores, opera Danielis Heynsii* (Leiden: Raphelengius, 1600), p. 2. Hence Kuiper's suggestion (Kuiper, 'Heinsius' *Auriacus*', p. 257), that Heinsius derived the theme of virtue vs fortune from Lucan is hardly probable, all the less since Heinsius avoided every allusion to civil war—which is by definition bad—, the actual theme of *Bellum civile* or *Pharsalia*.

33   There are some perfunctory similarities, for example a remark about the Tagus as a gold-bearing river (*Aur.* 71, Sil. XVI, 560, etc.); nor can conclusions be drawn from Silius' predilection for the adjective *Tarpeius* with regard to Jupiter (cf. *Aur.* 227, 286). It is not easy to explain this remarkable absence of reception of *Punica* in *Auriacus*. To attribute this to a difference in genres is not adequate: firstly, Heinsius also used material from other genres for his play (from the epics of Virgil and Ovid, and the pastoral poetry of Virgil) and, on the other hand, Silius' epic could easily have been echoed in the epic poem *Pro Auriaco sua*. More satisfactory is the assumption that Heinsius published Silius' work mainly on technical grounds, without being fully involved, as the unbalanced distribution of the annotations suggests. Even the suspicion arises that he merely published the notes of his teacher Scaliger.

vernacular—was published anonymously. This booklet was the beginning of the typically Dutch genre of the love emblem.³⁴

The publication of *Auriacus* meant a turning point in Heinsius' career, since it encouraged the curators of the University allow him to lecture on Horace.³⁵ On 9 September, one week after the final decision of the professors, Heinsius delivered his first public oration, in which he announced this course.³⁶ This meant for Heinsius the start of an academic career at Leiden University, in which he combined philological and other scholarly activities with the writing of poetry and an influential treatise on tragedy, *De tragica constitutione* (1611), which was published in an expanded and emended edition as *De tragoediae constitutione* (1642). In 1635 he published a second tragedy, *Herodes infanticida*.³⁷

---

34   *Quaeris quid sit amor, quid amare, Cupidinis et quid castra sequi?* (...) ([Amsterdam: Matthijsz and De Buck, 1601]). On Heinsius as its author, see Ronald Breugelmans, 'Quaeris quid sit amor? Ascription, Date of Publication and Printer of the Earliest Emblem Book to be Written in Dutch', *Quaerendo* 3 (1973), pp. 280–290, and Herman de la Fontaine Verwey, 'Notes on the Début of Daniel Heinsius as a Dutch Poet', *Quaerendo* 3 (1973), pp. 291–308. On the genre of the love emblem, see Hans Luijten and Marijke Blankman, *Minne- en zinnebeelden: Een bloemlezing uit de Nederlandse emblematiek* (Amsterdam: Amsterdam University Press, 1996), esp. p. 15. See on the emblem book and Heinsius as a Dutch poet also Karel Porteman and Mieke B. Smits-Veldt, *Een nieuw vaderland voor de muzen: Geschiedenis van de Nederlandse literatuur 1560–1700* (Amsterdam: Bert Bakker, 2008), pp. 179–189.

35   In the minutes of the meeting of 8 May 1602 is recorded: "Insgelicx van wegen Daniel Heynsius student der Universiteit geproponeerd sijnde, als dat hy wel van meyninge soude sijn om hem selven te exerceren ende om te thoonen wat vruchten hy in dese universiteit gedaen hadde, te doen enige publycque lessen in poesi, by aldyen sulcx met het goet gelyeven van de voors[eiden] C[uratoren] ende B[urgemeesteren] gescyeden conde, soo ist dat de voors[eiden] C. ende B. onderricht sijnde van de goede genegentheit des voors[eiden] Heynsii ende eensdeels gesyen hebbende sijne bequaemheit in dyen deel uyte Tragedia auriaca by hem gemaect, hebben t selve geconsenteert [...]." Quoted after Molhuysen, *Bronnen*, p. 142. For the decision itself, see *ibid.* pp. 408–409 (appendix 351). On 28 April, according to the *Acta Senatus*, Dousa had recommended him, see *ibid.*, p. 138. On 3 June the Senate discussed the decision of the curators and burgomasters, but postponed the case because of the absence of some of the professors. Only on 2 September Heinsius received the requested permission, see *ibid.*, p. 139 ("E.d. decreta est Danieli Heinsio ad edendum specimen suae eruditionis in re poetica, hora 4ᵃ in auditorio Philosophico").

36   Published in Leiden by Raphelengius in 1602; see also Daniel Heinsius, *Orationum editio nova* [...]: *Accedunt Dissertationes aliquot* [...] (Leiden: Elzevier, 1642), pp. 572–581.

37   See on that tragedy above, p. 3 and n. 11.

2   Genesis and Printing of *Auriacus* and Its Performance

Auriacus was printed in quarto format in 1602. On December 18, 1601, the play was already finished or almost finished. For on that day Scaliger wrote to Casaubon: "Soon I will write to you more, when I will send you the tragedy by Heinsius".[38] Moreover, in his own draft manuscript Grotius' poem *Iambi* follows on from *Abfuit Heinsiades*, which is dated after the beginning of August 1601 and is in turn followed by the poem *Crede mihi, Pottei,* of December 1601.[39] This indicates that Heinsius has written his tragedy in the autumn or winter of 1601. In which month it was printed cannot be determined with certainty. Since Heinsius' request to be allowed to lecture on Horace was for the first time on the agenda of the meeting of the University curators on 8 May (on that occasion they saw the book), it would have been printed before that time.[40] A further indication of this is a letter from Casaubon to Scaliger, dated 12 June 1602, in which the French scholar thanks his friend for a copy of *Auriacus* that he received a few days earlier.[41]

Heinsius does not seem to have been very satisfied with the printer of the *Auriacus* Andreas Cloeck (or Cloucquius). After the list of corrigenda (the *menda typographica*) he expresses his regret that the printer has hired an ignorant typesetter without any knowledge of Greek accents whatsoever.[42] However, such a complaint had become a commonplace[43] and although the edi-

---

38 Paul Botley and Dirk van Miert (eds), *The Correspondence of Joseph Justus Scaliger* 4 (Geneva: Droz, 2012), p. 150: "Propediem uberius tibi scribam, quum mittam Tragoediam Heinsii". See also Grotius, *Dichtwerken/Poetry* I, 2, 2B (Assen: Van Gorkum, 1977), p. 238. The passage can be found in Scaliger, *Epistolae* 1627, vol. 1, p. 198 (*Epist.* 63).

39 For the *Iambi*, a preliminary poem to *Auriacus*, see below, pp. 102–112.

40 Cf. above, n. 35.

41 See Isaac Casaubon, *Epistolae* (The Hague: Maire, 1638), *Epist.* 447; Botley and Van Miert (eds), *The Correspondence of Joseph Justus Scaliger* 4 (Geneva: Droz, 2012), p. 312: "Accepi nuper Heinsii tui tragoediam." The editors annotate: "Scaliger, too, owned a copy: 'Dan. Heinsii Auriacus Tragoedia. Leid. 1602', see *The Auction Catalogue of the Library of J.J. Scaliger*, ed. H.J. de Jonge (Utrecht: HES Publishers, 1977), p. 35."

42 See below, p. 126.

43 Cloeck, who worked in Leiden as of 1599, mainly produced small editions of collected poetry. Grotius would later be seriously disappointed by his typesetters and correctors at the publication of his *Poemata collecta* (1617). On that occasion Cloeck showed himself a skilful printer, who adroitly added a section. Perhaps he proposed to Heinsius to insert a later written passage, the Maurice scene, as a quire. On Cloeck, see Eyffinger, *Grotius Poeta*, pp. 175–198, esp. pp. 177–182. For a list of his editions, see *ibid.*, p. 257, n. 147. About the addition of the quire in Grotius' poems, see *ibid.*, pp. 197–198.

tion is not faultless, it is not really that bad.[44] There are many mistakes in the accentuation of Greek words; as far as is known, there were no corrections on the press. Heinsius was probably actually disappointed, but some exaggeration may have been involved too.

After the book had been printed, but before it was bound, a four-page quire was inserted containing a scene in which Prince Maurice occurs that covers two pages. On the other two pages of the quire, Heinsius had a passage printed that was to be inserted after l. 1575, and a separate poem on the doves that were mentioned in ll. 1805–1811. Also the typography and the page numbering indicate clearly that these four pages are inserted later: The pages are set in roman, whereas the rest of the text of *Auriacus* is in italics. And following on Inquisitio's clause on p. 84, the page containing the poem Διονύσῳ τῷ ἀρίστῳ, bound immediately after the quire, is numbered 85.

Heinsius dedicated his tragedy to the States of Holland and West Friesland. He received f. 200 in return, which was just below the average of f. 260.[45]

One of the questions to be asked about such a play is whether it was actually performed and if so, how many times. It certainly was performed, but we do not know how often. In a letter of 25 January 1602 students asked the Senate of the University to be allowed to stage Plautus' *Amphitryo*. One of their arguments was:

> Because we noticed that an *actio* of a tragedy is being prepared, and because, for other reasons but also in itself, we believe that such a tragedy would be somewhat boring if it were not enriched by another piece, or painful and bitter if it were not softened by adding a cheerful comedy, and the listeners, who would be affected and dejected by the death of that great Hero, by seeing a merry comedy could be cheered up again. Especially for these reasons we use the opportunity to ask that the expenses

---

44 I counted some 80 typographical errors or misreadings, 40 of which are mistakes in orthography, 30 in punctuation, 5 in capital or lowercase letters, and 5 in page numbering and custodes. But this is liable to subjectivity. Moreover, Heinsius' hand is hardly legible.

45 See on this Piet J. Verkruijsse, 'Holland "gededieeerd": Boekopdrachten in Holland in de 17e eeuw', *Holland* 23 (1991), pp. 225–242, esp. 238; Marijke Spies, 'Betaald werk? Poëzie als ambacht in de 17e eeuw', *Oud Holland* 23, (1991), pp. 210–224; it also added to someone's cultural capital, see Karl Schottenloher, *Die Widmungsvorrede im Buch des 16. Jahrhunderts* (Münster: Asschendorffsche Verlagsbuchhandlung, 1953) Reformationsgeschichtliche Studien und Texte, 76–77; Saskia Stegeman, *Patronage and Services in the Republic of Letters: The Network of Theodorus Janssonius van Almeloveen (1657–1712)* (Amsterdam, APA-Holland University Press, 2005), esp. pp. 282–293 and 328–333, and the commentary below, pp. 292–293.

and costs that would otherwise have been spent on the tragedy would also be applied for our use, without any damage to the public welfare.[46]

This passage must refer to *Auriacus*. From 30 December 1595, after student riots at the staging of a play, theatre performances at the University had been limited, and were subject to approval of the rector and four *assessores*.[47] Therefore, the students took the opportunity of the *actio* of *Auriacus*, for which the rector and the assessors apparently had given permission, and to ask for a subvention for their own performance. Another indication for an actual staging of the tragedy can be found in the 'Amico lectori', where Heinsius calls as a witness the subregent of the States College Petrus Bertius, who "actioni huius Tragoediae primae praefuit". In this context *actio* can refer to a performance or a declamation.

There was a tradition of performing Seneca's tragedies in the Netherlands, in the sixteenth century in and around the Latin school at Deventer, as well as in Utrecht, Middelburg, Dordrecht and Leiden. Also at Leiden Academy Senecan plays were staged, as well as comedies.[48] We know that Justus Lipsius had his Leiden students perform Seneca's *Medea* in 1590, whereas the Rector of the Latin school Snellius performed 'four tragedies and a comedy' by Euripides and Plautus. The year after Lipsius brought Seneca's *Agamemnon* and Plautus' *Cap-*

---

46   Molhuysen, *Bronnen*, p. 407*, appendix 349: "Quare cum videremus Tragoediae cuiusdam actionem institutam, eaque videretur nobis cum aliis de causis tum per se sola otiosa futura, nisi alterius etiam fabulae accessione locupletaretur; aut odiosa et insuavis, nisi hilaris comoediae appulsu temperaretur, et per mortem magni illius Herois affecti auditorum animi et collapsi comica quadem suavitate rejicerentur; arripuimus commodam hanc occasionem nos, eo nimirum potissimum, ut sumtus illi et dispendia, quae alioquin soli essent Tragoediae impendendi, ad nostrum quoque usum sine ullo publico detrimento converterentur [...]". Cf. also Molhuysen, *Bronnen*, p. 134. On this issue, see also Johan M. Koppenol, *Leids heelal: Het loterijspel (1596) van Jan van Hout* (Hilversum: Verloren, 1998) Doctoral thesis Leiden, pp. 123–124. The Senate could not prohibit the students to attend performances, since Leiden was often visited by English 'strolling players', see A.G.H. Bachrach, 'Leiden en de Strolling Players', *Jaarboekje voor de Geschiedenis en Oudheidkunde van Leiden*, 1968, pp. 29–38, and the Leiden rederijkers also staged plays, see, e.g., Koppenol, *op. cit.* pp. 121–122.

47   See Molhuysen, *Bronnen*, p. 88: "Decretum praeterea, ne ullae deinceps Comoediae aut Tragoediae habeantur, nisi ex sententia Magnifici Rectoris et Quattuor Assessorum" ("Moreover it is decided that from now on no Comedies or Tragedies may be performed without the permission of the Rector Magnificus and the Four Assessors"). The Letter of Dedication with its stress on the moral-didactic function of tragedy as a derivative of philosophy therefore also fits in this quarrel about theatre.

48   Asmuth, 'Die niederländische Literatur', pp. 238–239, 245.

tivi and *Pseudolus*, whereas in 1592 Sophocles' *Aiax* and Euripides' *Rhesus* were scheduled. Lipsius staged Aristophanes' *Plutus* on 7 June 1595, Seneca's *Troades* the day after, and Plautus' *Miles gloriosus* on 9 June. In he same year students performed Sophocles' *Aiax*, Seneca's *Hercules furens* and Plautus' *Captivi* for the States of Zeeland.[49] The Acts of the Academy Senate mention that plays were performed 'on the public square beneath the Library', a room of 10 by 26 metres and 6 metres high, and they list the characters and the actors. As might be expected, both the female and male characters were played by (male) students. Moreover, it is ordained that performances should be held in holidays or on days off, to prevent other students or professors to be disturbed by the noise.[50] The students acted 'valde eximie'.[51] However, we do not know *how* the plays were performed: as a declamation or with props and scenery. Some acting must have been involved.

The text itself contains explicit and implicit stage directions. For instance, the heading of Act II, Scene 1, mentions Inquisition carrying a torch and a chalice of human blood, and getting drunk. In Scene 2 of the same act, Loisa has the child Frederick Henry on her lap. Characters see their collocutors weep, rush around, have a pale face, etcetera, see, for instance ll. 490–493, where the *senex* asks Loisa: "Why are your mouth and bosom lukewarm and humid by the shedding of tears, why does a flood of tears flow from your eye and does the usual red colour of your beautiful cheeks disappear?" As can be deduced from the questions of the Praefectus, the Sicarius is walking around with a pale face, everything in him betraying intense emotions (ll. 800–810). In ll. 405–414 Inquisition conducts her troops, which when staged must have been impressive. The same may hold for the scene where she is mixing a poisonous drink (ll. 1473–1493), and the hissing snakes that are mentioned in ll. 1497–1501. Again, these features may have been shown, but we just do not know.

Heinsius might have thought of having a second, revised edition published. Leiden University Library has a copy of *Auriacus* with manuscript annotations by Heinsius himself for the purpose of this second edition. From a letter by Hooft to Heinsius of 19 April 1610, in which the magistrate offers a laudatory poem in Dutch for an "anderden druck" (a second edition), can be con-

---

49   See also Koppenol, *Leids heelal* (n. 46), p. 123.
50   H.J. Witkam, *De dagelijkse zaken van de Leidse Universiteit van 1581 to 1596*, 10 vols (Leiden, 1970–1975), vol. 1, part 1, pp. 4–6; vol. 9, pp. 71, 101, and 137, and vol. 10, part 2, pp. 128–129.
51   Everardus Bronchorstius, *Diarium sive Adversaria omnium quae gesta sunt in Academia Leydensi (1591–1627)*, ed. Jacob C. van Slee (The Hague: Nijhoff, 1898), p. 91, quoted after Koppenol, *Leids heelal*, p. 123.

cluded that Heinsius was considering it around that year.[52] This new edition, however, never materialized.

3   The Political-Historical Context

The murder of William I, Prince of Orange (1533–1584), which is the subject matter of *Auriacus*, is part of the Dutch Revolt, or Eighty Years' War (1568–1648). The play contains references to this 'grand story', which below will be put in their historical context and related to Heinsius' sources, without giving a full description or analysis of the Revolt.

It comes to no surprise that Heinsius treats William of Orange and the assassination from a Dutch perspective. This accords with the sources he chose, some of which are very easily traceable. Also oral tradition was an important source. His father had been involved in the war as a result of his position in the Council of Flanders and of his conversion to Calvinism. Also his patron Janus Dousa had an active role in the Revolt as a protagonist in the Siege of Leiden and may well have informed him. One of the most specific allusions in *Auriacus* (ll. 1805–1811) was part of this siege, viz. the use by Dousa himself of doves to transfer messages.[53]

Heinsius took part of the material for his tragedy from an epic on William of Orange, Benedicti's *De rebus gestis Guilielmi* (1586), evidenced by several similarities, of which the reference to the Zeeland admiral Ewoud Worst is the most striking one.[54] However, it is also salient that references to the religious aspect of the war are absent from *Auriacus*; even the character 'Inquisitio', a personification of the Spanish Inquisition, does not mention any religious issues. With his play and the choice of its title, Heinsius apparently took sides in the contemporary discussion on the causes of the Revolt, "religionis erga" or "libertatis erga", in favour of the latter.[55]

---

52   See below, pp. 47, 54 and 57. Part of the handwritten annotations to the liminary poem 'Pro Auriaco sua' and its text in the *Poemata* of 1606 coincide, which means that either the poem was adjusted according to the manuscript—and then Heinsius would have made these revisions of *Auriacus* before or in 1606—or the manuscript notes were taken from the edition, which, however, seems to be less likely.

53   *Aur.* 1805–1811.

54   *Aur.* 1803.

55   The few instances of possible reception by Heinsius of the historiography of the Dutch Revolt, such as Pieter Bor's *Oorspronck, begin ende aanvang der Nederlantsche oorlogen* [...] (1595) and his *Vande Nederlantsche oorloghen, beroerten ende burgerlijcke oneenicheyden* (1601), or Emanuel van Meteren's contemporary history in German, which appeared

For the events in and around the Prince of Orange's court in Delft Heinsius based himself on the official report that was in accordance with the resolutions of the States General, *Een verhael vande moort.*[56]

3.1   The Dutch Revolt

Auriacus deals with a short episode from the long war between the Netherlands and the Habsburg rulers. In 1555 Charles V abdicated in favour of his son Philip II.[57] Charles' power had met with only moderate resistance because, as a native of Ghent, he was considered an indigenous ruler. It stiffened, however, with the assent of the 'foreigner' Philip (who was born in Spain) to the throne, culminating in a struggle for freedom that 'officially' started around 1568. However, before then the Habsburg centralization policy had brought about a change in the tax system, and in religious matters the emergence of the Reformation had provoked a repressive reaction from the Roman Catholic Church and the Habsburg Empire. In the 1560s Philip had introduced a new division of the dioceses and ordered that the new bishops should be doctors in theology. This was a blow to the higher nobility, who until then had distributed ecclesiastical offices among themselves. This measure provoked the resistance of this group, including a nobleman with the most possessions in the Netherlands, William Count of Nassau, who inherited the title Prince of Orange from his uncle René of Châlon.[58] In 1564 the members of the high nobility in the Council of State (who formed the 'League of Noblemen') felt themselves set aside by the appointment of jurists in the Council. Therefore, they addressed the governor of the Netherlands, Philip's half-sister Margaret of Parma, with demands regarding the expansion of the jurisdiction of the Council of State. Although Margaret inclined to give in to their demands, Philip ignored them.

---

in 1598 in a Latin translation (*Historia Belgica nostri potissimum temporis Belgii* [...]) and in 1599 in a Dutch translation (*Belgische ofte Nederlantsche historie, van onsen tijden* [...]), are too general to be decisive.

56   See below, pp. 18–21.

57   For a general overview of the Low Countries in the second half of the sixteenth and the seventeenth centuries, see, for example, Geoffrey Parker, *The Dutch Revolt* (London: Penguin, 1977); Jonathan Israel, *The Dutch Republic: Its Rise, Greatness and Fall, 1477–1806* (Oxford: Clarendon Press, 1998), and Helmut G. Koenigsberger, *Monarchies, States Generals and Parliaments: The Netherlands in the Fifteenth and Sixteenth Centuries* (Cambridge: Cambridge University Press, 2001). A view of the Dutch Revolt from a Spanish perspective is given by Yolanda Rodríguez Pérez, *The Dutch Revolt through Spanish Eyes: Self and Other in Historical and Literary Texts of Golden Age Spain (c. 1548–1673)* (Oxford, etc.: Peter Lang, 2008).

58   Mentioned in *Aur.* 1262. Although the principality of Orange was small, with this inheritance William became a sovereign prince, equal to kings and emperors.

Moreover, there was opposition against the Spanish Inquisition—an institute to 'inquire' about and punish heretics.

In the meantime the lower noblemen, united in the 'Compromise' (Covenant) of the Nobles, also protested; they did so against the severe persecution of heretics. In April 1566 this Compromise presented a petition to Margaret. The persecution and a famine were the breeding ground for iconoclasms that transferred from France in August of that year. Margaret gave in: overt preaching of reformatory ideas was allowed and the Inquisition would be abolished. Gradually she rescinded these measures, probably on Philip's orders.[59] Thereupon the king replaced Margaret with the Duke of Alba (Alva).

The 'Iron Duke' came to the Netherlands in 1567 as head of the army in the rank of captain general. As a governor he instituted the Council of Troubles to put the rebels to trial and he introduced new, very unpopular taxes.[60] These measures made him the personification of all evil for Dutch people. Furthermore, during his 1572 campaign Mechelen was plundered, Zutphen's inhabitants were stabbed, hanged or drowned in the river IJssel, and the town of Naarden was massacred. The following year, burghers of Haarlem were bound back-to-back and thrown into the Haarlemmermeer.[61] However, the most hated institution was the Inquisition, which was thought to be incredibly cruel and the numbers of whose victims grew to very great heights. Moreover, its torture practices and implementation of capital punishment were notorious.[62]

Officially the revolt is said to have started with the Battle of Heiligerlee on 23 May 1568, in which William's brother Adolph died.[63] However, the battle hardly had any direct consequences. William then successfully sought for allies in the Netherlands and among French Huguenots under the leadership of de Coligny. It was agreed to invade the territory from three sides: Orange from the German lands, the Huguenots from France and the Sea Beggars, patriotic pirates under the command of impoverished Dutch lower nobility, from the North Sea. In 1572 they captured the town of Den Briel, while William took Mechelen and held a campaign in Brabant.[64] At sea the Zeeland admiral Ewoud

---

59   Cf. *Aur.* 1297: "Ruptumque regi foedus" ("the treaty broken by the king").

60   On Fernando Álvarez de Toledo, the third Duke of Alba, see William S. Maltby, *Alba: A Biography of Fernando Alvarez de Toledo, Third Duke of Alba, 1507–1582* (Berkeley, etc.: University of California Press, 1983) and Henry Kamen, *The Duke of Alba* (New Haven, CT: Yale University Press, 2004).

61   For such cruelties, cf. *Aur.* 1298–1305; Alba is alluded to in *Aur.* 88, 710, 1121 and 1306. For that matter, the Dutch revolutionaries, esp. the 'Sea Beggars' were as cruel.

62   There was a 'Black Legend' about this Inquisition, which acts as a character in *Aur.* II, 1.

63   Mentioned in *Aur.* 1260, but see the comm. *ad loc.*

64   *Aur.* 1942 probably refers to this campaign.

Pietersz. Worst was successful,[65] and William's brother Louis occupied Bergen in Hainaut. However, the expected support from France failed to come after St Bartholomew's Day Massacre on 23 and 24 August 1572, when thousands of Huguenots, including de Coligny, were killed.[66] Thus, in the end William's plan failed and Alva made the aforementioned counter-attacks.[67] Some Dutch pro-Spanish enclaves, such as the Episcopal city of Utrecht and Amsterdam, supported the Spaniards.[68] Nevertheless, Alba's mission eventually was ineffective, partly because there were no more money shipments from Spain after Philip became engaged with the threat of the Turks.[69]

Yet the Revolt was not always a success. In 1573 the town of Leiden was in serious danger of being captured during a siege that lasted until its relief in October 1574,[70] during which doves transferred messages between the besieged led by Dousa and the Sea Beggars led by Admiral Boisot.[71] It was also a drawback for the Revolt that in the Battle of Mookerheyde (April 1574) William's brothers Louis and Henry died. By then the provinces of Holland and Zeeland, where no battles were fought, experienced an enormous economic and cultural growth. This growth increased because many Protestants from the southern provinces fled to the northern ones, particularly after the 'Spanish Fury' of 1576. That year Spanish soldiers plundered several cities after the payment of their salary stagnated. This was a result of Spain's tight financial situation, since it had to fight against both the Turks and the Netherlands. In this period the States of Holland and Zeeland handed over great powers to William of Orange. In the Pacification of Ghent of November 1576, in which the southern, Habsburg provinces allied with Holland and Zeeland, Prince William was acknowledged as 'Stadtholder' of these two provinces, which effectively made him their ruler. The Pacification was not acknowledged by Philip II, who sent Alexander Farnese, Duke of Parma, a hardliner, to the Netherlands to become Governor-General. This meant the division between the southern and the northern part in the Unions of Arras (south) and Utrecht (north), both concluded in 1579. William did not sign any of them, because he still strove for a union of north and south, with

---

65   See *Aur.* 1803 and comm.
66   William would marry Louise, Gaspard de Coligny's daughter, who had been married before with another Huguenot, Charles de Téligny, who also died on St Bartholomew's Day. References can be found in *Aur.* 1210; see also the comm. *ad* 1166–1222.
67   Cf. *Aur.* 1942 and the comm.
68   *Aur.* 1120–1122 and the comm.
69   Perhaps this is alluded to in *Aur.* 94, which says that the "ferarum victor" fears William of Orange.
70   Cf. *Aur.* 110–126 and the comm. *ad Aur.* 1805–1811.
71   *Aur.* 1805–1811.

some form of freedom of religion. However, he found no support in this aim and was forced to join the Union of Utrecht. In *Auriacus* the concept of *patria*, which was foremost one's own town, village or region, included the southern provinces, expressing Heinsius' hope that the States General and Maurice would liberate his native soil from the Habsburg repression.[72] For after the suppression of the revolt in the southern provinces by the Spanish, Protestant Flemish, such as Heinsius' parents, had to flee, going mainly to the Republic,[73] but also to other countries, for instance England, where the Heinsius family also settled for a short time, France and the West and East Indies.[74]

The Habsburgs reacted severely to the Revolt, by launching a military campaign led by the Duke of Parma in the southern provinces, which were now under the direct rule of the King of Spain and were reconquered and re-catholicized. Meanwhile in 1580 Philip II also reacted politically by banning William.[75] The prince reacted by publishing his *Apologia* (1581). This defence— but at the same time an attack on Philip—involved a religious problem: in the Bible, Romans 13, it is stated that one should obey the government. The pretence presented by William was that if a lord did not fulfil his obligations, the legitimate representative of the people might revolt against him, as was the reasoning of the so-called "monarchomachae".[76] In accordance with these ideas, the States General renounced Philip as sovereign of the Netherlands in the *Placcaet van Verlatinghe* (1581).[77] In *Auriacus*, Philip is presented as 'tyrannus', which positions Heinsius as a sympathiser of the monarchomachae.[78]

The provinces now had to find a new monarch, and found him in France. They offered the sovereignty of the Netherlands to the Duke of Anjou. However, as a Catholic Frenchman he did not enjoy broad support and when he failed to re-conquer the southern Netherlands, he returned to France and died

---

72   The first two chorus songs are spoken or sung by Flamish exiles, who stress that they long for their *patria*. Heinsius gives *patria* also a philosophical, stoic interpretation: the whole world is one's country, see *Aur.* 607–608.

73   See Briels, *Zuidnederlanders.*

74   Cf. *Aur.* 219–229.

75   Cf. *Aur.* 261–281, esp. *Aur.* 275 "fulmine".

76   The most important writing that expressed the ideas of these 'monarchomachae' was the *Vindiciae contra tyrannos*, see Geurts, *Opstand in pamfletten*, pp. 142–146, and A.C.J. de Vrankrijker, *De motiveering van onzen opstand: De theorieën van het verzet der Nederlandsche opstandelingen tegen Spanje in de jaren 1565–1581* (Utrecht: HES, 1979 [= Utrecht, s.n., 1933]) Doctoral thesis Amsterdam, 1933, pp. 133–163, esp. 144–163.

77   *Plakkaat van Verlatinge*, ed., trans. and ann. M.E.H.N. Mout (Groningen: Historische Uitgeverij, 2018²; 2006¹). For another vision, see Bettina Noak, *Politische Auffassungen im niederländischen Drama des 17. Jahrhundert* (Munster, etc.: Waxmann, 2002) Doctoral thesis Berlin.

78   See *Aur.* 71: "Tagi tyrannus"; 952: "odium tyranni"; 1084: "fraudes tyranni".

there in 1584. This was a blow for William's prestige, since it was he who had invited Anjou to the Netherlands. He left Antwerp, where he stayed, in 1583 for Middelburg and then Delft, which had been his residence since 1572; this was a sign of the crumbling of his ideal of a general union. The States intended to endow him with the dignity of Count of Holland on 12 July 1584, which would make him the sovereign of these provinces, but William was assassinated two days earlier.

3.2 *The Assassination*

By then, William of Orange had already survived several murder attacks. The best known is that by Jean de Jaureguy (18 March 1582). His third wife Charlotte de Bourbon took care of the wounded William, but died herself from exhaustion.[79] On 12 April 1583 William married Louise de Coligny, daughter of the Huguenot leader Gaspard de Coligny and widow of Charles de Téligny, who both had died in the St Bartholomew's Day massacre. In 1582, the Frenchman Balthasar Gérards from Vuillefans (Franche-Comté) decided to follow up Philip's ban and kill Prince William.[80] That year he left for the Netherlands. Halfway he heard that William would already have died by the hand of Jean de Jaureguy, so he stayed in Luxemburg, but after he learned that his target was still alive, he pushed on. His plan was to go to the Prince, in the guise of a fleeing Huguenot to gain access to him and win his trust, and then kill him. Beforehand he had received absolution from a Jesuit priest and permission from Parma. In May 1584 he arrived in Delft, where he managed to speak to the court preacher Loyseleur de Villiers, to whom he told his 'Guyon story':

> That his name was François Guyon, that he was born in Besançon, and always had been a loyal servant of the Prince, since he was Viscount of Besançon and the most powerful Lord of Franche-Comté; that he had always wished to serve William, but especially since the death of his father, who was born in Lyon, but married in Besançon; there, after the assault on the Lord of Beaujeu, a Protestant nobleman in the Duchy of Burgundy, committed in Besançon, his father had been imprisoned because of an evil suspicion, since he adhered to the Reformation, and was executed; that for that reason from then on he wished to leave the

79 On this attempt to kill William, see *Bref recueil de l'assassinat, commis en la personne du Très Illustre Prince, Monseigneur le Prince d'Orange, Conte de Nassau, Marquis de la Vere, etc par Iean Iauregui Espaignol* (Antwerp: Plantin, 1582).

80 See for this and the following *Een verhael vande moort*, Frederiks, *De moord van 1584*, pp. 57–82: "De confessie en verhooren", and pp. 26–41.

place, both because of the disgrace resulting from his father's death, and fundamentally because his conscience forced him to go to a place where the Protestant religion was practiced, (and) to serve the Prince, and that on account of that conviction he had left two years before with a good horse and weapons to serve here in this country.

Dat hy was ghenoemt Fransois Guion, ende gheboren tot Bezanson, ende dat hy altijdts hadde gheweest een goethertich dienaer vanden Prince, om dat hy was Burchgraue van Bezanson, ende de machtichtste Heere van Hooch-Bourgoigne, dat hy oock altijdts goede begheerte hadde ghehadt om hem dienst te doen, maer sonderlinghe zedert de doodt van sijnen vader, die tot Lions gheboren was, maer gehouwet tot Bezanson, waer dat nae den aenslach vanden Heere van Beaujeu, Edelman vander Religie van het Hertochdom van Bourgoigne, die ghedaen wert op de stadt van Bezanson, sijn voorseyde vader door quaet vermoeden ghevanghen hadde gheweest, midts dat hy vande Religie was, ende ter doot ghebrocht wordt, soo dat hy sedert den seluen tijdt, soo wel om de schande die hy hadde wt oorsake vande selue doot, als oock principalijck, om dat sijn conscientie hem dwonck te comen ter plaetse daer men de Religie oeffende, groote begheerte hadde hem van daer te vertrecken, om den Prince te dienen, ende dat hy tot dier meyninge ouer twee jaren van daer vertrocken was met een goet peert ende wapenen, om hier te lande in dienst te comen.[81]

De Villiers transferred the message to Prince William, who was sceptical. He had Gerards/Guyon sent on an envoy to France. But when on 10 June the Duke of Anjou died, Gerards was commissioned to bring the news to Delft.[82] At his arrival he got access to the Prince and could have killed him if he had had his weapons. He stayed in Delft until he could carry out his plan. He was sent to France again, but protested because 'he did not have fitting socks and shoes'. For that purpose he was given twelve crowns, but from that money he bought guns, gunpowder and bullets.

10 July 1584 was his D-day:

On 10 July he waited until the Prince of blessed memory came down to have lunch, and approaching the same Prince, he asked him for a passport, which he asked (as my Lady the Princess very well noticed) with

---

81   *Een verhael vande moort*, in: Frederiks, *De moord van 1584*, pp. 63–64. The murderer told this story in spring, see Motley, *Dutch Republic*, p. 889.

82   See *Aur.* 819: "maximae interpres rei".

a trembling voice and being afraid, so that the Lady asked my Lord the Prince who he was, and said that he had an evil appearance; the Prince answered that he wished him to leave, which would be arranged.

Op den thienden dach wachte hy dat den Prince, saligher gedachten, af quam om te gaen eten, ende commende by den seluen Prince, heeft hem een passepoort gheeyscht, d'welcke hy was eysschende (gelijck mijn Vrouwe de Princersse seer wel merckte) met een beuende stemme ende verbaest zijnde, in voegen dat de selfste Vrouwe mijnen Heere den Prince vraechde, wie dat hy was, ende dat hy een seer quaet ghelaet hadde, waer op dat den Prince antwoorde, dat hy sijn affscheydt begheerde, dwelck hem soude ghemaect worden.[83]

The murderer carried the two guns fastened to his belt, with his cloak flung over his right shoulder:[84]

Towards the end of lunch he was seen walking around near the stables that are behind the house, to the walls of the town, and standing at the door of the room where the Prince had eaten, and when he came out, he came to the Prince and pretending to ask his passport [the travel allowance he had asked for], shot him with a pistol. The Prince, feeling that he was hit, only said these words: *Lord God, have mercy upon my soul, I am severely hurt; Lord God, have mercy upon my soul and these poor people*; after having said these words, he began to stagger, but his knight held him, and eventually he was put on the stairs, where he did not speak anymore, only when my Lady the Countess of Schwarzburg, his sister, asked in High German, if he would not put his soul in the hands of Jesus Christ, he answered in the same language: 'Yes', and has never spoken again.

Teghen het eynde vander maeltijdt sach men hem wandelen ontrent de stallingen, die achter dat huys staen, streckende naer de wallen vander stadt, ende staende aen de deure vande sale daer den Prince gheten

---

83   *Een verhael vande moort*, in: Frederiks, *De moord van 1584*, pp. 67–68.

84   See 'De confessie en verhooren', in: Frederiks, *De moord van 1584*, p. 38: "Il s'est retourné à la court, ayant les deux pistoles chargées pendues a sa ceinture au coste sinistre, laissant son manteau pendre de son espaule droicte, affin que le[s] voyant au descouvert on n'eust supeçon qu'il avoit lesdictes pistoles au coste senestre desoubz son manteau" (He returned to the court, with two charged guns on his belly, on the left, while he had his cloak flinging from his right shoulder. In this way, people seeing them would not be suspicious that he would have them under his cloak). See also *Aur.* 1596–1599.

hadde, soo hy soude wtcomen, is hy by den Prince ghecomen, ende de maniere makende van zijn passepoort te eysschen, heeft hem met een sinckroer doorschoten. Den Prince ghevoelende dat hy ghetreft was, en seyde anders niet dan dese woorden: *Heere Godt weest mijn siele ghenadich, ick ben seer gequetst, Heere Godt weest mijn siele, ende dit arme volck ghenadich*: dese woorden ghesproken hebbende, soo begonst hy te suyselen, maer sijn schiltknecht heeft hem vast ghehouden, ende wert ten laetsten op de trappen neder gheset, waer dat hy niet meer en sprack, dan soo mijn Vrouwe de Grauinne van Swertzenborch sijn suster in Hoochduyts vraechde, Oft hy sijn siele niet en stelde inde handen Christi Jesu, soo antwoorde hy inde selue tale, Jae, ende en heeft noyt meer ghesproken.[85]

The Prince was taken care of by the (supreme) Equerry Jacques de Malderé. His body was laid on the table, but he could not be saved. In the meantime William's knights chased the murderer.[86]

Heinsius uses these elements for his drama, but adjusts them to his dramaturgy. Thus, he makes the murderer tell the 'Guyon story' on the day of the assault— probably to preserve the unity of time—, and elaborates on the murderer's hesitations and fear.[87] In *Auriacus*, too, the murderer asks for a passport.[88] Like Louise de Coligny in *Een verhael vande moort*, Loisa in *Auriacus* has suspicions about the man's appearance.[89] Heinsius also makes the Prince say his traditional famous last words, in Latin, and makes his sister appear.[90]

Yet, Heinsius does not entirely follow this official report. In contrast to the report, the murderer carries the guns under his cloak.[91] Also, he omits the question of William's sister whether he would commend his soul to Jesus and his answer. He simplifies the Guyon story.[92] For instance, he does not mention the

---

85 *Een verhael vande moort*, in: Frederiks, *De moord van 1584*, p. 68.

86 See *Aur.* 1738–1751. This Malderé (see on him Nanne Bosma, *Balthasar Gerards: Moordenaar en martelaar* (Amsterdam: Rodopi, 1983), p. 77, and L.J. van der Klooster, 'Drie gelijktijdige berichten over de moord op Prins Willem van Oranje', in: *Jaarboek Oranje-Nassau Museum* (The Hague, etc.: Vereniging Oranje-Nassau Museum, 1984), pp. 37–83, esp. pp. 43–44) may be the model for the 'praefectus' in *Aur.*, if this praefectus is thought of as an actual person.

87 *Aur.* 1720–1734.

88 *Aur.* 1731–1732.

89 *Aur.* 1591–1594.

90 *Aur.* 1737–1738 and 1864–1865, resp.

91 *Aur.* 1596–1599.

92 *Aur.* III, 1, and see also Heinsius, *Auriacus*, ed. Bloemendal.

report of the death of Anjou, since his failed leadership taken up on request of Orange would diminish William's heroism, and instead concentrates on the murder itself. A striking role is given to the baby of William and Louise de Coligny, Prince Frederick Henry, born in January 1584, who is carried and addressed by Louise (Loisa).[93]

After William's death, the leadership of the revolt was taken up by William's son Maurice, who at that time was studying at Leiden. The study of classical authors helped Maurice to reform warfare, which led to considerable victories. Around 1598, after ten successful years, Maurice gave the Republic its final shape; he was said to have 'closed the garden of Holland'. In that year Philip III, who was more moderate than his father and more prone to negotiating, entered the throne. During the following years, 1598–1601, the war stagnated. An expedition by Maurice was stopped near Oostende (1600). His successes in the past make his absence in *Auriacus* all the more striking. But perhaps Heinsius blamed him for giving up the southern provinces.

4   The Literary Context

4.1   *The Theoretical Model: Scaliger*

Modern criticism of renaissance drama mainly focused on rhetoric and the moral instruction that the playwrights with their work tried to offer, in embellished language and varied subject matter (*copia verborum* and *varietas rerum*).[94] Those playwrights were inspired by the ten plays written by or attributed to Seneca, and by the theoretical background given by Julius Caesar Scaliger in his *Poetices libri septem*, posthumously published in 1561.[95] His son, the Leiden professor Joseph Scaliger, propagated the work of his father. The *Poetica* was well-known and witnessed seven editions up to 1617.[96] Scaliger's

---

93   William's other sons, Maurice and Philip William (who lived in Spain as a hostage), are hardly or not mentioned in the tragedy. See also below, p. 31.

94   Mieke B. Smits-Veldt, *Samuel Coster ethicus-didacticus: Een onderzoek naar dramatische opzet en morele instructie van Ithys, Polyxena en Iphigenia* (Groningen: Wolters Noordhoff and Forsten, 1986), and *id., Het Nederlandse renaissance-toneel* (Utrecht: HES, 1991).

95   A modern edition in Julius Caesar Scaliger, *Poetices libri septem: Sieben Bücher über die Dichtkunst*, ed. and trans. Luc Deitz, Gregor Vogt-Spira and Manfred Fuhrmann (Stuttgart-Bad Canstadt: Frommann-Holzboog, 1994–2011) 5 vols.

96   Two editions were issued in 1561 ([Lyon]: Antoine Vincent, and Geneva: Jean Crespin) and editions were also published in 1581, 1586, 1594 (all three in Geneva with Pierre de Saint André), 1607 and 1617 (both with the Heidelberg printer Commelin). On the history of its printing, see Scaliger, *Poetica/Dichtkunst* 1, pp. xvi–xxxi.

definition of tragedy is alluded to in the beginning of the Letter of Dedication to the States,[97] where the nature and aim of tragedy is presented in opposition to Aristotle's definition of poetry as μίμησις (imitatio, representation), and consistent with Horatian terms:

> The aim of poetry is not representation, but to offer education in a pleasant form, which brings people's moral consciousness to right reason. This consciousness should bring people to a perfect way of life, which is called Bliss.

> [...] non est poetices finis imitatio, sed doctrina iucunda, qua mores animorum deducantur ad rectam rationem, ut ex iis consequatur homo perfectam actionem, qua nominatur Beatitudo.[98]

This instruction mainly focuses on emotions. Tragedy, according to Scaliger in his famous definition, represents gruesome events that happen(ed) to high-ranking characters, described in a lofty style.[99] The outcome may be unhappy, but that is not necessarily the case.[100] For Scaliger the outcome is connected

---

97   See *Aur.* 1–9 and the comm. In the letter of dedication to his edition of Hesiod (1603), Heinsius also used Scaligerian rather than Aristotelian formulations, see Meter, *The Literary Theories*, pp. 67–74. In his oration *De utilitate quae e lectione Tragoediarum percipitur* (between 1609 and 1612; in: Heinsius, *Orationes* (1642), pp. 376–386) he described the structure of a drama in Scaligerian terms, too, see Meter, *o.c.*, pp. 158–159. On the influence of Scaliger in Leiden, see Marijke Spies, 'Scaliger en Hollande', in: *Acta Scaligeriana: Actes du Colloque International organisé pour le cinquième centenaire de la naissance de Jules-César Scaliger (Agen, 14–16 septembre 1984)* (Société Académique d'Agen, 1986), Recueils des Travaux de La Société Académique d'Agen 3, 6, pp. 157–169, esp. 157–159.

98   Scal. *Poet.* VII, 2, pp. 347aC–D, in: Scaliger, *Poetica/Dichtkunst* 5, p. 494, ll. 9–12; cf. *ibid.* VII, 3, pp. 347bD–348aC, in: Scaliger, *Poetica/Dichtkunst* 5, pp. 498–501: "Vtrum poeta doceat mores an actiones", where the answer is that the poet comes to good actions through ethical instruction. Cf. also Hor. *Ars* 333–334: "Aut prodesse volunt aut delectare poetae | Aut simul et iucunda et idonea dicere vitae", and *ibid.* ll. 343–344: "Omne tulit punctum qui miscuit utile dulci | Lectorem delectando pariterque monendo."

99   Scal. *Poet.* VII, 3, p. 348aB, in: Scaliger, *Poetica/Dichtkunst* 5, p. 500, ll. 7–11: "Docet affectus poeta per actiones, ut bonos amplectamur atque imitemur ad agendum, malos aspernemur ob abstinendum. Quare erit actio quasi exemplar, aut instrumentum in fabula, affectus vero finis", and *Poet.* I, 6, p. 11bB–C, in: Scaliger, *Poetica/Dichtkunst* 1, p. 130, ll. 4–7: "In Tragoedia Reges, Principes, ex urbibus, arcibus, castris. Principia sedatoria, exitus horribiles. Oratio gravis, culta, a vulgi dictione aversa, tota facies anxia, metus, minae, exilia, mortes."

100   Scal. *Poet.* III, 97, p. 146aB–C, in: Scaliger, *Poetica/Dichtkunst* 3, p. 34, ll. 2–5: "Est autem eventus aut infelix, aut cum infortunio coniunctus. Malorum laetitia in lucrum, bonorum moeror in laetitiam, sed cum periculo aut damno exilii, iudicii, caedis, ultionis."

with poetic justice.[101] By placing the fall of heroes in a moral framework, the audience may draw the right conclusions with regard to right moral conduct on the basis of dealing appropriately with emotions. These lessons are supported by *sententiae*, or aphorisms, which are, "so to speak, the columns and pillars on which the dramatic structure rests", and they "offer an explicit formulation of the universal truths that are propagated through the entire action."[102]

For Scaliger the probability of the events is essential.[103] This also has consequences for the choices made with regard to time and place in drama, for a too quick change of place is not realistic. Thus he concludes that the duration of the action in a tragedy is usually 6 to 8 hours. Moreover, truth and probability are important to achieve the rhetorical aims of delighting and moving the audience in order to teach them.[104] Examples of tragic events are, according to Scaliger, "kings' commands, murders, instances of despair, hanging, banishment, orphanage and incest, fires, fights, blinding of eyes, weeping, wailing, complaints, funerals, eulogies and elegies."[105]

In his *Auriacus* Heinsius closely adheres to Scaliger's ideas about poetry, although he does not make this explicit. In the Letter of Dedication to the States he stresses the didactic aspect of tragedy, which has to bring the audience to "knowledge of correct behaviour in moral and political issues" ("moralis civilique scientia").[106] Furthermore, *Auriacus* contains many *sententiae*, although these may also have been inspired by Seneca's tragedies. There are gruesome events, including the murder of Orange itself, which evoke reactions

---

101   See Joel E. Spingarn, *A History of Literary Criticism in the Renaissance* (New York: Columbia Universy Press, 1954), pp. 51–52.

102   Scal. *Poet.* III, 96, p 145aD, in: Scaliger, *Poetica/Dichtkunst* 3, p. 28, ll. 14–15: "[Sententiae] sunt enim quasi columnae, aut pilae quaedam universae fabricae illius", cf. Smits-Veldt, *Samuel Coster*, p. 32 and n. 88, and, on *sententiae* and the exegesis of this passage, *ibid.*, pp. 56–58. The last quotation is (in translation) taken from Smits-Veldt, *Samuel Coster*, p. 32.

103   Scal. *Poet.* III, 96, p. 145bA, in: Scaliger, *Poetica/Dichtkunst* 3, p. 28, ll. 22–23: "Res autem ipsae ita deducendae disponendaeque sunt, vt quam proxime accedant ad veritatem". Cf. Robortello's statement that tragedy presents events "quae multum accedunt ad veritatem ipsam", quoted after Spingarn, *o.c.*, p. 95.

104   See Scal. *Poet.* III, 96, p. 148bA and C; Scaliger, *Poetica/Dichtkunst* 3, pp. 28, ll. 22–23, and 30, ll. 11–14, and for the probability demand, cf. Hor. *Ars* 338–340: "Ficta voluptatis causa sint proxima veris, | Ne quodcumque velit poscat sibi fabula credi | Neu pransae Lamiae vivum perum extrahat alvo."

105   Scal. *Poet.* III, 96, p. 144bC, in: Scaliger, *Poetica/Dichtkunst* 3, p. 24, ll. 17–21: "Res tragicae grandes, atroces, iussa Regum, caedes, desperationes, suspendia, exilia, orbitates, parricidia, incestus, incendia, pugnae, occaecationes, fletus, ululatus, conquestiones, funera, epitaphia, epicedia."

106   "Illustrissimis ...", ll. 11–12.

from the main characters: emotional ones from Loisa and stoic-calm ones from Auriacus. These reactions are put in words that express Stoic attitudes towards emotions. Also, the structure of *Auriacus* can be analyzed in the Scaligerian categories of *protasis* (the part indicating the subject), *epitasis* (the part with the complications) and *katastasis* (the part with an unexpected return of rest, possibly presenting deaths and exile).[107] William's death is an instance of "mors", which evokes a dirge ("epicedium") by Libertas, who then goes into exile, just like the Flemish immigrants went into exile.

4.2   *The Classical Model: Senecan Drama*

Traditionally, ten Latin tragedies are attributed to the first-century Roman philosopher Lucius Annaeus Seneca, which—with one exception, the *fabula praetexta Octavia*—are based on Greek mythology.[108] However, the authorship of some of these plays has been disputed and it has been assumed they have been written by two or even more authors. It is now also disputed if the plays were written for performance or as closet dramas.[109] In the early modern period, they were seen as plays for performance, and in fact were staged by pupils and students, also at Leiden University.[110] In any case, they are highly rhetorical in their manifold figures of speech and thought, and other embellishments. Early modern readers expected to learn Stoic lessons from them on the best way to deal with adverse circumstances and sought comfort "in publicis malis", as Justus Lipsius calls it in the title of his immensely popular *De constantia in publicis malis* (*On Constancy in Times of Public Evil*, 1583). Seneca's philosophical writings were well known through, for instance, the edition of Erasmus, as were his plays, which this humanist published in 1514.[111]

---

107   Scal. *Poet.* III, 96, pp. 146a–149a, in: Scaliger, *Poetica/Dichtkunst* 3, pp. 24–54.

108   Much has been written about these dramas. See, for instance, Regenbogen, 'Schmerz und Tod'; C.J. Herington, 'Senecan Tragedy', in: Niall Rudd (ed.), *Essays on Classical Literature: Selected from Arion* (Cambridge, etc.: Heffer/New York: Barnes and Noble, 1972), pp. 170–219 [= *Arion* 5 (1966), pp. 422–471]; Charles D.N. Costa, 'The Tragedies', in: *id.*, *Seneca* (London, etc.: Routledge and Kegan Paul, 1974), pp. 91–115; Asmuth, 'Die niederländische Literatur'; and Roland Mayer, 'Personata Stoa: Neostoicism and Senecan Tragedy', *Journal of the Warburg and Courtauld Institutes* 57 (1994), pp. 151–174. Heinsius himself made an edition in 1611, in which he included annotations by Joseph Scaliger, see Sellin, *Daniel Heinsius and Stuart England*, p. 234, Checklist no. 290.

109   See Dana Ferrin Sutton, *Seneca on the Stage* (Leiden: Brill, 1986) and Thomas D. Kohn, *The Dramaturgy of Senecan Tragedy* (Ann Arbor: University of Michigan Press, 2013).

110   See Asmuth, 'Die niederländische Literatur', esp. pp. 238–239, and H.J. Witkam, *De dagelijkse zaken van de Leidse Universiteit*, 10 vols (s.l.: s.n., 1969–1975), vol. 9, p. 71: Lipsius is given money for the costs of a performance of Seneca's *Medea*. See also above, p. 11.

111   See Asmuth, 'Die niederländische Literatur', pp. 238–240.

The tragedies are characterized by horror and awe, and gruesome events happening to lofty persons.

Seneca's tragedies have some formal characteristics in common. They can be divided into five acts, the first one often being the shortest.[112] In *Auriacus* the acts are divided into numbered scenes, indicating the exit or entrance of one or more characters. The metre of the action scenes is the iambic trimeter. The first four acts are concluded by a chorus, consisting of several, 'stichicly' (without variation in metre) used metres. There is hardly any dialogue between the chorus and other characters, and in their lyrical-descriptive or moralising songs the chorus does not always react directly to the action.

In the action scenes monologues and stichomythia stand out. The plays also contain *domina-nutrix* scenes and their variants: dialogues between an emotional main character and a soothing additional character. The emotions sometimes are aroused by dreams.[113] Stylistically, the dramas contain many *sententiae* providing moral statements. The monologues have rhetorical features, elaborating on one passion, state of mind, or motif. Hence, the characters become somewhat unhuman, being either entirely good, such as Hercules in *Hercules Oetaeus*, or entirely bad, like Medea in the eponymous tragedy. The plays were written from a Stoic perspective, giving models or anti-models for behaviour. They teach that, in contrast to their protagonists, in prosperity one should exert *temperantia*, in adversities *constantia*. The cruel events often are not part of the action, but told by a messenger. The atmosphere of horror is evoked by a Fury, for instance in *Thyestes*, or a ghost, as in *Agamemnon* and *Octavia*.

Most Senecan plays begin *mediis in rebus*, with a monologue that creates an atmosphere or is pathetic, rather than giving an exposé of the pre-history of the events. Frequently, the third act is the climax of the play, containing a crucial confrontation that shows the emotions of the main characters at their height. The structure is generally loose, the scenes being compartmentalized actions in themselves, without the one logically following from the other.

Auriacus is in most respects a Senecan tragedy: it has a five-act structure, in which the scenes are quite loosely connected, the choruses are pathetic, and

---

112   In the manuscripts there is no such a division, but it was readily made, the more so because of Horace's remark, *Ars* 189–190: "neve minor neu sit quinto productior actu | Fabula quae posci volt et spectata reponi." See also William Beare, *The Roman Stage: A Short History of Latin Drama in the Time of the Republic* (London: Methuen, 1964³), pp. 196–218. Already in early modern editions, for instance in the Basel 1529 (Henricus Petrus) edition, such a division was made.

113   Such as the dream of Andromacha in Sen. *Tro.* 438–460.

the first act is the shortest. The play also contains many *sententiae* (in print often indicated by commonplacing marks in the margin). The main characters are portrayed having only one emotion or state of mind: Auriacus having Stoic constancy, Loisa being in fearful sorrow, the murderer in despair. There is a Fury-like character, Inquisitio (II, 1 and IV, 1), there are *domina-nutrix* (IV, 2, and V, 1), and *domina-senex* scenes (II, 2), there is a (short) messenger speech (IV, 3). Act III (scene 2) contains a crucial dialogue between Auriacus and Loisa.

4.3   *The Practical Models or Anti-models: Neo-Latin Drama until 1600 and Rhetoricians' Drama*

In the Low Countries, as in other parts of Europe, Latin drama written by *rectores scholae* or teachers flourished.[114] Accordingly, in the Netherlands humanist drama started in the classroom. Initially the schoolmasters had classical plays—especially comedies by Plautus and Terence—performed by their pupils, but gradually they began writing their own plays, mostly in Terentian vein, but with a Christian content. In the Netherlands Guilielmus Gnapheus wrote a play on the Prodigal Son (Lk 15, 11–32), *Acolastus* (1529), as did Georgius Macropedius in his *Asotus* (1537). The same Macropedius wrote a play on the theme of *Everyman*, called *Hecastus* (1539).[115]

This type of play is characterized by its loose structure, the scenes being situational, which means that the time and place of each scene are set according to the situation and the information in one scene does not necessarily correspond to that in another. The plots are often simple, but the characterizations excellent and the humour apt. The pieces have speed and action, and in most cases a moral-didactic or religious-didactic goal. Often they contain choruses, probably in imitation of Seneca's dramas.[116]

---

114   See Jan Bloemendal, 'Neo-Latin Drama in the Low Countries', in: Bloemendal and Norland, *Neo-Latin Drama and Theatre*, pp. 293–364, and Fleurkens, 'Schooltoneel tijdens de renaissance' (n. 21).

115   On Macropedius, see Henk Giebels and Frans Slits, *Georgius Macropedius 1487–1558: Leven en werken van een Brabantse humanist* (Tilburg: Stichting Zuidelijk Historisch Contact, 2005); see also Raphael Dammer and Benedikt Jeßing, *Der Jedermann im 16. Jahrhundert: Die Hecastus-Dramen von Georgius Macropedius und Hans Sachs* (Berlin and New York: Walter de Gruyter, 2007) Quellen und Forschungen zur Literatur- und Kulturgeschichte, 42; Henk P.M. Puttiger, *Georgius Macropedius'* Asotus: *Een Neolatijns drama over de Verloren Zoon door Joris van Lanckvelt* (Nieuwkoop: De Graaf, 1988) Doctoral thesis Nijmegen, and Jan Bloemendal (ed.), *The Latin Playwright Georgius Macropedius (1487–1558) in European Contexts*, special issue of *European Medieval Drama* 13 (2009).

116   See Georgius Macropedius, *Bassarus*, ed. Rudolf C. Engelberts (Tilburg: H. Gianotten, 1968) Doctoral thesis Utrecht, p. 45.

With respect to the situational structure and the moral-didactic aims, this type of Neo-Latin play is similar to contemporary rhetoricians' dramas in the vernacular; both can be compared to morality plays.[117] Leiden humanists strongly opposed this often allegorical type of drama, that, moreover, was written by people who in their view (according to the contemporary stereotype) were incompetent due to alcoholism and a lack of talent.[118] They also objected to Neo-Latin school drama, which, they thought, had similar literary shortcomings. They did so by treating the same subjects in a tragic, 'better' way. Thus, Grotius wrote his *Adamus exul*, which had been the subject of a *fabula* by Macropedius (*Adamus*, 1552), and a Joseph play (*Sophompaneas*, 1535), which had been treated in comedies written by the Amsterdam rector Cornelius Crocus (*Ioseph*, 1535), Macropedius (*Iosephus*, 1544), and the Haarlem rector Cornelius Schonaeus (1592). In the same way, Heinsius dramatized the murder of William of Orange, which had been the inspiration for two dramas: Toussaint du Sel's *Nassovius* (*Nassau*, 1589) and Caspar Ens' *Auriacus, sive Libertas defensa* (*Orange, or Liberty Defended*, 1599).

The South Netherlandic poet Panagius Salius (Toussaint du Sel or Sailly) has remained rather unknown. He earned some fame with his *Vedastiados* (Douai, 1591), an epic on the first Bishop of Arras (Atrecht), Vaast. He published it after his return from Paris, where he had been a classics tutor in a home for bursal students. Perhaps he was inspired to write a tragedy after an encounter with George Buchanan. His *Nassovius: Tragoedia* (1589), counting 753 lines, is the first tragedy written on the assassination of William of Orange.[119] At the time of

---

117   On this drama, see, e.g., Willem M.H. Hummelen, *De sinnekens in het rederijkersdrama* (Groningen: Wolters, 1958) Doctoral thesis Groningen, esp. pp. 21–22 and 401–404; Bart Ramakers, 'Dutch Allegorical Theatre: Tradition and Conceptual Approach', in: Elsa Strietman and Peter Happé (eds), *Urban Theatre in the Low Countries, 1400–1625* (Turnhout: Brepols, 2006), pp. 127–147; on some of its functions, see Anne-Laure van Bruaene, '"A wonderfull tryumfe, for the wynnyng of a pryse": Guilds, Ritual, Theater, and the Urban Network in the Southern Low Countries, ca. 1450–1650', *Renaissance Quarterly* 59 (2006), pp. 374–405. On the rhetoricians as a social phenomenon, see Arjan van Dixhoorn, *Lustige geesten: Rederijkers in de Noordelijke Nederlanden (1480–1650)* (Amsterdam: Amsterdam University Press, 2009) Doctoral thesis Amsterdam, 2004.

118   See the comm. on the Letter of Dedication to the States, l. 135, below, pp. 298–299.

119   To be found in *Panagii Salii Audomarensis varia poemata* (Paris: [Denys du Pré/Dionysius] a Prato, 1589), dedicated to Parma. The edition made by B.A. Vermaseren in 'Een onbekend drama van katholieke zijde over de moord op Prins Willem I', *Bijdragen en mededelingen van het Historisch Genootschap (gevestigd te Utrecht)* 67 (1949), pp. 121–156, is unreliable. See also his 'Humanistische drama's over de moord op de vader des vaderlands', *Tijdschrift voor Nederlandse taal- en letterkunde* 68 (1951), pp. 31–67. On the pro-Spanish tenor of the play, see Duits, *Van Bartholomeusnacht tot Bataafse opstand*, pp. 95–96. Its title *Nassovius*

the publication, the Roman Catholic author was part of humanist circles in the Roman Catholic, pro-Spanish town of Arras, so he must have had the intention to support the Spanish-Habsburg cause and denigrate the rebellious leader of the revolt. The play was published in Paris as part of a collection of *Poemata*, so it is likely not to have been very well known in the northern Netherlands. Maybe Heinsius' patron Janus Dousa had a copy, since Salius devoted a poem to him. In any case, both dramas have hardly anything in common except for the five-act structure with choruses, William's wife telling of a dream, and the chorus reflecting on the vicissitudes of fortune, all typical characteristics of Senecan tragedy.[120] The differences are more striking: In Salius' drama one of the characters is Orange's general Hohenlo; according to the rhetoricians' tradition the murderer, who in the play is mentioned by name (Gerardus), deliberates with the allegorical character Ratio (Reason). Also the role of Loisa differs: in *Nassovius* she makes her husband fatally promise to stay at home, and her emotions are the cause of a spontaneous miscarriage.[121] But the most important difference is, of course, the judgement of Orange: a hero in *Auriacus*, a rebellious villain in *Nassovius*.[122]

Kaspar Ens or Caspar Casparius, conrector of the Latin school in Delft, reworked this local subject matter of Delft into a drama that was to be staged by his pupils: *Princeps Auriacus, sive Libertas defensa*, published also in Delft by the

---

     (*Nassau*) already is a depreciation of William of Orange, since as Count of Nassau he was just one of the German nobles, whereas the title Prince of Orange made him Philip II's equal in rank.

120   The following instances are the similarities I found between *Nassovius* (*Nas.*) and *Auriacus* (*Aur.*), which all can be traced back to their indebtedness to Seneca's drama: *Nas.* 333: "pavet animus" and *Aur.* 481–482: "pavet mens"; *Nas.* 346: "effare" and *Aur.* 489: "fare"; *Nas.* 435: "Numerus tuetur Principem, melius fides" and *Aur.* 571–574: "Firmo maritus urbium munimine, | Totoque clusus Nerei regno sedet, | Pelagoque cuncto tutius quod arbitror: | Amore populi"; the signs mentioned in *Nas.* 470 and the chorus in *Aur.* III, 3; in *Nas.* 482–489 and 490–497 is told that Calpurnia and Colignia (Louise de Coligny) dreamt about the death of their husband, Caesar and Orange, in *Aur.* 1545–1572 Loisa tells the nurse that in a dream she saw her husband die; *Nas.* 563 and *Aur.* 772; *Nas.* 708–717 and *Aur.* 1743–1750.

121   *Nass.* 450; 667–694 and 730–742. Cf. Lia van Gemert, '"Hoe dreef ick in myn sweet": De rol van Louise de Coligny in de Oranje-drama's', *De zeventiende eeuw* 10 (1994), pp, 169–180, esp. 171–172. There are more differences. In *Nas.* 510 the murderer is coming to Delft by ship; in *Nas.* 530–531 he is bringing a letter in which the death of Anjou is reported; both elements are lacking in *Aur.*

122   Even the titles show the difference in esteem: *Nassovius* refers to Nassau, qualifying William as one of the many counts in the German lands, subject to the emperor and the king; *Auriacus* to the principality of Orange, which made William a sovereign ruler, equal to the king of Spain (see also above, n. 119).

printer Bruno Schinckel in 1599.[123] This drama of 1090 lines is an educational play with the allegorical features of rhetoricians' dramas. The very choice of the characters and their names makes this clear: Alastor (Avenging Ghost, the devil) opens the play. The protagonist Princeps (the Prince of Orange) has as his antagonist Tyrannus (the tyrant Philip II), who is advised by Eubulus (Good Advice) and Ahitophel (an unreliable advisor), whereas Princeps is helped by Eusebius (Piety).[124] At the same time these names frame the play as a Christian piece of theatre.[125] Ens also puts the events in a Christian context in the Letter of Dedication to the Ministers of Holland and Zeeland, in which he emphasizes that, even though it will open up old wounds, the story of the murder should be told as a logical consequence of God's command to Israel to pass on to posterity the exodus from Egypt.[126] Thus, as he implies, the sorrows of the Prince's death and the blessings of God's mercy—the economic prosperity and the military successes of Maurice—should be passed on to posterity.[127]

---

123   Modern edition in Caspar Ens, *Princeps Auriacus (1599) (De prins van Oranje)*, ed. Jan Bloemendal and Jan W. Steenbeek (Voorthuizen: Florivallis, 1998); for a facsimile, see https://reader.digitale-sammlungen.de/resolve/display/bsb11103648.html (accessed October 2018). It was probably ready in 1598, witness the Letter of Dedication, dated 1 October 1598. See also Bloemendal and Norland, *Neo-Latin Drama and Theatre* (n. 21), p. 344, and Janning, *Der Chor im neulateinischen Drama* (n. 11), pp. 227–228.

124   It is obvious that Alastor should be equated with the devil from ll. 87–89, where he says that the woman has bruised his head, but he bruised her heel, cf. Gen. 3, 15; for Ahitophel, see 2 Sam. 15, 12 and 31, and 16, 15–23. The position of the good and bad counsellor is also a feature of rhetoricians' drama, see Marijke Spies, 'De "declamatio" bij de humanisten: Bijdrage tot de studie van de functies van de rhetorica in de renaissance', *Rhetorica* 8 (1990), pp. 91–93. The Tyrannus quotes in l. 393 Philip's motto "nec spe, nec metu".

125   Stachel, *Seneca und das deutsche Renaissancedrama*, p. 138, points at the religious and political impact Casparius wished to make.

126   "Quod enim populum Israeliticum Deus iussit ut quae in Aegypto contra Pharaonem per Mosen et Aronem praeclare et admirabiliter fecisset, liberis suis narrarent eorumque memoriam quam sanctissime conservatam ad omnem posteritatem propagarent, ad nos etiam pertinet, qui nec pauciora nec minora ab eo beneficia accepisse fatemur", Ens, *Princeps Auriacus*, ed. Bloemendal and Steenbeek (n. 123), p. 30.

127   The classis of Haarlem gave him a reward for this dedication, see Jacob A. Worp, *Geschiedenis van het drama en van het tooneel in Nederland* (Rotterdam: Langerveld, [1970] [= Groningen: Wolters, 1903–1907]), 1, p. 224, basing himself on G.D.J. Schotel, *Tilburgsche Avondstonden* (Amsterdam: J. Stemvers, 1850), p. 290. Stachel, *Seneca und das deutsche Renaissancedrama*, p. 138, demonstrates the reception of Marcus Antonius Muretus' *Iulius Caesar* (written in the 1540s; published in 1552): the formulations have a striking resemblance, cf. *Princ. Aur.* II, 1 ("Quid restat ergo quidve nostro nomine | Dignum exhibere mundus hic queat amplius?") and *Iul. Caes.* I ("Quid ergo restat quidve dignum Caesare | Subacta tellus exhibere amplius potest?"), which cannot be found in Seneca's tragedies. On pp. 138–140 he discusses the Seneca reception in *Princ. Aur.*

The author of the play, the Prussian-born Ens, was working in the Nether-
lands from 1596 to 1599. In the German lands, he is known as a translator of
Spanish picaresque novels into Latin, especially *Lazarillo de Tormes* and Mateo
Alemán's *Guzmán de Alfarache*, and as a historian.[128]

The title and the elaboration of the topic suggest that Heinsius knew *Princeps Auriacus*, but he went his own way in implicit criticism of his predeces-
sor, even though there are similarities, such as the occurrence of a dream.
But whereas in *Auriacus* it is Loisa who dreams that her husband will die,
evoking a sinister atmosphere, in *Princeps Auriacus* the tyrant dreams that a
tree is eradicated by two lions, which is explained as Holland and Zeeland
overcoming him. From the hole a twig is rising, which will become a tree,
an overt allusion to Maurice's motto "Tandem fit surculus arbor" (Eventually
a twig becomes a tree). This expresses the same idea as the subtitle, *Libertas
defensa* ('Liberty Defended'): Maurice will defend Dutch liberty, whereas Heinsius' outlook is more tragic: *Libertas saucia* ('Liberty Wounded'). And while
in *Auriacus* nothing is said about Philip William, William's son in Spain, he
is extensively addressed in *Princeps Auriacus*. Overall, Casparius wrote a pre-
dominantly rhetorician-like play in Latin, a Christian school drama; Heinsius a
Senecan, Stoic university tragedy.

4.4   An Epic Source of Inspiration: Benedicti's De rebus gestis Guilielmi (1586)

Georgius Benedicti Wertelo (or Joris Benedictusz. Wertelo), possibly a native
of Delft, wrote an epic about Orange two years after the assassination. He
attended the newly founded university of Leiden, where he began studying
the *artes* in 1577 before turning to theology. He met several outstanding figures
working at the university, such as Janus Dousa, Petrus Bertius and Justus Lip-

---

128   On Ens, see Wilhelm Kühlmann, 'Ens, Caspar', in: *id.* (ed.), *Killy Literaturlexikon: Autoren
       und Werke des deutschsprachigen Kulturraumes*, 2nd revised ed., vol. 3 (Berlin: Walter de
       Gruyter, 2008), pp. 285–286, and Walther Ludwig, 'Zwei spanische Romane, lateinisch
       bearbeitet von einem Deutschen, in Amsterdam gedruckt für einen Danziger Buchhänd-
       ler: das *Vitae humanae proscenium* von Caspar Ens (1652)—eine Menippeische Satire',
       Neulateinisches Jahrbuch 8 (2006), pp. 129–176. See on the play also Bloemendal and Nor-
       land, *Neo-Latin Drama and Theatre* (n. 21), pp. 344–345. A decade later, Ens also wrote
       a history of Prince Maurice: *Mauritiados libri VI, in quibus Belgica describitur, civilis belli
       caussae, illustrissimi ac fortissimi herois Mauritii Nassovii, etc. natales et victoriae explican-
       tur* (Cologne: Lutzenkirche, 1612), see https://gdz.sub.uni-goettingen.de/id/PPN805011103X
       (accessed October 2018). Before his *Princ. Aur.*, he had written about the Danish king Fred-
       erick II: *Rerum Danicarum Friderico II. inclitae memoriae, rerum potiente, terra marique
       gestarum Historiae* (Frankfurt a.M: Fischerus, 1593).

sius. He continued his theology studies at Cambridge. In 1586 he came back to Leiden, but moved on to study at Heidelberg. Dousa inspired him to write poetry, including *De rebus gestis Illustrissimi Principis Guilielmi, Comitis Nassovii etc.* (*The Military Operations of the Most Distinguished Prince William, Count of Nassau, etc.*), published by the Leiden printer Johannes Paetsius (Jan Paets) in 1586.[129] *De rebus gestis* is a Virgilian epic in two books respectively of 692 and 572 lines. It is written from an Orangist perspective, as would be expected from a member of the Leiden circles he moved in, but also from a Christian Providentialist viewpoint: God wants Orange to protect his country.

There are some striking similarities between *De rebus gestis* and *Auriacus*: in both works the Fury Alecto intervenes in the action and the allegory Inquisitio appears; in the epic the Fury Tisiphone is going to the Netherlands under the name Proscriptio (Ban) and incites the murderer when he hesitates, just as in Heinsius' tragedy. After Orange has died, it is Religio who takes his soul in a chariot to heaven, situating him near the constellation of Boötes.[130] His bier is placed there, while the Dutchmen are standing around it.[131] However, unlike *Auriacus*, the epic stresses the religious aspect of the war against the Habsburg empire, and also more than in the play *De rebus gestis* alludes to topical issues.

5   Summary and Structure

I, 1 (1–185): **Orange.** Auriacus (Orange) invokes Nature and night, and presents himself as the ideal person to save the country, since he controls his passions. Hence, he can take action against the Spanish tyranny in a sensible way. He portrays himself as a (Stoic) sage, who knows the transience of human life and the divine origin of the soul. He also positions himself in a line with classical expellers of tyrants, and compares the Spaniards with the Hydra, one of the monsters that Hercules had to defeat. Philip II resembles Eurystheus, the king who commissioned Hercules to accomplish the twelve canonical deeds. Fortune is like the goddess Juno, Hercules' evil stepmother. Thus, Heinsius makes Auriacus indirectly equate himself with Hercules.[132] He is not

---

129   A modern edition in Georgius Benedicti, *De Krijgsdaden van Willem van Oranje*, introd., trans. and ann. Coll. class. c.n. E.D.E.P.O.L. (Leiden: Dimensie, 1990).
130   Cf. *Aur.* 2034–2038.
131   Cf. the last scene (before the Maurice insert) of *Aur.*, where Libertas is bewailing Orange. For the allusion to Admiral Worst, see below, n.l. 1803.
132   For Hercules as a 'Stoic hero', see, e.g., Sen. *Ben.* IV, 8, where his suicide on the pyre is a sym-

meeting danger for his own sake, but because his country called him. To bring his country peace, he waged war.

I, 2 (186–242): **Chorus of old Flemish exiles**. A chorus of exiles from Flanders say farewell to their country in lyrical and dramatic phrases. Harsh fate drove these old men from their lovely countryside life. They expect that their children and even unborn foetuses will be exiles. All people, old and young, have to leave without knowing where to go: Walcheren, Holland, England, France or India, each country having its own problems. In old days, peace reigned in Flanders and people saw their grandchildren grow up safely, but now the situation has changed.

II, 1 (243–414): **Inquisition with three Furies**. Drunk with human blood, Inquisitio says that the Spaniards have summoned her from the underworld and added her as a fourth to the three Furies. The Pope has brought her out of her dwelling with his bolts of lightning, made by Romans who are not as martial as in former times. But the Batavians resist her power and with their ships they defy storm and rain. Therefore, Inquisitio is sent to them to convert them. She invokes Bacchus, saying that the best wines are not good enough to quench her thirst; only blood will satisfy her. She summons the Spaniards and her sisters to make haste with massacres. Also she urges the stars and the moon to find someone who will be able to frighten the Dutch. She herself will march on with evil powers, including Rage, Envy, Cruelty and Deceit.

II, 2 (415–610): **Louise and old man**. Loisa invokes Day and addresses her baby son (i.e. Frederick Henry): as a baby he does not yet need to worry about the blows of fate, but soon he will have to face the dangers connected to power. As a caring woman, she is very worried by a dream, the content of which she does not yet tell him. Then the old man tries to calm her, telling her that dreams are lies and mirror the worries of the day. As a reason for comfort he adds that the Prince is defended by a solid fortress: the water line (lands flooded as a defence line), and even a more solid one: the love of his people. Loisa opposes that the Prince is a foreigner. The old man replies that princes do not know any boundaries, since the whole earth is their fatherland, the entire heaven their home. Although Loisa knows all this, she remains afraid.

---

bol for Stoic *ekpyrosis* (the downfall of the world in a purifying fire, to rise again). See also Cornelia C. de Vogel, *Greek Philosophy: A Collection of Texts with Notes and Explanations, III: The Hellenistic-Roman Period* (Leiden: Brill, 1973), p. 55, no. 905b; pp. 57–58, no. 908b; p. 68, no. 924a, and E.L. Bassett, 'Hercules and the Hero of the Punica', in: L. Wallach (ed), *The Classical Tradition: Literary and Historical Studies in Honor of Harry Caplan* (Ithaka, etc.: Cornell University Press, 1966), pp. 258–263. On Orange as a Stoic hero, see Bloemendal, 'Hercules'.

II, 3 (611–737): **Chorus of Flemish exiles.** Now the Flemish exiles address the sweet west wind, which creates an idyllic atmosphere. Anxiously they wonder where they will end up. It hardly matters, if only in that country there are no Spaniards. That will be their new fatherland. The carefree night has been replaced with the worries of the day. Simplicity has left them and is dwelling far away. They praise the cricket, who does not know the Spaniards, for his carefree life. They themselves as humans have many worries, although fate afflicts simple people less than the great ones. They prefer to live in small houses, which will safeguard them from much misery.

III, 1 (738–1048): **Murderer and commander.** Now the murderer is in Delft, engaged in an inner conflict: he wishes to accomplish the crime, but does not really dare. A big woman, screeching and swinging a torch, whom he has seen in his dream, is his witness that he will execute his plan. The commander of the guard wonders why this stranger is wandering about so restlessly. The murderer feigns that it is only with much difficulty that he manages to tell what he experienced. After the commander's insistence he gives an account of the death of his father who was brought to the stake for the sake of freedom, faith, and hatred for the Spanish tyrant and the pope. The soldier advises him to take service with the prince and thus to avenge his father. The murderer would like to do this, even though he is weakened by grief for his father. Then he wishes to go to the Prince, who is just arriving.

III, 2 (1049–1340): **Orange and Louise.** Auriacus tries to calm his wife with the argument that in the past there had been a cause for fear, but not anymore, since the water is between him and Philip. This water stopped the king, which was however necessary, since the more a ruler gets, the more he wishes for. Then he asks to see the baby. Not comforted, Loisa expresses her fear: although the enemy is far away, she is afraid because of her experiences: on St Bartholomew's Day initially everything was quiet, yet she lost her father and her husband. Then she orders the baby to be brought. Auriacus addresses the baby and Loisa: if something would happen to him, the baby will have to avenge him. Loisa should tell him about the heroic deeds of his father, raise him for war and keep the fire alive that already is burning within him. Now it is time for lunch.

III, 3 (1341–1405): **Chorus of native Hollanders.** The chorus has seen the moon shrouded in clouds and asks if this would be an ill omen, but considers this kind of signs lies. For the moon is a source of life, since new life is created from her marriage to the sun in spring, while the birds whistle the wedding music; flowers, corn and grapes are the children from this marriage. Then the chorus again mentions the ominous signs, seeing a comet near the Little and Great Bears, a bad omen for tyrants, not for simple people.

IV, 1 (1406–1502): **Murderer, Inquisition and Furies.** In a monologue the murderer expresses his fear to carry out the deed and finally decides to perform the evil act. During his speech Alecto urges her sister Megaera—without the murderer noticing it—to incite him. Then Inquisition summons her sisters to collect all kinds of poison in order to motivate the murderer.

IV, 2 (1503–1595): **Louise and nurse.** Loisa expresses her fear to the nurse, by whom she is urged to moderate her emotions: Loisa is not allowed to move her husband by her tears. Then she finally tells her dream: she saw her husband full of blood dying in her arms. The nurse is not able to reassure her with the remark that dreams are lies. Loisa sees the murderer and asks the nurse who the unusual guest with the evil face is. Before the nurse can answer, Loisa continues that she has to go inside the house to do the housekeeping and take care of the baby.

IV, 3 (1596–1751): **Murderer, Orange, soldier and chorus of servants.** The murderer has hidden the pistol under his cloak and is already picturing how he will cause the prince a horrible death. At the prince's arrival he delivers a monologue about the impermanence of life: in nature everything changes into something else. In the midst of all these changes, man is the only one who realizes this. Even though there are many natural causes of death, he has added one, by guns and bullets. Whole cities are the victims of this. The killer now knows that the moment of the attack has come, but then he is afraid again. However, he encourages himself. He asks the prince for a passport, shoots and flees. The prince speaks his last words: "Great father, have mercy upon my people and me" (1737–1738), and dies. A choir of soldiers sets off in pursuit of the murderer.

IV, 4 (1752–1818): **Chorus of native Hollanders.** The chorus of native Hollanders breaks into a song of praise of their people who tamed the sea and the Spaniards. With their ships they fearlessly go to far-away shores, following the stars that tell how the Hollanders gain victories at sea, and which role the doves played in the siege of Leiden as a means of communication. Then they break off their praise because they hear cries in the town, which frightens them.

V, 1 (1819–1911): **Louise and nurse.** Loisa weeps before her nurse. Tyrants can feel safe, since Fortune has used all its powers on her. Again she is a widow. She wishes to go and see if her husband shows some sign of life. But the deep grief of her husband's sister (the Countess of Schwarzburg) makes her realize that there is no hope left. Her nurse advises her to control the first impulse of sorrow, time will heal the wound. Her words are in vain and Loisa faints. Then an unspecified chorus addresses her with reproaches: she is mourning, which in fact befits the chorus more, since she has lost a husband, which often happens, whereas the chorus have lost their ruler. Fortune simply pours out her powers on high-ranking people. Every time he sets, the god of the sun Phoebus blushes for every grief people cause each other.

v, 2 (1912–2105): **Liberty.** Wounded Libertas addresses the earth, sea and sky: they, too, should bewail the prince, since his death means a loss to the entire cosmos. She also addresses the citizens: the prince was invincible and his death confirms this, because a ruse was necessary to overcome him, as was the case with some heroes from the Trojan War. Agamemnon and Achilles endured battle, but were treacherously murdered in their own houses. She calls upon the whole nature to mourn the death of this hero. The Dutch must wear mourning clothes, and wrap the town in mourning garments during a procession in which the stars and planets also participate. She leaves her liberty cap and her hair with the corpse as tokens of mourning and will go to far-away places where only wild animals live, not people.

v, 3 (1–41): **Maurice.** Then Prince Maurice in a monologue says he cannot mourn his father because he must avenge him. He complains about his youth, because this means he cannot take revenge, but says he will do it later. He asks Liberty to stay and not despise his youth. He asks the souls of his father and ancestors the same question. His father must wait for him to attack the Spaniards by ship, overcome them and kill them to avenge his death.

The structure of the drama is quite loose: scenes from William of Orange's last day are only partly ordered chronologically, without following from each other. For instance, scene II, 2, the dialogue of Loisa and her nurse, does not logically result from Inquisitio's monologue. Each scene is a tableau in itself with an elaborate atmospheric description. This too situates the play in a primarily rhetorical-Senecan tradition.[133] Just as in Seneca's dramas, the play contains quite a few monologues and some scenes in which Loisa is in dialogue with confidents: an old man and her nurse. Such a *domina-nutrix* scene also regularly occurs in the tragedies of the Roman playwright. The play also has dream *récits*, already known from classical literature, one by Loisa, one by the murderer.[134]

---

133   This structure also fits in the loose composition of ancient Roman comedy and Latin school drama and rhetoricians' theatre. See on features of Seneca's tragedies, for instance, Eckard Lefèvre, *Der Einfluss Senecas auf das europäische Drama* (Darmstadt: Wissenschaftliche Buchgesellschaft, 1978), pp. 41–66, and Smits-Veldt, *Samuel Coster*, pp. 64–69.

134   See Leendert Strengholt, 'Dromen in Vondels drama's', in: *Verslag van het zevende colloquium van docenten in de neerlandistiek aan buitenlandse universiteiten [...] 27–31 augustus 1979* (The Hague and Hasselt: Internationale Vereniging voor Neerlandistiek, 1980), pp. 25–40, and Wisse A.P. Smit, *Van Pascha tot Noah: Een verkenning van Vondels drama's naar con-*

The first act is loosely related to the plot and its function is mainly to invoke the atmosphere of a confident hero in imminent danger. The opening scene resembles that of Seneca's *Hercules Oetaeus*: in both scenes the protagonist portrays himself as a Stoic hero. The following chorus is also arousing emotions, since the Flemish old men are shown in their misery. In the second act the action is started by Inquisitio summoning her sisters to find someone who will kill the Prince, followed by a *domina-senex* dialogue, a scene which is typical of the second act in Seneca's drama.[135] The chorus with its glorification of idyllic Flanders is hardly connected to the rest of the act.

At the beginning of the third act someone has been found to kill the Prince. At first this future murderer is walking around hesitantly, next he is addressed by the commander to whom he tells his untrue 'Guyon story'. The second act, a dialogue between Auriacus and Loisa, shows his constancy, and thus the third act shows in a crucial confrontation the emotions or state of mind of the protagonist, just as in Seneca's drama.[136]

The first scene of act IV is divided into two, almost simultaneous situations: the murderer still wavering between the wish to accomplish his deed and fear, and Inquisitio urging her sisters to prepare a poisonous drink. In the next scene the two situations are, so to speak, connected in the story of Loisa's dream, in which she saw her husband die. Then the murder takes place,[137] followed by the reactions to it, just as in Seneca's *Hercules Oetaeus*: the chorus, at first unaware of the disaster, then reacting terrified, Loisa wailing before her nurse,

---

tinuïteit en ontwikkeling in hun grondmotief en structuur. Vol. I: Het Pascha—Leeuwendalers (Zwolle: Tjeenk Willink, 1956) Zwolse reeks van taal- en letterkundige studies 5 A, pp. 190–195. On these kinds of stock elements, see Richard Griffiths, *The Dramatic Technique of Antoine de Montchrestien: Rhetoric and Style in French Renaissance Tragedy* (Oxford: Clarendon Press, 1970), who dubbed them 'set pieces'. Griffiths also discerns a larger structure, a 'string' of set pieces, about which he is not quite clear. On the one hand he assumes that the set pieces are related only through the subject of the play and very loosely connected, on the other hand he states that they receive added value—what value remains implicit—by their position towards other set pieces and that a drama is a 'mammoth set piece' in which the separate parts are placed in balance, see *ibid.* pp. 35, 73 and 81.

135   Cf. Jo-Ann Shelton, *Seneca's Hercules Furens: Theme, Structure and Style* (Göttingen: Vandenhoeck und Ruprecht, 1978) Hypomnemata: Untersuchungen zur Antike und zu ihrem Nachleben, 50, pp. 17 and 23.

136   See, for instance, Annette M. Baertschi, 'Drama and Epic Narrative: The Test-Case of Messenger Speech in Seneca's *Agamemnon*', in: Ingo Gildenhard, Martin Revermann (eds), *Beyond the Fifth Century: Interactions with Greek Tragedy from the Fourth Century BCE to the Middle Ages* (Berlin: Walter de Gruyter, 2010), pp. 249–268, esp. p. 260.

137   For the catastrophe taking place immediately after the truth has been revealed, cf. Lefèvre, *Der Einfluss Senecas* (n. 133), p. 46.

who in vain tries to calm her, a lamentation of wounded Liberty, and, finally, Mauritius wishing to avenge his father.

In fact, there are two story lines in *Auriacus*: the first featuring Louise de Coligny and William of Orange, both reacting to the blows of fate; the second showing the search for and finding of a murderer, with the Inquisition and her sisters as a kind of mythological-allegorical figures. Both lines converge in the assassination itself, and in Liberty's lamentation.

6   Characters

The portrayal of the characters in *Auriacus* also conforms to that of the Senecan-Scaligerian tradition of early Renaissance drama. A playwright in this Senecan tradition is not concerned with giving a psychological portrayal of characters with developments, but with the representation of a character according to one passion.[138] His aim is showing interesting moral questions and the reactions of several 'types' to the vicissitudes of life.[139] In the representation of the characters, Heinsius in *Auriacus* fits in the theoretical model of Scaliger and his 'doctrina iucunda', especially with regard to the passions.[140]

The eponymous hero is Auriacus, a Latin name for Orange, referring to William, Count of Nassau, Prince of Orange (1533–1584). This protagonist is characterized as a wise prince, who embodies the main virtues of Stoic philosophy. This is made clear in the opening lines of the play, in which he invokes Nature as organizing principle of the world, causing changes of fortune and playing a game with people. The soul of such a prince sees heaven, which brings about a positive ambition, in his case the wish to save his country.[141] His virtue causes him to defy dangers, but mainly to control his emotions, in the way of Stoic ἀπαθεία. His Stoic virtue is the summary of four cardinal virtues, viz. practical wisdom (*prudentia*), courage (*fortitudo*), self-control (*temperantia*) and justice (*iustitia*).[142] In this attitude Auriacus resembles Hercules as portrayed in Seneca's *Hercules Oetaeus*. This is done implicitly by Auriacus himself, when

---

138   See, for instance, Smits-Veldt, *Samuel Coster*, pp. 43–46.

139   See Donald A. Stone, *French Humanist Tragedy: A Reassessment* (Manchester: Manchester University Press, 1974).

140   Scal. *Poet.* VII, 3, p. 348aB, in: Scaliger, *Poetica/Dichtkunst* 5, p. 500, ll. 7–9 (also quoted above, n. 99): "Docet affectus poeta per actiones, ut bonos amplectamur atque imitemur ad agendum, malos aspernemur ob abstinendum."

141   Cf. Sen. *Med.* 222–225: "Hoc reges habent | magnificum et ingens, nulla quod rapiat dies: | prodesse miseris, supplices fido lare | protegere."

142   See Francis H. Sandbach, *The Stoics* (London: Chatto and Windus, 1975), pp. 41–45.

he equates the Spaniards with the Hydra, and Fortuna with Juno,[143] and by Libertas who also refers to 'the grandson of Alcaeus', i.e. Hercules (ll. 2055–2057), and by pointing at the impact of the loss of the hero, which affects the whole world.[144] These references to Hercules are deliberately made, since the demigod was a Stoic hero *par excellence*.[145] Auriacus is portrayed in a literary-philosophical way, which detaches him to some extent from political topicality. The function of the character is to present Orange and his sons as the legitimate rulers of the Netherlands, and to show him as an *exemplum* of constancy.

His antagonist is Loisa, Louise de Coligny (1555–1620), the fourth wife of William of Orange and, as told, daughter of Gaspard de Coligny and widow to Charles de Téligny, who both died in the Paris St Bartholomew's Day massacre on the night of 23–24 August 1572. She is worried and full of grief, fearing the dangers of the court. In her—understandable and easy to sympathize with—grief she is the anti-model for dealing with passions, in contrast to her husband. One of the causes of her fear is a dream she had at the end of night, a circumstance that heightens its credibility, for in classical and early modern literature dreams seen at daybreak are considered more reliable.[146] Her behaviour resembles that of Andromacha in Seneca's *Troades*, when she sees the ghost of her deceased husband Hector, that of Hector's mother Hecuba in the same play, who is full of grief and sorrow, and that of Amphitryon's wife Alcmene and his daughter-in-law Megara, Hercules' wife, in Seneca's *Hercules Oetaeus* and *Hercules furens*.[147] The function of her character is to support the *iacturae demonstratio* of William of Orange.

The third main role is for the murderer, the *sicarius*. He is of course a wicked man, but wavering between the wish to fulfil his deed and fear. Although in

---

143 See above, p. 32.

144 Cf. Sen. *H.O.* 758–762.

145 See, for instance, Bassett, 'Hercules and the Hero of the *Punica*' (n. 132), pp. 259 and 270 (who even calls Hercules "the 'patron saint' of the Stoics"), and Gotthard Karl Galinsky, *The Herakles Theme: The Adaptations of the Hero in Literature from Homer to the Twentieth Century* (Oxford: Blackwell, 1972), pp. 167–184, ch. 8 ('Seneca's Herakles').

146 See Fokke Veenstra, 'Dromen zonder Freud', *Spektator* 4 (1974–1975), pp. 582–610, esp. pp. 590–591, and Leendert Strengholt, 'Dromen in Vondels drama's', in: *Verslag van het zevende colloquium van docenten in de neerlandistiek aan buitenlandse universiteiten* [...] *27–31 augustus 1979* (The Hague and Hasselt: Internationale Vereniging voor Neerlandistiek), pp. 25–40.

147 Grotius in his *Iambi* 74–76 made these comparisons as well. He also contrasted Loisa's role with those of Deianira, who caused Hercules' death, and Medea, Phaedra and Clytemnestra, who all killed relatives or had them killed (her children, Hippolytus and Agamemnon, resp.). Finally, he opposes Louisa to Juno, who maddened Hercules. In contrast, Loisa is a "sancta femina" (*Iambi* 77).

reality the man's name was well known, in *Auriacus* he remains anonymous, probably to emphasize the tragedy's more 'timeless' character. Just like Loisa's, the murderer's inner feelings are visible through outward signs, as the commander notices (ll. 800–806): he has a hesitating step and uncertain foot, he wanders aimlessly back and forth, he has an undefined, white colour, vibrating eyebrows and collapsed cheeks. The *sicarius* himself indicates that he is driven by divine powers—these will turn out to be Inquisitio and her sisters, the Furies—and by fate.[148] But it is also 'Spain' and specifically Philippus who inspired him, as well as 'Rome', i.e. the Pope and the Curia, the Roman Catholic Church. Inquisition and her sisters are in this view the accomplices of fate. Just like Loisa, he has seen a dream, and his description of that dream makes clear that he saw *Inquisitio* and her retinue. His fanaticism increases after he is handed the poison. The functions of this character are on the one hand to contrast Loisa, to bring forth the action, on the other hand to show that it is the King of Spain and the Roman Catholic Church that incited the murder of the Prince. He can be compared to villains in Seneca's drama: Thyestes who ate his own boys, slaughtered and roasted by Atreus, Theseus who caused the death of his son Hippolytus, and Oedipus, the murderer of his father, or the murderers Atreus, Aegisthus and Tantalus.[149]

Furthermore, there are supporting roles of the *senex*, the *nutrix*, the *praefectus* and an *armiger*. The *senex* (old man) speaks to Loisa in act II, scene 1. His main characteristic is his wisdom. He is so to speak her 'philosophy teacher'. Hence, his function is to show how to correctly deal with emotions, but he also gives Loisa the opportunity to express her feelings and illuminate her strong emotions. His role can be compared to that of the *senex* in Seneca's *Troades* (ll. 409–518), where he is in dialogue with Andromacha, who has seen the ghost of her husband Hector. However, this Senecan *senex* only has three lines, asking a question or giving very short advice. Heinsius seems to have amplified this role.[150] The *nutrix* (nurse, 'nanny') of *Loisa* is an old, wise woman who, as a confident, can listen to her lamentations and give her good advice. It is to her that Loisa tells her dream. The old woman also tries to console her. Such *domina-*

---

148 This may well be the Stoic fortune as ordering principle of nature, or providence, *Ratio*, God, see Sandbach, *The Stoics* (n. 142), pp. 79–82 ('Fate and Providence'), and Thomas G. Rosenmeyer, *Senecan Drama and Stoic Cosmology* (Berkeley, etc.: University of California Press, 1989), pp. 68–69. I do not assume, as Becker-Cantarino, *Daniel Heinsius*, p. 122, that the classical idea of fate is blended with Christian providence.

149 See also Grotius, *Iambi* 112–113.

150 See Smit-Veldt, *Samuel Coster*, p. 71. This *domina-senex* scene is identical to a *domina-nutrix* scene, which will be discussed in the next section. Cf. also Sen. *Oed.* 784–882, where a 'senex Corinthius' tells Oedipus of his descent.

nutrix scenes have become a fixed pattern in Seneca's tragedies and in early modern Senecan tragedy.[151] The nurse tries to calm the state of mind of her foster child and bring him or her to *temperantia*, fitting well in Stoic attitudes toward emotions. The *praefectus* is also a minor character in *Auriacus*, who is in dialogue with the murderer.[152] He, too, is well versed in Stoic philosophy and tries to calm the *sicarius*. After the villain has told his story of the 'unjust death' of his father, he advises him to join the Prince, which is an example of tragic irony. This is one of his functions; another is to give the murderer a chance to tell his stories. The character of a *praefectus* occurs in Senecan tragedy only once, in the Pseudo-Senecan history play *Octavia*. But in *Phaedra* and *Thyestes* a *satelles* occurs, in *dominus-satelles* scenes that are similar to a *domina-nutrix* scene.[153] This is also the case in *Auriacus* for the *sicarius-praefectus* dialogue, although the connection between both interlocutors is looser. In IV, 3 a soldier (*armiger*) occurs. Immediately after the assassination he urges his comrades to chase the murderer. The *chorus satellitum* does not hesitate for a moment to do so.

Furthermore, there are mute characters (κωφὰ πρόσωπα): servants around the prince, others who bring the baby prince Frederick Henry on stage, and an old woman carrying him. But the most striking mute character—not mentioned in the *Personae tragoediae*—is the young prince himself, who was born on 29 January 1584 and thus half a year old. The occurrence of the baby introduces pathos, with both Loisa and the audience. Another function of the baby is to bring hope.[154] Grotius in his *Iambi* compares Frederick Henry with Hector, Hyllus, Philisthenes and Poeas' son Pyrrhus. The comparison with Hector is especially interesting since he was valued highly in the early modern period.[155]

---

151 On the *domina-nutrix* scenes, see Konrad Heldmann, *Untersuchungen zu den Tragödien Senecas* (Wiesbaden: Steiner, 1974) Hermes: Zeitschrift für klassische Philologie: Einzelschriften, 31, pp. 108–149; see also Jan W.H. Konst, *Woedende wraakghierigheidt en vruchtelooze weeklachten: De hartstochten in de Nederlandse tragedie van de zeventiende eeuw* ([Assen: Van Gorkum], 1993) Doctoral thesis Utrecht, pp. 79–80, Smits-Veldt, *Samuel Coster*, pp. 66–67 and 295–296, and Fokke Veenstra in P.C. Hooft, *Baeto*, ed. F. Veenstra (Zwolle: Tjeenk Willink, 1954) Zwolse drukken en herdrukken, 11, pp. 53–55.

152 It is not likely that Heinsius had an actual person in mind, but if so, it would have concerned Jacques de Malderé, see above, p. 21 and n. 86.

153 See Heldmann, *o.c.*, p. 111, n. 300.

154 In fact, Maurice, born 14 November 1567, and sixteen years of age at the time of the murder, would have been a more likely candidate to bring hope, but Heinsius was convinced that he could not have him appear in the drama, see below, p. 44.

155 See L.M. Gilbert, 'What is new in Hooft's *Achilles en Polyxena*?', *Dutch Crossing* 36 (1988), pp. 3–38, and 37 (1989), pp. 3–52, esp. pp. 40–41. In one of the chorus songs in Hooft's *Achilles en Polyxena* she discerns an apotheosis of William of Orange in the character of Hector.

Loisa mentions William's sister Catharina, Countess of Schwarzburg, who is not mentioned in the list of *dramatis personae*.[156]

Next to these characters, four allegorical figures or noetic characters (τὰ νοητά) appear. Heinsius himself explains that they are: "affects that are presented on the stage in human clothing and decoration".[157] These are *Inquisitio* and her 'sisters' the Furies Alecto, Megaera and Tisiphone. Inquisition is vice incarnate, who leads her armies and makes the poison to incite the murderer to his evil act. With this representation of passions Heinsius imitates Seneca's tragedy, in which the characters' psychology can also be represented by supernatural forces.[158]

Heinsius does not mention *Libertas saucia* (wounded Liberty) as one of the noetic characters, but as an 'ordinary' one. Yet, one could imagine her as a personification, too. The function of her appearance is to show poetic justice, which at the same time is a kind of apotheosis: the Prince will be lamented by his people, but also be led into heaven, because he is a hero worth following. In this way, the tragedy is also a mirror for princes.

---

156   See also above, pp. 20 and 35, and below, p. 521.
157   Daniel Heinsius, *Epistola, qua Dissertationi D. Balsaci ad Heroden Infanticidam, respondetur*, ed. Marcus Zuerius Boxhornius (Leiden: Elzevier, 1636), p. 46: "Poetas, cum in Dramate inducunt Furias, non aliud repraesentare, quam Personas νοητάς, hoc est affectus, qui in Scena habitu humano et hoc apparatu exhibentur"; see also Leo, 'Herod and the Furies' (n. 11). See also Heinsius, *De tragoediae constitutione*, ch. 17, p. 238: "Quae quod a poetis, cum non sint, esse fingantur, νοηταί dicuntur" (Because they are conceived by poets to exist, whereas they do not, they are called 'invented'; cf. Daniel Heinsius, *On Plot in Tragedy*, trans. Sellin and McManmon, p. 134: "When these are introduced by poets, they are called noetic characters, since they do not exist except insofar as they occur in the mind").
158   See Shelton, *Seneca's Hercules Furens* (n. 135), p. 22, who concludes that Seneca's "use of a goddess in the opening scene is simply a technique which allows him to present to the audience processes not normally visible to humans, and to explore, therefore, the psychology of his characters." The three Furies also appear in other dramas, such as *Gorboduc* (1561), where a *tableau vivant* at the beginning of Act IV says: "First, the music of hautboys began to play, during which there came forth from under the stage, as though out of hell, three Furies, Alecto, Megaera and Tisiphone, clad in black garments sprinkled with blood and flames, their bodies girt with snakes, their heads spread with serpents instead of hair, the one bearing in her hand a snake, the other a whip, and the third a burning firebrand, each driving before them a king and a queen, which moved by Furies, unnaturally had slain their own children", see Thomas Sackville and Thomas Norton, *Gorboduc or Ferrex and Porrex*, ed. Irby B. Cauthen, Jr. (London: Edward Arnold, 1970), pp. 44–45, quoted after Nigel Smith, 'English Revenge Drama and the Arminian Crisis in the Dutch Republic: *The Revenger's Tragedy* and Theodoor Rodenburgh's *Wraeckgierigers treur-spel*', *Renaissance Studies* (forthcoming).

Auriacus contains six passages with choruses, consisting of specified groups: Flemish exiles in I, 2 and II, 3; indigenous Hollanders in III, 3 and IV, 4; servants (*chorus satellitum*) in IV, 3; and an unspecified one in V, 1.[159] All choruses sympathize with the Prince of Orange.

The chorus of Flemish exiles, who turn out to be elderly people, are shown in an emotional state: they will have to flee their beloved country for unknown, unattractive regions, in contrast to their peaceful homeland Flanders.[160] The chorus of indigenous Hollanders is also highly involved in the action and full of fear. At the end of Act IV, the chorus, still unaware of the awful event, sings the praise of the Dutch who have conquered the sea as well as the Spaniards, and are now heading for the Indies, since their own country became too small for them. After this passage of tragic irony the ode stops, because the members of the chorus hear a frightening noise. The *chorus satellitum* chases the murderer and they now are, just like the *armiger*, soldiers in the guard of William of Orange. The unspecified chorus in Act V tells Loisa not to mourn, since she has lost her husband, which is common, but their prince is gone, and therefore they rightly burst into lamentations. This chorus consists of William's subjects and therefore probably is the gathering of the previous choruses.[161]

Part of the choruses in *Auriacus* do not have a function as *dramatis personae*, in the sense that they continue the action—such as the Flemish and the Hollanders with their lyrical choral odes—, but part does, such as the chorus of servants and the unspecified chorus, as well as the last part of the choral ode in IV, 4 (ll. 1815–1818). They function to increase the pathos by relating the horrors of the Spanish tyranny, to comment on the action (the chorus lines just mentioned for instance), or to give (moral) instruction, such as the unspecified chorus who tells the audience how to deal with passions.[162]

---

159 See also Janning, *Der Chor im neulateinischen Drama* (n. 11), pp. 229–231.

160 Walcheren and Holland, which are at war (ll. 219–220), England that is far from the world (ll. 225–226), the sun-burnt Indies (l. 227), and France that is afflicted by civil war (ll. 228–229).

161 The indication of this chorus in the 1602 print ("CHOR.") can be an abbreviation of Chorus or Chori, but Heinsius may not have cared about the composition of the chorus, see E.M.P. van Gemert, *Tussen de bedrijven door? De functie van de rei in Nederlandstalig toneel 1556–1625* (Deventer: Sub Rosa, 1990) Deventer Studiën, 11, Doctoral thesis Utrecht, p. 64, on the small value that some authors attached to the exact identity of the chorus; on the often occurring lack of specification of the chorus in Neo-Latin drama, see Janning, *Der Chor im neulateinischen Drama* (n. 11), p. 45.

162 On these functions, see also Janning, *Der Chor im neulateinischen Drama* (n. 11), p. 45. The pathetic function is in line with Scaliger's description in *Poet.* III, 96, p. 146bC, in Scaliger, *Poetica/Dichtkunst* 3, p. 36, l. 28–p. 38, l. 2: "Erat aurem multiplex officium chori. Interdum

It remains a question how many people constitute the choruses. In Dutch contemporary drama choruses consist of one or two persons,[163] whereas the Italian Jesuit Bernardino Stefonio in his letter on the staging of his tragedy *Crispus* in 1603 tells us that the choruses consisted of sixteen boys.[164] But the latter is a school drama, in which the author/director obviously wishes to engage a maximum of students. However, there are reports of Jesuit choruses numbered as many as fifty people, using the supposed size of Aeschylus' chorus before the *Eumenides* as their precedent. The choruses are discussed in Martin Delrio's *Syntagma tragoediae latinae* (1593), who mentions the number of sixteen for ancient tragedy.[165]

The function and position of the choruses in *Auriacus* are in line with the treatment of the chorus in Seneca's tragedies: they are fairly independent, but thematically involved in the action.[166]

As said above,[167] at the end of the play a quire is inserted, in which Mauritius (Prince Maurice of Orange, 1567–1625) is presented. Initially, Heinsius says in the 'Amico lectori', he did not wish to include him in the drama, since Maurice was not at Delft at the time of the murder, and he wished to adhere to the unities of time and place, referring both to literary composition and historical truth. Moreover, he continues, a baby evokes more pathos than an adolescent.[168] Perhaps more reasons can be adduced: Maurice as the son of William and Anna of Saxony does not fit the interdependence of the other characters; or Maurice's policy to give up the southern provinces in order to secure the northern ones, which would constitute the Republic. He had 'closed the garden of Holland', that is: protected (only) the northern provinces. But on the advice of friends—probably Scaliger and Grotius—Heinsius introduced him in the second instance as a *deus ex machina*, offering hope: Maurice will avenge his father and thus restore "wounded liberty". This may not have fitted in

consolatur, aliquando luget simul, reprehendit, praesagit, admiratur, iudicat, admonet, discit ut doceat, eligit, sperat, dubitat. Denique chori omninio est ἠθοποιία et πάθος."

163 See Van Gemert, *Tussen de bedrijven door?*, pp. 125–126.

164 Stefonio writes, August 1604 (quoted from Janning, *o.c.*, p. 48, n. 16): "Ma che diro dei Cori? Il suo numero era di sedici giovanetti ..." (But what should I say about the choruses? Their number were sixteen boys). However, generally Jesuits had far more skilled schoolboy-players available than others.

165 Martinus Antionius Delrius, *Syntagma tragoediae latinae in tres partes distinctum* (Antwerp: Plantin-Moretus, 1593), Ch. 7, 'De choris', pp. 14–17.

166 On the choruses in Seneca's plays and their reception in Neo-Latin drama, see Janning, *o.c.*, pp. 29–31, and on their reception in the early modern period, see Van Gemert, *Tussen de bedrijven door?* (n. 161), pp. 31–47.

167 See above, p. 10.

168 See above, p. 41.

Heinsius' concept of tragedy well, consistent with Julius Caesar Scaliger's idea of a tragedy having an "exitus infelix".

7   Style

With regard to style, too, Seneca was Heinsius' main model of inspiration. This was in line with the preference at Leiden University for a pathetic-rhetorical mannerist style.[169] In prose this found its expression in Asianism (or Neo-Atticism), a pointed style which prevailed with Leiden authors in the last quarter of the sixteenth and the beginning of the seventeenth centuries, especially with Justus Lipsius.[170] In drama Seneca was the standard. Heinsius also imitated his style, but he applied its stylistic features in a larger number and more intricately than the model.[171] Thus a complicated, sometimes even twisted style emerged, fitting with Heinsius' penchant for poetic fantasy.[172]

Seneca's style is characterized by many rhetorical means, aiming at a short, pointed phraseology, including *stichomythia*, in its strictest form a passage of words in which the opposing speakers are allotted one line every time they speak, in which they often repeat one word of the other person ('Stichworttechnik').[173] It also accumulates elements, such as words, sentences or thoughts, in a form of *amplificatio*.[174] This can also be seen in tricolons, elaborated com-

---

169   On this predilection, see Meter, *The Literary Theories*, p. 18.

170   See Eduard Norden, *Die Antike Kunstprosa vom VI. Jahrhundert v. Chr. bis in die Zeit der Renaissance* (Leipzig: Teubner, 1898), 2 vols, pp. 251–299; Morris W. Croll, 'Juste Lipse et le mouvement anticicéronien à la fin du XVIe et au début du XVIIe siècle', *Revue du seizième siècle* 2 (1914), pp. 200–242 (also in J. Max Patric and Robert O. Evens (eds), *Style, Rhetoric, and Rhythm: Essays by Morris W. Croll* (Princeton: Princeton University Press, 1966), pp. 7–43), and Gilbert Highet, *The Classical Tradition: Greek and Roman Influences on Western Literature* (New York: Oxford University Press, 1985 [= Oxford: Oxford University Press, 1949¹]), ch. 18 ('Baroque Prose').

171   On Seneca's style, see, e.g., Canter, *Rhetorical Elements*; Gustav A. Seeck, 'Seneca's Tragödien', in: Eckard Lefèvre (ed.), *Das römische Drama* (Darmstadt: Wissenschaftliche Buchgesellschaft, 1978), pp. 378–426, esp. pp. 393–402 ('Der neue Stil'); Elaine Fantham, *Seneca's Troades: A Literary Introduction with Text, Translation, and Commentary* (Princeton: Princeton University Press, 1982), pp. 24–35, and Rosenmeyer, *Senecan Drama and Stoic Cosmology*, for instance pp. 43–47.

172   See Meter, *The Literary Theories*, p. 20.

173   This term is coined by Bernd Seidensticker, *Die Gesprächsverdichtung in den Tragödien Senecas* (Heidelberg: Carl Winter, 1969), pp. 25–26. If the speakers get only part of a line, it is called 'antilabe'.

174   On these 'Häufungen', see Karl O. Conrady, *Lateinische Dichtungstradition und deutsche Lyrik des 17. Jahrhunderts* (Bonn: Bouvier, 1962) Bonner Arbeiten zur deutschen Litera-

parisons,[175] and hyperboles. A similar effect of pathos and *varietas* is aimed at in Seneca's use of stylistic figures, *sententiae* and the exploitation of the horrific. Another feature of his style is display of learning. In these matters, Seneca stands in the tradition of Ovid, with whom he plays a game of *aemulatio*. All these features—that are to be expected in a tragedy that is usually written in a lofty style—can also be found in Heinsius' tragedy, but to such an extent that it seems to aim at *obscuritas*.[176] Heinsius employs many *hyperbata*, inversions, *apostrophes*, metaphors, antitheses, and similar figures of thought, and of expression and display of learning.[177]

In this case, we have two sources in which Heinsius himself explicitly and implicitly evaluates his own style. In chapter 16 of *De tragoediae constitutione* he criticizes stylistic aspects of *Auriacus*: Now he would not call sleep the 'mimic of the day' or 'frisky actor'.[178] But his criticism also concerns other *iuncturae*:

> ... and similar things that, not through our own fault but that of the age, escaped us in the tragedy approved by many during our youth (although I snip at my own vineyard) or at least young manhood. Although things of this sort are universally pleasant and delightful, they are not universally fitting. But just as to hit on good and lucky metaphors is, as was very well said by the Philosopher, a sign of a luckily gifted, not an ordinary, nature, so properly to judge of the metaphors that are peculiar to this sort of expression does not fall to the lot of everyone. In the past, I used to have a passion, and that an immoderate one, for many of Aeschylus' metaphors, some of which I would now avoid in embarrassment and shame.[179]

---

tur, 4 (esp. pp. 128–156 and 215–220), and Heinrich Lausberg, *Handbuch der literarischen Rhetorik: Eine Grundlegung der Literaturwissenschaft* (Munich: Hueber, 1960¹), §§ 665–687.

175   See, e.g., the comparison with a lion, ll. 1012–1041.

176   On *obscuritas*, see Norden, *Die antike Kunstprosa* (n. 170), pp. 251–299; Riet Schenkeveld-van der Dussen, *Duistere luister: Aspecten van obscuritas* (Utrecht: Rijksuniversiteit Utrecht, 1988).

177   For a detailed analysis of Heinsius' style in four passages, see Heinsius, *Auriacus*, ed. Bloemendal, pp. 136–146. For figures of thought and of expression, see Lausberg, *o.c.*, §§ 755–910 and 604–754, resp.

178   Heinsius, *Trag. const.*, pp. 216–217: "Neque somnum, *mimum diei*, aut *ludibundum histrionem*; neque Iberum *universi candidatum*, vel Neptunum *continentis helluonem*"; *Aur.* 544, 1103 and 1648.

179   See Daniel Heinsius, *On Plot in Tragedy*, trans. Sellin and McManmon, p. 121; Heinsius, *Trag. const.*, pp. 216–217: "Et similia, quae olim adolescentibus nobis (ut vineta caedam meam)

The reference to Aeschylus is remarkable, since the tragedies of this ancient Greek playwright were not yet well known around 1600, but Heinsius probably by then only had a general acquaintance of his work, although he and Hugo Grotius were interested in Greek tragedy and *Tragoediae selectae* of the three Attic playwrights had been published in Paris, 1567.[180] Perhaps his knowledge was as superficial as Thomas Legge's who may have been inspired for his Cambridge trilogy *Ricardus Tertius* by the structure of Aeschylus' *Oresteia*. Heinsius also admired Lucan and his epic.[181]

The annotations Heinsius wrote in his own copy, mainly concern style too. In the first two acts there are many of them, but then they become scarcer. Often they concern the purity of imagery. Therefore, the author changed "in se fluentes" into "in se euntes" (l. 3), or "eduxit pedem" (said of a hand!) into "stravit viam" (l. 65). In ll. 69–73 William of Orange addresses his own heart: will Philip without punishment "collum premat", but since one cannot 'press the neck' of the heart, it becomes: "nobisne semper" (will he suppress us every time without being punished?).

8   Metres

The metres used in *Auriacus* are found in Seneca's tragedies, too.[182] The metre mostly used for the action is—as in Seneca's tragedies—the iambic trimeter, in which fewer substitutions are possible (only in the first foot of a measure (v-v-)); some parts are written in trochees, which indicates a heightening of pathos.

---

in tragoedia tantopere tum eruditis probata, exciderunt, vitio non nostro, sed aetatis iudicio. Quia cum ubique delectent, non ubique decent. Sicut autem recte transferre felicis indicium est naturae, ut praeclare a philosopho est dictum, ita quae translationes, cui sint peculiares elocutioni, recte intelligere, non est cuiusvis. Multas Aeschyli impotenter tum amabam; quasdam verecunde ac pudenter nunc praeteream." For the Philosopher, cf. Arist. *Poet.* 1459a6. See also Meter, *The Literary Theories*, pp. 259 and 264.

180   On Aeschylus in the Renaissance, see Monique Mund-Dopchie, *La survie d'Eschyle à la Renaissance: Éditions, traductions, commentaires et imitations* (Leuven: Peeters, 1984).

181   See Meter, *The Literary Theories*, pp. 71.

182   On metres, see Hans Drexler, *Einführung in die römische Metrik* (Darmstadt: Wissenschaftliche Buchgesellschaft, 1978 [= 1967]) and Friedrich Crusius and Hans Rubenbauer, *Römische Metrik: Eine Einführung* (Munich: Max Huebner, 1967⁸ [= 1929]).

8.1   *Conspectus metrorum*

Act I
Scene 1   1–185   iambic trimeters
Chorus   186–190   sapphic hendecasyllables
           191–192   glyconaeans
           193–241   anapaestic dimeters
           242   anapaestic monometer or adonius

Act II
Scene 1   243–276   iambic trimeters
           277–386   trochaeic catalectic tetrameters
           387–414   iambic trimeters
Scene 2   415–610   iambic trimeters
Chorus   611–737   anapaestic dimeters (and monometers in ll. 667,
                           706 and 725)

Act III
Scene 1   738–1048   iambic trimeters
Scene 2   1049–1340   iambic trimeters
Chorus   1341–1363   choriambs
           1364–1372   iambic catalectic dimeters
           1373–1384   dactylic tetrameters
           1385–1392   dactylic pentameters
           1393–1399   dactylic hexameters
           1400–1404   hendecasyllables
           1405   anapaestic monometer or adonius

Act IV
Scene 1   1406–1472   iambic trimeters
           1473–1502   trochaeic catalectic tetrameters
Scene 2   1503–1521   anapaestic dimeters (and monometers in ll. 1516
                           and 1521)
           1522–1544   iambic trimeters
           1545–1575   anapaestic dimeters
           1–25   anapaestic dimeters (and monometers in ll. *4, 6, 17,
                           18, 20, 22* and *24*)
           1576–1590   iambic trimeters
           1591–1595   anapaestic tetrameters

Scene 3	1596–1738	iambic trimeters
	1739–1742	trochaeic catalectic tetrameters
	1743–1751	iambic trimeters
Chorus	1742–1814	hendecasyllables (and adonians in ll. 1755, 1768, 1773,1780, 1786, 1791, 1797, 1811, 1814)
	1815–1818	iambic trimeters

Act v		
Scene 1	1819–1888	iambic trimeters
	1889	extrametrical exclamation
	1890–1899	anapaestic dimeters (and monometers in ll. 1896 and 1898)
	1900–1911	iambic trimeters
Scene 2	1912–2105	iambic trimeters (and extrametrical exclamations in ll. 1927, 1936, 1962, 1967, 1978, 1988, 1997, 2015, 2024, 2033, 2051, 2067, 2082, 2089 and 2105)
Scene 3	1–41	iambic trimeters

9   Reception of *Auriacus*

Heinsius' first tragedy was highly praised in his own times and the play itself was reworked in Latin and in Dutch. Moreover, its merits were seen abroad, and it enjoyed a favourable reception in the German lands and France. This happened in spite of Heinsius' own evaluation, who considered it a juvenile work, which he did not include in his *Poemata*. Neither had he reissued it.

The first tokens of praise can be found in the preliminary texts to *Auriacus* itself. Topical as they may be, the laudatory poets praise the play and its author highly for their literary qualities and for the choice of subject. The Leiden Professor of Greek Bonaventura Vulcanius and the founder of the university Janus Dousa praise Heinsius' talent with which he competes with the ancient playwrights.[183] Vulcanius, Janus Gruterus, Dousa and the independent scholar Petrus Scriverius[184] are surprised that he was able to write such a tragedy at such a young age, and according to his companion Hugo Grotius,

---

183   See pp. 92–99.

184   On him, see Michiel Roscam Abbing and Pierre Tuynman, *Petrus Scriverius Harlemensis (1576–1660): A Key to the Correspondence, Contacts and Works of an Independent Humanist* (Leiden: Foleor, 2018).

he surpasses the four Greek tragic authors Aeschylus, Sophocles, Euripides and Lycophron.[185] The Professor of Hebrew Coddaeus calls Heinsius—quite complimentarily—Seneca's equal.[186] He even surpasses Seneca: "Cordoba was defeated in Ghent".[187] He does so in the ancient playwright's grand style, and by his choice of the elevated subject, fitting to an elevated genre. Orange is a better subject for a tragedy than mythology, since it is history, truth, and not fiction, a lie.[188] Heinsius' tragedy will give Orange eternal fame and so to speak eternal life.[189] And vice versa will Orange's fame illuminate Heinsius.[190] Heinsius' tragedy is compared to—and surpasses—Marcus Antonius Muret's *Iulius Caesar* (1554), George Buchanan's *Iephthes* (1554) and *Baptistes* (1576), Hannardus Gamerius' (Van Gameren's) anti-Catholic tragedy *Pornius* (1566), and Caspar Casparius' (Kaspar Ens') *Princeps Auriacus* (1599).[191]

Another token of the Dutch reception of *Auriacus* is the sum of 200 florins that the States of Holland and West Friesland gave Heinsius as a reward or as compensation for the costs—and because they were pleased with the choice of the subject—, probably on the instigation of Janus Dousa.[192] When he asked the Grand Pensionary (raadspensionaris) Johan van Oldenbarnevelt for a recommendation of the play, this reward may have been implied.[193]

In the Low Countries, the play was also imitated. The politician and Neo-Latin author Rochus Honerdus seems to have written another Latin tragedy *Auriacus*, that remained unpublished and has been lost.[194] The *Maria Stu-*

---

185 Grotius, *Iambi* 20–24.

186 Coddaeus, Πρὸς ... Δανιὲλ Εἴνσιον, Ἐπίγραμμα 10, below, pp. 100–101.

187 Grotius, *Iambi* 53: "Victa Gandae Corduba."

188 See Dousa, *In eandem* 11–12 and 13–17, resp. (see Appendix I, [19]), and Scriverius, *Elegia* 25–33 (Preliminary texts, [13]).

189 See Scaliger, *In Auriacum Danielis Heinsii* 10, and Vulcanius, Εἰς τὸν Δανιέλος Εἴνσιου Αὐραϊκάρχην 13–14 (Preliminary texts, [4] and [6]).

190 Vulcanius, *ibid.* 7–12.

191 Dousa, *In eandem* 29–10; Grotius, *Iambi* 42–47; Scriverius, *Elegia* 53. On Gamerius, see, for instance, Judith Rice Henderson, 'Humanism and the Humanities: Erasmus's *Opus de conscribendis epistolis* in Sixteenth-Century Schools', in: Carol Poster and Linda C. Mitchell (eds), *Letter-writing Manuals and Instruction from Antiquity to the Present: Historical and Bibliographic Studies* (Columbia, SC: University of South Carolina Press, 2007), pp. 141–177, esp. pp. 165–166; *NNBW* 8, pp. 582–583 (J. Fruytier); *Biographie nationale de Belgique* [etc.] 7, 471–472; Bloemendal, 'The Low Countries', pp. 337–338.

192 On such 'honorary sums' for dedications, see above, p. 45 and below, pp. 292–293.

193 This undated letter could have been written in 1602 (if so, it concerned the publication of *Auriacus*) or in 1603 (in that case it may have had to do with Heinsius' appointment at Leiden University).

194 See Schotel, *Tilburgsche avondstonden* (n. 127), pp. 295–297. The existence of the tragedy is known from a poem by Heinsius: *In Rochi Honerdi ... Thamaram et Auriacum, Tragoedias,*

arta, published as *Maria Graeca* (Antwerp, 1623), by Heinsius' distant relative Jacobus Zevecotius heavily draws on *Auriacus*.[195] The opening lines are quite similar, even though the priest Zevecotius clearly Christianizes the tragedy:

> Rerum beate rector, et magni parens
> Natura mundi, Vitaque et Lex omnium
> In se fluentes quae trahis rerum vices
>> *Aur.* 1–3

Blessed ruler of the earth, creator of the great universe, Nature, Life and Law of everything, who cause the successive vicissitudes of fate and in an idle game play mockingly with the human race, divine majesty of the vast sky.

> Rerum beate Genitor et magni potens
> Dominator orbis, cuius aeternum tremit
> Natura Numen, quique decreto semel
> Tenore flectis labiles rerum vices
>> *Maria Stuarta/Maria Graeca* 1–4

Blessed Creator of the earth and mighty ruler of the world, for whose eternal divine power Nature quivers, and who steer the undulating vicissitudes of the world according to the path you once established.

Whereas in *Auriacus* it is Inquisitio (in II, 1) who encourages the murder of the protagonist, Orange, in *Maria Stuarta/Maria Graeca*, it is Haeresis (Heresy) who does so (also in II, 1) to kill Mary (Stuart, or the Byzantine princess), and whereas in *Auriacus* Libertas mourns the death of Orange and flees, in *Maria Stuarta/Maria Graeca* Fides does so after the death of Mary.

The officer in the army of Prince Maurice and Leiden rhetorician Jacob Duym reworked *Auriacus* into Dutch in his *Het Moordadich Stvck van Balthasar*

---

in: Heinsius, *Poemata auctiora* (Leiden: Franciscus Hegerus, 1640), pp. 111–112 [= *Poemata Latina et Graeca* (Amsterdam: Johannes Janssonius, 1649, pp. 100–101). On Honerdus, see *NNBW* 8, 817–819.

195   For a modern edition, see Jozef IJsewijn, 'Jacobus Zevecotius: Maria Stuarta/Maria Graeca, tragoedia: A Synoptic Edition of the Five Extant Versions', *Humanistica Lovaniensia* 22 (1973), pp. 256–319. On Zevecotius' drama, see now James A. Parente, Jr., 'Latin and the Transmission of the Vernacular: Multilingualism and Interculturality in the Tragedies of Jacob Zevecotius', *Renaissance Studies* (forthcoming).

Gerards, begaen aen den Doorluchtighen Prince van Oraegnien, 1584 (*The Murderous Deed of Balthasar Gerards, Committed to the Illustrious Prince of Orange, 1584*).[196] It explicitly professes itself as an imitation of *Auriacus*.[197] Duym Christianized the eponymous hero and changed Heinsius' tragedy of fate into a martyr play. These changes were partly due to the fact that in the quarrels around 1605 whether the war against Spain should be continued or peace should be negotiated, Duym sided with the 'war-side', which makes the choice for the subject of the murder of William of Orange as a martyr for freedom quite obvious. Moreover, he, like Heinsius, originated from the Southern Netherlands. After he had been imprisoned by the Spanish after the Fall of Antwerp, he settled as a poet and historian in Leiden, where he was one of the members of the Brabant chamber 'D'Oraigne Lelie'. It may come to no surprise that he dedicated the play to Frederick Henry. As a rhetorician Duym added the allegories *Bloed-dorst* (Blood-thirst), *Spaenschen Raed* (Spanish Council) and *Heymelijcken Haed* (Secret Hatred), and a prologue and epilogue, spoken by the *Dichtstelder* (Poet). He also divided the choruses, that of Flemish old men into people from Flanders and Brabant (subdivided into *Overicheyd* (Government), *Edel-lieden* (Noblemen) and *t'Ghemeyn Volck* (the Common People), and into *Coopman* (Merchant) and *t'Ghemeyn Volck*, respectively). The Hollanders are also divided into two groups: *Steden* (Cities) and *t'Ghemeyn Volk*.[198] He compressed the play from Heinsius' 2100 into 1350 lines.

Gijsbrecht van Hogendorp brought the subject back to Delft and to Amsterdam through his *Truer-spel Van de Moordt, begaen aen Wilhem by der Gratie*

---

196   It was first published in his *Ghedenck-boeck, het welck ons leert aen al het quaet en de grooten moetwil van de Spaignaerden en haren aenhanck ons aen-ghedaen te ghedencken* ... (Leiden: Haestens, 1606). The collection contained six history plays: (1) *Een Nassausche Perseus, verlosser van Andromede, oft de Nederlandsche maeght*; (2) *De nauwe Belegheringhe ende wonderbaerlijck ontset der Stad Leyden*; (3) *Het Moordadich Stvck*; (4) *De Belegheringhe ende het overgaen der Stad van Antwerpen*; (5) *De cloeck-moedighe daed van het innemen van 't Casteel ende Stad Breda*; and (6) *Een bewijs dat beter is eenen goeden Crijgh, dan eenen gheveynsden Peys*. A new edition was made by L.F.A. Serrarens and N.C.H. Wijngaards in Jacob Duym, *Het Moordadich Stvck van Balthasar Gerards, begaen aen den doorluchtighen prince van Oraignen, 1584. Vergeleken met Auriacus sive Libertas saucia (1602) van Daniel Heinsius* (Zutphen: Thieme, [1976]) Klassiek letterkundig pantheon 218. See also Appendix II, [9a].

197   'Tot den Lezer', Duym, *Het Moordadich Stvck*, ed. Serrarens and Wijngaards, p. 62: "Hier sal u goetwillighe Leser voor ghestelt worden het leelijck ende moordadich stuck van Balthasar Gerards begaen aen den persoon van den Prince van Oraingnen, het welck over sommighe jaeren is in den Latine ghesteld gheweest, by den Hoogh Vermaerden Professoor ende Poët Daniel Hensio, in sijnen Auriaco: Die het selfde seer fray ghevonden ende met veel schoone Poetische spreucken verciert heeft, ..." See also Appendix II, [9a].

198   These divisions have to do with Duym's political choice, making clear that the entire people, i.e. municipal governors, noblemen and commoners, were engaged in the war.

Gods, Prince van Oraengien, etc. (Tragedy of the Murder, Committed to William, by the Grace of God Prince of Orange, etc.; Amsterdam: Cornelis vander Plasse, 1617).[199] It was performed at Delft in 1616, where Van Hogendorp was a member of the local rhetoricians' chamber, and it saw a reprise on 24 September 1617 at the occasion of the opening of the Amsterdam rhetoricians' chamber 'De Nederduytsche Academie'.[200]

The first two acts of *Truer-spel* are entirely Van Hogendorp's own invention; acts III to V are adaptations of Heinsius' play. In this Dutch play Stoic-Christian convictions prevail, in contrast to the Stoic ideas that dominated *Auriacus*. Van Hogendorp extended the play to 2650 lines. Whereas Heinsius focused on Auriacus/Orange, Van Hogendorp concentrated on the murder itself and the reactions it aroused. On the other hand, he followed Heinsius in his rhetorical style and technique, whilst intensifying it.

Like Duym, Van Hogendorp was a soldier, in Maurice's guard. Unsurprisingly, he dedicates his tragedy to this son of Orange. He certainly knew Heinsius' tragedy, but also those of Duym and Casparius. Since the latter play was staged in Delft, where Van Hogendorp had joined the Chamber, he may well have read it.

Not only in drama but also in other poetry Heinsius' play was adapted. In his *Ethopoeia illustrissimae principis Louisae interfecto marito* (1609) the courtier and diplomat Constantijn Huygens represents Louise de Coligny's fierce emotions after her husband's death. The poem contains many allusions to *Auriacus* or quotations from it. This was certainly possible, since he owned a copy of the play.[201] Literature and reality here convened, since Huygens knew Louise personally and saw her on an almost daily basis.[202]

---

199 Modern edition by F. Kossmann in *De spelen van Gijsbrecht van Hogendorp* (The Hague: Nijhoff, 1932), pp. 45–175.

200 See F.C. van Boheemen and Th.C.J. van der Heijden, *De Delftse rederijkers 'Wy rapen gheneucht'* (Amsterdam: Huis aan de Drie Grachten, 1982), pp. 130–135, esp. 135; on pp. 133–134 van Boheemen and van der Heijden list the stage properties that the Delft chamber bought for the performance of van Hogendorp's tragedy; see also Mieke B. Smits-Veldt, 'De opening van de "Neerlandtsche Academia De Byekorf": Melpomene presenteert Gijsbrecht van Hogendorps *Orangien-tragedie*', *Spektator* 12 (1982–1983), pp. 199–214, esp. 199.

201 See [W.P. van Stockum (ed.)], *Catalogus der bibliotheek van Constantijn Huygens verkocht op de Groote Zaal van het Hof te 's-Gravenhage 1688* (The Hague: Van Stockum, 1903) [original title: *Catalogus variorum & insignium in omni facultate & lingua librorum, bibliothecae nob. amplissimique viri Constantini Hugenii* [...] (Hagae-Comitis: Troyel, 1688)], p. 27, no. 20, under the 'Libri miscellanei in quarto'. Here published in Appendix II, [8].

202 See Constantijn Huygens, *Mijn jeugd*, trans. Chris L. Heesakkers (Amsterdam: Querido, 1987), pp. 30–32, and cf. Van Gemert, *Tussen de bedrijven door?* (n. 161), p. 179, n. 13.

Besides through direct imitations and adaptations, *Auriacus* enjoyed an influential reception also in a more general way. The magistrate and playwright Pieter Cornelisz. Hooft greatly admired Heinsius. In a letter of 16 April 1610 he tried to obtain the Leiden professor's friendship and therefore sent him a laudatory poem in Dutch for a second edition that would possibly be issued.[203] In the same period, he highly praised Heinsius' *Auriacus* in his *Reden vande Waerdicheit der Poesie* (*Oration on the Dignity of Poetry*), which must be dated between 1610 and 1615. Why Hooft sought a relationship with Heinsius is unclear, but it was at a moment in his life that he had obtained some social status and when a relationship would in fact be established, this would be on the basis of some equivalence.[204] Of course he recognizes, in modesty, the distance between the famous poet-professor and the still unknown, ambitious young man who has not yet written his own tragedies. It is in this light that we should read the opening sentence of the letter: "Ick en ben geen schrijver" ("I am not a writer"). The request did not have any effect.[205] The poem itself is preserved in a fragment of 108 lines, which are already imposing; they have a complicated structure and are written in the lofty alexandrine metre. The theme, the battle of the Dutch for their freedom, the engagement with the Dutch people and their suffering, and the admiration of William of Orange may have appealed to Hooft.[206]

It may well have been *Auriacus* that inspired Hooft to write tragedies on 'national' history, such as his *Geeraerdt van Velsen. Treurspel* (Amsterdam: Willem Jansz. Blaeu, 1613) on the conspiracy of Gerard van Velzen and others against the Count of Holland, Floris v, in 1296.[207] In this play he introduced three allegorical figures: *Twist*, *Bedroch* and *Ghewelt* (Quarrel, Cheating and Violence). One cannot maintain that these allegorical figures directly 'stem' from *Auriacus*—they were also elements in other plays by rhetoricians—, but

---

203 The letter and the poem are edited in Hooft, *Briefwisseling*, 1, p. 124. See also Eddy K. Grootes, 'Hooft en Heinsius', in: *Uyt Liefde geschreven: Studies over Hooft, 1581–16 maart-1981* (Groningen: Wolters-Noordhoff, 1981), pp. 89–100. See also above, pp. 12–13.

204 Grootes, *l.c.*, p. 92.

205 One letter from Heinsius to Hooft has been transmitted. It was sent on 28 March 1615, to thank Hooft for friendly having sent him a "franchois boecsken" (a little book in French). In return, Heinsius sent him a copy of his *De tragica constitutione* (1611).

206 Grootes, *l.c.* (n. 203), p. 96.

207 On the literary works written about this event, see Jan Willem Verkaik, *De moord op Floris v* (Hilversum: Verloren, 1996) Middeleeuwse studies en bronnen, 47, Doctoral thesis Utrecht, 1995. A new edition of this play (and of Hooft's *Baeto*) in P.C. Hooft, *Geeraerdt van Velsen. Baeto, of oorsprong der Hollanderen*, ed. Henk Duits (Amsterdam: Bert Bakker, 2005).

it helped that Heinsius introduced Furies in his history play.[208] At the end of the play the river Vecht appears with a long monologue predicting the history of Holland and the coming of William of Orange. The scene is somewhat loosely connected to the action, but may have been motivated by the Maurice scene at the end of Heinsius' tragedy.

Hooft's *Baeto, oft Oórsprong der Hóllanderen. Treurspel* (*Bato, or the Origin of the Hollanders, a Tragedy*) stages the revolt of the Batavians against the Romans in 69 AD. It was written in 1617, but not performed and published until 1626, again with Hooft's uncle, the famous Amsterdam printer and publisher Willem Jansz. Blaeu. For the structure of this play he may have been inspired by Heinsius' *De tragica constitutione* (1611), an appendix to the Leiden professor's translation of Aristotle's *Poetica*, but also by his *Auriacus*.

Through *Geeraerdt van Velsen*, Heinsius' first tragedy also had some impact on Joost van den Vondel, whose *Gysbrecht van Aemstel* (1637) was inspired by Hooft's play.[209] However, any direct reception of *Auriacus* by Vondel is unlikely, because of both Vondel's partial knowledge of Latin and his highly ambivalent attitude towards the house of Orange after the putsch of Maurice and the subsequent murder of Johan van Oldenbarnevelt in 1618.

Not only in the Low Countries, but also abroad Heinsius' tragedy was read and received well. Heinsius and his patron Joseph Scaliger contributed to this fame themselves. Scaliger promised Casaubon to send him the tragedy and he assured Jacques-Auguste de Thou that Heinsius would send him a copy.[210]

---

208   See Theo Hermans, 'P.C. Hooft: The Sonnets and the Tragedy', *Dutch Crossing* 12 (1980), pp. 10–26, esp. 16–23.

209   One of the modern editions in Joost van den Vondel, *Gysbreght van Aemstel*, ed. Mieke B. Smits-Veldt (Amsterdam: Amsterdam University Press, 1994).

210   Scaliger to Casaubon, quoted above, n. 41 (which he received 'recently' as he wrote on 12 June 1602: "Accepi nuper Heinsii tui tragoediam", Botley and Van Miert (eds), *The Correspondence of Joseph Justus Scaliger* 4, p. 312), and Scaliger to de Thou, 22 January, 1602: "Heynsius vous envoiera bientost la tragedie", Botley and Van Miert (eds), *The Correspondence of Joseph Justus Scaliger* 4, p. 176. See also Scaliger's letter to Casaubon, 2 July 1602, Botley and Van Miert (eds), *The Correspondence of Joseph Justus Scaliger* 4, p. 319: "De Heynsio magis mirareris, si et adolescentem nosses, et eius poematia legisses, quae aliquando edet in publicum" ("*et* eius poematia", i.e. in addition to his tragedy); see also Appendix II, [3a] and [3b]. Ghent University Library (G 6845) owns a copy with a hand written dedication to Jacque de Thou: "Nobilissimo Amplissimoque Viro Jacobo Thuano supremi Galliarum senatus praeside, dedit dedicavitque autor." The copy of the Bayerische Staatsbibliothek contains a dedication to Dr. Nicolaas Seyst, Pensionary of the town of Leiden: "Prudentissimo, Doctissimo, et Amplissimo Viro Nicolao Seystio Celeberrimi Lugduni Pensionario domino et patrono honorando dedit dedicavitque autor."

In 1608 the German playwright Michael Virdung from Jena stated that in Germany there was no real tragedy. Only abroad there were some praiseworthy attempts, but "of the living only one (may he continue) has flown with the flight of his mind over the level of our age", referring to Heinsius and his *Auriacus*, whom he had also praised in a letter to Janus Gruterus on Seneca and the Greeks in 1602.[211] According to Paul Stachel, some traces of *Auriacus* can be seen in Virdung's *Thrasea* (1609), but these are too slight to draw any conclusions.[212]

The remark in the 'Amico lectori' about the division in acts is quoted by the German playwrights Theodorus Rhodius and Andreas Gryphius.[213] And the Neo-Latin author Rhodius from Asselheim was inspired by Heinsius' tragedy to write his martyr drama on Orange's father-in-law de Coligny, *Colignius* (1614).[214]

Heinsius has also been known and read in England, for instance by Ben Jonson, who met him in 1613;[215] in France his treatise on tragedy, *De tragica constitutione* (1611) was widely read, among others by Jean Racine, who owned a copy of the treatise.[216]

211   Stachel, *Seneca und das deutsche Renaissancedrama*, p. 41 and n. 2; for the letter, see Alexander Reifferscheid, *Briefe G.M. Lingelsheims, M. Berneggers und ihrer Freunde* (Heilbronn: Henninger, 1889) Quellen zur Geschichte des geistigen Lebens in Deutschland während des 17. Jahrhunderts, 1, Brief no. 3, pp. 6–7, Michael Virdung to Ianus Gruterus, esp. p. 6, ll. 21–23: "Me quidem ab hoc scribendi genere modo non deterruit visa nuper Heinsii vestri Auriacus tragoedia, ita me Musae, vel super ipsum antiquorum cothurnum".
212   Stachel, *o.c.*, p. 48. On Virdung, see Markus Mollitor, 'Virdung', in: *Killy Literaturlexikon* (n. 128), 12, p. 35.
213   Stachel, *o.c.*, pp. 131–132. On Rhodius, see Wilhelm Kühlmann, 'Rhodius', in: *Killy Literaturlexikon*, 9, p. 426; Janning, *Der Chor im neulateinischen Drama* (n. 11), pp. 256–269.
214   Stachel, *o.c.*, pp. 132–134; see also Hans-Gert Roloff, 'Klassizismus im deutschen Drama um 1600: Beobachtungen an der Tragoedia Colignius des Theodor Rhodius', in: *id., Kleine Schriften zur Literatur des 17. Jahrhunderts: Festgabe zum. 70. Geburtstag*, ed. Christiane Cämmerer a.o. (Amsterdam, New York: Rhodopi, 2003) *Chloe*, 35, pp. 187–199. A modern edition in Johannes Bolte, *Coligny/Colignius, Gustav Adolf/Gustavus saucius, Wallenstein/Fritlandus: Drei zeitgenössische lateinische Dramen von Rhodius, Narssius, Vernulaeus* (Leipzig: Hiersemann, 1933), Bibliothek des Litterarischen Vereins in Stuttgart, Sitz Tübingen, 280.
215   David McPherson, 'Ben Jonson Meets Daniel Heinsius', *English Language Notes* 14 (1976), p. 105; see also Sellin, *Daniel Heinsius and Stuart England*, pp. 147–153.
216   Edith G. Kern, *The Influence of Heinsius and Vossius Upon French Dramatic Theory* (Baltimore: Johns Hopkins Press, 1949), and Paul R. Sellin, 'La pathétique retrouvé: Racine's Catharsis Reconsidered', *Modern Philology* 70 (1973), pp. 199–215.

10   This Edition

The basis of this edition is the first and only printed edition of 1602: DANIELIS HEINSII / AVRIACVS, / *siue* / LIBERTAS SAVCIA, / Accedunt eiusdem / IAMBI / *Partim morales, partim ad amicos, partim / amicorum causâ scripti.* / [*Impressum*] / LVGDVNI BATAVORVM, / Apud Andream Cloucquium, / sub signo Angeli Coronati. / ANNO M.D.CII.[217] I preserved the spelling of the original printing. Obvious typesetting errors (or the typesetters' misreadings of Heinsius' difficult handwriting) have been corrected.[218] The punctuation has been changed to modern standards.[219] The accent marks in Latin have been retained;[220] those in Greek have been standardized. Grotius' liminary poem *Quis ille tanto* [...] has been edited by B.L. Meulenbroek; consultation of his remarks and the manuscript (UBL Pap. 10) made clear that in some instances another reading than Meulenbroek's should be chosen.[221] In the *apparatus criticus* the changes Heinsius proposed in his own copy (UBL 754 B 34) are recorded, also in their genesis and subsequent stages of development. No distinction has been made between corrections made in haste ('Sofortkorrekturen') and other changes.[222]

---

217   Sellin in his Checklist, *Daniel Heinsius and Stuart England*, pp. 213–215, nos 66, 67 and 87 gives other editions of *Auriacus* from 1608 (no. 66) and 1649 (67 and 87). However, he found them mentioned in M. Henning Witten, 'Scripta Heinsii', in: *id., Memoriae philosophorum, oratorum, poetarum*, II. (Frankfurt: Martinus Hallervord, 1679), pp. 197–201; nor Sellin, nor I have found them, so they are likely to be nonexistent.

218   On the editorial practices with regard to Neo-Latin texts, see Tom Deneire, 'Editing Neo-Latin Texts: Editorial Principles; Spelling and Punctuation', in: *ENLW*, pp. 959–962.

219   On punctuation in early modern Latin printings, see Johanna Greidanus, *Beginselen en ontwikkeling van de interpunctie, in 't biezonder ín de Nederlanden* (Zeist: Vonk, 1926) Doctoral thesis Utrecht, pp. 189–244, esp. 206–219 and 227–231; Margareta Benner and Emin Tengström, *On the Interpretation of Learned Neo-Latin: An Explorative Study Based on Some Texts from Sweden (1611–1716)* (Göteborg: Acta Universitatis Gothoburgensis, 1977) Studia graeca et latina gothoburgensia, 39, pp. 25–26; Piet Steenbakkers, 'First Excursus: Meyer and Diacritics', in: *id., Spinoza's Ethica from Manuscript to Print: Studies on Text, Form and Related Topics* (Assen: Van Gorcum, 1994), pp. 20–25.

220   See Piet Steenbakkers, 'Towards a History of Accent-Marks in Neo-Latin', in: *id., Spinoza's Ethica from Manuscript to Print*, pp. 71–101.

221   See Grotius, *Dichtwerken/Poetry* I, 2, 2 A/B, pp. 236–238.

222   In the liminary poem 'Pro Auriaco sua', part of the changes in Heinsius' own copy found their way into the editions of his collected poetry of 1603 and especially 1606.

10.1   *Sigla Used*

A	*editio princeps* Leiden 1602
MT	*Menda typographica*
L	copy UB Leiden sign. 754 B 34
a, b, c	stages in the author's annotations
del.	*delevit* (erased)
sublin.	*sublineavit* (underlined)
rest.	*restauravit* (restored)
n.l.	*non legitur* (illegible)
post corr.	*post correctionem* (after correction)
add.	*addidit* (added)
postea	later
om.	*omittit* (omitted)
in margine	in the margin

The commentary traces quotations from and allusions to classical authors and explains historical references. The events recorded in *Auriacus* are in line with the official reports of the States General, for which references to *Een verhael van de moort*, the most complete account of this official version, are used.

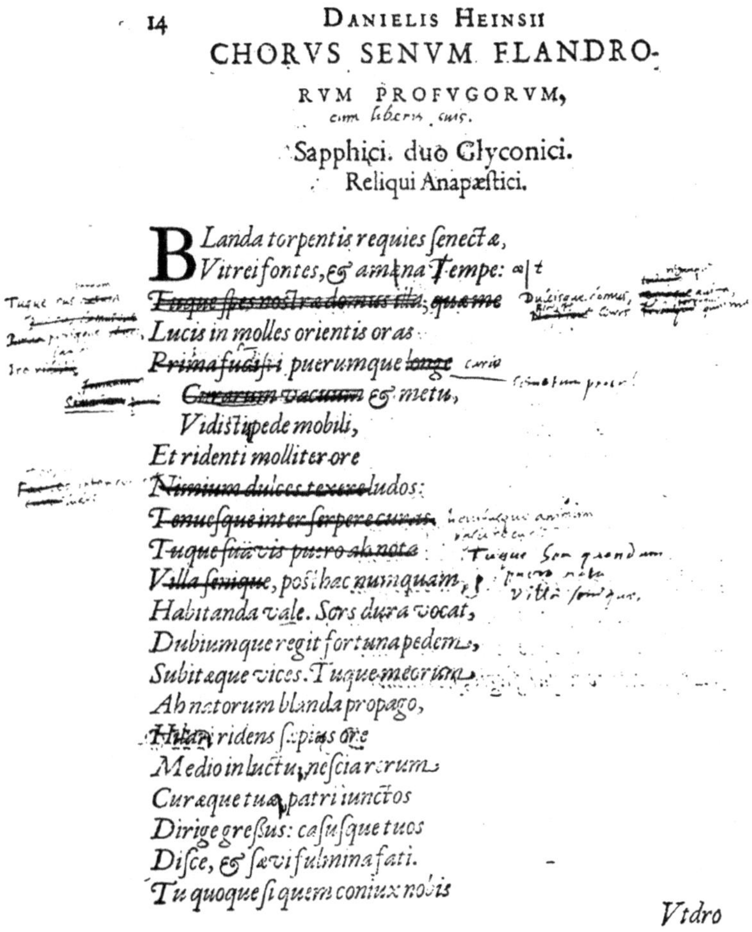

14 **DANIELIS HEINSII**
CHORVS SENVM FLANDRO-
RVM PROFVGORVM,
cum liberis suis.

Sapphici. duo Glyconici.
Reliqui Anapæstici.

Blanda torpentis requies senectæ,
Vitrei fontes, & amæna Tempe:
Tuque spes nostra domus illa, quæ me
Lucis in molles orientis oras
Prima fudisti puerumque longe
Curarum vacuum & metu,
Vidisti pede mobili,
Et ridenti molliter ore
Nimium dulces texere ludos:
Tenuesque inter serpere curas,
Tuque suavis puero ah nota
Villa senique, posthæc numquam,
Habitanda vale. Sors dura vocat,
Dubiumque regit fortuna pedem,
Subitæque vices. Tuque mecum una,
Ah nætorum blanda propago,
Hilari ridens sapias ore
Medio in luctu, nescia rerum
Curæque tuæ patri iunctos
Dirige gressus: casusque tuos
Disce, & sævi fulmina fati.
Tu quoque si quem coniux nobis

Vidro

FIGURE 3   Daniel Heinsius, *Auriacus sive Libertas saucia* (Leiden: Andreas Cloucquius, 1602)
UNIVERSITY LIBRARY LEIDEN 754 B 34, P. 14

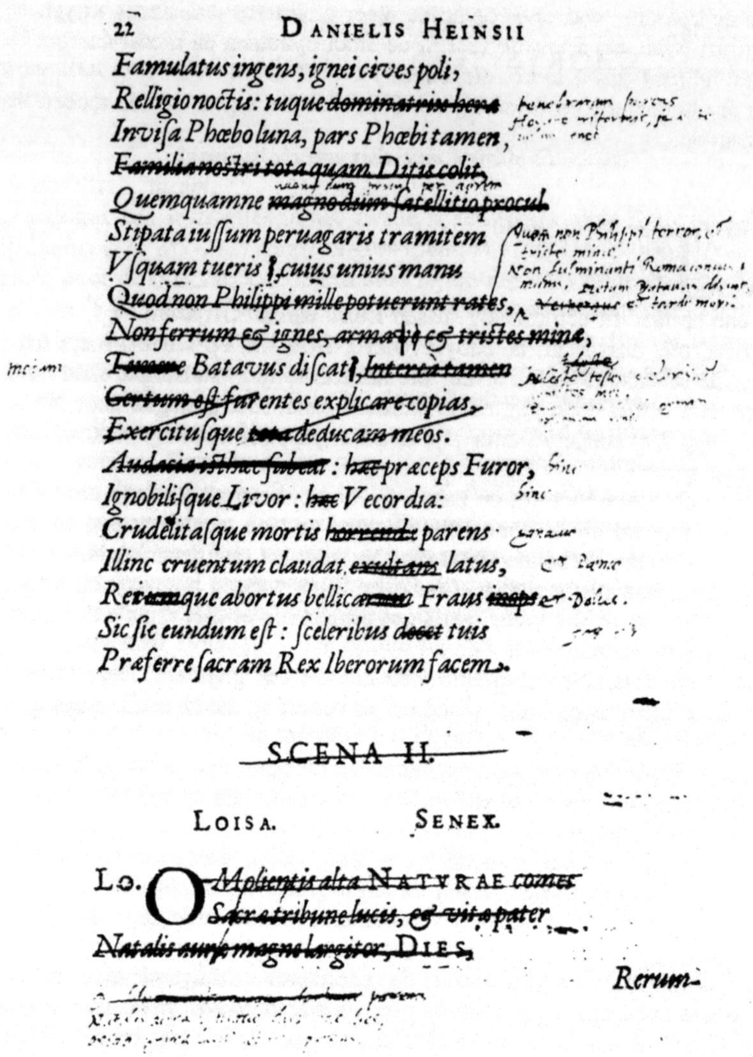

22   DANIELIS HEINSII

Famulatus ingens, ignei cives poli,
Relligio noctis: tuque ~~dominatrix hera~~
Invisa Phœbo luna, pars Phœbi tamen,
~~Familia nostri tota quam Ditis colit~~
Quemquamne ~~magno dum satellitio procul~~
Stipata iussum peruagaris tramitem
Vsquam tueris? cuius unius manu
Quod non ~~Philippi mille potuerunt rates,~~
Non ferrum & ignes, ~~armat & & tristes minæ,~~
~~Tuæque~~ Batavus discat? ~~Interea tamen~~
~~Certum est fur~~entes explicare copias.
Exercitusque ~~tota~~ deducam meos.
~~Audacia isthæc furbeat~~: hæc præceps Furor,
Ignobilisque Livor: ~~hæc~~ Vecordia:
Crudelitasque mortis ~~horrenda~~ parens:
Illinc cruentum claudat ~~exultans~~ latus,
Re~~rumque~~ abortus bellica~~rum~~ Fraus ~~inops~~
Sic sic eundum est: sceleribus ~~docet~~ tuis
Præferre sacram Rex Iberorum facem.

SCENA II.

LOISA.   SENEX.

Lo. O ~~Molientis alta~~ NATVRAE ~~comes~~
      ~~Sacra tribune lucis, eg vita pater~~
Natalis ~~cuius magno largitor~~, DIES,
                                                    Rerum

FIGURE 4   Daniel Heinsius, *Auriacus sive Libertas saucia* (Leiden: Andreas Cloucquius, 1602)
UNIVERSITY LIBRARY LEIDEN 754 B 34, P. 22

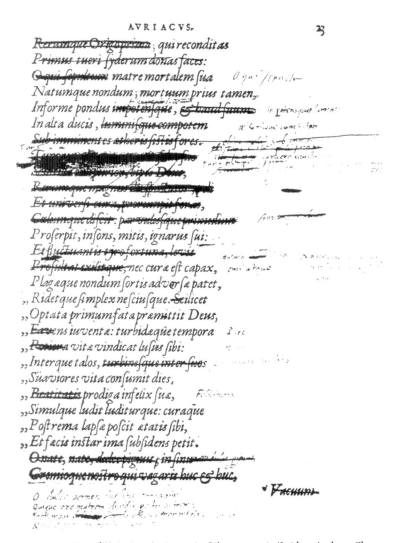

Text and Translation

∴

Conspectvs siglorvm

A   Daniel Heinsius, *Auriacus, sive Libertas saucia, accedunt eiusdem Iambi, partim morales, partim amicorum causa scripta* (Leiden: Maire, 1602).

MT   Menda Typographica, in: Daniel Heinsius, *Auriacus, sive Libertas saucia, accedunt eiusdem Iambi, partim morales, partim amicorum causa scripta* (Leiden: Maire, 1602), (unnumbered p.).

L   Daniel Heinsius, *Auriacus, sive Libertas saucia, accedunt eiusdem Iambi, partim morales, partim amicorum causa scripta* (Leiden: Maire, 1602) the copy (UB Leiden, shelf number 754 B 34) with manuscript notes by Heinsius himself.

© KONINKLIJKE BRILL NV, LEIDEN, 2020 | DOI:10.1163/9789004425361_003

DANIELIS HEINSII

AURIACVS,
Siue
LIBERTAS SAVCIA,
Accedunt eiusdem
IAMBI
Partim morales, partim ad amicos, partim
amicorum causâ scripti.

[Printer's Mark]

LVGDVNI BATAVORUM,
Apud Andream Cloucquium,
sub signo Angeli Coronati,
Anno MDCII.

Daniel Heinsius'

Auriacus
or
Liberty Wounded
Added are his
Iambs
partly moral, partly written to friends,
partly because of friends

[Printer's Mark]

Leiden
By Andreas Cloeck
under the sign of the Crowned Angel
1602

[1]   ILLVSTRISSIMIS, NOBILISSIMIS, AMPLISSIMIS,
Potentissimisque HOLLANDIAE ET Westfrisiae Ordinibus,
Dominis suis Magnificis.

ILLVSTRES ORDINES

Inter reliqua monimenta quibus vel humanum se efferre ingenium, vel acuere
industria consuevit, una Tragoedia Regium sibi nomen vendicat, vel quod
reges heroasque ac principes in scenam ea deducat, vel quod non nisi regales
sublimesque atque ab omni vulgari dicendi genere remotos spiritus admittat.
5   Gravissimam eam dignissimamque omnium scriptorum esse multis argumen-
tis probarunt Romani et ante eos disciplinarum autores Graeci. Ac ne apud vos
rationes e Grammaticorum scholis adferamus, duplici modo eius dignitatem
tuetur eius princeps Sophocles, tum quod senex eam scripsit, tum (quod pro-
prie ad vos spectat) quod Reipublicae praefectus.
10   Vnum tamen est quod mirari saepenumero soleam, sublimia nimirum illa
ingenia, quae non sine singulari eruditione ac praesertim sapientiae illius,
quam Moralem Civilemque dicimus, rerum praeterea cognitione et industriâ
se ad hoc scribendi genus contulerunt, cum solam Tragoediam omnes vitae
humanae casus, fortunas, pericula, eventa rerum, consiliorum exitus amplecti
15   statuerent, prudentiae praetereà magistram esse, eâ tamen ad fabularum vani-
tatem, ac rerum deliria abusi sint, nec sibi vel res gestas aeui sui, vel imperatores
subiectum esse maluerint, quam Oedipodas, Aiaces, Medeas caeteraque quibus effaeta anus antiquitas credulitati hominum turpissime illusit.
Ego verò, Illvstrissimi Ordines, Tragoediam vobis offero meam, imò
20   vestram: quod in eâ meum est, trado vobis; quod vestrum est, vt gratum sit id
quod offero, efficiet. Ita simul quod in reliquis Tragicis deplorari solet effugi,
viamque mihi ad benevolentiam vestram praeparavi.
Ego autem simul et de opere et de operis argumento cogitare coepi, seu
potius argumento dignum opus quaesivi, simulque invêni. Nec enim tam fac-
25   torum gestorumque sterilis vestra Batavia est, ut in eâ materies scribendi quae-
ratur quam inueniatur citius. Hoc vobis affirmare liquidò possum, nihil ab
antiquis Philosophis pluris olim, hoc vno scribendi genere, factum esse. Hinc

---

Tit. Ante Illustrissimis *add. L* Dio Chrys. In oratione περὶ κάλλους 272 locum sub de pulcherrimo
de tragoedia veterum τούτου δὲ αἴτιον τὸ μὴ πάνυ φιλεῖν τοὺς τραγῳδοὺς, μηδὲ ζηλοῦν· ἐπεὶ οἶδα ὅτι
αἰσχρόν ἐστιν ἐν τραγῳδίᾳ τοὺς νῦν ὄντας ὀνομάζειν etc.

[1]   **To the Illustrious, High-born, Noble and Mighty States of**
          Holland and West Friesland, their High Representative Councils.

Illustrious States,

Compared to the other writings that human talent industriously uses to elevate or hone itself, only tragedy claims the predicate royal, because it presents kings, heroes and princes on the stage, or because it admits merely royal and lofty characters void of any form of colloquial language. That it is the most serious and dignified of all literary genres has been proven with many arguments by the Romans and before them by the Greek authors on the disciplines. And to refrain from giving you argumentations from the rhetoricians' schools, it is its prince Sophocles who defends its dignity in two ways, because he wrote it as an old man, and because he did so—this affects you in particular—as a ruler of the State.

Nevertheless, there is one thing about which I am constantly wondering, namely that the undoubtedly great talents who have dedicated themselves to this literary genre—not without extraordinary knowledge, especially of so-called moral philosophy and politics, and, moreover, with erudition and zeal—abused it for meaningless stories and foolish histories, although they believed that only tragedy treats all the vicissitudes of human life, fate, dangers, events and consequences of decisions and, moreover, is a master of wisdom, and that they did not rather choose heroic deeds or rulers of their own time as subjects, than people such as Oedipus, Ajax, Medea[1] and other material with which antiquity as an old woman who gave birth to too many children shamelessly ridiculed people's credulity.

But, Illustrious States, I offer you my tragedy, or rather yours. What is mine in it, I offer it to you. And your share in it will ensure that what I offer will be pleasant to you. In this way I avoided at the same time what is usually regretted in other tragic poets, and paved the way for gaining your benevolence.

After all, at the same time I started thinking about writing a tragedy and about the topic for it. Or rather, I was looking for a genre that was worthy of the subject and at the same time I found it. For your Holland is so rich in events and acts of war that one finds a subject matter almost before it is searched for.

I can assure you that the old philosophers in the past did not hold any literary genre in higher esteem than this very one. From this genre, those in power, from

---

1 Oedipus and Ajax were protagonists of plays by Sophocles (ca. 496–406 BC); Euripides (ca. 480–ca. 406 BC) wrote a *Medea*.

imperatores, hinc duces prudentiam apud Graecos suam hauriebant; haec illa
disciplina est, quam illi per excellentiam doctrinam dicebant; hinc Tragici quo-
30   tiescunque in theatrum prodirent publicè, docere ab Atheniensibus dicebantur; hinc Aristotelis, hinc Carystij, maximorum virorum περὶ διδασκαλιῶν, id est
de disciplinis libri. In ijs Rex philosophorum ille tempus actionis vniuscuius-
que Tragoediae diligentissime notarat. Ille sapientiae ac voti humani terminus Plato et scripsit eam, et quicquid in Philosophia postea reliquit nobis, ad
35   normam Tragicam et antiquorum τετραλογίαν direxit, vt omittam quod Dio-
nysiis quoque certasse feratur. Omitto reliquos minorum gentium Philosophos, omitto magnum Euclidem, qui omnem propemodum quam in sapientiae
cognitione operam collocarant, ad vnum hoc studium contulerunt.

    Quod si eam proptereà quisquam (vt sunt sinistra hominum hoc tempore
40   iudicia) minoris putet, quod ad poeticen referatur; eum nos, ILLUSTRISSIMI
ORDINES, per ea conuincemus, quae ipse miratur maximè, modo ne ità rerum
ignarus sit, vt ab ipsâ Philosophiâ vitae humanae Reginâ abhorreat. Homeri
tempore, qui vnus è tam profundâ temporis antiquitate nobis relictus est,
Philosophiae nomen ne fando quidem auditum fuit vnquam. Fuerunt tamen
45   illo tempore, qui et rerum causas, principia, motus, ortus, materiem, et pul-
cherrimae denique machinae huius rationes inquirerent, et quae vera demùm
sapientia est, fuêre et qui de moribus, de rectè instituendâ hominum vitâ age-
rent, non publici modò, sed et privati morum magistri, quos aetas illa simplicis-
sima ἀοιδοὺς sive cantores dicebat. Illi matronarum thalamis absentibus maritis
50   praeficiebantur, Regum liberos instituebant, mores formabant hominum, virtutis causam agebant, omnia denique philosophi habebant, praeter nomen.
Idipsum apparet ex illo cantore qui belli Troiani temporibus Clytemnaestram
seruauit, dum in expeditione cum reliquis Graeciae proceribus esset Agamemnon, quo interfecto tandem illâ potitus est Aegystus.

55   Non adferam vobis somnia aegrorum, ILLVSTRISSIMI ORDINES, neque id
quod volo poëtarum testimonijs probabo, vt plerique hodie solent, qui tum

this genre, rulers from the Greeks drew their views, this is the education they called science par excellence. That is why the Athenians said that the tragic poet, every time he staged a piece, gave instruction. This was the source of the books of Aristotle, the source of those of Carystius,[2] the greatest men *Peri didascalioon*, that is, in the area of education. In his books the prince of philosophers has carefully recorded the time of every tragedy.[3] The famous summit of wisdom and of what a man aspires to, Plato, also wrote a tragedy and all he left us in philosophy, he directed to the norm of the tragedy and the tetralogy of the ancients,[4] not to mention that he would have joined in the competition at the Dionysia. I leave aside the other philosophers of less important people, I leave aside the great Euclid,[5] who devoted all efforts they spent on studying wisdom, precisely to studying this particular genre.

Now if someone (since the judgement of people of this time is contentious) would hold it in lower esteem because it belongs to poetry, we will convince such a person, Very Serene States, by what he admires the most, if at least he is not so ignorant that he even abhors the queen of human life, philosophy. In the time of Homer, the only one left to us from early antiquity, people did not even know the term philosophy. Yet there were people at that time who were looking for the causes, principles, movements, origins, matter of things, and finally at the beautiful structures of this building, and what is true wisdom, there were people who wrote treatises on morals and about the proper organization of human life, not only in public, but also as private teachers in ethics.

That primitive time called them *aoidoi* (singers). They supervised the bedrooms of housemothers when their husbands were away from home, taught kings' sons, formed the morals of the people, argued for moral quality; in short they were philosophers in all but name. The truth of this is evident from that singer who guarded Clytemnestra in the time of the Trojan War, as long as Agamemnon was on expedition with the other nobles of Greece; Aegisthus won her only after the singer was murdered.

I will not mention to you the dreams of the sick, Very Serene States, nor will I prove what I want with testimonies from poets, as many people today are wont

---

2 The Greek grammarian Carystius (2nd c. BC) was the author of a work *Peri didaskalioon* (*On the Dramatic Poets*).

3 It was Aristotle (384–322 BC) who in his *Poetics* described the time of the action of a play.

4 The dialogues of the Greek philosopher Plato are grouped in squares: 'tetralogies', just like the three tragedies (trilogy) and the satyr play at the dramatic festivals.

5 It is not quite clear which Euclid is meant here—the mathematician, the Socratic philosopher or the grammarian.

demum rem factam habere arbitrantur, cum Peripatheticam aut Stoicam philosophiam aut quamlibet eius partem testimonijs ex eâdem sectâ petitis com-
probarunt.

60   Quod res est dicam: vox ᾄδειν sive cantandi ita à veteribus sumpta fuit teste
Geographo vt φράζειν sive dicere significaret. Ea quae à nobis et ab illo dicuntur,
ita se habere probant doctissimae Graecorum magistrorum Glossae, et certius
multo quod dicturi sumus.

Septem enim illi Graeciae sapientes nondum tamen philosophi dicti, metra
65   quaedam de moribus ediderunt quae ᾄσματα seu ᾀδόμενα (si modo idem vtrun-
que) dixerunt in quibus et vestigia vocis ἀοιδὸς animaduertimus, et quid illis
propositum fuerit manifestè videmus. Talia primus eorum Thales, talia Chilo,
talia Pittacus, talia et Bias, et Cleobulus et caeteri. Nam magnum illum legisla-
torem Atheniensium, cuius statuta quoque Populus Romanus missis in Grae-
70   ciam Sp. Posthumio Albo, T. Manlio, P. Sulpicio Camerino legatis diligentissime
descripsit, ad Elegias et omne fere poëmatum genus se demisisse praetereo,
reliquos etiam sapientes ad σίλλους et alia praetermitto.

Nec enim id ego nunc ago, quod à vulgo poetarum toties tractatum fuit, vt
Poëticen extollam, quam illi non intelligunt, cuiusque vsum antiquissimum
75   ignorant. Aequissimum peto, ILLVSTRISSIMI ORDINES, vt quò tendit mea per-
ueniat oratio, Philosophiam vt laudari patiantur ab illis postulo. Atqui eam illi
in ore habent, nec difficulter id impetrabimus. Deinde, vt nobis respondeant,
quantùm à philosophiâ facultas poetica abfuerit, cum axioma à philosophis
pronunciatum fuit, quod beneficio Geographi adhuc habemus, quo negatur
80   poëtam bonum esse posse, qui non prius vir bonus sit. Nam inter illam Zenonis
definitionem aliquid interesse fortasse dicerent, cum humanarum diuinarum-
que rerum imitatio Poëtice esse dicitur.

60–63 Quod res est—dicturi sumus A: Quis Pherecyden ignorat ante Pythagoram, eiusdem prae-
ceptorem, Empedoclenque Parmeniden ante Socratem non aliter ex instituto philosophiam trac-
tasse: nam Linum Musaeum Orpheum, quos solos cum Homero inter sapientes in Apologia sua
Plato recenset, ut antiquiores praetereo. L.   64 enim A: deinde L. ‖ philosophi *scripsi*: phili-
sophi A.   67 videmus. A: videmus. A [Quare a *b*] vulgo certe [, Laertio *b*] teste, praeter [per *b*]
contemptum poetae dicti sunt: et ab eo tempore quod laudis erat, vitio dedit [stultitiaque *del.*]
pessimus sapiendae iudex populus. L.

to do, who think they have only done with a case when they have proven Peripatetic or Stoic philosophy, or a small part of it, as being true with testimonies derived from the same philosophical school.

I will tell you how it is: the word *aidein* (to sing) was used by the ancients in such a way, according to the geographer, that it meant *frazein* (to tell). That this is the way it is with what is said by us and by him, is made plausible by the most learned glosses of the Greek teachers, and much more by what I am going to say.

After all, the seven sages of Greece (who were not yet called philosophers) wrote some texts in the form of verse about moral issues, which they called *aismata* (songs) or *aidomena* (chants) (assuming that both are the same). In these words we notice traces of the word *aoidos* (singer) and we see clearly what they had in mind. Such verses were written by the first of them, Thales; such verses were also written by Chilo, Pittacus, Bias, Cleobulus[6] and others. For I pass over in silence that the great lawgiver of the Athenians, whose statutes were also accurately copied by the Roman people after the mission of Spurius Posthumius Albus, Titus Manlius and Publius Sulpicius Camerinus to Greece, did not deem it beneath his dignity to write elegies and almost every poetic genre;[7] nor will I mention that the other philosophers did not feel themselves superior to the writing of satires.

Nor shall I do now what has been done so often by the mob of poets,[8] namely that I praise poetry, which those poets do not understand nor know how old its practice is. I have a very fair wish, Very Serene States, that my argument reaches its goal, I ask their permission to praise philosophy. Well, they always talk about it and we will achieve this without difficulty. Then I ask them to answer my question of how far away poetic competence is from philosophy, since the axiom has been posited by philosophers (which we still have, thanks to the geographer)[9] in which it is denied that a poet who is not first a good man can be good. One might perhaps say that there is a difference with Zeno's[10] definition when it is said that poetry is the depiction of the divine and human world.

---

6   The philosophers from Thales to Cleobulus, five of the seven sages, explained their theories in poetry.

7   The lawgiver of the Athenians Solon (639–559 BC) was also one of the seven sages; he reorganized the constitutional system of Athens, and wrote poetry. In 456–454 BC a delegation of Posthumius, Manlius and Sulpicius went to Athens to make inquiries about Solon's legislation.

8   This 'mob of poets' probably refers to the rhetoricians.

9   The geographer is Strabo (ca. 66 BC–ca. 21 AD), who is mentioned a few lines below.

10   Either the founder of the Stoic school of philosophy Zeno of Citium (ca. 334–ca. 262 BC) or another Greek philosopher, Zeno of Elea (5th ca. BC).

At me Hercule quantum mihi laborandum hoc tempore esset, si Oratoriâ
facultate antiquiorem eam esse contenderem, nisi me eâ molestiâ et inuidiâ
85   cui vix ferendae essem, à Strabone subleuatum scirem, qui tam certis testimonijs Oratoriam facultatem à Poëticâ oriundam probat, quam à Tragicâ gravitate
familiarem characterem Comicum. Nec hoc agimus, vt in Aristidis reprehensionem incurramus qui false ridet eos, qui solutam orationem vinctâ posteriorem
putant. Verùm enimverò satis coacta est illa oratoris calumnia et quae nobis
90   etiam ampliùs hac de re cogitandi ansam praebuit. Nam quae de Cadmo, Pherecyde, Hecataeo dicuntur, eruditos saltem fugere non debebant. Habet ergò
ad oratoriam illa se, vt ad filiam mater, ad philosophiam autem olim, sicut illa
se ad quamlibet sui partem.

Quòd autem hodiè pro pellice sedeat, quòd ab hominibus trivialibus, indoc-
95   tis, barbaris, prostituatur, non magis genuinae huic quicquam detrahit, quam
castissimae illi Abradatae apud Xenophontem vxori, Phryne, aut Lais aliqua,
aut si quid his impudentius. Nomen ei à Platone illud quod ad nostram vsque
permansit aetatem inditum grauissimi scriptores testantur. Idem tamen, quod
in ore est omnibus quicunque diuinam hanc facultatem oppugnare solent, è
100   Republicâ suâ exegit eos.

Nos verò ad illa, ILLVSTRISSIMI ORDINES, videte, quam breviter respon-
deamus. Primò enim, si illam Rempublicam Platonis recipiamus, exigendus erit
ante omnes ipse fundator, cuius ipsa soluta oratio, vt et Herodoti, nusquam à
poësi abhorret, nisi quis eam modo poësin esse existimet, quae numeris pedi-
105   busque vincta est; quod si concedamus, ne ἄμετρα quidem poësis erunt, imo
ne quaedam fortasse ἔμμετρα, ac ne ipsi Dithyrambi; non quod à vulgari verborum in metris, sed metrorum inter se iuncturâ abhorreant, ac ne ᾄσματα forsan
philosophorum.

89–90 et quae—ansam praebuit A: nec quisquam ignorat argumenta servire Graecos. L.   103
ipsa soluta oratio A: ipsum dicendi genus L.   104 abhorret A: recedit L.

But good heavens, how many efforts should I make if I were to claim that poetry is older than rhetoric, if I did not know that I was freed from that burden and the barely endurable jealousy by Strabo, who also proves with reliable evidence that rhetoric comes from poetry, as comedy with its spoken language stems from severe tragedy! I do not aim to expose myself to the criticism of Aristides,[11] who falsely ridicules the people who believe that prose is younger than poetry.

The accusations of the orators have truly accumulated enough and given me sufficient reason to think more about this issue. What has been said about Cadmus, Pherecydes and Hecataeus[12] should not have escaped the scholars. So poetry relates to prose like a mother to her daughter, but to philosophy she has for a long time been related as it relates to each part of itself.

The fact, however, that she would have descended to the level of courtesan today, that she would be thrown down by vulgar, illiterate and barbarous people, does not detract from her being a real lady like a Phryne or a Lais[13] or something even more impudent than this to that very chaste wife of Abradates at Xenophon.[14] That this title, which has remained until our time, has been given by Plato,[15] is attested by the greatest writers. It was he who also banished them from his state, something which all those who combat this divine art never cease to relate.

As far as I am concerned, Serene States, see how short my answer is. First of all, if we reinstate that state of Plato, the founder himself above all will have to be expelled, whose prose itself, like that of Herodotus, nowhere differs much from poetry, unless someone considers to be poetry only what is bound in meter. If we accept that blank verses will not be poetry, not even some metric verses, nor will the very dithyrambs[16] (not because it is the ordinary connection of words in meters, but because it lacks the connection of the meters itself) and perhaps not even the songs of the philosophers.

---

11   The Greek rhetor Aelius Aristides (129–189 AD).

12   The Greek historians or *logographoi* ('storytellers') Cadmus of Miletus (perhaps fl. 550 BC), Hecataeus of Miletus (ca. 550 BC–ca. 476 BC) and Pherecydes of Syrus (near Miletus, ca. 450s BC) were allegedly the first authors writing prose.

13   Phryne (b. ca. 371 BC) was a Greek hetaera (courtesan); Lais was the name of two Greek courtesans of Corinth, one during the Peloponnesian war, the other at the time of Demosthenes.

14   The Greek general and historian Xenophon in his *Cyropaedia* sings the praises of Panthea, the chaste wife of Abradates.

15   In his *Politeia* in particular, Plato criticized poetry and excluded poets from his ideal state.

16   Initially dithyrambs were songs in praise of Bacchus; they were considered to be the precursors of tragedy.

Deinde, vt Platonis ciues simus, recipienda erit mulierum communitas, et
110 reliqua, vt certum sit nihil ad eversionem Reipublicae plus conferre, quam eius
constitutionem. Sed ego me hercule tam facile eius Politiam in bene constitutâ
urbe esse posse concedam, quam Idaeas in naturâ. Quod si proptereà poëtas
ille in vrbe sua non fert, quod adulteria Deorum et praelia introducat Homerus,
metuo ne in eam artem impingat, cuius scientiam profitebatur, ratiocinandi
115 nimirum. Nam illud aut peccatum non est, aut si est, vnius tantum. Scimus
enim non Grammaticos modò, sed et Platonis discipulos, quae in vniuersum
de Dijs ab Homero dicuntur, ad naturales rationes referre solere. Quod si, vt
diximus, Homerus peccauit, poëtae vitium est, non poetices, et quidem illius
tantum. Nam omnes ob eam causam poëtas exigere tale est, ac si quis omnes
120 Philosophos exigat quod Plato ibi male argumentetur. Omitto interim, Platonem eum quem è Republica sua exigit vbique diuinum dicere. Clemens certè
ille est, qui Homerum ex vrbe sua in caelum exulatum mittit et in Deorum
numero citius esse patitur quam suorum.

Iam autem ad vos venio, ILLVSTRISSIMI MAGNIFICIQUE VIRI, ORDINES
125 POTENTISSIMI, quibus in vindictam Nobilissimo AVRIACI sanguini debitam,
vix vniversum sufficit Hispanorum nomen. Ducem vobis vestrum offero. Quid
admiramini? Vt benevolentiam vestram favoremque conciliem, titulum inspi-
cite. AVRIACVM fero. Percussit sat scio, foditque pectus vestrum nominis illius
recordatio, mentemque subijt illa, quae vobis communis cum illo fuit, in tutan-
130 dis aris, focis, liberisque vestris pietatis imago. Videte quantum spei concepe-
rim: quod vix totis operibus quidam consequuntur, solâ operis inscriptione me
consecutum video. AVRIACVM vobis fero; atque vtinam ne talem. Vtinam et
viueret ille et ego non haec scriberem! Cum vero ille si vixisset diutius nihil
praeter nominis immortalitatem propositum habuisset, quae Musarum nostra-
135 rum ope nonnihil eget, agedum, id mortuo, si fieri possit, tribuamus, quod
vnum ille, si vixisset, expeteret.

Ambulet ergò in cothurno deinceps, quoniam in huius terrae ambitu, quam
vel vniversam animo suo angustam semper iudicauit, ambulare diutius non
potest. Ambulet in animis, in pectore, in manibus iuuentutis vestrae et tenellis
140 animis patriae amorem imprimat, adultis propugnationem eius defensionem-
que. Videat posteritas vestra, ILLVSTRISSIMI VIRI, discant liberi, quanto vobis

---

117 *Post* solere. *add. L* Nec Platonis [praeceptoris sui *b*] sententiam admittere sed excusare: neque
de omni Republica ea accipere, quae in sua probat Plato: *n.l.* [usquam fuisset, *b*: quam nusquam
esse posse, *c*] confitetur legislator.   123 *Post* suorum. *signum add. L.*   124 Illustrissimi *scripsi:*
Illustrissmi *A.*   130 focis liberisque vestris *A*: focisque *L.*   130–132 Videte—video *A*: *del. L.*
132 fero *A*: offero *L.*   133 et ego—scriberem *A*: nec ego vobis haec offerrem *L.* ‖ ille *A*: *del. L.*
135 ope nonnihil eget *A*: opem implorat *L.* ‖ agedum *A*: nos *L.*

Moreover, in order to become citizens of Plato, we will have to accept the common property of women and the rest; thus, certainly nothing contributes more to the fall of the state than its establishment. Of course, I will admit that his regulation state can as easily exist in a well-ordered city as the Ideas in reality. But if he does not tolerate poets in his city, because Homer describes adultery of gods and their struggle, I am afraid that he will go against that skill of which he has knowledge, namely that of reasoning. Because that is no mistake, or if it is, only the fault of an individual. After all, we know that not only the interpreters, but also the pupils of Plato, generally tend to reduce what Homer says about the gods to principles of nature.[17] If, however, as I said, Homer made a mistake, it is a mistake of the poet, and his own mistake, not of poetry. To keep all poets away for that reason is the same as if someone would keep back all philosophers because Plato is following a wrong reasoning here. Next, I leave aside the fact that Plato everywhere calls divine the poet he rejects from his state. Mild is at least the man who banishes Homer from his city to heaven and allows him to belong to the number of the gods rather than that of his citizens.

But now I am addressing you, Very Serene and Supreme Lords, Powerful States, for whom hardly all Spaniards are sufficient for the revenge owed to Orange's noble blood. I offer you your leader. Why are you surprised? Look at the title so that I win your goodwill and favour. I offer you Orange. I am sure that the memory of his name shocked and pierced your heart and that the thought of piety that you shared with him in protecting your altars, houses and children came to your mind. Look how much hope I cherish: what some people hardly achieve with their work, I see myself having achieved with only the title of the work. I bring you Orange, and ah, if it were not in this form, but he were alive and I did not write this! Since, however, if he had lived longer, he had had no other endeavour left than that of the immortality of his name, for which he hardly needs the help of my poetry, come on, let us grant him if possible after his death the only thing what he had wanted to acquire if he had lived.

Let him henceforth walk on a buskin, since he cannot wander about on this globe, which he, in its entirety always judged too small for his mind. Let him walk around in the spirit, the heart and the hands of your children and let him imbue the young souls with the love for the homeland, and in his wake and his defence. Let your offspring see, Very Serene Gentlemen, let your children

---

17   In the *Iliad* and *Odyssey* that are attributed to Homer the gods are described as cheating, quarrelling and committing adultery. The Alexandrian philologists tended to interpret these stories allegorically; in such an interpretation, the gods are considered principles of nature.

diuinum illud LIBERTATIS nomen steterit, quod non nisi virtute et fortitudine
paratur, frugalitate et industria retinetur. Excelsi illi animi, mortisque contemp-
trix pro patriâ virtus, latius se fundat, quam vbi nata est. Nec tam angustis
145   limitibus diuini hi motus ausaque regia cohibeantur, vt in eâdem terrâ et exti-
tisse et sepulta esse videantur.

Agedum maris imperator, BATAVE, iam te appello, cui pro patriâ mori posse
dulcius fuit semper, quàm in eâ. Tu populi Romani triumphorum, victoriarum,
ouationum, omnium denique particeps fuisti, praeterquam ruinae. Tu à terrae
150   dominis, Romuli nepotibus bellum gerere posse didicisti, velle omnes docuisti.
Tu vitam, tu hunc spiritum, tu hanc lucem pro libertate semper venalem habui-
sti. Tu artem ab alijs, ausus à te mutuatus es, ita vt mortem melius inferre illis, tu
promptius subire potueris. Illis imperium terrae tempus ademit, tibi maris reddidit. Tu foris Oceano, domi socijs, vbique tibi imperas. Tu, quod olim frustrà
155   Xerxes tentarat, Neptuno compedes iniecisti; cumque alij sive reges, sive principes ultrà populos imperium suum extendere non soleant, tu etiam in ventos
obtines, inuentumque tibi aliquid praeter hominem, quod parêre sciat. Accipe
principem tuum, BATAVE, sed morientem, qui cum omnia saluti tuae impen-
disset, se quoque impendit. Accipite, viri, et recordamini, in terrâ vestrâ nihil
160   vnquam vindicasse Iberum sibi, praeter fraudem, cuius vnius artis pudenda
est scientia. Agedum, BATAVE, quod solum pro tuis in me beneficijs possum,
Musas meas consecraui tibi, quoniam chartae solae, cum ferrum, aes, et chalybs non possint, diuturnitatem annorum, et saeculi violentiam perrumpunt.

Ego cum bonis exutus omnibus, laribus et praedijs meis, nihil Hispanorum
165   tyrannidi, communis relligionis ergò, praeter infelicem hanc animam subdu-
xissem, et si quam spem in parentibus, miserrimis et ipsis repositam haberem,
tu me excepisti, fovisti, amplexus es ac, quod mirum maximè, vestrum benefi-
cium maius mihi fecit Hispanorum crudelitas.

164–184 Ego cum ... habuit A: *del. L.*

learn how much the name of Freedom has cost you, which is not attained but by moral quality and prowess, and retained by frugality and zeal. Let the excellence of his exalted spirit, which despises death for his homeland, spread wider than where it was born. And let these divine deeds and princely enterprises not be enclosed in such narrow borders that they appear both to have come into being and to be buried in the same country.

Come on then, ruler of the sea, Dutchman, I now address you, for whom it has always been sweeter to die for than in your homeland. You have participated in the triumphs, the victories and ovations, yes to everything of the Roman people, except for its fall. You have learned from the rulers of the earth, the grandsons of Romulus,[18] to be able to make war; you yourself have taught all to want it. You have always been willing to sacrifice your life, this breath and this light for freedom. You have received the skills from others, the courage from yourself, in such a way that you could kill them better and you could be killed with greater willingness. Time has taken away their power over the earth, it has given you the power over the sea.

Abroad you rule over the ocean, at home over your allies, and over yourself. You have enchained Neptune, something that Xerxes had tried in vain.[19] Although others, whether kings or emperors, do not allow their power to reach beyond people, you even possess power over the winds, and you have found something beyond men that knows how to obey you. Hollander, here is your prince, but in his dying hour, who after having sacrificed everything for your salvation, also sacrificed himself. Listen, Sirs, and bring into your mind that in your country the Spaniard has never appropriated anything but deceit, the only art for the knowledge of which one must be ashamed.

Come on then, Hollander, I have dedicated my poem[20] to you, the only thing I can return for your benefits to me, since only paper breaks the long series of years and the violence of time, whereas iron, bronze and steel are not able to do so. When, deprived of all my goods, house and land, I had withdrawn nothing from the tyranny of the Spaniards for the sake of the common faith than only my poor soul, and if I had any hope in my parents, it was still in them while they themselves were most unfortunate, have you taken me in, cherished and embraced me.[21] And, what is most surprising, the cruelty of the Spaniards has made your benefaction even greater for me.

---

18   The Romans who lived in the city founded by Romulus, supposedly in 754 BC.

19   The Persian king Xerxes I (518–465 BC) is told to have 'punished' the sea by throwing 'chains' (viz. pontoon bridges on the Hellespont) in it.

20   Lit. 'my Muses', a reference to his own tragedy *Auriacus*.

21   At the age of three, his parents fled with Daniel Heinsius from Ghent to the northern Netherlands, ending up in Voorburg, near The Hague.

Inter reliqua et illud accedit, quod in Academiâ vestrâ tot iam annos ver-
170 satus sim, in quâ et illud vobis, vt primariae causae, asscribendum puto, quod
in hâc terrâ vestrâ tot summorum virorum familiaritate vsus sim, ac praesertim
trium Heroum, in quorum tempora me incidisse gloriari soleo: Iosephi Scaligeri
(ac quantum hoc nomen Dij immortales?), omnis scientiae, omnium literarum,
omnium linguarum, totius non Europae modò, Viri, vt generis splendore prin-
175 cipis, quem vos, cum vnum modò eodem tempore in hoc vniuerso Phoenicem
posse esse sciatis, in Bataviâ vestrâ vivere voluistis, vt imperium simul Maris
apud vos sit, et Literarum. Pauli praeterea Choarti, Christianissimi Gallorum
regis apud vos Oratoris, cuius nomen praeterquam quod vobis propemodum
sacrum sit, liceat et illud mirari mihi, virum tam Illustrem non de omni erudi-
180 tione modò iudicare posse, sed et primas in eâ tenere; et Iani Dousae, Senatoris
vestri, Curatoris nostri, viri incomparabilis, qui cum de totâ litteraturâ iam olim,
nuperrimè etiam de patriâ suâ optimè mereri cepit, et tanquam parum sit quod
infelici hoc aeuo literas restituit, nuperrimè etiam Bataviam suam restauravit,
qui me filij loco semper habuit.
185 Itaque diutius vel animi grati, vel debiti officij testimonium desyderare vos
passus non sum, nec idoneum magis hoc tempore argumentum Patriae vestrae
Vobisque reperire potui, quam fatalem illum Patriae parentis casum, quem
penitus amisissetis, nisi in Filio viueret. Qui vobiscum, tot Illustria Hispanorum capita Dijs Manibus, Paternae necis vltor mactare cepit, quem ut Deus
190 immortalis nunquam in Tragoediâ partes habere permittat, optabo; in reliquis
verò parenti simillimum, vel virtute, vel animi magnitudine sibi, vobis nobis-
que conseruet. Ego verò intereà hoc qualecunque committo vobis.

Nobilitatis vestrae addictissimus Cliens
DANIEL HEYNSIUS.

---

185 Itaque *A*: Quare *L*.

In addition, among other things, I have been at your Academy for so many years. There, in my opinion, I especially owe it to you that I have become familiar with so many excellent men in your country and especially with three Heroes, whose contemporary I boast to be: Josephus Scaliger[22] (what an important man, great gods!), a man who is the first in all science, all literature, all languages, not only of all Europe, as he is by his illustrious descent. You wanted him to live in your Holland, knowing that only one phoenix can live in this universe at the same time, so that at the same time you have dominion over the sea and that over literature. Moreover, Paul Choart,[23] the ambassador of the most Christian king with you. Apart from the fact that his name is almost sacred to you, I might wonder that such an illustrious man cannot judge only about every branch of science, but also plays the first role in it. And Janus Dousa,[24] member of your States, our curator, an unequalled man. He has since long been propitious for the whole literature, and also very recently for his homeland, and if it was not enough to restore literature to its old level in these unfortunate times, he has only recently restored Holland. He has always treated me as his son.

Therefore, I did not endure that you should do any longer without proof of my gratitude or of the due service, and I could not think of a theme that is more appropriate for your homeland than that fateful death of the father of the Fatherland, whom you would have lost completely, if he did not live on in his Son.[25] Together with you, he has already offered many illustrious Spaniards to the gods of the underworld as an avenger of the murder of his father. I will pray that the immortal God will ensure that he never has a role in a tragedy. However, in the rest He may preserve the image of his father either in bravery or in greatness of mind, for Himself, for you and for me. However, in the meantime I trust this work to you, whatever its quality.

Your Honorary's most humble servant
Daniel Heinsius.

---

22   The French classicist and scholar Josephus Justus Scaliger (1540–1609) was a professor at Leiden University who also knew languages of the Middle East; Heinsius was one of his favourite students.

23   Paul Choart de Buzenval (ca. 1550–1607) was the French ambassador in The Hague.

24   Janus Dousa or Jan van der Does (1545–1604) was founder of the Leiden academy and a patron of Heinsius.

25   Viz. Prince Maurice (1567–1625).

[2]   ΙΩΣΗΠΩΙ ΣΚΑΛΑΝΩΙ τῷ Ἰουλίῳ τοῦ πάνυ
        ΔΑΝΙΗ῾Λ ῾Ο ῾ΕΙ῾ΝΣΙΟΥ εὖ πράττειν.

Τὸν Ἀνάχαρσιν λέγεται, ὦ Διογενές, τὸ πρῶτον ἐκ Σκυθίας Ἀθήναζε παιδείας ἐπιθυμίᾳ
τῆς Ἑλληνικῆς ἀφικνούμενον, τῷ Τοξάρει, Σκύθῃ καὶ αὐτῷ ὄντι καὶ ὁμοεθνεῖ, Ἀθήνη-
σιν ἐς λόγους ἐλθεῖν. Τὸν δέ, παιδείας τε ἅμα, καὶ φύσεως εὖ ἔχοντα, τἆλλα δὲ καὶ τῶν
Ἀθηναίων λόγων οὐ παρέργως ἁπτόμενον, οὐδὲ δυσπρόσοδον ὄντα, ὡς εἰκὸς ἄνδρα
5   τῶν τῶν πολλῶν καὶ δημοτικῶν, τῶν τε ἐκεῖ ὀκταπόδων (τοῦτο γὰρ τοῖς ἀπόροις ἐν
     Σκύθοις τοὔνομα κεῖσθαι λόγος ἔχει) τὸν ἔρωτα τοῦτον καὶ ζῆλον φίλου ἀνδρός, ὃν οὐ
     πρὸ πολλοῦ ἦρα καὶ αὐτὸς τὴν Ἑλλάδα ἰδεῖν, οὐδαμῶς ἐν παρέργῳ θέμενον, πολλὰ
     καλὰ κ᾽ἀγαθὰ ὑποθέσθαι· οὐ μὴν ἀναδειξάμενον τἆλλα, οἷς ἐκεῖνον μάλιστα φιλο-
     φρονούμενος ξυνίει, εἰπόντα δὲ μόνον· εἰ ἕνα μέν, ὦ φιλότης, τῶν τῇδε ἀνδρῶν φίλον
10 κτήσαιο, εὖ ἴσθι πᾶσαν τὴν Ἑλλάδα οὐ μόνον ἔχων ἐν αὐτῷ, ἀλλὰ καὶ πάντα τὰ παρ᾽
     Ἕλλησι θέας ἄξια ἰδὼν καὶ ἐμπορευόμενος. Καὶ ταῦτα μὴν περὶ τοῦ Σόλωνος ὁ Σκύθης,
     ὀρθῶς γε λέγων ἐκεῖνος.
     Ἐγὼ δέ, ὅτε τὸ ἐπεδήματα τῇ πόλει ταύτῃ, σοὶ κατὰ δαίμονα ἐντυχών, μονονουχὶ
     θεὸς ἐν ἀκαρεῖ χρόνου γεγενημένος ἔδοξα, πλὴν ἀλλὰ καὶ πάντων ὀλιγωρήσας, καὶ
15 τῶν πάνυ τοῖς πολλοῖς περιβλέπτων καταγελάσας ἀτεχνῶς, τὸ κεφάλαιον εἰδέναι τῶν
     τῇδε ἀγαθῶν.
     Τὸ δὲ νῦν εἶναι, ἐπείγε τὸν κόθορνον, μείζω ἢ ὥστε νεανίᾳ καὶ οἵῳ ἐμοὶ πρέπειν,
     περικεῖσθαι κινδυνεύω, ἐν μυριάνδρῳ ἐμαυτὸν θεάτρῳ καθίσας δόξω, εἰ σύ γε τὴν
     δίαιταν ταύτην ἐπιτετραμμένος, καὶ τὸν τῶν ἄθλων νόμον ἐγχειρισθείς, κατὰ τὰ σοὶ
20 δοκοῦντα τὴν ψῆφον φέροις, οἷς ἂν μόνος σὺ διαγινώσκοις ἀγαπήσειν.
     Οὐ μὴν οὐδ᾽ ἕωλόν τινα ἔφεσιν ἀγωνιοῦμαι, οὐδὲ δικαιολογήσομαι, κἄν τι ἁμαρτὼν
     ἅλω, οὐδέ, τὸ τῶν ὑπευθύνων ἐκεῖνο, λόγον τῶν τετολμημένων ὑφέξομαι· ὥσπερ οὐ
     πάνυ μοι μέλον, εἰ καὶ εὐτελῆ τινα, καὶ σεμνότητος τραγικῆς ἄξιον, ἢ μεγαλόφρων ἐν
     οὐδέν, ἣν μόνον ᾖ τε ἡλικία ἡμῶν, καὶ τὸ ἡδέως περὶ τὰ τοιαῦτα ἡμᾶς διακεῖσθαι, σοὶ
25 διὰ σπουδῆς ᾖ· οὐ γὰρ τὸν Εὐριπίδην ὅλον, ἢ καὶ τὸν τραγῳδόν, νὴ τὸν Διόνυσον, τὸν

---

3 Τὸν δέ *A*: Τόνδε *L*.   5 τῶν τε *scripsi*: τῶντε *A*.   18 καθίσας *scripsi*: καθίξας *A*.   19 τὸν *L*: τὴν *A*.
20 ἀγαπήσειν *scripsi*: ἀγαπήσων *A*.   24 ἤ τε *scripsi*: ᾖτε *A*.

[2]   **Daniel Heinsius sends Josephus Scaliger,**
                       the son of the Famous Julius, his greetings.

Son of the gods,[26] the story goes that when Anacharsis[27] first travelled to Athens from Scythia out of an interest in Greek culture, he got into conversation with Toxaris, also a Scythe and a compatriot. This man was well-educated and healthy in body and among other things he had seriously participated in the debates of the Athenians; he was not a-social, as your pasture would expect from a man from the mob and from the people, one of those 'eight-legged friends' (because according to the stories in the Scythians this is the name for the poor). He found his friend's desire—namely to see Greece, a desire he had himself cherished not long before—certainly not unimportant, but gave much excellent advice, not by showing everything that he had understood would do him a great service, but by saying only: "My dear, if you only had a chance to make friends with one of the men in this place, then be convinced that you do not have only all of Greece in him, but also have seen everything that is worth seeing among the Greeks and made it your own". By this, the Scythe meant Solon, and he was right.

But when I first arrived in this city as a stranger and by a happy chance met you, I almost thought I had become a god in a moment, but even that I knew the essence of all good of this place, with neglect of all others and simply laughing at the people whom the mass admires highly.

For now, because I run the chance of wearing a stage boot that is too big for a boy like me, I'll be sitting in a ten thousand-person audience, and I will, if you—and you're entrusted with the decision, you've got the rules of the match in your hands—would cast your vote as you see fit, be satisfied with any judgement you make as sole judge. And I will certainly not appeal afterwards and advocate my case, even though I should be caught on mistakes; nor will I, what is the task of those responsible, account for my enterprise, since I do not care if it is ordinary and there is nothing in it that is worthy of the ceremony of the tragedy, if you only would take into account my age and the fact that I deal with such matters as a hobby. For I have not devoured the entire Euripides, or, by

---

26   Lit. Diogenes (son of a god), an honorary indication of Joseph Scaliger and perhaps meant
      to be an allusion to the name Joseph (God increases).
27   It is the Greek satirist and rhetorician Lucian (ca. 125–after 180 AD) who in his *Scytha* tells
      the story of the Scythian philosopher Anacharsis (6th c. BC), who came to his compatriot
      Toxaris in Athens, who advised him to make friends with the sage Solon.

σὸν καραπεπώκαμεν, οὐδὲ τὰ τοῦ Ὁμήρου, κατὰ τὸν Αἰχύλον, τεμάχη, ἀπὸ στόματος
εἴποιμεν, ὥστε ὑποδραματουργεῖν σοι. Μάλιστα δὲ τοῦ θάρσους ἡμῖν, τό τε τῆς ἀφορ-
μῆς τὸ μέγα, καὶ τὸ τῆς ὑποθέσεως τὸ λαμπρὸν συλλαμβάνεται, καίπερ πολλάκις τῶν
ἔργων τοὺς λόγους οἵους δήποτε ὑπερφθεγγομένων.

30   Οὐ γὰρ κατὰ Μηδείας, ἢ Ἑκάβας, ἢ καὶ Αἴαντος νὴ Δία μαστιγοφόρους τὸ πρᾶγ-
μα, ἢ τὰς ἄλλας τερατείας, καὶ μαγγανείας ποιητικάς, πάνυ ἀλλόκοτα μυθίδια ὄντα,
παιδῶν ψυχάς, ἔτι περὶ τὸ βρῦν καὶ τὸ μαμμᾶν σπουδαζόντων, καὶ τὴν Μορμὼ καὶ τὴν
Λαμίαν δεδιότων, ἐκπλήττειν δυνάμενα· περὶ δὲ τῶν ἡμεδαπῶν, τῶν τε Αὐρανσίου τοῦ
μεγάλου πάλαι πεπραγμένων, καὶ μάλιστα περὶ τῆς τοῦ βίου αὐτοῦ καταστροφῆς πᾶς
35   ὁ λόγος, ὃν καὶ ἐπιγράφεται.

Σὺ μὲν οὖν ὀβέλισον τὰ πολλά, καὶ καταδίκασον, ὡς οὐκ ἔστιν ὅ τι ἂν ἄλλο ποιήσας
μᾶλλον χαρίσαιό μοι· οὐ γοῦν δεοίμην σοῦ γε τὸ κωμικὸν τοῦτο,

Τῶν ποιητῶν εἶναί με λέγειν ἑκατὸν σταδίοισιν ἄριστον,

οὐκ, εἴ γε καὶ χύτραις λημῶν τυγχάνοιμι, ὀλεθρίων γὰρ ταῦτα, μόνοι τε ἐλλόγιμοι εἶναι
40   φασκόντων, καὶ σοφόν τι χρῆμα, καὶ ἄκρον ἐν παιδείᾳ γενέσθαι πεπεισμένων· τὰ δ’
ἐμὰ μετρίως ἔχει πάντα, καὶ νέος ἔτι κομιδῇ ταῖς Μούσαις ἅμα, καὶ τῇ τούτων ἀδελφῇ
τῇ βελτίστῃ πενίᾳ προσφιλοσοφῶ.

Σὺ μὲν οὖν οὐκ ἂν φθάνοις ταῦτα ποιῶν· ἐγὼ δὲ τὴν τραγῳδίαν τὴν ἐμὴν ἐκδιδόναι
μοι δοκῶ, οὐδὲν δέον ταύτην, ὥσπερ τὴν Ἀκρισίου, παρθενεύεσθαι, καθάπερ ἱερειάν
45   τινα τῇ θεσμοφόρῳ ἀνατρεφομένην, ἀλλὰ κοινόν, φασι, κτῆμα γενέσθαι. Τί γὰρ ἂν
καὶ πάθοι τις, ὁπόταν φίλοι ἄνδρες καὶ εὐδόκιμοι βιάζοιντο; Ἢν γοῦν ἕν δρᾶμα τοῦτο
γραψαίμην μόνον, πρὶν τὴν ὑπήνην ἀνέρπειν, περὶ τὸ στόμα τοὺς κροτάφους τε (οὕτω
γὰρ τῶν ποιητῶν τινος μέμνημαι λέγοντος) τοῦτο πρὸ ὁδοῦ ἐς τὴν παιδείαν ἔσομαι
ποποιηκὼς ὑπέρευγε ποιῶν τά τε ἄλλα, καὶ ὅτι ἐμβαδίων δεόμενος περιπατῶ, μικρὸς
50   ὢν καὶ πηχναῖος, καὶ ταῦτα μὲν δὴ ταῦτα· ὁ δὲ κάκιστα μιασμάτων ἀπολούμενος

---

27 Μάλιστα L: μάλιστα A. ‖ τό τε scripsi: τότε A.   33 τῶν τε scripsi: τῶντε A.   37 γοῦν scripsi:
γοῦ A.   39 μόνοι τε scripsi: μόνοιτε A.   48 πρὸ ὁδοῦ scripsi: προοδοῦ A.

Dionysus, your tragedian,[28] nor can I, in order to speak with Aeschylus, recite whole rags of Homer by heart[29] so that I cannot stand in your tragic shadow.

Especially the greatness of the courage and then of the endeavour and the radiance of the subject are seized upon by me in defence, although often the actions override the words, however they may be.

For it is not about people like Medea, or Hecuba[30] or also, by Zeus, the whip-bearing Ajax[31] or the other tall stories and magic arts of the poets, which are bizarre stories and can frighten children's souls who are still busy drinking and eating and are scared of Mormo and Lamia;[32] but the whole piece deals with national matter, namely the earlier heroic deeds of the great Orange and especially with the disastrous end of the life of the man, after whom it is also named.

You, then, tick off most faults and give a strict judgement, because you would not be able to please me with anything else: at least I would not like to ask you (to speak with the comedian), that you say "I am miles ahead of the other poets", even if I were hopelessly overconfident. Because that characterizes worthless people, people who think that they alone count and people who are convinced that they have a monopoly on wisdom and are the summit of erudition. In my case, all circumstances are modest, for I am still very young and still under the tutelage of the Muses, and of their sister, poor poverty.

You could not do this early enough. I am strongly thinking of publishing my tragedy, because it is not necessary that it remains in chaste seclusion, like the daughter of Acrisius,[33] like a priestess who was brought up for the Thesmophoria,[34] but it has to become common property as it is called. Because what else would someone do when dear and honoured men are killed? If this was the only play I would write, before the beard covered my chin and temples (for I remember that one of the poets expresses it thus), I will thereby have made a useful contribution to my development, while I do especially well that I walk around and ask for dramatic boots, although I am small and a thumb long; but enough about this. Let, as far as I am concerned, jealousy shrink, which should

---

28 Of Euripides (480–406 BC) seventeen plays are extant. This is a quotation from Lucian's *Juppiter tragoedeus* 1.
29 According to Athenaeus in his *Deipnosophistae* (VIII, 39), Aeschylus (525–456 BC) said of his tragedies that they contained whole pieces of Homer.
30 Two tragedies written by Euripides.
31 A tragedy by Sophocles.
32 Mormo and Lamia were ghosts, used as ogres to frighten children.
33 Acrisius tried to prevent his daughter Danae to become pregnant by locking her up. Zeus penetrated her as a golden rain.
34 The Thesmophoria were a festival to honour Demeter; it was accessible to women only.

φθόνος ἐμοῦ ἔνεκα, οἰμωζέτω, μηδ' ὥρασιν ἵκοιτο, τὸ προσωπεῖον, ὃ μεταξὺ τραγῳδῶν
περιβέβλημαι, μορμολυττόμενος, καὶ γενναίως μὰ Δι' ὑπ' ἐμοῦ ἐκτραγῳδούμενος.
"Ερρωσο

Διογενές μοι Ἰουλιάδη μέγα φέγγος Ἀχαιῶν,

55   καὶ Βακχεῖον τοῦτον ἄνακτα, σήμερον Διονυσίοις τραγῳδοῖς ἀποκηρυττόμενον, ἀποδέχου.

perish most miserably, and let them flee out of fear of the mask which I have set up during the writing of my tragedy, and now it has, by Zeus, considerably been cast by myself in a bad light.

Goodbye, Son of the gods,[35] son of Julius, great fame of the Greeks and accept this Bacchic lord,[36] today openly proclaimed to the Dionysian tragedians.

---

35   Diogenes, see above, n. 26.
36   An intricate metonym for the *Auriacus*: the Bacchic lord is the Prince of Orange, here presented in the genre dedicated to Bacchus, tragedy.

[3]   IN HISPANUM ET BATAVUM.

Δημοβόρος κόσμου ποτ' ἐέλδετο παντὸς Ἴβηρος
    Ἰσχανόων Κελτῶν, ἰσχανόων Λιγύρων.
Οἷον ἀπάντα φόβησεν· ἐδείδιε πᾶσα δέ μιν χθὼν
    Οὐρανίης ὅσση κεῖται ἐν ἀγκαλίσιν.
5   Φλανδριακοὺς δ' ἐμὸν ἔθνος ἀεικέα μήσατο ἔργα,
    Οὐδὲ πόνου λῆζις πὰρ μίη, οὐδ' ἀλέη·
Παισὶ κακὸν φρονέεσκε καὶ ἀνδράσι, ῥέζε δὲ λίην
    Νήπια καὶ ἁπαλὰς αἴσυλα παρθενικάς.
Αἵματι δ' ἡμετέρῳ ἰδίη ἐρύθρηνεν ἄρουρα,
10   Πάντα δὲ μόρμυρεν βένθεα, καὶ ποταμοί.
Τοὺς δὲ μέτα κρατεροῖο καθιππεύεσκε Βαταύου,
    Νηυσὶν ἁλὸς ταμίην ᾗσιν ἐποιχόμενος.
Ὠκεανὸς δ' ἑὰ τέκνα σαώσατο, μήδετο δ' εὐθὺς
    Κύματα δειλαίῳ ἀμφιχέαι Βατάβῳ.
15   Αὐτὰρ ὁ βῆ πατέειν διερῷ ποδὶ νῶτα θαλάσσης·
    Ἐκ δ' ἔριν, ἐκ δ' αἰνοὺς φευγέμεν ἐχθοδοποὺς.
Ζεύγνυτο δ' ἅρμα θοὸν, ἀνεμοτρεφὲς, οἷο χαλινοὶ
    Πείσματα, τοί δ' ἵπποι λαίφεα, καὶ ὀθόναι.
Τῷ πίσυνος διὰ πόντον ἐλαυνέμεν ὦρτο καὶ ὕδωρ,
20   Ὦρτο δὲ καὶ ταχέων πρόσθε θέειν ἀνέμων.
Μὰψ δ' ἀνέμων ταμίησιν Ἴβηρ ἀνεμώλιος ἔτλη
    Μαρνάνεμος δεινῷ ἀντιάειν πολέμῳ.
Πολλὰ δὲ τοὺς ἀπέλεθρος Ἄρης ξυνέηκε μάχεσθαι
    Ὕδατος ἀρχαίης γῆς τ' ἐπὶ κοιρανίης.
25   Κόσμου δ' ἀντιπάλαιο μόνος περίγεντο Βατοῦος.
    Ἀνδρομέης ἤτοι ἐξεφάνη γενεῆς
    (Γῆς ὕπερ ἐν Πόντῳ, Πόντου δ' ὕπερ ὅρμενος ἐν γῇ)
    Ἀντίβιος κεῖνος ἀμφίβιος Βατάβος.

3 ἀπάντα scripsi: ἐ πάντα A.   27 ὕπερ scripsi: ὕπερερ A.

[3]   **On the Spaniard and the Hollander**

The Spaniard, who bleeds the people, formerly longed for the whole world, and set his sights on France and Italy. How much did he frighten everything; the whole world, which lies in the arms of Uranus,[37] was afraid of him. Against my people the Flemings he devised wrongdoings, there was no end to the misery, there was no escape. He projected violence against children and adults, he even committed all too foolish crimes against weak girls. Our own fields turned red from our blood, all the depths and rivers bubbled from it.

After them he marched against the powerful Hollander, while he attacked the lord of the sea with his ships. Oceanus, however, protected his children and immediately made sure to wash the unfortunate Hollander with high waves.

But he entered the crests of the sea with a swift foot, and fled the battle and the fearsome enemies. He controlled the fast chariot, fed by the winds. Its reins were ropes, the horses were sails and tarpaulins. Putting his trust in them, he made up his mind to march over the sea and the water, to sail out quickly before the fast winds.

In vain the powerless Spaniard has dared to take up to struggle fighting in a formidable war against the lords of the winds.[38] The awe-inspiring Ares brought them together to fight much about both the domination of the sea and the sovereignty on land. The Hollander on his own conquered the hostile world. He truly stood out over the human race (in the sea he stood up in defence of the land, on the land in defence of the sea), the offensive Hollander living in both regions.

---

37   I.e. under the sky.
38   A reference to the destruction of the Spanish Armada which was defeated by the English and destroyed by a storm in 1588.

[4] ·   IN AVRIACVM
                          DANIELIS HEINSII.

Melpomenae sacrum facit Heinsius. Ore fauete
    Dum quatit Aeschyleo pulpita picta pede.
Cede Sophoclaei carmen regale cothurni,
    Cedite Cecropijs plausa theatra choris.
5 Principis ille vicem subitam, strictumque dolosè
    Non expectato fulmen ab hoste canit,
Et fixum in patriâ, dum figitur induce, vulnus.
    Hanc tibi nulla dies tollet, Ibere, notam.
Grandiloquisque Heynsi numeris, quae dedecus vna est
10   Mors tibi, Nassovio vita perennis erit.

       Iosephus Scaliger Iulij Caesaris Filius.

Tit. B Iosephus Scaliger, Iul. Caes. F., *Poemata omnia, Ex museo Petri Scriverii* (Leiden: Raphelengius, 1615), p. 54 (KB 759 K 1).   2 Aeschyleo *B*: Aschyleo *A*.   9 Heynsi *A*: Heinsi *B*.

[4]   **On Daniel Heinsius'** *Auriacus*

Heinsius makes a sacrifice to Melpomene;[39] be quiet while he is shaking the colourful scene with Aeschylean foot. Make way, royal song of Sophocles' tragedy, make way, theatres that resound with Greek choruses. He sings the sudden death of the Prince, the pistol cunningly unexpectedly drawn by the enemy, and the wound inflicted on the fatherland by being inflicted on the leader.

Not one single day will take away this shame from you, Spaniard. Because of the lofty verses of Heinsius, death, which is pre-eminently a disgrace to you, will mean eternal life for Nassau.

Joseph Scaliger, the son of Julius Caesar.

---

39   I.e. he writes a tragedy, Melpomene being the Muse of tragedy.

[5]   IN EANDEM.

GRAECORVM gravitas ab acumine victa Latino est,
    SCALIGERO in Tragicis Iudice Hypothesibus.
Arbitrio cuius vni data palma Poëtae
    Prae tribus Argolicis Vatibus Ausonio.
5   Laus SENECAE haec, cui maiestas, cui spiritus ac vis
    Cura, nitor, cultus, omnia plena DEO.
At vetera haec; nostrâ sed tempestate Poëtae
    Personam Tragici qui ferat, ecquis erit?
MVRETVSNE? Sed hic quid ad Orgia BVCHANANI,
10   CAESARIS is, IEPHTAE conditor iste suae?
AESCHYLEO argumenta vides indicta Cothurno,
    Nec CLITÛS NATO cognita, nec SOPHOCLI.
Et dubitas, vtrum antistent mendacia veris?
    Illane, an haec pluris sint faciunda tibi?
15 Quae tantum ijs, quantum SALLVSTI pagina ficto
    LVCI ASINO aut MARSI praestat AMAZONIDI.
At quantum Historijs cedunt Acroâmata, tantum
    HEINSIADI assurgunt pulpita cuncta meo;
HEINSIADI, cui tota HELLAS, cui poplite flexo
20   Submittit fasces PINDARVS ipse suos.
Materiem quaeris? GVILLELMI hîc funera (Lector)
    PRINCIPIS Hesperiâ fraude peracta leges.
Dùmque leges, aequare rei mirabere Ephebum
    Pondera Romuleis sic potuisse modis.
25 Forsitan et dicas: Proavito qui Lare pulsus
    Talia Leidensi scripsit in Exsilio,
Quid faciet, Patriae compos si quando futurus?
    Lux (precor) ô fatis sit prior illa meis.

Tit. B Ianus Dousa, *Echo, sive Lusus imaginis iocosae quibus Titulus Halcedonia* [...] (The Hague:
Nieuland, 1603) pp. 69v–70v (KB 188 D 14); *C* Ianus Dousa, *Poemata pleraque selecta* [...] (Leiden:
Basson, 1609), pp. 148–149.   4 *ad* tribus Argolicis Vatibus *in marg. add. B C* Aeschylo, Sophocle,
atque Euripide. ‖ *ad* Ausonio *in marg. add. B C*: Senecae Tragico.   10 Iephtae *A*: Iephtes *B C.* ‖
conditor *A*: editor *B*, Editor *C.*

[5]   **On the same**

The gravity of the Greeks was overcome by the Latin acumen in the opinion of Scaliger in his reflections on tragedy.[40] In his opinion, a poet from Italy deserves the victory over the three Greek tragic poets. This honour befalls Seneca, with his grandeur, liveliness and dynamism, his thoroughness, lustre and refinement, all inspired by the deity.

That as far as antiquity is concerned; which poet will wear the tragic mask in our time? Muret? But how can he be weighed next to the biblical drama of Buchanan, the former the author of *Julius Caesar*, the latter of *Jephthah*?[41] You will see subjects that have not been addressed in Aeschylus' theatre and are still unknown to the son of Clyto and Sophocles.[42] Do you still doubt whether fiction is preferable to truth and whether you should regard the former higher or the latter? Facts are as far above fictions as Sallust's work is above the *Ass of Lucius*, or the *Amazonis* of Marsus.[43]

Just as stories make way for Histories, so the entire audience stands up for my good friend Heinsius. Heinsius for whom the whole of Greece, for whom even Pindar[44] strikes the flag.

You ask for the subject? Here you can read (Reader) about the murder of Prince William, committed with Spanish ruses. While reading you may be surprised to find that a young man has been able to adequately express the important content in Latin verses. You might say that if someone who, expelled from his ancestral home and living as an exile in Leiden, has written something like that,[45] what will he perform if he ever lives in his fatherland again? Ah, if only I could experience that day! And you could add: a poet to whom the

---

40   Julius Caesar Scaliger (1484–1558), the father of Heinsius' teacher Joseph Scaliger, in his *Poetices libri septem* (1561) attaches more importance to the Latin tragedy by Lucius Annaeus Seneca (ca. 4 BC–65 AD) than to that of the Greek tragic playwrights Aeschylus, Sophocles and Euripides.

41   The French humanist Marc Antoine de Muret (1526–1558) wrote a tragedy *Iulius Caesar* (1591), the Scottish poet George Buchanan (1506–1582) wrote a tragedy for the school in Bordeaux where he taught: *Iephthes sive votum* (1544).

42   The son of Clyto is Euripides. Heinsius chose a historical subject, not mythology as the Greek tragic poets had done.

43   The Roman historian Sallust (86–ca. 35 BC) was known for his earnestness; Heinsius puts him above the story of *Lucius and the Ass* by the Hellenized Syrian satirist Lucian (ca. 125–ca. 180 AD); of the Roman poet Domitius Marsus (d. between 19 BC and 12 AD) the title of an epic poem *Amazonis* is known. Again, history is put above mythology.

44   The Greek poet Pindar (ca. 518–446 BC) was greatly appreciated in the Renaissance.

45   Heinsius as a child fled from Ghent, in Flanders, to end up a student in Leiden.

Et licet haec addas: Cui tantum indulsit Olympus,
30   Materiem hanc meritò legerat ipse sibi,
Nec verbis nec rebus vbi sua pondera desint.
      Ne longum faciam, singula conueniunt.
VATE suo ut PRINCEPS, dignus sic PRINCIPE VATES,
      AVRIACO HEINSIADES, HEINSIADE AVRIACVS.

IANVS DOVSA NORDOVIX
Hagae comitis scripsi.

Olympus donated so many talents rightly chose this subject, because both his style and his material possess weight.

In short, everything is in balance. The Prince was given the appropriate poet, the Poet the Prince who suited him, Heinsius is worth Orange, Orange Heinsius.

Janus Dousa from Noordwijk. Written in The Hague.

[6]   Εἰς τὸν Δαν<ιέλος> τοῦ Εἰνσίου
                            ΑΥΡΑΙΚΑΡΧΗΝ.

Ἔρρετ' Ἰβηρομανεῖς, σφέτερον κακὸν ἀμφαγαπῶντες,
    Δίζυγα δουλοσύνην, σώματος ἠδὲ νόου.
Ἄμμιν ἀλεξίκακον θεὸς ὤπασεν Ἡρακλῆα,
    Ἡνίοχον γλυκερῆς δέξιον εὐπραγίας,
5 Αὐραικῆς ἀρχὸν, μέγαν ἰθυντῆρα Βαταύων,
    Ἰσπανῶν θάμβος, καὶ δέος Αὐσονίων.
Κεῖνον, ἐλευθερίης ταμίην, καὶ Βελγίδος ἄλκαρ,
    Δισσὸν δουλοσύνης ἄχθος ἀπωσάμενον·
Μούσαις καὶ Χάρισιν πεφιλημένον ΕΪΝΣΙΟΣ ἔρνος
10 Ταῖς δ' ἱεραῖς γέρασεν Μνημοσύνης σελίσιν,
    Ἄφθιτον ἀμφιέσας μεγαλήτορος Αὐραικάρχου,
    Ἀΐδιον τ' ἰδίῃ εὐκλείην κεφαλῇ.
Ζώσι γὰρ ἐσσομένοισι τ' ἀγάκλυτος ἔσσεται αἰὲν
    ΚΕΙΝΟΥ εὐεργεσίη, ΕΪΝΣΙΟΥ εὐεπίη.

BONAVENTURA VVLCANIVS.

---

9 Χάρισιν *scripsi*: χάρισιν *A*.   10 Μνημοσύνης *scripsi*: μνημοσύνης *A*.

[6]   **On Daniel Heinsius'** *Prince of Orange*

Go away, you cursed Spaniards, who embrace your mischief with love, double slavery, of body and spirit.

The deity gave us a Hercules[46] who averted disaster, a skilful bringer of sweet fortune, the Prince of Orange, the great captain of the Dutch, the fear of the Spaniards, the terror of the inhabitants of the Occident.

He, the lord of liberty, the protector of the Hollanders, who dispelled the burden of double slavery, is honoured by Heinsius, a child loved by the Muses and the Graces, with the holy writings of Mnemosyne,[47] and thus loaded the imperishable and eternal fame of the proud Orange on his own head.

In current and future generations, Orange will always be famous for his own merit and by the praising words of Heinsius.

Bonaventura Vulcanius

---

46   Just like Hercules in Greek mythology defeated monsters, the Prince of Orange stops the monstrous Spaniards.

47   Mnemosyne is the mother of the Muses; Vulcanius refers to Heinsius' poetry, especially his *Auriacus*.

[7]   Idem Bonaventvrae Vvlcanii.

Τῶν παλαιῶν Σοφόκλης μέγ' ὑπείροχός ἐστι τραγῳδῶν,
    Τῶν νυνὶ δ' ἔξαρχος ΕΊΝΣΙΆΔΗΣ πέλεται.
Κείνου πατρὶς ἔην τῆς Ἑλλάδος Ἑλλὰς Ἀθῆναι,
    Τούτου Φλανδριακῶν Γάνδα πόλις πόλεων.
5 Ἐν τραγικῆς ἀμφοῖν σοφίης κλέος· ἀλλὰ Σοφόκλης
    Δρέψατο τοῦτο γέρων, ΕΊΝΣΙΆΔΗΣ δὲ νέος.

―――――――
1 τραγῳδῶν scripsi: τραγῳδῶν A.   3 Ἑλλὰς scripsi: ἑλλὰς A.

[7]   **A similar poem by Bonaventura Vulcanius**

Sophocles far excels the antique tragedians,[48] Heinsius is the leader of the contemporary ones. The father's city of the former was the Hellas of Hellas, Athens, and of the other it was the city of Flemish cities, Ghent. Both are famous for their handsome tragedies, but Sophocles got that fame in old age, Heinsius in his youth.

---

48   Sophocles was considered to be the most profound of the three Greek tragic poets.

[8]   Πρὸς μέγαν τὸν ποιητὴν τραγῳδὸν,
                       ΔΑΝΙΕΛ Εἵνσιον,
                       Ἐπίγραμμα.

Εἵνσι' Ἀρουσιόνων ὅτ' ἀείδεις Ἀρχὸν ἀγαυῶν,
   Σφόδρα ποσήκουσάν σοι τιν' ἔχεις πρόφασιν·
Ἠὲ διεξελθὼν τὰ ἐκείνου φαίδιμα ἔργα,
   Ἠὲ σφαγὴν κείνου πρὸς μέτρ' ὀδυρόμενος
5 Πάντα λέγεις μετρίως γε (μέτρον δ' ἐνὶ πᾶσιν ἄριστον)
   Θαμβεῖ, ἀχεῖ, θρηνεῖ πᾶς ὅ γε ταῦτ' ἀναγνούς.
Πράγματα δεινά γε μὲν τοῖς σοῖς ὑποκείαται ὕμνοις,
   Ἀλλὰ τεαὶ λέξεις εἰσ' ἔτι δεινότεραι·
Εἴ ποτε Πυθαγόρα εὖ πάντα τὰ δόγματ' ἔχουσιν,
10   Ἡ ψυχὴ Σενέκης εἰς βίον αὖθις ἔπτη.

   G. CODDAEUS.

[8]   **Epigram on the great tragic poet Daniel Heinsius**

Heinsius, when you praise the prince from the family of the proud Oranges, you have a goal that is right for you; whether you are treating his radiant deeds, or you are grieving his cruel death in meters, you say everything to measure (and measure is best in everything).

Everyone reading this is upset, lamenting and wailing. Formidable actions are the subject of your poetry, but your words are even more formidable: if ever the doctrines of Pythagoras are true, the soul of Seneca has come back to life.[49]

G. Coddaeus.

---

49   The Greek philosopher Pythagoras of Samos (ca. 570–495 BC) held the doctrine of the transmigration of souls. Seneca's soul has so to speak migrated into Heinsius.

[9]   IAMBI
                    LIBERTATI SAVCIAE
                       HEYNSIANAE,
    In quibus, praeter alia, quae in hoc, quaeque in Senecae Dramatis
                personae illustres omnes conferuntur.

    QVIS ille tanto PVLPITVM motu quatit,
    Et insolenti tundit ORCHESTRAM pede?
    Quanquam furentem motibus fallax tegit
    PERSONA vultum, Faexque detonantia
5   Furatur ora, non lates, HEYNSI, tamen,
    Te certus index prodis: augustum jubar
    Dispellit atrae nubilum caliginis,
    Centumque noctes luce perrumpit suâ.
        At nos parentis vana Terrae pondera
10 Frustrà tenebris indies victricibus
    Luctamur: omnes ludit incassum labos,
    Vt ille paruus ales abreptum fugâ,
    Et navigantem vasta Inanis aequora
    Sequi parentem sperat et pennas quatit,
15 Aurasque plausu captat affectans iter
    Strepitque; tandem pronus in nidum cadit.
    Tu Daedaleïs ocior volatibus,
    POETA, Caeli scindis alatus vias,
    Plebémque et ipsos plebis obtutus procul
20 Post te relinquis. Iam SOPHOCLEN praeteris,
    Iamque EVRIPIDEN fultus alâ remige,
    Séque author olim triplicis PROMETHEI
    Victúm fatetur, quique CASSANDRAM dedit
    Caeco furentem versuum volumine.

_____

Tit. B Grotius manuscript UBL Pap. 10, fol. 4v–5r; *C Poemata collecta*, 1617; pp. 230–234; *D Poemata collecta* Leiden 1639, pp. 200–204; *E Poemata collecta* London 1639(1), pp. 230–234; *F Poemata collecta* London 1639(2); *G Poemata collecta* Leiden 1645, pp. 168–172; *H Poemata collecta* Amsterdam 1670, pp. 161–164; *P* The *Poemata collecta* editions.   *Tit.* Senecae *A: n.l. A*, poeta [Impressa in Tragoedia *b*] *B*, TRAGOEDIA HEINSII *P*.   3 furentem motibus *A*: trahentem [furentem *b*] cuneos [pulpitum *b* motibus *c*] *B*.   8 sua *A*: sua nova *add. et del. L*.   10 indies *A*: subditi [indies *b*] *B*.   11 ludit *A*: torquet [ludit *b*] *B*. ‖ labos *A*: labor *B P*.   13 vasta *A*: magna *B*.   14 et *A: om. P*. ‖ quatit *A P*: aquit [quatit *b*] *B*.   15 iter *A P*: viam [iter *b*] *B*.   18 Caeli *A P*: caeli *L*, Caelum [Caeli *b*] *B*.   21 Iamque Euripiden *A*: Euripidenque *P*.   22 olim *A P*: ille [olim *b*] *B*.   24 versuum *A*: carminum *B P*.

[9]   Iambs on The Wounding of Liberty by Heinsius,
                      in which, among other things, all lofty
                      characters which appear in this drama
                      and in that of Seneca are compared

Who is the one who shakes the pulpit so violently and makes the stage shake
with his extraordinary chorus dance? Even though a deceitful mask covers your
face raging with passions and the face-paint hides your reverberating mouth,
yet you cannot hide, Heinsius. Unmistakably you betray yourself: your high-
luminous reverberation disperses the cloud of darkness and breaks with its
light through the deep-dark night.

But we, a useless burden to Mother Earth, in vain wrestle against the darkness that daily overwhelms us: our senseless toil is mocking all of us, like that
young bird trying to follow his father who has flown up and sails through the
immeasurably thin airspace. It strikes with its wings and, flapping, tries its best
to go into the air in its urge to fly, but finally falls forwards into the nest screaming.

You cleave the orbits faster than Daedalus on his flight, winged poet, and
you leave the crowd and her gaze far behind you. On the wick of your wings,
you are already outrunning Sophocles and Euripides. Even the one who once
created the trilogy Prometheus gives in,[50] and he who made an ecstatic Cassandra appear in his book full of dark poetry.[51] Not satisfied that you see them

---

50   The *Prometheus vinctus* was written by Aeschylus.
51   A reference to the *Alexandra* or *Cassandra* of the Hellenistic Greek poet Lycophron (3rd
      c. BC), who also wrote tragedies.

25 Nec hos, nec omnes caeteros IONICI
    Fastus THEATRI, multa quos nobis dies
    Invîdit, aevique impotens iniuria,
    Longè tueri terga sectantes tua
    Contentus ultrà tendis, et Caelo natas
30 Sublimiori, déque summo vertice
    Priscum LATINAE despicis SCENAE decus,
    CHORAGIVMQVE praeter ANNAEI volas.
        O CYCNE FLANDER, me simul tecum rape
    Per candicantis caerulas aethrae vias.
35 Ignava quanquam torpidum moles premit,
    Et surgere ultrò pondere obsessum vetat,
    Tuâ levatus quolibet dextrâ sequar,
    Supráque nubes ibo, quas crassus vapor
    In nos adurget. Diligam SPECTACVLO
40 Propinquiores siderum metae FOROS,
    Vbi serena semper et purus dies.
        Hîc prisca cernam provocantem saecula
    Prodire nostri temporis TRAGOEDIAM:
    Non hanc, IEPHTHAE quae Triumphales manus
45 Caede immerentis inquinavit filiae,
    REGISVE mensis ora BAPTISTAE dedit
    Tacere verum nescia, vt falsum loqui,
    Sed HEYNSIANAM, nata quae serò licet
    Retrò tot annos laude praevortit novâ.
50 Iudex sedebit DOVSA, judex SCALIGER
    Haeres paterno destinatus muneri.
    HEROA nostris hunc, et hunc felix Deus
    Seruavit annis, justa ne saeclo rudi
    Nostris deessent VATIBVS praeconia.
55 Vox una binis: VICTA GANDAE CORDVBA.
    Applaudit omnis MAXIMI CIRCI CHORVS.

---

26 multa *A P*: longe [multa *b*] *B*.   28 Longè *A*: Procul *B P*.   29 natas *A P*: natans [natas *b*] *B*.   31 Priscum *A P*: M [Priscum *b*] *B*.   35 premit *A P*: premat [premit *b*] *B*.   36 obsessum *A P*: oppressum [obsessum *b*] *B*.   44 Non hanc *A P*: At non [Non hanc *b*] *B*.   46–49 Regisve—novâ *A P*: Quae nata sero finis humani ingeni [*add.* Regisve—novâ *in marg. b*] *B*.   48 nata *A P*: serius [nata *b*] *B*.   49 Retrò—novâ *A*: *om. P*. ‖ laude *A P*: luce [laude *b*] *B*.   55 Corduba *P*: corduba *A*.

and all the others who made the fancy of the Greek playwrights, but who are withheld to us by the long passage of time and the immense injustice of the centuries, following you on a great distance, you strive even more, you float in a higher canopy and from the highest peak you look down on the ancient ornament of the Latin scene and you surpass the splendour of Seneca.

Flemish swan,[52] take me with you along the blue seams of the radiant ether. Although a cumbersome slowness paralyses and oppresses me and prevents me from standing up on my own strength, I will raise my feet, follow you everywhere, and transcend the clouds that lay a dense mist on me. Before the performance I will choose a seat closer to the turning point of the stars, where it is always clear and the daylight shines.

Here I will see a tragedy appear on the scene, one of our time, which can compete with that of antiquity. And not the piece in which Jephthah after his triumph has sullied his hands by the murder of his innocent daughter, or the drama in which the head of the Baptist who could not conceal the truth nor speak lies is on the king's table,[53] but that of Heinsius which, although it has arisen only recently, retroactively surpasses many generations by its fledgling fame. Dousa will judge this, and Scaliger,[54] who is destined as heir for his father's office. The auspicious God has kept both heroes for our years to prevent our poets from missing deserved tribute in this unruly time. Both share the same verdict: Cordoba was defeated in Ghent;[55] the whole crowd in the busy theatre applauds.

---

52 An allusion to Heinsius' Flemish descent, and his melodious poetry, as the song of a swan; Heinsius was called the Ghent nightingale.

53 I.e. the tragedies *Iephthes sive votum* (1544) and *Baptistes sive calumnia* (written before 1544, published 1577) by the Scottish humanist who worked in France, George Buchanan (1506–1582).

54 Janus Dousa, Dutch and Neo-Latin poet and founder of the University of Leiden, was a patron of Heinsius, as was Joseph Scaliger, professor at the same university.

55 Heinsius, stemming from Ghent, surpassed the Roman tragic poet Seneca who was born in Cordoba.

Formae micantem celsioris lumine
Miratur ire magnus ALCIDES DEVM,
AVRANSIOQVE cedit (at nulli priùs)
60 Dolétque rursum REGIS HISPANI scelus.
Incedit alto parte ab Eoâ Poli
PRINCEPS COTHVRNO, nam tremit VESPER gradum,
Et sentit hostem. Nunquid ATRIDE pudet?
Bis quinque TROIA messibus constat tibi,
65 Huic unus annus plus decem TROIIS dedit;
Hoc par, scelestâ fraude quòd victor cadis.
Vidit MYCENA per scelus caesum DVCEM,
Vidêre DELPHI. PATRIA ô quanto mades
Cruore! Non hoc eluat RHENVS nefas,
70 Non MOSA vasto pronus incumbens mari,
Non qui propinquus menstruo motu tumens
NEPTVNVS agris parcit HOLLANDIS Pater,
Seséque arenis arcet, atque hostem salo.
      Cerno LOISAE SYRMA. Talis HECTORIS
75 Coniunx parensque, talis ALCMENE fuit
AMPHITRYONIS uxor, et prior NVRVS.
OENEIS autem casta sanctae Feminae
Veretur ora, tollere et vultum simul
Formidat omnis, quae sui sexus cohors
80 Transgressa Leges: noxium AEETAE genus
LEDAEQUE proles, et noverca VIRBII,
Materque ORESTIS, et viri Mater sui,
Et ipsa IVNO. Stirpis antiquae decus
Materna parvum ducit HENRICVM manus.
85 Alludit illi magnus Argivûm metus
Futurus HECTOR, Fata si vitam darent;
Alludit HYLLVS, et Coronati patris

---

57 micantem *A P*: nitentem [micantem *b*] *B*.   58 Deum *A*: Ducem [Deum *b*] *B*, ducem *P*.   59
Auransioque *A*: Arausioque *P*.   62 *In marg. add. B* Compet. Sol Syrmae Coth. *n.l.* Inq. ebria
Libertas Buch Senec. 1005 ?   65 *In marg. add. B* tempus [*Scena b*].   69 hoc *A P*: vix [hoc *b*]
B. ‖ Rhenus *A P*: *n.l.* [Rhenus *b*] *B*.   73 Seséque *A P*: Seque [Seseque *b*] *B*. ‖ hostem *A*: hostes *B*
P.   75 Coniunx, parensque *A P*: Thebaea coniunx [Coniunx, parensque *b*] *B*.   76 prior Nurus
A: nurus prior *B P*.   77 sanctae Feminae *A*: sanctae [sanct *del. b*] coniugis *B*, sanctae coniugis
P.   80 Aeetae *A–C E–H*, Aetae *D*.   83–90 Stirpis—Poeantiusque *A P*: *add. in marg. B; postea
add.* et Coronati patris Phocaea proles *B*.

In admiration Alcaeus' great grandson[56] sees a god ascend, who shines with the light of an even higher figure, and for Orange he returns, which he has done for no one before. He should once again regret the crime of a Spanish king. There, on a high stage boot, the prince appears at the eastern horizon; the Occident trembles for his step and regards him as the enemy. You are not ashamed, though, son of Atreus?[57] Troy cost you ten years, he has been handed over ten Troys in one year. But the similarity is that after your victory you die by criminal deception.

Mycenae has seen how its captain died through crime, likewise Delft. O hometown, how much blood has flown! The Rhine cannot cleanse this crime, nor could the Meuse, even if it would pour into the immeasurable sea with full force, nor could Father Neptune, who rising nearby in his tidal movement spares the Dutch fields, and would keep himself at a distance through the dunes, and the enemy through his water.

I see the dragging robe of Louise.[58] Thus were Hector's wife and his mother, thus were Amphitryon's wife Alcmene and his first daughter-in-law.[59] But the daughter of Oeneus[60] is afraid of the subdued face of this impeccable woman, and the whole crowd who have violated the laws of her sex are equally afraid to lift up their eyes: the criminal child of Aeetes and Leda's daughter, the stepmother of Virbius, the mother of Orestes and the mother of her own husband and even Juno.[61] Her mother's hand leads the ornament of the old generation, the young Henry.[62] The great fright of the Argives reminds one of him, he would become a Hector if fate allowed him to live long enough.[63] Hyllus reminds of him, and the child of the crowned father who resides in Phocis; and

---

56   Hercules.

57   Agamemnon, who after a siege of ten years took Troy. William of Orange took many cities in one year, viz. 1572. Both were killed treacherously: Agamemnon by his wife Clytemnestra and her lover Aegisthus, William by Balthasar Gerards.

58   Louise de Coligny (1555–1620), William's fourth wife.

59   Hector's wife Andromache and his mother Hecuba mourned for him; as did Hercules' mother Alcmene (married to Amphitryon) and his first wife Megara for their son and husband.

60   Oeneus' daughter Deinanira killed her husband Hercules.

61   Medea, daughter of Aeetes, killed her children; Leda's daughter Helena was the cause of the Trojan war; the stepmother of Virbius (another name for Hippolytus) was Phaedra, who had her stepson killed; Orestes' mother Clytemnestra killed her husband; Oedipus unconsciously married his mother Iocaste; Juno tried to have Hercules killed.

62   Frederick Henry (1584–1647), son of William of Orange and Louise de Coligny, was 6 months of age at the time of the murder.

63   Just like young Astyanax, who would resemble his father Hector in later life, thus Frederick Henry will take up the duties of his father.

PHOCAEA proles, iam puer PHILISTHENES,
Iam meta TROIAE PYRRHVS exspectat parem,
90 POEANTIVSQVE. Dira COCYTI vada,
Et aestuantes igne permisto lacus
HISPANA ERINNYS linquit, humanus sitim
Cuî sedat vnus sanguis: hoc illi merum est,
Haec pôcla MONSTRO. Cerno pro taedis rogos,
95 Cerno secures. Ipsa ad aspectum soror
Horret MEGAERA; defluit flagrum manu,
Fugitque tortis anguis implexus comis.
    At ille magni PARRICIDA PRINCIPIS
Pone hîc scelestum perfidus volvit gradum.
100 Fuit THYESTES impiâ factus dape
Natis sepulcrum. Segregem THESEVS nova
Castum per agros filium sparsit nece,
Patrem cecîdit, mistus est Matri OEDIPVS;
Sed inscientes: primus hic sibi placet,
105 Gaudetque, quanto nullus erravit, malo.
Quicunque, Famae punctus antiquae notâ
Crudelis audis, patruus, Frater, parens,
ATREV, nepotes Patris heu dirum genus,
AEGISTHE, quíque semper arentes aquas
110 Sempérque captas arboris foetae fugas,
Gaudete: vestra maius absolvit scelus.
Inuentus hic est, cujus vnus PATRIAM
Trajecit ictus. Quis, Dij, tantum nefas
Ausus jubere! Non LYCVS, neuter CREON,
115 Non hoc ULYSSES saeuus in parvos quoque,

89 Pyrrhus *B P*: Purrhus *A*.   91 *In marg. add. B* Inq. serp. Lib. sicarius.   93 Cuî *A P*: Huic [Cui
b] B.   99 Pone hîc *A P*: Retro [Pone hic *b] B*.   100 factus *A P*: captus [factus *b] B*.   101–102
Segregem Theseus ... Castum ... filium *A P*: Durus Aegides [Segregem filium Theseus *b*] ... Natum
[Castum *b*] ... segregem [filium *b] B*.   102 *In marg. add. B* Atreus Tantalus Aegisthus Eteocles
Polynices.   104 sibi placet *A P*: voto capit [*n.l. b* sibi placet *c] B*.   105 Gaudetque *A P*: Audetque
[Gaudetque *b] B*. ‖ quanto ... malo *A P*: quantum [quanto *b*] ... nefas [scelus *b* nefas *c* malo *d] B*.
107 Crudelis *A–C E–G*: Caudelis *D*. ‖ audis *A P*: audes [audis *b] B*.   108 Atreu—genus *A B: om.
P*. ‖ Patris heu dirum *A*: Matris et Patris [Patris heu dirum *b] B*.   110 Sempérque—foetae *A P*:
Foetaeque [Plenaeque *b* Semperque *c*] ... semper [foetae *b] B*.   111 vestra *A P*: vestrum [vestris
b vestra *c] B*. ‖ *In marg. add. B* Lycus, Creon, duplex, Ulysses, Calchas, Iason, Tiresias, Strophi-
lus.   112 *In marg. add. B* Antigone Orestes Cassandra *n.l.* Tiresias Iason ? Iole.   113 Trajecit *A
P*: Transegit [Traiecit *b] B*.   115 hoc *A P*: ipse [hoc *b] B*. ‖ parvos *A P*: parvus [parvos *b] B*.

the youthful Philisthenes and Pyrrhus who meant the end for Troy, see in him their equal, as well as the son of Poeas.[64] The Spanish Fury[65] leaves the terrible pools of the Cocytus and the boiling, fire-mixed lakes. Only human blood can quench her thirst: that is for that monster pure wine, that is what she drinks. I do not see flares, but pyres and axes. Even her sister Megaera[66] shudders at the sight; the whip falls out of her hand, the serpent intertwined in her head of hair is fleeing.

But he, the murderer of the great prince, walks here in the background hatching crime. Thyestes has become the grave for his sons by his godless meal. Theseus scattered his impeccable son in pieces across the fields with an unheard murder, and Oedipus killed his father, had intercourse with his mother, all in ignorance.[67] He is the first to be full of himself, who finds joy in a misdeed as great as no one has ever committed in error. All of you and those branded by an old fame have the name to be cruel—uncle, brother, father—you Atreus, and you, grandsons of your own father, o gruesome race, you Aegisthus, and you who try to seize the ever-dripping water and the ever-evading fruits of the trees, be glad: a greater crime has pardoned yours.[68] Here is the man who has shot the fatherland with a shot; who, good Gods, has had the courage to order such a crime? Not Lycus, and not one of the two Creons, not

---

64   Hyllus, son of Hercules and Deianira, mourned for his father; Pylades, son of King of Phocis Strophios; Philisthenes or Pleisthenes, the second son of Thyestes, was slaughtered by Atreus; Pyrrhus, son of Achilles, showed his courage at the downfall of Troy; Poeas' son Philoctetes accompanied Hercules.

65   The Spanish Inquisition, presented as an Erinys, a deity of vengeance; the Erinyes were equated with the Roman Furies, the deities of fright and vengeance.

66   Megaera was one of the Furies.

67   Without realizing, Thyestes ate the meal his brother Atreus prepared for him, consisting of his own sons; Theseus unintentionally killed his son Hippolytus, and Oedipus his father Laius, marrying his mother.

68   Cruel murderers from Greek mythology: Atreus who killed the sons of his brother Thyestes; Eteocles and Polyneices, the grandsons of their own father since they were the children of Oedipus and his mother Iocaste, who stood up against each other; Aegisthus who killed his uncle Agamemnon; Tantalus who murdered his son Pelops and gave him to the gods as a meal.

Et in puellas; ipse nec fluxâ fide
Amans IASON: AVREI sed VELLERIS
Possessor alter. Nec tua hoc, CALCHA, licet
Cruenta semper praecinunt Oracula,
120   Senéxue aruspex caecus, aut MANTO monet:
Sed qui superbus RVPE TARPEIA sedet,
Et è QVIRITVM COLLIBUS SEPTEM tonat.
Vidésne? Pulcram rasa LIBERTAS comam,
Et PILEATA, turpe proculcat jugum.
125   Sed pectus, eheu, SAVCIVM vulnus gerit
Quod antè PRINCEPS. PATRIAE raptum PATREM
Seséque luget. Ora commendat dolor,
Decétque luctus. EURYTVM sic Filia
Cum lacrimaret, et Parentales Rogos,
130   Sibique lapsum patrij Regni decus;
Sic cum doleret vera se quondam nimis
Cantâsse PHAEBAS, staret et jam Troïcas
Supra ruinas, et cadaver Regium;
Tamen placebant. Talis ELECTRE fuit
135   Caeso parente. Nata talis OEDIPI
Caeco parente. Siquis est sensus super,
Curis nec VMBRAS exuit Mortalibus
Donata DIVIS MANIBVS Felicitas,
Restátque quòd non atra LETHE sorbeat,
140   SALVE BATAVIS Ductor AVRANSI tuis
VLTORE NATO, VATE FELIX HEINSIO.

H. GROTIVS IVRIS CONSVLTVS

116 ipse—fide *A P*: perfidus quamquam fuit [ipse nec fluxa fide *b*] *B*.   118 Nec—licet *A*: nec licet Calchas tua [nec tua hoc Calcha licet *b*] *B*.   118–122 Nec tua—tonat *A*: Ecquis immite hoc sacrum | Aut caecus augur aut ferus Calchas docet? *P*.   119 praecinunt *A*: hoc monent [praecinunt *b*] *B*.   120 aruspex caecus *A*: caecus augur *B*.   126 Princeps *B P*: Princps *A*.   126–127 raptum ... luget *A P*: luget [raptum *b*] ... raptam [luget *b*] *B*.   128 Eurytum *A P*: Euryti [Euritum *b*] *B*.   130 Sibique lapsum *A P*: Fratremque tota [Sibique lapsum *b*] *B*.   131–132 vera se quondam ... Cantâsse *A P*: sancta se veram ... fuisse [vera se quondam ... Cantasse *b*] *B*.   132 Troïcas *A*: Troicas [Pergami *b*] *B*: Pergami *P*.   133 *Post lineam* Sub his sepultum, Pergami [Troico *b*] et flagrans rogo *add. B*: Sub his sepultum Troico flagrans rogo *P*.   134 placebant *A*: placebat *B P*.   140 Ductor Auransi *A*: dux Arausiade *P*.   *Subscriptio* Hugo Grotius Iuris Consultus *A*: *om. P*.

Ulysses even though he was cruel to little boys and girls; not Jason either, that unreliable lover, but the second owner of the Golden Fleece.[69] Even your oracles, Calchas, however bloodstained they always were, have not predicted this. Even the old blind seer or Manto did not instigate this, but the man who proudly has his throne on the Tarpeian rock and throws his bans from the seven hills of the Quirites.[70]

Look at that! Freedom, with her beautiful tresses cut off and the hat of freedom on her head, tramples the shameful yoke. But ah, her wounded chest shows an injury that the prince had before: she mourns the Father of the Fatherland who has been taken away from her, and herself. Sorrow beautifies her features and mourning becomes her. Thus was the daughter of Eurytus, when she wept for him, and for the stake where her father died and regretted that the splendour of her father's kingdom had escaped her.[71]

Thus was the priestess of Phoebus when she mourned that previously she had predicted the truth too much and was already on the ruins of Troy under which the corpse of the king was buried.[72] Yet they experienced sympathy. Thus was Electra when her father was murdered, thus was also Oedipus' daughter when her father had become blind.[73]

If there is still some feeling, if the bliss imparted to the dead does not get the realm of shades rid of human worries, and if something remains that is not swallowed by the grim Lethe,[74] then stay with your Hollanders, captain Orange, blessed in your son who is your avenger and in your prophet Heinsius.

H. Grotius LLM.

---

69 Lycus had the father and two brothers of Hercules' first wife Megara killed; Creon of Corinth who had Medea banned and Creon of Thebes who eventually had his niece Antigone executed; Ulysses or Odysseus wanted to have the little son of Hector Astyanax thrown from the walls of Troy and through the ruse of the wooden horse caused the death of many young children of Troy; Jason, the leader of the Argonauts, got hold of the golden fleece with the help of Medea, but abandoned her and thus indirectly caused the death of his sons.

70 Calchas was the priest of the Greeks at the camp near Troy; the blind seer Tiresias and his daughter the prophetess Manto. The actual instigator was the Pope who is in Rome.

71 Iole mourned for her father Eurytus who had been killed by Hercules.

72 The priestess of Phoebus Apollo, Cassandra, mourned for the fall of Troy and the death of King Priam.

73 Electra incited her brother Orestes to avenge the death of their father Agamemnon, who had been killed by his wife Clytemnestra and her lover Aegisthus; Oedipus' daughter Antigone remained faithful to him when he had struck out his eyes.

74 Lethe, the river of oblivion, which made the souls of the deceased forget everything.

[10]   IN EANDEM.

Effoetâ vegetum sibi cor superasse senectâ
   Saltato Sophocles arguit Oedipode.
At vegetae sibi cor canum anticipare iuuentae
   Saltato docuit Heinsius Auraico.
5 Heroïs tragico dùm magni fata cothurno
   Aptat, et Orchestrae refricat attonitae.
Fortia facta virûm aut crudelia dicere fata
   Ausus maturi, sed tamen est iuuenis.
Ast actum rebus dare, res aequare cothurno
10   Ausus maturi, at solius ille senis.
Perge annos, Heinsi, ingenio, spem vincere coeptis,
   Nisu te, nisus strenuitate moras.
Perge, inquam, ignavae postscenia spernere vitae,
   Faustae spectatus cum fremitu caveae.

   Iacobus Gruterus.

[10]   **On the same**

Sophocles proved that his heart was resilient at a venerable age because he was performing Oedipus.[75] But Heinsius has shown that he already has a venerable heart in his resilient young years because he is showing Orange on stage. By setting the fate of the great hero on the footing of a tragic buskin,[76] he recalled it to the baffled audience.

His courageous attempts to describe the brave acts of men or their cruel fate are from someone who is mature, while he is young himself.

In the case of that other poet the attempt to represent events in action and to put them on stage, was that of a ripe man, but that attempt was from an old man.[77]

Continue, Heinsius, to surpass your years with your talent, and the expectations one has of you with your undertakings and yourself with your vigour, and to overcome with your urgency the postponement of your attempt. Do continue to despise the wing of unimportant life, if you are watched with loud acclaim of all spectators.

Iacobus Gruterus.

---

75   Sophocles wrote his tragedy *Oedipus Coloneus* at an old age; it was performed posthumously.
76   The cothurn or buskin is the footwear of the tragedy, hence metonym for the tragic genre.
77   The old man refers to Sophocles again.

[11]   A MONSIEUR DE HEINS
                              Sur sa Tragedie.
                                 STANCES.

Parmy tant de soleils dont l'Immortelle flamme
Pour avoir trop de lustre offence mes deux yeux,
Ozeray-ie eslever les glaces de mon ame
En forçant la nature enter la terre aux Cieux!

5   *De Heins* il suffiroit que ta gloire suivie
De ces perfections vint arrester mes pas
Sans qu'vn si grand ozer pour finir mon envie,
Me fit voler si haut, pour retomber si bas.

       Ce miracle du Ciel qui trop grand tirannise
10 L'orgueil des beaux esprits, forzez de l'adorer
Non, ie ne le puis voir, que mon ame surprise
Au cours de mille effrois ne se laisse emporter.

       Pourray-ie voir aussy l'honneur de la *Hollande*
Sans avoir de cent peurs mes esprits agitez
15 Et ce ieune flambeau dont la gloire est si grande,
Et dont ia l'Orient lance tant de clartez!

       Mais le sort est iecté vne perte honorable
Au moins courronera vn superbe vouloir,
C'est vivre que mourir d'vne mort agreable,
20 Et puis vn bel envy vaut mieux qu'vn bas pouvoir.

       Ie veux comme ie peux, *o Soleil, o bel Astre*
Qu'vne langue *Françoise* esclate ton honneur
Et bien si ton merite enfante mon desastre,
Pour vn si beau subiect i'aimeray mon malheur.

---

1 dont *scripsi*: d'ont *A*.   10 *In marg.* Scaliger.   13 *In marg.* Dousa.   15 dont *scripsi*: d'ont *A*. ‖
In marg. Grotius.   16 lance *scripsi*: l'ance *A*.

[11]   **Stanzas to Mr Heinsius about his Tragedy**

If only I dared to raise among so many suns with which the Immortal flame[78] hurts my two eyes, because they have too much light, the mirrors of my soul, so to force nature to connect earth and Heavens.

Heinsius, your fame, which has these effects, would be enough to make me keep my step without so great an attempt to carry out my aim making me fly me so high, to fall back so deeply.

[*in marg.*: Scaliger] This great miracle of Heaven that dominates the pride of people with taste, compels admiration. No, I could not see him without my soul being carried away, overwhelmed by a thousand instances of astonishment.[79]

[*in marg.: Dousa*] Ah, if only I could also see the glory of Holland, without my mind having to bear a thousand fears, [*in marg.*: Grotius] and that young torch whose fame is so great, and of which the East is already so vivid.[80]

But the lot of fate has been cast, an honourable loss will at least crown an exalted effort; life is only to die a pleasant death, and furthermore a good effort is worth more than a small skill.

I want as much as possible, o Sun, o beautiful Star,[81] to add to your glory in the French language and even if your merit produces my downfall, I would love my misery for such a beautiful purpose.

---

78   The immortal flame is either the sun or God.
79   Josephus Justus Scaliger (1540–1609), professor at Leiden University and teacher of Hein-
      sius.
80   Janus Dousa (1545–1604), the founder of the Leiden Academy and patron of Heinsius;
      Hugo Grotius (1583–1645), younger friend of Heinsius and comrade in literature.
81   Daniel Heinsius, the author of this *Auriacus*.

25   Qu'on ne me parle plus de ceste bande *Grecque*
        D'vn *Sophocle, Euripide*, et tant de grands esprits,
        Qu'on ne m'allegue plus le tragique *Senecque*
        Et ceux-la dont le temps a mangé les escrits.

        De Heins les va biffant, en son ame incognüe
30   Pour son stile empoulé, ne se fuit que des yeux.
        Ces antiques cerveaux rampent dedans la Nüe
        Au lieu que de son front il va toucher les Cieux.

        Ses mouvemens choisis tiennent sous leur empire
        Le plus determiné de nos plus beaux desirs.
35   Et nostre ame emportee au flot de son bien dire
        Fait lascher quand et luy, des larmes et des soupirs.

        Lorsque triste il despeint la *Liberté blessée*
        Parle perfide bras, qui meritoit cent Croix:
        O Dieu combien nostre ame est doucement percée
40   Par le charme plaintif, de sa divine voix!

        Il semble que ie voy une *Femme* mi-morte
        Qui iette de martire vne sueur de sang,
        Vne vivante *Mort* que la douleur emporte
        Et qui tient un *Enfer* attaché à son flanc:

45   Quand rouge de courroux de la gent *Espagnolle*,
        Il va les cruautez exprimant brusquement,
        Vne rude *Furie* à nostre ame s'envole
        Qui la transforme en ce, qu'elle soit iustement.

        Il semble que ie voy un supplice une rage,
50   Une fiere *Enyon* qui se paist de sanglots:
        Un perfide *Affronteur*, qui au lieu de courage,
        Loge la trahison au milieu de ses os.

---

35 Et *scripsi*: En *A*.   36 des[2] *A*: *del. L.*

Do not talk to me any more of that Greek gang, of a Sophocles, Euripides and all those great minds. Stop relating to me the tragedian Seneca and all those writers of whom time has consumed their scriptures.

Heinsius will surpass them, in his unprecedented soul, because of his rich style, he only flees the eyes. The ancient brains will creep around in the Mist as he will touch Heaven with his head.

His exquisite passions hold the most specific of our most beautiful emotions in their grasp. Our minds, carried away by the flood of his eloquence, let tears and sighs escape when he does too.

When he sorrowfully portrays the Wounding of Freedom by that faithless arm, which would deserve it to die a thousand deaths, o God, how much our mind has been gently pierced by the plaintive charm of his divine voice!

It looks like I see a half-dead Woman sweating martyrs' blood, a living dead who is carried away by grief and that keeps Hell at her side.

When red with rage he rudely displays the cruelties of the Spanish people, a grim Fury[82] flies into our soul which brings her into the right state of mind.

It seems as if I see a torment, a frenzy, a proud Enyo[83] who feeds on sobbing, a faithless Deceiver who, instead of showing courage, hides treason in his heart.

---

82   In *Auriacus* the Spanish Inquisition is presented as the fourth of the three Furies, deities of vengeance.

83   Enyo, the Roman goddess of war.

Heureuse mille fois ô *Belgique Province*,
De voir par vn *Achille* vn si grand tort vengé,
55   Et pour eterniser la valeur de ce *Prince*
Le voir d'vn autre *Homere* encore loüangé.

Comme l'vn en exploicts est vn *Foudre* de guerre,
Qui peut mesme avec *Mars* debatre le *Laurier*,
L'autre qui ne cognoit de pareil en la *Terre*
60   Va desia dans le *Ciel* paroistre le premier.

Belle ame que le Ciel d'vne douce influence,
Anima de grandeur, on void par cest escrit
Qu'vn si galand *Esprit* n'est rien que *l'Eloquence*
Et *l'Eloquence* rien, qu'vn si galand *Esprit*.

65   Mais d'autant que ie sçay qu'vne chose divine,
Se conçoit beaucoup mieux qu'elle ne se despeint,
De Heins pour l'admirer il faut que ie termine,
Le fil de mon discours, d'vn extaze non feint.

D. de Licques.

A thousand times happy, o Dutch provinces, to see that an Achilles[84] avenged such a great injustice and that in order to immortalize the value of this Prince he was once again praised by a second Homer.

Just as the one in his heroic deed is a war lightning, who could even fight with Mars for the laurel wreath, the other person who does not find his equal on earth, is already the first in heaven.

Beautiful soul who animated heaven by a sweet inspiration with grandeur, one sees in this writing that such a gallant spirit is nothing but eloquence and eloquence nothing but so gallant a spirit.

But because I know that one can experience something divine much better than describe it, in order to admire Heinsius I have to break the thread of my argument into unfeigned ecstasy.

    D. de Licques.

---

84   Prince Maurice will avenge his father, just like Achilles took revenge for the death of his friend Patroclus at the Trojan War; Heinsius is the Homer who will sing of the deceased William of Orange.

[12]   AMICO LECTORI.

CONSTITVERAMUS, amice lector, Tragoediae nostrae ea, quae tam de Graeco,
quam Latino charactere Tragico satis prolixè notaveramus praefigere, quae
nunc secundae editioni reseruamus, in quâ, ex amicorum consilio, quaedam
explicabimus, quorundam etiam, in quibus Hellenismi vestigia premimus,
5   rationem reddemus. Nunc properamus. Tu vera his fave, ac reliqua, quae in
Graecos autores notauimus, expecta. Hâc certè aetate, quae lubrica est, ab his
exordiri placuit. Et vt alibi lusimus:

      Ἡ μὰν ἄριστός ἐστι βουλευτὴς χρόνος,
      Γέρων δικαστής, πολλὰ νουθετῶν ἀεὶ
10   Ὅστις τελείῳ δὴν ὑπεζύγη πόνῳ.

Praeterea est quod te velim: si quis malit distinctiones scenarum, quas hic
praeter morem adhibitas videt, praetermittere, nobis haud inuitis id faciet.
Hîc autem id factum est, quod sciamus non omnia illa τμήματα inter Actus,
scenae vicem obtinere posse, ἀλλὰ τι καὶ ἐν τῇ τραγῳδίᾳ τῶν τῆς ἀρχαίας κωμῳ-
15 δίας παραβάσεων τάξιν ἔχειν aliquâ ex parte. Graeci autem ne maiores quidem distinctiones notare amant. Liberum hoc ergo est. Pag. 20. Qui volet
pro *tabum tabem* legat; nos non ita temere Seruio credimus, nec putamus
vetitum esse τῇ εὐθείᾳ vti, aut αἰτιατικῇ, nihil enim certi afferunt γραμματικῶν παῖδες; nam vt ille δίπτωτον, sic auctor Glossarij veteris μονόπτωτον esse
20 vult, et modo *tabo* λύθρῳ exponit, et αἵματι νεκροῦ, modo tabo (ubi tabum
legendum fortasse) λύθρος, αἷμα νεκροῦ. At hae sunt ἐπιπολάζουσαι λόγων ἔρι-
δες. Pag. 21 primam in *Iberi* contra morem meum producere malui, quam à
sensu recedere, quod cum tam Graecis quam Latinis poëtis in appellatiuis
liceat, in proprijs mihi licere putaui; quod si quis aliud malit, substituat vel

[12]   **To the Benevolent Reader**

I had decided, benevolent reader, to have my tragedy preceded with my rather extensive notes on the nature of Greek and Latin tragedy; I will now keep this for a subsequent edition, in which I will explain some things on the advice of friends and will also account for some characteristics with which I have followed in the footsteps of the Greeks. Now I continue. You, however, lend your willing ear to this and await the rest of the comments I made about the Greek writers. In any case, I wanted to start this in this time, which is uncertain. And as I have said elsewhere:

> The best adviser is time, the old judge, who, always correcting a lot, has long strived for a perfect job.

Moreover, I would like to say the following: if someone prefers to abandon the division into scenes that he sees as being applied against every custom, he will not do so against my will. Here, however, it has been applied, although I know, that not all those parts within the companies can take the place of a scene, but that something in the tragedy in a sense also has the place of the *parabases*[85] of the old comedy. But the Greeks did not even like making larger divisions. This is therefore free.

Whoever wants it, may read on p. 20 for *tabum tabem*. I do not just believe Servius[86] and do not believe that it is forbidden to use the nominative or the accusative; after all, the grammarians give nothing conclusive. For while Servius says that the word has a form for two cases, the author of the old *Glossary* claims that it only has one case, and now declares *tabo* as 'with dirt' and 'with the blood of the dead', then again he declares *tabo* (where perhaps *tabum* should be read) as 'dirt' and 'the blood of the dead'. But these are altercations on the surface.

On p. 21 I would rather elongate against my habit the first syllable of *Iberus* than deviate from the meaning; what both the Greek and the Latin poets are allowed in substantives, I thought I was allowed to do in proper names.

---

85   The *parabasis* is the part of a play in which the chorus directly addresses the public.

86   Servius is the fifth-century commentator of Virgil.

25   *illius*, vel *Hispani*, modo nobis nostrum permittat. Haec moneo, ne quis nobis
     inscijs id factum existimet. Sed haec leuia sunt, καὶ οὐδενόσωρα. Sequitur gra-
     uius.

     Absoluto hoc opere admonitus sum ab amicis quosdam mirari, cur in Tra-
     goediâ meâ partes potius comiti Henrico, quam Serenissimo Principi nostro
30   Mauricio dederim; ego primo non respondi, sed risi imperitiam hominum,
     donec audivi quosdam etiam graviores esse, quos haec cura coquat. Quibus
     verba vno et altero rationem reddam. In laudes Magni illius Principis effu-
     sum hoc ipso opere me fuisse videbit, quicunque praefationem meam Heroi-
     cam quam huic operi praefixi inspicere dignabitur, vt deinceps facturus sum,
35   *dum spiritus hos reget artus*. Atqui, dicent illi, cur ibi potius quam in cothurno.
     Audite, et credite.

     Existimavi ego in re tam recenti mentiendum non esse; atqui Serenissimum
     Principem tum temporis absentem fuisse scimus; secundò Tragoedia ea tan-
     tum (quod multos ignorare scio, atque *hinc illae lachrymae*) quae aliquot horis
40   gesta sunt complectitur, nunquam vltra diem extenditur, quod multi doctissimi
     viri hoc tempore neglexerunt, etiam apud antiquos nonnulli, quos tutius repre-
     hendere licet quam imitari. Cum tam breuis igitur hîc sit periodus et (vt hac
     voce ita vtar) pericomma, quis locus est absenti? Quod si aliquis aliter arbitre-
     tur, ad doctiores provoco, quibuscum hac de re multum egi, vt testabuntur cum
45   alij multi, tum Magnus Heros noster, Clarissimus Bertius qui actioni huius Tra-
     goediae primae praefuit, καὶ ὁ θαυμάστος Grotius. Quod si illi rationibus vicerint,
     ostendam me non Tragoedias modo scribere posse, sed et διασκευὰς, vel verius
     ex Heinsio Simonides fiam. Non negabunt etiam πάθος in Tragoedia maius
     infantem mouere quam iuuenem aut adolescentem. Ne autem quis pertinaciae
50   me accuset, introducemus, cum publicè haec Tragoedia nostra Lugduni Batavo-

If someone prefers something different, let him put *illius* or *Hispani* instead, provided he allows me my solution. Do not let anyone think I did this unconsciously. But these are insignificant and trivial things. The following is something more important.

After I had finished this work, I was made aware by friends that some people wondered why in my tragedy I did assign a role to Frederick Henry, but not to our Serene Prince Maurice.[87] At first I did not answer, but laughed at the stupidity of the people, until I heard that there were also some people of more authority whom this concern tormented. I will answer to them in a few words. Anyone who deigns to read my epic introduction, which I have precede the play, will see that I have just exhausted myself in this poem in praise for that great Prince, as I intend to do afterwards, 'as long as breath will control my body'. But still, will they say, why rather there than in the play itself? Hear and believe.

I thought that in such a recent event I should not violate the truth; now, however, I knew that the Illustrious Prince was absent at the time; secondly, a tragedy only includes that (I know that many are ignorant of this and 'hence those tears') which happens in a few hours, and it never spans more than a day, something that many scholars of this time have neglected, but also some of the ancients, who can be reprimanded safer than imitated. Since this period and (to use this word in this way) this *pericomma* is so short, what place is there for one who is absent?

If someone thinks differently, I refer to the scholars with whom I spoke a lot about this matter, such as, besides many others, our Great Hero, the glorious Bertius who was the patron of the first performance of this tragedy, and the miraculous Grotius will testify.[88] If they convince me with proofs, I will show that I can write not only tragedies, but also rhetorical pieces of art, or rather, I will become from Heinsius a Simonides.[89] They will not deny that a baby in a tragedy also evokes more pathos than a boy or an adolescent. However, in order to avoid being accused of obstinacy, when this tragedy of mine will be shown in public in Leiden, I will introduce the role of that great avenger of ours and in

---

87   Frederick Henry (1584–1647), the infant child of William and his last wife, Louise the Coligny, and Maurice (1567–1625), the son of William and his second wife Anna of Saxony.

88   The great hero can refer to Joseph Scaliger (1540–1609), the 'super professor' of the Leiden Academy; the Flemish theologian, historian and geographer Petrus Bertius (1565–1620) was subregent of the Staten College, a boarding school, affiliated with Leiden University for students of theology who studied with a scholarship; Hugo Grotius (1583–1645), a student at Leiden University, was a friend of Heinsius.

89   *Diasceuae* are rhetorical pieces of art, written by such figures as the Greek poet Simonides of Ceos (ca. 556–468 BC).

rum repraesentabitur, personam magni illius Vindicis nostri et loco vt putamus satis idoneo, magis tamen ex iussu eorum quam primo instituto nostro. Quod si placeat non verebimur etiam ea cum reliquis edere, vt appareat tanquam θεὸς ἀπὸ μηχανῆς. Atque ita in hac tempestate magnos illos διοσκούρους coniugemus.

a place we deem suitable, but more on their authority than to my initial plan. If it pleases, I will not hesitate to publish it with the rest, so that he appears as *deus ex machina*.[90] And so in this tempestuous time I will link those great sons of the gods[91] together.

---

90   The figure who brings the unexpected denouement.
91   Through a comparison the sons of Zeus, the Dioscuri Castor and Pollux, Maurice and Frederick Henry are honoured.

[13]   MENDA TYPOGRAPHICA
                    AB OPERIS COMMISSA SIC EMENDA
                              LECTOR:

In epistula Graeca punctum ante, καὶ ταῦτα μὲν, Pag. 18. Vers 7. *compos*, ibidem
penultima ipsa p. 25. v. 22 pro PR. Lois. p. 38. v. 19. *seculum*. p. 46. v. 9. *luctu* p. 49.
v. 17. *turbidâque aspergine* p. 54. p. 52. v. 13. *hîc*. v. 1 *ignarae* ibid. v. 5 *vinculo*. p. 56.
v. 14. *suffundes*. p. 62. v. 6. pro Au. scribe. AI. p. 65. v. 16. pro Au. pone Nu. ibid.
20. v. *illud*. p. 70. v. 26. pro Lois. Sic. p. 78. v. 27. *gemimus* p. 80. v. 10. *reddidit*. p. 81.
v. 5 *purum* p. 84. v. 10. *aditum*. p. 85 οὐ μὰ Δί· At p. 86 dele punctum post *ego*. Sic.
pag. 58. ξυλοκόποι et ξύλαθ᾽.

                      Monendus item de mendis commissis
                              IN IAMBIS

Pag. 90 Vers. 2 *Consessus*. v. 18 inter p. 103. v. 19 *Coloniamque*. p. 104. θεὸς εἴμι
v. 31. *hyeme*. ibid. v. ultima *inuideres*. p. 107. v. 12. *Graecum*. ibid. v. 16 οἶς p. 108.
v. 20. *Venus*. ibid. v. 26 *sine*. p. 111. v. 24. *gemmata*. p. 112. v. 13. *iuuentae*. p. 119
Aeschyleas. p. l.v.6.d a in elegia Dousae. p. 234. v. 12. *Principe*.

Amice lector, haec notavimus, quaedam minuta scientes praetermisimus,
quaedam etiam fortasse inscij, quae humanitati tuae committimus. Quod
vereor ne factum sit eò magis, quod Typographus noster ad haec homine mer-
cenario vsus sit, et ὅλης τῆς τυπογραφικῆς πραγματείας ἐπείρως ἔχοντι, maxime
vero Graecorum, ac praesertim accentuum; vnde fortasse videbis alibi τὶς et
τὶ pro τίς et τί. Item ὧς et similes ineptias, quas tute facile emendabis. Nec
enim haec tanti sunt vt moneantur. Sic pag. 45. v. 12. punctum tolle post *satis* et
alibi.

[13a]   **Typographical Errors**
                    Made by the typesetters, which
                    should be corrected thus, dear reader

[Then follows a list of typos with their corrections in the *Auriacus*]

[13b]   **The reader should also be made**
                    conscious of mistakes made in the Iambs

[Then follows a list of typos with their corrections in the *Iambic verses*]

Dear reader, we have noted these mistakes, we have deliberately passed on certain trifles, to other ones perhaps even unconsciously. We leave this to your kindness. I fear that this has happened the more, since our printer has hired somebody who had no experience in typesetting, but least of all in Greek, especially in the accents. That is why you might read somewhere *tis* and *ti* instead of *tís* and *tí* and such oddities, which you can correct easily. After all, they are not so important that they have to be pointed out. This is why in p. 45, l. 12 [= l. 1035] and elsewhere you should remove the dot after *satis*.

[13]   P. SCRIVERII
                    IN AVRIACVM Danielis Heinsii
                 Splendidissimi sibique jucundissimi Poëtae
                              Elegia.

    Ite procul Curae, durum genus, ite Labores,
        Non mea nunc vestrâ compede crura sonent.
    Ille ego jam tandem meus à Praetore recessi,
        Et data sunt Musis otia laeta meis:
5   Mitior adfulsit nobis Deus. Ilicèt omnis
        Turba puëllari non satis aequa choro.
    Ilicèt. Ad vetereis en me juvat ire Sororeis,
        En iuvat in lusus et mea sacra vehi.
    Non tamen ut Volusî referam deliria nostri,
10   Sive adeò fastus, Brassica vane, tuos.
    Non tanti pascale pecus, non Hispo Tragûrus,
        Ad stomachum Crambe nec facit ista meum.
    Me meus ad parteis vocat Heinsius, illa piorum
        Delicies hominum, deliciesque Deûm.
15 Illius (ô Musae) liber ad sua cornua venit,
        Purpureoque omni lumine parte nitet.
    O quis nunc turpi possit torpere veterno,
        O quis nunc tacitas possit habere fideis?
    Non ego, qui nulli faveam magis. Ite Vacerrae.
20   Heinsius est solus, qui mihi carmen erit.
    Quem modò quem parvo versare Crepundia nisu
        Vidimus, et planum sollicitare pedem,
    Insurgit Tragicis evinctus crura Cothurnis,
        Aeschyleumque aequo pondere Syrma trahit.
25 Non tamen hic Epulas Tereî, non saeva Thyestis
        Fercula, non Bacchas, non Athamanta sonat,
    Non Scyllas, non quae docuit ludibria vanus
        Ennius, aut Ennî, vanus et ipse, Nepos.

----

12 stomachum *scripsi*: stomachnm *A*.

[14]   Elegy by Petrus Scriverius
                          on *Auriacus* by Daniel Heinsius,
                 the dazzling poet who is highly appreciated by him

Go far away, Worries, hard race, go away Troubles, my legs may not rattle with your shackles now. I finally am a master of my own time and have left the Praetor,[92] and my welcome free time is now devoted to my Muses:[93] God shines for us more mildly. Get rid of every mess that does not have enough sympathy for the virgins' group. Get rid of it!

Look, I would like to go to the old Sisters, look, I want to go to my poetry and my sacred business. But not to praise the gaze of our Volusius[94] or your big bombast, vain Brassica.[95] For me no grazing cattle,[96] no horny Bockenberg,[97] and also heated Cabbage[98] is nothing for my stomach. I am called to my duty by my dear Heinsius, the darling of righteous people, the darling of the Gods.

His book, O Muses, is nearing completion and shines with radiant light on all sides. O, who could sink into shameful lethargy, o, who would be able to silence his lyre now? In any case, I do not, because I do not cherish admiration for anyone else. Get rid of you, Slug-heads. Heinsius is the only one who will be worth a song to me.

The man I just saw handle his Toy[99] with childish attempt, and stampede, stands up with his calves in the buskin of the tragedy and he equals Aeschylus' tragedy in dignity.

Yet he does not tell of meals by Tereus, no cruel dishes of Thyestes, no Bacchants, no Athamas, no Scyllas, nor the nonsensical stories told by the nitwit

---

92   I.e. public life, or the courtroom.

93   The Muses, goddesses of poetic activity, are here used metonymically for the poetry.

94   The author of *Annals* Volusius is ridiculed by the poet Catullus for his long-windedness.

95   The historian Jacobus Brassica or Jacob Cool († 1637).

96   Perhaps an allusion to the rhetoricians.

97   The *hispo tragurus* is an allusion to the historian Pieter Cornelisz. Bockenberg (1548–1617); Scriverius had a quarrel with Cool and Bockenberg on the use of sources in historiography.

98   Crambe (cabbage) may refer to Juvenal's expression *crambe repetita* (old cabbage) and at the same time to Jacob Cool (the Dutch 'cool' meaning cabbage).

99   Toy is *crepundia*, which can mean rattle as a children's toy, but probably is also an allusion to Heinsius' annotations on Silius Italicus' *Punica*, the *Crepundia Siliana* (1601).

Longè alia, ô, nostris iuvat exhibuisse Theatris,
30   Digna vel Orchestris, magne Quirine, tuis.
Ingenteis canit ille Animos, dominosque Batavos
        Aligero secum tollit in astra gradu.
Semideumque Heroa canit, feliciter; unum
        Triste, quòd Hispanos detegat ille dolos.
35   Triste, quòd in Scurram pugnet pius. ô Dolor! ô Dî!
        Quàm scelus hoc ipsi non licuisse velim!
Viveret Auriacus, Patriae Pater, optimus Heros
        Viveret, et felix Belgia tota foret.
Belgia iam longis bellis concussa ruinis
40   Belgia, quae belli nîl, velut antè, gerit.
Vota sed haec tantùm. Fuit, ah, fuit! îlicet, ah! ah!
        Quo servata fuit Belgia, pulsus Iber;
Vixit. At, ô Cives, quid eum vixisse dolemus?
        En quo iam primum vivere possit habet.
45   Heinsiadem dico, quo nullus acutior umquam,
        Quo gravior nullus splendidiorque fuit.
Credite, non soli numeros miramur Ephebi,
        Et juvenem tanto posse tumore loqui.
Iuliades stupet ipse, stupet gravis ille Senator
50   Noster Hiantéae Dousa sititor aquae.
Iure bono: mala multa mali perpessus Iberi,
        Exemplum Tragici iam puer exsul erat.
Caspari procul ite leves, procul ite Gameri,
        Non facit ad Vatem pagina vestra meum.

Ennius or his Cousin, also a nitwit.[100] He wants to see completely different subjects in our Theatres, which are worthy of even your Theatre, o great Roman.[101] He sings of exalted Men, and brings the mighty Hollanders with him to the stars with his winged feet. He sings of an almost divine hero, with success! The only sad thing is that he unfolds the Spanish tricks. The sad thing is that the pious man fights a Villain. O Grief! O Gods! How would I have longed to see that this crime had been thwarted by him! Then Orange, the Father of the Fatherland, would still live, then the excellent Hero would still live, and the Netherlands would be happy in their entirety. The Netherlands that have been ravaged by protracted war violence, the Low Countries that are waging an unprecedented war.

But these are merely wishes. He is done, done! All is over, ah, with the man through whom the Netherlands are saved and the Spaniards are expelled far away. His life is over. But, fellow citizens, why do we mourn that his life is over? See, he has a man through whom he can really live for the first time now. I mean Heinsius. No one was ever more discerning, no one ever more exalted in his style and more glorious than he. Believe me, I am not the only one to admire the Young Man's verses, and admire that a young man can speak with such a lofty style. The son of Julius himself[102] is astonished, just like our weighty Senator, Dousa, who yearns for Hyantic water.[103] Rightly so: after experiencing a lot of misery from the wicked Spaniards, he was, like a true tragic figure, already an exile as a young man. Go away, light-hearted people like Casparus, go far away, people like Gamerius,[104] your writings will be nothing in comparison to my Poet. Go away, dry writers, go away, chatters;

---

100   Here Scriverius lists several mythological subjects which were cast in the form of a tragedy: Tereus who unintentionally ate his son Itys, a story on which the Attic playwrights Sophocles and Philocles both wrote a play; Thyestes who (also unwittingly) ate his sons, the subject of a tragedy by Seneca; the *Bacchantes*, a play by Euripides, on these frantic female worshippers of Bacchus; Aeschylus, Sophocles and Euripides wrote tragedies (now lost) on the story of Athamas who was driven crazy at the instigation of Juno; Scylla was a dangerous rock that had to be circumnavigated by Ulysses; the Roman playwrights Quintus Ennius (239–169 BC) and his nephew Marcus Pacuvius (220–131/130 BC), both of whom had written dramas.

101   I.e. Seneca.

102   I.e. Josephus Justus Scaliger (1540–1609) the son of Julius Scaliger.

103   'Hyantic' water is a metonym for Boeotian water, i.e. water from Boeotia where Mount Helicon with the source of the Muses is, so ultimately a metonym for poetry.

104   The German translator of Spanish novels Caspar Casparius or Caspar Ens (1568/1570–c. 1649/1652) as a Delft deputy headmaster wrote a tragedy *Princeps Auriacus, sive Libertas defensa* (1599), and Hannardus Gamerius or Hannard van Gameren wrote a play *Pornius* (Munich 1566; reprinted Antwerp 1568).

55 Cedite ieiuni scriptores, cedite blenni:
    Scîlicèt huîc palmas Grotius ipse tulit.
   Provocet antiquas haec una Tragoedia chartas,
    Quas modò cumque Hellas, Romaque dives habet.
   Sed nunc erubui de tanto dicere Vato,
60   Cùm mihi tàm parvus perstet in ore sonus.

for Grotius himself has brought him the honorary palm. This one Tragedy can compete with all ancient writings, both those of the Greeks and those of the rich Romans.

But now I am ashamed to speak about such a great Poet, since my voice does not carry far enough.

[15]   DANIEL HEINSIVS
PRO AVRIACO SVA.

AVRIACI cineres, debellatrixque tyrannûm
NASSOVIVM stirps magna deûm. Tuque aequa parenti
Progenies immensa tuo; seu fulgida caeli
Metiris spatia, aut aequalem in pulvere circum
5 Aemulus Euclidae veteris deducis, et astra
Igneaque aurati percurris lumina mundi,
Tranquillae leve pacis opus; seu fervidus inter
Tympanaque fremitusque virûm provectus, Eoâ
Purpureus galeâ, et niveis conspectus in armis
10 Spumantem pertundis equum, dum vertice summo
Nutat apex, tremulique adverso flamine coni
Cristaque turbato circum tremit horrida vento,
MAVORTI dux nate tuo; seu sulphure et atro
Terribilem Iovis igne manum, flammataque coeli
15 Nubila, et ardentis sonitus imitaris Olympi,
Immensumque novo perterres fulmine mundum
Oceani terraeque potens, vindexque parenti
Tandem nate tuo, tumulique exactor et umbrae
Ingentisque animae. Tuque indignatus Iberum
20 Aequoreae regnator aquae, magnoque QVIRITI
Acta per aequaevos confundens nomina fastos
Aeterni comes imperij, consorsque laborum,
Tum quoque, cum rerum dominum, ingentesque secures
Victaque Romanas tremuit GERMANIA virgas,

Tit. B Daniel Heinsius Gandensis, *Elegiarum lib. III. Monobiblos* [...] (Leiden: Maire, 1603), pp.
256–261; *C* Daniel Heinsius, *Poematum nova editio auctior emendatiorque* [...] (Leiden: Maire,
1606), pp. 286–290.   1–49 Auriaci cineres—pectus *post corr. del. L.*   1 debellatrixque tyrannum *A*: umbra indignata tyrannos *B C.*   2 Nassovium—deûm *A*: Nassoviûmque heroum animae *B*, victricesque heroeum animae *C.*   3–4 Progenies—aequalem *A B*: Stirps immensa tuo,
seu pulchro *L C.*   7 leve pacis *A B*: virtutis *L C.*   10–15 dum vertice summo—ardentis *A B*:
quem Bructera tellus | Horruit, et ponti domino summisit Iberus; | Huc ades, et pictis galeam
submitte cothurnis, | Qua te cura tenet, seu iam flammantia coeli | Nubilia, seu magni *C.*   13–14
Mavorti dux nata tuo ... Terribilem *A*: Terribiles inter fremitus ... Armatam *B.*   17 Oceani terraeque potens *A B*: Oceano terraque ultor *C.*   20–21 Aequoreae—fastos *A B*: Magnae rector aquae
quem non virtutis egentem | Aspect Romanis iunxerunt praelia fastis *C.*   23 ingentesque *A B*:
magnasque *C.*   24 Romanas *A B*: venturas *C.*

[14]   **Daniel Heinsius in defence of his *Auriacus***

Ashes of Orange, and great descendant of the divine Nassaus who have sub-
jected tyrants. You too, great scion, the equal of your father, whether you cross
the brilliant spaces of heaven, or draw a symmetrical circle in the sand, competing with the ancient Euclid, and racing past the stars and the fiery lights
on the golden sky,[105] an easy activity in quiet peacetime, whether you progress
energetically between the drums and the cries of men, with a rosy glow over
your helmet in a brilliant gleam and eminent in shining white arms set spurs
to your foaming horse while on top of your head a swaying crest is moving,
and when the wind blows the quivering plumes and the bushy helmet forest
around it move back and forth in the strong wind, captain, son of your father
Mars, or with sulphur and black fire imitate the terrible hand of Jupiter, the
thunderclouds in the sky and the rumbling of the flaming Olympus, and with
a new kind of lightning terrify the immense world, lord and master of ocean
and earth, son that eventually will be the avenger of your father and demand
satisfaction for his grave, his shade and his immeasurable soul.

     And you, who are angry with the Spaniard, ruler over the sea surface, and
who associate your name, carried for as many years, with the great Roman,
companion of the eternal realm, partaker of his efforts, also at that time, when
vanquished Germania trembled for the lord of the world, the enormous axes

---

105   The great scion is Prince Maurice, who was interested in mathematics, in which the
      Greek Euclid (b. 308 BC) excelled; Maurice was taught by the Flemish mathematician who
      resided in Leiden Simon Stevin (1548–1620); he was also interested in astronomy.

25 O BATAVE, immensi maris accola, divitis undae
   Vasticies, regum metus. O qui turgida Ponti
   Inter et horrentes hybernis motibus Haedos
   Montesque fluctusque et caeruleam AMPHITRITEN
   Prodigus humentes vitae moderaris habenas,
30 Veliferumque levi volitantem flamine currum
   Aeolios inter fremitus, atque horrida monstra
   TRITONASQVE vagos, tempestatumque furores,
   Et concurrentes diverso e carcere fratres
   HIPPOTADAE genus indomitum, Boreamque Notumque
35 Oceano mirante vehis, postremaque THVLES
   MEMNONIAMQVE domum et magni Titanis egentem
   Praetergressus humum, multumque errantis IACCHI
   AMPHITRYONIADAEQVE extremo in littore metas;
   Huc agedum spectator ades, dum ingentibus ausis
40 Ignauam calcamus humum, audacesque iuventa
   Tollimur, et priscos vaga mens se tollit in Actus,
   Horridaque ingenti percurrit pulpita socco,
   Et thyrso percussa venit, qua nobilis ante
   Mens GROTI divina mei, quae corpore parvo
45 Cincta, per immensas rerum diffunditur oras
   Causarumque vias, diu interclusa tenebris
   Dirigit ardenti BATAVVM vestigia passu:
   Orchestramque invectus eo. Quo tigride raptum
   Pampinea trahis attonitum per nubila pectus,
50 Magne MIMALLONIDVM genitor? Date vela BATAVI
   Surgenti date vela. Feror, feror. Ebrius Evan
   Semivirâ cinctus choreâ et bacchantibus Euoe,

26–38 Vasticies—metas *om. B C: add B post lineam* 25 Fortibus exultans spoliis et divitis undae.
39–43 Huc agedum—*ante A B:* Huc spectator ades: si non incognita vobis | Pectora concepere
deum, fretique iuventa | Tollimur, et pulchris inclusit crura cothurnis | Excelsae virtutis amor. Qua
fortiter ante *C.*   39 ingentibus *A:* fortibus *B.*   40 audacesque *A:* fretique *B.*   42 Horrida—
socco *A: del. L.*   45–46 Cincta—tenebris *A B:* Circum clausa licet, diu intercepta tenebris *C.*
47 ardenti *A B:* audaci *C.*   49 Pampinea—pectus *A B: del. L,* Tollis ovantem animum, medioque immittis Olympo *C.*   52–53 et bacchantibus—Sileno *A B:* nixusque cothurno *C.*   52
bacchantibus *A C:* bacchantibsn *B.*

and the Roman power,[106] o Hollander who live by the great sea, plunge the rich water, and frighten kings. O you who in the middle of the stormy sea, the horrifying storms of the Kids and Mountains,[107] currents and the dark blue Amphitrite without caring for your life handle the moist reins.[108] You ride a sail-carrying car that flies through a light breeze, amidst the roar of Aeolus, the horrifying monsters and the roaming Tritons, the raging storms, the brothers racing from various dungeons, the unbridled race of the grandson of Hippotes, and Boreas and Notus, while the Ocean looks at it in admiration.[109] You have sailed past the distant Thule, the house of Memnon and the empire that the great Titan never sees, and beyond the area where Bacchus came on his far journey and the furthest coasts of Amphitryon's descendant.[110]

Come on, be present as a spectator, while in my great recklessness I will set foot on as yet untrodden ground and raise myself up in youthful rashness, and while my restless spirit dares to practise the age-old genre of Drama, running with pounding buskin over the horrifying boards and, chased by a thyrsus, entering territory where once the divine spirit of my noble friend Grotius, notwithstanding his short stature, earned fame across the immense orbits of the world and the expanses of the universe, and with his own energetic stride led the footsteps of the Hollanders, who for a long time had been in darkness.[111] I'll go on that stage. Where do you haul my haunted heart, dragged along on a vine-twisting tigress, past the clouds, great leader of the Bacchantes?[112]

Hoist the sails, Hollanders, hoist the sails for me on my high flight. I'm dragged along, dragged along. In drunkenness, Euhan wields his signs, sur-

---

106   The Romans used Batavian (Dutch) auxiliaries at the time that the Dutch territory was part of the Roman Empire as *Germania inferior*.

107   The *Haedi* are the constellation of the Kids in the hand of Auriga, the Wagoner; the Mountains perhaps indicate the large constellation Auriga.

108   Amphitrite as a sea goddess is used as a metonym for sea.

109   Aeolus, the grandson of Hippotes, is the god of winds; Tritons are sea gods; Boreas and Notus are the gods of the north and south winds respectively.

110   The island of Thule—identified with Iceland—was situated in the north; Memnon was the King of Ethiopia, his house indicating the south; the empire that the Sun never sees may be the land south of the equator; Bacchus in his wanderings reached India, the east; the coasts of Amphitryon's descendant Hercules are the Strait of Gibraltar (the Pillars of Hercules), the west.

111   By writing and publishing his *Adamus exul* (1601) Hugo Grotius had revived the neglected genre of tragedy in the Low Countries.

112   I.e. Bacchus, the leader of the 'Mimallones' or Bacchantes.

Et madido Satyrûm gemitu, et nutante Sileno
Signa movet, motusque animi ferit, imaque cordis
55   Excutit, et totum distillat ab aethere NONNVM.
Cernitis? Immenso trepidant proscenia motu
Sub pedibusque exultat humus (spectate BATAVI):
NASSOVIVS dux magnus adest, ac lumina caelo
Tollit, et ingentem defigit in aere vultum;
60   Non fraudes mens alta pavet, non fata necemque,
Degeneremve heroa dolum. Non invidet hosti
Fallere posse suo: soli hoc concedit *Ibero*.
O fatum! O crudele nefas! Sors improba! CVNCTAS
ADMITTIT FORTVNA MANVS. NON ABNVIT VLLI:
65   ANGVSTVM EST VIRTVTIS ITER. Mauortius ille
Ardor, et augusti vis pectoris; ille tot ante
Exuvijs, titulisque ducum sublimis; ab hoste
Vulnere qui pulchro meruit confossus, et ictu
Caedi posse suo (superi et crudelia fata),
70   Latroni servandus erat! Patriaeque ruinam
Duxit, et ingenti tremefacta BATAVIA motu
Externas invicta manus, SICVLVMQVE tyrannum
Horruit, et sero venturum è littore regem.
     Cernitis ardentem piceâ fuligine taedam
75   Foemineosque habitus, et tetrae virginis ora,
Sanguine fumantis calido, et serpentibus hydris
Colla per horrentesque comas? Prorumpit Erinnys,
Alteraque ALECTO Siculis emergit ab oris.
Estne aliquid supra stridentia colla Megaerae
80   Tisiphonenque Dei! Quod nec Iovis ille ferarum
Immitis domitor, genitorúe PALAEMONIS olim
Horruit, aut Diris ultricibus actus ORESTES
Per scenas DANAVMQVE choros? Nec GRAECIA nempe

---

54 motusque animi ferit *scripsi*: motusque animi serit *A B*, mentemque animi ferit *C*.   58 Nassovius dux magnus *A B*: Nassoviae dux gentis *C*. ‖ dux magnus adest *A B C*: *del. L*.   59 ingentem
A B: audacem *C*.   75 Foemineosque *B C*: Feminosque *A*.   83 nempe *A B C*: quondam *L*.

rounded by a half-male host, by people who, drunk, shout Euhoe[113] and by the drunken support of Satyrs and by the gaggling of Silenus;[114] he brings my soul into ecstasy, shakes the depths of my heart, and lets the whole Nonnus drip from the ether.[115]

Do you see it? The stage shakes with a great movement, the dust rises under the feet (look, Hollanders): the great leader Nassau[116] is there, he points his eyes to the sky and keeps his big eye tightly focused on the air. His lofty heroic mind is not afraid of deception, fate and death or shameful ruse. He does not deny his enemies that they are able to deceive: this is something he only allows the Spaniard.

O fate! O cruel crime! Angry fate! Fortune admits everyone. She does not reject anyone, but narrow is the path of courage. That glowing figure of Mars, the strength of his exalted chest, he, formerly exalted for his great spoils and royal titles, which he deserved by being pierced by the enemy with a beautiful wound and the possibility of being killed with a blow that suits him (gods and cruel destiny!), had to be kept for a bandit![117]

He caused the collapse of the fatherland, and the invincible Holland trembled in a great turmoil and shuddered for foreign hands and the Sicilian tyrant and the king who would come late from the coast.[118]

Do you see the burning torch with its jet-black smoke, the figure of a woman, the face of a horrible virgin, steaming with fresh blood and water snakes around her neck and wild hair? A Fury jumps forward, a second Alecto pops up from the coasts of Sicily. Is there something worse than the hissing neck of Megaera and Tisiphone, good gods![119] Something which the hard-hearted tamer of Jupiter's wild animals or the father of Palaemon had previously feared, or Orestes, who was pursued by the vengeful Furies, as staged in tragedies and told in the chorus songs of the Greeks.[120] All of Greece alone was not

---

113   Euhan of Euan is another name for Bacchus, hence his followers shouted 'Euhoe'.

114   Satyrs and Silens were among the followers of Bacchus.

115   The fifth-century Greek poet Nonnus had written an epic *Dionysiaca*; in 1610 Heinsius would write a commentary on it together with Petrus Cunaeus (1586–1638).

116   William, Prince of Orange, Count of Nassau (1533–1584).

117   The bandit is Balthasar Gerards, Orange's murderer.

118   In Antiquity the 'Sicilian tyrant' was Phalaris (see Hor. *A.P.* 463); here it indicates Philip II, who was also King of Sicily (from 1554 onwards).

119   These lines refer to the Spanish Inquisition, in the tragedy added as a fourth to the three avenging goddesses, the Furies Alecto, Megaera and Tisiphone.

120   In Greek mythology Athamas' son Palaemon shivered for the Furies who made him mad; Orestes fled them, as depicted in plays by Aeschylus.

In Fvrias satis una fuit. Maiora Batavi
85　Vidimus, et toto pelagi seclusimus aestu.
　　　Cernitis indigno perfossum vulnere pectus,
Oraque torpentesque genas? En nobilis atro
Sanguine suffusa est Divae morientis imago:
Libertas iacet, ite viri, complexaque funus
90　Magnanimumque heroa tenet, gemituque Batavam
Cum domino conclamat humum trepidumque Leonem
Deserit, et nostris properat vestigia terris.
Quo gressum, quo Diva moves? Adeone Deabus
Venturi mens caeca sua est? Necdum altera rerum
95　Argumenta tamen, necdum exultantia campis
Agmina, victricesque Aqvilas, natumque tonantem
Circum castra vides? Quantum tibi restat, Ibere,
Sanguinis! Immensam Frisiorvm e littore nubem
Et coniuratum video descendere Geldrvm,
100　Mattiacvmqve undae domitorem, altique Batavvm
Contemptorem animi. Pater ipse è littore Nerevs
Ingentes populis animos et corda ministrat.
Illum indignantem multùm, multoque furore
Indomitum, totumque in littus cogere Pontvm
105　Et vastam spumantis aquae sustollere molem
Aspiceres; undae auderet quod credere Vesper
Et Siculas frustra Batavis immittere puppes.
　　　O animi, ô proles Neptvnia, nataque rebus
Pectora. Tempus erit (me si vis inclyta fandi
110　Surripiat cinerique meo, et mortalibus umbris,
Fatalesque colos extra, atque ignobile lethum
Constituat tumuli ignarum et caliginis atrae)
Quo clades Thvrnovda tuas, lethumque Philippi
Nobile, et Eoi perruptas littoris oras
115　Expediam ingentis voti reus, armaque et enses
Nassovios: iuxtaque aeterni nominis Hvgo
Ibit et ereptum patriae donabit Erasmvm.
Illi junctus ego (si quid tamen, haec quoque si quid
Carmina venturis valeant promittere saeclis)
120　Illi junctus ego, motusque animosque virorum
Armaque fortunasque et rerum ingentia cepta

84　Furias *A C*: furias *B*.

big enough for the Furies. We Hollanders have seen worse things and we have tamed them with the whole surf of the sea.

Do you see her breast pierced with a disgraceful wound, the face and the stiffened features of her face? Look, the noble figure of the dying goddess is dripping with black blood: Freedom has been felled. Out of the way, men: she holds the body of the magnanimous hero, and besides her lord she also laments Holland; she leaves the Lion[121] trembling and hurries away from our countries. Where are you going, Goddess, where?

Is the mind of goddesses so badly informed of the future? And do you not yet see the proofs of the events, not yet the cheering columns on the fields, the conquering armies and the son who goes about on the camp thundering? How much blood do you still have, Spaniard!

I see an immense dust cloud coming from the coasts of the Frisians, descending on the loyal Gelderlander, the Zeelander, the tamer of water, and the Hollander, who does not count his high life. Father Nereus[122] himself gives these peoples great courage and valour from the coast. You could see him indignant and untameable by great rage drive the whole Sea to the shores and see a huge mass of foamy water rising, because the Occidental ventured to step on the waves and send Sicilian ships to the Hollanders in vain.

O courageous men, o offspring of Neptune, hearts born for action. Time will come (if the famous power to speak pulls me from the grave and the shadows of the deceased and puts me outside the fateful spinning distaffs and unworthy death, unfamiliar with the grave and the black nebula), Turnhout,[123] that I will relate your defeat and the renowned death of Philip[124] and the victory on the shores in the east, bound by a great vow, and the weapons and swords of the Nassaus: next to me Hugo[125] with his eternal name will go and he will give the deceased Erasmus[126] back to the fatherland.

Next to him I will (if at least this poetry too can predict something, predict something for the future times), next to him I will tell about the actions and courage of men and their wars and fate, and the great undertakings among

---

121   On maps the northern part of the Low Countries was depicted as a Lion, hence a metonym for the Netherlands.

122   Nereus, a sea god.

123   The capture of the city of Turnhout in 1596 was an important exploit of Maurice.

124   Philip II, who was also Lord of the Netherlands.

125   Hugo Grotius (1583–1645).

126   Grotius will become as great as the humanist Desiderius Erasmus (1466–1536).

Per populos urbesque feram, magnique THVANI
Limina, et extremam CELTAE properabimus oram,
Et fines Ligurum, et praedivitis ostia RHENI.
125   Intereà Heroës patrij, Tuque arbiter horum
CAESARIS invicti stirps, AENEADVMQVE ruinis
Et sortis rabie, et crudelibus altior annis
Regnorumque minis. Pater, ô pater, annue ceptis,
IVLIADE, dux magne meis, caveaeque Senator,
130   Incipe cessanti fremitus indicere turbae,
Ambiguosque ciere foros, vulgique tuentis
Per cuneos late geminandas ducere voces.
Ipse ego pacatae folijs evinctus Olivae
Sacra feram, Heroasque tuos, et magna ciebo
135   Nomina, VERONAEQVE deos, Manesque parentes,
CAESAREOQVE aeterna feram solennia busto.
Tu quoque tu, cui fata virûm, multumque labantem
Victuris patriam fas est committere chartis,
BOISOTI pars magna tui, quo praestite nobis
140   Inclyta LVGDVNVM domitum defendit Iberum.
Fas sit, fas sit, DOVSA, mihi tam grandibus atras
Praesidijs nebulas, sit caligantia fati
Pondera, et umbrosae tenebras perrumpere terrae,
Sordentesque hominum curas, vique alite mentis
145   Aethera vicinum legere, et sublimia rerum,
Inque SOPHOCLAEAS animum demittere Musas.
     At tu ingens anima, et nostris innixa cothurnis
Tendis ovans per inane, soloque emissus, Ibero
Terribilis spolio, et Mauris indutus opimis
150   Immensum moliris iter, quaque aera late
Tundis et heroo praevertis nubila passu

---

123 Limina *A B*: Limen *L C*.   124 fines Ligurum, et praedivitis *A B C*: Ligurum fines, et divitis *L*.
126–129 Caesaris—magne meis *A B*: Stirps Hetrusca [*Thyrrhena bL* Tyrrhena *C*] deûm [Deûm *C*]
quem non fortuna parentum, | Hausit [Traxit *C*] et ingentes [aeternos *C*] animi corruperit [com-
pescerit *bL* compescuit *C*} ignes. | Iuliade, si sacra tuis indiximus aris, | Magne pater, tum cum
caeli regione serena | Aeternos inter stellas ardebis honores, | Aut pulchras proavorum animas,
pater annue ceptis | Et felix succurre meis *L C*.   134 Heroasque tuos *A B*: gentesque tuas *L C*.
137 labantem *A B C*: *del. L*.   142 sit caligantia fati *A B*: caecasque [semperque *b*] evadere terras [curas *b*] *L*, caecamque evadere terram *C*.   143–145 Pondera—rerum *A B*: *om. C*.   143 et
umbrosae *A B C*: *del. L*.   144–146 Sordentesque—Musas *A B C*: *post corr. del. L*.   146 Inque *A*
B C: Adque *L*. ‖ Sophoclaeas *A B*: Sophocleas *C*. ‖ demittere *A B C*: p..ellere *L*.

peoples and in cities, and rush to the area of the great De Thou[127] and the farthest coast of France and the area of Italy and the mouth of the abundant Rhine.

In the meantime, ancestral heroes and you, ruler over them, offspring of the invincible Caesar,[128] exalted above the remains of the descendants of Aeneas[129] and the madness of fate, the cruel years and the threats of kings; Father, o father, favour my undertakings, great leader, son of Julius,[130] Senator of the theatre, begin to make the crowd applaud when they hesitate and encourage the wavering banks and encourage the spectators on the seats to express their approval twice as loudly.

I myself will, wreathed with the leaves of a tamed Olive,[131] bring offerings and summon your heroes and big names and the gods of Verona, the Shade of your father and forever annual commemorations for the grave of Caesar.[132]

And you, you too, who have the opportunity to entrust the destiny of men and the declining fatherland to permanent writings, great comrade of your Boisot,[133] under whose leadership the famous town of Leiden tamed the Spaniards and stopped them. Please allow me, Dousa, under your great protection, to break the black clouds, the obscured weight of fate, the dark fog of the spiritual kingdom and the unimportant cares of people, and grant me to fly on the powerful wings of the mind in the proximity of the ether and the top of the world, and make my mind reach freely to Sophocles' Muses.

But you, great spirit, go around leaning on my buskin and cheering through the thin space, apart from the earth, and lent a daunting aspect by the Spanish booty that you sport and the harness of the conquered Moor that you bear, you undertake the immense journey, and wherever you enter the air and walk past the clouds with the pass of a hero and knock on the door of the

---

127   The French statesman and historiographer Jacques-Auguste de Thou (1553–1617).
128   Joseph Scaliger (1540–1609), son of Julius Caesar Scaliger.
129   I.e. the Romans, whose empire had been founded by the Trojan prince Aeneas.
130   I.e. Joseph Scaliger.
131   The olive as a symbol for poetry.
132   Heinsius will bring tribute to the grave of Julius Caesar Scaliger in Verona.
133   Louis Boisot (ca. 1530–1576) played an important part in the relief of Leiden in 1574.

Auratique fores premis aetheris; omnis ab alto
Cedit IBER, umbramque tuam tremit, ipsaque late
Flammea turbato subsidunt sydera vultu.
155 Sis felix, natumque diu securus ab alto
Barbaricas cernas poscentem in praelia turmas,
Et patrios multo pacantem sanguine Manes.

golden ether, every Spaniard gives way from the high sky and shivers in front of your shadow and even the fiery stars languish in confusion. Be happy, and look carefree from the high heaven to your son who challenges the barbaric troops to a battle and brings peace to the Shade of his father with much blood.

PERSONAE TRAGOEDIAE

AVRIACVS.	SICARIVS.
INQVISITIO.	PRAEFECTVS.
TISIPHONE.	NVTRIX.
ALECTO.	ARMIGER.
MEGAERA.	CHORVS SATELLITVM.
LOYSA.	LIBERTAS SAVCIA.
SENEX.	

Κωφὰ πρόσωπα sunt Satellites qui personam Principis stipant, Famuli qui infantem Comitem adducunt, et Gerula quae eundem gestat. Nam reliqua Dramatis repraesentatio, καὶ τὸ πρέπον ostendet. Talia sunt et τὰ νοητὰ quae Actu secundo inducuntur, quorum habitus facillime ex pictorum modernorum tabulis, aut antiquorum numismatis partim; partim inscriptionibus, et symbolis cognoscetur. CHORI priores duo Flandrorum profugorum sunt; posteriores Batavorum ἐνδημοῦντων, viriles omnes.

Characters of the Tragedy

Orange	Murderer
Inquisition	Commander
Tisiphone	Nurse
Alecto	Soldier
Megaera	Chorus of servants
Louise	Wounded Liberty
Old Man	

Mute characters are the servants surrounding the prince, servants who bring the baby count and an old woman who carries him. As far as the further scenery of the drama is concerned, decorum will show. This also applies to the *allegorical figures* who perform in the second act; their appearance can easily be learned from paintings by modern painters or partly from antique coins, partly from inscriptions and tokens. The first two choruses consist of Flemish exiles, the last of *indigenous* Hollanders. All choruses are male.

ACTVS PRIMVS.

Princeps Avriacvs.

Rerum beate rector et magni parens,
Natvra, mundi, Vitaque et Lex omnium
In se fluentes quae trahis rerum vices,
Iocoque inani ludis humanum genus,
5   Lateque fusi sancta maiestas poli.
Et tu minorum sacra mater ignium
Nox, quae diei lucidam premis facem,
Silentiumque rebus indis, et polo
Faces perennes, languidosque syderum
10 Donas recursus, Hesperasque lampadas,
Orbesque magnos igne deducis vago,
Vsamque nunquam vultibus Phoeben suis
Pro fratre reddis aurei ducem chori.
Ergon' caduca nata gens mortalium
15 Brevis fugacem currere aetatis viam,
Inter minaceis intonantis impetus
Fortunae, et atras sortis infestae manus
Lususque rerum? Labitur velox dies
Ipsisque ab annis mensibusque ducimur,
20 Fatique summam pervenimus orbitam,
Denascimurque semper, et finem suum
Breves citato provocant anni gradu.
At igneae lux alta mentis, et vigor,
Scintillaque acres pectoris tundens fores,
25 Et ille tardi spiritus dux corporis
Aeternitatis inclytam affectat viam,
Coelumque lambit, motibusque ingens novis
Sese lacessens impetu emergit suo,
Terramque supra fertur, et quicquid videt
30 Mortale ducit, terminosque transilit
Metasque rerum, corporisque odit moras,

Tit. ACTVS PRIMVS *A: del. L.*   3 se fluentes *A:* se cadentes [sese euntes *b*] *L.*   8 indis *A:* addis
L.   9 syderum *A:* siderum *L.*   14 Ergon' *A:* ergo *L.*   26 affectat *A:* scandit *L.*   27 ingens *A:*
ultro *L.*

ACT I

The Prince of Orange

Blessed ruler of the world, creator of the great universe, Nature, Life and Law of everything, who cause the successive vicissitudes of fate and in an idle game play mockingly with the human race, divine majesty of the vast sky.

And you, holy mother of the smaller fires, Night, who extinguish the bright torch of the day—you bring silence to the world and place in the sky the eternal fires, the stars with their slow circulation, the Light of the Evening Star,[134] you let the huge planets, the wandering stars, take their job, you make Phoebe,[135] who never shows her own shape, instead of her brother, the head of the golden choir.

Is the perishable race of mortals then really born to take the fleeting course of a short life, under the threatening attacks of furious Fortune, under the black hands of hostile fate and the erratic course of events? Time passes by quickly, through the years and months itself we are carried away until we finally reach the end of the path of Fate: we die every moment and the short-lived years call their end at a swift pace.

But the lofty light of the sparkling spirit, its power, the spark that smashes at the door of the fierce heart, the breath of life that rules the slow body, goes the famous way to eternity. He touches the sky, stirring himself up to unprecedented efforts, raises himself through his own energy and rises above the earth; he considers everything that he sees to be perishable, he transcends the boundaries and limitations of the world and hates the obstacle that the body forms. He despises death and without being warned that he is stopped

---

134   The evening star, Venus.
135   Phoebe, the moon, as the sister of the god of the sun Phoebus, the leader of the stars.

Lethumque calcat, propriumque ad aethera
Ignarus atrâ corporis premi lue
Exultat, emicatque, nec sese capit.
35 Pars illa nostri est; caetera, ipsa quae dedit,
Tellus reposcit, iureque exigit suo
Sese prementem corporis foedi struem,
Onusque mentis. Magnus hinc rerum parens
Coeli micantem fornice aurato domum
40 Et hinc et inde fudit, altaque atria
Discriminata gemmeo astrorum choro
Spectanda late vultibus nostris dedit,
Vt illa magni purior lux pectoris
Infixa terrae sit licet, terram premat
45 Coelumque cernat semper, et sese erigat.
Hinc illa dia laudis emergit sitis,
Ardorque honorum semper in maius ruens,
Comes ducumque principumque, quos procul
Supraque rerum culmen evexit favor,
50 Et annuentis blanda Fortunae manus
In alta duxit. Belgia his cervicibus
Inclinat incubatque et invitum trahit
Seges laborum vasta, patriaeque onus
Fluctusque nostrae. Sancta libertas vocat,
55 Et servitutis faeda detrectat iuga
Mens nata magnis, nec sibi, sed omnibus
Quoscunque regis insolens premit tumor,
"Comesque rebus prosperis ferocia."
Sic divus ille fascium dux et parens
60 Autorque quondam Brutus, et magni patres,
Togata turba, Martis aeternum genus,
Diu labantem fulciere regiam
Sanctae nepotes Iliae, sic et ferox
Aristogiton faustaque Harmodii manus
65 Caelo superbum prospere eduxit pedem.

32–34 Lethumque—capit *A*: *post corr. del. L.* ‖ ad ... Exultat *A*: in ... Effertur *L.*   39 micantem
fornice *A*: superbam marmore *L.*   41–42 Discriminata gemmeo ... late *A*: Distincta late [circum
b late *c*] flammeo ... circum *L.*   47 maius ruens *A*: *del. L.*   62 Diu labantem fulciere *A*: Fero-
cientem sustuelere *L.*   64 faustaque Harmodii manus *A*: Harmodique dextra *L.*   65 eduxit
pedem *A*: stravit viam *L.*

by the despicable, disastrous body, he elevates himself to his own ether, jumps up and does not withhold himself.

That part is ours; the rest is reclaimed by the earth, which has given it itself, and under personal right it demands the pile of the ugly body that oppresses itself and is a burden to the mind. That is why the great creator of the world has produced everywhere the radiant house with the golden sky and the high dwellings,[136] scattered with the sparkling chorus of stars, in our field of vision to look at them, with the aim that the purest light of the big heart, even though it is attached to the earth, despises this earth and always looks up to heaven and raises itself up.

This is the source of that divine thirst for fame and the glowing passion for honours that always has new ambitions, qualities of leaders and sovereigns who have risen high above the top of the world in the generosity of Fortune in its leniency, and are highly exalted by its friendly hand.

The Netherlands are resting on these shoulders as a heavy burden, an enormous amount of efforts drags me against my will, as well as the burden and the turbulent times of my homeland. Holy Freedom calls; my mind, born into great things, rejects the shameful yoke of slavery, not for itself,[137] but for all who are oppressed by the insolent lust of the king[138] and "his ferocity accompanying prosperity".

Thus, once the excellent leader, founder and initiator of the consulate Brutus,[139] the great fathers, the people with the gown, the eternal lineage of Mars, the descendants of the holy Ilia,[140] supported the long-wavering empire, thus the sturdy Aristogeiton as well as Harmodius[141] with his successful actions have prosperously put their proud foot in heaven.

---

136 I.e. heaven.

137 Since he is a servant to the fatherland.

138 I.e. Philip II.

139 Lucius Iunius Brutus is said to have expelled the last king of Rome Tarquinius Superbus and thus instituted the republic and the consulate.

140 The founder of Rome, Romulus, was a son of Rhea Silva, also called Ilia, and Mars.

141 Aristogeiton and Harmodius († 514 BC) were the Athenian tyrannicides who killed the tyrant Hipparchus.

Eundum, eundum est. Haud capit motus leveis
NASSOVIORVM sanguis, et vanas moras,
Periculorum provocator, et sui.
O cor, tibine vincula et ludos ferox
70 Impune nectat hostis et collum premat
Tagi tyrannus, aureo exultans vado,
Opumque nixus robore ingenti? Licet
Soloque Pontum iungat, et caelo mare,
Terramque circa spumea eructans vada
75 Ille aestuantis caerulus regni pater
In nos resurgat, orbe concusso licet
Vtroque ab axe turbidus caeli fragor,
Atlasque latè pondere excusso tremens
Viam recuset, ibimus tamen, neque
80 Servire nostrum est. "Regiâ tendens viâ
In dura virtus sponte prorumpit; neque
Cedens prementi subtrahit collum deo,
Seseque fato semper opponit suo
Vis alta mentis." Nec tamen primordia
85 Nunc prima restant: iacta sunt fundamina
Bellique magna prosperi praeludia,
Motusque vasti. Dexteram hanc ter inclytus
Novit Philippus, Albaque; et si quod ferox
Saevumque pectus arbiter lucis vagae
90 Phaebus, comantem respicit condens facem,
Haec Hydra nostra est. Surgit in laudes meas
Faecunda rerum messis et manum vocat
Virumque poscit. Tremuit Alceiden fera;
At nos ferarum victor. Est et aspera
95 Nobis noverca, premere quae excelsas solet
Fortuna mentes impetusque. "Sed tamen
Virtute sortem qui sapit pessundabit.

---

69 O cor, tibine *A*: Nobisne semper *L*.   69–73 O cor—mare *A*: Imus Batava, nulla vis retro
trahet | (Amplector aras [aras *b*] sancta libertas tuas) | Aususque [Cursumque *b*] sisto: incubet
collo licet [incubet collo licet *b*] | Tagi tyrannus: aureo incumbens vado, [Tagi tyrannus: terraque
oppugnans suas *b* Tagi tyrannus: cuncti praecludant viam, *c*] | Opumque nixus robore ingenti
licet [Caelumque [Caelumque *c*] vires iunget et tellus suas *b*] *L*.   87 vasti *A*: tanti *L*.   87–92
Dexteram hanc ter inclytus Novit ... manum *A*: Novit hanc [Hanc sensit *b*] olim manum Ingens
... dextram *L*.   90 Phaebus *A*: Phoebus *L*.   95 excelsas *A*: magnas *L*.

I have to go, I have to go. The blood of the Nassaus, which challenges dangers and itself, cannot tolerate unimportant actions or useless inertia. Oh heart, will the impetuous enemy throw you in chains and mock you with impunity, and will the tyrant of the Tagus,[142] overconfident with his water rich of gold and bearing on the great crab of his riches, subject you with impunity? Even though that dark-blue father of the bustling realm[143] makes the division between sea and land and between sea and sky blur, as he bursts out frothy waves around the earth, and he rises up against me, even though a violent cloudburst at both poles, and the trembling of Atlas[144] as he shakes his load on me, choke the earth, yet I will go; it is not in my nature to be a slave. "Because it travels a royal road, virtue rushes out of itself on dangers and without departing it wrestles away from a god who oppresses her, and always the exalted power of the mind opposes its fate."

But it is not about the first beginnings: the foundations of and the great preparations for a prosperous war and an enormous revolution have been laid and struck. The thrice famous Philip has come to know this right hand, as have Alva,[145] and every impetuous and cruel man whom Phoebus,[146] who determines the movement of the light, watches when he stores his radiant torch; they are my Hydra.[147] A rich harvest of problems comes to my praise, calls me to action and demands virile courage.

The wild animals trembled for Alceus' grandson, but for me even the besieger of the savages trembles. I too have an evil stepmother,[148] Fortune, who usually suppresses exalted spirits and ambitions; "a wise man, however, will

---

142 I.e. Philip II.

143 I.e. the god of the sea, metonymically the sea itself.

144 Atlas, one of the Titans, was punished with bearing the globe.

145 Fernando Álvarez de Toledo, 3rd Duke of Alba or Alva (1507–1582), who was governor of the Netherlands 1567–1573.

146 Phoebus, the god of the sun.

147 The Hydra was one of the monsters defeated by Hercules, the grandson of Alceus.

148 The stepmother of Alceus' grandson Hercules Juno—since he was the son of Jupiter and Alcmene—had Hercules carry out difficult assignments.

Heramque inanem pectori subdet suo,
Ausisque magnis, strennuâque adoreâ
100 Premet superbam casuum potentiam.
Speique vana blandioris praemia,
Dolosque et artes, vimque pellacis deae
Quae incerta semper sponte promittit sua,
Pectusque frustra credula astrictum tenet
105 Lubens recidet, et bonis praesentibus
Ventura ducet; ipse Fortunae parens."
Nec ansa multi defuit periculi,
Eurystheusque nomini incumbit meo,
Et solus auget, perfidâque Iber manu
110 Prodest nocendo. Caetera haud quicquam moror,
De me triumphum primus ingentem tuli:
Idemque victor solus, et victus fui,
Motusque vanos pectoris molem mei,
Aestusque et iras impetusque subdidi
115 Deo mihique. Latius virtus nequit
Efferre gressus. Omnium victor fui
Meique. Testor nobile heroum genus
Nostrorum et ausus, sanguinemque et inclytas
Vmbras meorum, sanctiora nomina
120 Et vos Batavûm semper invictas manus,
Et te Batavae magne virtutis parens
Ductorque Nereu; caerulo qui gurgite
Spumantibusque semper exundans vadis
Lubens Ibero caerulam opponis viam;
125 Victoriarum primus hic gradus fuit,
Vicisse memet. "Regna namque sceptraque
Mirarierque cuncta quae vulgus solet
Regesque, sortis blandientis alea est,
Cassumque nomen, larva magnarum modò,
130 Et umbra rerum, principum crepundia,
Ducumque. Prima haec cura virtutis, neque
Vincendus hosti est qui sibi prius fuit."

---

103 incerta *A*: vana *L*. ‖ sua *A*: sibi *L*.   127 Mirarierque *A*: *del. L.*

overcome his fate through his virtue, he will subdue that unsteady mistress to himself and suppress the proud power of vicissitudes by great daring and fierce victory. He will gladly banish the empty rewards of the all too seductive hopes, the wiles and layers and the power of the devious goddess who is always, unsolicited, ready to give her uncertain promises, and with gullibility unsuccessfully straps his heart up, and he himself will, if the good possibilities are present, give guidance to his own future. Thus he brings about his own destiny".

I did not lack any cause for danger, a Eurystheus[149] threatens my good name; he and no one else makes me famous and with his faithless deeds, the Spaniard benefits me by harming me.

I do not care about the rest: first I have achieved a great triumph over myself. I alone was both besieger and besieged: I have subjected the ineffective emotions that oppress my heart, the passions and impulses of anger to God and to myself. Virtue can not go further. I have overcome everything and myself. I call to witness the noble lineage of the heroes on our side, and the courageous deeds, the blood and the famous shades of my relatives, holy names;[150] and you, always invincible crowds of the Dutch and you, great creator and leader of the Dutch courage, Nereus,[151] who by always bursting your banks with your dark blue stream and with your foamy waters, with pleasure put your dark blue road against the Spaniard: this was the first step of my victories, to have conquered myself. "After all, kingship and sceptre, and all that people and kings usually admire, are the die of flattering fate, an empty cry, only a delusion and a shadow of great things, toys of princes and leaders. This is the first concern of virtue; and he cannot be overcome by the enemy who was first overcome by himself." For the benefit of himself he has taken

---

149   The King of Mycenae who, at the behest of Juno, commissioned Hercules to perform the canonical twelve works.

150   William's brother Adolph (1540–1568) was killed in the Battle of Heiligerlee, his brothers Louis and Henry in the Battle of the Mookerheyde (1572).

151   The god of the sea, a metonym for the sea.

Vincique posse sponte praeripuit sibi;
Ne restet ulli, consilique pondere
135 Lascivientem saepius pressi manum
Ardore Martis, impetusque mobiles
Sese solutis efferentes vinculis
In se reduxi, turgidosque spiritus
Et has superbas regii ardoris notas
140 Virtute strinxi. "Principum hîc mentes calor
In prona ducit, visque feruentes ciet
Et ira motus; fraena sed magis sua
Et acriorem poscit hic legem furor."
Sic aestuantis pervagator Africae
145 Venator olim, feruidum venabulo
Premens leonem victor intentat minas
Libys, feramque versat, et tergum ferox
Quatit feritque deprimitque. Olli fremens
Spumas ab imo pectore eructat dolor,
150 Seseque tollit, bilis haud capax suae,
Scintillaque ardens lumine absistit vago,
Iubaeque moto corpore erectae tremunt,
Venabulumque mandit, et superbus it
Et huc et illhuc vinculi ignarus sui.
155 At ille contrà pastor, insultans procul
Feram lacessit, illa sese, et ingruit.
Iraque certat alter, alter ictibus,
Potentiorque cedit invitus licet,
Captumque tandem sentit et sese leo
160 Summittit hosti. Mentis illa regiae
Imago viva est. Surgit et sese erigit
Sublimis ille pectoris magni vigor,
Iniuriarum censor, et vindex sui,
Altasque in iras fertur, et morae inscius
165 Erumpere ardet. Sic minax Divûm pavor,
Fuliginoso sub specu versat latus
Ingens Typhoeus, Aetnaque exultans tremit,
Magisque semper fata tentantem premunt.

---

141 ferventes *A*: sublimes *L*.   154 Et ... et *A*: Modo ... modo *L*.   162 vigor *A*: tumor *L*.

away the possibility of being conquered in advance, in order to deprive another person of this opportunity.

Because of the weight of my insight, I often have stopped my hands that are longing to wage war, as well as the desire to move that flares up if it is not restrained, and reduced them to a mere desire, and I have curbed with my virtue my urge to act, and these proud traces of royal fervour.

"On the one hand, ardour is a good incentive for sovereigns, and power and fervour intensify violent emotions, but on the other hand that passion must be curbed more and it should be constrained longer."

Thus, a nomad from hot Africa, a hunter, a Libyan, sometimes triumphantly threatens an impetuous lion by cornering him with a hunting spear; he fatigues the animal and hits, strikes and breaks the proud back. The roaring pain causes the animal to raise foam deep out of his chest, it stands up, because it cannot withhold its gall, from its rolling eyes flaming sparks flash, and the mane, standing upright, tremble by the shocks of the body: it bites the spear and goes proudly back and forth, not paying attention to what hinders him. The shepherd, on the other hand, defies the beast from a distance, and that incites itself and mounts a counter-attack. One fights with his turbulence, the other with blows. The animal with more power gives in, albeit reluctantly. The lion notices that he has finally been overcome and submits himself to the enemy.

That's a vivid picture of the spirit of kings. The lofty power of the great heart that punishes injustice and avenges itself, stands up, rises and quickly makes its emotions flare up and without delay consumes itself out of desire. Thus the threatening terror of the gods, the enormous Typhoeus,[152] turns around in his grimy cave, the Etna vibrates excessively: anyone who puts it to the test is increasingly suppressed by fate.

---

152   In Greek mythology Typhoeus, a monstrous creature, son of Tartarus and Gaea, is struck with lightning by Jove who throws the Etna over him.

Nec sponte nostra Martis in discrimina,
170   Licentiaeve spe subacti venimus;
Communis ista patriae sed vox fuit,
Iussumque, cui nos hoc litare sanguine
Et iustum et aequum est. "Poscit hoc tranquillitas
Et pace dempta panditur paci via,
175   Necessitasque est ipsa Mavortis parens.
Bellumque tandem ne sit, esse convenit,
Pacemque gignit. Incipitque ut desinat
Haec una rerum." Caeterûm hic dux maximus
Et vir profecto est, patriaeque commodis
180   Servire natus. "Fervor ille impos sui
Virtutis altum nubilo obfuscat diem,
Solemque menti demit et lucem suae.
Ardetque semper, imperatque plurimis,
At servit uni, seque nolentem trahit,
185   Et servitutem qui fugit, sibi dedit."

CHORVS SENVM FLANDRORVM PROFVGORVM.

Sapphici. Duo Glyconici.
Reliqui Anapaestici.

Blanda torpentis requies senectae,
Vitrei fontes, et amaena Tempe:
Tuque spes nostrae domus illa, quae me
Lucis in molles orientis oras
190   Prima fudisti puerumque longe
     Curarum vacuum et metu
     Vidisti pede mobili,
Et ridenti molliter ore

---

173 iustum *A*: ius *L*.   *Tit. Post PROFVGORVM add. L* cum liberis suis.   187 amaena Tempe *A*:
amoena tempe *L*.   188 Tuque—me *A*: Tuque rus notum [parvum *b*] puero, domusque Parva
[patriaeque sedes *b* Lares *c*] | [Dulcisque domus, regnaque [taedaque *c* regnaque *d*] aucta, |
Nostrique [Blandaque *? c*] Lares tectaque [terraque *c*] quae me *b*] *L*.   190 prima fudisti *A*:
Ire vidistis [primi fudisti *b*] *L*.   190–191 longe Curarum vacuum *A*: curis semotum [immunem
b semotum *c*] procul *L*.   192 vidisti *A*: vidiisti *b*] *L*.

Not on my own initiative did I go into danger of war, or driven by hope of debauchery, but I was called by the voice and the command of the common fatherland, for which it is fair and equitable to sacrifice my blood. "This is what peace demands and by taking away peace the way to peace is opened; necessity itself is the father of war. For that there be no war at last, it fits that there is war now, it brings forth peace. This is the only thing in the world that is starting to stop." He[153] is the most important leader of the others and certainly a figure of power, and born to serve the interests of the fatherland. "That uncontrolled glow obscures the high light of virtue with a cloud and deprives the sunlight of its own mind. He is always glowing and commands many people, but is a slave of one,[154] and drags himself against his will. And while he flees slavery, he has imposed it on himself."

Chorus of old Flemish exiles

Sapphic verses, two glyconees, the rest anapests

Attractive resting place for stiff old age, crystal-clear springs, sweet Tempe,[155] you, the house on which I have set my hopes, which in the beginning have made me enter the lovely places of the rising light and as a boy have seen me free of worry and fear playing games, dancing and sweetly laughing, and seeing me crawling amidst unimportant worries. And you, pleasant country

---

153   That is, someone who has conquered himself.
154   I.e. himself, the god or the fatherland.
155   Flanders is compared to the lovely valley of Tempe in the northern Greek region of Thessaly.

Nimium dulces texere ludos,
195   Tenuesque inter serpere curas.
Tuque suavis puero ah nota
Villa senique, posthac numquam
Habitanda vale. Sors dura vocat,
Dubiumque regit fortuna pedem
200   Subitaeque vices. Tuque meorum
Ah, natorum blanda propago,
Hilari ridens saepius ore
Medio in luctu; nescia rerum
Curaeque tuae; patri iunctos
205   Dirige gressus, casusque tuos
Disce, et saevi fulmina fati.
Tu quoque si quem coniux nobis
Vtero gestat nescia faetum,
Natus nondum, tamen exul eris,
210   Patriamque fugis nascendus adhuc,
Et tibi paena vitâ prior est.
Lachrymas tellus, lachrymas tellus
Patria tellus, ultima nostri
Dona doloris impressa tene.
215   Poscimur, ah ah, nos relliquiae,
Genus effaetum, saturumque aevi,
Quibus infelix spiritus aegrè
Placidam ducit luminis auram.
Pars aequoreas Walachrûm sedes,
220   Aut horrentem Marte Batavum,
Et spumantem littoris oram
Patris Oceani, visam nunquam
Ibimus eheu; assueta prius

194–197 Nimium—senique A: Faciles [Tenuos b] inter crescens curas [ludos b'] Lenibusque ani-
num pascere curis | Tuque heu quondam puero nota | Villa senqiue L.   209 Natus A: Vivus L.
215 ah, ah A: olim L.   216 aevi A: sui L.   222 Patris—numquam A: Patris Oceani, canamque
domum | Quam tu crudeli murmure semper | Boreae fratres visam numquam [Patris Oceani,
canamque domum | Cui crudeli mumure semper | Boreae fratres, genus indomitum, | Supe-
rincumbunt, vastique gemitus visam numquam b] Canamque domum, cui crudeli | Murmure
semper Boreae fratres | Superincumbunt, vastaquae gemitus [tristesque gemitus d animaeque
leves e] | Maris insanis [Aetheris alti d] lethumque gradu | Propriore lachrymas tellus [vastique
d tristesque gemitus e; postea del.] | Lachrymas tellus, lachrymas tellus | Patria tellus, patria tel-
lus [ultima nostri d] | Dona doloris impressa tene c]. Primum add. L hos versus [b c] post Oceani,
postea ad campis.

house, that I, ah, knew as a boy and as an old man, and in which I will never live afterwards, farewell.

Hard fate calls me, chance and the unexpected course of events govern my hesitant steps. And you, oh, my dear children who laugh so often in the midst of lamentation, you who are unaware of the circumstances and your gloomy situation, follow your father, and learn what your destiny is and how cruel fate will fire its lightning bolts at you. You too, if my wife still unknowingly carries my child in her belly, even if you are not yet born, you will still be exiled: you flee your homeland, although you still have to be born, and you receive a punishment before you get life. Land, save my tears, land, my tears, my homeland, save the last gifts of my sorrow in yourself. Alas, alas, we, the surplus, an emaciated race, exhausted, have to leave, we, whose unhappy breath with difficulty inhales the friendly winds of the light of life.

Some of us will live on watery Walcheren, or in Holland, which shows the rough appearance of war, on the foamy coast of the beach of father Oceanus, which we have never seen before, we, a people who used to live in quiet

Placidis, ah, gens vivere campis:
225 Pars caerulei gurgite Ponti
Toto avulsos orbe Britannos,
Aut incoctum solibus Indum.
Pars sudantem proprio semper
Sanguïne Gallum. Miseri, miseri,
230 Quos incertum dubiumque vocat!
Pax Flandriacas placido tenuit
Foedere gentes, patrioque foco
Veterum fluxit vita parentum,
Et tranquillo tutus in aruo
235 Vidit teneros ire nepotes
Avus et lepidam currere turbam;
Qui vicinum cerneret agrum
Peregrinus erat. Patria tellus,
Patria tellus, saxaque et antra,
240 Et cognatae vallibus umbrae,
Patria tellus, Flandria, nostros
Imbibe questus.

ACTVS II. SCENA I.

Inquisitio cum tribus Furijs facem et calicem
humani sanguinis gestans inebriatur.

INQVISITIO.

Lucem perosa, lucis immunis Dea,
Tetrumque noctis improbae ludibrium
245 Tot imminentes Tartaro rupi fores,
Caliginemque, magna Paenarum parens,
Crudelitatis nata, quam ferox Iber

---

224 ah, gens *A*: turba *L*.   225 Ponti *A*: ponti *L*.   234 tutus *A*: natus *L*.   235 Vidit *A*: tuetur
? [*n.l. b* Vidit *c*] *L*.   236 Avus et lepidam *A*: lepidamque domi *L et add. L* Securus [*Spectabat b*]
avus: nescius undae | magnique maris, nescius Austri.   242 *add. sub* Imbibe questus. *et postea*
del. L: CHOR. LIB. Sequimur | Genitor quocumque vocas, | Gressusque tuos pede non segni |
Premimus, turba non indocilis | Ducere primos luctibus annos.   244 Tetrumque *A*: Novumque
L. Post corr. L: Tandemque nata noctis ignavae soror.   245 rupi *A*: fregi *L*.   246 Paenarum *A*:
Poenarum *L*.

fields. A part will go to the British, isolated from the whole world by the whirlpool of the dark blue sea, or to the sun-burnt Indies. Some will go to France, which is always dripping with its own blood.[156] We are unfortunate, unfortunate, who are called by uncertainty and peril.

Peace held the Flemish people in a placid bond, the life of our ancestors lingered at their own hearth: safely in the quiet field a grandfather saw his young grandchildren and the sweet crowd run; who looked at a neighbouring field was already a stranger. Fatherland, fatherland, rocks and caves, and you, shady valleys, fatherland, Flanders, absorb our complaints in you.

ACT II, SCENE I

Inquisition with the three Furies[157]
She is carrying a torch and a chalice of human blood, and gets drunk

Inquisition

I who have a disgust of light, a goddess devoid of light and a horrible whim of the evil night, I have forced the many doors that protrude above Tartarus and the darkness, I, great mother of the Punishments and child of Infidelity, now for the first time brought to the upper world by the proud Spaniard

---

156 Referring to the Wars of Religion in France, finding their culmination in St Bartholomew's night.

157 The Furies or Erinyes, the three goddesses of avenge, Megaera, Alecto and Tisiphone.

Primum sub auras duxit, et ferro et face
Quartam profanis addidit sororibus,
250 Noctisque alumnis, Graia queis primum manus
Vibrare saevas dexterâ indulsit faces:
Serpentibusque vinxit, et collum dedit
Atris draconum pullulare nexibus.
Gaude, Megaera, nata iam soror tibi est,
255 Iovisque nigri primus infernum genus
Perseidosque squallidas faetu domos
Iber scelestus auxit; ille Erinnyas
Treis mutuavit perfidus, quartam dedit.
Hispana tellus, scilicet vesper tuus
260 Foecundus ipse noctis exemplo fuit.
Emerge, rumpe, caede; claustraque et feros
Caliginosae pande Naturae lares,
Lethique sedem discute et lucem tuam
Mens atra disce. Testor anguineum caput,
265 Et te, Megaera, teque noctis arbiter,
Et qui redundans igne Cocytos vago
Luctu tremendam flebili tundit domum,
Meque ipsa tandem (Numine hoc maius nihil)
Patremque Iberum; pallidas Ditis domos
270 Imperuiasque mortis horrendae vias,
Phlegeton cruento quicquid ambit alueo
Invita liqui. Nunc tamen ferox pater
Tarpeia saxa cui patent, et inclyta
Vastae ruina gentis, è reconditis
275 Exciuit antris fulmine invitam trahens,
Quod non Pyracmon crudus, aut Brontes pater,
Aut claudicantis dextera effinxit Dei,
Non Siculus ignis, aut caminorum globi
Vndantis Aetnae, flammeique vortices.

---

249 profanis *del. L.* 250–251 queis ... indulsit *A*: quas ... iussit *L.* 250 manus *del. L.* 261–262 Emergit—Caliginosae *A*: Perrumpe terrae et claustra, et insana manu [Emerge in auras, claustraque umbrosae domus *b*] Reconditosque *L.* 263 discute *A*: desere *L.* ‖ tuam *A*: novam *L.* 264 Mens atra disce *A*: Admitte pectus [vultus *b* pectus *c* vultus *d*] *L.* ‖ anguineum *A*: iusus ? *L.* 266–267 Et qui—domum *A*: Quique involutus igne Cocytus vago, | Vapore tristem fumeo nubem trahit, | Nomenque luctu vincit infelix suo, *L.* 268 Numine *A*: numine *L.* 269 Ditis *scripsi*: ditis *A.* 270 horrendae *A*: ignavae *L.* 272–275 Nunc—trahens *A*: Traxit invitam licet | Pater Latinus, traxit, et coelo dedit, | Datumque coelo fulmine afflavit suo, *L.*

and by fire and sword added as fourth to the impious sisters, the foster children of the night, to whom the Greeks first attributed the property of sowing the torches of destruction in their right hand, as they coiled serpents round them, and had their necks swarming with black writhing snakes.

Be happy, Megaera, you've now got a sister: the first one who has augmented the hell brood of the black Jupiter and the filthy dwellings of Persa's grand-child[158] with offspring, has been the criminal Spaniard; the treacherous one has created a fourth after the model of the three Erinyes. Spain, your evening, pre-eminently fertile with darkness, was of course an example to him.

Go to the upper world, break, pound and open the bolts and the gruesome house of nature that is hidden in the dark. Search the house of death and get, black spirit, acquainted with your light. I will take to witness the serpent's head, you, Megaera, and you, lord of the night; and the Cocytus, the torrent that pounds the frightening house with crying lamentation,[159] and finally myself (there is no greater Deity) and my Spanish father: against my will I have left the pale dwellings of Dis and the impassable roads of the horrifying death, all that is washed around by the Phlegethon with its blood-red bed.[160] Now, however, my savage father who has access to the Tarpeian Rock[161] and the famous ruins of the awe-inspiring people, summoned me with lightning from the remote caves and dragged me against my will. This lightning was not made by the rugged Pyracmon, Father Brontes or the right hand of the lame god, not in the Sicilian fire or the furnaces and the fiery vortices of the erupting Etna,[162] but by the

---

158 I.e. Pluto, king of the underworld and brother of Jupiter, and Hecate, queen of that realm, granddaughter of Persa and daughter of Perses.

159 The meaning of the name of Cocytus is 'river of lamentation'.

160 Phlegethon means 'burning', 'blazing'.

161 A metonym for Rome; from the Tarpeian Rock on the *mons Capitolinus* criminals were thrown headlong. There the 'savage father', the Pope, has his see.

162 Pyracmon and Brontes are two of the Cyclopes, giants who are children of Uranus and Gaea, on Sicily where they work as blacksmiths for Vulcan, the lame god, who has his forge under the volcano Mount Etna.

280   At Martiorum dissipata rudera
     Vrbisque funus, et solum Quiritium.
     "O quanta curas fata mortaleis agunt!
     O quantus urbes regnaque incumbens Deus
     Ludens fatigat dissipatque, turbines
285   Rerum fateri cogor invita." (O pater
     Tarpeie, natae liceat hoc unum tuae:)
     Magni cohortes Romuli, nati Deûm;
     Arx alta rerum, gens Camillorum ferox,
     Orbis voratrix illa, regnorum lues
290   Et universi compos, et tandem sui,
     Ah, tot triumphis aucta pene, quot viris,
     Et tot ruinis urbium vitans suam,
     Illa, illa regum nata Septimontium
     Calcare fastus, insolensque nominis
295   Regalis una, spiritusque, pro pudor,
     Regum cinaedis paret, et monstro Deo.
     Cui fulmen illud obsoletus Iuppiter
     Sepultus arce Iuppiter Minoia
     Haereditatis lege rellictum tulit.
300   At contumacis vis rebellatrix tamen
     Acres Batavi corde versat impetus,
     Radicitusque fixa libertas sedet
     Gentis profanae, patriaeque ardens amor
     Animos feroces tundit, et subigit sibi.
305   Vidi perustos sole candenti patres,
     Piceosque voltus funibusque atram manum,
     Ruptasque nubes, et procellosas Iovis
     Magni ruinas provocare audax genus,
     Vndaeque legem dicere et venti minis.
310   Vidi, ipsa vidi, cum feri vis Africi
     Tempestuosa torsit hybernum mare

---

283 O ... O *A*: Heu ... Heu *L*.   285–286 invita—tuae: *A*: et tristes vices *L*.   287 cohortes *A*: nepotes *L*. ‖ nati *A*: pulli *L*.   288 ferox *scripsi*: ferax *A*.   290 compos *MTL*: compes *A*. ‖ tandem *A*: sero [victrix *b*] *L*.   291–292 Ah ... vitans *A*: Quae ... evasit *L*.   295 spiritusque, pro *L*: spiritusque; Pro *A*. ‖ pro pudor *A*: mollibus *L*.   298 arce Iuppiter Minoia *A*: *post corr. del. L*. ‖ Iuppiter *A*: Iupiter *L*.   301 Acres *A*: Altos *L*.   305–306 patres ... voltus *A*: viros ... patres *L*.   306 funibusque atram manum *A*: turbidasque Austri minas [invium ventis salum, *b*] *L*.   308 Magni ruinas ... audax genus *A*: Leni carina ... turbines *L*.   310 ipsa *MT*: ipse *A*.

meagre remnants of the descendants of Mars, the remains of the city and the bare ground of the Quirites.[163]

"O, how powerful are the destinies that cause the cares of men, oh, how great is the god who puts cities and empires under heavy pressure, plays with them, dumps them and destroys them: however terrible I think it is, I must confess that the world is upside down." (Tarpeian father,[164] do not blame your daughter for saying this:) The great cohorts of Romulus, sons of gods, a high fortress for the world, proud people of the Camilli,[165] who conquered the earth and destroyed kingdoms, the master of the world and finally also of themselves, oh, who are rich in almost as many triumphs as great men, and by destroying many cities avoided their own devastation, that people born to trample on the pride of the kings of the seven hills, the only one who is not familiar with the name and spirit of the kingship (o shame!), now obeys the catamites of princes and a monster of a god.[166] A sealed Jupiter, buried in the Minoan castle,[167] bequeathed him his lightning in accordance with inheritance law.

On the other hand, the rebellious power of the recalcitrant Dutch generates energetic impulses in their hearts. The sense of freedom of the heretical people is firmly rooted in them: fervent patriotism beats on their pride and submits them to itself.

I have seen them, the men scorched by the bright burning sun with their tanned faces, the pitch-black hand on the ropes, the people who dared to defy the cloudbursts and the destructive storms of the great Jupiter and to lay down the law to the water and the threatening winds. I have seen, with my own eyes, that this people, even when the turbulent hurricane hell of the savage Africus[168] ravaged the wintry sea, trod on the waves, and pounded the crests of the

---

163 Quirites is a solemn term for Romans as civilians.

164 For Tarpeian father see above, n. 161.

165 Camillus is a cognomen in the *gens* Furius; *camilli* were also noble youths employed in the sacrifices of the Flamen Dialis, or in religious offices in general, who should be perfect and healthy.

166 Derogatory terms for the Pope and members of the Curia.

167 The Cretans showed a grave of Jupiter on their island.

168 I.e. the south wind.

Insistere undae, dorsaque aerato pede
Fluvij rapacis tundere, et crudum gelu
Acresque lapsus, ac per undantes sinus
315   Calcata tutam lympha praebebat viam.
Ollis sepulchrum pontus, aulaque est ratis,
Agnatus ingens Aeolus, Nereus pater,
Forisque cives, hospitesque sunt domi.
Ilhuc remittor, et vetus colonia
320   Mutanda restat; deerat haec sedes mihi.
Parere certum est; maximum explevi scelus
Maiusque restat. Semper antiquum parum est.
Angusta sacris quaelibet tellus meis
Viam relaxat. Aridas sitis premit
325   Squallorque fauces: sanguine hic opus novo est.
Pace hoc, Lyaee, pace fas hoc sit tua,
Dux Thyadum nocturne; non curae mihi
Nyseïo qui colle distillat latex,
Tuusque si quid languido fallax gradu
330   Maron procaces inter exhaurit choros,
Interque Panas, virginesque Menadas,
Et aestuantes Liberi succo Deos.
Non si Falerni quicquid vuarum est tui,
Quod Setia usquam, vel Velitrarum colunt
335   Dumeta; non si tota vinorum parens
Albana tellus, Caecubique honos cadi
Descendat in me: carior sitis premit,
Paruumque nescit; pluris hic liquor mihi est,
Merumque Ibero nuper inventum meo
340   Cruor, Cruor, Cruor. Quid, o fallax Iber,
Cessas? Nec atrae sanguine undanti viae
Sanieque tristes squalidâ rigent domus?
Nondum recentes mens cadaverum strues,
Tabumque cernit; pure sudantes novo

314–315 ac per undantes sinus ... praebebat *A*: perque spumantes sinus [perque *b* ferreisque cal-
cibus *c* ut per undanes sinus *d*] ... praeberet *L*.   315 Calcata *A*: Subacta [Calcata *b*] *L*.   319
Ilhuc *A*: Illuc *L*.   324–325 Aridas ... Squallorque *A*: Squallidus ... Aridasque *L*.   331 Menadas
A: Maenadas *L*.   336 honos *A*: flos *L*.   343–344 mens cadaverum ... cernit *A*: mente caesorum
... cerno *L*.

dragging stream, the ice-cold water and the buzzing waves with a copper-clad ship, and actually the water on which they stepped provided a safe path through the sea bed. The sea is their grave, a ship their court; the great Aeolus is related to them and their father is Nereus;[169] abroad they are at home, in their own country they are strangers.

I am sent there and I have to move to the old colony:[170] I have not yet settled in this place. I am determined to obey: I have carried out a very great crime and a larger one remains to be committed. The previous crime is always too small.

Every country, however small, opens the way for my sacrifices.[171] Thirst and dirt are tormenting my dry throat: that's why I need fresh blood. Please excuse me, Lyaeus, please, nocturnal leader of the Thyades; I do not care about liquor that seeps from the hill Nysa, nor about everything your Maron drinks, while he wags slowly in the middle of the undisciplined choruses, the Fauns, Maenad girls and the gods heated by the juice of Liber.[172] I do not care about all your Falernian grapes or the products of Sezzia or of the vines of Velitrae; even if the whole mother region of the wines, the Albanian country and the fame of the Caecubian wine barrel would disappear in my gullet,[173] I do not care about it: an overly picky thirst torments me and does not want to drink normal wine.

More valuable to me is this liquid, the unmixed drink, recently introduced by my Spaniard: blood, blood, blood. Why do not you hurry, sneaky Spaniard? Are the roads not yet black with running blood and the houses are not yet awfully stiff with dirty, tainted blood? I do not see any piles of fresh corpses from which the dirty moisture is dripping.

---

169   Aeolus is the god of the winds; Nereus a sea god.

170   The 'old colony', either since it was part of the Habsburg empire since 1477, or because it was a former colony (and, in fact, not anymore in 1584, when William of Orange was murdered, nor in 1602, when *Auriacus* was written).

171   *Sacra*, i.e. the sacrifices, or 'Holiness' as an allusion to the term Holy Office for the Inquisition.

172   Lyaeus, or Bacchus, was leader of the Thyades; he was supposed to have been born in Nysa on Mount Meros in India. Maron refers either to the instructor of the young Bacchus, or to the hero of sweet wine in Homer. The Fauns (lit. Pans) and Maenads were gods of woods related to Bacchus, who is also called Liber, and his priestesses respectively.

173   The *Falernus ager* in Campania, the cities of Setia (Sezzia) and Velitrae in Latium, and the region around Alba Longa and Caecubus in Latium all were famous for their excellent wines.

345 Nondum revulsis ossibus pallent agri.
Cessas Ibere, fluctibus, ferro et face
Rerum coactas vortere in sese vices?
Adsum. Quid hoc est? Scaeve sacrorum pater
Frustran' cruentum Tartaro emisi pedem
350 Et hospitalem nocte mutavi diem?
Nunquam supernos sobria accessi deos,
Et luce fuluam solis aurati comam,
Terrasque vidi; sanguinis gustu novi
Efferre sese suevit optatum scelus
355 Mensque ipsa factis saeva praeludit suis.
Nunc hic redundans sanguine humano calix
Feram cruore musteo sedet sitim,
Cordisque totas imitus mergat vias,
Mentemque tollat, quicquid et clemens, pium
360 Nobis relictum, molle, pacatum fuit.
Bacchare certum est: en iuvat, iuvat, iuvat
Laxare mentis fraena. Quid segnis stupes
Gens atra terrae? Tuque germânum caput,
Megaera, nocte nil geris dignum tua?
365 Patrisque verum dextera probas genus?
At o quid atrum nubila involuunt diem?
Meque ipsa perdo? Flexaque in sedes novas
Caliginosus lumina obducit situs?
Errantque tristes luce subducta pedes?
370 Et ominosus poplitum labat gradus?
Vestigijsque turbida incertis tremens
In luce lucem quaero, et in die diem?
Nosco furentes sanguinis poti notas,
Nosco. Cruoris hocce munus et meum est,
375 Mentemque secum mysticus tollit furor.
Incerta certum mens tamen voluit nefas.

---

348 scaeve *A*: saeve [magne *b*] *L*.   351 supernos *sublin. L*. ‖ accessi *A*: invasi *L*.   354 sese ...
optatum *A*: sese ... insanum [sese ... indictum *b* semet ... indictum *c*] *L*.   356 redundans *A*: *del.*
L.   358 Cordisque ... imitus *A*: Saevique cordis *L*.   358–362 Cordisque—fraena *A*: *Post corr.*
Imasque cordis impii mergat vias, | Mentemque tollat: quicquid et clemens pius [pium, *b*]| Nobis
relictum [Mentemque tollat quicquid et clemens *n.l.* [pium *c*] Ani- | Adhuc relictum pectore sub
imo latet. [Animo relictum mite, paccatum latet. *C*] | Bacchare certum est [Nil usitatum *n.l.* [vol-
uimus *d*] vires novas *c*]] saevusque trepidet Belga *b*] *L*.   368 obducit *A*: involvit *L*.   374 hocce
munus *A*: munus illud *L*.   375 Mentemque—furor *A*: *del. L*.

The fields do not sweat fresh pus yet and are not yet white with boned bones. Don't you hurry, Spaniard, to carry out well with water, sword and fire, which should be done anyway?

Here I am now. What is this? Perverse executor of my rituals,[174] have I put my bloody foot out of the Tartarus for nothing and have I exchanged the night for the hospitable day for nothing? I was never sober when I entered the upper world and saw the light yellow halo of the golden sun and the earth: through a swallow of new blood, the desire for murder usually becomes overconfident and a cruel spirit prepares for its misdeeds.

Now let this chalice overflowing with human blood quench my thirst with fresh blood: let it flow to the depths of my heart and take away my mind and all that is kind, pious, gentle and peaceful in me.

That it comes to a Bacchanal is certain: see, I would like, very gladly, to slacken the reins of my spirit. What strikes you dumb, black people of the earth? And you, my very own sister Megaera, do you carry nothing that is worthy of your darkness? And do you not show yourself a true offspring of father through your actions?

But oh, suddenly it becomes dark around me, I lose control of myself, and my eyes, focused on an unknown place of residence, are covered by a dark mist! And do my feet wobble through my sadness now that I do not see anything anymore? And are my knees knocking ominously? And am I trembling in confusion with uncertain steps in light, the light and by day, the day? I know the signs of frenzy of drinking blood, I know them. This gift of blood has now also been granted to me: a bacchantic frenzy turns off my mind. Although my mind is insecure, it is still considering a well-defined crime.

---

174   The king of Spain who introduced the Inquisition in the Low Countries.

Terra coelum, noctis atrae regia, et vastum mare
Explicate trina vires regna, et occultos dolos.
Adsumus sacris, Philippe, vindices dignae tuis.
380   Victima ingens, victima ingens, victima hacce dextera
Concidet, qualem nec ille perfidas Teucrûm rates
Mortuus victor poposcit Ilia emergens humo,
Cum feras minax Pelasgum turba soluebat rates.
Nos Batava terra, Ibero nomen horrendum, vocat.
385   Poscimur? Quid o moramur? Quò nequit fallax Iber
Tendere, huc fraudes dolique tendere Iberi queunt.
Magnae sorores, Atthidos sacrum genus,
Priscisque Erechtei Cecropisque finibus
Cognata turba, si quid antiquum manet
390   Viresque vobis tempus asscripsit novas,
Quaerendus ille, qui ferox, vecors, furens
Aut genere Iberus (alterum sat est tamen),
Aut mente fuerit, quique pectore vnico
Solus profanas quattuor gestet Deas.
395   O flammei ignes, tuque pallentis Deae
Famulatus ingens, ignei cives poli
Relligio noctis, tuque dominatrix hera,
Invisa Phoebo luna, pars Phoebi tamen
Familia nostri tota quam Ditis colit,
400   Quemquamne magno dum satellitio procul
Stipata iussum pervagaris tramitem
Vsquam tueris? Cuius unius manu
Quod non Philippi mille potuerunt rates,
Non ferrum et ignes, armave et tristes minae,
405   Timere Batavus discat? Intereà tamen

---

380 victima—dextera *A*: victima ingens, victima hac ingens manu *L*.   381 Concidet *A*: Quaeritur *L*. ‖ ille *A*: olim *L*.   382 emergens *A*: surgens *L*.   384 Nos—vocat *A*: *del. L*.   386 Iberi *A*:
illius *L*.   389 Cognata *A*: Agnata *L*.   393 pectore vnico *del. L*.   394 gestet *A*: condat *L*.   397
dominatrix hera *A*: tenebrarum parens | Hecate triformis, sane [sive ?] te caelum tenet, *L*.   399
Familia—colit *A*: *del. L*.   400 magno—procul *A*: magnum dum procul per aerem *L*.   403–404
Quod—minae *A*: *post corr.* L: Quos [Quem *b*] non Philippi terror, et tristes minae, | Non fulmi-
nanti Roma concussit manu, | Metum Batavus discat, Vesperque [et tarde *b*] mori.   404 armave
A: armaque *L*.   405 Timere *A*: Metum *L*. ‖ Intereà tamen *A*: *del. L*.

Earth, sky, palace of the black night, and immeasurable sea, three kingdoms, unleash your powers and hidden wiles. Philip,[175] I stand ready as a worthy protector of your sacrifices. A great, a huge victim will fall through my hand, a victim greater than the sacrifice that the triumphant of the Trojans after his death demanded from the unfaithful ships, when he ascended from the ground of Ilium[176] at the moment when the threatening Greeks were about to release the proud ships.

The Netherlands, for a Spaniard a chilling name, call me; does one desire my arrival? What do I hesitate? Where the sneaky Spaniard cannot go, there is space for the Spanish tricks and stratagems.

Great sisters, sacred family of Attica, group from the old area of Erechtheus and Cecrops:[177] if something of old times is left and there is time you find new ones.

You have to find someone who is fierce, mad, furious and either of origin or of disposition (one of them will suffice) Spaniard, and who on his own has the four horrible goddesses in his one heart.

O fiery flames, great servants of the pale goddess, inhabitants of the fiery sky, holy crowd of the Night, and you, ruler, Moon, never seen by Phoebus,[178] yet a part of him, who is worshipped by the whole house of our Dis,[179] when you take your course through the sky surrounded by a large crowd of servants, do you see somebody through whose hand alone the Dutchman can learn to fear, something that a thousand ships of Philip, or his sword and fire, weapons and hard threats failed to do?

---

175 Philip II (1527–1598), King of Spain 1556–1598, lord of the seventeen provinces of the Netherlands 1555–1598.

176 The shade of Achilles demanded the life of Polyxena; Ilium was a poetic name for Troy.

177 The 'great sisters', the Furies stemmed from Greece, here indicated by Attica, the region around Athens, as pars pro toto, which in mythical times was led by kings Erechtheus and Cecrops.

178 The Moon is never seen by Phoebus, the sun; the notion of hatred in 'invisa' remains implicit.

179 Dis is another name of Pluto, king of the realm of shades, hence a metonym for underworld.

Certum est furentes explicare copias,
Exercitusque tota deducam meos.
Audacia isthaec subeat: haec praeceps Furor,
Ignobilisque Livor, haec Vecordia,
410 Crudelitasque mortis horrendae parens
Illinc cruentum claudat exultans latus,
Rerumque abortus bellicarum Fraus inops.
Sic sic eundum est: sceleribus decet tuis
Praeferre sacram, Rex Iberorum, facem.

SCENA II.

LOISA. SENEX.

LOISA.
415 O molientis alta NATVRAE comes,
Sacrae tribune lucis, et vitae pater
Natalis aurae magne largitor, DIES,
Rerumque Origo prima, qui reconditas
Primus tueri syderum donas faces.
420 O qui sepultum matre mortalem sua
Natumque nondum, mortuum prius tamen,
Informe pondus impotensque et haud suum,
In alta ducis, luminisque compotem
Sub imminentes aetheris sistis fores.
425 Tunc expeditus carcere infelix suo
Scintilla coeli purior, bipes Deus,

406–407 Certum—meos A: Adeste [Adeste b] testes sceleris, et comites mei | Praesensque sacris agmen obscenum veni L.   408 Audacia isthaec subeat A: del. L.   409 haec ... haec A: hinc ... hinc L.   410 horrendae A: ignavae L.   411 exultans A: et Poenae L.   412 Rerumque ... bellicarum Fraus inops A: Reique ... bellicae Fraus et Dolus L.   413 decet A: fas sit L.   Tit. SCENA II A: del. L.   415–418 O molientis—prima A: O fluctuantis magna fortunae parens [Natalis aura: tuque dux vitae dies, | Origo prima lucis, aetatis parens, b] L.   419 Primus—faces A: del. L.   420 O qui sepultum A: del. et rest. L.   422–423 impotensque, et haud suum ... luminisque compotem A: impotensque syderum [impotensque luminis b] ... aetherisque compotem L.   423–429 luminisque—primulum A: post corr. del. L.   424 Sub—fores A: Sub imminentes elicis caeli [Sub imminentis ambitu sistis b] fores L.   425 Tunc—suo A: Tunc [Ibi b Tunc c] sorte [paulis primum b] [Tunc ille [nempe e] primum carcere eductus suo d] L.   426 Scintilla—Deus A: Aeternitatis [Imago coeli, b] curaque ingentis Dei, L.

In the meantime I have decided to set up my raging troops and I will carry my armies with full dedication. Let Audacity come here, blind Frenzy, base Envy and Madness, and let Cruelty, processor of the horrifying death and impotent Deceit, a misrepresentation of warfare, at last cheeringly close the bloody flanks. Exactly in that formation we must advance: it is fitting, King of the Spaniards, to carry a holy torch for your crimes.

SCENE II

Louise, Old Man

Louise

O Day, companion of Nature who sets the heavens in motion, you who administer the sacred light, father of life and great, gentle giver of the breath of life, primordial Origin of the world, who is the first to see the still hidden celestial light. O, you who take the mortal child, buried in his mother, although not yet born yet died before, a formless mass, impotent and still without grip on itself, into the height and grant it the full possession of the light under the high ports of the ether. Then, to his misfortune he breaks out of his dungeon in freedom, a bright spark from heaven, a god on two legs,[180]

---

180   As a prince and as a human being gifted with reason the baby is divine.

Rerumque magnus ille spectator, poli
Et universi cura, prorumpit foras
Coelumque discit, parvulusque primulum
430   Proserpit, insons, mitis, ignarus sui,
Et fluctuantis tyro fortunae, levis
Prosultat exilitque, nec curae est capax,
Plagaeque nondum sortis advorsae patet,
Ridetque simplex nesciusque. "Scilicet
435   Optata primum fata praemittit Deus
Favens iuventae, turbidaeque tempora
Potiora vitae vindicat lusus sibi,
Interque talos, turbinesque inter suos
Suaviores vita consumit dies
440   Beatitatis prodiga infelix suae,
Simulque ludit luditurque, curaque
Postrema lapsae poscit aetatis sibi,
Et faecis instar ima subsidens petit."
O nate, nate, dulce pignus, in sinu
445   Gremioque nostro qui vagaris huc et huc,
Vacuumque leni transigis risu diem,
O dulcis aetas! "Scilicet primum est Deus
Novisse cuncta, proximum tamen, nihil."
O nate, nate, mox in adversum mare
450   Aestusque vastos, principumque munia,
Et imminentem purpurae ferociam,
Motusque regni deferende; nunc modo
Securitatis aureae regnum tenes:
Satellitemque praeter innocentiam
455   Nullum tueris, tutus hoc uno satis
Quod esse nescis, laetiorque. "Nec potest
Vllum timere, nate, quem nullus timet."

---

429 Coelumque discit *A*: Auramque ducit, *L*.   431–432 Et fluctuantis—exilitque *A*: infans
nescius [inscius *b*] vitae sibi | Insana nescit [cernat *? b*] fata | Notaeque nondum tyro fortunae,
sibi | Indulget emicatque *L*.   431 tyro *A*: tiro *L*.   436 Favens *A*: Parcens *L*.   437 Potiora *A*:
Meliora *L*.   438 turbinesque inter suos *A*: et minuta gaudia *L*.   440 Beatitatis *A*: Felicitatis *L*.
444–445 O nate—et huc *A*: O nate, matris dulce pignus [O dulce germen inclytae propaginis *b*]
| Quique ore matrem dividis gestu patrem; | Utrumque dulci [blanda ib *dulci c*] vincis ignorantia,
| Nunc e parentis pendulus sinu tuae *L*.   446 Vacuumque leni *A*: Leni morantem *L*.   447 Est
Deus *A*: bonum est *L*.   455 Nullum tueris *A*: Nullum fatigas *L*.

the great spectator of the world, the care of the whole expanse, and gets to know heaven.

At first, the little one crawls around innocently and lovely, unaware of himself. It still has to learn how fortune can change and jumps and darts lightheartedly and unconcernedly. It is not yet exposed to the blows of throw-backs, laughs naively and innocently. "The deity first sends prosperity, because he is kind to youth. The best period of turbulent life is claimed by play, and with the dicing and turning-rollers, life wastes the pleasant days and wastes his own happiness. At the same time it plays and is played with: sorrow demands the rest of the slipping life and settles down on the bottom like dregs."

O child, child, sweet pledge of love, jumpy boy on my loving lap that with a sweet smile, unconcernedly spend your day, oh sweet age! "It is best to know everything, just like the Deity, but the second best to know nothing." O child, child, who will soon be exposed to the stormy sea, the immeasurable surf, the duties of princes, the aggressive pride of the Purple and the turmoil of power, now you have only a realm of golden insouciance and you have no servant than innocence, sufficiently safe, right because you are unaware of your existence and cheerful. "He does not have to be afraid of anyone, child, for whom no one is afraid." Not yet "that usual fever of kings and princes" seizes

Nondumque sensus illa pertentat tuos
"Regum ducumque febris, ardor imperi
460   Et possidendi cuncta porrigo levis."
Cuniculosque pectore occultos agit
Ambitio fraudum mater, aut opum furor,
Tuumque ducis quicquid aspicis, Deo
Vicinus uni proximusque. Nate mi,
465   Si forte somno molle reclinas caput,
Artus sopore lacteo victus iaces
Extraque motus, ciuicumque extra metum, et
Tempestuosa casuum tonitrua,
Somnumque spiras melleum, mitem, levem
470   Tranquillitatis unicum testem tuae;
Quiesque lenes tuta perrepit genas,
Thorusque qui te, parue, diffusum tenet
Genu sinusque est: thalamus hic unus tibi est,
Et pes cubili sufficit noster tuo.
475   O invidenda regibus mens! Ah ferè est
Vt ipsa sortem mater invideat tibi,
Annosque similes speret, atque aevum sibi
Cunasque dulces, nesciumque aulae diem
Fraudem timentis semper, aut fraudis minas.
480   Quin et querelis ne qua pars desit meis,
Et falsa terrent, trepidaque horrentem pavet
Mens noctis umbram, et ille curarum Sopor
Exactor acer dissipatorque omnium,
Pater mearum est, curaque haec illam premit,
485   Et somniorum dubia succedit fides:
Diemque nox lacessit, et noctem dies.

Senex
Dignata magno principis princeps thoro
Taedaeque columen, nata magnanimi patris
Maioris uxor, fare, quid reconditus

---

460 cuncta porrigo levis *A*: quidlibet fallax amor *L*.   461 Cuniculosque—agit *A*: Nondumque
vota spesque perduxit [corrumpit *b*] tuas *L*.   463 ducis *A*: credis *L*. ‖ aspicis *A*: aspicio ? *L*.
464 Nate mi *A*: Tum levi *L*.   467–468 et Tempestuosa *A*: et Improborum *L*.   471 tuta *L*: tutae
A.   477 sibi *L*: tibi *A*.   482 Sopor *A*: sopor *L*.   489–491 Fare—sinusque *A*: Fare, quid pal-
lor vagus [Fare, quid pallor gravis *b*] | Tristesque [Tristisque *b*] maestas obsidet maeror genas |
Sinusque guttis *L*.

your senses, nor "the burning desire for power and the fickle tendency to possess everything". Ambition, the mother of deception, or the raging desire for wealth do not yet dig hidden trenches in your chest. You consider everything you see to be yours, almost equal to that one deity.

My child, if you sometimes lay your head softly asleep, you are lying there, your members overwhelmed by a milky sleep,[181] without tossing, without the fear of grown-ups and without the thunderous thunderstorms of vicissitudes. You are absorbed in a honeyed, soft, regular sleep, an unmistakable proof of your ease. An unconcerned calmness creeps up your soft cheeks and the cradle you lie on, little one, is a knee, a bosom: this is your only bedroom and my legs can still be your bed.

Oh, soul to be envied by kings! Alas, it is almost as if your own mother envies you and wishes to be as young and unconcerned as you and would like to lie in a soft cradle and not yet be acquainted with the court, which always fears deceit or threats of deceit.

Yes, to complete my misery: even things that are not there scare me. My mind trembles with fear of the horrible nightly darkness, and sleep, which otherwise dispels and scatters all worries, causes it to me. One concern directly follows the other and a first hesitant belief in dreams follows: what I see at night makes me uneasy during the day and what I experience during the day, unsettles me at night.

Old Man
You, princess, worthy of marriage to the great prince, the mainstay of marriage, the child of a proud father, the wife of an even greater man,[182] tell

---

181   The sleep of a baby after having drunk milk.
182   Louise de Coligny (1555–1620) was the daughter of the nobleman and Huguenot leader Gaspard II de Coligny (1519–1572); her first husband was another Huguenot leader Charles de Téligny (ca. 1535–1572), who were both killed in the St Bartholomew's Day massacre on 24 August 1572; her second husband was William of Orange.

490   Vultum pererrans obsidet pallor? Quid os
      Guttis sinusque tepidus effusis madet?
      Et lachrymosus lumine exundat liquor?
      Ruborque blandis solitus excessit genis?
      Meroris ah quae causa? Mentis abdita
495   Exonera et aegrum pectus.

      LOISA
                              Omnia et nihil.

      SENEX
      An ipse sese nescit infelix dolor?

      LOISA
      Ambiguus urit millies; certus semel.

      SENEX
      Sortis flagello quisquis adversae stupet
      Ictuque subito pallet, hic merito pavet,
500   Causam doloris, et cicatricis suae,
      Vulnusque, dum scit.

      LOISA
                              Plura dum nescit tamen,
      Nescitque quantum lugeat caecus dolor,
      Lugetque quantum nescit, id luget tamen.
      Simulque sese nescit, et modum sui.

      SENEX
505   "Ventura quisquis luget, haud luctum sibi
      Seseque luctu servat, at praeoccupat
      Quod vitat ultrò, provocatque quod fugit,
      Gaudetque maerens, et lubens miser fuit."

---

492 exundat *A*: erumpit *L*.   493 Ruborque—genis *A*: *del. L*.   494 Meroris ah quae causa? *A*:
Invitaque hument ora? *L*.   495 Louisa *scripsi*: Lo *MT*, Pr. *A*.   496 An ... nescit *A*: Et ... fallit *L*.
506 praeoccupat *scripsi*: praeocupat *A*.

me, why is your whole face so utterly pale? Why are your mouth and bosom lukewarm and humid by the shedding of tears, why does a flood of tears flow from your eye and does the usual red colour of your beautiful cheeks disappear? Ah, what is the cause of your sadness? Tell your deepest thoughts and relieve your sick heart.

Louise
Everything and nothing.

Old Man
Or does your unhappy grief sometimes not know itself?

Louise
If the cause is unknown, sadness consumes you a thousand times; if it is known, only once.

Old Man
Who is stunned by a setback of chance and faded by being hit unexpectedly, is rightly afraid, because he knows the cause of his grief and of his scar, the wound.

Louise
But when blind grief does not know more things and does not know how bad his grief is and mourns everything that it does not know, then it mourns anyway. At the same time, the grief knows neither itself nor its size.

Old Man
"Whoever mourns the future, does not at all keep mourning at a distance, and does not save himself from mourning, but on the contrary, he reaches in advance what he avoids, and calls out what he evades. He enjoys his grief and revels in his misery."

LOISA
Succubuit animus: poplites trepidi labant,
510 Simulachraque oculis noctis illudunt meis,
Seseque late spargit ignarus dolor,
Et ominosus corda pervolitat sopor.

SENEX
At falsus ille est.

LOISA
                    Falsus, at veri pater,
Praenunciusque.

SENEX
                    Fluxa noctis est fides.

LOISA
515 At non diei.

SENEX
                    Terret et noctis diem
Formido, seque vanus insinuat metus,
Vmbratilique somnus imponit dolo,
Noctuque fallit; at die terret tamen,
Partemque lucis poscit, et regnum suum
520 Transcendit audax, imperique limites.
Humanus acres spiritus motus habet,
Interdiuque feruet, et sese rapit,
Metuque pallet gaudioque diffluit
Quietis expers, corporisque terminum, et
525 Adiudicatas lege NATVRAE vias
Perrumpit alis nixus huc illhuc suis,
Exorbitatque semper, et quicquid potest,
Simulque quicquid haud potest, versat tamen,

524–525 et Adiudicatas *A*: Et destinatas *L.*   526 alis—suis *A*: alis nixus intentis suis [alis tran-
silitque inanibus *b*] *L.*   528 haud *A*: non [haud *b ex. del.*] *L.* ∥ Donec iugales abluit Phoebus
suos [At cum facem [micantem *c*] Phoebus extinxit facem, *b*] | Cum [Tum *b*] pictus aer aureis
sororibus | Phoebes relucet, languidoque lumine | Currum parentis amovent [advehunt *b*] leves
n.l. fratres ..stos, *? add. L post 536, postea post 533.*

Louise
I am fainting: my trembling knees knock and visions play for my eyes, an unde-fined grief spreads over me and an ominous dream rages through my heart.

Old Man
But that is deceit.

Louise
Deceit, but it accomplishes and predicts something that is a truth.

Old Man
The night is unreliable.

Louise
But not the day.

Old Man
Fear that arises at night also frightens the day, and unnecessary fears enter; through deceptive dream images sleep tells stories and deceives at night, but still inspires fear during the day, demands part of the day and boldly exceeds his domain and the limits of his power.

The human mind has strong emotions. During the day it glows, sweeps itself up, is pale with fear and revels restlessly in joy. It breaks the border of the body and the roads assigned by the law of Nature, by floating up and down on its wings, and always deviates from the track. It goes wherever it can go

Agilisque passim fertur, et meta est sibi.
530 Adestque et absens rebus, et praesens abest,
Erratque latè, seque pandit illa vis,
Hauritque formas elicitque, visaque
Pererrat, imbibitque, et in sese trahit.
Tunc illa luci furua succedit parens,
535 Polumque pullis incubans amictibus
Hinc inde obumbrat, induitque caeca nox,
Corpusque stringit, liberat mentem tamen,
Lucisque viua suscitat vestigia
Seminaque rerum, imaginesque, fomites
540 Motus diurni, ruminataque excitat,
Mentemque multum gaudia inter et metus
Adhuc vagantem volvit, et circumuenit,
Caliginisque ludit in postscenio
Mimus diei, ludibundus histrio,
545 Proteusque vitae futilis Somnus pater,
Verisque falsa miscet, atque vtrique se.
Ceraeque adinstar mollis, impressas tenet
Mens et figuras, et vagas rerum notas,
Redditque nocte, quicquid excepit die,
550 Laruataque altos somnia incutiunt metus.
At cum diei roscidum redit iubar,
Et imperator aetheris magni subit
Sol, aureamque dividit terris comam;
Fugit timoris causa, non timor tamen,
555 Et somniorum profuga vanescit cohors,
Nihilque restat, at nihil gemimus tamen,
Id quod quoque ante cum fuit, nusquam fuit,
Quodque esse falsò reris, at verè doles.

LOISA
Experta metuo.

---

537 Soporque lenta pectus invadit face, | Tunc ille mentem [Pectusque victum *b* Animumque
victum *c*] lenis expugnat Deus, *add. L.*   539 Seminaque *A:* Umbrasque *L.* ‖ imaginesque; fomites *A:* fomitesque languidos *L.*   543 postscenio *sublin. L.*   544 ludibundus *sublin. L.*   550
incutiunt *A:* inducunt *L.*   556 at *A:* hoc *L.*

and even where it cannot, and it focuses on everything and determines its own limit.

Although absent, the powerful mind is present at the events, and although present it is absent, it wanders far and wide and spreads, sucks in images, evokes them again, and wanders around along what is visible, absorbs it and remembers it. Then the black mother[183] follows the light and overshadows the sky everywhere, wrapping itself in dark robes. The dark night clothes itself in darkness and pinches the body, but releases the spirit and evokes vivid light traces, the seeds of events, the images, the fuel of the daytime motion, and lets them light up again. It turns the mind that is still tossed to and fro between joy and fear, confused, deceiving and playing in the wings of darkness, mimic of the day, frisky actor; and sleep, father of idle life, as a Proteus[184] mixes lie with truth and itself with both, and just like soft wax, the mind holds the impressions and the rapidly vanishing stamps of the events and transmits at night what it caught during the day; nightmares cause deep fears. But when daylight returns with its dew and the lord of the great aether, the sun, rises and spreads its golden hair over the world, the cause of fear flees, but not fear itself and the fleeting horde of dreams disappears; nothing remains but nevertheless we sigh about nothing, about what also before it was, was nowhere, of which you mistakenly think it exists, but about which you truly have sorrow.

Louise
I am afraid from experience.

---

183   I.e. the night.
184   Proteus had the gift of prediction but tried to escape giving prophecies by taking different
      forms.

SENEX

           "Saepius favet sibi
560   Error dolusque, nubiloque deprimit
Rationis ignem."

LOISA

          'Decipi in malis iuvat
Fallique dulce est.'

SENEX

           "Falsa dum latent tamen
Ut vera laedunt."

LOISA

          Aetheris beate rex
Quid ah perennis imber, et lachrymae leves
565   Cogente nullo sponte prorumpunt sua?
Si quâ minaris imminesque saeva sors,
Sperare liceat: bis ferus mordet dolor,
Venturus, et cum vênit; et praesens nocet,
Idem et futurus.

SENEX

          Pallidum excutias metum
570   Ducemque vitae lenioris spem fove.
Firmo maritus urbium munimine,
Totoque clusus NEREI regno sedet,
Pelagoque cuncto tutius quod arbitror:
Amore populi.

LOISA

          Haud tangit externos amor,
575   Peregrina nemo imperia diu subdit sibi.

SENEX

"Angustiore principis mentem viri
Meta coercet, patriam quisquis suam

---

563 beate rex *A*: magni pater *L*.   567 bis ferus *sublin. L*.   572 clusus *A*: clausus *L*.

Old Man
"Often mistakes and ruse support each other and obscure the light of reason with a cloud."

Louise
In misery it is a pleasure to be deceived and agreeable to be misled.

Old Man
Because the falsity is hidden, it still hurts as if it were the truth.

Louise
Blessed king of the aether, ah, why do eternal rain and light tears spring without any pressure if you, cruel fate, in some way or other threateningly are hanging over our heads; then one may still hope so much, yet cruel grief hurts twice: when it is coming and when it has come; it brings misery, not only when it is there, but also when it is expected.

Old Man
Ban pale fear and cherish hope, bringer of a more pleasant life. Your husband is enclosed in a strong fortress of cities, in the whole realm of Nereus[185] and in something I consider safer than the whole sea: the love of his people.

Louise
That love does not concern foreigners; no one submits a foreign realm to himself for a long time.

Old Man
"Whoever grants him only his own fatherland closes the mind of a monarch in too narrow boundaries: the people have falsely concocted the territory of

---

185   The god of the sea, a metonym for sea.

Assignat illi. Vana natalis soli
Plebs spacia finxit, et solo leges dedit.
580 At culmen ille dignitatis et caput,
Deoque magno pene par, et pro-Deus
Princeps vagatur, municepsque totius
Diffusa latos aemulatur mens polos,
Coelique adinstar semper in motu suo est.
585 Natale magni principis quaeris solum?
In orbe natus ille, patria est ei
Quaecunque soli, terminusque quicquid est.
Seseque terris aequat unus omnibus
Generosus ardor ille, et herous vigor.
590 Polusque quicquid caerulo amplexu tenet
Illius urbs est: civitas isthaec patet
Qua magnus aether, quaque flammantes globi
Et aureorum vasta signorum via."
Titana magnum cernis, vt pleno gradu
595 Superbus altum metiatur aethera,
Coelique partem teneat, et totum petat;
Viaeque magnae per novas semper licet
Adveniat oras; advena haud usquam est tamen,
Quocunque namque tendit, in domo sua est;
600 Seu purpurato cum renatus atrio
Cubile coeli pandit, et lucis fores,
Auroque crispam roscidus tollit comam,
Seu cum diurnâ membra defessus viâ
Dulceis in ulnas Thetyos fertur suae,
605 Axemque utrumque novit et neutrum colit.
Sic feruor ingens, mensque magnorum ducum.
"Vbique civis ille et inquilinus est,
Quicumque princeps."

LOISA
                    Omnia et scio, et dolet
Timere posse, dum dolet, timeo tamen,
610 Metusque causae nescius, causa est metûs.

---

579 leges *A*: *del. L.*   581 et pro-Deus *A*: *del. L.*   589 Generosus *A*: Sublimis *L.*   600 purpurato *A*: purpurante *L.*   604 Thetyos *A*: Tethyos *L.*   606 feruor ingens *A*: *n.l.* [ardor ingens *b*]
L.   607 inquilinus *A*: *sublin. L.*

the birthplace and imposed laws on the ground. But a prince is the top and the head of dignity, almost like the great Deity, and as a God he wanders about, and his omnipresent mind as a citizen of the universe reaches as far as the broad poles, and like heaven it is always in its own movement. You ask for the native soil of a great prince? He is born in the world, the whole earth is his homeland and the universe is his boundary. That generous glow, heroic courage, reaches on its own as far as all countries. All that holds the celestial pole in his blue embrace is his city: that is the place for him to live, wherever the great sky, wherever the flaming spheres and the vast orbit of the golden signs are."[186] You see the great Titan,[187] how he proudly traverses the high aether with a firm step, occupies a part of the sky and wants to cover it entirely; even though he always goes through unprecedented areas of the grand orbit, yet he is nowhere a stranger, for wherever he goes, he is in his own house; or, when he is reborn in his purple-red room, storing the bed of heaven, opening the doors of the light, and full of dew lifting his garland intertwined with gold, or when he grows tired of limbs in the sweet arms of his Tethys[188] by the journey of the day, he knows both axes and lives in neither of them. Thus are the great glow and the spirit of great princes. "Every monarch is citizen everywhere and at home everywhere."

Louise
I know all that and it makes me sad that there is the possibility of fear, but while it is grieving, I fear, and the fear is, because it does not know the cause, the cause of fear.

---

186   I.e. the stars and the constellations.
187   Titan, the god of the sun.
188   Tethys, a sea goddess, a metonym for sea.

CHORVS.

Anapaestici.

O qui levibus vectus habenis
Virides subter roris genitor
Laberis herbas, violasque inter,
Et trepidantes tepido circum
615 Sole myricas thalamum figis
Blande Favoni, pastusque levi
Nectare ludis, sive per altas
Lenibus alis laberis undas,
Seu per gelidas specuum latebras
620 Montesque procul tenui serpis
Humore pater, qua lascivas
Tityrus insons subducit oves,
Iuxtaque suas blanda Amaryllis
Supputat agnas, et tibi dulcem
625 Felix Thyrsi condit avenam,
Gens immitis nescia fati
Sortisque vagae. Quam palantes
O verne pater prendimus oram?
Placitas certe liquimus ante
630 Dilecta tuas Flandria sedes;
Sed tamen unà liquimus atri
Nomen Iberi. Patria est nobis
Quicquid saevus nescit Iberus.
Salvete tamen vos ignotae
635 Littora terrae. Tuque o lucis
Aurea mater, tandem maestis
Reddita terris, o quae caecâ
Tenebras tristes, Aurora parens,
Proscribis humo, cum sperato
640 Phosphorus audax exilit ore,

---

612 subter *A*: inter [circum *b* inter *c*] *L*.   614 trepidantes ... cricum *A*: sudantes ... semper *L*.
617 ludis *A*: vivis i Li.   619 Roscidaque antra volucurum domos *add. L*.   621 lascivas *A*: secu-
ras *L*.   623 blanda Amaryllis *A*: con [*n.l. b* aurea Phyllis *c*] *L*.   628 prendimus *A*: tangimus *L*.
629 liquimus *A*: fugimus *L*.   630 Dilecta *A*: Umbrosa [Erepta *b*] *et postea del. L*.   631 liquimus
A: fugimus *L*.   640 audax *A*: *del. L*.

Chorus of Flemish Exiles

O, you who glide in a light chariot on the green grass, creator of dew, and set down a dwelling between violets and rustling tamarisks in the beneficent warmth of the sun, gentle Favonius,[189] and play, feeding yourself with sweet nectar; whether you slide on soft wings over the deep sea, whether you penetrate far and away with your damp haze in cold, dark caves and mountains, where Tityrus innocently grazes his frisky sheep. Next to him the sweet Amaryllis counts her lambs and makes a melodious reed flute for you, happy Thyrsis,[190] a kind of people unfamiliar with hard fate and uncertain destination.

Which coast will we reach on our wanderings, father of spring? We have, in any case, beloved Flanders, left your places that were so dear to us.

On the other hand, at the same time we left everything that was horrible Spaniard. For us, a homeland is everything the cruel Spaniard does not know. Yet hail you, coasts of an unknown land, and also you, golden mother of light, finally returned to the afflicted lands, oh, you who dispel the gloomy darkness of the dark earth, mother Aurora, when Phosphorus boldly leaps

---

189   Favonius, the west wind.

190   Tityrus, Amaryllis and Thyrsis are pastoral names.

Cogitque suos undique fratres
Roseae invitos cedere luci,
Et sydereas ducens turmas
Mox redituras in castra sua
645 Iam dididicit Hesperus esse,
Et mutato nomine fallax
Altera solus munia poscit.
Fugiuntque suos sydera lusus
Veniente die; nos tranquilli
650 Munera somni, partesque suas
Regnaque rursus dolor invadit,
Tristisque labos, subitoque atrae
Circum volitant agmine curae.
At Simplicitas sedes hominum
655 Sera reliquit, Taurosque colit,
Et Massagetas, gentesque feras,
Nostrisque procul exulat oris.
Ibi quisque suae est auriga domus,
Peregrinantes quisque vagasque
660 Incolit aedes, sic mutarum
Tranquilla colit saecla ferarum.
Cernis, cernis per inane leves
Nare columbas, expersque metus
Placida ut campos perrepat ovis,
665 Tuque ô tepidi conscia veris
Quae nocturno carmina fundis
Ebria rore;
Quae sub tremulis Zephyri tenui
Flamine ramis, tua tecta colis,
670 Paruosque lares, nutantesque
Strepitu tenui suspirantis
Leniter aurae, florumque leves
Incolis umbras blanda cicada.
Non te trepido quatit infelix
675 Turbine Mavors. Non te querulae
Denso cingunt murmure lites.
Non vanorum Iongè sequitur

---

642 Roseae invitos *A*: Croceae [Roseae *b*] sensim *L*.   643 sydereas *A*: sidereas *L*.   652 labos
A: labor *L*.   654 Simplicitas *A*: simplicitas *L*.

forth with the face we have looked for and forces his brothers on all sides against their will to give way to the pink light—while leading the throngs of stars that will soon return to their camp, he has already learned to be Hesperus[191] and, his name changed but his nature just the same, deceitfully demands different functions.

The stars leave their game at the dawn of the day, we leave the gift of the peaceful sleep, and the pain and hard effort take up their task and their realm again: horrible worries circulate in a column.

But finally, Simplicity has left the human houses and is with the Taurians and with the Massagetes,[192] wild tribes, and lives in exile far from our regions. There is every driver of their own house and each one lives in a wandering nomadic dwelling house. In this way he takes care of the quiet offspring of animals without speech.

You see, really, the fast pigeons fly through the air, and how the sheep graze peacefully, free of fear, over the fields. You, o confidante of the warm spring, you sing those songs drunk with nocturnal dew, you who build your house under branches that rustle in the soft breeze of Zephyr[193] and who live in a small house that waves under the gentle whizzing of a soft sighing breeze, and in the light shadows of the flowers, dear cricket. You do not attack the disastrous Mars with a nervous whirl. You do not surround yourself with litigation accompanied by intense murmurs, you do not follow an unreliable

---

191 Aurora is the goddess of dawn; the planet Venus is both the morning star Phosphorus and the evening star Hesperus.

192 The Taurians were a Thracian tribe in what is now Crimea, the Massagetes a Scythian nomadic tribe, both considered to be uncivilized.

193 I.e. the gentle west wind.

Turba clientum, regnumque tenes
Secura rosas, inter et herbas,
680   Et tibi si qua est Curia, tantum est
Flos, aut tenuis culmen aristae.
Haec aula tibi, regiaque, illhic
Ius agricolis, et venturae
Tempora lucis lepido pandis
685   Leniter ore, blande Senator:
Nec te clusis tristia cingunt
Maenia portis. Non crudelis
Vrbem placidam, sedesque tuas
Invadit Iber, quaeque per auras
690   Tenui sudant flumine guttae,
Tibi sunt blandi dona Lyaei.
Mulgensque leves caelitis undae
Garrula succos, roseos Phaebum
Cum iungit equos matutinâ
695   Prima salutas obvia voce,
Felixque optas iterum coeli
Succedat iter. Tu secura
Pacis alumna, Tu daedaleae
Filia terrae. Tua sunt viridis
700   Gramina campi; tuus omnis ager.
Felix, Felix! Quotiesque tuas
Vaga cernis opes, plenâ, plenâ
Dulcia solvis Gaudia voce.
Nec divitias caelare suas
705   Sustinet illa teneri cordis
Pura voluptas.
Comes agricolis, Tu messorum
Rapido durum solis in aestu
Solaris opus. Non tibi saevi in-
710   Notuit Albae nomen, Iberque.

---

680 Curia *A*: curia *L*.   685 Leniter *A*: Moliter iLi.   686 Nec *A*: Non *L*. ‖ clusis *A*: clausis
L.   696 Felixque *del. et rest. L*.   698 daedaleae *L*: Dedaleae *A*.   702 Vaga cernis *A*: Miraris
L.   703 Gaudia *A*: gaudia *L*.   705 illa *A*: intus *L*.   709 Solaris *A*: comitaris *L*. ‖ *Post* opus
add. L: blandoque sono [strepitu blando *b*] | Et perpetua garrula [sedula *b*] voce | Donec serus,
rubicunda tegat | Lumina vesper, dea [pontique Deae *b*] | Gens Oceani aerata Phoebum | Redu-
cens rursum, maris auratis | Abluit undis. patriaeque manes | Secura tuae, civis ubique.   710
in-Notuit *A*: Notuit *L*.

army of unreliable servants, you are a carefree king between roses and grass, and if you have a court, it is only a flower, or the top of a thin culm. This is your court and your palace, here you remind, softly in friendly language, dear senator, the farmers of their duty and you announce the time of the coming of the light. You do not surround hard walls with closed gates. The cruel Spaniard will not invade your peaceful city and your homes. The drops that seep through the air in a thin stream are like gifts of a sweet Lyaeus[194] for you, and while your loose tongue milks the gentle juices of the rainwater, you are the first to greet Phoebus[195] with your chirping in the morning when he takes his pink horses and you wish him that the journey through heaven is successful again.

You are the carefree foster daughter of peace, you are the daughter of the colourful earth, yours is the grass of the green field, yours is the entire cropland. How blessed you are! As often as you see your riches during your tour, you express your sweet joy with a loud, overflowing voice. The pure pleasure of your delicate heart cannot conceal its riches. Fellow for farmers, you soothe the hard labour of the mowers in the vehement heat of the sun. You do not know the name of the cruel Alva,[196] nor the Spaniard.

---

194   Lyaeus, 'deliverer from care', one of the names of Bacchus.
195   Phoebus, the god of the sun.
196   Fernando Álvarez de Toledo, 3rd Duke of Alva or Alba (1507–1582), the 'Iron Duke', governor of the Netherlands 1567–1573.

Nos perfidiae Gens tetra tuae
Nos ludibrium casibus, ah ah,
Lususque sumus. Nos vrgentis
Premit insultans turbo procellae.
715   "Leviora levis Fortuna videt,
Parvaque parvos fata lacessunt.
Homines curis Gens nata sumus.
Superi, Superi, quisquis multos
Ordine cives, gentesque regit;
720   Plures metuit. Superi, superi,
Quisquis multas vndique terras,
Gentesque suis subdidit armis;
Plures poscit." Vos crudeles
Genus infidum posthac nobis
725   Ite, tyranni,
Aulaque fraudum perfida nutrix.
"Nimium multis immensa patent
Limina curos." Mea tecta omnes
Angusta metus, tenui excludent
730   Culmine, sic, sic, locus baud nimius
Domino; at curis, non vllus erit.
Regnumque meum est, domus exilis,
Larque suauis, populique mei,
Lepido circum concurrentes
735   Ordine nati. "Nimium, diui,
Labitur ille, qui cum mundi
Totius alto corruit ictu."

---

711 Nos *scripsi*: Non *A*. ‖ Gens tetra tuae *A*: gens foeda tuae [tristesque doli *b*] *L*.   712–713
casibus ah ah Lususque *A*: sortis iniquae Fatique *L*.   713–714 Nos—procellae *A*: Nos insanae
[urgentis *b* incertae *c* Semper *d* subito *e* semper *f*] ǀ Vindicat [Opprimit *b*] ingens ioca ruinae
[turbo procellae *b*] [Nos incerto ǀ Feriunt semper vulnere Divi. *c*] *L*.   715 Fortuna *A*: fortuna *L*.
717 Gens *A*: gens *L*.   728 omnes *A*: suos *L*.   729 tenui *A*: parvo [humili *b*] *L*.   733 suauis *A*:
pudicus *L*.

We, we are an object of ridicule, horrible people, for your faithlessness, and a toy, ah, ah, for fate. We are choked by the defiant hurricane of a seething storm. "Light fate sees lighter things and a small lot torments lower people. We humans are a people born for worries. Great gods, everyone who dominates countless numbers of subjects, fears even more. Great gods, everyone who has subjected many countries and nations around the world with his weapons, demands more." You, cruel tyrants, disloyal race, go away from now on, you too, unreliable court, that is deceiving. "Large palaces are open to too many worries." My little house will keep all fear outside of its low shelter. In those circumstances there will not be too much room for the master of the house, but no room for worries, and so my kingdom is a small home and a pleasant house, and my people are my children, running around in a charming chorus. "Gods, deep is the fall of him who pulls the whole world with it."

ACTVS. iii. SCENA. i.

Sicarius. Praefectus.

Quo? Quo? Quis urges? Huccine anne illhuc feror?
Vtroque certe: saeva tempestas dei
740   Intus redundans cordis exercet salum,
Exaestuatque mens; et incertus ferit
Ardens tremensque pectoris votum tumor,
Sedemque mentis hinc et hinc pessum trahit
Metus, tenaxque consili ingentis furor,
745   Cordisque caecis impetita fluctibus
Casura nutat vis, retroque corruit,
Incerta quonam, quodque factura annuit
Fecisse nondum luget, insultans sibi,
Praeponderatque vtroque et vtroque imminet,
750   Inobsequensque pectoris magni ciet
Motum reluctans fervor, et premi negat,
Redireque ardet rursus, et rursus nequit.
Sic cum profundis auctus in praecordijs
Telluris imae, daedaloque viscere
755   Magnae parentis ignis occultè furit,
Notique saevis Africique follibus
Nutritur ardor, latiusque promouens
Vulcanus intus flammeas agit vias,
Crateraque altum matris occulto in sinu
760   Molitur, aestuatque, et immensum sibi
Iter resurgens flamma molitur foras,
Caelumque poscit, impetu minor suo,
Donec pauentem totus inuadit diem,
Ruptoque hiatu mugit, et tetro e specu
765   Inauspicatus victor exundat vapor.
Quo voluor, effluoque? Quo praeceps traho
Voti ruinam consilique? Quid tremens
Felicitati terga mens vertis tuae?
Exurge pectus, masculique spiritus

Tit. SCENA. i. *A: del. L.*   738 illhuc *A:* illuc *L.*   740 exercet *scripsi:* excercet *A.*   742 tumor
A: timor *L.*   743 mentis *A:* cordis *L.*   768 vertis *A:* vortis *L.*

ACT III, SCENE I

Murderer, Commander

Murderer

Where should I go? Where? Who are you who drive me? Will I be pulled one way or the other? Certainly in both directions. The savage storm of the god is tearing the bustling sea in my heart. My spirit is in a violent wavering: an ambiguous impulse, of fervent desire and fear, meets the vow of my heart. On the one hand, it is fear that confuses my mind, on the other, a desire that holds on to the enormous plan. My heart, otherwise so steadfast, attacked by blind turmoil, waves, about to fall, and falls backwards. Insecure what to do, it repents that it has not yet done what it promised, and curses itself. It tilts its weight to both sides and longs for both: there is an irrepressible drive in my big heart, impetuous, indomitable, and then it burns again with desire to return, but cannot do that either.

In the same way, hidden in the heart of the deepest of the earth and in the restless interior of the great mother, a fire rages. Due to the aggressive bellows of the Notus and the Africus,[197] the heat is fed, and to spread it Vulcan makes blazing roads from within.[198] He forms a deep crater in the lap of mother earth and makes it burn. The swelling fire takes an immense path out and now the pressure behind it is too big, it wants to go into the sky, until it penetrates into fullness the daylight that has become frightened, unexpectedly triumphantly opening the gaping, and the blazing of the horrible cavern dumps outside.

Where am I and where does my eruption go? Why do I, rushing, break my desire and plan? Why do you, my spirit, turn your back on your success? Come

---

197   I.e. the south and south-west winds respectively.
198   Vulcan having his forge under Etna. This is a vivid description of a volcanic eruption.

770   Recollige aestus; si quid elapsum tibi est,
        Duplo reprende. Iam feror, certe feror,
        Quis? Quo? Quid? Vnde? Visa, portenta horrida
        Obtestor, et vos atra mentis omina,
        Quaeque vmbra vultus nocte delusit meos,
775   Seu numen, aut quid numini advorsum fuit;
        Perstat, sedetque fixa mens, nihilque quam
        Mortem videre restat huius, aut meam.
        Ergo, ergo tandem, quo ruinosus furor,
        Ardentibusque palpitans cor motibus
780   Ingentis undae, quoque lanx vergens diu
        Sententiarum, lubricique turbinis
        Propendet, inclinatque, quòque mens vaga,
        Hospesque magni pectoris rapit deus,
        Et nox dolorum seminatrix omnium,
785   Gradum capesso, turbidisque fluctibus
        Ventisque totam fervidis dedi ratem.
        Vidi, ipse vidi, prima vix nascens dies
        Dubium recenti luce spargebat polum,
        Diesque nocte mixta, nox erat die,
790   Secumque magnos exigebat impetus
        Rerumque vastas mens futurarum vias,
        Blandae quietis nescia, haud sui tamen;
        Immane celsi corporis vastique onus
        Notoque maius foeminae ingentis tuor.
795   Ast illa gressu pallida elato furens,
        Vultuque nostro turbida incumbens thoro,
        Ter fulgurantem dexterâ excussit facem
        Vocemque rupit. Sequimur, ô sequimur, Dei,
        Spondetque mens itura quâ nescit viâ!

PRAEFECTVS

800   Quo fluctuantes insolens gressus refert
        Titubante passu temerè, et incerto pede
        Ambiguus hospes? Creperus haud quaquam color,
        Exanguis, amens, et profundi luminum
        Placent recessus, et supercilij tremor,

---

783 rapit *A*: ducit *L*.   786 fervidis *A*: *del. L*.   791 vastas *A*: primas *L*.

on, my heart, exhort and gather all your energy again: if something has slipped away from you, take it back twice. I'm already running, surely.

Who? Where to? What? From where? I call the horrifying faces and omens to witness, you, black signs of the mind, misleading dream that appeared to me at night, whether it was a god, or just the opposite: my plan stands firm and is steadfast, there is nothing left for me to see than his death or mine. Well then, finally I go in the direction where the devastating desire and my fiercely beating heart want to go in a stormy movement, where the long-standing scale of my considerations tilts and lapses, and where my indecisive mind, the god who is in my great heart lives and the night that sows all worries drags me: I have entrusted my whole ship to the unsteady waves and the furious winds.

I have seen it, with my own eyes: hardly the early dawning of the morning sprinkled the vacillating sky with new light and the day was mixed with night, the night with day, and my spirit was filled with great urgency and thought about the grand courses of the future, unfamiliar with sweet rest, but perfectly aware of itself, or I behold the extraordinarily tall figure, the lofty, immense body of an overwhelming woman.

But she loomed pale and raging. As she bent over my bed with a confused face, shrieking she waved three times a lightning torch with her right hand. I follow, o, I follow, gods, and my spirit solemnly promises that it will take the unknown path.

Commander
Why does this unusual guest indecisively, with hesitating step and uncertain foot wander aimlessly back and forth? His undefined colour, white and mad, his deeply receding eyes, the vibration of his eyebrow, his cheeks

805 Nimioque ceu furore labentes genae,
    Vecordiaeque proditor, vanus timor.
    En metuit, en, trepidatque, maestaque huc et huc
    Flectit reflectitque ora, nec satis sibi
    Lucique credit; maximum hoc pectus scelus
810 Metuit paratve.

SICARIVS
                    Quo feror? Rursus dolos
Mens necte et astus, et procellas pectoris
Fluctusque cohibe.

PRAEFECTVS
                        Siste. Quo gressus agis?
Cuias? Quis? Vnde?

SICARIVS
                    Tristis, infelix, miser.

PRAEFECTVS
Quo versus ergo?

SICARIVS
                    Nominis ter inclyti
815 Nassoviorum pridem, et augustae domus
    Cuius trophaea primus emergens dies
    Stupet, ultimusque praelia, et bellum ferox,
    Motusque Iberi regis, et tristes minas,
    Minister adsum, maximae interpres rei
820 Admissus olim, profugus, extorris; patre
    Patriaque viduus.

PRAEFECTVS
                    Nunc tamen quonam moves?
Aut quas in oras tendere est animus tibi?

---

811 necte *A*: conde *L*.

collapsed by violent emotion and his senseless fear, which betrays insanity, do not please me at all.

Look, he is afraid, he is trembling and turns his sad face now here, now back again, and he does not trust himself and the daylight: this person is either fearing or planning a very great crime.

Murderer
Where am I drawn? My mind, cogitate again stratagems and ruses and lie down and control the storms and turbulences in my heart.

Commander
Halt. Where are you going? What is your homeland, who are you and where are you from?

Murderer
Sad, unhappy, miserable.

Commander
Where, then, are you going?

Murderer
I have been here for a long time as a servant of the thrice famous Nassaus and their lofty house. About their victories the start of the day is stunned by its rise and about their fights the end of the day, as well as the fierce war and the warfare of the Spanish King and his chilling threats. Permitted a while ago as a messenger of a very important matter, I am here now as a refugee, banished, deprived of my father and my fatherland.

Commander
But where are you going now? Or what area do you plan to go to?

SICARIVS
Quo sors agit, Deusque, quo miseri solent.
Patriam reliqui, patriam rursus peto,
825   Semperque terras has vel has mutavimus,
Sortemque numquam. Vbique cum fui, fui
Vbique miser. Hoc vnicum restat mihi.
Miseriam eundo transveho passim meam,
Nusquam relinquo.

PRAEFECTVS
                              Quo parente? Qua domo?
830   Quis generis autor?

SICARIVS
                              Per secunda te precor
Gentis Batavae fata, perque nescia
Spei metusque corda, et inuictam manum,
Excussaque ante regis infesti iuga,
Domitamque ponti fluctuantis regiam
835   Aestusque canos, inuiamque semitam
Magno Philippo, et Hesperuginis duci,
Per has perennes turbidasque lachrymas,
Quas fluere cernis, perque tabentes genas,
Singultibusque rupta tot suspiria,
840   Animique vulnus, quemque nulla forsitan
Solis corusci nata delebit dies
Solitum dolorem. Sic genus Nereïum
Marisque dominos discat infelix Iber,
Longaque terras ambiat propagine
845   Faecunda rerum turba gens Neptunia,
Annosque laude, saeculumque viribus
Post se relinquat parua stirps Nassouia,
Tacere liceat, tabidique vulneris
Lenem cicatrix squallida obducat notam.
850   "Memoria doloris ipsamet saepe est dolor."

---

845 gens Neptunia *A*: *del. L.*   846 saeculumque *MT L*: saecalumque *A*.

Murderer

Where destiny and God lead me; where unhappy people usually go. I have left my homeland, I am looking for a homeland again, I changed again and again my country, but never changed fate. Wherever I was, I was unhappy everywhere. This is the only thing that is left to me. On my journey I carry my misery everywhere, nowhere do I leave it behind.

Commander

Who is your father? What is your family? Who is your ancestor?

Murderer

By the prosperity of the Dutch people, by the hearts that are unfamiliar with hope and fear, by the invincible hand, by the formerly shaken yoke of the hated King, by the conquered residence of the wavy sea, the foaming surf, the path that is impassable for the great Philip, the Prince of the Evening, by these unbroken and intense tears that you see flowing, by these damp cheeks and by the many sighs interrupted by sobbing, my soul's wound and the grief to which I am now accustomed and which will probably be cancelled by no day, child of the brilliant sun. As the wretched Spaniard gets to know the lineage of Nereus, the lords of the sea, and the people of Neptune[199] in a long line of generations and with an abundance of heroic facts goes around the earth and leaves behind the little tribe of the Nassau in fame for years and leaves a whole century in power: allow me to keep silent and let the rough scabbing form a soft scar over the stinking wound. "Often the memory of grief in itself is a reason for sadness."

---

199   The people of the sea (Nereus and Neptune as gods of the sea) are the Dutchmen, more specific the Hollanders.

PRAEFECTVS
Tacito dolori nulla succurrit dies.

SICARIVS
Obliuione corruit solâ dolor,
Virtute maior, auxilique nescius.

PRAEFECTVS
Phoebeïam quicumque detrectat manum,
855   Dolore pressus sit licet; causa est tamen,
"Vulnusque semper auget, et semper gemit.
Malisque gaudet ille, qui solus dolet."

SICARIVS
"Dies mederi cui potest, solus potest."

PRAEFECTVS
"Breui mederi longa non solet dies."

SICARIVS
860   "Lugere didicit ille, qui luget diu,
Aetate sensim summa decrescunt mala,
Diuque magnum quod fuit, fit et leue,
Viresque sumit tempore, et perdit suas."

PRAEFECTVS
"Frustra latebit usque."

SICARIVS
                         "Quicquid alteri
865   Frustra refertur, tutius frustra latet."

PRAEFECTVS
Sperare opem qui nescit, auxilium potest.

---

856 semper gemit *A*: luget suum *L*.   857 Malisque—dolet *A*: *del. L*.   858 Sicarius *scripsi*: Sic
L, Sis *A*.

Commander
Concealed grief never gets help.

Murderer
Only by forgetting does sadness diminish, moral quality cannot remedy it and no help avails.

Commander
Whoever withdraws from the contact with Phoebus[200] may be overwhelmed by grief, yet he is also the cause of it, "he always makes his wound bigger and ever sighs. He who mourns in solitude enjoys his misery".

Murderer
"Whom time can cure, does not need any help."

Commander
"It is not the custom of a long time to bring a quick healing."

Murderer
"Whoever mourns for a long time has learned to mourn and over time the greatest misery gradually declines. What has been great for a long time is also becoming light again, gaining strength with time and losing it again."

Commander
"He will hide everywhere in vain."

Murderer
"What one tells to another in vain can be hidden more safely in vain."

Commander
Who cannot put his hope in his own strength can hope for help.

---

200   I.e. daylight.

SICARIVS

Age, post dolores rursus infelix, age
Et fortis esto mens in aerumnas tuas,
Et ante quicquid asperum, durum tibi
870   Abominandum, noxium, aduersum fuit,
Dicendo reuoca. Citius ardentem poli
Titan relinquet orbem, et occasu suo
Praeuertet ortum, citius aetheris vagam
Regina noctis luna dediscet viam,
875   Laudes Batauus Martias, fraudes Iber,
Quam fata sicco lumine evolvam mea.
Eheu me! Eundem principem lucis diem
Curaeque vidi, vix et in cunis suis
Fefellit atras vita fortunae manus,
880   Et blandientis primus aetatis lepor,
Vernumque vitae tempus, et tranquillior
Ridentis aeui leniorque semita,
Crescentibusque tempus accreuit malis,
Pariterque curas auxit, et sese dies,
885   Et effluentes aemulus cursu dolor
Aequavit annos. Hei mihi natus fui
Simul, miserque.

PRAEFECTVS
                    Quae tot in te nubila
Imbresque rupit ira fortunae suos?

SICARIVS
Vnus dolores plurimos vexit dolor.
890   Vidi vapore fumeo ambustum caput
Miseri parentis, membraque infelicibus
Populata flammis, ipse spectator mei
Doloris aderam: parvus, inscius, rudis
Quotacunque turbae pars euntis, huc et huc
895   Visurus ibam, sortis ignarus meae.
Vidi reciso stipite et multa comâ

---

868 esto *L*: est o *A*.   893 inscius *A*: ignarus *L*.   895 ignarus *A*: *del. L.*

Murderer

Come on, after suffering once again unhappy, come on, your mind must be fortified against your misery, and you have to recall what used to be difficult, hard, horrible, harmful and unfavourable for you. Rather, the fiery Titan[201] will leave the glowing celestial circle and precede its rise under its precursor, rather the moon, the queen of the night, will renounce her wanderings along the aether, the Dutchman his warfare and the Spaniard his strokes, than that I will tell my fate with dry eyes. Woe to me! On the same day I saw the light of life and the beginning of care, and already in the cradle my life I barely escaped Fortune's black hands, nor did the initial charm of the lovely age, the spring of life, and the quiet, sloping path of a radiant life course; over time the growing misery increased and with the progress of life itself my worries increased. My smart kept pace with the fleeing years. Alas, I was already miserable at the time of my birth.

Commander

What resentment of Fortune has released so many of her cloud-strikes against you?

Murderer

One pain has brought countless sorrows. I saw the head of my unhappy father burnt, surrounded with a smoke column, and his members destroyed by the miserable flames. I was present in person to look at my grief: small, ignorant, inexperienced, a very small part of the swarming mass, I went looking at it here and there, still unconscious of my destiny. I have seen that in

---

201   The god of the sun.

Ramalibusque roborum ingentem pyram
Strui sub auras, nemoris immensi luem.
Dum iactor, et me confluentis impetus
900   Fremitusque turbae voluit, et secum procul
Populi procellas inter, et magnum fori
Vndantis agmen, civiumque murmura
Motusque, perdit error; inveni patrem
Iam perditurus, teque vidi, haud denuo
905   Visurus vnquam, vita, spes, opes meae
Animique fulcrum languidi, o dulcis parens,
Olli trementes horridus tortor manus
Hinc inde ferro, duplicique compedum
Frustra labantes strinxerat vinclo pedes,
910   Instansque crebris verberum vibicibus
Senile multo vulnere vrgebat latus,
Canaeque largo sanguine vndabant genae,
Et illa sacra temporum nix, vltima
Labentis aevi messis, et fessae seges
915   Extrema vitae, rore sudabat novo,
Cruenta multùm, puluerisque squallido
Infecta coeno, morsque iam toto viri
Errabat ore saeva, vicina, imminens,
Et ante funus, funus infelix erat,
920   Iterum futurus morte, nunc mortis metu.
Penè et dolori spiritus cedens suo
Effugit hostem, seque furatus sibi est,
Mortemque propera morte vitavit suam.
Bis impeditas sustulit caelo manus,
925   Et bis remisit rursus et frustra fuit,
Gemitumque ab imo pectore ingentem trahens
Lachrymasque inanes, flebili erupit sono:
Tu purioris magne regnator poli
Caelumque factis omnibus praesens meis,

---

901 et—fori A: et me confluentis impetus | Fremitusque turbae voluit, et magnum fori L.   903
Motusque—error A: Caecusque tuus poscit error [Caecusque perdit [ducit c] error b] L. Post
corr. habet L: Dum iactor, et me confluentis impetus | Populi, procellas inter et caecum fori |
Undantis agmen, civiumque murmura | Motusque perdit [ducit b] error. [Dum iactor insons,
hucque et hinc illuc feror, | Pariterque turbam pariter et votum sequor | Forique euntis agmen b]
L.   904–905 haud—unquam A: postmodo Nunquam videndum L.

the open air a huge pyre was built from a clean chopped pile, a stack of leaves and oak chips, the miserable remnant of an immense forest.

While I was pushed back and forth, and while the hustle and the noise of the congregating crowd dragged me along and the uncoordinated journey took me far amongst the swirls of the people, the great procession of the undulating mass in the square and the grumbling and the movements of my fellow citizens, I found my father whom I would soon lose. I saw you, whom I would never see again, my life, my hope, my strength and the strut of my languishing soul, oh dear father. The ruthless executioner had unnecessarily tied the two trembling hands with iron and the staggering feet with a double foot buoy. By inflicting upon him many lashes, he tormented the body of the old man with many wounds. His grey-haired cheeks dripped with a lot of blood and the holy snow of time, the last harvest of the passing time, the final crop of the weary life,[202] sweated uncommon dew, heavily bleeding, stained with filthy dust mud. The cruel death came all over the face of the man, near, threatening. Before he was a dead corpse, the unfortunate one already was a corpse: he would be a second time because of death, now he was already because of his fear of death.

Almost his mind, yielding to his grief, had fled the enemy, left for its own salvation, and had avoided his determined death by a quick death. Twice he raised his bound hands to heaven and twice he lowered them again, and it was in vain. He let out a huge sigh from his chest, shedding fruitless tears and exclaiming complacently: "You, great governor of the clear celestial pole, heaven, present in all my deeds, which irradiates everything because you cover

---

202   The holy snow of life [...] all indications of his grey-white hair.

930 Et cuncta lustrans, cuncta quod circum tegis,
     Antestor, inquit. Cernis haec? Cernis? Trahor
     Et vos meorum gens pusilla liberûm
     Pudicaque uxor, o mea, aeternùm vale.
     Extremus ore frigido haerebat sonus;
935 Tortor cruentas inijcit collo manus,
     Vitaeque cursum rumpit, et voci sonum.
     Flammisque trepidum tradit, eminus tamen,
     Maiorque letho paena fit lethi mora,
     Morique nescit, quodque postremum fuit:
940 Negata mors est ipsa, morienti tamen.
     Tandem misertus ipse prorumpit vapor
     Ambitque vultum, dum fuit vultus tamen,
     Vnaque luce carceri et letho fuit
     Addictus ille, binaque infelix tulit
945 Mortisque damna compedumque et, o nefas,
     Nullius vnquam fraudis aut doli reum
     Idem beatum vidit, et cinerem dies.

     PRAEFECTVS
     Et quae furoris causa tam subiti fuit?

     SICARIVS
     Quaecunque vobis, quaeque tot quondam expulit
950 Laribus paternis, sancta libertas, fides,
     Pietasque pura: cuncta praeterquam scelus,
     Odium tyranni, rituumque adulteri
     Regis sacrorum, frausque Romani patris.
     Exin dolores inter et suspiria
955 Miserae parentis, degere aetatem in malis
     Penuriaque, flebilem ingressa est viam
     Puerilis aetas, liberisque reddita
     Pro patre rapto sola paupertas fuit.

---

930 Et cuncta lustrans … quod *A*: Si cuncta lustras … si *L*.   931 Cernis—Trahor *A*: *del. L*.   932
gens pusilla *A*: parvi gregres [*sic*] *L*.   934 haerebat *A*: errabat *L*.   936 voci *A*: vocis *L*.   937
tamen *A*: licet *L*.   938 paena *A*: poena *L*.   939 Morique nescit *A*: Diu imminentis *L*.   941
ipse prorumpit *A*: colla circundat *L*.   942 tamen *A*: *del. L*.   948 Et quae *A*: Ecquae *L*.

everything around: I take you as a witness", he said, "do you see this? Can you see? I'm being taken away. And you, my little children, and you, o my impeccable wife, forever goodbye".

The last word faltered in his chilled throat, the executioner struck the bloody hands on his neck. He squeezed his breath and his voice, and gave him convulsing up to the flames, but kept himself at a distance. A greater punishment than death itself became the postponement of death, he could not die. And what was worst: death itself was denied him, although he was dying. At last the wretched fire flickered and surrounded his face as long as it was still a face, and one day he was given to the dungeon and to death. The unfortunate man suffered a double sorrow: death and chains. O horror: he who was never accused of any deceit or any ruse was happy and brought to ashes on the same day.

Commander
What was the cause of that totally unexpected rage?

Murderer
Every cause that exists for you, and which has driven many far away from their father's house: holy freedom, faith, pure piety, in short everything, except crime; hatred of the tyrant and the adulterous King with his holy rites, and betrayal of the Pope in Rome. The result is, under the sadness and sighing of my unfortunate mother, a life of misery and poverty. My young life has turned into an agony and we children only got poverty in exchange for our snatched father.

PRAEFECTVS
Opes quis autem sustulit misero suas?

SICARIVS
960 Qui vitam.

PRAEFECTVS
            Eone peruicax mentis tumor
Legisque certae ignarus erupit furor?

SICARIVS
Saeuitum in omne est ordine infelix genus,
Paterque saeva morte multatus iacet,
Vitaque mater; paenaque illi mors fuit,
965 Huic munus esset, quotque liberos parens
Totidem doloris liquit haeredes sui,
Opumque nullos.

PRAEFECTVS
            Surge et aduerso feras
Sortis malignae corde prouoca minas,
Fatumque contra pectore excelso preme.
970 Campoque aperto Martijsque legibus
Inuade Iberum, cuncta fraus absit procul
Ignota Batavis; exulat nostris adhuc
Hoc nomen oris: artis haud Mavors eget.
Virtutis altae robore et forti manu
975 Ferroque tantus expiandus est cruor
Animique motu. Poscit vltricem manum
Nati cinis paternus, et virum vocat,
Puerum nequibat; quicquid effluxit tuis
Ignouit annis. Nunc age, vltorem para
980 Natum parenti: magnate moles premit.
Tune vt sepulchri debitor tanti, queas
Haurire lumen, siderumque ardens iubar?
Ah creditores patrios manes habes,
Teque vmbra poscit illa, te cinis ciet,

---

960 tumor *A*: calor *L*.   961 ignarus erupit *A*: nescius *L*.   962 Sicarius *scripsi*: Sis. *A*.

Commander
Who has deprived the unfortunate of his wealth?

Murderer
He who took his life.

Commander
Is that the reason for the eruption of that stubborn emotion, that erratic frenzy of yours?

Murderer
All members of my unhappy family are each of them badly treated: my father died, punished with a cruel death, my mother was punished with a cruel life. For him death was a punishment, for her it would be a gift. My father left all his children with an inheritance of sorrow, not of possessions.

Commander
Get up, challenge the savage threats of evil destiny, and bravely resist fate. Attack the Spaniard in the open field and according to the laws of war: keep any deceit, something unknown to the Dutch, far from you. This concept is still banned from these shores. Mars does not need cunning at all. So much blood must be enthusiastically avenged with great courage, with a brave hand, and with the sword.

The physical remains of your father ask for the avenging hand of his son and call him now that he is a man, because they could not do that when he was a boy. He has forgiven your past years. Now, come on, provide an avenger in the person of the son to your father: a heavy task is pressing on you. How can you, if you are in the debt of such an important dead person, see the light and the glow of the stars?

Ah, you owe it to the shadow of your father: his spirit calls you, his ashes excite you, mother earth itself calls you slow and is disappointed in you. You still

985   Et ipsa lentum terra te mater vocat,
Geritque frustra. Feruet aetatis calor
Sanguisque totas integer venas alit.
Vtrumne laudi pectus occallet tuum,
Speique totas vita praeclusit vias?
990   Exurge tandem, pectorisque feruidas
Effunde habenas, teque huic dedas duci
Nomenque Marti.

Sɪᴄᴀʀɪᴠs
                  Scilicet fixum est, placet.
Ergo vt iuventae largioris plenior
Pulsavit aetas limen, et lanuginis
995   Autumnus atras primus infecit genas,
Rebusque dignum tempus, et primordium
Maioris aeui, cum dolor, primusque honos
Potentiores pectori subdunt faces,
Vehuntque in altum, deprimuntue spiritus
1000   Motusque primos, fata iuraui tua
Miserande genitor, cladis et tantae necis
Futurus ultor. Nunc quoque, immensa licet
Vastaque mole dura paupertas premat,
Et eminentem saeva virtutis diem
1005   Nisusque condat, opprimatque, et arduos
Supplantet ausus, et resurgentem domet,
Plerumque magnis imminens conatibus
Imbelle pondus, et dolor penuriae
Aedilis altis additus virtutibus,
1010   Quoties parentis cumque praerepti tamen
Sensus cruentis cor fodit calcaribus,
Ceu ille longa membra defessus die
Bellator alto cornipes torpet situ,
Mauortis acres suetus inter impetus
1015   Glomerare gressus; ille dum tempus sinit
Annique, et aetas, it iuuenta feruidus

1004–1006 Et eminentem—domet *A: post corr. del. L.*   1004 saeva *A:* male *L.*   1009 Aedilis *A:* tyrannus *L.*

have the vibrant energy of youth and fresh blood flowing through all your veins. Or is your heart insensitive to fame and has life lost all hope? Get up and slacken the reins of your fiery heart, sign up yourself in the service of this captain and register with Mars.[203]

Murderer

Yes, I am determined to do that, I am. So when the older age of the older youth was nearing and autumn with the first stubble of a flax beard darkened my cheeks, when the time was right for action, the beginning of the older age, when the grief and the first glory set fire to the heart and blaze or suppressed the first enthusiasm, I swore by your lot, pitiable father, that I would avenge your ruin and so miserable death. Even now—albeit that bitter poverty weighs heavily on me and cruelly steals and suppresses the lofty light and the strenuous efforts of my courage, and albeit that the disarming burden of heavy deprivation and attendant sorrow, which often threaten to frustrate great undertakings, and to limit great heroic deeds, will make my difficult endeavours fail and, if I get to my feet again, restrain me—the thought of my father torn away too soon often pierces my heart with bloody traces, as a warhorse with horned feet and wearied limbs becomes limp after a long time in deep rest, even though he was accustomed to galloping under the fierce attacks of Mars. As long as time, years and age allow it, in youthful

---

203   I.e. enter into military service.

Enses micantes inter et ferri minas,
Ardensque gestit, toruus, et plenus sui,
Strepituque maior, auribus totis bibens
1020   Galeasque, vocesque, aeraque et neces virûm
Superba crurum ponderat volumina,
Tremitque palpitatque, et in numerum salit.
At nunc senectae pondus infelix licet
Suique vix pars, si tamen litui procul
1025   Tubaeque notum rursus hauriat sonum;
Inhorret armos, et tremor totos vetus.
Redux in artus, corpus immensum quatit,
Auremque sursum tollit, et terram ferit,
Annosque nescit, seque restituit sibi.
1030   Sic colla quamuis semper incumbens, graue
Onus fatigat, impetusque intercipit
Laudemque rerum "degener penuria
Virtutis umbra", et pertinax necessitas
Sublime dura cor retundens compede,
1035   Animique nascens lumen, et promtam satis
In bella dextram; sic quoque ardentes agit
Sublata motus mens, suasque ventilat
Libratque vires, copiamque. Et peruigil
Inusitata parturit molimina,
1040   Nec ille cassam laude sol praesens facem
Ducet sub vmbras. Singulos perdo dies
Si nil Iberus.

PRAEFECTVS
        Perge, sitientes patris
Restingue manes, sanguinem sanguis suum
Exposcit ille.

1025 hauriat *A*: accepit [excepit *b*] *L*.   1033–1035 Virtutis—satis *A*: Virtutis umbra: [Tristisque
egestas *b*] sic quoque occulto calet | Mens aegra motu, languidoque pectore | Inusitata parturit
molimina *L*; satis *MT*: satis. *A*.   1036 In bella dextram *A*: Necessitasve *add. et postea del. L.* ‖
ardentes *A*: ingentes *add. et postea del. L.*   1037 Sublata motus mens *A*: mens alta motus *add.*
et postea del. L.   1037–1039 Sublata—molimina *A*: *del. L.*

impetuosity he goes straight through flickering swords and their threatening iron, and fervently he moves freely, grimly, full of himself, allied by the noise, all ears for the sound of helmets, voices, bronze and the death of men; he looks at his huge, proud legs, vibrates, moves nervously and jumps into the line.

But even though now miserable old age presses upon him and he is hardly a small part of his former self, when he hears the familiar sound of the clarion and the trumpet again in the distance, his flanks still shudder and the old vibration comes back in all his limbs, he shakes his great body, pokes his ears and stomps on the earth, does not count his years and regains his strength—thus, although a heavy, heavy burden always tires me down, as well as "unworthy poverty, casting a shadow over courage", and a continual deprivation take away my lust for life and ambition by throwing my lofty heart, the rising light of my courage and my hand, willingly to wars, in hard chains, likewise also my exalted mind nevertheless has fiery emotions, it whips up its powers and faculties. Vigilantly he makes unusual efforts; the sun today will not extinguish its torch without having harvested praise. I am lost every day when the Spaniard does not suffer any losses.

Commander
Go, soak the thirsty shadow of your father, his blood demands others' blood.

SICARIVS

        Patriam versus trahor
1045 Nec illa nobis vana diffluet via:
Nunc ecce nostris praestitem conatibus
Heroa petimus, splendidae culmen domus.
En ipse celerem praeuius refert pedem.

SCENA. II.

AVRIACVS. LOISA.

Quid immerentes rori commendas genas,
1050 O dulcis uxor, maestaque amplexus fugis
Visusque nostros, nec suave purpurae
Hilarumque laetae mentis emergit iubar,
Vultumque pingit? Non vt ante, candida
Tibi serenus ora perstringit rubor.
1055 Sed maesta, sed deiecta, sed luctu grauis.
Sic illa Phoebi blande spoliatrix sui
Nocturna Phoebe pallet, et caecum caput
Obnubit atris implicata nubibus,
Poloque lumen tollit, et terrae polum,
1060 Trepidique torpent aetheris magni chori,
Suasque linquunt aurei fratres domos
Vigiles serenae noctis, et caeli cohors
Statione ruptâ. Non ita pridem tamen
Certe fatebor dulcis o consors thori,
1065 Non tanta lachrymis causa defuit tuis,
Cum perduelles inter et nostram manum
Paruo redundans alueo Rhenus stetit,
Vitaeque nostrae terminus flumen fuit,
Mortemque vidi semper et fugi meam.
1070 Certe fatebor quicquid huius est, mea,

1045 diffluet *A*: decedet *L.*   *Tit.* SCENA. 2. *Del. L.*   1049 rori commendas *scripsi*: rore commendas *A*: imbribus tingis *L.*   1051 Visusque *A*: Vultusque *L.*   1052 Hilarumque *A*: Blandum-
que [Purumque *b*] *L.*   1054 Tibi *A*: Circum *L.*   1055 Sed—grauis *A*: Humum tueris, oraque
in nubes [bus *b* rores *c* luctus *d*] eunt *add. et postea sublin. L.* ‖ luctu *MT* [vultu *b*] *L*: luctuis *A.*
1056 Phoebi *A*: *del. L.*   1057 Phoebe *A*: luna *L.*   1065 defuit *A*: *del. L.*   1070 quidquid huius
est, mea *A*: *del. L.*

Murderer

My fatherland draws me, and I will not let that road be closed. See, now I turn to the hero who is the guardian god of my company, the roof peak of a beautiful house. Look, he is already ahead of me and coming quickly.

SCENE II

Orange, Louise

Orange

Why, dear wife, do you submit your innocent cheeks to tears, do you eschew my embrace and look, and is there no pleasant and cheerful purple sheen, the hallmark of joy, that colours your face? You do not have a bright red colour, a sign of calm, on your white face, as before. But you are sad, dejected and full of sorrow. You are as pale as Phoebe who gently robs her brother Phoebus at night. She clothes and wraps his head in black clouds, so that it can no longer be seen, takes away the light and makes it invisible to the earth. The canals of the great sky are motionless of fear. The stars, those golden brothers, the watchmen over the clear night, the celestial crowd, break their guard post and leave their homes.

Yet it was not so long ago that I must certainly give in, my beloved, a good reason for your tears, when only the Rhine lay between the enemies and our army, in a narrow bed; the border between life and death was only a river and I constantly faced death and fled it.

All this I have to admit, my dear, and I will not encapsulate your sweet heart with meaningless, mendacious words and oracular language: no country

Nec dulce vanis dictionum fraudibus
Ambagibusue pectus inuoluam tuum;
Non vlla Iberum, meque sat tutò queat
Diuidere tellus, non Pyrenes si iuga,
1075 Idemque Celtas meque disiungat tuos,
Discriminataque Alpium cacumina,
Quacunque late cornibus caelum suis
Vicinus ambit, aemulumque verticem
Humerosque circum velat aestivo gelu
1080 Apex superbus, nubibusque aptum caput,
Terraeque quicquid continentis vspiam
Succumbit arcu flammeo ingentis poli,
Inhorruique semper, eminus licet,
Fraudes tyranni, comminus nunquam manum,
1085 "Timuique solo quod timore vincitur
Dolos et astus"; caetera haud quicquam sibi
In hoc profanus corde deposcet timor.
Non vlla tantum (testor hoc vnum deos)
Capax Iberi terra, sit simul mei.
1090 At nunc profundo spumeus regno pater
Tot aestuantes victor obiecit sinus
Molitus alta fluctibus diuortia
Sequester ingens arbiterque; solus hic
Horrere Ibero suadet, et nostro vetat.
1095 Primus Philippum patriam vrgentem viam,
Orbisque habenas mente voluentem suâ
Vidi tulique. Primus hoc voui latus,
Et prurientes totius fregi manus,
Ardore mundi. Per meae Batauiae
1100 Certe minas, et lacessitum caput
Maiora poscit. Sternit hanc votis suis,
Conatibusque rex superbus semitam,
Et vniuersi candidatus est Iber.
Gaudete reges, proximum polo genus,
1105 Aboriginesque caelitum magni duces
Divûm propago: tutor omnibus fui
Simulque noster. Cuncta defendi loca

1095 Philippum *scripsi*: Phllippum *A*.   1098 prurientes *A*: insolentes *add. et postea sublin. L.*

could form a sufficiently secure separation between the Spaniards and I, not even if the Pyrenees or all Alpine peaks, all high mountains that compete in height as neighbours of the sky and of which the clouded crown, flanks and peaks are cold even in the summer, and whatever continent there might be under the fire bow of the great sky, would form a secure separation at the same time for your French and myself. I always shuddered at the tyrant's wiles, even though they were far, but never for his army, even though it was close. "I feared what is only overcome by fearful caution, namely wiles and duplicity." For the rest, shameful fear on my heart will have no control. In short, not a single country (for only this thing I will testify to the gods) that contains the Spaniard could at the same time have me within its borders.

But now the foaming father with his deep empire triumphant with many rushing waves has blocked the road, because he has made deep separations with his currents, an immense intervening sole arbitrator. He is the only one who makes the Spaniards shudder and keeps us from shivering. I was the first to see and endure Philip when, in his father's footsteps, he held the reins of the world in his imagination. I have been the first to use my physical strength and to thwart his action when he was out for the whole world. To the shattered remnants of my Netherlands and my enraged head, he certainly demands something greater. The proud king makes a path here for his wishes and efforts, and the Spaniard desires everything.

Rejoice, kings, generation closest to heaven, great princes, descendants of celestials, sons of gods: I have all protected and at the same time myself. I defended all places when I regained ours. I have given the Dutch an avenger,

Cum nostra cepi. Vindicem Belgis dedi,
Munimen orbi, cumque rex mundo minax
1110 Soli patentem liber inuasit viam
Venturus vltra, primus obieci mare
Moramque feci. Terra non satis fuit;
Successit unda, coerulisque fluctibus,
Pontique saeuam gurgite repressi manum.
1115 "Namque inquietus feruor ille principum
Gliscendo surgit, seque tollit, et licet
Sit aemulator nullius, fiet suus
Regalis ardor, pluraque hoc vno petit
Quo plura restant, perque populorum rapax
1120 Crescit ruinas", quodque supremum reor,
Bellum sine hoste gessit Albanus furor,
Egitque cives in se et armauit suos.
At tu reposta lenior cura veni
O blanda coniux, mentis o vigor meae
1125 Eademque thalami, frontis et supercili
Nubem serena, laetaque in cultus redi
Habitusque veteres. Nunc in amplexus patris
Commune pignus veniat, et collum premat
Breuibus lacertis paruulum germen domus
1130 Natusque noster: sic iuvat, certe iuvat
Curis fathiscens, Belgiaeque pondere
Laxare pectus, otioque turbidam
Rigare mentem, lenibusque gaudijs.

LOISA
Metuo marite; plura non queo tamen,
1135 Metuo marite.

AVRIACVS
          Tristia et luctus graues
Remitte Iberis. Omen hoc nostros precor
Inuadat hostes.

1116 Gliscendo *A*: In magna [In alta *b*] *L.*   1129 paruulum germen *A*: germen antiquae *L.*   1130
Natusque—iuvat *A*: Stirpisque nostrae, iuvat impetus gravis [sic iuvat curis grave *b*] *L.*   1131
curis fathiscens *A*: cura *n.l.* [perenni *B* victum labore *c*] *L.*   1134 queo *A*: possum *L.*   1135
graues *A*: suos *L.*

given the world a defensive wall, and when the King threatened the world and, unhindered, travelled across everything under the sun and wanted to go further, I was the first to throw the sea over him and to force him to postpone his plan. Land was not enough, water came in its place: I pushed back his cruel army by means of the deep blue waves and the water of the sea.

"For the impatient turbulence of princes swells, surges and rises itself. Even though it is no one's competitor, the desire of a king will become its own competitor. Merely because there is more, it strives for more, and predatory as it is, desire increases by the destruction of peoples." And what I find worst: the fury of Alva waged a war without enemy, he incited his own citizens against each other and armed them.

But you, take care of yourself, calm down and come to me, my dear wife, oh you, the power of my spirit and my marriage, let the gloomy cloud of your forehead and eyebrows clear up and let return your normal cheerful state and appearance. Now let the common pledge of our love come to his father's lap and wrap his short arms around my neck, the little sprout of the house, our son; this is how I would like, very much like, to relax my heart that is fatigued by worries and the weight of the Netherlands, and to cool my depressed mind with peace and calm joys.

Louise
I'm afraid, husband. I am not able to do more: I am afraid, my husband.

Orange
Let the Spaniards mourn and grieve deeply. I pray that this omen affects our enemies.

LOISA

     Neutiquam frustra tamen
Timore vano fluctuatur cor meum;
Nec ante tanto. Qualis hybernas ferox
1140 Cum Corus auras, arbiterque fluctuum
Caecas profundo coerulo intentat minas
Insanus Auster, vimque praemittit suam
Venturus ipse; sensit aduentum dei
Thetys residens, summaque absentem licet
1145 Exhorret vnda, turbidaque aspergine
Cautes trementes inter alludit mare,
Refluitque rursus, seque sorbet et fremit,
Sensimque maius turget: undaque hinc et hinc
Terram flagellat dubia, vix credens sibi,
1150 Adhuc futuri plena, donec impotens
Caeli furentes pervagatur cardines
Pontumque verrit ventus, et nubem trahit,
Et incubantem fluctibus miscet polum,
Vadumque voluit, pallidique nauitae
1155 Pectus pauore soluit, et fluctu ratem.
Sic ante luctus luget, et fatum sibi
Indicit aeger mentis ignarae stupor.
Non me Lyaei dona, non mitis Ceres,
Ipsaeque dulces ante delectant dapes,
1160 Crescitque in ore lentus inuito cibus.
Victos nec artus vinculo mitis sopor
Leni pererrat, flebilesue luminum
Demulcet orbes. Cura non lapsu graui
Noctis profundae liquitur, sed in genis
1165 Infesta, pernox excubat. Tremo, tremo,
Metuo marite.

AVRIACVS

     Scilicet pacem tremis
Non arma quondam.

1144 Thetys *A*: Tethys *L*. 1145 turbidaque *MT L*: turbidoque *A*. 1157 ignarae *MT L*: igarae *A*.
1161 vinculo *MT L*: vinciulo *A*.

Louise

But my heart is absolutely not just tossed and turned, because of an unfounded fear; it has never been so intense. Like when the fierce Corus thrusts the wintry gusts, and the ruler of currents the raging Auster,[204] his blind threats at the dark blue depth; they send their violence ahead to come later; Tethys,[205] still calm, feels already the coming of the god, the surface of the water shivers for him, even though he is not there yet. The sea plays in a swirling splash between the trembling rocks and flows back again, swallows itself, buzzes and gradually swells to something bigger. The water strangles desperately against the land, while it barely knows where it is, already full of what is still to come, until the wind roams the raging celestial poles, blows over the sea, drags clouds with it, mixing the sky and the waves beneath it, stirring the water and the heart of the pale sailor through fear, and sinking the ship through the stream.

This is how the sickening paralysis of my mind that does not know what will happen is sorrowful for grief and announces fate itself. I no longer like the gifts of Lyaeus, the soft Ceres[206] or even the once delicious meals, and the food swells slowly in my reluctantly munching mouth. No sweet sleep wanders over my limbs, which would then be softly overwhelmed, or strokes my tear-stained eyes. My concern does not melt away in a deep sleep in the middle of the night, but viciously watches my cheeks all night. I shudder and tremble and am afraid, my husband.

Orange

Apparently you are shivering with fear of peace, but not of the guns of old.

---

204 Corus, the north-west wind; Auster, the south wind.
205 Tethys, the sea goddess.
206 Lyaeus ('deliverer from care') is another name for Bacchus, a metonym for wine; Ceres, the goddess of corn, a metonym for bread or food in general.

LOISA
                    Pace tranquilla viros
Perire didici. Pace tranquilla iacet
Quem non tot ictus, ciuiumque murmura,
1170   Quassumque regni corpus, et Celtae furor:
Non factionum saeua concussit manus,
Non Martis alta vis, et inclinans onus
Patriae mentis. Pace tranquilla iacet,
Bellique fmem vidit, et vitae suae.

AVRIACVS
1175   Secura metuis?

LOISA
                    Ne diu sint.

AVRIACVS
                    Siquid hic
Vsquam tremendum, siquid aduersum fuit,
Trans mare relictum est. Longa nos secat via
Simulque fraudes, et dolos. Toto mari
Distamus illhinc vnde metuendum fuit
1180   Quicquid timetur. Omne trans pontum est scelus
Vnaque Iberus.

LOISA
                    "Pax subinde decipit
Securitate, Marsque tutatur metu,
Cavetque semper arma, qui semper timet."
Testis maritus, testis et genitor fuit,
1185   Alterque natae monstrat, alter coniugi
Timere quauis fraude plus, quicquid latet.
Ille, ille, regni fulgor ingentis parens,
Potensque rerum, sacra vis Colignij,
Emancipatus horridae pendet neci,
1190   Interque terras et polum, neutrum tenet;
Vtroque dignus, impotens spectaculum
Sortis proteruae, sydera et caeli vagos

1192 sydera *A*: sidera *L*.

Louise
I have learned that in quiet times of peace people die. In calm peacetime, someone dies who has not been crushed by many battles, murmuring citizens, the
shocks of the empire, the frantic French, or the raging party gossip, nor the
fierce force of Mars or the crashing rubble of a fatherland doomed to destruction. In such a peaceful time of peace such a person is killed and he has seen
the end of the war and of his own life.

Orange
Are you afraid for safe times?

Louise
Yes, that they will last too long.

Orange
If there was something to fear here, if there was anything hostile here, it was
left on the other side of the sea. A long road separates us from the wiles and layers. By the whole sea we are separated from the party from which everything
fearsome was to fear. All crime is just like the Spaniards on the other side of the
water.

Louise
"Often peace deceives through carelessness and Mars protects through fear; he
who always fears is at least always on his guard against weapons." Witness to
this were my husband and my father; the one warns me as a daughter, the other
as a wife more than for any deceit to be afraid of everything that is hidden.

   He, my father, the splendour of a great empire, a mighty man, the inspired
De Coligny,[207] hangs there, the victim of a chilling death. Between heaven and
earth he lives in neither, although worthy of both. While in his weakness he
shows the brutality of fate, he takes the stars and the planets in heaven as

---

207   Gaspard de Coligny (1519–1572), one of the Huguenot leaders who were killed in the St
      Bartholomew's Day massacre; see also above, p. 179, n. 182.

Testatur ignes, duplici functus malo
Diuisque versum corpus, et terrae vicem
1195 Demonstrat ille, nec sepulchro clauditur
Caelo sepulchro tutus, et patriâ suâ.
Quis fata nescit, magne Theligni, tua?
Fossumque ferro pectus, et tristem necem?
His, his in ulnis ille, in hoc, in hoc sinu
1200 Vndans cruore triste demisit caput,
Oculosque morte iam natantes, collaque
In ora nostra flexa, et exangues genas,
Animaeque dulces ore languenti bibi
Abeuntis auras: pressus, elisus diu
1205 Inter lacertos, inter haerentes manus,
Interque vultus, spiritus fugit meos,
Quemque ipsa tenui, perdidi ereptum tamen
Misera maritum; concidit pondus graue
Vel sic tremendum perduellibus suis,
1210 Impune magna Guisiorum victima.
Hymen quot ille finis heroum fuit?
Haud cariores vlla gens vidit thoros
Emitue taedas ante quis pluris suas,
Regique regni dos cruor fuit sui.
1215 Quis metuit istos quisue trepidauit dolos,
Caecasque fraudes, et reconditum scelus
Aulaeque latebras? Horruit nemo necem
Nemoque fugit.

AVRIACVS
           Desine infelix metûs
Luctusque inanis, neue vanis irrita
1220 Te trade curis. Firmus à nobis locus
Defendit hostem.

LOISA
           Nullus hic hostis fuit.

1195 ille *A*: una *L*.   1196 tutus *A*: tectus *L*.   1219–1220 neue—curis *A*: nec libens inanibus
Succumbe curis *L*.

witnesses, in double misery, and turns his body alternately to the gods and to the earth; he is not safely locked in a grave, because heaven and his fatherland form his grave.

Who does not know your fate, great De Téligny,[208] your chest pierced by the sword, your hard death? In these arms, on this lap, he has laid down his sad head from which the blood gushed, his eyes already broken by death, his neck and pale cheeks to my face; I have drunk the sweet breezes of his breath, escaping from his languid mouth; for a long time being kicked and crushed, he expired in my arms, in my tireless hands and under my eyes. I, unfortunate, did lose by death the husband whom I held myself. His heavy weight collapsed, even in this shape horrifying to his enemies, he, a victim of the Guises[209] without them being punished for it. For how many heroes was that Wedding their end? No people saw a more precious marriage, no one ever before paid more for his wedding,[210] never was the dowry for a king the blood of his empire. Who was afraid or who trembled for the wiles and blind layers, the hidden crime and the sneaky acts of the court? No one feared a bloodbath, no one fled.

Orange
Unhappy wife, do not be afraid and needlessly sad, and do not give in inanely to senseless worries. A strong place will ward off the enemy from us.

Louise
There was no enemy here.

---

208 Charles de Téligny (ca. 1535–1572), the first husband of Louise who was also killed in the St Bartholomew's Day massacre; see also above, p. 179, n. 182.

209 The Guises were a branch of the House of Lorraine; members of this house had a leading role in the wars of religion and the St Bartholomew's Day massacre.

210 The St Bartholomew's Day massacre took place a few days after the marriage of the French king's sister Margareth of Valois to the Protestant Henry III of Navarre (the future Henry IV of France), hence it was also called the Paris Blood Wedding. In a series of assassinations thousands of French Protestants were killed.

AVRIACVS
Fuere et omnes.

LOISA
Vocibus certè tuis
Lubens remitto quicquid est, tamen, tamen
Metuo, marite. Perge famularis manus
1225   Paruamque patri sistite hic prolem suo.
Hic en hic ille est, dulcis effigies tui
Pariterque nostri, pars mei, pars et tui
Vtrumque iungit. Hunc ego quoties tuor
Quotiesque vultus cerno, et has paruas manus,
1230   Similesque patri luminis blandi notas,
Lachrymis invndo. Siquid aduersi ferox
Fortuna regno moliatur, aut tibi
In hoc suaue pars redundabit caput.

AVRIACVS
Accedat agedum. Nate, spes o nunc patris,
1235   Futurus vltor, Nate, Nate, surge, age
Laudum sititor, aemulusque patriae
Virtutis, aeuo maior; aetatem tuam
Transcende victor, temporisque vrge moram,
Annosque iam nunc supputent moestae tuos
1240   Matres Iberae. Nate, vt illud contuor
Sublime pectus, oraque et vultus meos,
Decusque latae frontis, et toruas genas,
Ingens Philippi crescit his terris pauor.
O nate, nate, dissipata nobilis
1245   Comae propago, et ille vagitus grauis
Elementa rerum spondet, et certam manum
Aususque magnos. Nate, si quae forte sors
Caeptam parenti durior rumpat viam,
Iterque rerum claudat atque exordia
1250   Ingentis orsus, Belgiaeque motuum;
Viduae parentis dulce solamen, patri

1243 his *scripsi*: hic *A*.   1249 atque exordia *A*: et primordia *L*.   1251 Viduae *A*: Maestae *L*.

Orange
All were enemies.

Louise
Oh, I certainly like to give all the weight to your words, yet I am afraid, my husband.—Go, group of servants and bring the little scion here for his father:—Here, look, here he is, your and at the same time my sweet image, part of me and part of you; he forms a connection between the both of us. Every time I look at him and see his face and these little hands and the sweet glance of his eyes that looks like his father's, I burst into tears. If the cruel Fortune has some misfortune for the empire or for you, part of it will affect this sweet head.

Orange
Come on, bring him here. Child, oh, now the hope of your father, once his avenger, child, child, come on, rise thirsting for fame and competing with the courage of your father, when you are older victorious over your age and hasten time. Let the sad Spanish mothers already now reckon with your years. Child, since I see that lofty heart of yours, features of your face, my image, your graceful broad face and your grim cheeks, the great fear of Philip for these countries grows.

O child, my child, the scattered implant of your noble hair and your violent screech guarantee the deeds, certain actions and large enterprises that you are in principle capable of. Child, if any hard-hearted fate would close the path taken by your father, the course of events, the first phase of his great undertaking and of the Dutch uprising, then be a sweet consolation for your mother, then widow, and make your father live on in your features, and

Vultu superstes esto, laudibus tibi.
Patremque matri redde, patriae virum.
At cum iuventae largior vis, liberas
1255   Totasque rebus Martijs pandet fores,
Sublimis ardor auctibus surgat nouis,
Seseque late fundat, et metum sibi
Mox regna subdat, iam triumphorum capax,
Avosque Diuos voluat, et magnum genus.
1260   Illhic Adolphi pectus altum, et indoles,
Tergoque numquam notus, aut fugae memor,
Dium Renatus nomen. O sanguis meus,
Eritne lux haec, quâ per vndantem sali
Deuectus aestum, per Bataua littora,
1265   Nereîque regna spumeum aerata secans
Sulcum carina, victor ardentem minis
Adhuc Iberum littore extremo trahas?
Patrique opima laetus, et victos lares
E puppe monstres? Nate, virtutis tuae
1270   Testem Batauum, Belgiaeque vindicem
Togae potentem, curiaeque purpuram,
Patresque magnos trado, et Ichnaeae decus
Sanctum senatum. Sic nec amisso patre
Futurus orbus. Nate, iam motus tuos
1275   Expectat hostis, quassaque Europae salus.
O nate, mundo conscio qui nascitur,
Latere nescit! Principem totus suum
Expectat orbis, oraque et vultus ducum
Annos sequuntur, gestaque et fortem manum
1280   Gliscentis aeui. Nate, magnanimus tibi
Binas Batauus monstrat armorum vias,
Terram salumque: semita haud vna est tibi
Modusque rerum, terraque angusta est nimis;
Vides et aequor: ipsa te in lucem trahit
1285   Natura nate, quodque supremum tamen
Felicitatis arbitror culmen tuae:

1259 magnum *A*: sanctum *L*.   1260 Illhic *A*: Illic *L*. ‖ altum, et *A*: altum et [altaque *b*] *L*.   1263
quâ *A*: cum *L*.   1265 secans *A*: trahens *L*.   1280 Gliscentis *A*: Nascenti [Surgentis *b*] *L*. ‖
Nate—tibi *A*: Nate, virtuti tuae *L*.   1283 Modusque *A*: Iterque *L*. ‖ terraque angusta *A*: terra si
parva *L*.   1285 nate *A*: rerum *L*.

yourself in your glorious deeds. Give your mother to your father and a man to the fatherland.

But when the greater strength of youth opens the doors for you completely and free for the military business, let a lofty fire rise in new growth and spread widely. It must subdue fear and then kingdoms to itself, already capable of victories. Let it bring the divine ancestors and the great race back to mind. From that race came the exalted heart and the courageous spirit of Adolf[211] and he who is never known in the back or thought of fleeing, René,[212] a godly name. O my own blood, will this be the day on which you sail through the undulating surf of the sea, along the coasts of the Netherlands and the empire of Nereus,[213] and by cutting a foamy furrow with a bronzed keel, triumphantly drag the threatening Spaniards off the coast, the day on which your father will, happy, show the honourable spoils and the conquered Lares from the stern? Child, I give you the Dutchman, the mighty avenger of the Dutch power, to witness your courage, the purple of the court, the great fathers and the ornament of the Ichnaeic, holy senate.[214] You will not be an orphan even if you have lost your father. Child, the enemy and the shocked well-being of Europe are already looking forward to your activities. O child, who is born with the knowledge of the world, cannot hide. The whole earth is looking forward to its leader, and princes are watching closely the years, deeds and brave actions of your growing age. Child, the generous Dutchman shows you a double way of warfare, the earth and the sea: there is not just one path or war for you, the land is too small, you also look at the sea: nature itself places you in the spotlight, my child. But what I consider the highest peak of your happiness: you overcome because you are pushed, you are called. That

---

211   Adolph of Nassau (1540–1568), William's brother who fell in the Battle of Heiligerlee.
212   William of Nassau inherited the principality of Orange from his uncle René de Châlon (1518–1544).
213   I.e. the sea.
214   The Ichnaean goddess Themis is the deity of justice, hence a metonym for law, which the 'holy senate', i.e. the States of Holland and West Friesland, or the States General, observe.

Vincis coactus, poscerisque. Hinc caerulae
Regnator vndae Cattus, hinc venti sciens
Fidum Walachri cor, et aetatis suae
1290   Profusor ingens Geldrus, et Friso minax
Cient morantem. Sis licet victor cito,
At vltor esse non nisi sero potes.
O nate, nate, tramitem o quantum tibi
Ingens parentis praeuij strauit labor!
1295   Quae o nate quondam nomina, o quantos leges
Mutantis aestus patriae, et fluxas vices,
Ruptumque regi faedus, et tetras dapes,
Dolosque Iberûm. Qualis excusso iugo
Turbatus atro Mosa spumauit vado,
1300   Stagno redundans turbido. Quantas pater
Superbus Honta, cornibus flexis, virûm
Strages cruento victor involuit sinu,
Cadauerumque mole praeclusus sibi
Quaesiuit in se sese, et ingentem viam
1305   Molitus extra gurgite vndanti fuit.
Qua primus Albae terror, audaci manu
Regina ponti, magna fraenatrix sali
Flissinga versos sensit exultans deos,
Soloque victas nomine exterrens aquas
1310   Curro marino vectus, et vastâ trabe
Per fluctuantem nauita erumpit viam,
Praedasque late verrit. At tu patriae
Foecunda nostrae, dulce solamen thori
Coniunx, memento per paterna paruulum
1315   Trophaea natum ducere, et Mauortios
Parentis ausus, armaque, et raucas tubas.
Sensimque in hastam surgat, inque puluere
Equi lupatis ora spumantis premat,
Armosque ferro calcet, et crudam niuem,
1320   Caelumque aperto vertice hybernum ferat:
Cum se pruinis turbidus laxat polus

1287–1288 poscerisque. Hinc caerulae ... undae A: Hinc procellosi maris ... audax L.   1295 Quae
o ... o A: Quae ... et L.   1295–1298 Quae—Iberûm A: Quae bella quondan, patriae quantos leges
| Mutantis aestus et repentinas vices, | Dolosque Iberûm. L.

is why the controller of the blue sea, the Dutchman, the loyal heart of the man from Walcheren, familiar with the wind, the great Gelderlander, who sacrifices his own life, and the ferocious Frisian urge you as you tarry.

Even if you quickly win, your revenge can only be too late. O child, my child, how great is the path that your father has gone before you with great effort and that he has paved for you! My child, what kind of a name you will read, what a great turmoil and unstable destiny of the conquering homeland, the treaty broken by the King, the horrible meals and wiles of the Spaniards. You will read how the Meuse has shaken the yoke and fiercely frothed with blood-black water, flooding from a turbulent pool; how large a slaughter of men the proud father Western Scheldt, victorious with his crooked horns in his blood-red bay, has harboured and how, blocked up by a pile of corpses, he could no longer see himself, had to search for himself, and with his maelstrom made a huge path outward. Where the terror of Alva first manifested itself, the Queen of the Sea, the great tamer of salty water Vlissingen, had jubilantly applauded by her courageous actions that the gods had turned; the skipper who by his name already scares the vanquished waters, riding on a sea-car, a large ship, chooses the spacious sea and drags away booty from everywhere.

But you, wife, fruitful for our fatherland, sweet consolation of marriage, tell the baby about the victories of his father and his brave warfare, weapons and penetrating sounding clarions. Let him gradually grow up to the military service and in a dust cloud a foam-brewing horse tighten the bit in the mouth, and give it the spurs on the flanks. Let him endure the inhospitable snow

Brumam lacessat primus, et spumans vadum
Nusquam tremiscens, pectore aduerso domet.
Exsuscitandus ardor ille est, indoles
1325   Ne forte tetro sacra torpescat situ,
Aut sub veterno regius lateat vigor.
Virtutis altae fomites claros tuor
O blanda coniux; vidimus nuper; meo
Cum forte iussu noster ille a limine
1330   Mota satelles arma vibrabat manu,
Mauortiasque miles inflabat tubas,
Arrisit ille, gaudiumque feruido
Admisit ore, vixque nutricis sinu
Sese remisit, emicansque dexteram
1335   Protendit, exilijtque et in ferrum ruit.
O nate, dignis scilicet crepundijs
Nassouiorum gente praeludis; neque
Iners paternum nube suffundes genus!
At nos suetae iam vocant, vxor, dapes
1340   Mediumque Phaebi currus inuadit polum.

CHORVS

Choriambici, Dimetri Iambici, Dactylici Pentametri, Hexametri Sapphici.

Frustran' sollicitis condita vultibus
Obscuris latuit Cynthia nubibus?
An lapsum miseris fataque gentibus,
Et belli dubios nunciat impetus,
1345   Et Mauortis opus? Fallere, fallere
Quisquis mente leuem vectus in aera
Adscribis nimiam syderibus fidem.
Namque illa emeritis pallida cornibus
Fratri blanda suo basia diuidit,
1350   Seque exinde nouis instruit ignibus,
Et Phoebi tepidos concipit halitus.

1338 suffundes *M T L*: suffendes *A*.   1339 suetae *A*: *del. L*.   1340 invadit *A*: ascendit *L*.

and the winter sky bareheaded in the first ranks to defy the winter chill and calm the foaming water without ever trembling.

The fire must be stirred up in him, to prevent his sacred nature from weakening through horrible rest, or his royal energy to become overwhelmed by indolence. I see the glowing fuel of the high courage, dear wife, I saw it recently; when that gatekeeper accidentally swung his arms with his hand and the soldiers blew the trumpet, he smiled, showed joy on his excited face, and had almost snatched himself from the nurse's lap. He lifted up, stretched out his hand, jumped off the lap and stormed at the violence of war. O child, you are already playing with toys that are worthy of the Nassau race. You will not shroud your ancestral family in idleness.–

But, woman, we are already called by the usual meal, the chariot of Phoebus enters the middle of heaven.

Chorus of indigenous Hollanders

Choriambs, iambic dimeters, dactylic pentameters, Sapphic hexameters

Is it without reason that Cynthia[215] has dressed herself in dark clouds, hidden from our anxious looks? Or does she really announce to the unhappy people their fall, fate, the dangerous attacks of war and the work of Mars? You are deceived, really, everyone who has seen the light air with the spirit and attaches too much faith to the stars. For she gives, now that her horns are being delivered, soft kisses to her brother, provides him with new light and takes the warm breath of Phoebus.

---

215   Cynthia or Diana, the moon goddess, a metonym for the moon.

Illinc dulcis humus parturit, et leuis
Humescit saturi penna Fauonij,
Illinc daedalei progenies soli
1355   Ridentes violaeque, et violae soror
Circum virgineis picta ruboribus
Florum nobilium dux Rosa nascitur.
Tellus vere nouo, iam genitalibus
Lucinam patitur faeta caloribus,
1360   Lucinam patitur veris, et obstetrix
Aspirat leuibus Cynthia mensibus;
Caelum nutrit amor, nutrit amor solum.
Constant faederibus omnia mutuis,
    Terramque magnus aether
1365   Amplectitur, suisque
    Gerit, fouetque in vlnis,
    Taedasque ouans quotannis,
    Redintegrat iugales,
    Et coniugem fatetur,
1370   Seseque miscet illi,
    Et in sinum beatae
    Se proripit maritae.
Tum volucrum toto vagus aethere
Dulcis hymen hymenaee sonat chorus;
1375   Pronubus exultat Zephyrus pater,
Syderaque aurata praeeunt face,
Et placidas caelum choreas agit,
Et domini praelucet amoribus,
Nuptaque in amplexum noua ducitur,
1380   Sponsaque regales aperit sinus,
Et varijs lasciuit amictibus,
Vtque suo placitura viro nitet.
Illinc flaua Ceres, et amabilis
Foemineus Bacchi refluit liquor.
1385   Vuaque sub tremulis pendula palmitibus
    Propter aquae dulcem luxuriat strepitum,
    Quae pariat maestis gaudia pectoribus.
    Tum vaga per tepidas exiliens latebras

1354 daedalei *scripsi*: Daedalei *A*.   1355 violaeque et *A*: violae tum *L*.   1357 Rosa *A*: rosa *L*.
1380 sinus *L*: senus *A*.

That is why the sweet soil is pregnant and the light-winged Favonius[216] becomes full of moisture. From it what the variegated ground generates and the colourful violins stem, from it is born the sister of the violin, the flower all around coloured with a virgin blush leader of noble flowers, the rose. The earth, already pregnant with fertile heat, is experiencing Lucina[217] in the new spring, she is experiencing Lucina, and the midwife of spring Cynthia[218] is favourable in the mild months. Love feeds the heavens, love feeds the earth. Everything is based on mutual treaties; the great aether embraces the earth, wears and cherishes her in his arms, renews cheering annually their marriage and recognizes her as a wife, has intercourse with her and penetrates the lap of his happy beloved.

Then a sweet-voiced chorus of birds swarming in the air sings "Hymen Hymenaee". And the bridal dungeon, father Zephyr,[219] cheers, the stars go with golden torch and the sky performs peaceful choral dances and lights the love affairs of their lord. The newly-weds are escorted to the embracement, the bride opens her royal garments and frolics in all kinds of cloaks, and shines as if to please her husband. From there the blonde Ceres sprouts and the sweet feminine moisture of Bacchus flows.[220]

The grape, hanging at the bottom of sagging branches, grows nicely next to sweetly sparkling water, to give joy to sad hearts. Then the lovely water, daughter of the golden sky, seeks out from warm shelters, running and gur-

---

216   Favonius, the gentle west wind.

217   Lucina or Juno Lucina was the goddess of childbirth, sometimes identified with Cynthia or Diana. 'To experience Lucina' therefore means 'to give birth'.

218   For Cynthia as the moon goddess, see above, n. 215.

219   I.e. the gentle west wind.

220   For Ceres and Bacchus as a metonym for bread and wine, see above, n. 206.

Aetheris aurati filia, dulcis aqua
1390   Garrula torrentem tentat iter per humum,
Arboribusque, suam, graminibusque, sitim
Sedat, et exiles soluitur in scatebras.
Vidimus horrendum caelo prodire cometen,
Qua validas auriga leuis moderatur habenas
1395   Lora regens axemque, polumque inuectus apertum
Lumina maioris turbatus conspicit Vrsae,
Quem licet armatus croceo qua fulgurat auro,
Palluit Orion, trepidoque exterritus ensis
Excidit, ingentique animum revocauit ab ausu.
1400   Regiae et fortes metuant tyranni;
"Nulla priuatis populis minantur
Sydera aut paruo pecudum magistro;
Parua non nouit polus; alta nutant,
Sorsque in occasum propriâ secunda
1405   Mole dehiscit."

ACTVS QVARTVS. SCENA I.

SICARIVS. QVATVOR FVRIAE, INQVISITIO, ALECTO, MEGAERA, TISIPHONE.

Ignosce victo Roma: cor retro salit
Fugamque versat intus. O sacerrimi
Tutela patris, votaque, et fides mea,
Et fibulati curiae sanctae patres,
1410   Superatus adsto: victus, ignauus feror,
Mihique cessi; pectus imbellis ferit
Tremor, quatitque, faedus, ignauus timor
Inuicta mentis maenia obsedit meae,
Et iam triumphum ducit: en victus trahor,
1415   Sed ante pugnam. Magne tot rerum vndique
Lustrator aether, cernis hanc tardam manum
In vota nostra? Quodque bis senis vaga
Mens egit annis vna vt arguat dies?
Dubitamus anime? Caeca consilia aduocas?

Tit. SCENA I. *A: del. L.*   1406 salit *A:* fugit *L.*

gling through the dry ground and quenches the thirst of trees and grass and dissolves in small pools.

We have seen a horrifying comet appear in the sky, where the fast Wagoner holds the reins firmly, with the straps steering the car. As he flies to the open air, he is startled by the stars of the Greater Bear, the Wagoner for whom Orion,[221] though armed, has faded at the place where he glistens of sapphire gold. Afraid as he is, the sword has fallen from his hands while he is scared to death, and he has refrained from a great venture.

Let palaces and strong tyrants fear, "the stars do not threaten private persons or the little shepherd, the sky does not know what is small, what is big, totters and prosperity opens up to a fall by its own weight".

ACT IV, SCENE I

Murderer, the four Furies: Inquisition
Alecto, Megaera, Tisiphone

Murderer

Forgive me that I am overwhelmed, Rome: my heart shrinks back and is about to flee. O protection of the High Father, my vow and word of fidelity, and fathers of the holy Curia with your ring,[222] I stand here as defeated: overcome by fear, cowardly, I am drawn, I have given in to myself. A disquieting vibration hits my heart and shocks it, a shameful, cowardly fear took over the invincible walls of my mind and already holds a triumphal journey: look, overcome I get dragged, but even before the battle.

Great aether, who oversees so much everywhere, do you see how slow my hand is to carry out my vows? And do you see how a day refutes what my vacillating mind has thought about for twelve years? Do you doubt, my mind? Do you call for advice that does not offer a solution? Here, you have to pass

---

221   The rise and fall of the constellation of Orion was associated with stormy weather.
222   The Latin *fibulatus* here means 'wearing a ring', since popes, cardinals and bishops wear a ring as a sign of their dignity or faith to the Church.

1420 Hac, hac eundum est. Cernis, has cernis fores?
Haec te beatum referet, aut nullum via.
Iam perge, perge hac. Omen haud quaquam placet,
Ter hoc labantem limine offendi pedem.
Recede rursus. "Haud capit periculum
1425 Angustior mens." Cede prohibenti deo
Ignaue, demens, nisibusque impar tuis,
Pactoque tanto. Cede age, gressum refer,
Haud solus ibis: dedecus comes tibi est,
Pudorque, sorsque aduersa, quaeque te diu
1430 Foedo subegit dura paupertas iugo.
Quid agimus? Haud si tota vis Mauortia,
Mucronibusque saeua destrictis cohors
Vndam minetur hinc et hinc flammam mihi,
Et quicquid vsquam est, telaque in nostrum caput
1435 Vibrata iam nunc impetu caeco ruant,
Premarque solus, spiritumque hunc hosticus
Cruore mersum tabido elidat furor;
Vsquam recedam. Praevius pes hic manet
Locoque fixus haeret; haud illum dei
1440 Totusque retro mundus incumbens agat,
Non si trecenae membra diuellant rotae.
Gaude, Philippe! Dextera o isthaec mea
Quot te trophaeis vna victorem creat?
Inermis hostem, magne rex, fundis tuum
1445 Absensque vincis. Flamina, et vos, o leves
Abite venti, dictaque et voces meas
Magno Philippo cedite, et rerum duci,
Suspendat arma. Praelij stat finis heic,
Belli supremum terminum haec claudit dies.
1450 Quo voluor amens? Vela mens impos tua
Lege, et furoris dirigas clauum tui.
Tun' ora vt illa et frontis augustae decus
Vultusque tantae conscius fraudis feras?
Nec victus ibis? Linguaque et vocis via
1455 Potentiori vincta torpebit metu?
Et inter ipsae facinus horrebunt manus?

1432 destrictis *scripsi*: districtis *A*.

by here. You see, do you see this door? That is the way that will make you bliss-ful, or unworthy. Go now, go here.

There is a sign that I do not like at all: three times I have stumbled my stag-gering foot against this threshold: go back! "A too fearful mind does not dare to take any risks." Devotion to the deity as opposed to you, coward, madman, who cannot handle your big business and appointment. Come on then, yield, return. You will not go alone: disgrace is your companion, as well as shame, adversity and bitter poverty that has long put you under a horrible yoke.

What to do? Even if there is a whole military force and a cruel company with drawn swords would threaten me on the one hand with water, on the other hand with fire and with all kinds of things that exist, if now the weapons hurled to my head would rush to me in blind speed, if I would be cornered by myself and the fury of the enemy would take my breath drenched in dirty blood, even then I am not going to withdraw. The front foot stays here and stays in place as if stuck. The gods and the whole world would not be able to drive him back, even though they did their best, even if three hundred wheels would tear my limbs apart.

Rejoice, Philip. Oh, this right hand of mine, with how many victories does this, and this alone, make you a victor? Great King, although unarmed you strike down your enemy and even absent you overcome. Wind gusts and you, gentle breezes, go and bring the words that I speak to the great Philip, the leader of the world, that he stows away the weapons. Here is the end of the battle, this day definitely puts an end to the war.

Where am I driven, out of control? Weak spirit, take your sails and keep the rudder of your fury straight. You, how can you wear that face and such an elegant, lofty forehead and face, if you are complicit in such a great crime? And will you, emotionally, not go? And will your tongue, the way for your voice, stifle, paralysed by the mightier fear? And will your hands themselves

Sudor trementes imbre pertentans graui
Dissoluit artus. Iunge, iunge et hunc tuis
Batauia titulis: victus accedo tibi.

ALECTO

1460   Cessas Megaera sanguine vndantem sacro
In ora taedam vergere? Et pectus ferum
Acherontis atro seminare toxico?

SICARIVS

Pudet coruscos flammei Solis, pudet
Videre vultus. Desere ingentem poli
1465   Sol magne cursum, desere, aut terras ego
Victus relinquo. Cernitis? Retro ruit;
Trepidusque clarum polluit Titan diem,
Comamque circum nubilo inuoluit suam,
Et ora nostra deserit. Mane, mane,
1470   Cedemus ipsi: quo moves? Tuam tibi
Terram relinquo, Phoebe: nos Pontus feret
Et hoc scelestum saxa collident caput.

INQVISITIO, ALECTO

MEGAERA TISIPHONE.
Trochaei.

INQUISITIO

Noctis ignauae propago pallidae Stygis deae,
Ite, turbidis lacerti squalleant serpentibus,
1475   Et veneni si quid vsquam Colchos extremo sinu
Phasias regno scelestum victa cum mouit pedem
Palluit, vel Pontus audax: quicquid vmbrosae domus
Cerberus latrator ingens ore conceptum fero
Inuias ructans sub auras, magnus Alcidae labos
1480   Gutture horruit trifauci, vique conspexit diem.

1460   Alecto *scripsi*: Al. *MT L*, Au *A*.

tremble under the crime? The gushing sweat penetrates my vibrating limbs and makes them powerless. Add me, Netherlands, add me to your list of honours: overcome with fear, I surrender to you.[223]

Alecto

Do you hesitate, Megaera, to keep the torch that is dripping with holy blood to his face and sprinkle his savage heart with the black poison from the Acheron?[224]

Murderer

I am ashamed to see the beautiful face of the fiery Sun, really. Great Sun, leave your vast sky, leave it, or I will leave the earth by fear. You see, Titan[225] storms back, vibrantly obscures the bright day, wraps his halo around in a cloud, and leaves my sight. Stay, stay, I will go myself: where are you going? I leave your earth, Phoebus Apollo:[226] the Sea will carry me and stones will crush this criminal head.[227]

Inquisition, Alecto, Megaera, Tisiphone

Trochees

Inquisition

Scions of the inactive Night, pale goddesses of the Styx,[228] go on your way, your arms must be scraped with writhing snakes, you have to leave all the poison for which the Colchians on that remote bay, or the daring Pontus, faded when the vanquished Phasian criminal left there;[229] everything that the awe-inspiring barker of the shameful house Cerberus, the great work of Alceus' grandson, with his ferocious beak seizes and bursts into the impassable shadowy realm and for which he shuddered with his threefold mouth—

---

223   His fear, so to speak, causes the siege of the Netherlands over this murderer.
224   The Acheron ('stream of woe') is one of the rivers of the underworld.
225   Titan, the sun god.
226   Phoebus ('the shining') Apollo, the sun god.
227   I.e. the murderer Balthasar Gerards himself.
228   In Greek mythology, the Styx is one of the rivers of hell.
229   A reference to Medea of Colchis (on the Black Sea); the Phasis is a river in Colchis.

Quicquid Inous maritus mente deiectus sua
Herculis iussu nouercae, cum patris furtum pij
Dactylos inter furentes, et Cabirorum choros
Tigridis fraenator Euan vagijsset; quicquid et
1485 Teste furtim noctiluca feruidae stillant equae;
Saeua quicquid è sepulchris saga nocturnis legit;
Aridi bubonis ossa, et exta ieiunae canis,
Et strigis iecur reuulsum, et pure conditum nouo
Faetidum bufonis inguen, et rubetarum cinis,
1490 Inter errores profanos mentis, et faedum scelus,
Et nefas, caedisque amorem, turbidasque lachrymas
Sanguine immistas recenti, languidisque luctibus
Et dolos, caecasque fraudes, aere versentur cauo.
Perfidum caput furentis mergite, et mentis viae
1495 Horrido spument veneno, perque Echidnaeus furor
Intimas serpat medullas, et profunda pectoris.
Densioribus colubri sibilate nexibus.
O mei, mei colubri, sibilo reconditum
Belgiae narrate funus. Instat infelix dies,
1500 Morsque prorumpens superbas tundit herois domos,
Vltimumque intentat ictum. Nescium sortis genus
Gaudia, ah, inter dapesque funus operitur suum.

SCENA ii.
Loisa. Nvtrix.

Quis me solos procul hinc, nutrix,
Vehat in saltus? Antraque nullo
1505 Peruia passu, vel desertas
Rupis latebras, inter querulos
Volucrum luctus? Iuuat obsessum
Lachrymis, nutrix, pascere pectus.
Iuuat ingenti soluere, nutrix,
1510 Fraena dolori. Iuuat ignarae
Soluere, nutrix, vincula mentis.

1500 prorumpens superbas tundit *A*: subrepens beatas pulsat *L*.   1502 ah … operitur *A*: *del. L*.
Tit. SCENA ii *A*: *del. L*.

he saw the day by force;[230] everything for which Ino's husband shuddered, deprived of his senses on the command of Hercules' stepmother, because the hidden child of the pious father, Euan, who controlled the tigers, had come up among the raging fingers and the Cabiri;[231] every poison dripping of the impetuous mares having the Moon as a secret witness; everything that a raging witch collects at night from graves: the bones of the dry night owl, the guts of a hungry bitch and the smashed liver of a night owl, the stinking pubic parts of a toad, seasoned with fresh blood, ashes of toads, together with pagan mindset, horrible wickedness, atrocities, murderousness and violent tears, mixed with fresh blood and relaxing mourning and wiles and blind deception, you must stir all of that in a bronze mixing vessel.

Immerse his faithless head so that he starts to rage, let the paths of his mind foam with horrifying poison and let Echidna's frenzy drip deep into his guts and the depths of his heart. Hiss in denser windings, snakes. Oh, my dear snakes, tell the Netherlands with hissing the unknown death. The unlucky day is imminent, and death that comes to the fore beats the proud house of the hero and threatens the last battle. The family, still unaware of their fate, ah, await under a merry meal death in her ranks.

SCENE II

Louise, Nurse

Louise

Who could bring me, nurse, far from here to remote forests, and to caves that cannot be trodden by foot, or to hidden recesses in the rocks, amid the plaintive lamentations of birds? I would like to surrender, nurse, my depressed heart to tears. I want to give free rein to my big grief. I would like, nurse, to release the bonds of my insecure mind.

---

230   One of the works of Hercules, grandson of Alceus, was to drag the three-headed watchdog of Hades from hell.

231   Ino was the wife of Athamas, King of Thebes; she tried to kill her stepchildren Phrixus and Helle, after which Athamas, maddened by Juno, killed her son Learchus; Euan is another name for Bacchus; the Cabiri were tutelary deities worshipped by the Pelasgians.

Felix quisquis cognita luget;
Late tendit dolor ignotus.
Abit in lachrymas mens caeca suas,
1515   Et congressus hominum dulces
Effugit. O quis
Mediae ereptam murmure turbae
Populos extra sistat et urbes.
O quis donet totos animi
1520   Promere motus, aut ignotas
Cernere curas!

NVTRIX
Alumna, vanis obsequi doloribus,
Mentemque magni masculam cessa viri,
Animumque maestis prouocare lachrymis.
1525   Qualis sonoris acta diu incudibus
Ferri rigentis massa, vel crudus chalybs,
Effossus alto desidis terrae sinu,
Venisque matris, multa quem frustra manus
Fabrûm fatigat, cum lacertorum graues
1530   Surgunt in ictus; ille vi tutus sua
Lacessit altos, et retundit impetus
Viresque cassas; postmodo exili tamen
Domandus igne. Talis herois viri
Mens alta, nullis quae labascit improbae
1535   Sortis ruinis, aut loco cedit suo
Virtute nixa, viribusque; lachrymis
Vanisque cedit faeminarum questibus,
Invictaque unus pectora eneruat dolor
Gemitusque sexus impotentis. "Lachrymae
1540   Luctusque causa quilibet prior sua
Rationis expers, mentis irritatio est,
Obsoniumque lachrymarum; nam sibi
Nimis subinde vanus arridet dolor,
Seseque pascit, ipse dum fomes sibi est."

1514 mens *A*: sponte *L*.   1524 Animumque *A*: Pectusque *L*.   1539–1544 Lachrymae—est *A*:
post corr. del. *L*.   1542 Obsoniumque—sibi *A*: Obsoniumque lachrymarum; dum sibi [Lachry-
maeque causa lachrymarum: dum sibi *b* queis sibi *c*] *L*.   1544 ipse dum fomes sibi *A*: ipse sic
fomes sui *L*.

Lucky is he who knows why he mourns, wide is the range of grief for what is unknown. My blind spirit casts out tears and flees the otherwise pleasant contact with people.

Oh, who could take me away from the noise in the middle of the crowd and put me outside peoples and cities? Oh, who could give me all my moods to speak or see my unknown concerns?

Nurse

Dear girl, stop to surrender to useless sorrows and to excite the powerful mind and soul of the great man with sad tears.

Like a lump of hard iron, long beaten on sounding anvils, or unprocessed steel, mined from the deep shot of the earth that slowly gives it up, and from the veins of the mother ground—the many hands of the craftsmen pound in vain when they get up to give heavy blows with their arms; the steel, safe because of its strength, defies the attacks from the height and the useless forces and rebuts them, but later it can be conquered by a small flame only—such is the high spirit of a heroic man who has not been caused to shake by wicked fate, nor departs from his place, based on his courage and strength; for the tears and unfounded complaints of women, he succumbs: only sorrow, the sighing of the weaker sex, paralyses inexpressible hearts. "Tears and any unreasonable pain that precedes her own reason stimulate his mind and are food for his tears; for useless sorrow often pleases itself too much and nourishes itself by being its own fuel."

LOISA

1545 Somnia nostros terrent visus
Atraque noctis (fallax vtinam)
Plerunque nouae nuncia curae
Sensibus imis ludit imago.
Vidi, nutrix (flebile noctis
1550 Procul omen eat), vidi, nutrix,
Maiora metu.
Rex astrorum luce renata
Tremulos noctis clauserat ignes
Phosphorus, et me domitor curae
1555 Victos somnus strinxerat artus,
Oculosque leui sopor occultè
Vinxerat vmbra.
Vidi trepidum maesta maritum,
Subiti largos distillantem
1560 Sanguinis imbres; vidi attonitos
Ceu vicinae necis adventu
Tendere vultus. Terque ingenti
Gemitu ducto concidit, inque
Pectore nostro late effusis
1565 Proruit vlnis. Vltimaque (inquit)
Munera, coniux, coniux, coniux,
Vltima nobis munera solue;
Trahor immensas retro, coniux,
Noctis ad umbras; at tu vero
1570 Crede sopori.
Sic effatus, procul aetherias
Fluxit in auras, somnusque simul.
Mihi cor gelido salit admonitu
Noctis amarae, curaque somni
1575 Somno, Nutrix, longior ipso est.

          Talis ad undas cum, Scaldi, tuas
          Prope fatali concidit ictu,
          Horrida multo sanguine, Nutrix,

1561 Ceu *scripsi*: Seu *A*.   1568 immensas *A*: *del. L*.   1575 *Post 1575 add. L. signum, indicans*
inseratum Talis ad undas cum Scaldi tuas.   3 Horrida *A*: *del. L*. ‖ Nutrix *A*: nutrix *L*.

Louise

Dreams frighten my gaze and the black vision of the night (if only that were deceitful), often the messenger of new care, plays deep in my senses. With my own eyes, nurse (may the sad nocturnal sign not come true), with my own eyes, nurse, I have seen things that are worse than what people fear. The king of the Phosphorus stars had stored the trembling fires of the night at dawn; the sleep, who subdues care, had gobbled me to the frightened party, and a slumber had covered my eyes in secret with a light shadow. Sad, I suddenly saw my husband shivering with drizzle of blood; and I have seen his bewildered face straining like the arrival of a near death. After three intense sighs, he died and on my lap he collapsed into my wide arms. "The last tribute", he said, "my wife, my wife, my wife, pay me the last tribute: I am being pulled away, my wife, into the immense shadow of the night; but you, believe in a true dream".

After having said this, he dissolved far away in the ethereal skies, and at the same time sleep did dissolve. My heart pounded through the chilly admonition of the bitter night: nurse, sorrow produced by sleep, lasts longer than sleep itself.

When he thus, Scheldt river, collapsed by a deadly blow at your water, he raised his head, shuddering by much blood, nurse. But why, gods, is this con-

Sustulit ora.

5   Quid tamen haec nunc iterum, Divi,
Cura recursat?
Ite sinistrae nubila mentis.
Felix modicos quisquis sentit
Pectore motus! Felix placidi
10 Rector aratri, felix teneri
Dux armenti. Viridi tutus
Ille sub umbra tepidos halat
Pectore somnos: lassior illic
Videt aequa suae somnia vitae.
15 Et modo dulces amittit oves,
Modo surreptam pallet avenam.
Haec domus illi,
Totaque res est.
"Felix quisquis tenuis tranat
20 Tempora vitae!
Felix quisquis modico sortem
Fallit agello!
Felix quisquis mediae fallit
Agmine turbae!
25 Numeroque latet tutus in ipso."

Nvtrix
Fidem sopori nescia asscribis tuo,
Noctisque fucum, et aemulos veri dolos
Alumna trepidas: somnij fallax parens
Spes est metusque, sensibus deme hos tuis,
1580 Excedet illud. Nauita exhorret fretum,
Venator imbrem: nocte vtrumque conditus
Vterque cernit, luce non credit tamen;
Dolumque noctis pura traducit dies.
Tibi mariti casta legitimi fides
1585 Pererrat animum, coniugisque copulae
Amor suauem pectoris sedem tenet,
Semperque metuit, noxque succedens tuas

---

10 teneri *A*: parvi *L*.   1576 Nutrix *scripsi*: Nu *MT L*, Au *A*.   1580 illud *MT L*: illu *A*.

cern now coming back again? Go away, clouds, from around my unhappy mind. Fortunate, everyone who knows only moderate emotions! Fortunate the calm ploughman, fortunate the shepherd who herds small cattle. In the shade under the green lover he breathes carefree and clothes his body in a warm sleep. When he is tired there, he sees dreams that are a reflection of his life. And now he loses beloved sheep, then again he is afraid that his shepherd's flute is taken away. This is his place of residence, this is his whole possession.

"Fortunate, everyone who spends the day as an insignificant man! Happy anyone who deceives fate with a small field! Fortunate, anyone who deceives it by standing in the middle of the crowd! He lives safely just because he hides in the crowd."

Nurse

You believe your dream in your ignorance, you tremble, my child, for deceit that appears at night and for tricks that are rivals of the truth. Hope and fear are the deceitful parents of the dream: take them out of your senses, and the dream will disappear. The sailor shudders before the flood, the hunter before the pouring rain: at night they both see when they are in bed, these two things, but during the day they do not believe them. The clear day keeps the deceptive thoughts that have arisen at night. You recollect the selfless fidelity to your lawful husband, love for the bond of marriage takes hold of your dear heart and is always afraid. The following nocturnal darkness, with its deceit, does not give

Et vmbra curas fraudibus versat suis,
Cum victa lenis membra decepit sopor,
1590   Sensusque somno dulce liquefacti iacent.

LOISA
Quis nouus ille, vel quibus ille,
Nutrix, Nutrix, vectus ab oris
Hospes nostram missus in aulam est?
Haud placet oris suspecta fides.
1595   Nos domus intro, pignusque vocant.

SCENA. III.

SICARIVS. AVRIACVS.
ARMIGER. CHORVS SATELLITVM.

Sic, sic eundum est; alterum chlamys latus,
Sclopumque velat, alterum fraudi patet
Fidemque facto praestat, et dolos tegit
Nihil tegendo; flammeis cor glandibus
1600   Et igne totas pectoris rumpam vias,
Sedesque vitae. Sensimus cassam fidem
Ferri scelesti: nuper effluxit sinu
Nisusque pene sica frustrata est meos.
Vtinam reuulsis viscerum radicibus
1605   Liceat cadentis pectus etiamnum tremens,
Suisque vulsa è sedibus praecordia
Monstrare viuo, cernat vt partem sui,
Mortemque viuus discat infelix suam,
Pereatque saepe: vel calentes sanguine
1610   Tractare venas, extaue obscenae cani
Lanianda ferro soluere, aut volucribus
Escam profanis; cura nunc duplex premit,
Necem tyranno molior, vitam mihi,
Perque alta praeceps vrbis erumpam vada,

1588 *add. et postea del.* L: Cum pictus aer flammeis sororibus | Phoebes relucet, aureaeque fulgu-
rant | Coelo choreaeque.   1589 Cum *A:* Tunc *L.*   *Tit.* SCENA. III. *A: del. L.*

your worries a rest, when the soft sleep has secretly taken possession of your overwhelmed limbs, and your senses, relaxed through sleep, lay down softly.

Louise

Who is this newcomer, or rather: from which region came that guest who has been sent to our court, nurse? I don't like his suspicious face. The household and our child, the pledge of our love, call us inside.

SCENE III

Murderer, Orange, soldier, Chorus of servants

Thus, thus I must go: one side with the pistol is covered by a cloak, the other is open for deceit, confers confidence in the deed and covers the wiles by covering nothing: I will crush his heart with flaming bullets and completely destroy the ways of his chest, the seat of life, with fire. I have learned not to put too much trust in the criminal metal; the dagger recently fell out of my pocket and almost thwarted my efforts. Ah, if only I could root out his bowels, and while he fell, tear his heart still rumbling and his lungs off their place and show them to him while he is still alive, that he sees part of himself and in deep misery learns of his death while he is still living and dies often thereafter: or if only I could take his blood-warm veins in my hand or cut his entrails with metal to tear them by a hideous bitch or food for horrible birds. Now I suffer from a double concern: I plan death for that tyrant and life for myself, I will flee head-on through the deep grass of the city and cross the water with a brave heart.

1615 Liquidamque forti corde transmittam viam.
      Vtinam ter ille, morte funestâ, horridâ,
      Nouaque semper, ictibusque millibus
      Fundendus esset. Vna mors poenae parum est,
      Nec digna nobis. O dies, o o dies,
1620 O vna votis metaque et finis meis;
      Prompti subimus. Debitum sacrum tibi
      Votumque dudum, magne, Belgarum caput
      Mactamus Alba. Mente funestam iuuat
      Versare caedem: bis iuuat, bis sanguine
1625 Gaudere eodem: parua moriendi mora est;
      Diu cogitando longior fiet tamen.
      Crudelitatis tempus extendam meae,
      Maiusque reddam. Pectore ingenti exigam
      Scelus futurum. Sic per vrgentem ferar
1630 Populi coronam; sic satellitij minas,
      Vultusque fallam; colla sic labens sua
      Et palpitantes morte demittet manus;
      Sic triste multa caede succumbet latus;
      Sic imminente victus horrescet nece,
1635 Toruusque totas pallor inuadet genas.
      Adhuc moramur? Trahimur, en pectus salit,
      Notamque ceptis tesseram dedit meis.
      Vocamur. Euge: cura Diuorum sumus
      Totumque votis annuit caelum meis.
1640 En, ipse rara cinctus ingentem manu
      Aulam relinquit, atriumque turbido
      Inuadit ore, feruidisque gressibus,
      Et sponte letho pronus occurrit suo.

      AVRIACVS
      Dies diei cedit, atque annum nouus
1645 Reducit annus, vltimusque saeculi
      Finis, futuri primus est aeui gradus,
      Voratque terram pontus immenso sinu,
      Ingens Batauae continentis helluo.
      At terra pontum rursus in sese trahit,
1650 Vlcisciturque, et destinatas fluminum

1619 o o *scripsi*: O O *A, del. L.*

Ah, if only he could be killed three times with a deadly, chilling and every time new death and with a thousand beats. One death is too little a punishment and in my opinion unworthy. O day, oh, o only limit and end for my vows, I am willing to go. Great Alva,[232] I slaughter the sacrifice that you owe and is longed for by you: the head of the Netherlands. It pleases me to think over the deadly murder: it pleases twice to be happy about the same blood twice. The time of his death will be short, but by thinking about it for a long time it will take longer.

I will stretch and extend the time of my cruelty. I will think about the future crime with heart and soul. Thus, I will rave through the intrusive circle of the people, thus, I will lead the threats and the sight of the bodyguard. Thus, falling, he will lower his neck and lower his death-convulsing hands. Thus, his grief-like body will collapse by many deadly shots, thus, he will be overwhelmed by fear of the threatening death shuddering, and an awkward pallor will completely occupy his cheeks.

Do I still hesitate? I am pulled forward, look, my heart pounds and has given the well-known legitimacy to my ventures. I am being called. Well done! The gods are concerned about me, the whole heaven agrees with my vow. Look, he leaves the big court, surrounded by a small escort, goes into the courtyard with his face confused and runs quickly and of his own accord to his death.

Orange

One day makes way for the other, a new year dissolves the old and the end of a generation is the first step of a new era. The sea, the great devourer of the Dutch mainland, swallows up the land in its immense bosom. But the country, in its turn, sucks the sea again, avenges itself, empties the roads of the rivers destined for the grey father, and so takes possession of the drink

---

232   On the Duke of Alva, who was governor of the Netherlands and was felt to conduct a reign of terror, see above, nn. 145 and 196.

Cano parenti praeuia exhaurit vias,
Praeoccupatque caeruli potum senis.
Sic cuncta sese lege nascendi premunt,
Pereuntque rursus vt resurgant denuo,

1655 Mutatque tempus cuncta, nil perdit tamen,
Semperque formas interim versat nouas
Veteresque soluit, cunctaque vt pereant simul
Simul reseruat, cum tot annorum graui
Pressus ruina, rursus in sese labans

1660 Dehiscet orbis, et superba machina
Magni quae in vlnis fixa requiescit poli,
Reuulsa priscum diruetur in chaos,
Eritque rursum mundus ille, quod fuit
Cum nullus esset. Interim constans tamen

1665 Natura solitas sedula retexit vias
Expers quietis, ocijque nescia,
Pensoque iussas admouet semper manus,
Suetumque fusum voluit. Has inter vices
Quotacunque rerum, totiusque pars, Homo

1670 Excelsa mente vota percurrit sua,
Morique trepidat, cuncta cum cernat tamen,
Sortemque solus discit, et nescit suam.
Idemque vitae sanguinisque prodigus,
Crudusque lethi machinator est sui.

1675 Cumque imminentis tanta sit fati via,
Aditusque mille, mille pereundi modi,
Audaxque Pontus, terraque in nos et ferus
Coniuret aether, flammaque et spumans aqua;
Mors arte creuit, ingenique munera

1680 In nos, et ipsas vertimus fati manus.
Quodcunque durus mille sub fornacibus
Fuliginosis, aeris exercet faber,
Neci paratur. Mille syluarum comae
Lethoque nostro vasta decrescunt iuga.

1685 Illinc tot arma, telaque magno graues
Emuntur enses: sternere haud gratis licet;
Preciosa mors est, cumque tot restent ferae,

1656 interim *A*: artifex *L*.   1659 labans *A*: cadens *L*.   1682 exercet *scripsi*: excercet *A*.

of the deep blue old man. Thus all things succeed each other through the law of birth and death, to rise again. Time changes everything, but does not erase anything. In the meantime he thinks up new forms and dissolves the old ones and so that everything may go together, he keeps it together, when the world, pressed by the heavy fall of the years, will collapse again and when the proud structure that rests motionless in the arms of the great heavens, will tear open and dissolve in his old chaos and the cosmos will be what it was when there was no cosmos. But in the meantime Nature is constantly rescuing the ordinary ways, restless and steady and, as ordered, always brings her hands to work and turns the ordinary spool.

Between these changes, man, only a small part of the world and of the whole, with his lofty mind contemplates what he wishes, and is afraid to die, but because he sees everything, he is the only one who knows his fate and does not know it. Man also generously treats his own life and blood lavishly and violently is the cause of his own death. Although the orbit of imminent fate is so broad and there are a thousand accesses, a thousand ways to die, and although the dangerous sea, the earth, the cruel ether, the fire and the foaming water conspire against us, by human invention there are still ways to die added: we turn the gifts of the mind, and even the hands of fate against us. All the bronze that a rugged smith works under in thousands of smoky stoves is destined for killing: a thousand crowns of forests and large hills are cut down for our death. That is why many weapons for defence and assault and heavy swords are bought for a lot of money: one cannot kill for free. Death is expensive, and although there

Tot monstraque, hominem fundit infelix homo,
Cedemque iactat, seque delegit neci,
1690   Cum multa posset, placuit hoc uno sibi,
"Factumque longa temporis propagine,
Nobis triumphus, quod fuit quondam scelus."
Hac lege virtus effera armorum parens
Sese tuetur; talis ingentis soli
1695   Fatalis ille subiugator et ducum
Altum Quirinus extulit terris caput,
Persenque Hydaspen, Bactraque, et saevum Schyten
Rupemque falsi pendulam Promethei
Prouectus olim, Caspiumque vltra mare,
1700   Et fabulosis asperas Tirynthio
Bacchoque rupes, Hesperumque limitem,
Et parciorem terruit ferro diem.
Hac lege fortis quilibet semper fuit,
Vt saevus esset. Hactenus tenui tamen
1705   Grassata mors est saeua per terras via,
Per nos adaucta est; liberos morti sinus,
Et vela tota pandimus Belgae manu.
Prius irreperto, totque retro saeculis
Inusitato teximus lethum modo,
1710   Dum fulminantis sulphure et flamma Dei
Imitamur ignes; pressus ingenti vapor
Caelum ruina terret, elisa globo
Mundus cavernas laxat, atque ingens humus
Circum pauoris conscia immensi tremit,
1715   Populosque late verrit, et totum simul
Inuadit agmen. Parua quin etiam loquor;
Necantur vrbes, saxaque et moles deûm:
Nocetur orbi, totque nostra haec maenia
Evertit aetas, prisca quot fudit viros.

SICARIVS
1720   Pudet fateri, pudet, at intremui tamen,
Nec lingua sequitur. Deseror rursus Dei,
Et me reliqui. Genua trepidanti labant,

1697 Persenque *scripsi*: Persesque *A*.   1720 Sicarius *scripsi*: Sic. *MT*, Loi. *A*.

are many wild animals and many monsters, unhappy mankind kills his fellow man and sows death and destruction; he has chosen himself to kill. Although he was capable of much, he pleased himself only by this and "in the long succession of time what was once a crime has become victory to us".

According to this law, hubris, barbaric mother of war, protects herself. In this way, the people of the Quirites,[233] destined by destiny to subjugate a large area and leaders, stuck their head high above the lands and did pass the Persians, the Hydaspes, Bactria, the fearsome Scythe and the hanging rock of the impostor Prometheus and sailed beyond the Caspian sea and the rough rocks at the mythical Tirynthian[234] and Bacchus, the western border,[235] and he frightened with his sword the places where the daylight is scarcer. To this law everyone was always brave, to be cruel.

Until now, violent death has crossed the earth along a narrow road; it has been widened by us. We Dutch with all our might freely hoist the sails for death. We produce death in a manner not previously invented and for many centuries unusual, because we simulate the lightning of the deity with sulphur and fire: the compressed glow makes the heavens afraid with its great destruction. When a bullet is shot, the world gets holes and a large piece of ground vibrates all around, because it has an immeasurable fear; the bullets wipe away people everywhere and storm at a whole division at once. And then I am talking about trifles. Whole cities are killed, rocks and giants of gods. The world suffers damage: our time now destroys as many cities as the earlier times killed men.

Murderer
I am ashamed to admit it, really, but still I fear and my tongue fails to speak. Again I do not control myself, gods, and am outside of myself. I shake, my knees

---

233   I.e. the Roman people, after Quirinus, the name of the deified Romulus.
234   I.e. Hercules.
235   The Hydaspes was a river in India (now the Jhelum river); Bactria was a region in central Asia; Scythia was a region also in central Eurasia; Prometheus having stolen the fire from the gods and having given it to mankind was bound to a rock in the Caucasus; the Caspian Sea also is in the Caucasus; the Tirynthian refers to Hercules who was raised in the city of Tiryns (in Argolis), here a metonym for the Pillars of Hercules, i.e. the Strait of Gibraltar, the west; Bacchus travelled to the east.

Quotiesque gressum protuli, retro feror.
Meliora volue, dicta modo constent tua,
1725 Vultumque finge; tempus en ipsum iubet,
Locusque cunctas facilis excludit moras.
Agedum incipe, agedum. Longa nos tandem dies,
Magnanime princeps (rursus in medio sonus
Defecit ore). Longa nos tandem dies,
1730 Magnanime princeps, patriam versus trahit:
At nunc fauoris obsides liceat tui
Mecum tabellas. Cecidit, en pronus labat.
Properemus, instat turba, nec reliquum sinit
Satellitum vis: pedibus hoc restat meis.

AVRIACVS
1735 O magne rerum genitor, en praeceps fluo,
Fluo, fluo, fluo, nec vlterius sinit
Mors ire voci. O maxime memento pater
Populi, meique.

ARMIGER
                    Pergite, o comitum manus,
Pergite, ah, ah, pergite, ah, ah, pergite: en celer effluit,
1740 Pergite ah furis scelesta persequi vestigia,
Ille postica cruentum saeuus emisit pedem,
Nos redundans sanguine atro triste fulcimus latus.

CHORVS SATELLITVM
Properemus: hac pars urgeat, pars hac ruat,
Pars tendat illhac, pars ad illa, pars ad haec,
1745 At pars vtroque, parsque iuratos duces
Proceresque sistat, parsque ne lateat dolus
Circundet vrbem, parsque ne pateat via
Vsquam scelesto; rupta, deserta, aspera
Latebras specusque semitasque et inuium,
1750 Scrutetur omne, ne quid occultum tegat,
Aut per prementes diffluat victor manus.

1738 Armiger *scripsi*: Am. *A*.

knock and every time I have cleared a hurdle, I retire. Think about what is better: let your words stand up now, put on your best mask of inscrutability. Look, the moment itself asks for it and the favourable occasion excludes any postponement. Come on then, start, come on.—

Gradually I begin after such a long time, generous monarch (again my voice stifles me in the throat), gradually I start after such a long time, generous prince, to desire my fatherland: would you now give me a letter of recommendation?—

He has fallen, see, he tumbles forward. I have to hurry, the crowd insists. The violence of the sentries leaves nothing else: this remains for my feet.

Orange
O great creator of the world, I fall, I fall down, and death does not allow my voice to speak any more. O highest father, please be gracious to my people and to me.

Soldier
Go after him, guards, quickly, oh, go on: look, he escapes quickly. Go on, oh, follow the criminal traces of that villain. The wicked man has gone through the back door with his bloody foot, I support the unhappy body, dripping with dark blood.

Chorus of guards
Quickly, come on: let part of us run this way, another part that way. Let part of us go another way: partly there, partly here, but at least on both sides a part: a part must stop the leaders of the conspiracy and instigators, part should surround the city to prevent the conspiracy from remaining hidden, part to prevent the criminal from finding an escape route. Ruins, deserted and rugged places, shelters, caves, paths, the impassable: search everything, so that no shelter will hide him or that he as a victor will slip through our hands in the pursuit.

CHORVS.

Hactenus magni domitor tyranni,
Hactenus vasti dominus profundi
Nerei rector Batavus, frementem
1755   Subdidit undam.
Ille vesanos Aquilonis imbres
Inter, et saeuas Boreae ruinas
Spumeum ridet mare, perque Iberum
Fertur et duras pariter procellas
1760   Victor amborum; per vtramque fati
Ille contemptor rate tendit Arcton;
Patria angusta est nimis, impotenti
Sole torrentem populatur Indum
Publicus mundi pauor: ite reges,
1765   Ille binarum dominus viarum est,
Caeruli fluctus equitator, ille
Turgidas inter nebulas, ferumque
Nascitur Austrum.
Vnda si rursus trepidumque castae
1770   Saeculum Pyrrhae redeat, gravesque
Fluminum lapsus, celeresque fontes
Iupiter laxet ferus, et furentes
Soluat in imbres;
Tutus horrendas maris inter algas,
1775   Inter et Protei pecus, horridasque
Eminens Phocas, et auara Cete,
Inter et blandas Thetidis sorores
Nabit optatas Batauus per vndas
Aemulus Glauci, patrijque fiet
1780   Incola ponti.
Patria huic tota est humus, est et aequor.
Patria huic nusquam est, et vbique, magni
Inquies mundi peragrator ille
Terminos rerum speculatur omnes,
1785   Cunctaque audendo subigit; periclo
Altior omni

1754 frementem *A*: superbam *L*.

Chorus of indigenous Hollanders

Up to now, the conqueror of the great tyrant, up to now, the lord of the immeasurable, deep sea, the driver of Nereus,[236] the Hollander, has controlled the roaring waves.

In the midst of the raging rains of Aquilo and the ferocious destruction of Boreas,[237] he laughs at the foaming sea and rages through the Spaniards and equally through hard storms, victorious of both. He who despises fate goes with his ship to both Bears. His homeland is too narrow and he plunders India,[238] blisteringly hot by the scorching sun, he, the general fear of the world. Make way, kings, he is the lord of two ways, rider on the dark blue sea, he is born between swollen mists and the ferocious Auster.[239] If the sea were to return again and the troubled times of the chaste Pyrrha[240] and the violent outburst of currents, and if Jupiter[241] would relentlessly release the fast-flowing springs and let its raging rain showers go, the Hollander will be safe in the midst of rough seaweed and elevated above Proteus' cattle,[242] the fearsome seals, amid the greedy sharks and the sweet sisters of Thetis[243] by the waves to which he has longed to swim like Glaucus,[244] and become a resident of his father's sea.

His homeland is all the land and even the sea. His homeland is nowhere and everywhere. Restlessly roaming the great world, he explores all ends of the earth and submits them by daring everything. He is above every danger. He

---

236   A sea god, a metonym for the sea itself.

237   Aquilo is the rough north wind; Boreas the north-west wind, often equated with the Aquilo.

238   I.e. India, and the Western and Eastern Indies.

239   I.e. the south wind.

240   For Deucalion and Pyrrha, being left as the only humans on earth after the flood, see Ov. *Met.* I, 313–347.

241   Here Jupiter as the weather god.

242   Proteus' cattle, the animals of the sea god Proteus—a poetic description of sea animals.

243   The sisters of the sea goddess Tethys are the Nereids, fifty beautiful daughters of the sea god Nereus.

244   In Greek mythology Glaucus was an old sea god with the gift of prediction; just like Proteus he could change himself into all kinds of forms.

Vesperumque atrum premit, et superbi
Impetus regis, spoliumque, opesque
Illius praesens rapit, et beatas
1790   Transvehit merces, medioque in hoste
Tutus ab illo est.
Pleiadum laetae praeeunt choreae,
Velaque aspectant, facilesque cursum
Dirigunt stellae, nimiumque mollem,
1795   Nec parem magnis animo Batauis
Omnis astrorum chorus aureorum
Ridet Iberum
Peruigil noctu; quotiesque rursum
Luce demissis subeunt tenebris;
1800   Praelia et pulsas referunt carinas,
Qualis immenso redeuns triumpho
Victor ingenti gelidum cruore
Strauerit Worstus mare, qualis ante
Viderit flexos iterum Penates
1805   Ire Lugdunum Patareia, quales
Aureae blandae volucres Diones
Mobiles olim tulerint tabellas
Consciae rerum, faciles ministrae,
Quas suo doctae precium Camaenae
1810   Mollium Dousae genitrix amorum
Miserat olim.
Totus arridet polus, et beati
Adnuunt Diui, fremituque magnus
Dissilit aether.
1815   Sed quid tumultu maenia ingenti tremunt,
Gemituque tota lachrymisque vrbs intonat?
Magnum minatur mutus et tacitus pauor,
Animumque terret cognitus nondum dolor.

1809 Camaenae *scripsi*: camaenae *A.*

oppresses the dark Occident and the attacks of the proud King,[245] drags his booty and riches quickly, transports merchandise that brings prosperity, and in the midst of the enemy he is safe for him.

Cheerful the Pleiades[246] in a circle walk and see the sails. The stars skilfully target the course of the Hollander and the whole reign of golden stars laughs at the Spaniard, too weak and not matching the great Hollanders in courage; at night they watch, but whenever they go back to daylight when the darkness is gone, they tell of fighting and expelling ships: how Worst,[247] triumphantly returning after a great victory, has covered the cold sea with a huge pool of blood, how in former times the Patareian goddess saw her restored house go to Leiden,[248] how the sweet birds of the golden Dione, aware of the situation and therefore willing attendants, once carried quick notes, which the lady of gentle love had previously sent to her Dousa as a prize for his learned Muse.[249] The whole heaven is gracious, and the blissful gods nod favourably, the firmament splintering in cheering.

But what do the walls vibrate with great noise and is the whole city sounding with groans and lamentations? Threateningly, a silent and noiseless fear is pervading everything, a grief of which I do not know anything scares me.

---

245   Occident here indicates Spain, its king is Philip II.

246   The Pleiades are the seven daughters of Atlas, chased by the hunter Orion and changed into doves by Zeus, and appearing as a constellation in the sky.

247   Ewoud Pietersz. Worst († 1573), a Zeelandic admiral.

248   A reference to the institution of the Leiden Academy; the Patareian goddess is the Muse, daughter of Apollo, named after Patara, a town in Lycia, which housed an oracle of Apollo.

249   These lines point at the doves (the birds of Dione) that were used during the siege of Leiden (1574–1575) to maintain contact between the besieged people in Leiden and the Sea beggars who were coming to rescue them. This was done by Janus Dousa, who played an important role at the siege and relief of Leiden; he was also a neo-Latin poet, hence the letters could be a 'prize for his learned Muse', his poetry.

ACTVS. v.

Loisa. Nvtrix.

Fortes tyranni, et quisquis excelsa procul
1820 Euectus arce, sortis optatae sedes;
Securus esto: tristia et fraudem, et dolum, et
Felicitati proximum quicquid mali est
Nusquam timeto: restat ulterius nihil;
Fortuna vires fregit in nobis suas,
1825 Nil servat alijs: perdidi patrem semel,
At bis maritum; vidit eadem nos dies
Viduas et orbas; vidua nunc rursus feror,
Si possem et orba. Relliquum est ipsi nihil
Sorti, vel in me. Quid meos cohibes sinus?
1830 Desiste nutrix. Quid meos luctus vetas?
Desiste nutrix. Quid meas premis manus?
Desiste nutrix. Quantus est, quantus dolor
Qui incipere nescit! Quid, quibusue lachrymis,
Quo, aut vnde primam luctibus sternam viam?
1835 Ibo, ibo nutrix, desine: ibo ibo, et ferar,
Vt si quid animae restet infelix sciam,
Amplectar artus, si quid, o si quid super
Experiar, ibo. Desine ah, nutrix, eo.

Nvtrix
"Alumna, primum pectoris motum rege,
1840 Violentus ille est: surdus est primus dolor,
Caecusque et amens, ipse nec cedit sibi
Mox longiori cedet aetati tamen."
Quid ah dolores tempori seruas tuos
Mox eluendos? Ipsa quin aetas tibi es?
1845 Quin ipsa longi temporis vicem subis
Et munus aeui, teque iam reddis tibi?

1837 quid, o *A*: quid est *L*.

ACT V

Louise, Nurse

Strong tyrants and everyone who has risen up on the lofty fortress of desired fate, do not worry. Do not be afraid of suffering, deceit and ruse at all, all the misery that is so close to happiness: nothing remains. Fortune has broken her powers on me, she does not save anything for others. I once lost a father, but twice a husband; the same day saw me a widow and an orphan.[250] Now I live again as a widow, and if it could be also as an orphan. Fate itself has nothing left over, not even to use against me. Why do you cling to my bosom? Nurse, stop. Why do you forbid me my grief? Nurse, stop. Why are you holding my hands? Nurse, stop. How big, how horrible is a grief that does not know how to start! To what or with what tears, where or from where should I first go through my mourning?

I'll go, I will go, nurse, stop! I'll go, I will go, and soon, to find out, unhappy me, if there is any life-spirit left in him. I will embrace his body to experience if anything, oh, if there is anything left. I'll go there, nurse, stop, ah, I'm going.

Nurse
"Dear child, control that first impulse of your heart; it is intense. Initially, grief is deaf, blind and out of sight and does not give way to itself, but soon it will step aside at the longer duration." Ah, why do you continue to cherish your sorrows while they will soon be washed away by time? Why don't you do for yourself what time will do for you? Why do you not take on the task of the long time yourself and do you not give yourself the gift that time will give you[251] and don't you come to yourself right now?

---

250   I.e. St Bartholomew's Day massacre, when she lost her father De Coligny and her husband
        De Téligny. See above, nn. 182 and 207–210.
251   I.e. oblivion.

LOISA

Desiste, nutrix. Cuncta nunc subeunt mala,
Veteresque curas suscitat recens dolor,
Desiste, nutrix; noster exemplo caret
1850   Paremque nescit, nescit aequalem dolor.
Tot dicta, nutrix, cassa tot solatia
Vocesque tolle. Desine, aut opem feras.
Reddas parentem, ne meum gemam virum,
Reddas maritum, ne meum gemam patrem.
1855   Quid prisca refero? Sufficit nunc vt gemam
Quod nunc peractum est. Languor hoc, nutrix, mihi
Hoc illa mentis visa spondebant meae.
Nunc nempe credor. Sera quam fides mihi est?
Properate famuli; cernite, an quicquam spei
1860   Nobis relictum est. Cernite, an vitae leuis
Modo restat aura. Lapsa relliquias legam
Vitae fugacis, oreque os illud meo
Gelidasque tepidi pectoris latebras premam.
Permitte tantum. Pallidis sed en genis
1865   Germana maestos illius gressus refert.
Mens nosse casus ardet et refugit suos.
Agnosco vultus. Loquitur infelix dolor,
Ille, ille sortis mutus est index meae.
Deficio nutrix, corpus infelix humi
1870   Lapsum, dehiscit, mensque sub tenebris latet
Vtinam aeuiternis. Caeca nox oritur mihi.
Sequimur marite.

NVTRIX

                    Concidit. Dolor sibi
Incumbit ipsi. Perdidit vires suas
Mens cum marito. Alumna, quid praeceps abis?
1875   Alumna, mentem recipe et extollas tuam.

CHORVS

Quid maesta luctu deficis, princeps, tuo?
Lugere nostrum est: munus haud recte meum
Praeoccupasti, munus inuadis meum.

1870–1871 tenebris … aeuiternis *A: del.* … perenni *L.*

Louise

Nurse, stop. All misery now comes to me and the new sorrow arouses worry
from the past. Nurse, stop; my sorrow is unprecedented and does not know its
equal, knows nothing even equivalent. Nurse, stop all those useless words of
comfort and advice. Stop or bring help. Give me back my father, so that I do not
have to sigh about my husband, or give me back my husband, so that I do not
have to sigh about my father. Why should I need to pick up the old sorrow? Now
I have enough to sigh about what has happened now. This was predicted, nurse,
by those visions in my sleep. Now I am really believed. How late did people start
to believe me? Quickly, servants, go and see if there is still some hope for me.
Go and see if there is still a bit of life air in him? If I have succumbed, I will
collect the remains of his fleeting life and kiss with my mouth that mouth and
the already cold cavities of the still warm chest. Give me that at least. But look,
his sister[252] comes sadly back with sad cheeks. My spirit desires to know its
destiny and flees it at the same time. I understand her expression. The painful
suffering speaks for itself; that indicates my fate without words. I die, nurse,
my unfortunate body, fallen to the ground, collapses and opens to my soul, my
mind is hidden in the darkness, if it only were eternal. A dark night rises in me.
I'm following you, my husband.

Nurse

She has fainted. Her smart intensifies itself. Her spirit lost its strength when she
lost her husband. Dear child, why do you faint? Dear child, come back to your
senses and do not let your head down.

Chorus

Why do you collapse, Princess, through your grief? It just fits us to mourn:
you have completely wrongly taken my task on you, you do what I have to do.

---

252   William's sister Catharina Schwarzburg-Nassau-Dillenburg (1543–1624) was at the court in
       Delft at the time of the assassination.

Tibi maritus occidit; princeps mihi;
1880　Plebeius iste luctus est, virum gemis
Commune nomen, nomen hoc vulgo patet.
Quaecunque noctem pura dispellit dies,
Flauamque Solis explicat magni comam,
Virum maritae demit, et natae patrem:
1885　Viduus, vel orbus, quisquis est, sortem gemit;
At inter omnes, occidit princeps mihi.
Quod nomen illi luctui inueniet dolor!
Quis luctus ah est ille qui dici nequit?
　　Ah ah ah ah.
1890　"O quam vario Turbine pessum
Gloria rerum sublimis abit?
Nempe insidiae, frausque, dolique
Sunt excelsae nomina sortis:
Lare priuati nequit exiguo
1895　Fortuna parens varium tuto
Voluere fusum.
Nimium magnae domui semper
Proxima, nulla est."
Hei mihi quantos aethere vectus
1900　Circum iugales Phoebus auratos agens
Casus tuetur, quotque scelerum nomina,
Dolosque caelo spectat, et fraudes suo,
Seram priusquam condat occumbens facem!
At nos profundas credimus solem tamen
1905　Ferri sub vndas: ille nostris fraudibus
Contaminatum diluit Ponto caput,
Vultusque terris subripit lubens suos.
Hinc ille puras fluctibus mergens comas
Rubore circum fulgurat tinctus nouo:
1910　Pudor ille nostri est; cernite aspectum Dei,
Pudibundus ille semper è terris abit.

1890 O *A*: Heu *L*. ‖ Turbine *A*: turbine *L*.

For you your husband died, for me my sovereign. Your grief suits someone from the people, you sigh for a man, a common term, a term that belongs to ordinary people. Every clear day that drives away the night and the blonde hair unfolds from the great sun, deprives a wife of her husband and a daughter of her father: everyone who has lost a partner or a parent sighs for his fate. But that applies to everyone. For me a monarch died. What words can my sadness find for that mourning? What kind of mourning, ah, is that unspeakable? Ah, ah, ah, ah.

"Oh, with what a capricious whirl the lofty fame of the world collapses into the deep? Truly, ambushes, deceit and wiles are the names of exalted fate; mother Fortune cannot turn the mobile spool into the small, safe house of a simple man. She does not exist here, because she is always very close to the house of a great one."

Woe to me; when Phoebus rides through the sky on his wagon decorated with gold, how many vicissitudes will he face and how much that is called a crime, and how many tricks and layers will he see from his heaven, before he leaves his torch in storage? But we believe that the sun plunges itself into the deep waves: he rinses his head in the sea that is deceived with our deceit and is happy to remove his face from the earth. When he then dips his clean hair into the waves, he blushes around with a red colour: that is shame about us. Notice the sight of God: he always leaves the earth full of shame.

LIBERTAS SAUCIA.

Tellus et aequor, languidique fluminum
Cursus et amnes, quique per Batauos, pater,
Trepidante multus, Rhene, prorumpis vado,
1915   Vndas ministra. Tuque qui terras tegis,
Magnoque maestus incubas aer solo;
Pluuijs perennes tristibus laxa sinus:
Lachrymis egemus. Lachrymas caelum tuas
Adiunge nostris. Vndique in nubes eas,
1920   Incumbe terris. Ipsa quin etiam tua
Duplicanda nox est: occidunt soles duo,
Tuus meusque: longa nox terras premat,
Vicesque solitas perdat infelix dies,
Facinusque condat. Hactenus malum tamen
1925   Lugere potuit quisquis aspexit suum,
Intraque luctus constitit metas dolor.
     Ah ah ah ah.
Maiora gemimus: nomen excessit dolor
Lachrymasque nostras, fletus haud noster sat est,
1930   Lugendus ipso maior est luctu dolor;
Minorque merito. Digna quis luctu queat
Lachrymare tanto? Quisue morientem queat?
Moriuntur omnes: funere illius iacent
Quoscunque tangit. Funus est quisquis videt,
1935   Et funus vrbs est, publicum funus iacet.
     Ah ah ah ah.
Spectate ciues: quisquis haud didicit mori
Hoc teste discat. Illa maiestas viri
Dictumque Marti pectus, atque horror soli
1940   Ingens Iberi, cuius occursum ferae
Tremuere gentes, cuius inuictam manum
Grudij feroces, concidit iacet, iacet.
Adeste ciues: lachrymas iuro meas,
Et illud atra caede transmissum latus;
1945   Inuictus ille est, saeua nec mors id negat,
Ipsumque lethum fraude superandum, docet

1926 dolor *A: sublin. L.*   1928 gemimus *MT*: geminus *A.* ‖ dolor *A: sublin.* [malum *b*] *L.*   1930
dolor *A: sublin. L.*   1937 Spectate *scripsi*: L. Spectate *A.*

Liberty, Wounded

Earth and sea, slow rivers and currents and you, Father Rhine, who rush through the Netherlands abundantly and with swirling current, pour your water. And you, who cover the nations and are saddened on the great earth, air, let your ever-humid reservoir flow freely in dreadful rains: I need tears. Heaven, connect your tears to mine. Form clouds everywhere, as a burden on the earth. Yes, even your night has to be doubled: two suns go down, yours and mine. A long night must cover the earth, the unfortunate day must lose its ordinary changes and hide the crime. Until now, anyone who saw his misery could mourn and the grief remained within the limits of mourning. Ah, ah.

I sigh for important matters: the sorrow is beyond words and my tears, my lamentations are not enough and the grief that I have to grieve is bigger than my mourning itself, and that is smaller than what it deserves. Who could shed tears that match grief so great? Or who could sufficiently bewail the dying? All people die, because of his death everyone dies who is touched by his death. Everybody who sees it, the whole city is dead, this death concerns all. Ah, ah.

Look, citizens, let anyone who has not learned to die, learn it by what has happened to him. The majestic man, who dedicated himself to Mars, the great fear of Spain, for whose coming even wild peoples, for whose invincible hand the fierce Grudians[253] shuddered, fell, died, passed away.

Come here, citizens: I swear by my tears and by the pierced side with black blood: he is invincible. Even cruel death does not refute this and the fact that the dead must be overpowered by deceit teaches that he could not be overcome.

---

253 The *Grudii* were a tribe in *Gallia Belgica*, here referring to the campaign of Orange in 1572 to Mechelen and Mons in Hainaut.

Nequijsse vinci. Talis immanis Phrygum
Metus Ilijque, Troia quem nutans decem
Tremuit per annos, vltimus Priami gener
1950 Sed iam sepultus: ille qui toruum Hectora
Potuisse vinci docuit, et mori simul;
Helenes mariti victima infelix iacet.
Talisque et alter ille Danaorum pauor,
Spoliator Asiae, ductor Argiuae manus
1955 Adultero seruatus et taedae suae,
Intactus alijs, fraude superatus fuit,
Sed post triumphum: concidit victor domi
Bello superstes. Funus, hoc funus iacet,
Fateor, Philippe, dextera scurrae tamen;
1960 "Non potuit aliâ, teque vincendo male
Victum fateris." Proh dolor, proh proh dolor.
    Ah ah ah ah.
"Priuata lachrymis damna defleri queunt,
At cum ruina totius quisquis iacet
1965 Gemendus illi est." Integer vires suas
Expromat orbis, concidit, iacet, iacet.
    Ah ah ah ah.
Ingens cauernis mundus euulsis fremat,
Gemitumque reddat. Tuque, tuque, o fulminis
1970 Potentioris magne librator Deus,
Percurre vastas aetheris tonitru fores;
Condi minore noenia tantus nequit.
Haec tuba sepulto praeeat, immanem polo
Quae eiecit Otum, quaeque flammarum patres
1975 Rursus parenti reddit caesos suae
Titanas olim. Vesper extremus tremat,
Ruptoque videat orbe quod fecit nefas,
    Ah ah ah ah.
At vos Batavûm corda, gens Neptunia
1980 Obnubite atris hic et hinc amictibus
Vrbem domosque; tota ferales gerat
Natura cultus, luctui angusta est nimis

1957 triumphum *scripsi*: trumphum *A*.   1959 scurrae *A*: tali *L*.   1970 Potentioris *A*: *sublin.*
L.   1972 Ah, ah, ah, ah *add. L.* ‖ noenia *A*: naenia *L*.   1979 Batavûm—Neptunia *A*: Batava
[parentis inclytum Nerei genus, *b*] *L*.

Such was the great terror of the Phrygians and of Ilium, for whom Troy staggered for ten years, the last son-in-law of Priam, yet he is now buried: he who showed that even the grim Hector could be conquered and at the same time that he could die, is dead, the unfortunate victim of Helena's husband.[254] In the same way, that other terror from the ranks of the Danaans, the one who took loot from Asia, the leader of the Argives, kept for an adulterer and his own wife, untouchable for others, was overcome by deceit, but after a victory: the victor, who had survived the war, fell at home.[255] Here too, is a dead person, this dead person, I acknowledge it, Philip, but fallen by the hand of a villain. "He could not be killed in any other way, and by overcoming in a wrong way you acknowledge your defeat." Ah, grief, ah, ah, grief. Ah, ah.

"Private losses can be bewailed with tears, but every time someone's death brings with him the downfall of the universe, he has to be bewailed by that." Let the whole world show its powers, he has fallen, died, gone. Ah, ah.

The big earth must thump with open caves and sigh. And you, oh great god[256] who are swinging the mighty lightning, rush forth through the great doors of heaven with your thunder. At the funeral of such a large man, no lesser funeral song fits. Let this thunder be the lamenting trumpet that goes before the dead, by which also the giant Otus was thrown out of heaven, and the defeated fathers of the flames, the Titans, were thrown back on their mother ground.[257] Let the extreme part of the Occident[258] tremble and see through the earthquakes the wicked man of his deed. Ah, ah.

But you, brave Dutch, people of Neptune,[259] obscure the city and the houses with dark mourning clothes everywhere: the whole of nature must wear mourning clothes, the crowd is too limited for mourning. When a passion-

---

254   I.e. Achilles, the terror of the Phrygians (Trojans) and Ilium (Troy), who killed the Trojan Prince Hector and married Polyxena, the daughter of the King of Troy, Priam; in his turn he was killed by Helena's lover Paris.

255   I.e. Agamemnon, leader of the Danaans (descendants of the King of Argos, Danaos, pars pro toto the Greeks) and the Argives (the inhabitants of Argos, poetical metonym for Greeks) at the expedition to Troy in Asia Minor. He survived the ten-year war, but was killed at home by his wife Clytemnestra and her lover Aegisthus.

256   I.e. Jupiter.

257   Otus, one of the Giants, who stormed Mount Olympus and the Olympian gods, but were vanquished and buried under volcanos. Here Heinsius seems to confuse the Giants and the Titans.

258   I.e. Spain, see above, n. 245.

259   I.e. the Dutchmen, or particularly the Hollanders, as a seafaring nation.

Humana turba; si quis armorum comes
Ostro superbum cornipes tollit caput
1985 Velamine atrum flebili radat solum,
Lugere non sat tota gens hominum sumus,
Accedat alter lachrymis nostris dolor.
     Ah ah ah ah.
Adeste ciues: patriae fulcrum iacet
1990 Sopore tristi victus. O fatum, o dolor
Haec illa sedes mentis, hoc illud caput
Prudentiarum viua, dum vixit, domus,
Excessit, abijt; restat illîus nihil
Nisi auferendum, nil nisi abdendum solo.
1995 Effodite tumulum, qui sit ambobus satis:
Tumulanda cives patria, et patriae est pater.
     Heu heu, heu heu.
Efferte funus. Praefica est magno duci
Natura rerum; funus hoc parui nihil
2000 Admittit in se: scilicet princeps Dei
Iacet: vniuerso nomen illud nascitur
Aequale mundo. Sequitur et retrò venit
Oceanus atra flebile redundans aqua,
Terramque pulsat tristis, et lachrymas agit,
2005 Vt ante spumas. Sydera, et caeli vagum
Comitetur agmen, pompa feralis veni
Stellae minores. Tuque qui caelum secas
Niueoque purum lacte distinguis polum
Aurate trames, caerula Heroum domus,
2010 Genijsque magnûm destinate principum
Dimitte, ciues, cras recepturus tuos;
Hodie vacabis, igneae caelum faces
Rellinquite omnes: Hesperus maneat tamen,
Scelus execrandum querimur Hesperij soli.
2015   Heu heu heu heu.
Tuque igneorum magne signorum, Leo,
Regnator, o qui flammeo motu minax
Chelas rapaces propter, et rictus feros

1998 funus *A*: *del. L.* ‖ est *A*: it *L.*   2000 Dei *A*: dei *L.*   2008 purum *L*: parum *A.*   2010
Geniisque magnûm *A*: Umbrisque magnûm *L.*

ate comrade puts his head proudly above the deck, he must wear a mourning garment that rubs along the black ground:[260] we, the whole human race, are not enough to weep. Let another expression of sorrow come to our tears. Ah, ah.

Be present, citizens: the strut of the fatherland lies down, overwhelmed by the hard-hearted sleep.[261] O fate, o grief, this renowned seat of the spirit, this famous head, during his life a living house of reason, has died, gone away; he has nothing left to do but what has to be buried in the earth, nothing but what has to be stored in the ground. Dig a grave big enough for both: citizens, your homeland must be buried and the father of your country. Ah, ah.

Carry his body to the grave. The lamenting woman for the great leader is nature: this dead endures nothing smaller. A prince of God[262] has died; such a person is by his birth the equal of the whole world. The Ocean follows and returns, mourning regrettably with black water, sadly beats the earth and now forms tears, like formerly foam.

Stars and procession of planets, be present, come funeral procession, smaller stars. And you who cut his shirt and pour the clear celestial pole with white milk, Golden way,[263] heavenly house of the Heroes, destiny for the souls of great princes, let your citizens go, whom you will get back tomorrow. Today you will be empty: fire flares, all of them leave heaven, but the Evening Star must stay,[264] we complain of a cursed crime of the Occident.[265] Ah, ah.

And you, great leader of the fiery signs, Lion, who with flaming movement threatening near the devouring Scorpion and the ferocious mounds of the

---

260   This refers to a war horse.
261   I.e. the eternal sleep, death.
262   Either a prince is divine by definition, or he is so because he is a 'ruler by the grace of God'.
263   I.e. the Milky Way.
264   The Evening star, the planet Venus, may stay as a sign of the crime committed at the instigation of the country of the Occident, Spain.
265   I.e. Spain, see above, n. 245.

Horrentis Hydrae caede viuacis sua
2020   Emergis altas igne vestitus iubas;
Defende nostrum: latius toruos polo
Protende vultus: o inauditum prius;
Leo Batauus tremuit, et fugam parat!
    Heu heu heu heu.
2025   Tuque a Tonante passa stuprum, at faemina,
Lycaone prognata, descendas licet,
Nostroque longam Nereo sedes sitim,
Et pellicatus eluas sordes tui,
Vt pura venias: si lubet, natum trahe;
2030   Vel cum sagittis: nulla fraus maior potest
Nobis timeri, concidit, iacet, iacet
Cui cauere nostra consueuit fides.
    Heu heu heu heu.
At tu, Boote, plaustra tantisper tua,
2035   Solitumque cursum cohibe, et in terras eas,
Mox axe funus illud extollas tuo,
Diuisque fraudes omnibus monstra nouas,
Artemque Iberam. Tuque vocalis Lyra
Fidibus remissis carmen infelix sona,
2040   Tuumque cantu demereri denuo
Delphina discas, iungat vt latus tibi,
Neptuniosque transuehat dorso choros
In iusta nostra. Tuque qui consors Lyrae
Illustre caeli, Cygne, praetentas iter,
2045   Nixusque in alas aureo emergis polo;
Fatale tristi voce moduleris melos,
Sed quale ripis flebilis Caystrijs
Tepidis in vndis morte vicina sonat,
Lateque canta; concidit, iacet iacet,
2050   Cor illud orbis, magna Belgarum salus.
    Heu heu heu heu.
Adeste, ciues. Quis feretro huic graues
Supponet humeros? Ponderi quis par erit
Molique tantae? Sidera haud vltra moror.

2025 a Tonante—faemina *A*: o Tonantis crimen infelix veni *L*.   2032 consueuit *A*: *sublin. L.*
2038–2043 Lyra ... Lyrae *scripsi*: lyra ... lyrae *A*.   2046 tristi *L*: triste *A*.   2050 illud *scripsi*:
Illud *A*.

chilling Hydra, rising up by its own slaughtering, lift up your mane, covered with fire, defend our lion:[266] stab your grim head further into the sky. Oh, something that has never been heard: the Dutch lion trembled and prepares the flight! Ah, ah.

You too, who have been afflicted by the Thunderer, but a woman, daughter of Lycaon, go down, lecture your long thirst with our Nereus and wash off the defilement of your extramarital relationship to come purely: if you want to, drag if you want your child with you,[267] or if necessary, come with your arrows. No greater deceit we can fear; fallen, died, gone is the one for whom our loyalty was to watch. Ah, ah.

But you, Boötes,[268] temporarily stop your carriage, do not abandon your normal job and come to earth; quickly bring up this dead man with your chariot and show all the gods the unprecedented deceit and the Spanish arts. You, sounding Lyre, make a sad song heard with limp strings and learn to oblige your Dolphin with your song to you, that he will join you and on his back bring the choruses of Neptune to our funeral.[269] And you, Swan, who just before the Lyre travel the radiant skies and rise floating on your wings in the golden sky, sing a dirge with a sad voice. But a dirge like the birds lamentably sing on the shores of the Caystrus in the lukewarm waves when death is near and sing it everywhere;[270] he has fallen, died, gone, the Heart of the world, the great salvation of the Dutch. Ah, ah.

Be present, citizens. Who will put his heavily loaded shoulders underneath this mortal, who will be able to cope with such weight and mass? I do not pay

---

266 The constellation Leo, but also a proleptic reference to the Dutch lion which is mentioned later in this sentence and again as *leo Batavus* (Dutch lion) in the next one—see also above, n. 121; the Scorpion is another name for the constellation Libra; the Hydra is the constellation of the Water snake.

267 Callisto, the daughter of Lycaon, who had been raped by Jupiter. In revenge, Juno changed her into a she-bear, whereupon Jupiter out of pity changed her into the constellation of the Great Bear; Mercury is her son.

268 Bootes is the constellation of the Bear-keeper, near the Wagon or the Great Bear.

269 The constellations of the Lyre and the Dolphin.

270 Cygnus, the constellation of the Swan; the King of the Ligurians with this name was changed to a swan and placed among the stars. The swan is also called the bird of the river Caystrus.

2055 Namque ille caelum qui labantis in modum,
     Similisque fesso magnus Alcides tenet
     Totus remisso lapsus occumbet genu.
     At tu pudicae magne Pleïones nepos,
     Tegeatice ales, inter errantes globos,
2060 Interque Diuos, inferosque, qui subis
     Totidem labores; huc auum sistas tuum,
     Illum potentes caelifer qui sustinet
     Defessus axes; mundus interea licet,
     Totumque ruptis postibus caelum ruat.
2065 Nihil moramur. Concidit, iacet, iacet
     Ille orbis ingens splendor, o fatum, o Dei,
         Heu heu heu heu.
     Spectate, ciues, pileum hic linquo meum
     Iuxta cadauer illud, vt sacras procul
2070 Secum sub umbras ille qui dedit ferat.
     Quin et capillum verticis messem mei
     Quem tum totondi, rasa cum primum coma
     Solenne sortis munus addecuit meae,
     Mando sepulto. Crinibus totum meis
2075 Vestire circum corpus infelix iuuat,
     Ah funus illud, funus illud o Dei.
     Nunc hoc fauoris munus extremum ferat,
     Quin me quoque ipsam; perdita a vobis eo
     Proscripta, ciues, exul a vobis eo.
2080 Valete, ciues, sancta Libertas abit.
     Spes nostra cecidit, concidit, iacet, iacet,
         Heu heu heu heu.
     Quo me immerentem mittitis, Di? Quo ferar?
     Gressumue referam? Sarmatarum vltra niues
2085 Tanaimque et Istrum, vel remotas horridi
     Boreae pruinas? Quo nec humanum gelu
     Indulget adytum, nec pedum vestigia
     Hominumue passus Schyticus adminit rigor?
         Heu heu heu heu.

2068–2070 Pileum—ferat *A: post corr.*: Pileum tellus sibi [habet *b*] | Funusque mando [linque *?*
b nostrum *? c*] quidquid illius fuit, | Umbris remitto, morsque crudelis tibi *L.*   2068 hic *A: del. L.*
2069 illud *A: additum n.l.* [additum *n.l.* suo *b*] *L.*   2076 Ah—Dei *A: del. L.*   2080 Libertas
scripsi: libertas *A.*   2087 adytum *A:* aditum *L.*

any further attention to the constellations. For that great grandson of Alceus,[271] who, like someone who seems to be tottering and tired, holds the heavens, will fall down completely with a slack knee. But you, great grandson of chaste Pleione, the winged one from Tegea[272] who have taken as much effort between the planets, between the gods and the underworld, put your grandfather here, the bearer of heaven[273] who wearily carries the heavy vault. Meanwhile, let the earth and the whole sky crash after the doors are forced. I'm not waiting. He has fallen, died, gone, the great light of the world, o fate, o gods. Ah, ah.

Look, citizens: here I leave my hat of freedom,[274] next to that body, that he[275] who has given it, takes it with him far into the holy underworld. Yes, even my hair, harvest from my head that I have shaved off, as soon as the shaving of my hair fits the ceremonial duties of my fate, I dedicate to the dead. I want to completely cover the unhappy body with my hair, oh, that corpse, that corpse. O gods. Let him now take this as a final gift from me, and also myself.[276] Lost, outlawed, I am going away from you, citizens, I am taking away exile from you. Farewell, civilians, holy freedom departs. Our hope has died, fallen, died, gone, ah, ah.

Where are you sending me undeservedly, gods? Where will I rush or direct my steps? Beyond the snow of the Sarmatians and the Tanais and the Ister, or the secluded winters of the chilling Boreas, where the cold does not allow people and where the Scythian freezing cold does not allow footsteps or people's passes?[277] Ah, ah.

---

271 I.e. Hercules.

272 I.e. Mercury, the son of Maia, who in her turn was a daughter of Pleione and Atlas; he was born in Arcadia where the city of Tegea was situated.

273 I.e. Atlas, Mercury's grandfather, who was condemned to hold up the earth.

274 The *pileus*, the hat of freedom, in Antiquity was a Phrygian bonnet, as a sign of freedom, but it is also to be seen on the tomb of William of Orange in the New Church of Delft.

275 I.e. William of Orange.

276 Libertas brings a sacrifice of her hair as was customary in Antiquity.

277 The Sarmatians were a Slavic people between the Vistula and the Don, used to indicate people who were living far away in the north; the river Tanais was in Sarmatia, the Ister is the Donau; Boreas is the north wind; Scythia a land on the Black Sea, known for its intense cold.

2090   Inter cauernas, vel ferarum tristia
       Spelea vultus obruam terra meos.
       Pertaedet hominum; perfidam fraudem et nefas,
       Tristeisque caedes cernere haud vltra queo.
       Valete terrae. "Tot truces inter feras
2095   Lupasque, et vrsas, et graues minacium
       Iras leonum, et ora toruorum boum
       Nil terra domino tristius gerit suo.
       Homo omne monstrum est: ille nam celat feras
       Quotquot timentur, ille crudeles leas
2100   Lupasque et vrsas, pectore obscuro tegit."
       Valete, ciues, sancta Libertas abit,
       Abiuit ille, quem videtis hic tamen,
       Abiuit ille, praeuium è terris sequor.
2105   Valete, ciues. Sancta Libertas abit.
       Heu heu heu heu.

                      FINIS

             PRINCEPS MAVRITIVS
             LVGDVNO REDVX.

       BATAVA tellus, coeruli sedes DEI,
       In hoc vocamur? Vna spem dies tibi,
       Nobis parentem sustulit. Felix cui
       Luctum fateri lachrymis licet suum.
   5   Cum patre nobis tollit et luctum DEVS.
       "Lachrymare magnus nescit Herois vigor,
       Nec illud altum nomen in pectus cadit;
       Lachrymare nescit, quisquis ulcisci potest."
       Lugete, cives. Quisquis hoc funus gemit
  10   Mecum orbus ille est. Iungit hic omnes dolor.
       Lugete, cives. Magna me fixum tenet
       Moles iuventae. Vos dolis, vos perfidae
       Crudelitati fraudibusque, ego meis
       Indignor annis. Magne terrarum parens

2101 Libertas *scripsi*: libertas *A*.

In the middle of the caves or the harsh dens of wild animals, I will cover my face with earth. I am disgusted by people; I cannot see any unfaithful deception, wickedness, and harsh murders. Goodbye, earth. Among the many ferocious beasts, she-wolves, she-bears, the fierce tale of stark lions and the ferocious heads of cattle the earth does not bear anything harsher than its own lord. Man is fully a monster: for he has in himself all the animals for which one is afraid, deep in his heart cruel lionesses, she-wolves and she-bears dwell.

Farewell, citizens, Holy Freedom leaves. He has already departed, whom you still see here, he has gone, I follow him who leads me away from the earth. Goodbye, citizens. Holy Freedom departs. Ah, ah.

THE END

Prince Maurice returned from Leiden

Dutch soil, residence of the deep blue God,[278] am I called to this? On a single day you have taken away your hope and my father. Happy is he who can show his mourning with tears. At the same time as my father, God also deprived me of mourning. "A generous hero cannot weep, that term does not fit with his high nature: he who can avenge cannot weep." Mourn, citizens. Whoever sighs for this death is an orphan like me. This sorrow connects us all. Mourn, citizens. The heavy burden of my youth stops me. You are indignant at the wiles, the unfaithful cruelty and the layers, I despise my younger years.

---

278   I.e. Nereus, god of the sea, who is at home with the Dutch people.

15 Cur tarda lento pergit Heroum gradu
    Aetas, nec ipsam protenus metam tenent
    Anni morantes? "O Devs, serò nimis
    Quicunque Divi nascimur, viri sumus!"
    At tu citatum, Diva, quo moves gradum?
20 Quid, Diva, nostrum profuga destituis solum?
    Per hunc paternum sanguinem, numen meum,
    Fraudemque, quam non tempus, aut anni graves,
    E pectore illo, non profunda saecula, aut
    Oblivionis genitor evellet dies;
25 O Diva, siste, Diva, nec parvas manus
    Aut hoc lacertos sperne; magnus incola
    Virtutis autor igneae hîc habitat Devs,
    Pectusque pulsat hoc, et invitus suis
    Latet sub annis, saeculumque despicit.
30   At vos parentis inclyti Manes mei,
    Tuque umbra, quae per aureas Deûm vias
    Orbemque nostris invium pedibus volas;
    Divis Paternis dic, et Heroae manu,
    Nassovijsque, civibus poli, Deis
35 Avoque magno, cuius ausa regia
    Idemque nomen indolem vocat meam;
    Spectet nepotem Genitor, et nostris adhuc
    Ignoscat annis. Tuque pacatus precor
    Tantisper esto, redditus donec mihi
40 Victor Batavâ Vesperum invadam trabe,
    Manesque Iberâ caede satiabo tuos.

FINIS.

---

23 pectore illo *A*: corde nostro *L*. ‖ profunda—aut *A*: *del. L.* 24 genitor *A*: mater *L*.

Great father of the earth, why does the life of heroes go so slowly and with a slow pace, and do the decelerating years not reach the final goal itself immediately? "O god, we who are born as gods, we are men too late!"

But you, Goddess,[279] where are you addressing your swift step? Why, Goddess, do you flee and abandon our country? To this blood of my father, to my majesty, and to deceit, that neither the time nor the heavy years will break from that heart, nor the innumerable ages or the course of time that brings oblivion: o goddess, remain, goddess, and do not despise these little hands or arms. Here[280] the great God trembles his house, causing fervent courage, He makes my heart beat and hides against his will deep in my years and looks down on my age.

But you, spirit of my famous father and you, his spirit flying past the golden orbits of the gods and the world that is impassable for our feet, tell my deified ancestors and that heroic group, the Nassaus, who live in heaven, the gods and my great grandfather, whose royal daring and name evoke my courage, that the ancestor must look to his descendant and still should forgive my years. And you, I pray, just be calm, until in the full possession of my strength I will triumph over the Occident[281] with a Dutch ship and fill your shadow with Spanish blood.

THE END

---

279   Heinsius makes Maurice address the goddess of liberty.
280   I.e. in me, Maurice.
281   I.e. Spain, see above, n. 245.

Commentary

[0]   Title Page

Auriacus, sive Libertas saucia was printed and published by Andries Cloeck (Andreas Cloucquius), who in 1602 had been active in Leiden for three years, from 1599 onwards; Eyffinger, *Grotius poeta*, p. 257, n. 147, offers a list of the works Cloeck published. Apparently the printer could not find good correctors: Heinsius complains about this in the 'Menda typographica' of *Auriacus*, and Grotius was not satisfied with the edition of his *Poemata collecta* (1617) either, see Nellen, *Hugo Grotius*, p. 210 and Eyffinger, *Grotius poeta*, pp. 153–297. See also p. 2, n. 43

In the double title Heinsius indicates the subject matter and the protagonist (Auriacus, William of Orange) and the theme (the wounding of Liberty), as is customary. In antiquity the two parts of the title were rather connected with *vel*, whereas in medieval Latin the conjunction *sive* was preferred. On this, see Arnold Rothe, 'Der Doppeltitel: Zu Form und Geschichte einer literarischen Konvention', *Abhandlungen der Geistes- und Sozialwissenschaftlichen Klasse: Alødemie der Wissenschaften und der Literatur* 1969, 10 (Mainz 1970), pp. 297–331.

In the title *Auriacus, sive Libertas saucia* Heinsius opposes his play to the piece of Casparus Casparius, *Auriacus, sive Libertas defensa*, in which God continues to protect the Low Countries after William of Orange's death, see also the intr., pp. 29–31. Grotius had already used the form 'Auriacus' in his *Scutum Auriacum* (1597, see Grotius, *Dichtwerken/Poetry* I, 2A, 1, pp. 59–69, snf I, 2 B, 1, pp. 40–49); for other Latin forms of the name of Orange, see the comm. *ad* Grotius, *Iambi* 57–73.

L In his own copy, Heinsius added a quotation from Dio Chrys.' *On Beauty* (*Discourses* 21), 11: "The reason for this is that I do not much care for the writers of Tragedy nor try to emulate them; for I know that it is a disgrace to mention people of the present day in a tragedy, but that it is some ancient event which I should have touched upon and one not very credible either" (trans. J.W. Cohoon, LCL). "Locum sub de pulcherrimo de tragoedia veterum" probably means something like: 'a place in the chapter "On the beauty, on Antique tragedy"'. I have not found the edition or florilegium in which the quotation is on p. 272.

[1]   Illustrissimis, [...] Hollandiae et Westfrisiae Ordinibus, Dominis
        suis Magnificis / Dedication to the States of Holland and West
        Friesland

1–18   Of all literary genres tragedy is the loftiest, as Romans and Greeks have
proved. Sophocles in particular did so because he wrote tragedies in old age and
as an administrator. Nevertheless, it is astonishing that the classical writers for
such a useful genre did not use subjects from contemporary history, but chose
useless inventions.

19–39   Heinsius has tried to avoid this problem by taking national material as
a theme. In ancient times people learned from tragedy. The fact that philosophers were involved in this genre proves that it generated philosophical lessons.

40–72   If someone were to hold tragedy in lower esteem because it belongs
to poetry, Heinsius objects that in early antiquity poetry and philosophy con-
verged, to such an extent that the philosophers were called 'singers'. He will
not prove this by using quotations from poets (they are not impartial), but
from Strabo, who told that singing and speaking (wisely) were synonymous.
The seven sages too gave their wisdom in poetry.

73–93   Heinsius will therefore not acclaim poetry, but asks permission to praise
philosophy. For these two are closely connected, since philosophers have stated
that a good poet must also be a morally good man. Zeno may say that poetry
is a representation of divine and human affairs, but it is older than rhetoric,
as Strabo already tells us. Therefore, tragedy is older (and better) than rhetoric
and prose, and part of philosophy.

94–123   Some people, Plato included, call it a hetaera. Therefore Plato banned
it from his state, an argument that many use. If that is true, he himself may be
banned too, for his prose is close to poetry. But Plato falsely keeps poetry out
of his state, because Homer describes adultery and quarrels among the gods.
That is the fault of a poet, not of poetry. Thus all philosophers should be kept
out the state, because Plato reasons incorrectly here.

124–137   Now Heinsius directly addresses the States, offering them William of
Orange; the title in itself will gain him their benevolence, although he had preferred that Orange would be still alive. The Prince had only one goal left in life:
immortality, and Heinsius will try to make him immortal through his tragedy.

137–146   Orange should walk onstage, because he cannot do so any more in
reality. Thus, he will be presented to the young and give them love for their
country, and take care that adults will continue to defend the fatherland. Moreover, the young will learn how costly freedom has been, and Orange's virtue may
not be buried with him.

147–163 The author then turns to the Dutch, courageous, prepared to die for their country and freedom, and having power over the sea. They will see their prince who was willing to give everything, including his life, for their freedom. They must realize that the Spaniards only appropriated deceit. To them he now dedicates his drama, because only literature can break through time and violence.

164–184 Heinsius has written the play in gratitude, for when as a child he came to the Netherlands, the Dutch lovingly received him. Through his studies at the Leiden Academy he became acquainted with celebrities of his age, the famous scholar and author Joseph Scaliger, the French ambassador and scientist Paul Choart de Buzenval and the member of the States and curator of the university Janus Dousa, not only a man with a literary gift and someone who has raised literature to a high standard, but also a person who has devoted his life to the fatherland. He has treated Heinsius as his own son.

185–192 Because Heinsius thought that the Dutch should receive proof of his gratitude, he decided to portray the death of Orange in a play. They would have lost all of Orange if it did not live on in his son, whom God may save. In the meantime, Heinsius offers this piece, whatever its quality, to the Dutch—and specifically the States.

In this dedication Heinsius defends tragedy, stressing its philosophical aspect and the possibility of providing insight, as well as his gratitude for the hospitality of the Dutch when he was expelled from Flanders. It may be related to the hostile attitude of Calvinist and Mennonite ministers towards the theatre, for whom he may have included some remarks on mythological fabrications the Greeks used for their drama, in contrast to his historical subject. This cautiousness was also needed on the part of the curators of the University, where in 1595 restrictive measures were taken for the performance of comedies and tragedies. See also Meter, *The Literary Theories*, pp. 36–38. Heinsius uses many authorities, but most arguments are taken from the *Geographica* of the Greek historian, traveller and Stoic Strabo (ca. 66 BC–21 AD), esp. Book I, where he deals with philosophy and poetry; see also the comm.

Except for ideological advance, such a dedication could gain financial support, which was quite usual. The young Heinsius received 200 guilders from the States of Holland, which was a fair amount, just below the average amount of 260 guilders (before 1580–1649), see Piet J. Verkruijsse, 'Holland "gedediceerd": Boekopdrachten in Holland in de 17e eeuw', *Holland* 23 (1991), pp. 225–242, esp. pp. 232 and 238. Moreover, such a dedication contributed to the prestige (in Bourdieu's words: cultural capital) of dedicator and dedicatee, see Karl Schottenloher, *Die Widmungsvorrede im Buch des 16. Jahrhunderts* (Münster:

Asschendorffsche Verlagsbuchhandlung, 1953) Reformationsgeschichtliche Studien und Texte, 76–77, esp. pp. 194–196; Saskia Stegeman, *Patronage and Services in the Republic of Letters: The Network of Theodorus Janssonius van Almeloveen (1657–1712)*, trans. Mary Kelly (Amsterdam, APA-Holland University Press, 2005), and Nina Geerdink, *Dichters en verdiensten: De sociale verankering van het dichterschap van Jan Vos (1610–1667)* (Hilversum: Verloren, 2012) Doctoral thesis Amsterdam.

The idea to dedicate this play to the States of Holland and West Friesland may have been suggested to Heinsius by his protector Janus Dousa, who himself was member of these States.

The form and structure of the dedication contains standard elements. See Stegeman, *op. cit.*, pp. 275–315, who mentions the form of a letter, the *captatio benevolentiae*, a passage on the good relationship between dedicatee and dedicator, and a praise of the dedicatee.

Salutation

Hollandiae   This is probably a *terminus technicus* for Holland as a political entity, since elsewhere *Batavus/Batavia, Catti* and *Belgi/Belgia* are used.
Domini   The members of the States, i.e. the "Gecommiteerde Raden", the deputies on behalf of the cities and the nobility.

The dignity of tragedy

1–9 *Inter reliqua monimenta—Reipublicae praefectus*   With his statement that tragedy presents royal persons, Heinsius is referring to Scaliger's definition (Scal. *Poet.* I, 6, p. 11b B–C; Scaliger, *Poetica/Dichtkunst* 1, p. 130.4–6): "In Tragoedia Reges, Principes, ex urbibus, arcibus, castris. [...] Oratio gravis, culta, a vulgi dictione aversa [...]". Furthermore, he refers to Sophocles, who is used as an argument to defend the dignity of tragedy, because he kept writing it in his old age, and did so as a city magistrate, cf. Cic. *Sen.* 7, 22: "Sophocles ad summam senectutem tragoedias fecit". For his writing in general service, see Charles Estienne's encyclopaedia, which gave an overview of what was known (Stephanus, *Dictionarium*, p. 406r): "Aequalis Euripidis et Periclis, cuius etiam quandoque collega fuit in praetura". On Sophocles see *RE* 2.R. 3, 1040–1094 s.v. Sophokles 1; on his political activities *ibid.* 1043–1044.

1–2 *ingenium ... industria*   For this literary-theoretical opposition between talent and effort, or education, in rhetoric and in poetics (*ingenium vs ars*) cf., e.g., Hor. *A.P.* 295–296 and 408–411, and the discussion of the latter passage in

Brink, *Horace on Poetry*, pp. 394–395; see also Joost van den Vondel, *Aenleidinge ter Nederduitsche dichtkunste*, ed. werkgroep Utrechtse neerlandici (Utrecht: Instituut De Vooys, 1977) Ruijgh-bewerp, 6, pp. 16–17. At the same time, it is a *topos* of modesty.

6 *Romani* Cf. Ov. *Trist.* II, 381: "Omne genus scripti gravitate tragoedia vincit".

6 *disciplinarum autores Graeci* Perhaps Heinsius is here already referring to the authors περὶ διδασκαλιῶν, see below, l. 31.

7 *Grammaticorum scholis* A *grammaticus* in antiquity was a man of letters and exegete, see, e.g., Cic. *Div.* I, 51, 116: "Sunt enim explanatores, ut Grammatici, poetarum"; see also *TLL* 6.2, 2171. Perhaps Heinsius is aiming at the scholastics, or the schoolmasters who spoke about poetry, but changed it into a system of rules.

        The subject matter for tragedies

10–18 *Vnum tamen est—turpissime illusit* The discussion on mythological stories must be seen in the light of the contemporary discussion on theatre at the Academy of Leiden. The amount of mythology in *Auriacus* shows that the remark was gratuitous, unless one should distinguish between subject and the use of mythology in an acceptable subject.

11–12 *sapientiae—dicimus* Here Heinsius deviates from the customary distinction (e.g. in Quint. XII, 2, 10) between *philosophia moralis*, *naturalis* and *rationalis*, but is following the division of Strabo (I, 1, 23). For *civilis scientia* as political science, see Cic. *Inv.* I, 5, 6. Cf. also Lipsius (*ILE* XVIII; 05 12 01) on the use of historiography which is "civilis atque moralis Philosophiae speculum aut exemplum".

13–14 *solam Tragoediam—amplecti* Cf. Donatus' definition of comedy (Euanthius/Donatus 5, 1): "Comoediam esse Cicero ait imitationem vitae, speculum consuetudinis, imaginem veritatis" (see also Diog. Laert. *Vitae* VII, 60) and Scal. *Poet.* I, 1, p. 11b: "Sola poesis haec omnia [i.e. what rhetoric and philosophy deal with] complexa est" (cf. Scal. *Poet.*, p. 3a D; Scaliger, *Poetica/Dichtkunst* 1, p. 70.25); cf. also *ibid.* I, 6 (Scaliger, *Poetica/Dichtkunst* 1, p. 128.26–27): "Tragoedia [...] in exemplis humanae vitae conformata".

17 *Oedipodas, Aiaces, Medeas* Sophocles wrote the tragedies *Oedipus Coloneus*, *Oedipus rex* and *Aiax*, Euripides the *Medea*.

The subject of this tragedy

19–26 *Ego vero—citius*   For the subject Heinsius considered his own interest, and the concerns of the dedicatee. By choosing historical matter he avoids mythology, since the past of the Low Countries has plenty of material for a tragedy.

20 *vestram*   'Yours', i.e. it regards the States, and their own, because of the dedication.

25 *Batavia*   Unlike in (for example) *Aur.* 1270, where it specifies the (northern) Netherlands, in this dedication (to the States of Holland and West Friesland) the region of Holland may be intended.

The use of tragedy

26–38 *Hoc vobis affirmare—contulerunt*   The fact that philosophers, at any rate Aristotle, held tragedy in high esteem is shown in his *Poetica* 1449b (ἔστιν οὖν τραγῳδία μίμησις πράξεως σπουδαίας καὶ τελείας μέγεθος ἐχούσης) and 1449a (ὀψὲ ἀπεσεμνύνθη). A source for the idea that *imperatores* or *duces* learnt their *civilis sapientia* by watching tragedy has not yet been traced, but see James A. Parente, Jr, '"Tragoedia Politica": Strasbourg School Drama and the Early Modern State, 1583–1621', *Colloquia Germanica* 29 (1996), pp. 1–11.

29–31 *hinc Tragici—dicebantur*   The point is that διδάσκω can be both 'to teach' and a *terminus technicus* for writing dithyrambs and other dramatic poetry, see LSJ s.v. διδάσκω III.

31 *Aristotelis*   In his *Poetica*.

31 *Carystij*   For Carystius as the author of a περὶ διδασκαλιῶν, see Stephanus, *Dictionarium*, p. 289; in antiquity Athen. VI, 235e: Καρύστιος ὁ Περγαμηνὸς ἐν τῷ περὶ διδασκαλιῶν (Carystius of Pergamus, in his treatise on the *Didascaliae*); see also *RE* 10, 2254–2255 s.v. Karystios.

32 *Rex philosophorum*   Arist. *Poet.* 1449b gives a day as the *tempus actionis*; however, it is debated whether he meant a day of 12 or 24 hours.

33–34 *Ille sapientiae ac voti humani terminus*   For the high esteem for Plato, see (for example) Stephanus, *Dictionarium*, p. 800: "Sublimis, apex philosophorum et columen dicitur Arnobio adversus Gentes lib. 1", and Quint. X, 1, 81: "Quis dubitet Platonem esse praecipuum sive acumine disserendi sive eloquendi facultate divina quadam et Homerica?"

34–36 *Plato et scripsit eam ... feratur*   For the fact that Plato wrote tragedies, see (for instance) Stephanus, *Dictionarium*, p. 357r: "Tragoediasque et poemata quaedam conscripsit". His dialogues were divided into groups of four (τετρα-λογίαι), which also indicates a series of four plays (three tragedies and a satyr play), see LSJ s.v. τετραλογία. Plato would also have joined a contest at the Dionysia and written tragedies for it.

36–37 reliquos minorum gentium Philosophos Besides Aristotle, Heinsius remains vague about other philosophers who wrote on tragedy. Pherecydes was a philosopher and tragic poet; Stephanus, *Dictionarium*, p. 547v.

37 Euclidem It is not fully clear which Euclid Heinsius refers to—the mathematician, the Socratic philosopher or the grammarian. The latter was quoted by the 12th-c. author Johannes Tzetzes in his Ἴαμβοι περὶ τραγικῆς ποιήσεως, see *RE* 6, 1003 s.v. Eukleides 6.

Philosophy and poetry used to be synonyms

39–54 Quod si eam—potitus est Aegystus Heinsius tries to convince possible sceptics who reject tragedy as poetry of its worth by pointing out the close connection between poetry and philosophy and the latter's worth, for which cf. Cic. *Tusc.* I, 64: "philosophia [...] omnium mater artium"; Heinsius may be referring to philosophy as normative for human behaviour. The Ionic natural philosophers, who searched for an ἀρχή, *rerum causae*, *principia* and *materies* of the cosmos and its *ortus* and *motus*, wrote their philosophical treatises in poetry.

On the other hand singers in ancient times were teachers in morals, and thus philosophers *avant la lettre*, which is proven by the bard who watched over Clytemnestra when Agamemnon was on a campaign to Troy. Aegisthus was able to get hold of her after he was killed, see Hom. *Od.* III, 253–275, esp. 267–268, but see esp. Strabo, I, 2,3: 'And Homer, too, has spoken of the bards as disciplinarians in morality, as when he says of the guardian of Clytemnestra: "Whom the son of Atreus as he went to Troy strictly charged to keep watch over his wife" [*Od.* III, 267–268]; and he adds that Aegisthus was unable to prevail over Clytemnestra until "he carried the bard to a lonely isle and left him there—while as for her, he led her to his house, a willing lady with a willing lover. [*Od.* III, 270–272]"' (trans. H.L. Jones, LCL). The remark on singers educating sons of kings, may well be an allusion to Strabo I, 2, 3: "That is the reason why in Greece the various states educate the young, at the very beginning of their education, by means of poetry; not for the mere sake of entertainment, of course, but for the sake of moral discipline" (trans. H.L. Jones, LCL). The poets are well equipped for this, the poet Homer already has all wisdom, according to Poliziano in his *Oratio in expositione Homeri* 9 (in: *Opera* II. Lyon 1533, pp. 63 and 65), and Heinsius in *De poetis et eorum interpretibus* (see Meter, *The Literary Theories*, p. 58).

46 *machina huius* See *Aur.* 1660 and the comm. *ad loc.*

> To sing is to speak wisely

55–72 *Non adferam—praetermitto* Heinsius will not use the testimonies of poets, but quotes Strabo (1, 2, 6): "[...] the fact that the ancients used the verb 'sing' instead of the verb 'tell' [meant that] the term 'sing' was to them equivalent to the term 'tell'" (trans. H.L. Jones, LCL). An extra argument, given in passing, is that the seven sages of Greek, including Solon, wrote 'ordinary' poetry too.

55 *somnia aegrorum* Cf. Cic. *N.D.* I, 42: "delirantium somnia" and the comm. by Pease *ad loc.*, 2, pp. 279–280. Heinsius will distance himself from poets in a Platonic poetic frenzy.

62 *doctissimae Graecorum magistrorum Glossae* These glosses have not been traced.

64 *Septem illi Graeciae sapientes* Solon, Thales, Chilo, Pittacus, Bias and Cleobulus. Heinsius does not mention the seventh, Periander. They would have written songs with moral philosophical lessons, cf. (for example) Stephanus, *Dictionarium*, pp. 967–968 s.v. Thales: "item poeta lyricus".

For the Roman embassy to Greece in 456–454 BC in order to copy Solon's laws, see Liv. III, 31: "missi legati Athenas Sp. Postumius Albus, A. Manlius P. Sulpitius Camerinus, iussique inclutas leges Solonis describere, et aliarum Graeciae civitatum instituta, mores, iuraque noscere". Solon can be used as an argument for the importance of poetry, since he wrote poems, e.g. the elegy in which he exhorts the Athenians to reconquer Salamis; see *RE* 2.R. 3, 946–978, on his poetry 951–955.

72 σίλλους Strabo XIV, 1, 28 uses the term for the poems of Xenophanes of Colophon. On *silloi*, see also *RE* 2.R. 3, 97–98.

***L* 60–63** Heinsius changes these lines into: "Who does not know that Pherecydes, before Pythagoras, his tutor, and Empedocles and Parmenides before Socrates, from the beginning dealt with philosophy in exactly the same way: for I will pass Linus, Musaeus and Orpheus, which Plato in his *Apology* counts as one with Homer among the sages, because they are too old". Heinsius shows off his erudition with this catalogue of pre-Socratic philosophers: the mythographer and cosmologist Pherecydes of Syrus (fl. 550 BC) (*RE* 24, 2025–2033 s.v. Pherekydes 5); the philosopher Pythagoras (6th c. BC), who established a religious community in which the Orphic idea of metempsychosis and numbers were the basis of life (*RE* 24, 171–209; he is supposed to have visited Pherecydes, *ibid.* 180); the statesman, poet and natural philosopher Empedocles, who in poetry enunciated the doctrine of four elements (*RE*, 2506–2512); Parmenides of Elea, who declared that there was one, unchangeable being (*RE* 18.2, 1553–1559); the Athenian philosopher Socrates, who in many dialogues of his pupil Plato is the interlocutor, and expresses among other subjects a cosmography (*RE* 2.R. 3, 811–890 s.v. Sokrates 5). In Plato's *Apology*, Socrates mentions Orpheus, Musaeus, Hesiod and Homer (Plato, *Ap.* 41A). Heinsius gives another list, probably because he was quoting by heart, and replace Hesiod with Linus, a famous mythological singer (Roscher 2.2, 2053–2063); Musaeus is also a singer from mythology, often mentioned together with Orpheus (Roscher 2.2, 3235–3237); Orpheus was famous as a singer and the founder of Orphism, a mystical movement whose tenets were expressed in poetry (Roscher 3.1.1058–1207).

L 67   Heinsius adds: "That is why, according to Laertius, they were despicably called 'poets': and from that moment on the people least able to make judgements about wisdom considered that which was praiseworthy as a mistake". See Diog. Laert. *Vitae* I, 12.

   Poetry is older than prose

73–93 *Nec enim—ad quamlibet sui partem*   Heinsius will not praise poetry but demands to be allowed to praise philosophy, for philosophy and poetry are closely connected, pointing to the definition that a good poet has to be a (morally) good man. Cf. Quint. XII, 1, 44: "oratorem esse virum bonum bene dicendi peritum". An objection could be that the foremost task of poetry is *imitatio* of divine and human affairs (Cic. *Tusc.* IV, 57: "Sapientiam esse rerum divinarum et humanarum scientiam cognitionemque"). However, Heinsius highlights that poetry is older (and implicitly better) than rhetoric, but Strabo has already done that, see Strabo I, 2, 5: '[...] it is impossible for one to become a good poet unless he has previously become a good man' (trans. H.L. Jones, LCL), and I, 2, 6: 'poetry was the source and origin of style [lit. rhetoric]' (trans. H.L. Jones, LCL).

73 *vulgo poetarum*   (1) inexpert *poetae vulgares*; (2) vernacular poets in general; (3) the rhetoricians who endlessly sang the praise of rhetoric without knowing either true poetry or the antiquity of its practice. Heinsius will also oppose the rhetoricians in his oration *De poetis et eorum interpretibus* (1603), see Heinsius, *Orationum editio nova: Auctior atque ita emendata, ut alia videri possit: Accedunt Dissertationes aliquot, nec unius argumenti* (Leiden: Elzevier, 1642), pp. 561–562, cf. Meter, *The Literary Theories*, p. 43. Later, in his verse dedication to Jacob van Dijck in Heinsius' *Nederduytsche Poemata* (1616), Scriverius

will fulminate against "de Reden-rijckers bend, en Rijmers" (the gang of rhetoricians and rhymers): "een volck dat veeltijdt is ontbloot van alle reden, | onmatich, onbesuyst, wanschapen, onbesneden" (a band, often without any reason, unseemly, rash, misshapen and ugly, ll. 105–106).

80–81 *Zenonis definitionem* Cf. Cic. *Off.* II, 5: "Sapientia autem est, ut a veteribus philosophis definitum est, rerum divinarum et humanarum causarumque, quibus eae res continentur, scientia" (cf. I, 153). Plato attributes this knowledge (ironically) to the poets in *Rep.* X, 598D–E: "'Does this mean, then', I said, 'that we must next examine tragedy and its leader, Homer, since we hear from some that these people understand all arts and crafts and all matters human in relation to virtue and vice and even to matters divine?'" (trans. C. Emlyn-Jones and W. Preddy, LCL).

Heinsius is probably pointing to the Stoic philosopher Zeno of Citium (ca. 336–264 BC), to whom is attributed the general Stoic saying (*SVF*, p. 15.3–5): "The Stoics maintain that wisdom is the knowledge of divine and human affairs" (and *ibid.* ll. 12–13; see also Cic. *Off.* I, 153).

85 *a Strabone* Strabo I, 2, 6.

87–88 *Aristidis reprehensionem* Aelius Aristides, rhetor from Mysia (129–189 AD); Heinsius may be referring to Aristides' *Hymn to Sarapis* (= *Or.* 45), 6–8. Translation in Donald A. Russell and Michael Winterbottom, *Ancient Literary Criticism* (Oxford: Oxford University Press, 1976), pp. 558–560, esp. 559.

88 *solutam ... vinctâ* As in ll. 104–105, poetry and prose are opposed as 'free' and 'bound', in verse.

90–91 *quae de Cadmo, Pherecyde, Hecataeo dicuntur* Cadmus is the mythical founder of Thebes who, according to Stephanus, *Dictionarium*, p. 144r s.v., "historiam invenisse et prosaicam orationem instituisse". Pherecydes is a philosopher and tragic poet, of whom Stephanus, *Dictionarium*, p. 547v wrote: "Hic primus soluta oratione traditur scripsisse [...] repudiato versuum nexu". The Milesian historian Hecataeus, according to Stephanus, *Dictionarium*, p. 547v, "primus soluta oratione historiam condidit". See also Strabo I, 2, 6: "Then came Cadmus, Pherecydes, Hecataeus and their followers, with prose writings in which they imitated the poetic art, abandoning the use of metre but in other respects preserving the qualities of poetry" (trans. H.L. Jones, LCL).

L 89–90 Heinsius suggests: "and everybody knows that the Greeks adduce proof for this", apparently suggesting that he needs not discuss this issue any more, but knows that it has already been treated.

Tragedy is no hetaera

94–123 *Quod autem hodie—quam suorum*   Now, however, tragedy is misused by poets not having the required skills. Heinsius may be referring to the rhetoricians and their morality plays, or specifically to the tragedies on the murder of Orange by Panagius Salius and Caspar Casparius, see intr. pp. 28–31. In any case, this abuse does not affect the value of tragedy itself.

Heinsius contrasts this value with the names Phryne and Lais, two famous courtesans in Athens and Corinth, resp. Stephanus, *Dictionarium*, p. 353r, s.v. Phryne, quotes Quint. II, 14, and (pp. 261v–262r, s.v. Lais) Prop. II, 6, 1: "Non ita complebant Ephyraeae Laidos aedes ad cuius iacuit Graecia tota fores". Tragedy is as chaste as Panthea, Abradates' wife, see Stephanus, *Dictionarium*, p. 4v s.v. Abradatas, and Xenophon, Cyr. 5, 6 and 7 passim.

It was Plato who called tragedy *pellex* (prostitute). However, he does not do this *expressis verbis*, but in *Rep.* X, 602C–608B he criticizes tragic poetry and in *Sophist.* 265b mimetic arts in general. For this criticism Plato has to be disputed. The first argument, *tu quoque* (hypocrisy), is that his own prose is poetic, and therefore he himself has to be banned from his own state, but then the term poetry should be taken in a broad sense, otherwise some ἄμετρα or even ἔμμετρα will not be poetry, nor the dithyrambs, of which people thought that they were the expression of Dionysian ecstasy, cf. Hor. *C.* IV, 2, 10–12: "Nova dithyrambos | verba devolvit numerisque fertur | lege solutis"; see also Carol H. Maddison, *Apollo and the Nine: A History of the Ode* (Baltimore: Johns Hopkins Press, 1960), e.g. pp. 12 and 333–335. In his discussion of the dithyramb, Scal. *Poet.* I, 46, p. 50A; Scaliger, *Poetica/Dichtkunst*, p. 398.25, calls it: "exsultans igitur, inconstans, et tumidum".

Then an *argumentum ad absurdum* follows: if we accept Plato's *State* women should become common property (*Rep.* V, 457C–D), which automatically leads to its downfall. A third argument, also *ad absurdum*, is that since Plato overgeneralizes when he states that all poets have to be banned for the mistakes of one of them, Homer, all philosophers should be kept out of the state because this philosopher is apt to reason wrongly. Moreover, Heinsius ironically adds, Plato calls the poets divine, so he expels them from his state into heaven, making him quite mild. Plato thus undermines his own position.

99–100 *e Republicâ suâ exegit eos*   Cf. (for example) Cic. *Tusc.* II, 27 "Recte igitur a Platone eiiciuntur ex ea civitate quam finxit ille" and see *Rep.* 398A, 598E–602C, and his *Ion.*

104–105 *soluta oratio ... numeris pedibusque vincta est*   Cf. l. 88.

111 *me hercule*   This exclamation gives the passage an ironic tone.

117 *naturales rationes* The grammarians, viz. the Greek allegorists—esp. Metrodorus of Lampsacus and Theagenes of Rhegium, as well as Strabo, Maximus of Tyrus (Heinsius will edit his works in 1607, see Sellin, *Daniel Heinsius and Stuart England*, p. 232) and Dio Chrysostomus—and Platonists applied allegorism to the Homeric epics. See such studies as Felix Buffière, *Les mythes d'Homère et la pensée Grecque* (Paris: Les Belles Lettres, 1956) and Pierre Levèque, *Aurea catena Homeri: Une étude sur l'allégorie Grecque* (Paris: Les Belles Lettres, 1959) Annales Littéraires de l'Université de Besançon, 27. For allegorism in Plato and before him, see J. Tate, 'Plato and Allegorical Interpretation', *Classical Quarterly* 23 (1929), pp. 142–154 and 24 (1930), pp. 1–10, for Strabo see *id.*, 'Cornutus and the poets', *Classical Quarterly* 23 (1929), pp. 41–45. For the reduction of the gods to natural principles, see (for example) Tate, *loc. cit.*, pp. 142–143.

121 *diuinum* Plato calls poets divine in several places, for instance *Meno* 81B; Homer is called divine in (for example) *Ion* 530B, Tyrtaeus in *Leg.* 629B. See also Kambylis, *Die Dichterweihe*, pp. 12–13.

L 117 Heinsius adds: "Furthermore, we know that they do not agree with the opinion of their master, but apologize to him and do not adopt everything that Plato approves of in his *State*; the legislator himself confesses that his state can never exist".

Orange will live on

124–146 *Iam autem ad vos venio—esse videantur* This tragedy will immortalize the murdered William of Orange, a topos discussed by Curtius, *European Literature and Latin Middle Ages*, pp. 476–477, excursus 9 'Poetry as perpetuation'. Heinsius connects this topos with the *locus communis* that the hero's fate should be an example for the spectators, their love for their country and their willingness to defend it. The tragedy will slacken the boundaries of time and space for Orange's fame and at the same time be a means for moral instruction. For a call to defend freedom, cf. Grotius, *Ordines federati* 90–93 (Grotius, *Dichtwerken/Poetry* I, 2A, 1, p. 129).

125–126 *in vindictam—Hispanorum nomen* An instance of hyperbole.

131 *quidam* Probably an allusion to Georgius Benedicti Wertelo and his epic, and Caspar Casparius and Panagius Salius and their dramas devoted to William of Orange. Heinsius may also refer to Janus Dousa, who in 1599 and 1601 published his *Annales* and thus safeguarded his position as historiographer of the States; maybe Heinsius aspired to such a position.

138 *vel vniversam—iudicauit* Cf. *Aur.* 576–608 and the comm. *ad loc.*

145 *diuini hi motus* These 'divine movements' are either acts or thoughts.

L 130–132 Heinsius will have wished to delete this remark because it interrupts the course of the argument; furthermore, if the words *totis operibus* refer to Benedicti's epic (see introduction, pp. 31–32), then he will have considered it less appropriate for the poet, who died in 1588.

          Praise of the Hollander

147–161 *Agedum maris imperator—pudenda est scientia* Through the Hollanders in general, Heinsius addresses the States, whose subjects are courageous seafarers and are willing to defend their country even at the expense of their own lives. He is playing with the meaning of *pro* in the expression "dulce et decorum est pro patria mori" (Hor. *C.* III, 2, 13): 'on behalf of', and 'in front of', therefore 'outside' the country, i.e. at sea. Cf. *Aur.* 305–318 and 1752–1814, q.v. For the play on words *pro patria-in patria*, cf. Cic. *Mil.* 104.

148–149 *populi Romani—ruinae* Heinsius was comparing the Romans and the Hollanders, both of whom were victorious; the Roman Empire, however, has fallen, whereas the Republic has not. Heinsius will have discussed this matter with Grotius, who was working on his *Parallelon rerumpublicarum*, a comparison of the Greek, Roman and Dutch societies. In Ch. III Grotius tries to prove that the Batavians were more like allies than slaves to the Romans: "Gentem Batavam et Civitatem saepe vocat Tacitus et Inscriptiones ex antiquissimis monumentis erutae. Non fuit itaque Batavia haec nostra Romanorum Provincia, aut externis, ut totus tunc Orbis fere, subiecta legibus, sed sui iuris Respublica", Grotius, *Parallelon*, ed. Meerman, 1, pp. 27–28. In this positive approach to the Romans Heinsius and Grotius were setting a trend, see Marijke Spies, 'Verbeeldingen van vrijheid: David en Mozes, Burgerhart en Bato, Brutus en Cato', *De zeventiende eeuw* 10 (1994), pp. 141–158, esp. 151.

150 *bellum gerere—docuisti* Cf. Grotius, *Parallelon rerumpublicarum*, Ch. 3 "Signum belli Batavici dabit gentibus" (Grotius, *Parallelon*, ed. Meerman, 1, p. 31).

155 *Xerxes* The story that the Persian King Xerxes tried to enchain the sea as a punishment for a storm is told by Hdt. VII, 53; see also Stephanus, *Dictionarium*, p. 449r: "compedes mari immisisse fertur". Stephanus mentions as his source Diog. Laert. *Vitae* I, 9.

160 *fraudem* The Spaniard's deceit is topical, cf. Heinsius *Pro Auriaco sua* 61–62 and *Aur.* 1946–1947.

As an exile welcomed in the northern Netherlands

161–168 *Agedum, Batave—Hispanorum crudelitas*   When Heinsius came to the Netherlands, he was received well by the Hollanders, i.c. the States of Holland and West Friesland. That is why he dedicates his play to them. Only literature can surpass the times and the violence, cf. Hor. *C.* III, 30 "exegi monumentum aere perennius". More specifically, Heinsius indicates that Orange has passed away, but his *Auriacus* can make him live on. The cruelty of the Spaniards even makes the benefaction of the Hollanders even more pleasant.

L **164–184**   In his own copy, Heinsius crossed out the reference to his exile, either because there was some aversion towards Flemish exiles, which may have increased because of the big influx, or because by the time the second edition was being planned, he had already integrated. Heinsius' career was delayed by his descent: only a year after the success of his *Auriacus* he was appointed *extraordinarius* in poetry, see also Hugo Grotius, *Dichtwerken/Poetry*, I, 2, 3A/B, pp. 36–37.

Leiden Academy

169–184 *Inter reliqua—semper habuit*   The greatest advantage of Heinsius' sojourn in the Netherlands is his contact—at Leiden University—with famous contemporaries: Joseph Scaliger, Paul Choart de Buzenval and Dousa. On Scaliger and Dousa see the intr. p. 4. Paul Choart, Seigneur de Buzenval was Ambassador in England and from 1592 onwards in The Hague, where he represented Henry IV ("Christianissimi Gallorum regis", ll. 177–178). He was part of the circle of the Leiden scholars and became a patron of artists and men of letters, among whom Grotius and Heinsius. In 1601 De Buzenval was recalled at his own request. He left on 30 October of that year, but returned to The Hague on 13 April 1602 and stayed there until his death. On him, see *DBF* 8, col. 1178–1179, Baguenault de Puchesse, "Un ami et un ambassadeur de Henri IV, Paul Choart de Buzenval (1551–1607)", *Annuaire-Bulletin de la Société de l'histoire de France* 46 (1901), pp. 109–118, Grotius, *Dichtwerken/Poetry* I, 2, 3A/B, p. 208 and Otto Schutte, *Repertorium der buitenlandse vertegenwoordigers, residerende in Nederland 1584–1810* (The Hague, Martinus Nijhoff, 1983) RGP, pp. 1–2. On the contacts between De Buzenval and Heinsius and Grotius, see also Eyffinger, *Grotius poeta*, esp. p. 72.

182 *nuperrime—mereri cepit* Heinsius is probably not pointing to Dousa's heroic actions in the Siege of Leiden (1574, see pp. 13 and 16) which even in 1584 cannot be called 'very recent', but to his historiography *Bataviae Hollandiaeque annales* (Leiden: Raphelengius, 1601), which had recently been published at the time of writing *Auriacus* (completed in December 1601, see intr., p. 9); the States had insisted on it for a long time already, see Vermaseren 1955, pp. 63–66.

183 *literas restituit* There are three possible interpretations of this combination: (1) Dousa restored literature to the level of Janus Secundus; (2) he is resurrecting Neo-Latin poetry in general; or (3) (as Jan van der Does) poetry in Dutch. On Dousa as a Dutch poet, see Jan Bloemendal, 'Janus Dousa als niederländischer Dichter', in: Lefèvre and Schäfer, *Ianus Dousa*, pp. 159–171.

184 *qui me—habuit* This remark is a token of gratitude towards and respect for Dousa, but at the same time implies the exhortation to other members of the States to follow Dousa's example.

Gratitude

185–192 *ltaque diutius—committo vobis* As proof of his gratitude Heinsius dedicates this tragedy on the death of William of Orange to the States. Fortunately the father lives on in his son, Maurice who will avenge his father. May God grant that he will live for the States. Heinsius ends with a short formula of modesty ("qualecumque"), which was already a topos in antiquity, see J. Janson, *Latin Prose Prefaces*, pp. 124–134.

190 *in Tragoediâ* As opposed to "in reliquis".

[2]   ΙΩΣΗΠΩΙ ΣΚΑΛΑΝΩΙ [...] / Heinsius to Scaliger

Summary

1–12 It is said that the Scythe Anacharsis, upon his arrival in Athens, had a conversation with his compatriot Toxaris and asked for all kinds of information. Toxaris advised him to get acquainted with Solon, who knew everything.

13–20 In the same way, when Heinsius arrived in Leiden he saw the most learned man in the world, Joseph Scaliger, who should judge his play.

21–29 If it lacks the required dignity, he should take into account Heinsius' young age, the fact that he is an amateur and does not have much knowledge. Moreover, Heinsius adduces his courage, the huge undertaking and the glorious subject.

30–35 The subject is no trifle, but national: the heroic deeds and violent death of Orange, the eponymous hero. A severe judgement is needed.

36–52 Heinsius does not ask for praise, which is impossible with regard to his youth, lack of experience and poverty. He would like to publish his tragedy quickly, for the murder of Orange has to be spoken and written about. Moreover, it will be part of his learning process.

53–56 He ends this second dedication with a farewell to Diogenes/Scaliger.

In this second letter, in which Heinsius quotes from Lucian and Aristophanes, the young author dedicates the play to Josephus Justus Scaliger, Julius Caesar Scaliger's son, as is stressed at the beginning and the end of the text. For Scaliger and Heinsius, see intr., pp. 4 and 7, on Heinsius' young age as an excuse, the comm. *ad* ll. 21–29.

Commentary

In Solon there is all of Greece

1–12 Τὸν Ἀνάχαρσιν—λέγων ἐκεῖνος Heinsius borrowed the story of the coming of Anacharsis to Athens and his visit of Toxaris for the greater part from Lucian. *Scytha* 1 and 3–5. For μπορευόμενος cf. also *Nigr.*, prol. 5.

1 Διογενὲς There may be three reasons for addressing Scaliger with 'Diogenes' (originating from god, or: having become a god). In the first place Diogenes can be a translation of the name Josephus (Joseph, JHWH shall increase, see *Gen.* 30, 24), a similar procedure as the translation of Daniel into "Theocritus (a Ganda)". The second possibility is that it is being used as an Homeric *epitheton* of kings and heroes, see *Il.* I, 337; IX, 106; XXI, 17; *Od.* II, 352. Thirdly this *epitheton* honours Joseph's father Julius Caesar Scaliger as a divine man.

Scaliger has to judge

13–20 Ἐγὼ δὲ—ἀγαπήσειν Just as Anacharsis in Athens found the culmination of all wisdom in Solon, in Leiden (called *Athenae Batavae*) Heinsius finds in Scaliger the most learned man of all times. Strictly speaking, Scaliger would have to be equated with Toxaris, since he came to Leiden from France; however, the comparison with Solon is more flattering. This interpretation is corroborated by the choice of words τὸ κεφάλαιον [...] τῶν τῇδε ἀγαθῶν, the same expression Lucian applies to Solon in *Scyth.* 5.

Heinsius stresses his status as emigrant and his youth. This is perhaps more than just a humanistic topos of modesty.

13 ὅτε τὸ ἐπεδήματα τῇ πόλει ταύτῃ Cf. Lucian. *Scyth.* 9.
14 ἐν ἀκαρεῖ Lucian. *Scyth.* 8.
15–16 τὸ κεφάλαιον εἰδέναι τῶν τῇδε ἀγαθῶν Cf. Lucian. *Scyth.* 5; this quotation is the sequel to that of l. 14.
18 ἐν μυριάνδρῳ—θεάτρῳ Cf. Lucian. *Nigr.* 18.
20 ἀγαπήσειν The participle ἀγαπήσων in Lucian cannot be combined with δόξω.

Lack of experience as excuse

21–29 Οὐ μὴν οὐδ'—ὑπερφθεγγομένων Heinsius will not defend himself if mistakes are found in the play. He merely asks for clemency on the basis of his age, dilettantism and lack of literacy. The task of writing such a tragedy is rather ambitious, but one's acts are more important than one's words, referring to the acts of both Heinsius himself and William of Orange, whose acts are greater than words can tell.

25–27 οὐ γὰρ τὸν Εὐριπίδην ὅλον [...] καραπεπώκαμεν, [...] ὥστε ὑποδραματουργεῖν σοι Cf. Lucian. *Iup. Trag.* 1 μηδὲ τὸν Εὐριπίδην ὅλον καταπεπώκαμεν, ὥστε σοι ὑποτραγῳδεῖν (v.l. ὑποδραματουργεῖν), which contains an allusion to Ar. *Ach.* 484.
25–26 τὸν τραγῳδὸν—τὸν σόν Heinsius is probably pointing to a predilection for Sophocles or Aeschylus on the part of Scaliger.
26–27 οὐδὲ τὰ τοῦ Ὁμήρου—εἴποιμεν See Athen. *Deipnos.* VIII, 39 and cf. *ibid.* epitome II, 1, p. 164.

An important subject

30–38 Οὐ γὰρ [...] ἄριστον This play is not about mythological stories (cf. the Dedication to the States, ll. 15–16), but about the *res gestae* of Orange and the end of his life.

30 Μηδείας, ἢ Ἑκάβας, ἢ καὶ Αἴαντος [...] μαστιγοφόρους Medea and Hecuba are the eponymous heroines of plays by Euripides, *Aiax* is a tragedy by Sophocles. Μαστιγοφόρος is the epithet for Ajax in the 'Argumentum' of the play. Heinsius had used it for a critic in the Dedication to Scaliger of his edition of Silius Italicus, p. 5.

31 τερατείας Cf., e.g., Isocr. *Panath.* 1 τοὺς τερατείας καὶ ψευδολογίας.

32–33 ἔτι περὶ—σπουδαζόντων Cf. Ar. *Nu.* 1382–1383.

32–33 τὴν Μορμὼ καὶ τὴν Λαμίαν δεδιότων The Mormo is a female monster to frighten children, the Lamia a monster eating human flesh. For 31–33 πάνυ ἀλλόκοτα—ἐκπλήττειν δυνάμενα, cf. Lucian. *Philops.* 2.

33 Αὐρανσίου Cf. below, Grotius, *Iambi* 59 "Auransioque cedit" and the comm.

38 Τῶν ποιητῶν—ἄριστον Cf. Ar. *Nu.* 430: τῶν Ἑλλήνων εἶναί με λέγειν ἑκατὸν σταδίοισιν ἄριστον.

Modesty, but a publication

39–52 οὐκ, εἴ γε—ἐκτραγῳδούμενος Scaliger has to make some haste with his judgement, for although *Auriacus* is not perfect, Heinsius will publish it (it will not remain hidden like Danae). It will be part of his learning process.

39 εἴ γε—τυγχάνοιμι Lucian. *Ind.* 23.

42 τῇ βελτίστῃ πενίᾳ πρσφιλοσοφῶ Lucian. *Gal.* 22.

43 οὐκ ἂν φθάνοις This expression indicates an urgent request, see LSJ s.v. φθάνω IV.2.

44–45 τὴν Ἀκρισίου [...] ἀνατρεφομένην Acrisius wished to prevent his daughter Danae from becoming pregnant, therefore he locked her in; Zeus penetrated her in the form of a golden rain; Danae gave birth to Perseus. See (for example) Stephanus, *Dictionarium*, p. 10v; Roscher 1.1, 213–214. She had to remain a virgin as a priestess at the *Thesmophoria*, see Lucian. *Timon* 17, 2.

47 πρὶν τὴν ὑπήνην—τοὺς κροτάφους τε An allusion to Hom. *Od.* XI, 319–320 and *ibid.* X, 279 (= *Il.* XXIV, 348). Cf. also Verg. *Aen.* VIII, 160: "tum mihi prima genas vestibat flore iuventas"; Lucr. V, 888–889.

51 μηδ' ὥρασιν ἵκοιτο A standard expression of cursing, see LSJ s.v. ὥρασι.

51 τὸ προσωπεῖον For the tragic mask, cf. below, Grotius, *Iambi* 4 'persona' and the comm.

Accept my tragedy

53–56 Ἔρρωσο—ἀποδέχου This letter of dedication is closed with the offering of the tragedy.

54 Ἰουλιάδη For this patronymic, cf. Dousa, *In eandem* 18 and the comm.

54 Διογενές μοι Ἰουλιάδη μέγα φέγγος Ἀχαιῶν This will refer to Scaliger's edition of Greek authors and his own literary works in Greek. For this hexameter, cf. Hom. *Il.* IX, 673: εἴπ' ἄγε μ' ὦ πολύαιν' Ὀδυσεῦ μέγα κῦδος Ἀχαιῶν (also X, 545;

ibid. X, 88 (also 555; XI, 511; XIV, 42; *Od.* III, 79, 202): εἶπ' ὦ Νέστορ Νηληϊάδη μέγα κῦδος Ἀχαιῶν.

55 Βακχεῖον τοῦτον ἄνακτα Ar. *Ran.* 1259, where it indicates Aeschylus; here *Auriacus* is meant, which is connected to Dionysus/Bacchus, as every tragedy is.
55 ἀποκηρυττόμενον Lucian. *Pisc.* 23. The meaning is that Scaliger should accept this tragedy in the style of Aeschylus, since it has now been made public.

[3]   In Hispanum et Batavum / On the Spaniard and the Hollander

Summary

The Spaniard used to have his eye on the whole world, including France and Italy. He committed crimes against the Flemish people: adults, children and defenceless girls. But when he attacked the Hollanders and went into the sea, the ocean protected them; the Spaniard's attempt did not work out. The Dutchman steals from the courts the rest of the people, because he fights and lives both on land and on the sea.

This poem describes the epic courage of the Hollanders or Dutchmen, and the likewise epic battle between them and the Spaniards. Heinsius underlines this epic nature by using specifically Homeric words from the *Iliad*. He also uses typically Homeric forms such as the iterative with -σκ- (φρονέεσκε, l. 7; καθιππεύ-εσκε, l. 11), and an optional use of the augment. Thus implicitly the war between the Spaniards and the Dutch is compared with that between the Greeks and the Trojans. The rhetorical tone is visible in the periphrasis (bear of the sea, l. 12), the *antimetabole* (l. 27) and the play on words ἀντίβιος—ἀμφίβιος, (l. 28).

Metre

The poem consists of elegiac couplets or distichs. For metrical reasons, the terms Βαταῦος (long second syllable, ll. 11 and 25) and Βατάβος (short second syllable, ll. 14 and 28) are used for 'the Dutch'.

Poet

The poem is not signed. Since it contains no praise for *Auriacus* or his poet, it is likely that it is written by Heinsius himself, even though it has not been included in the editions of the *Poemata*, but Heinsius was selective in this regard. Scaliger signed the following poem, perhaps leading one to suspect that this is also his; however, it too is not included in his *Poemata* from 1606.

Commentary

1 Δημοβόρος Hom. *Il.* I, 231.

2 ΚΕΛΤῶΝ [...] ΛΙΓΎΡΩΝ The Celts occur in Greek literature, the Ligurians do not; the latter, a tribe in *Gallia Cisalpina*, indicates (the north of) Italy, the *Celtae* are according to Caesar *B.G.* I, 1, 1 synonymous with *Galli*, indicating France. The politics of Charles V and Philip II were targeted at these lands. Spain and France engaged in a war of words over hegemony in Italy, for instance Charles V and Francis I in 1521–1526; Charles claimed Milan, Francis Navarra and Naples. Also under Philip II wars were waged between the two countries on their Italian claims, see (for example), Geoffrey Parker, *Imprudent King: A New Life of Philip II* (New Haven and London: Yale University Press, 2014), pp. 54–56; Louis Bertrand and Charles A. Petrie, *The History of Spain* (New York: Appleton, 1934), pp. 311–338; also Grotius, *Rex Hispaniarum* 25–40.

4 ἀγκαλίσιν In Homer only the form ἀγκαλίδεσσι occurs.

5 ἀεικέα μήσατο ἔργα Hom. *Il.* XXII, 395.

6 οὐδ' ἀλέη Hom. *Il.* XXII, 301.

7 φρονέεσκε Cf. Apoll. Rhod. *Argon.* IV, 1164 and Quintus Smyrnaeus (epic.), *Posthom.* XIII, 377, but Heinsius probably invented his own iterative form.

7–8 ῥέζε [...] αἴσυλα Hom. *Il.* V, 403.

9 Αἵματι [...] ἐρύθρηνεν ἄρουρα Cf. Hom. *Il.* X, 484 ἐρυθαίνετο δ' αἵματι γαῖα. The author uses the Attic variant of the verb.

15 διερῷ ποδὶ Hom. *Od.* IX, 43.

15 νῶτα θαλάσσης This *iunctura* occurs three times in Hom. *Il.*, for instance II, 159, and seven times in *Od.*

17 ἅρμα θοὸν Cf. (for example) Hom. *Il.* XI, 533 θοὸν ἅρμα.

17 ἀνεμοτρεφὲς Either 'swollen by the wind', as in Hom. *Il.* XV, 625, or 'hardened by the wind', *ibid.* XI, 256. The literal meaning is 'fed by the winds'.

19 Τῷ πίσυνος Hom. *Il.* XXIV, 295.

21 ἀνέμων ταμίῃσιν The lords of the winds are the Hollanders, who with their seafaring skills are masters of the winds. This theme is also in *Aur.* 305–317 and the chorus after Act IV, e.g. 1756–1761.

23 ξυνέηκε μάχεσθαι Hom. *Il.* I, 8 and VII, 210.

24 ἀρχαίης Is this a synonym of κοιρανίης (dominion, power, sovereignty), or should it be taken in the usual meaning of 'old'? If so, the question is whether it relates to γῆς or κοιρανίης.

[4]   In Auriacum Danielis Heinsii / On Daniel Heinsius' *Auriacus*

Summary

Heinsius has written a tragedy in the style of Aeschylus, and thus shades the theatre of Sophocles and the other Greek tragedians. The subject is the gun shot that killed the prince and wounded the fatherland. This shame will always stick to the Spaniards, partly through Heinsius' play, which also immortalizes Nassau.

Metre

The poem consists of elegiac distichs. Line 9 ends on a monosyllable, something that is usually avoided. The elision (una'st) renders this less disturbing, see Drexler, *Römische Metrik*, p. 86.

Poet

Josephus Justus Scaliger (1540–1609), who was a poet in Latin and Greek and a philologist; he worked at Leiden University from 1593 until his death. On him and his relation with Heinsius, who dedicated *Aur.* to him, see the intr., p. 4. See Grafton, *Joseph Scaliger*. Some Greek poems by Scaliger are edited and translated in *Bataafs Athene*, pp. 1–9.

The text is also included in Heinsius, *Poemata* (1647), p. 633.

Commentary

1 *Melpomenae sacrum facit* Heinsius brings a sacrifice to Melpomene, the Muse of tragedy, by having written a tragic play. For *sacra* related to literature, see *OLD* s.v. sacrum 3e.
1 *Ore favete* It was forbidden to disturb the Roman sacrifices with inappropriate words; therefore, the priest spoke the formula *favete linguis* (favour this with your tongues, i.e. do not say anything wrong, be silent). See (for example) Verg. *Aen.* V, 71: "Ore favete omnes" and Tib. IV, 6, 1: "Sint ora faventia sacris"; also *id.* II, 2, 1: "Quisquis adest, faveat".
2 *Dum quatit ... pede* Cf. Grotius' *Iambi* 1–2 "[...] quatit [...] orchestram pede".
2 *Aeschyleo* Cf. Grotius, *Iambi* 22–23 and the comm. *ad loc.*
3 *Sophoclaei carmen regale cothurni* For the comparison with the Greek tragedian Sophocles, cf. Grotius, *Iambi* 20 and see the comm. *ad loc.* For the

royal aspect of his theatre, cf. the Dedication to the States 2: "Vna Tragoedia Regium sibi nomen vendicat" and the comm. *ad loc.*

3–4 *Cede ... cedite*   Among other texts Prop. II, 34, 65 and II, 2, 13.

4 *Cecropijs*   Cecrops was the first mythic king of Athens, the adjective derived from that name "Cecropius" can be used as a metonym for Attic (Attica being the region around Athens where tragedy saw its blossoming), cf. Hor. *C.* II, 1, 12: "Grande munus Cecropio repetes cothurno".

6 *Non—canit*   Cf. Ov. *Her.* 6, 82: "Non exspectata vulnus ab hoste tuli".

7 *fixum in patria, dum figitur in duce, vulnus*   Cf. Grotius, *Iambi* 125–126, where Libertas has the same wounds as the Prince.

8 *hanc—notam*   Cf. Prop. III, 11, 36: "tollet nulla dies hanc tibi, Roma, notam", and Dousa, *In Auriacum* 52: "Tollet nulla dies hanc tibi, Maure, notam".

9–10 *Grandiloquisque—vita perennis erit*   The murder of the Prince will be a disgrace for the Spaniards, but for Orange himself eternal life, i.e. immortalization through poetry. For this literary topos, already occurring in Hom. *Il.* VI, 359, see Curtius, *European Literature and Latin Middle Ages*, pp. 476–477. The adjective *grandiloquus* is used by Quint. X, 1, 66 for Aeschylus; perhaps Scaliger also wanted to honour Heinsius in this indirect manner by comparing him implicitly with this Greek tragic poet.

10 *vita perennis erit*   A common combination in medieval Latin, already in Paulinus Nolanus, *Carm.* 31, 560, p. 327 and Venantius Fortunatus, *Carm.* VI, 5, 356, p. 146. See Schumann, 5, p. 682.

[5]   **In eandem / On the same**

Summary

According to Scaliger, Seneca surpassed the Greek tragic authors, but now the representative of tragedy is Heinsius, who outdoes ancient tragedy. He even outclasses Muret and Buchanan, even though they too treated non-fictitious subject matter. Heinsius outstands in two respects: he is a second Seneca, and he deals with a non-fictitious topic, and even the highest one, viz. the murder of Prince William. It is amazing that a young man can represent such an important subject in Latin poetry. He even does so while being an exile. What will he achieve when he is in his own country! Justly he chose this subject for its majesty keeps pace with the tragedy's style. Thus the poet Heinsius and the Prince of Orange match.

The poet's work contains relatively many words from Greek: *Hypothesibus* (l. 2), *orgia* (l. 9), *acroamata* (l. 17), *ephebum* (l. 23) and the Greek-like patronymic *Heinsiades* (ll. 18, 19, 34). Dousa may have used Greek vocabulary *ornatus causa*, but perhaps also because Heinsius had a predilection for Greek. In his use of other poetical means, such as metonymy and mythology, he was inspired by the poetry of the French Pléiade poets; for the use of mythology by these poets see Guy Demerson, *La mythologie classique dans l'oeuvre lyríque de la Pléiade* (Geneva: Droz, 1972) Doctoral thesis Paris 1970. For Dousa's contact with them, see Heesakkers and Reinders, *Genoeglijk bovenal zijn mij de Muzen*, passim.

Metre

The poem consists of elegiac distichs, with a *versus spondiacus* in ll. 9 and 23; the Roman Neoterics or *poetae novi* were fond of this procedure, see Drexler, *Römische Metrik*, p. 85.

Testimonies

This poem is also included in Janus Dousa's *Echo, sive Lusus imaginis iocosae* (The Hague: Nieulandt, 1603), fol. 69v–70v and his *Poemata pleraque selecta* (Leiden: Basson, 1609), pp. 148–149. For the text with a Dutch translation, see Heesakkers and Reinders, *Genoeglijk bovenal zijn mij de Muzen*, pp. 83–85.

Poet

Janus Dousa (Jan van der Does, Lord of Noordwijk, 1545–1604), Neo-Latin and Dutch poet, philologist, nobleman, statesman, co-founder and curator of the Leiden Academy. He played an important role in the development of the young Republic; as a commander of a militia, Dousa was one of the main figures in the Siege of Leiden. He is mentioned in *Aur.* 1810. On him and Heinsius, see intr. p. 4. On Dousa, see *NNBW* 6, 425–429; Chris L. Heesakkers, *Praecidanea Dousana: Materials for a Biography of Janus Dousa Pater (1545–1604): His Youth* (Amsterdam: Holland Universiteitspers, 1976) Doctoral thesis Leiden; Haitsma Mulier and Van der Lem, *Repertorium*, pp. 120–122; J.A. van Dorsten, *Poets, Patrons, and Professors: Sir Philip Sidney, Daniel Rogers, and the Leiden Humanists* (Leiden: Leiden University Press; London: Oxford University Press, 1962) Publications of the Sir Thomas Browne Institute, Leiden, General series, 2; Heesakkers and Reinders, *Genoeglijk bovenal zijn mij de Muzen*; Schäfer and Lefèvre, *Ianus Dousa*.

Commentary

Title *In eandem*   Sc. *tragoediam Auriacum*.
2 *Scaligero in Tragicis Iudice Hypothesibus*   In his *Poetica* Julius Caesar
Scaliger ranked Seneca above the three Greek tragedians, see Scal. *Poet.* VI,
6, p. 323b; Scaliger, *Poetica/Dichtkunst* 5, p. 274.10–13: "Seneca [...] quem nulla
Graecorum maiestate inferiorem existimo, cultu vero ac nitore etiam Euripide
maiorem. Inventiones sane illorum sunt, at maiestas carminis, sonus, spiritus
ipsius". A *hypothesis* was the summary of the plot of a tragedy, see Justina Gre-
gory (ed.), *A Companion to Greek Tragedy* (Malden, MA and Oxford: Blackwell,
2005), pp. 384–385. Probably Dousa uses the word in the sense of scientific treatise, i.e. the *Poetica*.
3 *palma*   A sign of victory carried by a Roman *triumphator*, also applied to
poets, see Verg. *Georg.* III, 12: "Primus Idumaeas referam tibi, Mantua, palmas".
4 *Argolicis ... Ausonio*   Dousa uses "Argolicus" (of Argos) as pars pro toto for
Greek, and "Ausonius" (from Ausonia, the lower part of Italy) as a metonym for
Roman.
6 *omnia plena Deo*   Cf. Verg. *Ecl.* 3, 60: "Iovis omnia plena".
9 *Muretus*   The French and Neo-Latin humanist author Marc-Antoine Muret,
whose writings included a Latin tragedy *Iulius Caesar* (1550), cf. l. 10 'Caesaris'; see Andreas Hagmaier, *M.A. Muret, Iulius Caesar: M. Virdung, Brutus:
Zwei neulateinische Tragödien: Text, Übersetzung und Interpretation* (Munich
and Leipzig: K.G. Saur, 2006).
9 *Orgia Buchanani*   The Scottish humanist George Buchanan wrote two tragedies, *Iephthes* (1544), and *Baptistes* (written before 1544, published 1577), edited
in George Buchanan, *Tragedies*, ed. Peter Sharratt and Patrick G. Walsh (Edin-
burgh: Scottish Academic Press, 1983). The word *orgia*, originally denoting
the secret rites for Bacchus, is here used metaphorically for a sacred, biblical
tragedy, on a sacred subject from Holy Writ. On Buchanan, see Ian D. McFar-
lane, *Buchanan* (London: Duckworth, 1981); Philip J. Ford, *George Buchanan:
Prince of Poets* (Aberdeen: Aberdeen University Press, 1982).
11 *Aeschyleo ... cothurno*   Cf. Scaliger, *In Auriacum* 3 "Sophoclaei cothurni", and
2 "Aeschyleo [...] pede"; for the comparison with Aeschylus, see also Grotius,
Iambi 22.
12 *Clytûs nato*   Euripides was a son of Mnesarchides (or Mnesarchos) and
Kleito, see *RE* 6, 1244.
12 *Sophocli*   See Scaliger, *In Auriacum* 3 and Grotius *Iambi* 20.
13 *mendacia veris*   Cf. *Illustrissimis* [...] *Ordinibus* 13–18. This is a variant on the
play on the words *ficta—facta*.
15 *Sallusti pagina*   The style and content of the works of the Roman historian Sallust (C. Sallustius Crispus, 86–35 BC), with their moral-political vision

and attention to virtue, were highly appreciated in Leiden. His style contains archaisms and (Sen. *Ep.* 114, 17): "amputatae sententiae et verba ante exspectatum cadentia et obscura brevitas"; cf. Quint. IV, 2, 45.

15–16 *ficto Luci asino* The works attributed to Lucian of Samostata include Λούκιος ἢ ῎Ονος. See *RE* 13, 1725–1777; on *Lucius* esp. 1748–1749.

16 *Marsi … Amazonidi* The epic *Amazonis* of Marsus, a poet (mainly of epigrams) from the Augustan period, mentioned by Mart. IV, 29, 8.

17 *Acroamata* ἀκροάματα are everything that is heard, and with pleasure, a play that is read, staged or sung (LSJ s.v. 1). In Latin this loan word indicated music or reading for entertainment at meals, see Lewis and Short s.v. acroama.

18 *Heinsiadi* Neologisms such as "Heinsiades", a patronymic in Greek style, occur so often that they do not seem to have a special meaning, but are used *metri causa*. Cf. Heinsius *Pro Auriaco suo* 129 "Iuliade"; see also Dirk Sacré, 'Neologismen in de neolatijnse poëzie', *Handelingen van de Koninklijke Zuidnederlandse Maatschappij voor Taal- en Letterkunde en Geschiedenis* 41 (1987), pp. 149–179, esp. pp. 159–160.

19 *poplite flexo* *Judic.* 7, 6.

20 *Pindarus* The Greek lyric poet of (for example) dithyrambs, Pindar (ca. 522–ca. 443 BC), was considered to be divinely inspired, see Hor. *C.* 4.2. See the comm. *ad Illustrissimis* [...] *Ordinibus* 92–122. For *submittere fasces* as *terminus technicus* for honouring high-ranked persons and submitting to them, see *TLL* 6.1, 304. Here, perhaps, an allusion is being made to Auson. 293, 3 "submittit cui rota suos Hispania fasces." On the reception of Pindar in the Netherlands, see René Veenman, 'De Thebaensche swaen: De receptie van Pindarus in de Nederlanden', *Voortgang: Jaarboek voor de Neerlandistiek* 13 (1992), pp. 65–90; on Pindar in the Renaissance, see Stella P. Revard, *Politics, Poetics, and the Pindaric Ode 1450–1700* (Turnhout: Brepols, 2010), and *id., Pindar and the Renaissance Hymn-Ode: 1450–1700* (Tempe, AR: Arizona Center for Medieval and Renaissance Studies, 2001) Medieval and Renaissance Texts and Studies, 221.

22 *Hesperia* The Occident is Spain, regarded as the west from Italy.

23 *ephebum* An ἔφηβος was a boy of ca. 18 years old who entered society, see *RE* 5, 2737–2746 s.v. ἐφηβία. The term is appropriate for the (21-year-old) Heinsius, since he will enter university life.

24 *Pondera Romuleis … modis Pondera* This phrase points to either the style or the subject. Cf. Cic. *De or.* II, 73: "Omnium sententiarum gravitate, omnium verborum ponderibus est utendum".

25–26 *Proavito qui Lare pulsus … in Exsilio* Heinsius mentions his exile in *Illustrissimis* [...] *Ordinibus* 163–168, and *Aur.* 186–242 and 611–714.

33–34 *Vate* For the sacral connotation of the word "vates", see Grotius, *Iambi* 141 and the comm. *ad loc.*

[6]   Εἰς τὸν Δαν[ιέλος] τοῦ Εἰνσίου Αὐραικάρχην / On Daniel Heinsius' Prince of Orange

Summary

The Spaniards are insulted because they embrace their mischief and subdue body and mind. The Dutch have a Hercules in Orange who brings prosperity and is the terror of the Spaniards. Heinsius has now immortalized Orange in poetry and thus earned fame. This ensures that Orange will remain famous for future generations, both on his own merits and through Heinsius' laudatory words.

The poem contains Homeric words, e.g.: Ἔρρετε (l. 1) Hom. *Il.* XXIV, 239; Δίζυγα (l. 2) *Il.* V, 195; X, 473; ἄλκαρ (l. 7), *Il.* V, 644; XI, 823; and the *epitheta*: ἀλεξίκακον (l. 3), *Il.* X, 20; μεγαλήτορος (l. 11) *Il.* V, 247, ἀγάκλυτος (l. 13) *Il.* VI, 463, alongside Attic forms such as εὐπραγίας (l. 4) and ἰθυντῆρα (l. 5, cf., for example, Apoll. Rhod. IV, 209) and Ἀΐδιον (l. 12). Epic language, however, prevails, cf. *In Hispanum et Batavum*.

Metre

The poem is written in elegiac distichs, with in the third line being a *versus spondiacus*.

Poet

Bonaventura Vulcanius (or De Smet, 1538–1614) studied law and medicine in Louvain. From 1581 to 1610 he was Professor of Classics in Leiden, where he taught Heinsius. He edited many Greek authors, often with a Latin translation. On him see Johannes Meursius, *Athenae Batavae, sive de urbe Leidensi et Academia virisque claris, qui utramque ingenio suo, atque scriptis illustrarunt, libri duo* (Leiden: Cloucquius: 1625), pp. 102–108; *Bataafs Athene*, p. 11; *NNBW* 10, 1143–1145; Helène Cazes (ed.), *Bonaventura Vulcanius, Works and Networks: Bruges 1538-Leiden 1614* (Leiden and Boston: Brill, 2010) Brill's Studies in Intellectual History, 194.

Commentary

Tit. Αὐραικάρχην For such a combination of Αὐράικος and ἀρχή, cf. Coddaeus Πρὸς μέγαν [...] 1: Ἀρουσιόνων [...] Ἄρχον.

1 Ἰβηρομανεῖς The suffix—μανης (of the verb μαίνομαι, to be mad), often means 'to be abounding in', see LSJ s.v. ἱππομανής. Here it may be a translation of or an allusion to "Maranos", a common nickname for Spaniards.

1 ἀλεξίκακον ... Ἡρακλῆα Just like in *Aur.* (intr. pp. 32–33) Orange is compared to Hercules, here as the one who keeps of ill.

7 Βελγίδος ἄλκαρ Cf. (for example) Hom. *Il.* XI, 822 ἄλκαρ Ἀχαιῶν.

9 Χάρισιν For the Graces as goddesses of grace, connected to the Muses, see Hes. *Theog.* 64 and Quint. I, 10, 21. See also Roscher 1, 873–884 and *RE* 3, 2163–2164.

10 Μνημοσύνης For Mnemosyne as the Muses' mother, see Hes. *Theog.* 54, and Roscher 2.2, 3076–3080; *RE* 15, 2265–2269.

10 Μνημοσύνης σελίσιν Cf. *CIG* 2237 σελίδες Μουσῶν. See also LSJ s.v. σελίς.

12 ἀγάκλυτος For this Homeric *epitheton*, see (for example) Hom. *Il.* VI, 436.

[7]   **Idem Bonaventurae Vulcanii / A similar poem by Bonaventura Vulcanius**

Summary

The Athens-born Sophocles stood out above the antique tragedian-poets, the Ghent-born Heinsius above the contemporary ones. There is, however, a difference: Sophocles wrote in his old age, whereas Heinsius does so in his youth.

Just like the previous poem by Vulcanius, it has a Homeric ring. For the comparison with Sophocles, see Grotius, *Iambi* 20 and the comm.

Metre

The poem consists of elegiac distichs.

Poet

For Bonaventura Vulcanius see above, p. 315 and intr. p. 4.

Commentary

2 ἔξαρχος This word is used by Homer for the one who raises a lamentation, appropriate for the author of a tragedy containing lamentations (of Loisa and Libertas).

[8]   Πρὸς μέγαν τὸν ποιητὴν τραγῳδὸν, Δανιελ Εἴνσιον, Ἐπίγραμμα /
        Epigram on the great tragic poet Daniel Heinsius

Summary

Heinsius, when you sing Orange people listen to you, and whether you are
singing his actions or his death, everything is in measure. The death of Orange
shocks everyone. The subject of your piece is a formidable act, but your style is
even more daunting: if metempsychosis is true, Seneca's soul is gone into you.

Just like in the previous poems, many Homeric words occur, with some excep-
tions, e.g. σφαγὴν (l. 4), μετρίως (l. 5) and πράγματα (l. 7).

Metre

The poem consists of elegiac couplets or distichs, the appropriate metre for
an epigram, see (for example) Gerhard Pfohl, *Das Epigramm: Zur Geschichte
einer inschriftlichen und literarischen Gattung* (Darmstadt: Wissenschaftliche
Buchgesellschaft, 1968) and Gideon Nisbet, 'Epigrams: The Classical Tradition',
in: *ENLW*, pp. 379–386.

Poet

Guilielmus Coddaeus (Willem van der Codde, 1575–1625?) studied Greek and
Hebrew at Leiden University, and Theology. In 1601 he was appointed Professor
of Hebrew, in 1617–1617 he was also Rector of the university. A Remonstrant, he
refused to sign the decrees of the Synod of Dordt, and was therefore suspended.
See *NNBW* 7, 305–306; *Bataafs Athene*, p. 35.

Commentary

1 Ἀρουσιόνων ... Ἀρχὸν   Prince of the Oranges. For the form Ἀρουσιόνων, see the
comm. *ad* Grotius, *Iambi* 57–73.
5 μέτρον   This indicates the metre and the measure or medium, cf. (for example) Hor. *C.* II, 10, 5: "aurea mediocritas", and see Otto, *Sprichwörter*, p. 216.
9–10 Πυθαγόρα ... δόγματ'   Pythagoras' doctrine encompassed belief in rein-
carnation (*RE* 24, 171–209; esp. 187–192). Plato would adopt this doctrine and
connect it to a winged soul, for instance in *Phaedr.* 249. Coddaeus refers to these
two issues in Ἡ ψυχὴ Σενέκης εἰς βίον αὖθις ἔπτη, i.e. in the body of Heinsius. For
the aorist form see (for example) Hom. *Battrach.* 208.

[9]   Iambi Libertati sauciae Heynsianae / Iambs on Heinsius' Wounding
         of Liberty

Summary

1–41 Praise be to *Auriacus* and its writer, who flies through the sky like a poet
'faster than Daedalus' and surpasses the Greek tragedian. He also surpasses the
Latin tragic poet Seneca. Grotius will choose a seat in the sky, for so high does
the flight that Heinsius go, on which he should take his friend with him.

42–54 Heinsius' tragedy is almost better than that of antiquity, but also surpasses the contemporaneous tragedies *Iephthes* and *Baptistes* of Buchanan.
Both Dousa and Scaliger agree that Heinsius surpasses Seneca by far.

55–95 Grotius compares the characters of *Auriacus* with those from Seneca's
dramas: Orange with Hercules and Agamemnon, his wife Louise with Hector's wife Andromache and his mother Hecuba, and with Alcmene, Megara
and Deianira, Hercules' mother and his two wives. The mute character Frederick Henry is compared with Astyanax, Hector's and Andromache's little child,
and with Hyllus, Hercules' son, and Philisthenes, Thyestes' second son, with
Pyrrhus, Achilles' son and with Philoctetes, Hercules' comrade, all of whom
have acted courageously.

96–120 For the murderer of relatives, Grotius chooses as parallels Thyestes,
Theseus and Oedipus, who, however, did not know that they were killing their
sons or father; the crime the murderer has committed is worse than that of
Atreus or Aegisthus. The Spanish King who gave the order surpasses Lycus, both
Creons and Ulysses or Jason, and even the seer Calchas had not dared to predict something as horrible, nor were the seers Tiresias or Manto able to exhort
to this deed, something which only the Pope could do.

121–135 Freedom, who has cut her hair as a sign of mourning and the hat of
freedom on her head, has traits of Iole who mourned for her father, and Cassandra, grieving over the destruction of Troy; furthermore, she resembles Electra
and Antigone, mourning their fathers.

134–139 If the shades are still concerned about what is happening on earth and
have not forgotten everything, the Dutch will bring salutes to Orange, blessed
as he is in his son as an avenger and in Heinsius as the one who sings a song of
praise for him.

This poem is very vivid, with the rhetorical means of the *sub oculis subiectio*
or *descriptio*, or *evocatio* such as: "cernam—prodire" (ll. 42–43), "incedit alto—
princeps cothurno" (ll. 59–60), "cerno Loysae syrma" (l. 72), "cerno pro taedis
rogos, cerno secures" (ll. 92–93), "at ille—gradum" (ll. 96–97) and ll. 121–126,

a description of the clothing of Freedom, who brings an offering of her hair and tramples the yoke. The frequency, however, suggests that this is not merely rhetoric, but that Grotius really did see or read the play. Cf. also the short poem he wrote for Heinsius in his complimentary copy of *Adamus exul* (Grotius, *Dichtwerken/Poetry* I, 1A/B, p. 311): "Heynsi vestustae restitutor Orchestrae, | Ornas cothurno qui pedes Sophocleo, | Primusque Syrmo vincis Euripideum | Et Aeschyleas et Lycophronis faeces".

Metre

The poem is in iambic trimeters, just like *Auriacus* itself. The metre suits the poem, which is not a particularly laudatory verse, nor an expression of personal feelings, for which the elegiac distich was the most suitable metre. See also Eyffinger, *Grotius poeta*, pp. 209–214.

Poet

Hugo Grotius (Huig de Groot, 1583–1645), jurist and Neo-Latin, Greek and Dutch poet, prose author, historian, theologian, ambassador and statesman, was already following courses in 1594, aged 11, at Leiden University, where he became a good friend of Heinsius. In 1598 he took part in an embassy to the King of France Henry IV and obtained a doctorate in law in Orléans. In 1601 he had published a Neo-Latin drama, *Adamus exul.* On him, see Nellen, *Hugo Grotius.*

For this commentary I drew on the material compiled in Grotius, *Dichtwerken/ Poetry* I, 2, 2A, pp. 150–159 and I, 2, 2B, pp. 236–249; I, 2, 2B, pp. 236–237 on mss and edd.: "Hs. Leiden, UB., coll. *Pap. A*, fol. 4v–5r. Printed in Heinsius, *Auriacus* (1602), pp. [XXI–XXIV]; *PC* 1617, pp. 230–234; Leiden *PC* 1639, pp. 200–204; London *PC* 1639(1), pp. 230–234; *PC* 1639(2), pp. 230–234; Leiden *PC* 1645, pp. 168–172; Amsterdam *PC* 1670, pp. 161–164". The variants are listed pp. 237–238.

Commentary

Heinsius has written a lofty play

1–8 *Quis ille tanto—luce perrumpit sua* Grotius imagines that his friend hides behind his drama, but that the darkness still breaks through the radiance of his glory.

1 *pulpitum ... quatit*   For the common metaphor cf. Grotius' poem of dedication to Brederode (Grotius, *Dichtwerken/Poetry* I, 1A, p. 319) 1 "Pulpita [...] quassata" and the parallels mentioned in Grotius, *Dichtwerken/Poetry* I, 1B, p. 220; for this metaphor in Latin literature, see Grotius, *Dichtwerken/Poetry* I, 2, 2B, p. 238.

2 *insolenti ... pede*   "Insolens" in this combination can mean (1) extraordinary, because it is Heinsius' first tragedy and one of the first in the Low Countries; (2) loud. Related to this is the interpretation of "pes": the foot clothed in the buskin, cf. the poem already mentioned, Grotius, *Dichtwerken/Poetry* I, 1A, p. 319: "tragico quassata cothurno", and p. 311 *Heynsi vetustae* [...] 3: "ornas cothurno qui pedes Sophocleo"; cf. also Meursius *In* [...] *Adamum exulem* 5–6: "Quippe pedem Tragico nemo insertare cothurno ausus", see Grotius, *Dichtwerken/Poetry* I, 1A, p. 31.

3 *motibus*   Either emotions or the movements of the tragic player Heinsius, just like in ll. 1–2 he made the stage shake and resound.

4 *Persona*   The tragic mask and the character, see (for example) William Beare, *The Roman Stage: A Short History of Latin Drama in the Time of the Republic* (London: Methuen, 1964), pp. 184–195 and 303–309 and Grotius, *Dichtwerken/Poetry* I, 2, 2B, p. 239.

4 *faexque*   See for this make-up Hor. *A.P.* 277: "quae canerent agerentque peruncti faecibus ora". For other, also contemporaneous parallels, see Grotius, *Dichtwerken/Poetry* I, 1 B, pp. 212–213.

4 *detonantia*   For *detonare* in the sense of reciting lofty poetry, see Stat. *Silv.* 2.7.65–66: "Albos ossibus Italis Philippos et Pharsalica bella detonabis" and Van Dam, *Statius Silvae, Book II*, p. 483 *ad loc.*

6 *jubar*   In this metaphorical sense also in Sen. *Tro.* 448: "vultus flammeum intendens iubar"; Mart. VIII, 65, 4: "purpureum fundens Caesar ab ore iubar".

7 *atrae ... caliginis*   Verg. *Aen.* IX, 36: "caligine volvitur atra".

We, the others, do not reach that high

9–16 *At nos—in nidum cadit*   Heinsius breaks through the dark, whereas our struggle against darkness is in vain. We try to fly high, but we do not succeed. Grotius uses a Homeric simile of a young bird trying to fly up but falling back into the nest. For the rarity of Homeric similes in Grotius' poetry, see Grotius, *Dichtwerken/Poetry* I, 2, 2B, p. 239.

10–11 *tenebris ... luctamur*   Cf. Stat. *Th.* XI, 522: "luctataeque diu tenebris".

14 *pennas quatit*   Cf. Ov. *Met.* IV, 677: "Paene suas quatere est oblitus in aere pennas".

15 *affectans iter* A common combination in Plautus and Terence; see (for example) Plaut. *Men.* 686 and Ter. *Heaut.* 301. For more parallels, see Grotius, *Dichtwerken/Poetry* I, 2, 2B, p. 240. Whereas the Roman playwrights used the expression metaphorically, Grotius takes it literally.

Heinsius flies high in the sky

17–32 *Tu Daedaleïs—volas* In his flight Heinsius goes higher than the classical tragedians Sophocles, Euripides, Aeschylus and Lycophron, as well as Seneca. The starting point for this metaphor may have been the expression 'the Ghent nightingale' for Heinsius, or the classical representation of the poet as a swan, e.g. Hor. *C.* IV, 2, 25: "Dircaeum [...] cycnum", i.e. Pindar; Virgil is called the Mantuan swan. Here it is not the poetic rapture that is at stake, but the notion of 'rising above'. The addition of "Daedaleis" suggests inspiration from Hor. *C.* IV, 2, 2–3: "ceratis ope Daedalea nititur pennis".

17 *Daedaleïs* For the architect Daedalus escaping with his son Icarus the island of Crete, see (for example) Ov. *Met.* VIII, 183–235.
19–20 *plebémque—relinquis* Here the thought is slightly different from Hor. *C.* III, 3, 1: "Odi profanum vulgus et arceo": it is not the people, but the ordinary poets (plebem) that he outpaces.
20 *Sophoclen praeteris* For the comparison with Sophocles (ca. 496–406 BC) see Scaliger (*In Auriacum* 3), De Licques (ll. 25–26) and Vulcanius (*Idem*, l. 5). See also the accompanying poem to *Adamus exul*, see Grotius, *Dichtwerken/Poetry* I, 1A, p. 311, whereas Grotius was praised like this for his *Adamus exul* by Dousa (*ibid.*, p. 29): "Qui Sophoclen Senecamque legis [...]". For more parallels, see Grotius, *Dichtwerken/Poetry* I, 2, 2B, p. 240.
21 *Euripiden* A similar comparison with Euripides was made by De Licques (p. 116, l. 26) and in Grotius' poem to his *Adamus exul*. In such laudatory poems Euripides is mentioned less frequently than Sophocles and Aeschylus.
21 *alâ remige* For this frequently occurring image, cf. (for example) Ov. *Met.* V, 558: "posse super fluctus alarum insistere remis".
22 *author olim triplicis Promethei* Of Aeschylus' trilogy on Prometheus, only *Prometheus vinctus* has survived. Aeschylus (see *RE* 1, 1065–1100 s.v. Aischylos 13) is mentioned by Scaliger (l. 2), Dousa (*In eandem* 11), Scriverius (*In Auriacum* 24) and Grotius in the poem to Heinsius to *Adamus exul*, Grotius, *Dichtwerken/Poetry* I, 1A, p. 311.
23–24 *quique—volumine* The Greek poet and grammarian Lycophron (3rd c. BC) from Chalcis on Euboea would have written many tragedies that are almost completely lost. The barely comprehensible poem *Cassandra* or *Alexandra* is

322						DANIEL HEINSIUS, AURIACUS: COMMENTARY

attributed to him. In the monologue of 1,474 lines Cassandra predicts the world history from the Trojan War to the time of Alexander the Great, see *RE* 13, 2316–2381; on *Alexandra* esp. 2325–2381. It had been published in 1597 by the Leiden Professor Johannes Meursius (*Lycophronis Chalcidensis Alexandra*). In this edition the Latin translation by Joseph Scaliger was included, entitled *Cassandra*.

24 *furentem* Cf. Sen. *Aga.* 724, where Cassandra says: "Cui bacchor furens", and Cic. *Div.* I, 39, 85: "Cassandra furens futura prospiciat".

25–27 *omnes—invîdit* Of many Greek tragedians neither plays nor even fragments have survived. Ionia is used pars pro toto for Greece.

31 *priscum Latinae ... Scenae decus* Perhaps Seneca is already meant, but probably these words refer to older Latin playwrights, esp. Ennius (239–169 BC) and Pacuvius (220–ca. 130 BC).

32 *choragiumque* For χορηγία cf. Plaut. *Capt.* prol. 61: "comico choragio"; Festus 1913, p. 45 "choragium: instrumentum scaenarum".

The flight of the swan

33–41 *O Cycne Flander—purus dies* The Flemish swan Heinsius, born in Ghent, should take Grotius with him on his high flight, above the clouds and to the shining turning point of the stars. As with lines 17–32, one may question the character of the flight, the flight of fame, the height of his talent and skills, or poetic rapture.

40 *siderum metae* Cf. Verg. *Aen.* V, 835: "Iamque fere mediam caeli nox umida metam contigerat".

40 *Foros* Cf. Liv. I, 35, 8: "Loca divisa patribus equitibusque ubi spectacula sibi quisque facerent; fori appellati". See also *TLL* 6.1, 1208–1209, esp. 1209.42–51.

Heinsius surpasses Buchanan and Seneca

42–56 *Hîc prisca—Maximi Circi Chorus* Heinsius' play is better than antique drama, i.e. by Seneca ("victa Gandae [the birthplace of Heinsius] Corduba [the birthplace of Seneca]"). Furthermore, Heinsius surpasses Buchanan's *Iephthes* (1544) and *Baptistes* (1577), on Judges 11, 30–40, and Mt. 14, 3–12; Mc. 6, 14; 17–29 and Lk. 3, 19–20 and 9, 7–9 resp. See also Dousa, *In eandem* 9–10 "Sed hic quid ad Orgia Buchanani? [...] Iephthae conditor iste suae?" A similar allusion in Dousa's poem for Grotius' *Adamus exul* (Grotius, *Dichtwerken/Poetry* I, 1A, p. 29), 20–21: "Fastus Scotia pone tuos. Ardua res, Iephten Scaenae ostentasse Latinae". On Buchanan's fame, see Grotius, *Dichtwerken/Poetry* I, 1B, pp. 15–16.

Dousa and Scaliger (l. 50) were both celebrities of Leiden University, cf. ll. 52–53 "Heroa hunc et hunc felix Deus servavit annis" (at the age of 56 and 61 resp.).

50 *Dousa* See his poem *In eandem*, above, p. 92–95.

50 *Scaliger* For his laudatory poem, see p. 90 "Melpomenae sacrum [...]".

51 *haeres—muneri* Cf. *Silva ad Cuchl.* 30–31 (Grotius, *Dichtwerken/Poetry* I, 2, 1A, p. 53): "quam iure suo suus obtinet haeres, Scaligerum dico". The heritage may be the humanistic education Joseph Scaliger got from his father, or his *Poetices libri septem* (Lyon 1561), in which tragedy takes an important place.

56 *Maximi Circi Chorus* In the Circus Maximus no plays were staged, but here the applause of a full house is meant (Grotius, *Dichtwerken/Poetry* I, 2, 2B, p. 243).

Orange and characters from Seneca's dramas

57–73 *Formae micantem—hostem salo* Orange is compared to Hercules as presented in Seneca's *Hercules furens* and *Hercules Oetaeus*. Strikingly, Grotius uses the Latin form *Alcides* in contrast to Heinsius who (*Aur.* 93) chooses the Greek form *Alceides*. In the Latin translation of Orange *Auransius* he also deviates from Heinsius' *Auriacus*, see Grotius, *Dichtwerken/Poetry* I, 2, 2B, p. 203 and cf. Coddaeus Πρὸς μέγαν τὸν ποιητὴν τραγῳδὸν 1 Ἀρουσιόνων. The form *Auraicus* also occurs, e.g. Benedicti, *De rebus gestis* I, 186: "Auraico [...] de nomine" and II, 409–410: "animamque recentem Auraici". The form *Aurasinus* is found in the minutes of the Leiden curators (e.g. Febr. 1580, Molhuysen, *Bronnen*, p. 10) who will have adopted it from Dousa's *Nova poemata* (1576), for instance in the poem of dedication *Illustrissimo Guilelmo Nassavio, Aurasiae principi* [...] 5: "princeps maxime et optime Aurasine". Grotius had used *Auriacus* in his poem *Scutum Auriacum* (1597).

The sentence "Doletque rursum regis Hispani scelus" contains a double allusion: to Philip II, in the case of Orange, and to the mythical Spanish King Geryoneus who attacked Hercules after he had stolen his cattle, see *RE* 7, 1286–1296; Roscher 1.2, 1630–1638.

Furthermore, Orange is compared to the Greek King Agamemnon, the eponymous hero of Seneca's tragedy. Like this general, Orange is treacherously murdered in his own house (cf. *Aur.* 1953–1958). The Greeks needed ten years to conquer one city, Orange conquered ten cities in one year (ll. 62–63), which refers to the year 1572, when many Dutch cities joined Orange, see also Grotius' poem on Pieter Bor's *Vande Nederlantsche Oorloghen* [...] (1601), *Si satis Hesperiae* 159–185, in: Grotius, *Dichtwerken/Poetry* I, 2, 2A, pp. 193–195.

61–62 *incedit—Cothurno* This is either a stage direction (Orange wears buskins), or—more likely—a metonym for Orange's playing a part in a tragedy. *Ab Eoa poli* (from the east) refers to Orange's German descent from the county of Nassau.

62 *tremit Vesper gradum* Cf. *Aur.* 1976: "Vesper extremus tremat". "Vesper" referring to Spain.

63 *Atride* On Atreus' son Agamemnon, see Roscher 1.1, 90–97 and *RE* 1, 721–729. See also *Aur.* 1953–1958.

66 *victor cadis* This oxymoron (to die a victor) better suits Agamemnon than Orange in 1584. See intr., pp. 14–18.

68 *Delphi* For the equation of Delft and Delphi in a play of words, see Johan Koppenol, 'De weg van Delft naar Delfi', in: Wouter Abrahamse a.o. (eds), *Kort Tijt-verdrijf: Opstellen over Nederlands toneel (vanaf ca 1550) aangeboden aan Mieke B. Smits-Veldt* (Amsterdam: AD&L, 1996), pp. 39–44. "Patria" may point to Delft, since Grotius was born there, or the region of Holland in general.

71 *menstruo motu tumens* This combination refers to the tides; cf. Grotius, *Ad. ex.* 274: "menstruus ordo", Grotius, *Dichtwerken/Poetry* I, 1A, p. 55.

Louise de Coligny and Frederick Henry

74–90 *Cerno Loisae syrma—Poeantiusque* Louise de Coligny, William's fourth wife (see intr., pp. 18 and 39), can be compared with several women in Seneca's tragedies: Andromache or Hecuba, mourning for their husband or son Hector, both presented in Sen. *Tro.* (Roscher 1.1, 344–345); Alcmene, Amphitryon's wife and by Jupiter the mother of Hercules, mentioned in *Herc. f.* 489–491 (Roscher 1.1, 246–249); Hercules' first wife Megara, saddened for the absence of her man, also in *Herc. f.* (Roscher 2.2, 2542–2546); Oeneus' daughter Deianira, Hercules' last spouse, who goes mad from grief after the death of her husband (*Herc. Oet.* 842–1030; see also Roscher 1.1, 976–978)—the fact that she had killed him (unconsciously) by giving him the poisoned cloth of Nessus, and committed suicide, enables Grotius to write that she does not dare face Loisa.

On the other hand there are antipodes, such as Medea, who killed her children to avenge her husband Jason's infidelity, as shown in Seneca's *Med.* (Roscher 2.2, 2482–2515). Or Leda's daughter Helen who was the cause of the Trojan War by committing adultery with the Trojan Prince Paris—unless Leda's other daughter Clytemnestra is meant, who, with her lover Aegisthus, killed her husband Agamemnon—later, her son Orestes (cf. l. 80: "mater Orestis") would avenge his father and kill her, see Sen. *Aga.* (on Clytemnestra see Roscher 2.1, 1230–1245). Another anti-example is Virbius' (Hippolytus who was killed and resurrected under the name of Virbius, see Ov. *Met.* xv, 497–544 and Roscher

6, 328–330) stepmother Phaedra who fell in love with her stepson, see Seneca's *Phaedra* (also *Hippolytus*). Nor is Louise like Iocaste, who unconsciously married her son Oedipus and committed suicide after having heard the truth, as told in Sen. *Oed.*, where, however, the suicide does not occur (see on her Roscher 2.1, 284–285). Finally, she is opposed to Juno who maddened Hercules and made him kill his children. This madness is the subject of Sen. *Herc. f.* (see also Roscher 2.1, 574–598 s.v. Iuno and 1.2, 2260–2265 s.v. Hercules).

The young Frederick Henry is compared to the future Hector, i.e. Hector's son Astyanax, cf. Sen. *Tro.* 413–415. In *Tro.* his mother Andromache tries to hide him, but he is discovered and bravely kills himself (in contrast to Euripides' presentation of a frightened Astyanax, see *RE* 2, 1866; Roscher 1.1, 660). Furthermore, Frederick Henry is compared to Hyllus, the son of Hercules and Deianira, who in *Herc. Oet.* must support the captive Iole—he too has to mourn for his father (Roscher 2.1, 977 s.v. Deianeira). The next comparison is to Pylades or Orestes, whose father Agamemnon had been killed. The indication "coronati patris Phocaea proles" can refer to Pylades, son of Strophius, King of Phocis— he and his father save Orestes from death, see Sen. *Aga.* 940–941 (cf. Ov. *Tr.* IV, 4, 71: "comes [...] Phoceus" [i.e. Pylades, who accompanies Orestes]). In that case Pylades would mourn for the death of his uncle Agamemnon, the father of his close friend—or to Orestes himself, who visited Phocis and mourned his own father. It is Sen., *Aga.* 910–940, who mentions that Strophius and Orestes together save Orestes. On the coming of Orestes to Phocis, see *RE* 18.1, 968 s.v. Orestes, and cf. Eustath. *Comm. ad Hom. Od.* III, 307 (ed. 1960 1, p. 129); Roscher 3.1, 955–1014 s.v. Orestes and. 3.2, 3319–3322 s.v. Pylades. Finally, Grotius compares Frederick Henry to Philisthenes (or Pleisthenes), Thyestes' second son, slaughtered by his uncle Atreus, see Sen. *Thy.* 726–727. It is not quite clear why he is mentioned here, since he died, not his father; perhaps Grotius puts him on a par with the son of Pelops of the same name (see Grotius, *Dichtwerken/Poetry* I, 2, 2B, pp. 245–246; Roscher 3.2, 2562–2563). Pyrrhus, the son of Achilles who helps to conquer Troy (*Tro.* 1154; on him Roscher 3.2, 3360–3363) and the son of Poeas Philoctetes, who accompanied Hercules and played a role as a messenger (*Herc. Oet.* 1607–1612; on him Roscher 3.2. 2311–2343), are the last ones, where it is more their heroic attitude that is stressed than the mourning for their fathers.

74 *Syrma* Cf. Dousa, *In Adamum exulem* 8: "syrma trahit". "Cerno Loysae syrma" can be paraphrased as 'I see that the character of Louise has a part in the play'.
77 *Oeneis* Cf. Sen. *Herc. Oet.* 583: "Oenei" [i.e. Deianira].
83 *Stirpis antiquae decus* The glory of the ancient lineage of the Nassaus (for which cf. Grotius, *In genealogiam illustrium Comitum Nassaviorum* in Grotius, *Dichtwerken/Poetry* I, 2, 2A, pp. 163–177) is Frederick Henry. For the expres-

sion, cf. Sen. *Tro.* 766: "o decus lapsae domus". For the carrying of the baby in
"materna—manus", cf. *Aur.* 415–486. However, according to the list of characters it is a "gerula" (old woman), who carries the baby: "[...] famuli qui infantem
comitem adducunt, et gerula quae eundem gestat".

86 *futurus Hector* Sen. *Tro.* 550–551: "Magna res Danaos movet, futurus Hector".

86 *Fata si vitam darent* Cf. Ov. *Met.* VII, 691–692: "si vivere nobis fata diu de-
derint", and Bömer, *Ovidius Metamorphosen* 3, p. 372 *ad loc.*

90 *Poeantiusque* For this form, see Sen. *Herc. Oet.* 1495: "genus Poeantium".

The Inquisition

90–97 *Dira Cocyti vada—anguis implexus comis* The Spanish goddess of
revenge leaves the underworld with a cup of human blood in her hand, for
which even her sister Megaera and her snakes shudder. Indeed in *Aur.* II, 1
the Inquisition is presented as the sister of the three Furies, arising from hell,
Aur. 243–281. According to the scene heading, and *Aur.* 356–358, she carries
a chalice of human blood. Only this can quench her thirst and is pure wine
for her (*Aur.* 324–340, esp. 339 "merum"). Megaera is one of the Furies mentioned in *Auriacus* by name (*Aur.* 254, 265, 364, 1460 and the heading of scene
IV, 1). The whip (not in *Aur.*) and the serpentine hairs (*Aur.* 252–253; 264) are
topical attributes of the Furies, see (for example) Ov. *Met.* IV, 454: "Deque suis
atros pectebant crinibus angues" (cf. the comm. *ad* 252–253), and Verg. *Aen.* VII,
451: "Verberaque insonuit". The words "pro taedis" refer to the torches that the
Furies often bear, see, for example, Verg. *Aen.* VII, 456–457: "Sic effata facem
iuveni coniecit et atro lumine fumantis fixit sub pectore taedas". In that case
the torches could burn in the background, which would reinforce the uncanny
atmosphere.

It is not quite clear what the *secures* refer to. They are no attribute of the
Furies, nor did the murderer use an axe. Perhaps it is to be interpreted as a
poleaxe.

90 *Cocyti vada* Cf. *Aur.* 266–267, and Sen. *Herc. f.* 686; 889; *Herc. Oet.* 1963.
92 *Erinnys* Cf. *Aur.* 257–258 and the comm. *ad loc.*

The murderer and the Pope

98–122 *At ille magni Parricida—tonat* In fact the murderer has no parallel:
Thyestes ate his sons, as told in Sen. *Thy.* (cf. l. 86; see Roscher 5, 912–914); Theseus killed his son Hippolytus, see Sen. *Pha.* (*Hippol.*); cf. l. 79 and Roscher 5,

678–760; Oedipus killed his father and married his mother, see Sen. *Oed.* (cf. l. 80 and Roscher 3.1, 700–746), but none of them knew what they were doing, whereas this murderer killed the *pater patriae* knowingly. He is more comparable with Atreus, Aegisthus, the brothers Eteocles and Polyneices, and Tantalus. For Atreus killing his nephews, see ll. 86 and 98 and the comm., and Roscher 1.1, 712–715; Aegisthus, the son of Thyestes and his own daughter Pelopea (Sen. *Aga.* 28–36), killed his uncle Atreus and Agamemnon, seduced his wife and expelled their son Orestes (Roscher 1.1, 151–153). The 'grandsons of their own father' are the sons of Oedipus and Iocaste, Eteocles and Polyneices, fighting each other for power over Thebes, see Sen. *Phoe.* 279–287 and 389–400, and Roscher 1.1, 1387–1389 and 3.2, 2661–2680; Tantalus prepared the body of his own son Pelops for the gods as a meal to test their omniscience, and was punished with eternal hunger and thirst (ll. 109–110). The grandfather of Atreus and Thyestes; his ghost speaks the prologue in *Thyestes*. On Tantalus, see Roscher 5, 75–85.

Then the focus shifts from the murderer to the commissioner. Lycus was the King of Thebes in Hercules' absence and longed for Megara, whose father and two brothers he had killed; see *Herc. f.* (and Roscher 2.2, 2186 s.v. Lykos 5). The two Creons are (1) the King of Corinth who ordered Medea's expulsion and gave his daughter Creusa to Jason, see Sen. *Med.*, and l. 80 and the comm., as well as Roscher 2.1, 1413–1415 s.v. Kreon 1; (2) a tyrannical king of Thebes, brother of Iocaste, appearing in Sen. *Oed.* He had seized power and finally ordered Antigone's execution, see Soph. *Ant.* and Roscher 2.1, 1415–1418 s.v. Kreon 2. Another similar commissioner is Ulysses who wanted to have Hector's little son Astyanax thrown from the walls, cf. ll. 85–86 and Sen. *Tro.*, e.g. 568–813 (on Ulysses see Roscher 3.1, 602–681). The "puella" is Hector's sister Polyxena, whose death was demanded by Achilles' shade, and she was actually killed by his son Pyrrhus (cf. l. 89 and *Aur.* 380–383 and the comm. *ad loc.*). However, Ulysses is also representative, so to speak, of all Greeks who, with the ruse of the wooden horse, caused the downfall of Troy, leading to the death or captivity of many Trojan women. Jason left Medea for Creusa, even though Medea had given up her home and family, and it was with her help that he had taken the Golden Fleece from her father Aeetes, cf. ll. 80 and 114. Philip II, however, himself bearer of the Order of the Golden Fleece who had knighted William of Orange as a Knight of the Fleece at the first gathering of the chapter on 17 Nov. 1555 (P.J. Blok, *Willem de Eerste, Prins van Oranje* (Amsterdam; Meulenhoff, 1919–1920), I, p. 37), did dare to give such an order. As often in *Aur.* mythology and reality meet.

Calchas, the respected seer in the Greek army at Troy declared that the death of Astyanax and Polyxena was necessary (see Sen. *Tro.* 360–370; Roscher 2.1, 921–924), whereas the blind old seer Tiresias had summoned the ghost of Laios who pointed to Oedipus as the murderer (Sen. *Oed.* 626–658; also Hom. *Il.* I, 69–101 and see Roscher 5, 178–207). The prophetess Manto was Tiresias' daughter, who accompanied her blind father (Sen. *Oed.* 290 and 303) and called for rehabilitation for Latona because of the insults Niobe had brought to her (Sen. *Aga.* 310–323). More *loci* in Grotius, *Dichtwerken/Poetry* I, 2, 2B, p. 248; see also Roscher 2.2, 2326–2329 s.v. Manto 2.

Behind the Spanish King is the Pope; see ll. 121–122, cf. *Aur.* 272–273: "ferox pater Tarpeia saxa cui patent", and 285–286 "pater Tarpeie", and the comm. *ad loc.* More *loci* are given in Grotius, *Dichtwerken/Poetry* I, 2, 2B, p. 248. The Tarpeian rock was on Capitoline Hill.

98 *Parricida* In the first instance this indicates the murderer of a close relative (Oedipus in Sen. *Oed.* 1002 and 1033, Hercules in *Herc. Oet.* 906), and in the second instance a murderer in general (*OLD* s.v. 1 and 2). Furthermore, it can indicate a high traitor (*OLD* s.v. 3). In *Aur.*, however, the murderer who appears in III, 1, IV, 1 and IV, 3 is called *sicarius* (a murderer with a dagger, an assassin). For *parricida*, cf. Val. Max. VI, 4, 5: "patriae parentis parricida", and Forcellini 1.5.2: "parricida dicitur interfector viri, qui summam imperii tenet, quasi patris patriae".

99 *pone—gradum* Another possible translation is: 'here in the background he treacherously divides his criminal step'.

100 *impiâ ... dape* Sen. *Thy.* 1034: "Epulatus ipse es impia natos dape".

101–102 *Segregem Theseus—sparsit nece* Cf. Sen. *Pha.* 1208–1209: "Morte facili dignus haud sum qui nova natum nece segregem sparsi per agros".

104 *sed inscientes* Cf. Sen. *Thy.* 1067–1068: "sed nesciens, sed nescientes".

109 *arentes aquas* Cf. Ov. *A.A.* II, 605–606: "In media Tantalus aret aqua", and Sen. *Thy.* 68: "recedentes aquas".

110 *sempérque—fugas* Cf. Sen. *Thy.* 69: "labrisque ab ipsis arboris plenae fugas".

116 *fluxâ fide* For this combination, see (for example) Tac. *Hist.* III, 48: "fluxa [...] fide" and II, 75: "fluxam per discordias militum fidem".

122 *Quiritum* See *Aur.* 281 and the comm., and Dousa's poem on *Ad. ex.* 13 (Grotius, *Dichtwerken/Poetry* I, 1A, p. 29 and the comm. Grotius, *Dichtwerken/Poetry* I, 1B, p. 15).

122 *Collibus Septem* Cf. Grotius *Orbis supremi* [...] 42: "septem quae sedens in montibus", i.e. of Rome (Grotius, *Dichtwerken/Poetry* I, 2, 2A, pp. 132–133).

122 *tonat* This combination admits two interpretations: (1) speaks with a thundering voice (*OLD* s.v. 3), or, more likely, (2) issues a ban (which was also called a banishing lightning, *WNT* 2, 951).

Libertas (Freedom)

121–134 *Vidésne?—caeso parente* In *Aur.* v, 2 (ll. 1912–2105) wounded Liberty speaks her lamentation. She has cut her hair and places it near the coffin as a sign of mourning (*Aur.* 2071–2075), just like her hat of freedom (*Aur.* 2068–2070). On the offerings of hair and hat, see the comm. *ad loc.* The fact that she 'tramples the disgraceful yoke' is not evident from *Aur.*, but the fact that she goes to free people in faraway regions inhabited only by animals (ll. 2083–2100) can lead to this conclusion. Nor is it clear in *Aur.* that she has the same wound as Orange, but in his death she is heavily wounded (*saucia*).

Grotius compares her to Iole who mourns her father Eurytes, killed by Hercules, whereas she herself was given to Hercules' wife Deianira to be a slave, see Sen. *Herc. Oet.*, and Roscher 2.1, 289–290. In *Herc. Oet.* 173–224 she mourns her sad fate. The seer Cassandra bewails the downfall of Troy and its king, her father Priam, see Sen. *Aga.* and Roscher 2.1, 974–985. Electra mourns the death of her father Agamemnon and incites her brother Orestes to avenge his father, see Sen. *Aga.*, and Roscher 1.1, 1235–1239 s.v. Elektra 4. Antigone refuses (Sen. *Phoe.* 51) to leave her father Oedipus after he has blinded himself, cf. l. 82, and see Roscher 1.1, 370–373.

132 *Phaebas* For the priestess of Phoebus (Apollo) Cassandra, cf. Sen. *Tro.* 34–35: "quaecumque Phoebas ore lymphato furens credi deo vetante praedixit mala". In Sen. *Aga.* 695–709 and 720–758 she makes her predictions.
134–135 Between these two ll. the ms. *Pap. A* has: "Sub his sepultum, Troico et flagrans rogo".

A plea to Orange

134–141 *Siquis est—Vate Felix Heinsio* If the dead are still concerned about the living, Orange can accept the congratulations offered to him. For the Epicurean thought, cf. Constantijn Huygens, *Epimikta* 121–122: "si quid est curae super mortalis aevi", cf. Constantijn Huygens, *Epimikta: Een rouwklacht in het Latijn op de dood van zijn echtgenote (1637–1638)*, ed. Jan Pieter Guépin (Voorthuizen: Florivallis, 1996), p. 28 and pp. 18–19. In *Genealogia* 225–226 Grotius also uses the concept: "si forsan adhuc mortalia curas, nec pietas Batavos erga, Guilielme, recessit", Grotius, *Dichtwerken/Poetry* I, 2, 2A, pp. 174–175. In Grotius, *op. cit.* I, 2, 2B, p. 281 these parallels are given: Verg. *Ecl.* 8, 35: "Nec curare deum credis mortalia quemquam"; Luc. VII, 454–455: "Mortalia nulli sunt curata deo"; Claudian. *Rapt. Pros.* III, 19: "Abduxere meas iterum mortalia curas". "Divis Manibus" is the Lucretian variant of "Dis Manibus", e.g., Lucr. III, 52. Also the River Lethe is referred to, whose water makes people forget everything (Roscher 2.2, 1956–1958). Orange is blessed twice: in the son who will avenge him, i.e. Frederick Henry, see *Aur.* 1234 "futurus ultor", and in Heinsius who sings his praise.

140 *Batavis*   See the comm. *ad Aur.* 1270, and Grotius' *Ode ad Henricum Frede-ricum*, Grotius, *Dichtwerken/Poetry* I, 2, 1A, p. 31 and the comm. in Grotius, *Dichtwerken/Poetry* I, 2, 1B, p. 19 *ad* r. 2 Βαταουια, where it is explained that 'Batavia' was the common word for the province of Holland, or for the core area of the Seven Provinces stretching up to the Waal and the IJssel.

140 *Auransi*   See l. 59.

141 *Vate*   This is the sacral word for poet; its meanings include 'seer' and 'di-vinely inspired poet' (*OLD* s.v.).

[10]   **In eandem / On the same [tragedy]**

Summary

With his *Oedipus*, Sophocles proved that as a venerable old man he was still young at heart, whereas with his *Auriacus* Heinsius proves that he is already respectable as a young man, by writing this lay that evokes the audience's emotions. Both wrote a full-term piece, but one was old, the other young. Heinsius is encouraged to continue to exceed the expectations that one has of him.

Just as in Vulcanius' second poem (see p. 98), Heinsius and Sophocles are put side by side. The young age of the one is opposed to the old age of the other, both hold an eminent place in their time and have a birthplace with a unique position, Ghent and Athens. In this poem the emphasis is on (1) the combination of respectability and resilience (ll. 1–4, an artful *antimetabole*) and (2) the maturity of their work (ll. 7–10). The lines 5–6, in which the emotive value of *Auriacus* is addressed, form a transition. The poem ends with the encouragement to continue writing drama.

Metre

The poem consists of elegiac distichs.

Poet

The poem is signed 'Jacobus Gruterus', but this was probably Janus Gruterus (1560–1627), who in 1584 became a *doctor utriusque iuris* in Leiden. He was a leading scholar and a meritorious poet in the vernacular and in Latin (his poems include *Manes Gulielmiani*, 1584). Moreover, in the *Iambi* added to *Aur.*, Heinsius included a dedication to Janus Gruterus (*Auriacus* 1602, pp. 106–107). In the copy it probably said 'Ia. Gruterus', which the typesetter may have resolved incorrectly. On him, see Forster, *Janus Gruter's English Years* and *NDB* 7, pp. 238–240 (Peter Fuchs).

Commentary

1–2 *Effoetâ—Oedipode* For the fact that the Athenian poet Sophocles still wrote poetry in old age (his *Oedipus Coloneus* being posthumously performed), see *Illustrissimis* [...] *Ordines* 1–9 and the comm. *ad loc.* For the contrast between the old Sophocles and the young Heinsius, see also *Idem Bonaventurae Vulcanii* 5–6.

5–6 *cothurno ... Orchestrae* For this buskin, the orchestra and their implication, see the comm. *ad* Grotius, *Iambi* [...] 2. Here the orchestra indicates the public.

10 *solius* The interpretation of this form involves a difficulty. It is gen. sg. to "senis" ('of an old man on his own'), but the combination "at solius" is the counterpart to "sed tamen" (l. 8), unless "solus" is to be regarded here as 'unique' (a unique old man).

13 *postscenia* Cf. *Aur.* 543 and Lucr. IV, 1186: "vitae postscaenia".

[11]   A Monsieur de Heins sur sa Tragedie. Stances / Stanzas for Mister
         Heinsius on his Tragedy

Summary

The poem runs, stanza by stanza, as follows: (1) If only De Licques dared to lift his eyes to bring earth and heaven together. (2) Heinsius' fame should stop him from trying: he would fall deeply. (3) Heinsius must be admired. (4) If only the poet could see Dousa and Grotius. (5) He has just set to write a poem, and although he does not succeed, he has tried it anyway. (6) He wants to honour this radiant star Heinsius with a French poem, even if it brings his own demise.

(7) The Greek tragedians, including Sophocles and Euripides, and the Roman tragedian Seneca are now done with. (8) Heinsius surpasses them with his beautiful style and flies out of sight while those antique writers keep crawling around in the mist. (9) With his portrayal of emotions, Heinsius brings the audience to emotion. (10) When he shows the injury of Freedom, he touches them deeply.

(11) A half-dead woman (Inquisitio) can be seen with hell on her side. (12) When Heinsius reflects the atrocities of the Spaniards, the spectators also become frantic. (13) A traitor enters, an Enyo. (14) Blessed are the Netherlands that such a great injustice was avenged by a second Achilles (Maurice) and that a second Homer (Heinsius) sings Orange. (15) This Achilles is as courageous as the god Mars, the other will also be able to take the highest position in heaven.

(16) Heinsius is endowed with greatness by heaven, and in his *Auriacus* one sees that eloquence and courtesy go together. (17) But because De Licques realizes that one can experience something divine better than describe it, he has to end his poem now in order to fully understand Heinsius' fame, though he is in fact really ecstatic.

The French is written in the *genus grande*, containing many mythological allusions and a syntax that is now and then obscure, to some extent resembling Pléiade poetry.

In Heinsius, *Poemata emendata* [...] (Leiden: Orlers and Maire, 1613), pp. 602–609 (and Heinsius, *Poemata emendata* [...] (Leiden: Maire, 1617), pp. 630–637) a poem of R.I. de Nerée is included. Some similarities between the two poems (e.g. *biffant*, De Licques l. 29, De Nerée l. 29; *empouze* De Licques l. 30, *empoulles* De Nerée l. 35 and the opposition of *pouvoir* and *vouloir*, De Licques ll. 18–20 and De Nerée ll. 19–20) suggest that De Nerée knew this poem.

Metre

This is a strophic poem in 'stances', in a verse of accents (4 accents per line).

Poet

David de Licques († 1616), a French nobleman, was probably the author of a biography of the Protestant leader Philippe du Mornay, *Histoire de la vie de Messire Phil. de Mornay Seigneur de Plessis Marly etc.* (Leiden: Elsevier, 1647). He also translated work by Du Plessis-Mornay in Latin. Thus, De Licques overtly took the sides of the Huguenots and Orange. Another poem for Heinsius by

De Licques is printed in Heinsius, *Poemata* (1613), pp. 610–612 and in Heinsius, *Poemata* (1617), pp. 638–640. On De Licques, see Christian G. Jöcher, *Allgemeines Gelehrten-Lexikon* 3. Ergänzungsband (Delmenhorst: Georg Jöntzen, 1810), col. 1779, on Du Plessis-Mornay *DBF* 12, 415–417 s.v. 43.

Commentary

1 *Immortelle flamme* The immortal flame as an expression for God is appropriate in the context of 'blinded eyes'.

3 *les glaces de mon ame* The mirrors of the soul are the eyes who can see heaven and earth in one glance and thus can, so to speak, combine them. For the eyes that mirror the soul, cf. Mt. 6, 22 and Lk. 11, 34; also Cic. *De or.* III, 221: "Animi est enim omnis actio et imago animi vultus, indices oculi".

16 *l'Orient* Grotius as a shining sun setting in the east.

17 *le sort est iecté* With this expression attributed to Caesar ("alea iacta est"), De Licques indicates that since he started this poem he should end it.

20 *vn bel envy—pouvoir* Cf. Ov. *Pont.* III, 4, 79: "Vt desint vires tamen est laudanda voluntas".

25–26 *bande Grecque ... Sophocle, Euripide* Cf. Grotius *Iambi* 20–26, for *Senecque ibid.* 31–32.

30 *stile empoulé* "Empouiller" actually means 'to sow'; the *stile empoulé* will be a 'rich style', in contrast to a "stile depouillé", a 'stripped [bare] style'.

33–36 In this stanza on the effect on the public, De Licques formulates the thought that a poet or orator who wishes to move the audience, should first be moved himself, cf. Hor. *A.P.* 102–103: "Si vis me flere, dolendum est primum ipsí tibi".

41–44 These lines point to the Inquisition, on whose hands is martyr's blood. Her hell is here 'tools of torture', but it is also inspired by the way Heinsius portrays her as a sister of the Furies. She is a living death, since she brings death, and looms from the realm of the dead.

47 *Furie* Here it is not the goddess of revenge that is meant, but the original meaning 'frenzy'. Like (9) this stanza deals with the effect on the public.

50 *Enyon* In Greek mythology, Enyo is a war goddess, equated to the Roman Bellona, see (for example) Petr. 120, 62: "feralis Enyo"; see *RE* 5, 2654–2655. She is *un supplice*, which may be an *abstractum pro concreto*, viz. a tormentor.

53–56 Maurice is compared with Achilles, the Greek hero who avenged the death of his friend Patroclus (Hom. *Il.* XVI); therefore, Heinsius can be equated with Homer, who sings this act of revenge (*Il.* XXII, 271–272; 331).

63–64 *Eloquence* and *galand Esprit* are interlinked, cf. Quint. XII, 1, 44: "oratorem esse virum bonum bene dicendi peritum".

[12]   Amico lectori / To the dear reader

Summary

At first Heinsius wanted to premise some notes concerning Greek and Latin tragedy, but he abandoned that idea. Anyone who decides to do away with the division into scenes and acts has the author's permission. He also makes a remark about the form *tabo/tabum*, engaging in a discussion about the possible cases of that word. This is followed by a typical philological defence of the extension of the first syllable of *Iberi*.

More important is the issue of why Maurice does not feature in the play, while Frederick Henry is mentioned and shown. Heinsius thought he had given sufficient praise to Maurice in the poem *Pro Auriaco sua*. There were two reasons for not including him in the piece: first, the Prince was absent at the time of the murder (Heinsius simply did not want to tell any untruth); second, the time spent in a tragedy may span only a few hours, so that Maurice, who was absent, would violate the unities of time and place were he to play a part. Heinsius has spoken about this with Bertius and Grotius. Moreover, a baby evokes more emotions than a child or a teenager. But in order not to give the impression of being stubborn, he had added Maurice as a *deus ex machina*.

Then some *errata* follow and an excuse for the many mistakes, especially in the Greek texts, due to an incompetent typesetter.

Commentary

3 *secundae editioni* A second edition of *Auriacus* was actually planned, see intr. pp. 12 and 54. However, this could also refer to another publication, which resulted in *De tragica constitutione*.

8–10 This short Greek poem, which Heinsius must have written before, has not yet been traced elsewhere. Line 10 is an adaptation of Soph. *Aiax* 24: τῷδ' ὑπε-ζύγην πόνῳ. For the thought, cf. Hor. *A.P.* 388: "nonumque prematur in annum". (Thanks to D.M. Schenkeveld)

11–16 Heinsius states that the indications of the scenes may be suppressed, since the Greek or Roman tragic poets did not divide their tragedies into scenes, nor acts. Cf. Scaliger, in: *In Q. Annaei Senecae tragoedias animadversiones*, published in in *Opuscula varia* (Paris: Drouart, 1610, but written before), p. 310: "Nam Senecae nullos distinctiones actuum reliquit, non magis quam Plautus, Terentius, tragici Graeci, Aristophanes". The remark by Serrarens and Wijn-gaard in Jacob Duym, *Het Moordadich Stvck van Balthasar Gerards* [...], ed. L.F.A. Serrarens and N.C.H. Wijngaards (Zutphen: Thieme, [1976]) Klassiek Letterkundig Pantheon, 218, p. 18, to the effect that it is unlikely that Heinsius wishes for the division into acts be abandoned, is in itself unlikely: he might wish to adapt to Greek and Roman customs.

15 παραβάσεων   The παράβασις was a part of the old comedy in which the chorus addressed the public and spoke about something beyond the subject matter (LSJ s.v. III and IV; *TGL* 6, 211–212).

c *tabum tabem*   Servius writes about the cases of "tabum" in his *Comm. in Verg. Aen.* III, 29: "*Tabo* corrupto sanguine. et est nomen casus septimi tantum, ut 'sponte' 'natu': quod si velis declinare, haec tabes, huius tabis dicis." Heinsius opposes the *Glossarium vetus* which treats "tabo" as a word with only one case, see Bonaventura Vulcanius, *Thesaurus utriusque linguae, hoc est Philoxeni aliorumque veterum authorum glossaria* (Leiden: Patius, 1600), there *Philoxeni Lexicon Latino-Graecum vetus*, p. 210: "Tabo αἵματι νεκροῦ λύθρῳ ἔστιν δὲ μονό-πτωτον" and below that, after "tabularium" and "tabidus", where "tabum" would be expected: "Tabo λύθρος, αἶμα νεκροῦ". This discussion on the cases of "tabo" is held by (for example) the grammarians Priscianus (Keil 2, 188.9), Charisius (Keil 1, 29.26) and Diomedes (Keil 1, 309.12–140).

18–19 γραμματικῶν παῖδες   Cf. Lucian. *Hist. Conscr.* 7: παῖδες ἰατρῶν; cf. Scal. *Poet.* I, 2, p. 4a; Scaliger, *Poetica/Dichtkunst* 1, p. 78.6: υἷες ἰατρῶν.

22–25   The form *Iberi* (*Aur.* 360) in the Leiden copy is actually changed into "illius". For the lengthening of syllables, see Dietmar Korzeniewski, *Griechische Metrik* (Darmstadt: Wissenschaftliche Buchgesellschaft, 1968), p. 23 (*productio epica*).

26–54 *Sequitur gravius ... coniugemus*   Here Heinsius discusses the question of the unities of time and place, which can be at odds with historical reality. Maurice was not in Delft at the time of the murder but in Leiden, and could not be at court in one day. These Aristotelian unities are also discussed in Scal. *Poet.* I, 6.

31 *quosdam etiam graviores*   Scaliger, Bertius and Grotius, mentioned in ll. 45–46. The young poet implicitly accuses them of "imperitia".

33–34 *praefationem meam Heroicam*   I.e. the poem *Pro Auriaco sua* written in the epic hexameter in which Maurice is praised.

35 *dum spiritus hos reget artus*   Cf. Verg. *Aen.* IV, 336.

39 *hinc illae lachrymae*   Ter. *Andr.* 99.

43 *pericomma*   A complete whole, see LSJ s.v. περίκομμα. In antiquity it was not used for a defined period of time.

45 *Magnus Heros noster*   Joseph Scaliger, the son of Julius Caesar, see Meter, *The Literary Theories*, p. 24, n. 169.

45 *Clarissimus Bertius*   Petrus Bertius (1565–1629) studied in London and Leiden, came to Leiden in 1592 and became a sub-regent and in 1606 Regent of the States College, for students of theology, where he taught philosophy. He organized the university's library and in 1595 the first printed catalogue appeared, compiled by him. He was a somewhat controversial person, who suffered in the student's revolt of 1594, but stayed. In 1600 he became Professor of Ethics by special appointment. "Clarissimus" is used for a professor. On Bertius see *NNBW* 1, 320–322; L.J.M. Bosch, *Petrus Bertius 1565–1629* (Meppel: Knips Repro, 1979) Doctoral thesis Nijmegen; and Wiep van Bunge et al. (eds), *The Dictionary of Seventeenth and Eighteenth-Century Dutch Philosophers* (Bristol: Thoemmes Press, 2003), 2 vols, pp. 86–89 (Henri Knop). In 1995 a reprint of the catalogue (*Nomenclator*) appeared, see Petrus Bertius, *Nomenclator: The First Printed Catalogue of Leiden University Library (1595)*, ed. Ronald Breugelmans and Jan J. Witkam (Leiden: Leiden University Library, 1995). Leiden University Library houses a copy of *Auriacus* (shelf number 1224 C 29) with a handwritten dedication for Bertius: "Clarissimo Doctissimoque Viro PETRO BERTIO domino suo honorando, grati animi debitum testimonium d.d. autor".

45–46 *actioni huius Tragoedia primae* For the multiple interpretations of this colon, see intr. p. 11.

56 ὁ θαυμάστος *Grotius* During his journey in France, King Henry IV had called Grotius "le miracle de la Hollande", and he was known as ὁ θαυμάσιος (Arthur Eyffinger, 'Hugo Grotius' *Parallelon rerumpublicarum*', in: Henk J.M. Nellen en Johannes Trapman (eds), *De Hollandse jaren van Hugo de Groot (1583–1621)* (Hilversum: Verloren, 1996), pp. 87–95, esp. p. 90).

47–48 διασκευὰς ... *Simonides* The Greek poet Simonides (ca. 556–468 BC) was known for such writings as his *apophthegmata* (*RE* 2.R. 3, 186–197 s.v. Simonides 2). A διασκευή is (rhetorical) ornament, see *TGL* 2, 1314.

53–54 θεὸς ἀπὸ μηχανῆς The *deus ex machina* is the character who brings the unexpected denouement, see (for example) Scal. *Poet*. I, 5, p. 11aA; Scaliger, *Poetica/Dichtkunst* 1, p. 124.24–25, Arist. *Poet*. 1454a37–b1 and Euanth. *Fab*. 3.2.

54 διοσκούρους The Dioscuri, sons of Zeus and Leda, the twins Castor and Pollux, were courageous warriors, the first as a horseman, the second as pugilist, see Roscher 1.1, 1154–1177. It is implied that the two brothers Maurice and Frederick Henry are both equally valiant.

[14]   In Auriacum Danielis Heinsii [...] Elegia/Elegy on Daniel Heinsius'
Auriacus

Summary

1–24 Finally Scriverius has time to devote himself to poetry. This not to praise a lesser poet, but the darling of men and gods: Daniel Heinsius. Now that he has written a tragedy in Aeschylus' style, one must start writing poems of praise.
25–40 Heinsius does not write about horrors, in fictitious stories, but about lofty men. Unfortunately, he must then also perform the wiles of the Spaniards and the villain against whom Orange had to fight. If he were still alive, the Netherlands, which is engaged in a long-lasting war, would be happy.
41–58 That was not to be, since Orange has died. But one does not have to worry about it that much: now he only really lives at the hands of Heinsius with his sharpness, exaltation of style and splendour. Not only Scriverius himself, but Julius Scaliger and Dousa also admire him highly. Rightly so, because as a true tragic figure Heinsius has gone through misery and is still passing it on as an exile. People like Casparius and Gamerius have to give way, their literary products are far behind that of Heinsius. Grotius himself considered himself a lesser poet than his friend, whose tragedy can compete with Greek and Roman drama.
59–60 Now Scriverius ends his poem, because his poetic talent is insignificant compared to that of Heinsius.

Metre

The poem consists of elegiac distichs.

Poet

Petrus Scriverius (Piet Schrijver, 1576–1660) was an historian, philologist and man of letters. He lived in Leiden as a private citizen, making editions of classical authors and writing historiographical works in Dutch and Latin. In 1616 he would publish and annotate Heinsius' *Nederduytsche Poemata*. On him see now Michiel Roscam Abbing and Pierre Tuynman, *Petrus Scriverius Harlemensis (1576–1660): A Key to the Correspondence, Contacts and Works of an Independent Humanist* (Leiden: Foleor, 2018).

Commentary

1–14 *Ite procul—deliciesque Deûm* Scriverius confesses his aversion to public life in the first lines. He did not hold any offices, his motto was *Lare secreto*. He prefers *otia laeta*, the unrestrained informal life that can be devoted to the study, in the sense of *loisir*. All this did not prevent him from participating in public debate and taking a position in the controversy between Dousa on the one hand and Bockenberg and Cool on the other. About this see Pierre Tuynman, 'Petrus Scriverius: 12 January 1576–30 April 1660', *Quaerendo* 7 (1977), pp. 4–45, esp., pp. 7–9 and 28–29, nn. 13–15; Roscam Abbing and Tuynman, *Petrus Scriverius Harlemensis*; also Grotius, *Dichtwerken/Poetry* I, 2, 3A–B, pp. 45 and 246; B.A. Vermaseren, 'De werkzaamheid van Janus Dousa Sr († 1604) als geschiedschrijver van Holland', *Verslag van de Algemene vergadering van het Historisch Genootschap en Bijdragen en mededelingen van het Historisch Genootschap* 69 (1955), pp. 49–107, esp. pp. 66–67; about Bockenberg see *NNBW* 6, 123–125; B.A. Vermaseren, 'P.C. Bockenberg (1548–1617), historieschrijver der Staten van Holland', *Verslag van de Algemene vergadering van het Historisch Genootschap en Bijdragen en mededelingen van het Historisch Genootschap* 70 (1956), pp. 1–81, and Herman Kampinga, *Opvattingen over onze vaderlandse geschiedenis bij de Hollandse historici der 16e en 17e eeuw* (Utrecht: HES, 1980 [= The Hague: Nijhoff, 1917]), pp. 31–33. In 1602, Daniel Heinsius published the collection *Iani Philodusi [...] Adversus nuperum Petri Cornelii Bockenbergii scriptum pro Iano Dousa N.D. Responsio*, a defence of Dousa and simultaneously launched an attack on Bockenberg and Cool (Tuynman, 'Petrus Scriverius', pp. 28–29, n. 15, Sellin, *Daniel Heinsius and Stuart England*, pp. 248–249, no. 404). Grotius also got involved in this Bockenberg polemic, see Grotius, *Dichtwerken/Poetry* I, 2, 3A–B, pp. 238–278. Thanks to R.C. Engelberts for his help with the exegesis of this passage.

1 *Ite procul—ite Labores* Cf. Tib. III, 6, 7: "ite procul durum curae genus, ite Labores". For other variations, cf. (for example) Janus Secundus *Iulia* I, 10, 1: "Ite procul maestum, lacrimae, genus ite querelae" (*Ioannis Nicolai Secundi Hagani Opera Omnia, emendatius et cum notís adhuc ineditis Petri Burmanni Secundi*, ed. Petrus Bosscha (Leiden: Luchtmans, 1821), 1, p. 69).

2 *Non mea—crura sonent* Tib. I, 7, 42: "crura licet dura compede pulsa sonent".

3 *à Praetore* The *praetor* as a legal official represents the administration of justice or public life.

6–7 *puellari ... choro ... vetereis ... Sororeis* For Muses as "puellae", cf. Prop. III, 3, 33: "novem [...] puellae"; for "sorores" cf. (for example) Prop. III, 30, 27 and Mart. IX, 42, 3: "doctae [...] sorores".

9 Volusî Volusius, a contemporary of Catullus (1st c. BC) had written *Annales*, which Catullus had slashed in poems 36 and 95 for being too long ("cacata charta", 36, 1) and garbage ("At Volusi Annales Paduam morientur ad ipsam et laxas scombris saepe dabunt tunicas"). Scriverius supports Dousa's attack on Bockenberg, who was also seen as long-winded, cf. Grotius' letter in *Responsio* (1603), quoted after Grotius, *Dichtwerken/Poetry* I, 2, 3A/B, p. 247: "Annales Tragorae cacata charta".

10 Brassica Here Scriverius interferes in the polemic against the historiographer Jacobus Brassica (Cool). Dousa had ridiculed him for his etymology of the name 'Holland'. When he edited the chronicle of his relative Reinier Snoy, despised by Dousa, Scriverius and Baudius, Brassica was attacked again (see, for example, Haitsma Mulier and Van der Lem, *Repertorium*, p. 72).

11 pascale pecus Perhaps Scriverius is pointing to 'the common herd of poets', as he did later in his preface to Heinsius' *Nederduytsche poemata*, but more probably he is aiming, here too, at Bockenberg and Cool, who according to Dousa leaned too much on the work of Snoy and followed in his steps like tame sheep.

11 Hispo Tragûrus For the name "Hispo", there a homosexual, see Iuv. 2, 50. The adjective "tragurus" is a combination of τράγος (he-goat) and οὖρα (tail) in analogy to the Homeric ἵππουρος (e.g. *Il.* VI, 495), another jibe aimed at Bockenberg (Tragoras, Tragomontanus or Hircimontanus), a relative of Brassica (Cool), for which Dousa used the soubriquet Brassica in *Echo* (1603), p. 4v, and see two poems in Janus Philodusus [D. Heinsius], *Adversus Petri Bockenbergii scriptum pro Iano Dousa responsio* [...] (Leiden: s.n., 1602), p. B3v and C4r, entitled 'In Hisponem'. Scriverius himself attacked Bockenberg in *In Tragoram*. After the first attacks in 1591, Bockenberg and Cool had responded in 1601, so the issue was topical.

12 Crambe See Iuv. 7, 154: "crambe repetita". A translation of the name Cool, see also Grotius, *Dichtwerken/Poetry* I, 2, 3A/B, p. 269, l. 12 and comm., p. 270. For "facere ad" in the sense of 'being qualified', see (for example) Ov. *Her.* 16, 192: "Ad talem formam non facit iste locus".

14 delicies hominum, deliciesque Deûm Cf. Lucr. I, 1: "hominum divumque voluptas".

15–24 Illius (o Musae)—Syrma trahit Scriverius is able to praise Heinsius, since one can only acclaim such a talent.

17 turpi possit torpere veterno Cf. Verg. *Ge.* I, 124: "nec torpere gravi passus sua regna veterno".

19 Vacerrae People such as Vacerra the birdbrain from Martial's epigrams, e.g. VIII, 69, 1–3; see also Liv. Andron. ap. Fest. p. 375 Müll. (*Com. Fragm.* v. 7 Rib.).

20 *qui mihi carmen erit*   Cf. *Aetna* 4: "Aetna mihi carmen erit".
21 *Crepundia*   This indicates the toys of the young poet, but alludes even more to Heinsius' *Crepundia Siliana* (1601), annotations to Silius Italicus' epic.
23 *evinctus crura Cothurnis*   Cf. Verg. *Ecl.* 7, 32: "suras evincta cothurno".
24 *Aeschyleum ... Syrma*   See Grotius, *Iambi* 22 and the comm.; for "syrma" *ibid.* 74 and comm.

25–40 *Non tamen hic—velut antè, gerit*   In view of the similarities between this passage and the Dedication to the States, Scriverius will almost certainly have seen it. Both Heinsius and he set mythological topics in opposition to patriotic, both sigh that the murder should not have happened, see *Illustrissimis* [...] *Ordinibus* 10–26 and 132–133.

25–30 *Non-tuis*   The subject of *Auriacus* is not taken from mythology, e.g. the "epulae Terei", the meal of Tereus whose wife Procne and her sister Philomela (his beloved) give him his own son Itys to eat, Ov. *Met.* VI, 412–674; Sen. *Thy.* 56, and Sophocles' *Tereus*, of which fragments are extant, see *RE* 2.R. 5, 719–721. Nor is it about the "saeva Thyestis fercula", the fare of Thyestes who ate his own sons, see Sen. *Thy.* as well as the fragmentarily transmitted tragedies of Sophocles *Thyestes* and *Atreus*, and *Thyestes* of Euripides; cf. the comm. *ad* Grotius *Iambi* 98–122, nor about *Bacchae*, cf. Euripides' tragedy of the same title; or on Athamas, who was made mad together with his wife Ino (see *Aur.* 1481 and the comm.), a story that was the subject of Sophocles' *Athamas* and Euripides' *Ino*, both surviving only fragmentarily. Nor does Heinsius speak about "Scyllae" (Hom. *Od.* XII, and, for example, Sen. *Med.* 350). The "ludibria" of Quintus Ennius (239–169 BC) point to his (lost) tragedies, which include a *Thyestes* (Cic. *Brut.* 20, 78), *Medea* and *Hecuba*, rather than his *Annales* (on Ennius see *RE* 5, 2589–2628 s.v. Ennius 3). His nephew was Marcus Pacuvius (220–131/130 BC). The titles of twelve plays and some fragments of them are extant, for instance through Cic. *Tusc.* I, 44, 106; see *RE* 18.1, 2159–2174 s.v. Pacuvius 6.
30 *magne Quirine*   This refers to (1) Romans in general, or (2) the Roman tragic author par excellence, Seneca.
32 *aligero ... gradu*   For the 'high flight' of the poet, cf. the comm. *ad* Grotius *Iambi* 17–32 and 33–41.
37 *Patriae Pater*   Cf. *Aur.* 1936 and the comm. *ad loc.* The same thought (if only Orange were still alive) can be read in the *Illustrissimis* [...] *Ordinibus* 132–133.

41–58 *Vota sed haec—dives habet*   The man who protected the Netherlands and expelled the Spaniards, has died. Probably "fuit" (l. 42) should be interpreted as *indicativus pro coniunctivo*; Orange did not protect the Netherlands and drive out the Spaniard, but, according to Scriverius, he would certainly have done so if he had been granted a longer life. Yet his death does not need to be mourned, Orange lives on through Heinsius. This is the literary topos of immortality through poetry, see the comm. *ad Illustrissimis* [...] *Ordinibus* 124–146.

45 Heinsiadem   For this Greek patronymic, see Dousa, *In eandem* 18 and the comm.

47 Ephebi   See Dousa, *In eandem* 23 and the comm.

49 Iuliades   For the formation of the patronymic, see above, l. 45, and Dousa, *In eandem* 18 and the comm. For this son of Julius, Joseph Scaliger, see also the dedication to him, l. 54.

50 Hianteae ... aquae   For the "Hyanteae sorores", the Muses, see Stat. *Silv.* II, 7, 8 and Van Dam, *Statius Silvae, Book II*, pp. 459–460. For the relation between Boeotia (*Hyanteus* [or *Hyantius*] is Boeotic), and the Muses, see Van Dam, *op. cit.*, p. 219. Scriverius presents Dousa as thirsting for water from the Pierian Spring, an old symbol for poetic activity, see Van Dam, *op. cit.*, p. 217 and Kambylis, *Die Dichterweihe*, pp. 23–30.

53 Caspari ... Gameri   Casparus Casparius (Caspar Ens, 1569–1642 or later), who wrote a *Princeps Auriacus, sive libertas defensa* (Delft: Bruno Schinckels, 1599), see ed. Bloemendal, and on Casparius, see Walter Killy (ed.), *Literaturlexikon: Autoren und Werke deutscher Sprache* 3 (Gütersloh and Munich: Bertelsmann, 1989), p. 266 (Wilhelm Kühlman), and Hannardus Gamerius (Van Gameren, fl. 1550s–1570s), who held a degree in medicine, was a teacher of Greek at the University of Ingolstadt, where he was also *poeta laureatus*; as the Rector of the Latin school in Tongeren, humanist and Neo-Latin poet, he wrote a play *Pornius: Tragoedia vere sacra, non minus elegans quam pia* (Munich: Adam Berg, 1566), see Bloemendal and Norland, *Neo-Latin Drama and Theatre*, pp. 337–338. The play was added to his *Bucolica* (Antwerp: Plantin, 1568). He also wrote polemical writings against Luther, and the *Vera et simplex narratio eorum quae ab adventu D. Ioannis Austriaci supremi in Belgio pro Catholica Maiestate gubernatoris* [...] *gesta sunt* (1578), which was translated into Dutch in the same year. On his play, see also Jozef IJsewijn, 'Annales theatri Belgo-Latini: Inventaris van het Latijnse toneel uit de Nederlanden', in: Jozef Veremans (ed.), *Liber amicorum Prof. G. Degroote* (Brussel: Koninklijke Zuidnederlandse Maatschappij voor Taal- en Letterkunde en Geschiedenis, 1980), pp. 41–55, esp. p. 47 on Gamerius *BNB* 7, 471–472 (thanks to R.C. Engelberts).

55 blenni   Plaut. *Bacch.* 1088 (βλεννός). For the line, cf. the famous verse of Prop. II, 34, 65: "Cedite Romani scriptores, cedite Grai". The *blenni* again point to Bockenberg (see the comm. *ad* 11); in Dousa's *Echo* (1603), p. 60v, a poem *In Blennum, cognomento Tragoram*, of which ll. 3–4 run: "Historia et Tragoras, duo sunt pugnantia: munus scilicet Historiae est, non nisi vera loqui". In the compilation *Iani Philodusi, Adversus* [...] *Bockenbergii scriptum* a Blennus occurs several times, e.g. pp. Cv and C2r; see Grotius, *Dichtwerken/Poetry* I, 2, 3A/B, p. 243.

56 *palmas* For the "palma" as a sign of victory for poets see Dousa *In eandem* 3 and the comm.

59–60 *Sed nunc—in ore sonus* Final lines with a modesty formula ('my talent is insufficient'). For a discussion of this literary topos, see Van Dam, *Statius Silvae, Book II*, p. 216; also Janson, *Latin Prose Prefaces*, pp. 124–134.

59 *erubui* A *perfectum praesens* or *resultativum*: 'I became red', i.e. 'I am ashamed'.

60 *parvus perstet in ore sonus* A combination of Prop. IV, 1a, 58: "parvus in ore sonus" and Ov. *Pont.* IV, 9, 92: "perstat in ore pudor".

[15]   **Pro Auriaco sua / For his Auriacus**

Summary

1–19 The ghost of Orange, who has fought tyrants, is invoked, followed by an invocation of his son Maurice, who is worthy of his father, whether he draws circles in the sand, shows himself in full armour on horseback on the battlefield or lets guns roar. This son will eventually avenge his father.

19–38 Next, the poet calls on the Dutch, who confront the Spaniard as if they were new Romans, and defy the sea and the winds. They travel all over the world.

39–55 They have to be spectators while the still young author has a play performed, with which he follows in the footsteps of Grotius. In poetic enthusiasm Heinsius is dragged along by Bacchus. The Dutch must facilitate his poetic flight with their sails.

56–73 The spectators see Nassau on the stage turning his face to heaven. His enemies needed to use deceit. Fortuna admits a cruel crime, and how narrow is the road to fame: Nassau, who deserved to die a heroic death on the battlefield, was spared to be killed by a brigand. This threw the Netherlands in turmoil and they feared the attack of the Spanish King.

74–85 The Dutch watching perceive Inquisitio, a second Alecto, to be more terrible than the Furies. The Dutch have seen off worse threats than the ordinary Furies and managed to tame them with the aid of the sea.

86–107 There is another dying figure on the stage: Freedom, who gathers the Dutch round their dead leader. She is in a hurry to leave their country. Heinsius urgently asks her to look at the good things, at the son who leads the armies to kill the Spaniards. Frisians, Gelderlanders, Zeelanders and Hollanders go to battle, assisted by the sea that stopped the Spanish fleet.

108–124 If Heinsius will have time left to live and speak, he will ever be able to sing the defeat of Philip and the victory of the Dutch in the Indies, and he will sing the arms of the Nassaus. Hugo Grotius will stand by his side and remind him of Erasmus. Together with Grotius, Heinsius will tell of courageous acts, triumphant victories through France and Italy and of the future richness of the red areas of the Rhine. If, at least, poetry has some predictive value.

125–146 He also invokes the support of Scaliger, who must tell the spectators that the subject is worthy of applause. He himself will then make a memorial sacrifice every year at the grave of Scaliger's father in Verona. Furthermore, he asks for the support of the friend of Boisot who helped Leiden stop the Spaniard, Dousa, under whose protection Heinsius would like to elevate his mind to write tragedies.

147–157 Heinsius urges the spirit of Orange to take flight and look down from heaven upon the earth. This will make the Spaniards tremble, just like the stars will do. Furthermore, Orange must respect his son who challenges the Spanish troops to battle and reconciles his father's shade with blood of the enemies.

This poem is transmitted in three sources: the edition of *Auriacus* 1602, and the *Poemata* 1603 and 1606. Furthermore, Heinsius annotated the copy in the Leiden University Library (shelf number 754 B 34). The changes he made in the Leiden copy are for the most part adopted in the *Poemata* of 1606, which suggests a date for these changes of somewhere between 1603 and 1606. In addition, the 1606 edition has changes that have not been made in the *Auriacus* copy. Under *L* the relevant changes from Heinsius' copy (often also adopted in the *Poemata* of 1603) are treated, under *C* the relevant *variae lectiones* of 1606.

Metre

The poem is written in dactylic hexameters, which ranks it in an epic tradition. In this tradition the invocation of Orange's ashes, and of Maurice, sits quite well, without the poem being an epic or even the beginning of an epic. On the dactylic metre see Eyffinger, *Grotius poeta*, p. 214. Line 28 is a *versus spondiacus*, l. 108 contains a hiatus.

Commentary

Heading

Pro Auriaco sua The preposition *pro* has a double meaning: 'preceding' and 'in defence of'. In the heading the tragedy *Auriacus* is intended, hence the female form of the possessive "sua", sc. tragoedia.

Invocation of William of Orange and Maurice

1–19 *Auriaci cineres—ingentisque animae* Firstly, Heinsius, in an epic style, calls for support for his endeavours, but not to the usual Muses (e.g. Hom. *Od.* I, 1, Verg. *Aen.* I, 8–11, Sil. I, 3–8). With the ashes of the Prince of Orange, it should be noted that *cineres* indicates the remains (cf. 'ashes to ashes'), irrespective of whether a cremation actually took place. The ashes are a metonym for Orange, hence: "debellatrixque tyrannum" (he who subjects tyrants, cf. Verg. *Aen.* VII, 651: "debellatorque ferarum"), the one who took up arms against the tyrant, Philip II. Furthermore, he is "Nassovium stirps magna deûm", literally 'the great stock of the divine Nassaus', but perhaps 'a large shoot of Nassau's stem' is intended. For the latter, the use of *stirps* as stem, cf. l. 126: "Caesaris invicti stirps". In the first case the whole stem fights against the tyrant, which is not impossible. Orange's brothers were very active in the Revolt. The fact that humans are called gods is not exceptional; consider Verg. *Ecl.* 1, 6: "Deus [i.e. Octavianus] nobis haec otia fecit", Cic. *Att.* IV, 16, 3: "deus ille noster Plato" and Lucr. V, 8: "deus ille [i.e. Epicurus] fuit, deus". Furthermore, Maurice (1567–1625), Count of Nassau, Prince of Orange, the son of William of Orange and Anna of Saxony is invoked. In 1587 he became Stadholder, Captain General and Admiral General of Holland, Zeeland and West Friesland. The period between the murder of Orange and the writing of *Auriacus* spanned the 'ten years' (1588–1598) full of successes. About Maurice, see *NNBW* 1, 1315–1318; Herbert H. Rowen, *The Princes of Orange: The Stadholders in the Dutch Republic* (Cambridge and New York: Cambridge University Press, 1988), pp. 32–55; Kees Zandvliet (ed.), *Maurits van Nassau* (Amsterdam and Zwolle, Rijskmuseum and Waanders, 2000); Nicholas Ridley, *Maurits of Nassau and the Survival of the Dutch Revolt* (New York: Routledge, 2020).

Maurice is a son worthy of his father, whatever he does. The division into three possibilities, introduced with "seu" (ll. 3, 7 and 13), is epic (e.g. Verg. *Aen.* VII, 880–881: "seu cum pedes iret in hostem seu spumantis equi foderet calcaribus armos"; Luc. VII, 19–23; Sil. XVI, 51–57), but also sacred, as if Maurice is invoked as one of the "Nassovii dei".

The interpretation of the first possibility (ll. 3–7) is not unproblematic. "Fulgida caeli metiris spatia", can mean: (1) 'you measure with your eyes the vastness of the sky', well suited to the mathematician Euclid; (2) 'you make an imaginary journey through heaven' (cf. Boeth. *Cons.* I, 2.C, r. 7). As an equal to Euclid (b. 308 BC; on him *RE* 6, 1003–1052), Maurice also drew circles in the sand. He did have a special talent for mathematics, following lessons with the Leiden professor Snellius and Simon Stevin (see J.G. Kikkert, *Maurits van Nassau* (Weesp: Fibula-Van Dishoeck, 1985), p. 26) and used them for strategies, see Eyffinger, *Grotius poeta*, p. 71; Grotius, *Dichtwerken/Poetry* I, 2, 3A/B, pp. 118–148, esp. 128–130, on Grotius' praise of Maurice's achievements in the field, and E.J. Dijksterhuis, *Simon Stevin: Science in the Netherlands Around 1600* (The Hague: Nijhoff, 2012), pp. 106–112. Stevin's teaching in particular stimulated Maurice's development, see H.H. Kubbinga, 'Stevin en Maurits', *De zeventiende eeuw* 10 (1994), pp. 93–102. Stevin and Maurice together published a *Mathematica*, which appeared in 1605–1606, but in 1602 was already being circulated in manuscript form. In addition, 'he runs along the stars and the fiery lights on the golden sky', that is to say he looks at the stars, a useful hobby more easily practised in peacetime (that is how I perceive "tranquillae leve pacis opus").

During wartime Maurice can go around as a classical captain with the accoutrements of such a man: a shining (copper) helmet, shiny weapons, a foaming horse and on his head an *apex* (helmet striker) and *coni* (the conus was the conical helmet tip onto which the *crista*, the helmet plume, was attached). See also below. Such headgear is more becoming of an antique captain and not quite so in keeping with the equipment of a sixteenth-century commander.

A third possibility is that he also goes into battle, but then with guns. These are described completely in classical terms: with 'sulphur' (gunpowder, cf. Kilianus, *Etymologicum*, p. 96 s.v. bus-kruyd: "pulvis sulphureus") and "ater ignis" (black fire, on this the comm. *ad Aur.* 263–264, but perhaps once again the black powder is gunpowder). Jupiter's lightning is imitated (metonymically marked with "manus", the hand with which they are thrown), the "flammataque caeli nubila", the thunderclouds and 'the sound of the burning Olympus', the thunder that accompanies the lightning struck by Jupiter thrown from Olympus. He is also 'lord and master of ocean and earth'. This aims at the function of Admiral General, to which Maurice was appointed in 1597 (J.C. de Jonge, *Geschiedenis van het Nederlandsche zeewezen* (Zwolle: Van Hoogstraten en Gorter, 1869[3]), p. 196).

This fight renders him his father's avenger. This theme will return in Maurice's speech at the end of *Aur.* and in *Aur.* 1002 (the murderer) and *mutatis mutandis* in *Aur.* 1247–1253 (on Frederick Henry).

4 *pulvere* Tradition has it that Archimedes drew circles in the sand, cf. Cic. *Fin.* v, 50 and Liv. XXV, 31, 9; also Sil. XIV, 677: "[...] meditantem in pulvere formas [...]".

5 *Euclidae* Instead of the usual genetive form "Euclidis" here an -ae form is used, in analogy to forms such as "Aeneades" (gen. Aeneadae) and "Hippotades" (gen. Hippotadae, see l. 34).

6 *lumina mundi* Cf. Cat. 56.1: "omnia qui magni despexit lumina mundi".

8 *tympana que* In the first instance, "tympanum" is a percussion instrument used in the worship of Bacchus and Cybele, which indicates something soft; however, what is meant here is the drums used on the battlefield.

8 *fremitusque virûm* Cf. (for example) Verg. *Aen.* v, 148: "fremituque virûm".

8–9 *Eoâ ... galeâ* The helmet is connected to Eos, dawn: (1) with a reddish glow like the morning red (thus in the translation); (2) early in the morning.

9 *niveis conspectus in armis* Cf. Verg. *Aen.* VIII, 588: "pictis conspectus in armis".

10 *spumantem ... equuum* Cf. Verg. *Aen.* VI, 881: "seu spumantis equi foderet calcaribus armos" and *ibid.* XI, 770: "spumantem agitabat equuum". "Tundere" here is also 'to give the spurs'.

10–12 *Nutat-vento* Cf. (for example) Verg. *Aen.* X, 270–271: "Ardet apex capiti cristisque a vertice flamma funditur et vastos umbo vomit aureus ignis".

15 *Olympi* Either (1) the Olympus as a metonym for heaven (*OLD* s.v. 1C; see, for example, Sen. *Herc. Oet.* 1907: "stelligeri [...] Olympi"), or (2) the mountain from which Jupiter throws his lightning bolts.

18 *exactor* In classical Latin a tax collector, in medieval Latin also 'someone who demands much' (*Lexicon Latinitatis Nederlandicae Medii aevi* 3.E, 418–419 s.v. exactor 4).

L 3–4   In his copy Heinsius changed these lines into: 'Immeasurable descendant, the equal of your father, whether you draw beautiful circles in the dust' and removed the crossing of heaven.

L 7   Here 'easy activity in calm peace' gives way to 'a work of courage'.

C 10–15   In 1606 this passage becomes: 'For whom Germany shuddered and who was sent by the Spaniard to the lord of the sea; be present here, and take off your helmet for the colourful buskins [the performance of this tragedy], as far as you are concerned, whether you imitate the thunderclouds in the sky or the rumbling of the great Olympus'. The "Bructeri" were a tribe on the right bank of the Rhine, between Cologne and Koblenz, see Friedrich Benedict, *Orbis latinus oder Verzeichnis der wichtichsten lateinischen Orts- und Ländernamcn: Supplement* [...] (Berlin: Schmidt, 1909) s.v. Bructarii.

L 1–49   Finally Heinsius strikes out this entire passage on Maurice and the praise of the Dutchmen. However, in the *Poemata* it was not removed.

Invocation of the (seafaring) Dutch

19–38 *Tuque indignatus Iberum—in littore metas* In these lines the Dutch are invoked in their capacity as assailers of the seas and brave warriors who, with their courage, frighten kings. For such praise of seafarers see *Aur.* 305–318, 1752–1814 and the comm. *ad loc.* This motif is mixed with the comparison between the Romans and the Dutch. Heinsius used it previously in *Illustrissimis* [...] *Ordinibus* 148–149; see the comm. *ad loc.* The passage is extremely stylized, with many mythological references, with high-poetic descriptions, e.g. l. 29 "Humentes [...] moderaris habenas" (on seafaring); l. 30 "veliferum [...] currum" (a ship); and with *abstracta pro concretis*, such as l. 26 "vasticies" (plundered state) for those who plunder, see also the comm. *ad loc.*, and l. 26 "metus" for the cause of fear.

20–21 *magnoque Quiriti—nomina fastos* A tentative paraphrase of this sentence could be: 'who have been associating your name with the Romans for so many years', i.e. whose history is as old and as glorious as that of the Romans. Thus it is, so to speak, synonymous with l. 22 "aeterni comes imperii". The complexity of the colon is increased by the indication "fastos", the lists of the consuls, in which the years are indicated, metonymically the years themselves. The dative *Quiriti* (a citizen of Rome) must be taken ἀπὸ κοινοῦ at "aequaevos" (from the same time as the Romans) and "confundens" (mixing with the Romans). For parallels with Grotius' *Parallelon rerumpublicarum*, written in the years 1600–1604, of which the third and fourth chapters in particular discuss the military aspects, see the comm. *ad Illustrissimis* [...] *Ordinibus* 148–149.

22 *consorsque laborum* Cf. Stat. *Th.* IX, 82: "consorte laborum" and *id. Silv.* V, 2, 35: "comitem belli sociumque laborum".

24 *Germania* This remark refers to the time when Germania, to which the territory of the Netherlands belonged, was under Roman rule (from 57 BC) and shuddered for "Romanas [...] virgas" (the "fasces"), often combined with "secures" as symbols of power. The fact that the Dutchmen 'shared in the eternal power' will have been discussed between Heinsius and Grotius when working on *Auriacus* and *Parallelon rerumpublicarum*. For the 'Batavian freedom', see Grotius, *Parallelon*, ed. Meerman, I, Ch. 3 and 4. Cf. also the comm. *ad Illustrissimis* [...] *Ordinibus* 148–149.

26 *vasticies* Cf. Plaut. *Ps.* 70 "voluptatum [...] vastities". Here the word is etymologically related to "vastare" ('to plunder', *OLD* s.v. 2a); it may refer to hijacking at sea, which the Sea Beggars did, sometimes with the official permission of William of Orange himself.

27 *Haedos* The rise and fall of the constellation of *Haedi* (two stars in Auriga) predicted storms, cf. Verg. *Aen.* IX, 668: "pluvialibus Haedis"; Ov. *Tr.* I, 11,13: "nimbosis [...] Haedis"; and see also Cic. *N.D.* II, 43, 110 and the comm. by Pease *ad loc.*, p. 821.

28 *Amphitriten* The name of the sea goddess, Nereus' daughter and Neptune's wife Amphitrite is here used metonymically for sea. For the *versus spondiacus* by this four-syllable word, see Bömer, *Ovidius Metamorphosen* 1, p. 21 and Ov. *Met.* I, 14. For this metonymical use of Amphitrite, see Bömer, *Ovidius Fasten*, p. 336 *ad* Ov. *Fast.* V, 731.

29 *moderaris habenas* Cf., e.g., Stat. *Th.* IV, 219: "moderatur habenas".

30 *Veliferumque ... currum* For this poetic metaphor, cf. Ov. *Met.* XV, 719: "veliferam [...] carinam" and Prop. II, 9, 35.

31 *Aeolios* For this use of the adjective of Aeolus, cf. Tib. III, 7, 58: "Aeolios [...] ventos", and *Aur.* 317; see also Roscher 1.1, 193–195 s.v. Aiolos 3.

32 *Tritonasque* For the Tritons, sea demons who serve other gods, cf. Verg. *Aen.* V, 824: "Tritones [...] citi", and Stat. *Ach.* I, 55: "armigeri Tritones", carrying Neptune's trident. See also Roscher 5, 1150–1207 s.v. Triton und Tritonen. The Greek accusative ending on -as is used here.

32 *tempestatumque furores* The same combination in the medieval Christian author Iuvencus III, 230, p. 88.

33 *carcere* For the *carcer* as the dwelling of the winds cf., for instance, Verg. *Aen.* I, 54. See also Bömer, *Ovidius Metamorphosen* 1, p. 593 *ad* Ov. *Met.* III, 596.

34 *Hippotadae* Hippotades, Hippotes' grandson, is Aeolus. See Hom. *Od.* X, 2: Αἴολος Ἱπποτάδης; Stephanus, *Dictionarium*, p. 20r: "Iovis filius et Sergestae (alias Acestae) Hippotae Troiani filiae, a quo dicitur Hippotades". Ovid uses this 'papponymicum' a few times, e.g. *Met.* XIV, 224: "Aeolon Hippotaden, cohibentem carcere ventos"; see also Bömer, *Ovidius Metamorphosen* 2, p. 200 *ad* Ov. *Met.* IV, 663–690 and Roscher 5, 193.

34 *Boreamque Notumque* For Boreas, see *Aur.* 1757 and 2086, for Notus, *Aur.* 756.

35 *postremaque Thules* Cf. Verg. *Ge.* I, 30: "ultima Thule". On this island and its identification with Iceland, see (for example) Stephanus, *Dictionarium*, p. 428v.

36 *Memnoniamque domum* For the 'house of Memnon' in Ethiopia, cf. Prop. I, 6, 4: "domos [...] Memnonias" and Luc. III, 284: "Memnoniis [...] regnis". On this king of Ethiopia, son of Tithonus and Aurora, see Roscher 2.2, 2653–2687. This is a way of saying that the Dutch sail to the far north and the south. The empire that the great Titan (the sun, see *Aur.* 594 and the comm.) never sees, refers to the East and West Indies, south of the equator.

37 *multum errantis Iacchi* On the wanderings of Bacchus, see (for example) Heinsius' *Lof-sanck van Bacchus* 453–460 and the annotations by Scriverius

(L.Ph. Rank, J.D.P. Warners, F.L. Zwaan, *Bacchus en Christus: Twee lofzangen van Daniel Heinsius* (Zwolle: Tjeenk Willink, 1965) Zwolse drukken en herdrukken voor de Maatschappij der Nederlandse letterkunde te Leiden, 53, pp. 156–157). The story of Bacchus' travel through India is told by Nonnus XVII, 192–289. See also Roscher 1.1, 1087–1089.

38 ***Amphitryoniadaeque extremo in littore metas*** Hercules, the son of Alcmene, Amphitryon's wife, a son of Alcmene and Zeus; see also the comm. *ad* l. 5 and Bömer's comm. *ad* Ov. *Met.* IX, 140. The "metae" indicate the Pillars of Hercules, i.e. the Strait of Gibraltar, cf. Luc. III, 278: "Herculeis aufertur gloria metis". In antiquity, Spain was the end of the world, cf. also Sil. XIV, 8: "extremumve diem terrarum invisere metas". So the Dutch reach to the east (Ethiopia and India) and the west (Spain).

C 20–21 In 1606 these lines become: 'Lord of the great water, not devoid of courage, who connected the fierce battles with Roman history [...]'.

Spectators at Heinsius' flight

39–55 ***Huc agedum—ab aethere Nonnum*** Heinsius invokes the people mentioned (the shade of Orange, the race of the Nassaus, Maurice and the Dutch) to watch his tragedy. In writing it, he is following in the footsteps of his friend Grotius, who had written the tragedy *Adamus exul* (1601). Heinsius needed divine inspiration.

39 ***Huc ... ades*** Cf. Verg. *Ecl.* 2, 45; 9, 39; 9, 43 "huc ades".
39 ***ingentibus ausis*** Val. Fl. II, 242.
40 ***ignavam calcamus humum*** Does the narrator tread the ground with his buskin (cf. Grotius *Iambi* 1–2), or does he trample the earth in order to fly higher? The latter is confirmed by the following ("audacesque iuventa tollimur"), but the former is corroborated by the fact that he is writing a tragedy (l. 41). A third possibility would be that he is entering untrodden ground, viz. writing a (Neo-Latin) tragedy, which was still highly unusual in the Netherlands.
42 ***horridaque—pulpita socco*** For the *pulpita* cf. Grotius *Iambi* 1: "Quis ille tanto Pulpitum motu quatit". They are called 'horrid' because of the horrid event that is shown, the murder of Orange. It could also point to stage fright. The *soccus*, the shoes of a comedy actor, are strange, but will refer to drama in general.
43 ***thyrso percussa*** For the thyrsus (the ivy staff of Bacchus) as an instrument for poetic rapture, see (for example) Ov. *Am.* III, 1, 23: "Tempus erat thyrso pulsum graviore moveri" (on writing a tragedy). See also *OLD* s.v. 1b.

43–48 *qua nobilis—invectus eo*   Grotius, with his (topical) small body, lives up to his name ('the great') and earns himself worldwide fame with his *Adamus exul*. They showed the Dutch the way to tragedy, a path that Heinsius will now tread. For "orchestram invectus eo", cf. Grotius, *Iambi* 2: "insolenti tundit Orchestram pede".

44 *corpore parvo*   See above, and cf. Ov. *Met.* VI, 142: "toto quoque corpore parva est" and Ps.-Ov. *De luco* 69: "Diogenes animo magnus, sed corpore parvo".

48 *Quo tigride raptum*   Cf. Hor. *C.* III, 25, 1–2: "Quo me Bacche rapis tui plenum". For the tiger as an animal connected to Bacchus, see (for example) Mart. VIII, 26, 8: "contentus gemina tigride Bacchus erat". The *pectus* of Heinsius is, so to speak, raptured by the god of wine with his tiger. The poet runs along the clouds which are like vineyards—also connected to Bacchus, indicated as the leader of the Mimallones, Bacchantes. This indication suits the poetic ecstasy Heinsius describes here. On poetic frenzy, see (for example) Curtius, *European Literature and Latin Middle Ages*, pp. 474–475, excursus 8 'The Poet's divine frenzy' and Jan-Pieter Guépin, 'Het enthousiasme van dichters', *Bzzletin* 144 (1987), pp. 47–64. The Bacchantes are referred to using their patronymic, probably *metri causa*.

50–51 *Date-vela*   The *Batavi* are summoned to help this cosmic voyage with their sails, an original merging of ecstasy and the reality of seafaring compatriots.

51–55 *Ferox-Nonnum*   Bacchus drags the poet enthusiastically and waves his *signa*, the thyrsus and the branches of grapes. This passage includes much mythology. Euhan is one of the cultic names of Bacchus, see (for example) Ov. *Met.* IV, 15. He is mobbed by a *semivira chorea*, either women who act somewhat manly or men who act femininely. Euhoe is a shout of the Bacchantes. Moreover, Satyrs and Silenus are joining the procession. The latter was (1) the educator of Bacchus, a drunk old man, or (2) the most famous of the satyrs, connected to Bacchus, for instance Verg. *Ecl.* 6, 14; see also Robert D. Williams' comm. in Vergilius, *The Eclogues and Georgics* (London: Macmillan; New York: St Martin's Press, 1979) *ad loc.* On Satyrs and Silenus, see Bömer, *Ovidius Metamorphosen* 2, p. 23 *ad* Ov. *Met.* IV, 25; Roscher 4, 444–531 s.v. Satyros und Silenos.

54 *signa movet*   Cf., for instance, Sil. XI, 517: "signa movemus"; Ov. *Fast.* VI, 764: "signa movere velim".

55 *totum distillat ab aethere Nonnum*   Nonnus was a fifth-century poet of *Dionysiaca*, an epic on Dionysus/Bacchus. He makes the product of the subject of Nonnus' poem stream, leading to poetic ecstasy and drunkenness.

C **39–43**   In the 1606 edition this became: 'Be present here as a spectator, if I have absorbed the familiar breast of the gods in me, trusting in my youth, and if the love of exalted masculinity has put my calves in beautiful stage boots, where

the divine spirit of my friend Grotius led the Dutch with power'. The 'untrodden paths' have disappeared, because Grotius had published his *Adamus exul*.
C 49 In 1606 the "pampinea nubila" are removed to make way for 'you lift my cheering spirit and put it in the middle of Mount Olympus'. Thus 'Quo' (l. 48) becomes an interrogative to "tigride".

Orange on stage

56–73 *Cernitis?—è littore regem* The motif that the hero (Orange) deserved an honourable death on the battlefield, but died ingloriously by a traitor's hand, is topical.

56 *proscenia* The *proscaenium* is the part of the theatre between the back wall and the *orchestra*, i.e. the stage, see (for example) Plaut. *Poen.* 17–18: "Scortum exoletum ne quis in proscaenio sedeat".
61 *invidet* This allows two interpretations: (1) he does not deny his enemies that they are capable of deceit; (2) he does not envy his enemies for that.
61–62 *hosti ... suo* This combination of "hostis" (state enemy) and this possessive pronoun (what one would expect at an "inimicus", personal enemy) seems strange, but in Orange state and person are united. For the thought that the enemy needs a ruse for which one has to be ashamed, cf. *Illustrissimis* [...] *Ordinibus* 160; cf. also *Aur.* 1946–1947.
63–65 *Cunctas—iter* The paraphrase of these lines could be: At Fortune, all people, good or bad, have their own chances, but virtue's path is narrow and therefore only few can enter it.
65 *angustum est virtutis iter* Cf. Sen. *Herc. f.* 437: "Non est ad astra mollis e terris via" and *ibid.* 201: "Alte virtus animosa cadit", as well as Sen. *Ira* II, 13, 1: "Nec, ut quibusdam visum est, arduum in virtutes et asperum iter est".
65–66 *Mavortius ... ardor* Cf. *Aur.* 136: "ardore Martis" and 1431: "vis Mavortia".
70 *latroni* In *Aur.* the murderer is called "sicarius", in Grotius *Iambi* "parricida". Here he is called *latro* (bandit), for the contrast with the honourable death a noble opponent should have made Orange die on the battlefield, with a secondary meaning of 'mercenary soldier', since Gerards was promised a reward for the murder (see intr. pp. 18–19).
70–71 *Patriaeque ruinam duxit* Either (1) the murderer brought ruin to the fatherland, in which case the expression is a variant of "ruinam dare"; or (2) Orange, leading a ruined fatherland.
72 *Siculumque tyrannum* Sicily belonged to Naples which was part of the Habsburg Empire and dominated by Philip II. Moreover, "Siculus" can be used to refer to the cruelty of some of Sicily's tyrants, esp. Phalaris, see *OLD* s.v. Siculus d. Less likely is the interpretation of "Siculus tyrannus" as the Pope.

73 *et sero venturum è littore regem* This may refer to the farewell of Philip II
and Orange and 1555, in which case it is both literal and metaphorical.

Inquisition

74–85 *Cernitis ardentem—seclusimus aestu* Now Heinsius points to the
appearance of Inquisitio as a Fury, a goddess of fright. In the play she appears
in II, 1 and IV, 1 (about her intr., pp. 40 and 42). It is remarkable that in the piece
Inquisitio is a sister of the Furies, the fourth Fury, but that these lines are not
specific on this, with the wording "altera Alecto". Her attributes: a burning torch,
fresh blood and snakes in her hair occurs in *Aur.* in the heading of the first scene
of Act 2 ("facem et calicem humani sanguinis gestans"), 251 ("vibrare saevas [...]
faces") and 252 ("serpentibusque vinxit") respectively. The Inquisition pops up
as a 'product' of the Roman Catholic Church in Italy, which is called Sicily pars
pro toto, cf. 72 "Siculumque tyrannum". This Fury is worse than the goddesses
of antiquity of whom the "domitor ferarum", Athamas and Orestes, were afraid.

79 *Estne aliquid ... colla* Cf. (for example) Ov. *Her.* 3, 131: "Est aliquid, collum
solitis tetigisse, lacertis"; however, the combination "est aliquid" is very common (Schumann, 2, p. 190).

80–81 *Iovis ille ferarum immitis domitor* Maybe this is Hercules, the son of
Jupiter, who has conquered wild animals, He was addressed by the Furies, see
Sen. *Herc. f.* 86–88: "Adsint ab imo Tartari fundo excitae Eumenides, ignem
flammeae spargant comae, viperea saevae verbera incutiant manus". For the
combination of "domitor ferarum", cf. Apuleius, *Apol.* 22, 81. The father of Palaemon ("genitorve Palaemonis") was Athamas. For the madness that Athamas
and his wife Ino were brought into by the Fury Tisiphone, see *Aur.* 1481 and
the comm. *ad loc.*

82–83 *Diris-choros* In Aeschylus' Oresteia trilogy (consisting of *Agamemnon*,
Choephori and *Eumenides*, 458 BC) Orestes is chased by the Furies to punish
him for the murder of his father Agamemnon, see Roscher 3.1, 955–1014.

83–84 *Nec Graecia—una fuit* The most probable interpretation of this sentence is that the Furies needed more space than Greece and expanded their
territory to the Low Countries. Other possibilities are: (1) Greece on its own
was not strong enough to withstand the Furies; (2) Greece on its own had not
enough imagination to think of something worse than the Furies, i.e. the Inquisition, invented by Spain.

84 *Batavi* Strictly speaking these are the Hollanders, and by extension the
Dutch. Heinsius, from Ghent, is not in fact a Hollander, but he identifies with
his new country.

Libertas (Freedom)

86–107 *Cernitis indigno—immittere puppes* Freedom appears on the stage
with a wound in her breast (cf. Grotius *Iambi* 125–126: "Sed pectus, eheu,
Saucium vulnus gerit quod ante Princeps"). She stands by the corpse and summons all the Netherlands to their lord (in her speech, v, 2, see, for example, the
repeated "adeste cives", and ll. 2068–2076 on the sacrifice of her freedom hat
and a lock of hair "iuxta cadaver illud", l. 2069). She leaves, as she announces at
the end of her clause (ll. 2077–2105). Contrary to the play itself, where it would
have been hardly possible, Heinsius objects that she should look at the good:
the chances of war are reversed, the Dutch armies, from Friesland, Gelderland,
Zeeland and Holland, win victories over the Spaniards. The sea came to their
aid by becoming impetuous when the Spaniards set sail (for the last paragraph,
see the comm. *ad In Hispanum et Batavum* 17). Moreover, these four states are
also mentioned in *Aur.* 1288–1290.

86 *vulnere pectus* I.a. Verg. *Aen.* XII, 5.

90 *magnanimumque heroa* For this not unusual combination, see (for example) Verg. *Ge.* IV, 476: "magnanimum heroum".

91 *cum domino* The lord of either Freedom or the Netherlands, in both cases
William of Orange.

91 *Leonem* The lion is also mentioned in *Aur.* 2016. For the concept of 'the
Dutch lion', see (for instance) Bram Kempers, 'Assemblage van de Nederlandse
leeuw: Politieke symboliek in heraldiek en verhalende prenten uit de zestiende
eeuw', in: *id.* (ed.), *Openbaring en bedrog: De afbeelding als historische bron in
de Lage Landen* (Amsterdam: Amsterdam University Press, 1995), pp. 60–100.

96 *Aquilas* The standards of a legion (*TLL* 2, 371–372), hence metonymically
the legion (army) itself.

97–98 *Quantum ... sanguinis* The Spaniards can still shed a lot of their own
blood, in other words Maurice and the Dutch can still win many victories.

100 *Mattiacumque* In humanistic Latin Zeelanders are regularly called "Mattiaci", from the assumption that they stemmed from the Chatti, whose capital was "Mattium" or "Mattiacum", see Grotius, *Dichtwerken/Poetry* I, 2, 1B,
p. 52 *ad* 20, and *ibid.* p. 28; also Kilianus, *Etymologicum*, p. 881 s.v. See-landers;
Stephanus, *Dictionarium*, p. 450r–v s.v. Zelandia, uses the etymology of the
word "maat" ('mate'): "Quod autem Mattiaci nominentur, non a loco, aut Duce
aliquo, sed a populari appellatione, atque usitato loquendi more enatum est,
nempe a Maat quae vox in quotidiano sermone Zelandico et congressu fami-
liari omnium actionum, contractuum, periculorum, ac totius voluntatis, con-
silii, laboris socium comitemque sonat, etc.". See also Cats, *Sinne- en minnebeelden*, ed. Luijten 3, p. 399, n. 79.

100–101 *altique ... contemptorem animi*   Two interpretations are possible: (1) not counting his own life; or (2) who despises arrogant people (i.c. the Spaniards).

101 *Nereus*   Cf. (for example) *Aur*. 122–124.

106 *Vesper*   For Spain as the land of the Occident, see *Aur.*, the speech of Maurice, l. 40 and cf. *Aur.* 259–260: "Hispana tellus, scilicet vesper tuus fecundus ipse noctis exemplo fuit" and the comm. *ad loc.* Cf. also (for example) Hor. *C.* I, 36, 4: "Hesperia [...] ab ultima" and see Nisbet-Hubbard 1, p. 402 *ad loc.*

107 *Siculas ... puppes*   See l. 72 and the comm. The fleet of the Spanish Armada is meant.

        The poet as seer

108–124 *O animi—ostia Rheni*   The exclamation on the brave Dutchmen adds pathos. If he is granted time to live, he will sing the praise of the defeat of Turnhout and the death of Philip II († 1598). If poetry has predictive power, the poet will speak of great endeavours and go to France, the country of de Thou, and to Italy and the estuary of the Rhine. He wishes to treat the history of all Europe insofar as it is connected to that of the Low Countries and the Habsburg Empire.

109–112 (*me si vis inclyta fandi—caliginis atrae*)   The sentence in parentheses should be read as a limitation (if I get the time) or as an adjuration (I will certainly get the time).

113 *Thurnouda*   In 1597 Turnhout was taken by Maurice, a psychologically important event, see John Lothrop Motley, *History of the United Netherlands From the Death of William the Silent to the Synod of Dort* (Rotterdam: J.G. Robbers, 1979), pp. 68–79, 881–886. For Grotius' poetry on this battle, see Eyffinger, *Grotius poeta*, pp. 48–49.

114 *Eoi perruptas littoris oras*   Either the victory of the Spaniards over the Muslims, or the eastern shipping of the Dutchmen. For *Eoa ripa* cf. Prop. IV(V), 5, 21.

116 *aeterni nominis Hugo*   Heinsius' friend Grotius; Heinsius plays with the name "Groot", i.e. 'important'. He will be considered as important as the great Desiderius Erasmus (1466?–1536). For the same praise by Dousa for De Groot as he enrolled at the university at the age of 11, see Anton D. Leeman, 'De klassieken en de Tachtigjarige Oorlog', in: Collegium Classicum c.n. M.F., *Miro Fervore: Een bundel lezingen en artikelen over de beoefening van de klassieke wetenschappen in de zeventiende en achttiende eeuw. T.g.v. het zestiende lustrum* (Leiden: Collegium Classicum, 1994), p. 6. *Donabit* may be an allusion to a passage in Grotius' *Parallelon rerumpublicarum* in which he praises Erasmus (*Paral.* 24, Grotius, *Parallelon*, ed. Meerman, 3, pp. 33–35).

118–119 (*si quid—saeclis*) Cf. Verg. *Ecl.* 9, 11–12: "sed carmina tantum nostra valent"; Verg. *Aen.* IX, 446: "si quid mea carmina possunt"; Sil. IV, 399–400: "si modo [...] carmina nostra valent"; Tib. II, 4, 19–20: "carmina [...] si nihil ista valent"; Verg. *Aen.* IX, 446: "siquid mea carmina possunt".

122 *Thuani* Jacques-Auguste de Thou (1553–1617), French statesman, historian and poet; on him, *Nouvelle biographie generale* 45, 255–262, and Ingrid de Smet, *Thuanus: The Making of Jacques Auguste de Thou (1553–1617)* (Geneva: Droz, 2006). De Thou was a friend of Joseph Scaliger, see John E. Sandys, *A History of Classical Scholarship, vol. 2: From the Revival of Learning tot the End of the Eighteenth Century in Italy, France, England, and the Netherlands* (Cambridge: Cambridge University Press, 1958), (for instance) p. 204, and maintained contact with Grotius (see Grotius, *BW* 1, pp. 19–20 [no. 24], a letter of 3 Sept. 1601 in which Grotius refers to de Thou's interest in tragedy) and Heinsius, see Eyffinger, *Grotius poeta*, pp. 22–24 and Grotius, *Dichtwerken/Poetry* I, 2 3A/B, pp. 11 and 43.

124 *fines Ligurum* For the *Ligures* as pars pro toto for Italy, see *In Hispanum et Batavum* 2 and the comm. *ad loc.*

Scaliger and Dousa

125–146 *Interea Heroes patrij—demittere Musas* Heinsius invokes two celebrities: he asks Joseph Scaliger to bring the audience to applause (a variant of the "plaudite" formula of comedy), and with Dousa's protection he wishes to break the 'darkness of the world' to get to the ether by writing tragedies. For the poetical flight, cf. Grotius *Iambi* 33–41 and the comm., for the reference to Sophocles *ibid.* 20 and the comm.

125 *arbiter horum* I.e. Joseph Scaliger (see comm. *ad* 126), who is "arbiter" of the "heroes patrii", since he had earned his fame with his work on chronology: *Opus novum de emendatione temporum in octo libros tributum* (Paris: Mamertus Patisson, 1583). He would corroborate his fame with the *Thesaurus temporum* (Leiden: Thomas Basson, 1606). On him, see Grafton, *Joseph Scaliger*.

126 *Caesaris ... stirps* For Joseph Scaliger, Julius Caesar's son, see above, p. 4. Cf. also "Iuliade" (l. 129) and "Caesareoque" (l. 136).

126 *Aeneadumque ruinis* The *Aeneades* are Aeneas' descendants or compatriots, the Romans, see (for example) Lucr. I, 1: "Aeneadum genetrix [i.e. Venus]", and Sil. I, 1–2: "gloria [...] Aeneadum".

128 *annue ceptis* Cf. Verg. *Ge.* I, 40: "audacibus adnue coeptis" and *id. Aen.* IX, 625.

133–134 *Ipse ego—sacra feram* Cf. Verg. *Ge.* III, 21–22: "Ipse caput tonsae foliis ornatus olivae dona feram" and *id. Aen.* V, 774: "ipse caput tonsae foliis evinctus olivae". On the poets' laurel wreath, see Kambylis, *Die Dichterweihe*, pp. 173–176 and Nisbet-Hubbard 1, p. 98 *ad* Hor. *C.* I, 7, 7.

135 *Veronaeque deos* The Della Scala family, from which Scaliger was said to descend, had its roots in Verona. See his *Epistola de vetustate et splendore Gentis Scaligerae* (Leiden, 1594).

136 *aeterna feram sollennia* Cf. Verg. *Aen.* IX, 626: "Ipse tibi ad tua templa feram sollemnia dona". Heinsius will celebrate an annual commemoration, as Janus Secundus had done for his lover Julia. His wreath will consist of olives, because he wishes to honour Scaliger for his Greek poetry, the olive being associated with Attica.

139 *Boisoti pars magno tui* Cf. Hor. *C.* III, 30, 6: "multaque pars mei" and Ov. *Her.* 3, 46: "Et fueram patriae pars ego magna meae". On the Sea Beggars' leader Louis de Boisot, Lord of Stuart, see Van der Aa 1, pp. 242–243; *NNBW* 5, 42–44. See Motley, *Dutch Republic*, pp. 577–579, on his role in the Relief of Leiden. The man who is now 'a great part of your Boisot' is Dousa, who collaborated with Boisot in Leiden's Relief. The "victurae chartae" are the small letters that were exchanged through doves between Boisot and Dousa (*Aur.* 1806–1811) or writings that will survive, i.e. the historiographical writing of Dousa Sr and Jr.

139 *praestite* "Praestes" is a religious term for a guardian god. In Heinsius' view Boisot is almost a saint. Cf. Dousa's long ode 'Ad Ludovicum Boisotum Batavicae Zelandicaeque classis Praefectum, Lugduni Batavorum urbis liberatorem' (*Odae* II, 1), in: *Nova poemata* (Janus Dousa, *Novorum poematum secunda Lugdunensis editio, plus dimidia parte, hoc est, novem librorum accessione recens locupletata et aucta.* (Leiden: In nova Lugduni Batavorum Academia, 1576), pp. Ciiv-Eiiiv).

140 *inclyta Lugdunum* "Lugdunum" (neuter) as "urbs" is treated as a feminine word.

141 *Dousa* On Janus Dousa Sr see the comm. *ad In eandem*. Heinsius asks him to be his patron. For the good relationship, see *Illustrissimis* [...] *Ordinibus* 180–184.

L et C 126–129   In the Leiden copy and in 1606 these lines become (passing over variants in Heinsius' own copy that do not have serious impact on the meaning): "Etruscan scion of the god, who has not been swept away by the fate of your parents, and who has conquered the enormous glow in your heart, son of Julius, if I have made sacrifices to your altars, great father, at the moment that you will shine in the bright celestial regions among the glorious stars or between the beautiful souls of the ancestors, father, favour my business and come to their aid for help". Heinsius adds the conviction, worded in (for instance) Cic. *Somnium Scipionis*, that the souls of good men get a place among the stars; see also the comm. *ad Aur* 23–45.

To Orange

147–157 *At tu ingens anima—sanguine Manes* Orange is now making a cosmic journey, supported by Heinsius' tragedy. Wearing the weapons that he has captured from the Spaniards, he terrifies the Spaniards and even the stars. From that high position he must then see his son Maurice, who is avenging his father with his warfare.

The cosmic journey is reminiscent of the *Somnium Scipionis*, the end of Cicero's *De republica*, in which the soul of the old statesman Scipio reveals the destiny of the human soul on earth and in heaven to the soul of his adoptive grandson Scipio. See also the comm. *ad Aur.* 23–45.

147 *cothurnis* The buskin of the tragic actor is here used both as a metonym for tragedy and as a (literal) part of Orange's clothing (ll. 148–149).
148–149 A paraphrase of these lines could be: "It is meant: 'you who look dire because of all the spoils you have won from the Spaniards, and are dressed in the oriental armour that you took from the Spaniards'." "Maurus" must be regarded as 'Moorish', i.e. 'Spanish'. Unless one ought to consider the Moroccan javelin from Hor. *C.* I, 22, 1–2: "Integer vitae scelerisque purus | Non eget Mauris iaculis neque arcu". "Opima" or "spolia opima" indicates the loot that one commander takes from the other in a man-to-man fight.
154 *Flammea turbato subsidunt sidera vultu* Literally: 'the flaming stars extinguish with a confused face'. This poetic formulation can be paraphrased as: 'even the stars get confused by Orange's triumph through heaven'. In "subsidunt", various aspects of the verb can play a part: kneeling (*OLD* s.v. 1), going to the side as a result of a shock (*OLD* s.v. 5) or waning (in brightness) (*OLD* s.v. 6), 'bleaching'.

Personae tragoediae / List of characters

Κωφὰ πρόσωπα For this term, cf. Mart. VI, 6, 2: "Κωφὸν Paula πρόσωπον amat", quoted by Scal. *Poet.* I, 13, p. 22aC; Scaliger, *Poetica/Dichtkunst* 1, p. 204.26–28: "In mutam personam ambigue lusit Martialis: Κωφὸν Paula πρόσωπον amat'". For a discussion of the several characters, see intr., section 6, pp. 38–45.

Act I, scene 1 (1–185)

Summary

The first act consists of a monologue by Auriacus/William of Orange.

1–51 Auriacus invokes Nature with various names, as well as the night; further-more, he reflects on the uncertainty of human existence, subject as it is to the vagaries of Fortune. Life is short, the spirit of man, however, reaches to heaven and despises death. The body may die, the spirit sees heaven, its destination, and rises. This is also the origin of ambition in princes and other high-ranking persons.

51–84 Now he is called by his homeland and Freedom to redeem the land of slavery, something that many have already done for him, such as Brutus, Har-modius and Aristogeiton. His origins also incite him: Nassaus do not hesitate. The enemy cannot remain unpunished for suppressing the Netherlands with deceit and ruse. Even if the cosmic forces were to oppose, he would go, for whosoever is courageous resists fate when it depresses him.

84–110 The issue at stake is no trifling matter: the preparations for a prosper-ous war have been made. Philip and Alva have learned of his actions. His great example is Hercules: both are incited to deeds, both by a tyrant, Eurystheus, or Philip II, both by instigation of a stepmother, Hera and Fortune respec-tively.

110–133 Because he manages to control his passions, a victory over himself, he almost feels invincible. This allows him to counter Fate and Fortune. It also ensures that he sees his elevated position in perspective, which was given to him by chance and could be lost again.

134–168 This victory over himself also led him to suppress the urge to wage war. Although this urge is an incentive for princes, it must be curbed by virtue. He compares the battle between virtue and the passions with a hunter who, after a battle, conquers a lion. A shorter simile sees Typhoeus, seated beneath Etna, and someone put to the test by fate being compared.

169–185 Auriacus/Orange did not go into the danger of war out of self-interest but rather to protect the fatherland. He started the war for the sake of peace, because peace is won with war. Through this insight, and because he has sub-jected his emotions to his control, he is the ideal protector of the fatherland.

Auriacus/Orange is presented as a man who, because of his Stoic virtues, is apt to defend freedom and his country. He is courageous, but controls his passions and will therefore act prudently. This is necessary since his enemy is not 'Spain', but Fortune. The struggle for freedom ultimately is a fight between virtue and

Fortune. Orange is confident that he will be able to protect the country. The prologue, which is somewhat separate from the rest of the play, does not give a factual 'exposition' but does contain allusions to the confrontation between him, and Philip II and Alva (ll. 70–72; 84–91). More important is his portrayal as a Stoic hero, in the same way that Hercules, who also prides himself on his deeds, is presented in Sen. *Herc. Oet.*

This first scene fits in with the prologues of some of Seneca's tragedies, such as the first scene of *Herc. f.*, which is preliminary and somewhat 'separate from the main action of the plot' (Fitch, *Seneca's Hercules Furens*, pp. 115–116). There, too, some background information is given, but not in an 'expository narrative'. The play beginning with a monologue is not unusual in Seneca's dramas (thus in *Tro., Med., Aga.* and *Herc. Oet.*). This is similar to Euripides, although the Greek playwright was more apt to address the audience and present the pre-history. Furthermore, monologues in Seneca's plays often are 'monologues intérieures' in which the state of mind of the protagonist is more important than the information he gives. Another feature that this monologue has in common with those of Seneca's plays is the portrayal of the protagonist in his final situation, without him developing (Eckard Lefèvre, 'Versuch einer Typologie des römischen Dramas', in: *id.* (ed.), *Das römische Drama* (Darmstadt: Wissenschaftliche Buchgesellschaft, 1978), pp. 1–90. 1978, pp. 51–52). Throughout the play Orange has the same ideas on defending his country; there is no *anagnorisis* in him.

Although the place of action is not made explicit, it should be the 'Princenhof' in Delft. It is spoken at dawn (see ll. 1–13 and the comm.).

Metre

The scene is written in iambic trimeters.

Commentary

Nature, God and fickle Fortune

1–5 *Rerum—poli* In this passage, the *Logos*, the Stoic, omnipotent Deity, is invoked, under the name of "Rerum rector", which can be a poetic description of Jupiter (e.g. 11, 60, and Sen. *Herc. f.* 205: "O magni Olympi rector et mundi arbiter"; Natura, the "parens magni mundi", "Vita et Lex omnium" and "fusi sancta maiestas poli"). Heinsius may have found this idea familiar in Stoic circles (that the deity bears many names) in Cleanthes' *Hymn to Zeus* 1–2: "Supreme of the gods, with names of countless names, who govern nature with eternal laws, its ruler", and in Sen. *Ben.* IV, 7, 1 and IV, 8, 3: "Quid enim aliud est natura quam deus et divina ratio toti mundo partibusque eius inserta? [...] et Iovem illum Optimum ac Maximum rite dices [...] Sic nunc naturam voca, fatum, fortunam, omnia eiusdem dei nomina sunt varie utentis sua potestate". The idea was also known in the sixteenth century—this passage is quoted by Lipsius in his *Physiologia stoicorum* III, 1, 9. See also (for example) Pohlenz, *Die Stoa* 1, p. 320 and Frank, *Seneca's Phoenissae*, p. 103 *ad* Sen. *Pho.* 82–85.

A similar view is given by the Christian author Lactantius—to prove the existence of God—in *Div. Inst.* I, 5: "Sive enim natura sive aether sive ratio sive mens sive fatalis necessitas sive divina lex sive quid aliud dixeris, idem et quod a nobis dicitur deus".

In this tradition, Heinsius seems not to worry too much about the differences that may exist between Nature and Fortune. "Iocoque inani ludis humanum genus" rather suits the changeable woman Fortune who plays with the human race, than Nature who rules everything according to fixed patterns, which are called "lex", such as in Sen. *Helv.* 6, 8: "ut lex et naturae necessitas ordinavit, aliunde alio deferuntur"; Lipsius *Const.* I, 16: "Aeterna lex a principio dicta omni huic Mundo, nasci, denasci, oriri, aboriri", and Grotius *Ad. ex.* 312: "legis aeternae vice".

The *vices* are somewhat ambiguous in this context—they can aim at the fixed changes in the cosmos, but here they will be the vicissitudes that befall the people through the fickleness of fortune (cf. Sen. *Tro.* 1145: "vagae rerum vices", see also Fantham, *Seneca's Troades*, p. 249 on *Tro.* 253 and *ibid.*, pp. 379–380). On Fortune in Seneca see, among others, Francis H. Sandbach, *The Stoics* (London: Hackett, 1975), p. 161, n. 21 and Rosenmeyer, *Senecan Drama and Stoic Cosmology*, p. 68.

With this apostrophe to Nature in many guises and with many names, Heinsius is also linking up with the ancient tradition of prayer, in which the gods are often called by many names and descriptions (e.g. Wisse A.P. Smit, *De dichter Revius* (Amsterdam: Uitgeversmaatschappij Holland, 1966) Doctoral thesis Utrecht, pp. 50–55 and Fitch, *Seneca's Hercules Furens*, p. 187), and which is not lacking in contemporary Neo-Latin drama (e.g. Buchanan, *Bapt.* 695–711 and *Iephth.* 431–443).

Fortune's 'games' are proverbial, see (for example) Sen. *Ep.* 74, 7: "ludos facere fortunam" or *Polyb.* 16, 2: "Fortuna impotens, quales ex humanis malis tibi ipsa ludos facis!"

For the (Stoic) cycle of merging things, cf. (for example) Lipsius *Const.* I, 16: "Eat hic rerum in se remeantium orbis quamdiu erit ipse Orbis". For more *loci* in Lipsius and Seneca in which this idea is expressed, see Van de Bilt, *Lipsius en Seneca*, pp. 77–78 and 119–121.

These lines have an interesting parallel in the third choral ode of Sen. *Pho.* 959–990, which also begins with the invocation of Nature as Stoic overarching deity: "O magna parens, Natura, deum tuque igniferi rector Olympi" (959–960) and continues with reflections on vicissitudes: "Res humanas ordine nullo Fortuna regit" (978–979; see Rosenmeyer, *Senecan Drama and Stoic Cosmology*, p. 72). This passage has been imitated by Boethius, *Cons. phil.* 1, carm. 5.

3 *rerum vices* Cf. Heinsius, *In miseros mortem optantes* 4: "digerit rerum vices" (Seneca 1601, p. H2v).

2 *Lex omnium* Grotius *Ad. ex.* 378.
L 3 Heinsius has eliminated the metaphor of the 'flowing' of *vices* and changed it into "cadentes" (falling), and in the second instance into "euntes" (merging into one another).

The night and its changes

6–13 *Et tu—chori* Auriacus/Orange addresses the night, with an emphasis on its ominous aspects: darkness and silence, though especially on the changes it brings. The fact that the moon goddess never shows her own shape (face) does, of course, refer to its phases, as in Grotius *Ad. ex.* 77: "quae varia lucis non suae alternans vices" and Janus Secundus, *Epist.* II, 4, 71: "et ora quater mutavit menstrua Phoebe". Yet through mythology an ominous undertone can be heard: at crossroads three-faced statues stood for the goddess Hecate (the moon goddess who called ghosts from the underworld and protected witches) as Hecate triformis or Trivia: Artemis, Selene and Hecate itself, see Ov. *Fast.* I, 141 and the comm. by Bömer's comm. *ad loc.*, p. 24; further Roscher 2.2, 3182–3184. The moon leads the stars instead of her brother Apollo, the sun. For his leadership cf. inter alia, Cic. *Rep.* VI, 17: "dux et princeps and moderator luminum reliquorum". For the notion that the moon is leading the rest of the stars, see Petron. *Satyr.* c. 89: "minora ducens astra"; cf. Sen. *Oct.* 389: "orbemque Phoebes, astra quem cingunt vaga" and Grotius *Ad. ex.* 324: "Et Luna ducens mille stellarum choros".

For this passage, Heinsius varies on his own *De fragilitate rerum* 9: "seseque rerum turbidae premunt vices" (l. 3: "in se fluentes [...] rerum vices"); 11: "orbe [...] vago" (l. 11: "orbes [...] vago"); 6 "lususque rerum, temporumque nascimur" (ll. 14–18: "nata [...] lususque rerum"); 10–11: "cunctisque ab annis mensibusque, et huc et huc provolvimurque ducimurque" (l. 19: "ipsisque ab annis mensibusque ducimur").

A time indication such as this, a stylized moment in the classical tragedy, is also widely developed in Seneca's tragedies. The play opens at (or just before) sunrise, witness the fact that Auriacus still calls the night, but the emphasis is on the changes. Although this is a natural beginning for a drama, there is no real parallel with the Greek playwrights. Only Aeschylus' *Agamemnon* opens at the same time. However, two tragedies by Seneca open at daybreak: *Oed.* 1: "Iam nocte Titan dubius expulsa redit" and *Oct.* 1–4 "Iam vaga caelo sidera fulgens Aurora fugat, surgit Titan radiante coma mundoque diem reddit clarum". This motif also occurs in Neo-Latin drama, but not in the opening scene, see Buchanan, *Jephth.* 238–239: "Aurora primum luce cum rosea polum perfudit" and Grotius, *Ad. ex.* 312–316: "Dies tenebras legis aëternae vice fugans resurgit: certus ordo temporum solis reducit aureum terris caput: stellis fugatis maius exoritur iubar; nox iussa luci cedit et Phoebo soror", cf. Grotius, *Dichtwerken/Poetry* I, 2, 2A/B, p. 56. See also Eyffmger in Grotius, *Dichtwerken/Poetry* I, 2, 5A/B, p. 33 and Grotius, *Dichtwerken/Poetry* I, 4, pp. 251–252. Such an indication of time stresses the temporal structure of a drama. Heinsius is being innovative by delivering it in an apostrophe.

10 *Hesperasque lampadas* A transcription of the Greek ἑσπέρας λαμπάδας, i.e. the stars, or the light of Hesperus, the Evening star (Venus, in which case "lampadas" is poetic plural), or the stars again, led by Hesperus (cf. Sen. *Med.* 878: "dux noctis Hesperus"). This interpretation accords with "orbes magnos igne [...] vago", which can indicate the planets and the stars in general (e.g. Sen. *Pha.* 962: "cursus vagos [...] astrorum"; *Thy.* 834: "vaga [...] sidere"; Lucr. V, 1191: "noctivagae [...] faces caeli", there of stars or of comets and meteors). For *lampas* with respect to stars, see *TLL* 7.2, 910.66–911.3. "Hesperas" is used *metri causa* instead of "hesperias".

Because in mythology Hesperus is the father of the Hesperides, whose apples Hercules had to steal, this may also be an indirect reference to that hero.

11 *igne ... vago* Cf. Grotius *Ad. ex.* 543: "lumine [...] vago" and Sen. *Herc. f.* 11: "passim vagantes" and Fitch, *Seneca's Hercules Furens*, p. 123 *ad loc.*

12 *Phoeben* Hesiod (*Theog.* 19 and 371) already presented Phoebe as the sister of Phoebus Apollo, though the Roman poets had also done so since the 1st c. BC. See also Stephanus, *Dictionarium*, p. 351v s.v. Phoebe: "eadem quae Diana sive Luna, a Phoebo fratre ita dicta".

L 8 In the Leiden copy "indis" (the night putting silence into things) is changed to "addis" (adding silence to things).

The unformulated transition to the sequel is the line of thought: Nature, you have so much power, why do not you prevent the human race from being mortal (and Orange from being killed)? Cf. for this also the aforementioned chorus song in Sen. *Pha.* 959–990, where there is also a shift from Nature who rules everything to volatile Fortune.

The threats of Fortune and the mortality of man

14–22 *Ergon' caduca—gradu* In this passage, an amplifying elaboration of "iocoque inani ludis" (l. 4), Fortune seemingly arbitrarily causes what happens and therefore it is not necessarily equated with fate. Rather, it is coincidence, as is "sors". These two are apparently synonymous for Heinsius, especially because "sors" has hands, as Lady Fortune, who "res humanas ordine nullo [...] regit" (Sen. *Pha.* 978–979). Heinsius will not have been aware of the inconsistency that lurks in the appearance of "fatum" in l. 20; for him, "sors", "fatum" and "fortuna" probably represent the same power, cf. the comm. *ad* l. 1. He is not the only one, see Kirchner, *Fortuna*, p. 2, pp. 168–169, n. 4 and pp. 41–45. Virgil already relates "fatum" and "fortuna" (*Aen.* V, 709–710: "Nate dea, quo fata trahunt, retrahuntque sequamur, quidquid erit, superanda omnis fortuna ferendo est").

Heinsius may have borrowed the fateful advancing years from the Stoics or the poets, e.g. Sen. *Ep.* 108, 24: "Non hoc animo legit illud egregium 'fugit irreparabile tempus' [Verg. *Ge.* III, 284]: vigilandum est; nisi properamus, relinquemur; agit nos agiturque velox dies; inscii rapimur [...]". The motif of the years that went on was not unknown in Roman poetry either, see Otto, *Sprichwörter*, pp. 112–113, Hor. *C.* II, 14, 1–2: "Eheu fugaces [...] labuntur anni" and Nisbet-Hubbard 2 *ad loc.*, pp. 226–227; Sen. *Herc. f.* 178–180 and 183–184: "Properat cursu vita citato volucrique rota praecitis vertitur anni; [...] at gens hominum flatur rapidis obvia fatis incerta sui". See also Secundus *Silvae* 2, 56: "O varios hominum casus"; Boeth. *Cons.* 2; Hor. *C.* I, 34, 12–16 and the comm. of Nisbet-Hubbard 1 *ad loc.*, pp. 383–386; Sen. *Thy.* 615–622.

Implicitly in ll. 16–18 the activities of "fortuna" and "sors" are criticized; for such reproaches, see Sen. *Herc. f.* 524–532 and Fitch, *Seneca's Hercules Furens*, pp. 256–257 *ad loc.* Also the idea of steadily dying is often seen in Stoic contexts; see (for example) Sen. *Ep.* 24, 19–20: "Cotidie morimur. Cotidie enim demitur aliqua pars vitae, et tunc quoque, cum crescimus, vita descrescit"; also Pohlenz, *Die Stoa* 1, p. 323; *id.* 2, p. 160.

16 *intonantis* For "intonare" with respect to Fortuna, see (for instance) Ov. *Pont.* II, 3, 24: "intonuit [sc. Fortuna]".

21 *denascimurque* In antiquity "denasci" is a rare and archaic word, see *OLD* s.v.; *TLL* 5.1, 522.63–65, which can mean 'to weaken'. But on contemporary monuments often the years of birth and death are indicated with "natus" and "denatus" (deceased). Lipsius uses the word for the passing of the world (*Const.* 1, 16). See also http://www.vii.com/~nelsonb/latin.htm (Latin Primer) and http://www.datadux.se/skolan/latin.htm (Latinska Termer).

22 *gradu* For the unusual combination of "gradus" and years, see Sen. *Herc. f.* 291: "tot per annorum gradus", cf. Fitch, *Seneca's Hercules Furens ad loc.*, p. 207.

The body may be perishable, but the soul lives on and can already get a taste of the future.

The high flight of the soul

23–45 *At igneae—erigat* This passage expresses ideas that were widespread in the Renaissance, and which are shown by, among others, Cicero at the end of *Rep.* (VI, 9–29, the *Somnium Scipionis*): Scipio the Elder tells his grandson in a dream that for statesmen who have been deployed for the commonwealth there is a place in heaven; if the deity has freed the soul from the dungeon of the body, that soul will go there. Therefore: "Haec caelestia semper spectato, illa humana contemnito" (Cic. *Rep.* VI, 20), cf. *Aur.* 38–45, and (for example) Plato, *Phl.* 246A–248E; Cic. *N.D.* I, 54 and Boet. *Cons.* IV, 1, where the soul also travels through the air. For such a view in Seneca, see Pohlenz, *Die Stoa* 1, p. 322 and Motto, *Seneca Sourcebook*, p. 61 s.v. death 32a. See also Von Moos, *Consolatio*, 3, pp. 176–178 sub d) "volatus ad auras". Heinsius described such a 'cosmic' voyage in the poem *De Deo* 26–30: "Mens alta perge, remige alarum procul trans claustra mundi, atque Herculis magni domos finesque summos, transque flagrantem aera tremulaque semper lumine ardenti polum evecta tendes, quicquid hic latet tuum est".

Heinsius here names the soul with "mens" (mind) and "spiritus" (breath) and virtually equates these two. Here he could be drawing on the Stoic view that the true essence of the soul is the spirit (Pohlenz, *Die Stoa* 1, p. 230, also Lipsius *Const.* I, 6, where the "ratio" is called "mens" or "animi mens"). This spirit is a 'spark' ("scintilla", l. 24) of the *Logos* or *Ratio*, and therefore also 'of fire' ("igneae", l. 23), cf. Lipsius *Const.* I, 5: "Clare in ea scintillantes reliquiae primi illius purique ignis [...] Emicant enim semper subsiliuntque illi igniculi".

As said, this thought that the mind is not hindered by boundaries, can also be found in other (Stoic) writings, such as Lipsius *Const.* I, 9: "Magnus enim rectusque animus non includit se istis ab opinione terminis, sed cogitatione et sensu totum hoc Vniversum complectitur, ut suum". Cf. also Sen. *Ep.* 41 on the divine mind in man, and see Van de Bilt, *Lipsius en Seneca*, pp. 113–114.

30–31 *terminosque—metasque rerum* I.e. the border between heaven and earth. The mind/soul surpasses the earth to enter the ether. This use of "terminus" deviates from Sen. *Herc. f.* 290 (cf. the comm. of Fitch, *Seneca's Hercules Furens ad loc.*, p. 207), where the border between world and underworld is intended. In *Aur.* the crossing of borders is (unlike Sen., see *loc. cit.*) no *hybris*, because the mind/soul arrives at its final destination, its own area ("propriumque ad aethera", l. 32). On the heroic ring of "ingens" (l. 27), see Austin's comm. *ad* Verg. *Aen.* IV, 89, p. 49 and Fantham, *Seneca's Troades ad* Sen. *Tro.* 181, p. 236. The several connotations of the word in Verg. *Ge.* are treated by J.W. Mackail, 'Vergil's Use of the Word *ingens*', *The Classical Review* 26 (1912), pp. 251–254.

31 *corporisque ... moras* On the body as a dungeon of the soul, see Von Moos, *Consolatio*, 3, pp. 175–176.

32 *propriumque ad aethera* In the Platonic view, the soul comes from the ether and returns to it. In the classical view (of Pythagoras, Aristotle and Ptolemy) this ether is the *quinta essentia*, the place where the seven planets and the *stellae fixae* are (P.E.L. Verkuyl, 'Kosmografische glossen bij *Naeniae* 141 (een Nenia?)', in: A.Th. van Deursen, E.K. Grootes, P.E.L. Verkuyl (eds), *Veelzijdigheid als levensvorm: Facetten van Constantijn Huygens' leven en werk: Een bundel studíes ter gelegenheid van zijn driehonderdste sterfdag* (Deventer: Sub Rosa, 1987), pp. 215–225, esp. pp. 219–220). In this view (also in the *Somnium Scipionis*), in which the souls of statesmen are placed in the Milky Way (catasterism), the ether is the soul's own. Even if "aether" is a synonym for "coelum" (*TLL* 1, 1149.66–83), this is still the soul's final destination. Such a view is not Stoic, for according to Stoics the soul is material and perishable, see (for example) Sen. *Ep.* 57, 7: "Nunc me putas de Stoicis dicere, qui existimant animam hominis magno pondere extriti permanere non posse et statim spargi, quia non fuerit illi exitus liber?"

39 *Coeli micantem fornice* Cf. Cic. *De or.* III, 40,162: "Coeli ingentes fornices"; Ennius (*Trag.* 319). For 39–41 cf. Heinsius *De Deo* 3–4: "Gemmata late caeruloque fornice suspensa mundi moenia immensi vides". For "micantem [...] domum", cf. Heinsius' *Ad impium* 13: "micantem lumine aeterno domum".

42 *spectanda late vultibus nostris dedit* Cf. Heinsius *Ad impium* 5–6: "obiecit illa vultibus nostris Deus spectanda semper".

43 *illa magni purior lux pectoris* Cf. Heinsius *De Deo* 31: "illa nostri purior pars".

L 26–27   Line 26 is made more specific, because "affectat" (striving for, endeav-
ouring) has become "scandit" (climbing). "Ingens" became "ultro", to introduce
an element of astonishment and perhaps also to get rid of the somewhat lost
"ingens" (at "spiritus"), which must be 'enormous', but here seemed to be 'with
great effort', a non-classical notion.

L 32–34   In the Leiden copy the expression "exultare ad" (jumping to) became
"efferri in" (being elevated to), making the image more logical. Eventually Heinsius deleted these lines.

L 36–37   Perhaps because it was an improper image, Heinsius deleted "strues"
for body; next, he changed the "exigit" (claims) in "iureque exigit suo" into
"extorquet" (extorts). Finally, he simplified the syntax by adding a verb (trahit)
and to express the thought of "iureque exigit suo" in the predicative "exactrix"
(she-claimer) and then in "extortrix" (she-extorter).

L 39   Why Heinsius replaced "micantem fornice" (the sky shining with a golden
arch) with "superbam marmore" (the sky proud of his marble) is not clear.

L 41–42   In these lines the author probably wished to get rid of "gemmeus
chorus", which led to 'the high dwellings, adorned everywhere with the fiery
chorus of stars'. For reasons of variation (l. 41 "late") in l. 42, "late" became "circum".

Ambition in princes

46–51 *Hinc—duxit*   The fact that the mind can see the sky, arouses a posi-
tively valued ambition in princes. Of course the monarch will not aspire to
earthly fame, but to "verum decus" (Cic. *Rep.* VI, 25), a place in heaven. That
is also the reason why this thirst for glory is "dia" (divinely inspired) because
it seeks the divine ether. In this passage, "favor" (l. 49) can be interpreted in
two ways: (1) is it Fortune's support (cf. "Fortunae favor", e.g. Sen. *Tro.* 269), or
(2) the "benevolentia populi" (the monarch must be loved by his people), one
of the two pillars of the royal power (besides "auctoritas") from Lipsius, *Politica* IV, 9? Focusing on action and the active life (a prince must attain fame)
is neo-Stoic (e.g. Gerhard Oestreich, 'Justus Lipsius als Universalgelehrter zwischen Renaissance und Barock', in: Lunsingh Scheurleer and Posthumus Meyjes, *Leiden University*, pp. 177–201, Hans Wansink, *Politieke wetenschappen aan
de Leidse Universiteit 1575–±1650* (Utrecht: HES, 1981) Doctoral thesis Leiden
1975, pp. 67–75 and Veenstra, *Ethiek en moraal*, pp. 45–48). Of course, he will
do this for the benefit of the fatherland, by dint of his virtue. This is again motivated by a "bonus animus", which participates in divine reason. That is a second
reason why the "laudis sitis" is called "dia". So it is with princes in general and so
is it with Auriacus/Orange. He also knows his (political) duties: a prince serves

his people and not the other way round (cf. Wansink, *op. cit.*, p. 78). For the metaphorical meaning of "sitis" see such sources as Iuv. 10, 140 "famae sitis".

Resistance against tyranny

51–58 *Belgia—ferocia* Commitment to the homeland, already highly valued by Cicero in *Somnium Scipionis* (e.g. *Rep.* VI, 13; VI, 16), is another quality Auriacus/Orange has, albeit reluctantly. The latter addition is strange at first sight— he should wish to devote himself to the fatherland. However, this indicates that Auriacus is not aiming at personal gain. Only because the fatherland and Freedom encouraged him is he committed to putting an end to the deterioration of (political) freedom by Philip. This king's crime is a result of his "ferocia". Apparently the monarch has not seen his happiness with a correct, Stoic view, and has lost sight of the *temperantia*. The passion that led to this is indicated by "tumor".

The addition to "ferocia" ('which used to occur in prosperity') can also be regarded as a *sententia*, hence the quotation marks before the line. Cf. for this thought Cato, *Orig.* 95a: "rebus secundis [...] superbiam atque ferociam augescere" and Sen. *Pha.* 204–207: "Quisquis secundis rebus exultat nimis fluitque luxu, semper insolita appetit. Tunc illa magnae dira fortunae comes subit libido".

Auriacus' "mens" is "nata magnis", through his descent (see also the comm. *ad* ll. 66–68) predestined to great deeds. The words "nec sibi, sed omnibus" can be taken with "nata" or with "servitutis foeda detrectat iuga"; the latter interpretation is supported by the fact that he is following the call of his country.

57–58 *tumor—ferocia* Often Seneca personifies passions, e.g. *Herc. f.* 28–29: "Saevus dolor aeterna bella pace sublata geret"; *Tro.* 282: "Ipse se irritat furor". Heinsius adopts this here and elsewhere; it is not the King who suppresses the Dutch, but his "tumor" and "ferocia".

Classical examples of resistance

59–65 *Sic—pedem* The first example is Lucius Iunius Brutus, who in 510 BC would have expelled the last king of Rome, the tyrant Tarquinius Superbus, and instituted the consulate and restored freedom. In the Renaissance this act was considered right and patriotic, see Geurts, *Opstand in pamfletten*, pp. 275–276, Mieke B. Smits-Veldt, 'De opening van de "Neerlandtsche Academie De Byekorf": Melpomene presenteert Gijsbrecht van Hogendorps *Orangientragedie*', *Spektator* 12 (1982–1983), pp. 199–214, esp. p. 203. See for Brutus *RE*

Suppl. 5, 356–369 s.v. Iunius and Stephanus, *Dictionarium*, p. 110v s.v. Brutorum familia. For the use of *exempla*, see Spies 1994.

The second example is the Romans in general, in a rhetorical *congeries* indicated as: "magni patres", "togata turba", with a stress on their sublimity, and "Martis aeternum genus", "sancta nepotes Iliae", in which their divine descent (Mars and Ilia [or Rhea Silvia] are the parents of Romulus and Remus, see also Stephanus, *Dictionarium*, p. 249). In the phrase "Martis [...] genus" the aspect of war is also extant, but a war to support ("fulciere") the country, here incorrectly indicated with the term "regia", for the Roman Empire was no kingdom any more after the expulsion of the kings.

His last examples are Aristogeiton and Harmodius, who, in a failed attack on the tyrants Hippias and Hipparchus, only killed the latter. Tradition has it that they turned from martyrs of freedom into its founders, because the expulsion of the Peisistratids (the two tyrants included) was in time equated with their attack (see Stephanus, *Dictionarium*, p. 70v s.v. Aristogeiton and *RE* 2, 930–931, s.v.). They are given an honourable mention in Cic. *Tusc.* I, 49. These two were less well known at the time of the Dutch Revolt and are not therefore mentioned by Geurts, *Opstand in pamfletten*, or others.

In rhetoric, historical examples were tried and tested to prove one's own point of view, see Bonner, *Roman Declamation*, pp. 61–62 and Nisbet-Hubbard 1 *ad* Hor. *C.* I, 12, 37, p. 157 and the references given there. They had a function in consoling people about the idea of the *similitudo temporum*, see Jeroen Jansen, 'Tacitus en de Opstand', *De zeventiende eeuw* 10 (1994), pp. 190–196, and (for Lipsius) Oestreich, 'Justus Lipsius als Universalgelehrter zwischen Renaissance und Barock', in: Lunsingh Scheurleer and Posthumus Meyjes, *Leiden University*, pp. 177–201, esp. p. 181.

61 *togata turba*   Cf. Grotius *Pont. Rom.* 46: "gentemque togatam".
62 *diu labantem fulciere regiam*   To solve the difficulties with regard to "regia", "fulciere" should perhaps be interpreted as 'sieging', 'suppressing', cf. Persius 1, 78: "Antiopa aerumnis cor luctificabile fulta"; for such a meaning in medieval Latin, see Du Cange 4, 624 who translates "fulcire" as "supplere", Gall. "remplacer". Besides "schoren", "steunen" (to support), Spanoghe 2, p. 48 also gives the meaning 'to stop' for "fulcire". Such uses are supported in antique texts as "ianuam fulcire" (to lock, *TLL* 6.1, 1503.59–62) and "pedibus pruinas fulcire" ('to trample', *OLD* s.v. 2). In which case, "regia" should be interpreted as 'kingdom' (*OLD* s.v. 3.b). Another possibility is to interpret "regia" as the palace of Numa Pompilius, who was considered a good king (with thanks to R.C. Engelberts). Then the line could be paraphrased as: Brutus and the Romans have ensured that the spirit of good kingship once again reigned. Because of these difficulties

it is likely that Heinsius decided to change the line into "inferocientem sus-
tulere regiam" (they have done away with rampant kingship).

The form "fulciere" is unusual. There is a late Latin perfect form "fulcivit"
(Inscr. ap. Mur. 466.3), which also exists in medieval Latin (Niermeyer IV, 2168
s.v.). Heinsius apparently wished to shorten the second syllable *metri causa*,
which is not impossible in such forms of the perfect. Moreover, he applied the
archaizing ending -ere (= -erunt).

63 *ferox* Heinsius often uses the word "ferox" (for instance, ll. 63, 69 and 88),
which can be used both *in bonam* (l. 63) and *in malam partem*. It indicates that
a man or an animal will not be tamed. It can be impetuous, arrogant (thus, for
example, Sen. *Herc. f.* 57) or belligerent (*TLL* 6.1, 566–570).

64–65 *manus—pedem* Here "manus" ('hand') is a metonym for 'deeds' (cf. l.
365). The imagery is quite 'wild', strictly speaking, as the hand sets foot in
heaven. For the interpretation of "educo" not only as a way out but also a way
up, see *OLD* s.v. 7b.

L 62 See supra, de comm. *ad loc.*

L 64 Heinsius perhaps wished to put the names of the two tyrannicides next
to each other and therefore removed "faustaque", and had to change "manus"
into "dextera" *metri causa.*

L 65 Perhaps due to the improper imagery "eduxit pedem" was changed into
"stravit viam" (the 'hand', 'paved the way').

The implicit transition is that if the admired examples were allowed to stand
up against their tyrants, then Auriacus certainly may, since Liberty called him.

Auriacus will be committed to his homeland anyway

66–80 *Eundum—nostrum est* As an incantation the words "eundum, eundum est" (l. 66) connect the following with the foregoing. Orange feels com-
pelled to go—instigated by the (positive) ambition of princes (ll. 46–51), stirred
up by the voice and circumstances of his homeland (ll. 51–54), driven by his
duty to freedom and his people (ll. 54–58), but above all necessitated by his
origin. The blood (gender or strength, see *OLD* s.v. sanguis 8/9 and 5) of the
Nassaus is energetic and defies the danger (ll. 66–68).

Auriacus/Orange asks himself the rhetorical question of whether the tyrant of
the Tagus (pars pro toto for Spain), Philip II, will cunningly overcome him with
impunity. He is called "hostis" and not "inimicus" (personal enemy). The gold
of the river is mentioned as a source of income for this king. The gold dust of

the Tagus is an antique topos (Stephanus, *Dictionarium*, p. 415r, *RE* 7, 1564.13–20 s.v. Gold; *RE* 2.4, 2025.31–63 s.v. Tagus; Bömer's comm. 1, p. 305 *ad* Ov. *Met.* II, 251 and Otto, *Sprichwörter*, p. 404). The pressing down of the neck (l. 70 "collum premat") was the ancient symbol for submission (*TLL* 3, 1660.61–1661.6 s.v. collum and Forcellini 2, 279 s.v. collum 3: "collum sumitur tamquam symbolum servitutis"), cf. Verg. *Aen.* XII, 356–357: "pede collo impresso" and Prop. II, 10, 15: "India quin, Auguste, tuo dat colla triumpho"; Claud. *VI Cons. Honor.* 648: "colla triumphati proculcat Honorius Istri".

The phrase 'Even if there is opposition, yet [...]' is a topos in which the exaggeration stems from the rhetorical tradition (Bonner, *Roman Declamation*, p. 165). This commonplace is also extant in Seneca's drama, e.g. *Pha.* 930–937 (Hippolytus, even though [*licet*] you hide on the other side of the Ocean, you will do penance) and *Herc. f.* 1326–1329 (Even though the whole sea is flowing over my hands, the blood will be stuck to it). The opposition can also come from an earthquake, here indicated by the trembling of the bearer of the skies Atlas. When Hercules has to get the apples from the Hesperides, one of his twelve works, he invokes his help. The naming of an earthquake as a movement on the part of Atlas fits in with the Herculean atmosphere evoked regarding Auriacus. Incidentally, the threat of the water is real; consider in this regard the many floods.

68 *provocator*   With this word Heinsius shows a similar predilection for unusual *agens*-words on -tor and -trix to that of Seneca, e.g. ll. 483 "exactor", "dissipator"; 806 "proditor"; 1236 "sititor" and "dominatrix"; 300 and 1307 "rebellatrix". On such formations, see Brink, *Horace on Poetry*, p. 236 *ad* Hor. *A.P.* 163, and for Seneca's uses of forms on -trix, see Fitch, *Seneca's Hercules Furens*, pp. 353–354.

69 *cor*   The apostrophe to one's own heart is not unusual in Seneca's drama, see (for example) Fantham, *Seneca's Troades*, p. 93. It is a figure of speech from rhetoric, see Bonner, *Roman Declamation*, p. 166. See also *Aur.* 264 ("mens") and 1429 ("animus"). In most cases this indicates a heightened emotionality, see Frank, *Seneca's Phoenissae*, p. 92 on Sen. *Pho.* 45. With the combination "vincula et ludos [...] nectar" (ll. 69–70), Heinsius uses "nectere" in a zeugma first in the sense of 'to make', rather than in the sense of 'contrive', as Sen. *Tro.* 523: "Nectit pectore astus callidos", see Fantham, *Seneca's Troades ad loc.*, p. 291. For parallels, see Frank, *op. cit.*, p. 114 *ad* Sen. *Pho.* 119–120: "dolos [...] nectens". See also Heinsius, *De Deo* 13: "lususque molles nectere" (*L. Annaei Senecae philosophi divini libelli quínque*, ed. Daniel Heinsius (Leiden 1601), p. H2r).

L 69–73 In the first instance Heinsius changed "O cor, tibine" into "Nobisne semper". Eventually, he changed the entire passage into: 'I'm going, Hollander. No power will withdraw me (I include your altars, holy freedom) and I will find its way, even though the tyrant of the Tagus tries to subdue me. All must block the way, the heavens and the earth will join forces'.

Virtue combats fate

80–84 *Regiâ—mentis* These lines, full of *sententiae*, provided with quotation marks, focus on an adage from Stoic philosophy: the sage will overcome his destiny by his virtue, e.g. Sen. *Ep.* 71, 30: "Sapiens quidem vincit virtute fortunam". See also the comm. on l. 97.

80 *Regiâ tendens viâ* The "regia via" is ambiguous: it can be the road taken by kings, their virtue facing dangers on its own initiative. Secondly, the words may be a paraphrase of an expression as in Sen. *Prov.* v, 10–11: "Per alta virtus it". Thus it can be an allusion to the upward path Hercules chose at the cross-roads.

81–82 *virtus ... prementi ... deo* Several times, Auriacus speaks of his *virtus* (e.g. ll. 81, 97, 115, 121 and 1237). This word has many implications and there-fore permits almost as many translations. It can be 'men's courage', but also has philosophical and social implications, allowing it to be translated by 'moral quality', 'moral autonomy', 'moral independence', 'moral ideal' or 'merit'; for Stoic virtue see, inter alia, Pohlenz, *Die Stoa* 1, pp. 258–259 and 314–315. The interpretation of *virtus* in this passage depends on the exegesis of "premens deus" (l. 82). This can be explained in two ways: it can be the Stoic god who, among other things, works as fortune or fate (cf. l. 1) and tries to overthrow men's spirit. The second possibility is that "deus" should be understood here as 'one in power' (*TLL* 5.1, 890.42–891.78), i.e. denoting the oppressor Philip. Given the sententious character of these lines, the first interpretation seems more likely. It is telling that "prementi [...] deo" is followed by (and repeated in) "fato [...] suo", against which a 'fierce spirit' stands.

Hercules (1)

84–96 *Nec tamen—impetusque* Here the heroism of Auriacus comes to the fore, as does his fighting spirit. The terms "fundamina" and "praeludia" (ll. 85–86) indicate the preparatory work for a war. If the passage is constructed logi-cally, the "prima primordia" (ll. 84–85) must indicate a stage before that. This could be the philosophical principle, the 'idea of war', or the war and the elab-

oration of the plans. The war is not small ("motusque vasti"), and will therefore
bring lifelong fame. It is probably necessary to think of Orange's warfare in
the years 1568, 1572 and 1579–1584. The fact that the events 'rise' to his fame
is a slight distortion of reality: the war had not been so successful for Orange.
See A.Th. van Deursen and Hugo De Schepper, *Willem van Oranje: Een strijd
voor vrede en verdraagzaamheid* (Weesp: Fibula-Van Dishoeck, 1984), pp. 126–
137 and 142–151. But perhaps the *possibilities* of achieving fame are intended.
Auriacus is a wise monarch who, with all his might, opposes oppressors, now
named: Philip and Alva. With all other savage men in Spain—for it is clear
that Philip and Alva are also *ferox* and *saevus*—, to him they are a hydra. This
animal was defeated by Hercules (see Roscher 1.2, 2769–2770). For example,
Auriacus' enterprise is given an antique parallel in Hercules (see pp. 104 and
43). A rich crop of *res* (events) gives him a chance to act as a brave warrior
and thus earn fame as a second Hercules. Such fame is a result of *virtus*, as
Cicero observed (Pohlenz, *Die Stoa* 1, pp. 272; 314–315) and that is how it is
with him. The evil stepmother of Hercules was Juno, Auriacus's is Fortuna. It
is a widespread theme in classical times, the Middle Ages and the Renaissance
(see, inter alia, Heitmann, *Fortuna und Virtus*, Kirchner, *Fortuna*, and Grotius,
Dichtwerken/Poetry I, 2, 4A/B, p. 370). Indirectly, emphasis is laid on Juno's position as a stepmother. This emphasis is typically Ovidian and Senecan, see Fitch,
Seneca's Hercules Furens, p. 129 *ad Herc. f.* 21. For the traditional image of the
evil stepmother, see Otto, *Sprichwörter*, pp. 245–246 s.v. noverca. The alignment
of Juno and Fortuna does not come entirely as a novelty, cf. Scal. *Poet.* III, 25,
p. 115bC; Scaliger, *Poetica/Dichtkunst*, p: 330.6–7: "Voluntas est Iuno, eadem (uti
dicebamus) quae et Fortuna. Coniunx et soror summi numinis". Heinsius had
used 'stepmother' for Fortuna in his poem *In miseros mortem optantes* 3: "leges
novercae".

Philip II was renounced as lord of the Netherlands by the States General in
1581. The 'iron duke' of Alva was considered to be the greatest enemy, who conducted a repressive policy after his arrival in August 1567, see also the comm.
ad l. 952.

85 *iacta sunt fundamina* Cf. Sen. *Pho.* 279–280: "Iacta iam sunt semina cladis
futurae" and Benedicti, *De rebus gestis* I, 425: "principium belli".
88–90 *si quod—facem* The idea of the sun seeing everything is a topos from
antiquity and the Bible, but here it is accompanied by the notion that the sun
would never set in the Spanish Empire, see (for example) Parker, *Philip II*, p. 159.
93 *Alceiden* The designation 'grandson of Alceus' for Hercules (Alceus as the
father of Hercules' stepfather Amphitryon) had been used since Hellenistic
poetry and was also regularly used by Sen., e.g. *Aga.* 815, see (for instance)

Bömer, *Ovidius Fasten*, p. 65 on Ov. *Fast.* I, 575. Here the transcription of the Greek Ἀλχεῖδης is used, which will be down to Heinsius' predilection for Greek.

94 *ferarum victor* The words "ferarum victor" may refer to Don Juan of Austria, the illegitimate son of Philip II, under whose leadership a victory was won over the Turks in the Battle of Lepanto (1571), and possibly indirectly to Philip. In 1574 this Don Juan was sent to the Netherlands as Commander in Chief (on him, see Motley, *Dutch Republic*, pp. 648–768 and Petrie 1967). Perhaps the words are referring to the murders of the Spaniards in the New World, to which much attention is paid in pamphlets, as an indication of the Spanish unreliability (Geurts, *Opstand in pamfletten*, p. 176). The phrase is also an allusion to Sen. *Herc. Oet.* 1989 where Hercules is addressed as "domitor magne ferarum" or Sen. *Aga.* 738 "victor ferarum" (here said of a lion). Or perhaps one should consider in this regard the sea god Proteus, who herds the undomesticated seals, and then indirectly to the sea (cf. the comm. *ad* 1775).

L 87–88 Perhaps the indication "ter inclytus" was too high an honour for Philip, hence the change into 'the awe-inspiring Philip has felt this hand'. A consequence was that "manum" in l. 92 was changed into "dextra" for reasons of variation.

L 95 The 'lofty spirits' became 'the spirits of great ones'. The idea is that Fortune pushes down the high-ranking, see the comm. *ad* ll. 23–45.

The wise man's victory over fate

96–106 *Sed tamen—parens* Fortune does not have the last word. Here again Heinsius provides a variation on a thought as shown in Sen. *Ep.* 98, 1–8: 'Do not fear the future, but be her master, the spirit is stronger than all the forces of fortune', esp. 98, 2: "Valentior enim omni fortuna animus est et in utramque partem ipse res suas ducit beataeque ac miserae vitae sibi causa est" and 71, 30: "sapiens [...] vincit virtute fortunam". The sententious lines (marked by typography) imply that Orange is also wise and will take charge of his own future and restrict Fortune's power. His instrument is his virtue, which, in the context of "ausa" and "adorea" alongside bravery, includes moral superiority. The struggle with Fortuna is described in warlike terms: "pessundare", "subdere", "premere potentiam".

In this passage too (cf. the comm. on ll. 14–22) several words are used interchangeably: "fortuna", "sors", and "casus" are in fact synonyms. They have some power, but the wise know the basis of this power: hope (perhaps a personification, see Pease, p. 1072 *ad* Cic. *N.D.* III, 47, or an instrument of Fortuna) with its idle promises of reward, and her ruses.

"Pectusque frustra credula astrictum tenet" (l. 104) is somewhat ambiguous. One can say that this Spes, who, gullible as she is, wants to keep her heart shut, but still hears what she does not want to hear. Also, the words allow the interpretation that they 'encapsulate' the heart of the wise, 'enchant' them with their credulity. In any case, he who knows this can resist his fate and give his own guidance on his future. Of course, this does not mean that fate is completely in his hands. It does imply that fate will not prevail over him. The instrument with which the battle can be fought is of course virtue. A key to understanding the nature of the struggle lies in ll. 110–116 (cf. the comm. on these lines): it is a struggle to control the passions. Whoever wins that battle is untouchable to the blows of fate and is, as it were, the creator of his own destiny by 'making' his future himself.

L 103   The *terminus technicus* for the promises of fortune is "vanus", for one knows for certain that its promises will not be kept.

Hercules (2)

107–110 *Nec ansa—nocendo*   The comparison with Hercules continues: Philip (or the Spaniards in general) is represented here as Eurystheus, the king who commissioned Hercules to carry out his efforts on behalf of Juno. Thus the Spanish King becomes an instrument in the hands of the authority that was compared with Juno: Fortuna. Adversity strengthens the sage (see Sen., *Ep.* 94, 74: "melius in malis sapimus"), so here too, formulated in an oxymoron: "prodest nocendo", where "Iber" indicates Philip II. The advantage is the fame that has been implied in "auget", to which an implicit object "nomen meum" has to be added. This bolsters the case for the interpretation of "nomini incumbit meo" (l. 108) as 'belittles my (good) name', rather than 'has it on my person'.

Victory over the passions (1)

110–126 *Caetera—vicisse memet*   In this passage, Auriacus gives his thoughts about the passions: these must be curbed in line with a Stoic model in order to achieve *apatheia*, freedom from passions (e.g. Pohlenz, *Die Stoa* 1, pp. 141–153). Heinsius does not make Auriacus pursue a strict form of *apatheia* (the complete elimination of emotions), but a more moderate one in which the passions exist, but are kept within limits (see also comm. *ad* ll. 140–143). These limits are determined by the *Logos*, the creator of the world and the leader and standard in the life of man (Pohlenz, *Die Stoa* 1, pp. 64–159), as "deo mihique" must be interpreted. The curbing of the passions is the task and concern of *virtus* (moral independence), which thus becomes invincible to others. Those others can at best do what *fatum* can; the sage overcomes his fate through his *virtus*, with which he tames his passions (ll. 96–106). The terms used are "motus vani", "aestus", "irae" and "impetus". They all indicate emotions. Here, therefore, "ira" is not an outburst of rage in a strict sense, but an excessive emotion that might have its origins in anger, cf. Verg. *Aen.* II, 575: "Subit ira cadentem ulcisci patriam" and Scal. *Poet.* III, 9, p. 88bD–89aA; Scaliger, *Poetica/Dichtkunst*, pp. 122.23–124.18. For the features of *ira* see *TLL* 7.2, 362.38–363.23. *Ira* often implies the avenging of injustice, another thing that is missing in this passage. *Impetus* (l. 114, also l. 136) plays an important role in the Stoic representation of the passions. Via Cicero it became the Latin equivalent of ὁρμή, see Tarrant, *Seneca Agamemnon*, p. 198 *ad* Sen. *Aga* 127 and *TLL* 7.1, 608.68–82. In this context, the *motus* have another meaning (i.e. 'violent emotions') to the one in l. 66 ("motus leves", 'actions').

The witnesses invoked by Auriacus form, as it were, ever larger circles: from the famous race of the Nassaus, their actions, blood and ghosts, via the invincible Dutch to the sea, which presents its water to the Spaniard. The latter probably refers to the Hollandic Water Line, see Hans Brand and Jan Brand (eds), *De Hollandse Waterlinie* (Utrecht: Veen, etc., 1986). In the Nassaus, one must consider Orange's brothers: Jan, Louis, Adolph and Henry who, like himself, toiled for the possessions of their family in the Netherlands.

Three of them died for the Dutch cause, Adolph in the Battle of Heiligerlee (1568) and Lodewijk (Louis) and Hendrik (Henry) on the Mookerhey (1574), hence "sanguis" and "umbrae". Through his self-restraint, William is able to follow in the footsteps of his aforementioned predecessors. In that regard, the invocation has no religious connotations, as invocations in classical drama, cf. (for example) Sen. *Oed.* 248–273 and Töchterle, *Seneca Oedipus*, pp. 279–280.

116 *efferre gressus* This combination is part of the epic diction of Virgil and Lucretius, adopted by Seneca, see Fantham, *Seneca's Troades*, p. 289 *ad* Sen. *Tro.* 518; cf. *ibid.* 616.

122 *Nereu* The sea being called after the sea god Nereus attests to Heinsius' predilection for metonymy. This metonym was common, see (for example) Stephanus, *Dictionarium*, p. 315v s.v. Nereus: "Figurate accipitur pro mare". Heinsius will elaborate on the theme of the seafaring Dutch in ll. 300–320, a clause of Inquisition, and the choral ode at the end of Act IV. The sea being "inundans" may again refer to the Hollandic Water Line, a series of areas in Holland and Utrecht that could be inundated in times of war. Furthermore, the Water Line played its part in the Siege and Relief of Leiden, see (for example) Motley, *Dutch Republic*, pp. 578–579, Reinier E. Dinger Hattink,

Leiden's nood en verlossing in de Spaanse tijd (Leiden: Brill, 1947) and Pieter Geyl, *History of the Dutch-Speaking Peoples, 1555–1648* (London: Phoenix Press, 2001), p. 138. For the vocative "Nereu" (l. 122), see Neue-Wagener 1, pp. 445–446.

122–123 *Nereu ... spumantibusque ... exundans vadis* Cf. Heinsius *De Deo* 17: "spumantibusque Neraea undantem vadis".

The vanity of power—*indifferentia*

126–131 *Regna—ducumque* Lines 126b–131 seem to interrupt the argument on the passions with thoughts on the vanity of power, given through the throw of a dice of fate, toy of princes. Since Auriacus/Orange knows that these matters— usually held in high esteem—are *indifferentia*, morally unimportant he is nei- ther worried nor happy. Power as a toy of fate and a plaything of princes is a widespread theme. In many ways it is said that Fortuna can easily take it away, see Otto, *Sprichwörter*, pp. 141–145, s.v. Fortuna, esp. 5, citing as an exam- ple (among others) Sen. *Aga.* 101–102: "Quicquid in altum Fortuna tulit, ruitura levat", to which it is often added that one would therefore be better off living a simple life (cf. ll. 728–735).

Victory over the passions (2)

131–168 *Prima—premunt* Controlling the passions and the attendant invin- cibility form the subject of these lines too. But with two limitations: they are only about Auriacus and only about one passion, namely the fighting spirit. This is favourably judged by princes—giving them courage and strength for the defence of the fatherland and for avenging injustice—but may, just like other passions, not go astray and must therefore be kept in check. The instrument for that is (still) virtue.

Two similes are of decisive importance in the passage: firstly, a long-winded Homeric comparison of a fight between a nomad and a lion. The lion compar- ison was a popular motif in epic and drama in ancient times. Scal. *Poet.* v, 3 and 14, pp. 229a–230a and 270b–271b; Scaliger, *Poetica/Dichtkunst* 4, pp. 172.18– 80.26 and pp. 510.1–18.24, gives a plethora of examples from Homer and Latin epics. Heinsius' starting point for this comparison could have been Luc. I, 206– 212 (also mentioned by Scal. *Poet.* v, 14, pp. 270bB–C; Scaliger, *Poetica/Dicht- kunst* 4, p. 510.22–27), where he compares Caesar with a Libyan lion. The cor- relation of the equation differs, despite some similarities in the use of words. Heinsius is comparing the (inner) passions instead of an external aspect as Lucan does.

This is in line with Seneca's use of similes. These do not provide information, but intensify, enliven. There is clearly a *tertium comparationis* (Wolf-Luder
Liebermann, *Studien zu Senecas Tragödien* (Meisenheim am Glan: Anton Hain,
1974) Beiträge zur klassischen Philologie, 39, pp. 85–110). In this case, the lion
and the passions, which are full of *ira* (more than just anger), have the ferocity of their combat in common; the hunter and the wise both use a weapon,
namely a hunting spear and the *ratio* respectively. The comparison does not
provide any additional information, but it does add much more weight to the
battle between *virtus* and the passions. Seneca also used the lion simile, esp. in
Herc. f. 939–952, but in that passage it marked the beginning of Hercules' madness, because he wants to have a place in heaven, in the constellation of Leo
(H.J. Mette, 'Die Funktion des Löwengleichnisses in Senecas Hercules Furens',
Wiener Studien 79 (1966), pp. 477–489). In terms of word use, the passage
has some similarities with Sen. *Oed.* 919–926, but such a comparison accen-
tuates Oedipus' despair. For the lion as a type of anger see Nisbet-Hubbard 1
ad Hor. *C.* I, 16, 15, pp. 210–211 and Van Dam, *Statius Silvae, Book II, ad* Stat.
Silv. II, 5, 1, pp. 371–372. Heinsius had already used a comparison with a lion
and a hunter in his *Apotheosis Georgii Paludani* (the glorification of Van den
Broeck, 1596), p. A7r–v. A struggle between lion and hunter as an image for
an inner struggle against the passions is found nowhere else but the nurse in
Sen. *Herc. Oet.* 241–242, which compares the frenzy of Deianira with that of a
tigress.

Something inconsequent is that the Libyan is both *venator* (hunter, l. 145)
and *pastor* (shepherd, l. 155). The impression is that two different people are
involved. The phrase "At ille contra—pastor" only reinforces this impression.
However, *pastor* refers to the relatively uncomplicated life that the hunter
leads. In ancient times Libya (Africa) is a topical place for lions, see Töchterle,
Seneca Oedipus, p. 585 *ad* Sen. *Oed.* 919.

The second comparison is with Typhoeus, the monster that overcame Zeus
and cut out the tendons of his hands. When the tendons were returned to Zeus'
arms, he crushed Typhoeus as a punishment and threw Mount Etna on him (see
Roscher 5, 1426–1454, 1437.24–57 and Bömer's comm. 1, pp. 526–527 *ad.* Ov. *Met.*
III, 303). He can be compared with the vigour of a "magnum pectus". As Etna
presses on the struggling Typhoeus, so fate impresses anyone who opposes it.
There seems to be a certain inconsistency here with the foregoing: the animal
(the passions) has been conquered, but Etna (fate) is the authority suppressing the monster (the passions). However, the ultimate victory is not for "fatum",
which can only suppress. Another possibility is to interpret "premit" as 'drives
forth', cf. Sen. *Ep.* 107, 11: "Ducunt volentem fata, nolentem trahunt", cf. also l. 184
"nolentem trahit". Etna, its fire, is used in Seneca's theatre as an image for pas-

sions, e.g. for the fury that Hercules must receive in *Herc. f.* 105–106 and for sorrow in *Pha.* 101–103, but Typhoeus has not yet been found in this role.

The metaphor of 'curbing' the passions (ll. 140 "strinxi" and 142 "fraena", also 362 and 1510), is not alien to the drama of Seneca, see *Tro.* 279 and Fantham, *Seneca's Troades*, p. 251 *ad loc.* The expression of pressing destiny could not be; cf., however, phrases such as "fata ducunt", e.g. Sen. *Prov.* v, 7.

L 162　In his copy the author changed "vigor" to "tumor", a word for drift, which he apparently thought more suited to "surgit et sese erigit".

War for peace in the homeland

169–178 *Nec sponte nostra—haec una rerum*　Here again the emphasis is on the fact that it is not Auriacus' own advantage spurring him on but the interests of the fatherland and its freedom (cf. ll. 51–58). His actions are *iustum*, legitimate, and *aequum*, socially and morally correct. For the motif "Dulce et decorum est pro patria mori" (Hor. *C.* III, 2, 13) in Scaliger, see Witstein, *Funeraire poëzie*, p. 107. With the sixteenth-century elite the dictum gradually took on a greater role, see Groenveld, 'Natie en nationaal gevoel', pp. 383–384. Cf. also "non nobis, sed patriae geniti", which Dousa recorded in an elegy to Peter Scriverius (*Poemata pleraque selecta*, Leiden: T. Basson, 1609), see Barbara Becker-Cantarino, 'Das Literaturprogramm des Daniel Heinsius in der jungen Republik der Vereinigten Niederlande', in: Klaus Gerber (ed.), *Nation und Literatur im Europa der Frühen Neuzeit: Akten des 1. Internationalen Osnabrücker Kongresses zur Kulturgeschichte der Frühen Neuzeit* (Tübingen: Niemeyer, 1989), pp. 595–626, esp. p. 600; this is an allusion to "Non nobis solum nati sumus ortusque nostri panem patria vindicat, partem amici" (Cic. *Off.* I, 7). The exact purport of *patria* for Auriacus/Orange (or for Heinsius) cannot be determined with precision. Groenveld, 'Natie en nationaal gevoel', pp. 379–380 assumed that for Orange the homeland consisted of both the northern and southern provinces, something that would have been appealing to the 'southerner' Heinsius (see comm. *ad* l. 210). See also intr. p. 17.

Furthermore, Auriacus gives a justification for the fact that he is waging war, namely to bring about peace. This is an amplifying elaboration on the adage: "Pax bello paritur" (Otto, *Sprichwörter*, p. 54) or "ex bello pax". For this dictum in emblematics, but often explained as 'weapons are turned into ploughshares' (e.g. Verg. *Aen.* VII, 636 and Isa. 2, 4), see Eddy de Jongh, *Een schilderij centraal: De slapende Mars van Hendrick ter Brugghen* (Utrecht: [Centraal Museum], 1980), p. 16 and fig. 25, and Karel Porteman, '13 januari 1566: Marcus Antonius Gillis van Diest schrijft, als eerste in het Nederlands, een uiteenzetting over het embleem: Embleemboeken in de Zuidelijke Nederlanden', in: M.A. Schenkeveld-van der Dussen a.o. (eds), *Nederlandse literatuur, een geschiedenis* (Groningen: Nijhoff, 1993), pp. 158–164, esp. p. 159. War is necessary (*necessitas*) for peace. In the case of *necessitas*, however, the (philosophically determined) necessity is not a synonym for fatum/fortuna, but denotes practical utility. The first words of this passage "nec sponte nostra" may evoke the words spoken by Aeneas to Dido, Verg. *Aen.* IV, 361: "Italiam non sponte sequor".

He who suppresses his passions is a suitable leader

178–185 *Caeterûm—sibi dedit* For the well-known motifs of the sage as prince and the prince as sage in Seneca's drama see, inter alia, Rosenmeyer, *Senecan Drama and Stoic Cosmology*, pp. 86–90 and Fantham, *Seneca's Troades*, p. 229. For the sage as a prince, see, e.g., Cic. *Fin.* III, 75: "Rectius enim appellabitur rex, quam Tarquinius, qui nec se, nec suos regere potuit: rectius magister populi (is enim est dictator), quam Sulla [...]". Such ideas were known in the Renaissance, cf. Lipsius *Const.* I, 6: "qui vere rex, vere liber, soli deo subiciere, immunis a iugo adfectuum et Fortunae" and Hooft's *Achilles ende Polyxena* (before 1601?) 783–786: "Maer diet gemoet in tegenspoet off noot | gestadich heeft en altoos even groot, | al heeft hij goet noch staet nochtans is hij | gheboren tot des werrelts heerschappij" ('But whosoever constantly and always has a high spirit in distress and adversity, is—even though he has no goods nor a high state—born to rule the world'). The fact that the sovereign is, on the other hand, wise is described by Veenstra, *Ethiek en moraal*, p. 27: 'At the top of the political pyramid is the monarch: in theory also morally the most eminent being on earth, a God on earth'. Opposite to this moral figure is the man who does not know how to control his passions and thus becomes 'a slave of one', namely himself, his emotions.

179 *Profecto* A relatively rare word in poetry, but occurring in (for example) Sen. *Aga.* 150 and Ov. *Met.* VIII, 72, see Tarrant, *Seneca Agamemnon*, p. 203 *ad loc.* "Impos sui" (l. 180, cf. l. 290 "compos sui" and 1450 "mens impos") occurs frequently in Plautus in the combination "impos animi", recurs in Seneca (*Aga.* 117 and *Ep.* 83, 10) and finally appears in the 2nd c. (Tarrant, *op. cit.*, p. 197 *ad* Sen. *Aga.* 117).

181 *obfuscat* See *TLL* 9, 533–534 s.v. offusco, esp. 533.57–68 for the figurative use of the word.

Act I, chorus Song (186–242)

Summary

186–198 The old Flemish exiles say farewell to their birthplace, which they will soon leave. They address this land and their home in idyllic terms.

198–211 They are called away by harsh fate without knowing where they must go. With a lamentation they address their children and the unborn foetus in the womb, which will also be in exile.

212–214 Then they cry; the fatherland has to imbibe and store their tears.

215–230 Old and tired as they are they must leave for various places, each with its own problems, facing an uncertain future.

231–238 Flanders used to be a wonderful and peaceful region.

238–242 The chorus end their lamentation by again invoking their homeland Flanders, which should imbibe their tears.

The *senes Flandri profugi* bewail the fact that they have to leave their beloved birth region, without knowing where they will be led to, which may indicate that they are bound to go. This would mean that the chorus does not fit in with the unity of place and is treated as an extra-dramatic entity. Their grief is accentuated in several ways: through the metre (see below); the many rhetorically and emotionally effective repetitions and apostrophes, notably to Flanders, their children and future children (for these devices see, for example, Konst, *De hartstochten in de tragedie*, pp. 96–98 and 102; for repetitions in antique lamentations see Nisbet-Hubbard 2 *ad* Hor. *C.* II, 1, 38, pp. 30–31, Alexiou, *Lament*, pp. 135–137 and Stefan Weinstock, *Divus Julius* (Oxford: Clarendon Press, 1971), pp. 352–353); and by stressing their old age (ll. 216–218) and the contrast with the peace they experienced in their young age. It is striking that the Flemish old men (Heinsius originated in Ghent, in Flanders), when leaving their homeland, will partly come to Holland, which apparently is not a part of their country, cf. Groenveld, 'Natie en nationaal gevoel', who also assumes that most people had a limited view of their 'fatherland'. This did not hold for Orange/Auriacus, see the comm. *ad* ll. 169–178. Flanders stretched from the Scheldt as the eastern border up to France, near Dunkirk and Cambrai. Ghent was a part of it, but the city of Antwerp, which belonged to Brabant, was not.

The chorus will consist of more people (cf. "Chorus senum Flandrorum profugorum"). However, the beginning of the song contains many singular forms (e.g. ll. 188 me; 190 puerum; 196 puero; 200 meorum; 204 patri). These, however, may have been used to show the old men's appropriation of the grief, for the plural forms are not lacking (e.g. ll. 188 nostrae; 207 nobis; 213 nostri; 215 poscimur; 241 nostros).

Probably Heinsius drew inspiration for this song from Verg. *Ecl.* 1. Some allusions can be traced to this pastoral song (ll. 198–199, 226), both poems speak of an exile to several places, see the comm. on ll. 197–198 and 219–229.

The song is structured as a ring composition. The beginning and the end (ll. 186–198 and 231–239, resp.) praise the peace in Flanders, whereas both 'halves' are ended by lamentations (ll. 212–214 and 238–242 respectively). In this structure, ll. 198–200 have a double function, ending the first part and serving as a transition to the next one.

Metre

As Heinsius himself indicates, the song is written in Sapphic hendecasyllabic verse, 11-syllable verses according to the scheme -v--- ‖ vv-v-x, ll. 186–190, two glyconaeans (--- ‖ vv-vx, ll. 191–192, indented in 1602) and anapaests (ll. 193–242), on which it should be noted that the last line can be read not only as anapaests but as an *adonius* (the closing line of a Sapphic stanza, -vv-x). These metres could all be found in Seneca's chorus songs, where they also appear stichically, see (for example) Drexler, *Römische Metrik*, pp. 140–141. The Sapphics and *glyconaei* are lyrical metres. The anapaest in Seneca and the Greek tragic poets is often associated with lamentations, cf. Fitch, *Seneca's Hercules Furens*, pp. 390–391.

Commentary

Scene heading

L Heinsius explicitly mentions the children (as mute characters, cf. 201), because they will answer the old men (cf. the comm. *ad* l. 242).

Carefree youth

186–198 *Blanda—vale* The home of the Flemings is a resting place for old age. Perhaps in the background Epicurean tones of a life in secrecy resound, cf. ll. 191 "curarum vacuum et metu" and 234 "tranquillo tutus in arvo". For the *requies* see, inter alia, Van Dam, *Statius Silvae, Book II*, pp. 209–210.

One of the elements of an idyll is the babbling brooks or little rivers, see (for example) the *locus amoenus* in Curtius, *European Literature and Latin Middle Ages*, pp. 195–200 and the literature mentioned by Hunink, *Lucanus Bellum Civile Book III*, p. 168. The founts are mentioned in Verg. *Ecl.* 1, 39 and 52 too. In this chorus song they are *vitreus*. This may be a reminiscence of Hor. *C.* III, 13, 1: "O Fons Bandusiae, splendidior vitro".

Furthermore, the country, Flanders, is called a *Tempe*. For the classical authors, the charm of the Tempe valley was its vegetation, see (for example) Cat. 64, 285–286: "viridantia Tempe, Tempe quae silvae cingunt super impendentes". Furthermore, a river flows through it, the Peneus (e.g. Ov. *Met.* I, 569: "per quae [...] Peneus volvitur"). By extension, Tempe is used for other, comparable valleys, see (for instance) Verg. *Ge.* II, 469; Ov. *Fast.* IV, 477; Stat. *Th.* I, 485; cf. Bömer's comm. *ad* Ov. *Fast.* IV, 477, p. 250; Curtius, *European Literature and Latin Middle Ages*, pp. 198–200; Stephanus, *Dictionarium*, p. 420r; *RE* 2.R. 5, 473–479.

Secondly, the house (*domus*) is addressed, but the interpretation of "spes nostrae domus illa" (l. 188) is ambiguous. A literal rendering (that hope of our house) does not clarify much. Perhaps it is possible to think of an *enallage*, so that the translation becomes 'our hope of that house', that is to say 'that house on which we had our hope'. Another possibility is to interpret *spes* as metonym for 'mother'. The paraphrase then reads: 'You, mother, who gave hope to our home by giving birth to children'. In the latter case, the clause "quae me— fudisti" (which made me see the light of day) would be more appropriate. However, because there are only local indications in the context "fontes", "Tempe", "villa", the first interpretation seems most likely. In addition, it is entirely possible to view the house as a 'cradle', 'which has driven me very early ["prima"] to the lovely paths of the rising light', a Lucretian formulation, e.g. V, 224–225: "cum primum in luminis oras nixibus ex alvo matris natura profudit", cf. *TLL* 9.2, 868.18–37.

The house also saw the ancients in their childhood, unlike, of course, the current situation, carefree and without fear "pede mobili nimium dulces texere ludos". In addition to the meaning 'very pleasant', "nimium dulces" (l. 194) has the connotation that the games were too pleasant when compared to the worrisome state in which they are at the moment. "Texere" ('weaving', l. 194) with "ludos" is daring and not attested to by authors from antiquity.

In an apostrophe the ancients turn to the *villa* as well, which was known to them as a boy and as an old man. Perhaps the "domus" (l. 188) and the "villa" (l. 197) are the same, but partly due to the repetition of "Tuque" there is a division between the two. The countryside house—the word *villa* itself evokes associations of a pleasant environment; see, inter alia, P.A.F. van Veen,

De soetícheydt des buyten-levens, vergheselschapt met de boucken: Het hofdicht als tak van een georgische literatuur (Utrecht: HES, 1985) Doctoral thesis Leiden 1960)—is said to be "suavis". Furthermore, the greybeards have lived there all their lives—until recently undisturbed. The opposition between *puer* and *senex* is elaborated. The *puer* is carefree (cf. ll. 190–195), the *senex* has lost his carefreeness and knows his circumstances. Now it becomes clear why the loveliness of the environment is accentuated: to make the departure ("posthac numquam habitanda") all the more painful.

The same situation is described by Virgil in his first *Eclogue*, where Meliboeus has to leave (see *ibid.* 75–76: "Non ego vos posthac viridi proiectus in antro dumosa pendere procul de rupe videbo"). This theme of the difference between former simplicity and present cares is not unfamiliar in the humanist tragedy and other Neo-Latin poetry, see Grotius, *Dichtwerken/Poetry* I, 4, p. 253 *ad Soph.* 13–43.

L 188–197 Heinsius amplifies these lines to: 'and you, dear house, increased kingdoms, [...] Lares and the country that gave me the chance [...] to start in the beginning [...], and have seen me far removed from worries [...] as I, growing up between playing, fed my spirit with gentle worries and you, countryside, oh in old times, when I was a child, known to me, and now that I am an old man [...]'.

Cruel fate

198–200 *Sors—vices* Just as in the opening scene, Heinsius does not seem to distinguish between *sors* and *fortuna*, and the *vices* as 'products' of *sors/fortuna* are not clearly distinguished either (see comm. *ad* 17). By identifying *sors*, *fortuna* and *vices* as the causes of their wanderings, the author connects this chorus song thematically with the opening scene. Fortuna leads their "dubium [...] pedem" (l. 199). Of course, such a connection is classical, cf. Sen. *Tro.* 255: "dubio gradu", but the literary parallel finds a justification in the uncertainty about the place where the exiles will end up (ll. 219–230), unless it is 'shaky steps'—unstable due to old age.

Exile for the children

200–211 *Tuque—prior est* This apostrophe to the children and to the possibly present unborn foetus, a very powerful means of evoking pathos, is to my knowledge without parallel. The fact that the foetus will go into exile before he sees the light of life is expressed in three ways (ll. 209–211): a convincing example of *amplificatio* and *variatio*, in "exul", "fugis" and "paena" and in "natus nondum, nascendus adhuc" and "vita prior", where ll. 209 and 210 are chiastic.

For the epic colouring of "patri iunctos dirige gressus" (ll. 204–205), see the comm. on l. 116; also cf. Verg. *Aen.* XI, 855: "huc derige gressum" and Sen. *Pho.* 120: "dirige huc gressus".

By following their father into exile, the children learn their *casus* (fate) and the "saevi fulmina fati". For this use of *fulmen* ('destructive force'), cf. Cic. *Tusc.* II, 27, 66: "Fulmina fortunae contemnamus licebit".

The fact that the wife of the *senex* might be with child seems to be a slight inconsistency. It is not necessary to speculate about the age of the old men or the wife—for the author their age will only be of importance for rousing pathos; the exile of the foetus serves the same purpose.

The exile is referred to in such terms as "poena", not a 'punishment', for fate does not know punishment or reward, but 'suffering'.

L 209   Heinsius changed "natus" into "vivus" in the Leiden copy, probably for reasons of variation with regard to "nascendus" (l. 210).

Lamentations (1)

212–218 *Lachrymas—auram* Here too everything should rouse pathos: the *repetitio* of "lachrymas" and "tellus", the *apostrophe* to "tellus", the *interiectio* "ah ah" and naming the old men "relliquiae" (only a shadow of themselves), "genus effaetum" and "saturum aevi"; after all it is true that their "infelix spiritus aegre placidam ducit luminis auram", cf. (for example) Lucr. VI, 1129: "spirantes mixtas hinc ducimus auras", but it is also attested by Seneca, e.g. *Herc. f.* 1142: "Quas trahimus auras?" See *TLL* 2, 1475.58–1476.10. For "auram ducere" as a periphrasis for 'breathing', see Bömer's comm. 1, p. 299 *ad* Ov. *Met.* II, 229–230. The expression "luminis auram" is also an allusion to Lucretius' phrase "in luminis oras" (passim).

Another instance of periphrasis is "patria tellus" (l. 213) for homeland, cf. Sen. *Pha.* 88: "Assyria tellus [i.e. Assyria]". Such metrically useful periphrasis can also be found in (for example) Verg. *Aen.* VI, 23: "Cnosia tellus [Crete]". In this case the periphrasis is useful because the "tellus" ('soil') is needed to hold the tears.

214 *impressa tene* Cf. Sen. *Pha.* 42–43: "dum signa pedum roscida tellus impressa tenet".

215 *poscimur* Cf. Verg. *Aen.* VIII, 533: "ego poscor Olympo"; see also *OLD* s.v. 3a.

L 216   "saturum aevi" becomes "saturum sui", retaining the general meaning.

Places of exile

219–230 *Pars—vocat* The various destinations are mentioned in a *distributio*. This list will have been inspired by the aforementioned pastoral song by Virgil in which Meliboeus also lists possible exiles (ll. 64–66). Heinsius adopts part of the last line (l. 66) almost literally (l. 226) and paraphrases another word ("sitientis", l. 64) with "incoctum solibus" (l. 227).

Is this list purely inspired by the literary source, or does it have an historical origin? The immigration of South Netherlanders to Zeeland and Holland (the Fleming Heinsius also ended up there) is sufficiently known (e.g. Briels, *Zuidnederlanders*). The fact that the Flemish people were accustomed to living in the quiet fields (ll. 223–224) is not strange from a literary point of view—the shepherds in Virgil's poems had the same environment. Historically, Flanders, with its port cities, was no stranger to the sea. People from Ghent, however, including the Heinsius family, whose town was situated in the fields, could consider themselves 'strangers to the sea' (see Briels, *op. cit.*, pp. 26–29). The departure to England is determined not only literarily (see above) but also historically, as witnessed solely by the fact that the Heinsius family was in Dover and London for some time (Ter Horst, *Daniel Heinsius*, p. 13). Some Flemings played a major role in the trips to the (West and East) Indies. A few others stayed in France, including Heinsius himself. In the poem *Hipponax* he writes: "Sed me superbus hostis [...] Britanniasque Galliasque, vix natum, lustrare adegit. Hinc recepit errantem, regalis Haga, post Walachriae littus" (Heinsius, *Poemata Latina et Graeca* [...] (Amsterdam: Janssonius, 1649), pp. 89.17–21). On the emigration of southern Dutchmen to France, see Briels, *op. cit.*, e.g. pp. 31 and 36. For England as a refuge for Flemish people see Briels, *op. cit.*, passim.

Each hospice, designated by its inhabitants, gets its own addition. The "Walachrum sedes" (the residence of the Walchers, pars pro toto for Zeeland) are 'sea dikes', very suitable for the province of Zeeland with its islands and peninsulas. Holland (the Hollander) is "Horrentem Marte". This can be 'the rough Dutch warrior' (see Verg. *Aen.* x, 237: "horrentes Marte Latinos") or Holland 'which shows the rough appearance of war' (*TLL* 6, 2976.70–2977.34). Although elsewhere "Batavus" may have been used for Dutchman, here the term is limited to the province of Holland, which is mentioned alongside Zeeland, and/or Walcheren.

The British are shut off from the whole world by the sea. The literary source (Verg. *Ecl.* 1, 66 "toto divisos orbe Britannos") has already been mentioned. In ancient times, England was a symbol of the far north, see Horace (*The Odes*, ed. Kenneth Quinn (Basingstoke: Macmillan, 1980) *ad C.* III, 4, 33, p. 251), a connotation that suits this tragedy.

The "Indus" can represent India as well as the Indies. From a literary point of view, the interpretation of India is more obvious, because this country does occur in ancient times as an Eastern and heat-ridden country, e.g. Ov. *Met.* I, 778: "positosque sub ignibus Indos"; Sen. *Med.* 484: "perusti Indiae populi" and Cat. 45, 6: "Indiaque tosta"; and in the adaptation of Scaliger (Scaliger, *Poemata propria* (Leiden: Raphelengius, 1615), p. 16: "tostos solibus Indos"). At the end of the sixteenth and the beginning of the seventeenth centuries, however, every region that is not Africa, Europe and the Levant (the Near East), is referred to as 'the Indian countries', which thus comprise the East and West Indies, including China, Japan and India. The Flemings also played a major role in the companies before the VOC (1602), which sailed from Zeeland and Amsterdam to the "Indies" in the 1690s (see Jurriën van Goor, *De Nederlandse Koloniën: Geschiedenis van de Nederlandse expansie 1600–1975* (The Hague: Sdu, 1994), pp. 15–51).

France (Gallum, Frenchman, resident standing metonymically for land) is said to be 'dripping with its own blood', a periphrasis for the internal religious disputes that plagued the country every now and then and which erupted in the St Bartholomew's Day massacre, cf. comm.

The mentioning of all these places is a preparation for and illustration of the closing sentence "Miseri, miseri quos incertum dubiumque vocat!" (ll. 229–230) This sentence is of course primarily concerned with the "senes Flandri profugi", but its formulation lends it a sententious character. As is often the case in Seneca's theatre and in the Neo-Latin drama based on it, the *sententia* closes a passage (on this, see Eyffinger in Grotius, *Dichtwerken/Poetry* I, 2, 5A/B, p. 35).

219 *Walachrûm*   Secundus used the variant "Valachria", *Epist.* I, 1, 9 (Bosscha 2, p. 26). Stephanus, *Dictionarium*, p. 447v and 450r–v does use "Walachria" (s.v. Walachria and Zelandia).

221–222 *spumantem litoris oram patris Oceani*   The foam from the surf is in an enallage transferred to the coast.

227 *incoctum solibus Indum*   Cf. Sil. XVII, 632: "incocti corpora Mauri". Cf. also Sen. *Oed.* 122–123: "et flamma propiore nudos inficit Indos", and see Töchterle, *Seneca Oedipus*, p. 225 *ad loc.*

L 222   Heinsius adds some lines; by repeating ll. 212–214, he intensifies the lamentation: 'the grey house, where the brothers of Boreas are constantly throwing themselves with their cruel roar, and the light blowing off the high sky, country, keep my tears, my country, my tears, my country, the last gifts of my sorrow in you'.

The peaceful situation in Flanders

231–238 Pax—peregrinus erat The carefree state of the Flemings is formulated in various ways. They live in peace. The *pax* is the state of peace, but
perhaps the original meaning 'peace treaty' (*TLL* 10.1, 864.41–866.24) is made
explicit by "placido foedere". The praise of peace is sung by such figures as Tibul-
lus (I, 10), who also points out that in peacetime people can continue to live in
their own homes. Heinsius describes this with "patrioque foco veterum fluxit
vita parentum": the focus is actually the inner part of the house, the seat of the
Lares (*TLL* 6.1, 988.2). This 'sacred place' has always been in the possession of
the family, as is indicated here.

Then the gaze shifts from the house to the yard, where grandfather saw his
grandchildren (again the emphasis on the immutability and the 'line of generations') run. The end of this passage is intriguing: what exactly does 'whoever
saw a neighbouring field was a stranger' mean? It is likely that this refers to the
low degree of mobility, so that even neighbouring areas were unknown to people. This makes their concern about the departure all the more understandable.
But perhaps the author is playing with the etymology of *peregrinus* (per-ager,
traveller from one field to another). Other possibilities include everyone being
familiar with one another, or everyone being so satisfied with their living that
they do not pay attention to one another's possessions.

L 234–236 The word "tutus" becomes "vivus". Line 236 was changed with an
addition: 'and a grandfather looked at the dear crowd of the house, unfamiliar
with water and the enormous sea, unfamiliar with the Auster'.

Lamentations (2)

238–242 Patria—questus For the *repetitio* as a means to rouse pathos, see
above, p. 384, and for the periphrasis "patria tellus". "Nostros imbibe questus" is
a variation on the theme "lacrimas [...] patria tellus, ultima nostri dona doloris
impressa tene" (ll. 212–214), where the 'questus' as *abstractum pro concreto* indicate the tears.

L 242 Heinsius added the children's answer to the chorus song (which, on
reflection, was deleted again): 'We follow you, father, wherever you call us,
and we willingly follow in your footsteps, a crowd that is not inexperienced
at spending the first few years in mourning'.

Act II, Scene 1 (243–414)

Summary

This scene consists of a monologue spoken by Inquisitio, the personification of the Spanish Inquisition.

243–281 Inquisitio, with the three Furies, emerges from the underworld in a drunken state, with a torch and a chalice of human blood. She introduces herself as a hellish power that has been added by the Spaniard as the fourth sister to the Furies. Against her will she has left the underworld, brought to that end by the Pope with the help of his (compared to the classic thunders of Jupiter) miserable lightning.

282–299 This observation leads her to the exclamation of how great the cares of the people are and how heavily the deity oppresses cities and kingdoms. The Romans, once a glorious people who had subdued the world, now obey "regum cinaedi" and a monstrous god, the Pope, who possesses a measly lightning.

300–320 The Dutch are the opposite: they have an ingrained sense of liberty and a healthy degree of patriotism. Furthermore, they defy the elements at sea: they are at home there. Inquisitio now has to leave for their country.

321–362 She will respond to the call to carry out an even greater crime than she has already committed. Now she has a great thirst that cannot be quenched by exquisite wines, but only by human blood. That is why she urges the Spaniards to press ahead with committing murders. If they do not, she has left the underworld for nothing. She has never been sober when coming to the upper world. Now she is already embarrassed at the thought of crime, and is herself drinking blood from the chalice, so that the last bit of friendliness disappears and she lets herself go completely.

362–376 The inhabitants of the underworld are dumbfounded and Megaera is also inactive. Inquisitio is about to faint, enraptured by the drink. In spite of this, her thoughts remain fixed on the crime.

377–386 Then it emerges what the crime will be: she calls earth, heaven and sea to witness her avenge Philip and a great victim will fall in the Netherlands, whither she is called. Even though the Spaniard cannot get there, his wiles and layers can reach the country.

387–405 Somebody capable of carrying out that ruse and that murder has to be found. Her sisters, the Furies, must find someone sufficiently vindictive to look after the Spanish cause. She asks the stars and the moon to help with the search. This man will have to frighten the Dutch, which Philip has not succeeded in doing with his many ships, weapons and threats.

405–414 In the meantime Inquisitio will prepare her armies, consisting of abstractions that personify evil. This army will carry a torch for the crimes of the Spanish King under her charge.

In contrast to Auriacus, this Inquisitio does not control itself. Emerging from the underworld with her torch and cup in her hand, she must leave a deep impression. She is a drunken, filthy woman, who only thinks of quenching her bloodthirstiness with the blood of a huge victim, implicitly but undoubtedly Auriacus/Orange. She is cast in an evil light in all possible ways: she is conceived by the Spaniards, whose name in this piece, written from a Dutch perspective, obviously has a negative sound. She was driven from the underworld by the Pope with his lightning, which might be construed as representing the papal ban (see comm. *ad* ll. 275–281). During her soliloquy she becomes more and more drunk, but continues to think of crime. Through all this an atmosphere of calamity is evoked and the scene thus enhances pathos. The scene also functions to increase the dramatic tension. A murderer has to be found, the net around the Prince closes.

Metre

The scene is written in iambic trimeters. However, ll. 377–386 are in trochaic catalectic tetrameters (eight trochees or their substitutions, with the last trochee shortened), which are occasionally used in Seneca's plays, see Drexler, *Römische Metrik*, pp. 135–136. This change of metre was indicated by indenting. The tone of these ten lines is somewhat more solemn, accentuated by the metre.

Commentary

Scene heading

Inquisitio cum tribus Furijs For the idea to add the Inquisition as fourth Fury to her 'sisters', Heinsius may have been inspired by reading some lines of a 1597 poem by Grotius, *Scutum Auriacum* 65–67: "Hic Furiis Sacra Inquisitio stabat addita quarta tribus face et omni armata veneno, 'Vre seca' clamans, famuli longo ordine mille" (Grotius, *Dichtwerken/Poetry* I, 2, 1A, pp. 65–67). Also in book II of Benedicti's epic *De rebus gestis* Inquisitio appears as Fury, see intr. p. 32.

A virago from hell

243–253 *Lucem—nexibus* Inquisitio presents herself as 'goddess of darkness', added to the Revenge goddesses. Such a presentation with periphrases is not alien to Heinsius' style, and finds parallels in, for example, Sen., *Herc.f.* 1, where Juno presents himself as "Soror Tonantis". Furies also occur in Seneca's dramas, e.g. *Herc. f.* 86–88; cf. further Verg. *Aen.* VII, 323–405, where the Fury Allecto is summoned from the underworld; in Ov. *Met.* IV, 432–562 it is Tisiphone who does her hellish work (see also the comm. *ad* IV, 1, pp. 207–208). Furthermore, the Furies occur in, inter alia, Sen. *Herc.f.* 982–986; the prologue of *Thy.*, where the shadow of Tantalus emerges from the underworld; *Med.* 958–964; *Aga.* 759–768. One can also think of Eur. *Hec.* 1–58, where the ghost of Polydoros emerges from the underworld; however, both passages have nothing in common except for this looming. Another possible source of inspiration may have been book IV of Torquato Tasso's *Gerusalemme liberata* (1581); see on the influence of *Gerusalemme liberata* in England Dana F. Sutton, 'Milton's *In Quintum Novembris, anno aetatis 17* (1626): Choices and Intentions', in: Gareth Schmeling and Jon D. Mikalson (eds.), *Qui miscuit utile dulci: Festschrift Essays for Paul Lachlan MacKendrick* (Wauconda IL: Bolchazy-Carducci Publishers, 1998), pp. 348–375, esp. 358–359.

The darkness of Inquisitio may have been inspired by the 'Black Legend', the anti-Spanish myth who elaborated on the devilish machinations of Inquisition (see, for example, Koenraad Wolter Swart, 'The Black Legend during the Eighty Years War', in: John S. Bromley and Ernst H. Kossmann (eds.), *Britain and the Netherlands*, V: *Some Political Mythologies* (The Hague: Martinus Nijhoff, 1975), pp. 36–57, and Judith Pollmann, 'Eine natürliche Feindschaft: Ursprung und Funktion der schwarzen Legende über Spanien in den Niederlanden, 1566–1581', in: Franz Bosbach (ed.), *Feindbilder: Die Darstellung des Gegners in der politischen Publizistik des Mittelalters und der Neuzeit* (Cologne, etc.: Böhlau Verlag, 1992) Bayreuther historische Kolloquien, 6, pp. 73–93; Hugo De Schepper, 'La "Guerra de Flandes": Una sinopsis de su Leyenda Negra (1550–1650)', *Foro Hispánico* 2 (1992). Contactos entre los Paises Bajos y el mundo Ibérico, pp. 67–86 and intr., p. 15, n. 63). As often, mythology and reality meet: as a sister of the Furies she is expected to be a character from the underworld, in the dark. The 'genealogy' in "Poenarum parens", "Crudelitatis nata" (ll. 246–247) mirrors reality as experienced by a sixteenth- and seventeenth-century Dutchman: the Inquisition descended from Mercilessness and Cruelty, and the causes of Punishments. The latter points to the burning of heretics; the *Poenae* in mythology are also known as goddesses (*OLD* s.v. 1d); the former relates to the 'Black Legend', since the Spanish Inquisition was considered to be ruthless.

It is this monster who breaks out of Tartarus, the lower part of the underworld, which possibly here is pars pro toto the entire underworld (Roscher 5, 121–128 s.v. Tartaros). It is not only Inquisitio that is a 'child of darkness', also her sisters, the Furies whose number in classical mythology eventually became three: Alecto, Megaera and Tisiphone, are "noctis alumnae", cf. Ov. *Met.* IV, 451–452 and Bömer, *Ovidius Metamorphosen* 2, p. 154 *ad loc.* and p. 160. Cf. also Benedicti, *De rebus gestis* I, 43: "Hesperiae Furias regionis alumnas" and *ibid.* II, 173–174: "filia caecae noctis".

Heinsius gives them their traditional attributes—torches and snakes—but omits the (also topical) whip, adding that Greek literature gave them these instruments, pointing to the equation of the Roman *Furiae* with the Greek *Erinyes* (see, for example, *RAC* 8, 699–722, esp. 701, and Roscher 1.2, 1559–1564). For the usual hair of snakes, see also l. 1474 and, for example, Janus Secundus *El.* III, 1, 10 (Secundus, *Opera Omnia*, ed. Bosscha, vol. 1, p. 158) "sistere et anguinae sibila dira comae".

244 *tetrumque noctis improbae ludibrium*   This line can mean (1) 'awful object of ridicule, brought forth by and an instrument of malicious night', or 'awful monster, which causes the ridicule of malicious night'.

245 *rupi fores*   Cf. Sen. *Herc. Oet.* 458–459: "discussi fores umbrasque Ditis" and Verg. *Aen.* VII, 622: "Belli ferratos rumpit Saturnia postes".

248 *primum sub auras duxit*   This can be interpreted in two ways: 'to bring to the world' (e.g. Ov. *Met.* V, 640–641: "Ortygiam, quae me [...] superas eduxit prima sub auras"); a counterargument would be that she opens the doors herself (l. 245) and that she never entered the upper world sober (l. 351). Another possible interpretation is 'to cause to see the light of day' (see *TLL* 2, 1475.57–1476.10).

248 *et ferro et face*   For this expression, see (for example) Sen. *Tro.* 1073 Stephanus, *Dictionarium*, p. 231v s.v. Hercules.

249 *profanis*   'Pagan' or 'wicked'.

L 244   First Heinsius changed "tetrumque" into "novumque" then he changed the whole line into: 'the last-born sister of the cowardly night'.

L 250–251   The syntax altered from 'to whom [...] assigned [...] to waving torches' into 'who let [...] wave torches'.

The underworld

The representation of the underworld, with its nebulae, houses and doors, is topical. Heinsius mentions the "Tartaro imminentes fores" (l. 245), the "caligo"

(l. 246, cf. *OLD* s.v. 1.b, Verg. *Aen.* VI, 267, Ov. *Met.* IV, 455, Lucr. III, 304), later the "Perseidos squallidae domus" (l. 256; cf. ll. 262 "caliginosae Naturae lares" and 269 "pallidas Ditis domos"). He will also mention the rivers Cocytos (l. 266) and Phlegethon (l. 271). Furthermore, Inquisitio came from "recondita antra" (ll. 274–275). At the end of the scene (ll. 405–414) she brings abstract evil powers into formation, apparently at the entrance to the underworld where Inquisitio is located, who just forced the door to that same underworld. The 'uncanny' atmosphere of the underworld is its most traditional aspect, see Roscher 6, 63–64, s.v. Unterwelt, sub 36. Hades as a house with doors is also well known (Roscher 6, 65–66, sub 39). The rivers include the Cocytos and the Phlegethon (ll. 266 and 271; also Roscher 6, 67–70, sub 41–42; for the hellish gods or abstractions, *ibid.* 76–78).

Heinsius chooses from the many possibilities, for which Senecan dramas could be a source of inspiration. See Fantham, *Seneca's Troades*, pp. 268–270 for a description of the underworld in Sen., Verg. *Ge.* IV, 467–486 and *Aen.* VI. The underworld in *Aur.* is (like Seneca's drama) closer to the more traditional view of *Ge.* than that of *Aen.*

Sister of the Furies

254–260 *Gaude—exemplo fuit* Inquisitio now addresses her sister Megaera ('the grudging'), Seneca's favourite Fury (*Herc. f.* 102; *Med.* 963; *Thy.* 252; *Herc. Oet.* 1006; 1014, see Fitch, *Seneca's Hercules Furens*, p. 152). Heinsius takes over this predilection, see ll. 265, 364 and 1460. Dis is here called "Iuppiter niger" (l. 255; cf. Sen. *Herc. Oet.* 1705 "nigri [...] Iovis"; Sil. VIII, 116 "nigro [...] Iovi"), his wife "Perseis" (l. 256), the granddaughter of Peras, and daughter of Persa's son Perses, i.e. Hecate, identified with the queen of the underworld Proserpina, see Roscher 1.2, 1885–1910 s.v. Hekate; 3.2, 1985 s.v. Perseis; 3.2, 1982–1983 s.v. Perse. For 'Perseis' to indicate Hecate, see Roscher 3.2, 1985, no. 3; cf. Hes. *Th.* 409–415; Sen. *Med.* 814 and Ov. *Met.* VII, 74: "Ibat ad antiquas Hecates Perseidos aras", and Bömer's comm. 3, pp. 220–221 *ad loc.*

The "Iovis[que] nigri [...] infernum genus" (l. 255) to which Inquisitio is added consists of all inhabitants of hell, rather than of possible children of Dis and Hecate, since the Furies also belong to them, not being descendants of the royal couple.

For the circumlocution "Hispana tellus" (l. 259) with its 'evening full of darkness', see the comm. *ad* l. 213. The country is addressed in an apostrophe, which points to a heightened emotionality. For the darkness of the Spanish night, one could think of the 'Black Legend' (see above, the comm. *ad* ll. 243–530).

255 *Iovisque nigri ... infernum genus* Cf. Sen. *Herc. Oet.* 1704–1705: "[...] mortis infernae locus [...] nigri regna [...] Iovis", and *Oed.* 597–598: "Ditis feri exsangue vulgus".

256 *squallidas* For this word ('scaly' and 'dirty'), see *OLD* s.v. 2 (also 'awful', 'full of lamentations'). It is often used with respect to the underworld, see (for example) [Verg.] *Culex* 333: "squalida Tartara"; Sen. *Med.* 742: "squalidae Mortis specus" (see also Seneca, *Medea*, ed. C.D.N. Costa (Oxford: Clarendon Press, 1973), pp. 137–138 *ad loc.*).

> She has to leave the underworld, unwillingly

261–281 *Emerge—Quiritium* Now Inquisitio does not address Megaera (l. 254) or Spain (l. 259), but herself, leaving the underworld, to 'get to know her light', which implies a contrast with "lucis immunis dea" (l. 243) and the daylight. "Lucem tuam" cannot point at light in the underworld, which is dark (Roscher 2.1, 63–64), but cf. the oxymoron in Verg. *Aen.* VII, 456–457: "atro lumine" (said of torches in hell). Perhaps "tuam" should be taken to be proleptic: 'the daylight with which you will be familiar soon'. For reasons of clarity Heinsius changed "tuam" into "novam" in his own copy.

For the involuntary departure from the underworld, she invokes witnesses, first the "anguineum caput" (the head of the snake, or the head tunicated with snakes—in both cases an allusion to the snakes that the Furies have in their hair, Roscher 1. 2, 1559–1564, esp. 1563).

Then she addresses her sister Megaera (see the comm. on l. 254) and Dis (periphrastically "noctis arbiter", l. 265), and mentions the Cocytus (the river of lamentation), explained by "luctu [...] flebili", l. 267, cf. l. 271.

She also calls herself as a witness, and her Spanish father (cf. ll. 247–248), Tartarus, the pale house of Dis (see Fantham, *Seneca's Troades*, p. 268 and Sen. *Herc. f.* 717a), and the Phlegethon (the burning river, cf. "cruento [...] alveo", l. 2710, cf. Stephanus, *Dictionarium*, p. 351r). See also Secundus *Silvae* 2, 91 (Secundus, *Opera Omnia*, ed. Bosscha, 2, p. 176): "per Phlegetonteas audacem spargere flammas artificem"; in antiquity already in Sen. *Pha.* 1227: "Phlegethon igneo vado"; *Thy.* 73: "Phlegethon [...] igneo [...] freta" and 1017–1018: "ardenti freto Phlegethon harenas igneus totas agens".

Her departure has been caused by the "ferox pater Tarpeia saxa cui patent" (ll. 272–273). For the Tarpeian rock on the Capitoline Hill, from which criminals condemned to die were thrown, and for Jupiter, hence called "Tarpeius pater", cf. Prop. IV, 1, 7 (and Liv. VI, 20: "Damnatum tribuni de saxo Tarpeio deiecerunt"; *RE* 2. R. 4, 2330–2331); Silius Italicus had a predilection for the adjective; see also comm. on Grotius *Iambi* 121; Luc. I, 195–196: "O magnae qui moenia prospicis urbis Tarpeia de rupe, Tonans [...]"; and see Hunink, *Lucanus Bellum Civile Book III*, p. 98. The 'ferox pater' indicates the Pope, who has control over Rome and is equated with Jupiter. The metonym "Tarpeia saxa" for Rome is functional: the Pope has the power over life and death through Inquisition. See also Benedicti, *De rebus gestis* I, 19: "Tarpeia solitus de rupe tonare". Cf. also Grotius, *Pontifex Romanus* 94–95: "dira minantis fulmine linguae" and the dedication to the States General in this poem, l. 25 (Grotius, *Dichtwerken/Poetry* I, 2, 1A, p. 75). Finally, Inquisitio calls the Roman people "inclyta vastae ruina gentis" (ll. 273–274), in which the adjectives should be taken in an enallage ('the awesome remains of what used to be a famous people').

The Pope's instrument is lightning, another parallel with Jupiter. Whereas his weapons are made in the ovens of Mt Etna by Vulcan and his personnel, the Cyclops Pyracmon and Brontes (cf. Verg. *Aen.* VIII, 425, and Verg. *Ge.* IV, 170–173), those of the Pope are made by "Martiorum dissipata rudera, urbisque funus, et solum Quiritum" (l. 280), where the Roman Catholics are a pale shadow of the once martial Romans. The lightning alludes to the ecclesiastical ban, also called lightning. The ban against William of Orange was issued by Philip II.

The demise of Rome is topical, cf. Janus Vitalis, *Roma prisca*, ll. 1–2: "Qui Romam in media quaeris, novus advena, Roma, et Romae in Roma nil reperis media" and the famous expression "Roma fuit", for which see Bernhard Kytzler, *Roma aeterna: Lateinische und griechische Romdichtung von der Antike bis in die Gegenwart* (Darmstadt: Wissenschaftliche Buchgesellschaft, 1984), passim.

263 *discute* The verb "discutere" means 'to shatter', but also 'to search' (*TLL* 5.1, 1374). In the formulation "lethi sedem" the second meaning would seem to prevail. However, because she has to see the daylight, it might well be 'to break out'. For the thought, cf. Sen. *Herc. Oet.* 458–459: "Discussi fores umbrasque Ditis".

264 *mens* Addressing one's own heart, which can be traced back to Homer, is common in Seneca's tragedies and often indicates an inner conflict. On this, see Williams, *Tradition and Originality*, pp. 461–463; also *Aur.* 69, 769 and 1419. On its possible philosophical implications, see Tarrant, *Seneca Agamemnon*, pp. 194–195 *ad* Sen. *Aga.* 108 and Rosenmeyer, *Senecan Drama and Stoic Cosmology*, pp. 184–187.

264 *Testor* Cf. Sen. *Oed.* 14: "caelum deosque testor" and see Töchterle, *Seneca Oedipus*, p. 152 *ad loc.*; also *Aur.* 117.

278–279 *caminorum—vortices* Cf. Verg. *Ge.* I, 472–473: "Vidimus undantem ruptis fornacibus Aetnam, flammarumque globos".

L 261 This line was made more explicit by transforming it into: 'Go to the upper world, open the bolts of the home of shades, the remote house of Nature'.

L 263 The somewhat ambiguous "discute" became "desere". For the change of "tuam" into "novam" see above, the comm. *ad* 261–281. With the change in l. 264, the colon becomes: 'face, allow a still unknown light'.

L 266–267 These two lines became three: 'and the Cocytus, the swirling current of fire, which from its smoky vapour forms a sad cloud that overcomes its hapless name with its lamentations'.

L 270 The adjective "mortis" becomes "ignavus" ('inactive', or 'making inactive').

L 272–275 The translation of the changed version runs: 'My Latin father took me along, although I did not want to; he drew me and exposed me to heaven and after he had done that, he inspired me with his lightning'.

    Fate rules: everything is turned upside down

282–299 *O quanta—tulit* In an *exclamatio* Inquisitio speaks some *sententiae*, typographically indicated with quotation marks (see the comm. *ad* l. 58), the first on fate and what it ordains, which is often negative, the second on the "Deus" who eventually destroys cities and kingdoms. This Deus is likely a synonym for the all-ruling Stoic deity, cf. the comm. on ll. 1–5; an extra argument for this interpretation could be that in his 1601 Seneca edition Heinsius also (though inconsistently) prints "Deus" with a capital, from the idea that Seneca is an "anima naturaliter christiana". Another possible interpretation would be 'ruler', i.e. Philip II (see the comm. on l. 82), a third to consider it "furor", cf. Sen. *Pha.* 184–185: "Vicit ac regnat furor potensque tota mente dominatur deus". The third *sententia* 'the world is upside down' constitutes the transition to the next, risky statement to the effect that the formerly brave Romans obey unworthily.

    Here, too, the Romans are indicated in several ways: "magni cohortes Romuli" (l. 287), accentuating their courage in war, "nati Deûm" (l. 287), with emphasis on the divine descent of Romulus and Remus from the war god Mars (cf. ll. 61 and 63), or perhaps the descent of Aeneas, the 'arch-founder' of Rome (from Venus) is at play. The Romans also were the "arx alta rerum" (l. 288), a metonym for the leading (and 'protecting') role they assumed, as well as "orbis voratrix illa" (l. 289), with a negative connotation, just like in "regnorum lues" (l. 289). In the indication "gens Camillorum ferox" (l. 288) there is an allusion to the troops of Marcus Furius Camillus who took the city of Veii and defeated the Gauls in 390 BC (see Liv. V, 19, 2 sq.; Cic. *Rep.* I, 3, 6; Stephanus, *Dictionarium*, p. 125r s.v. Camillus), where the stress again is on their bravery and martial spirit. Furthermore, they were "universi compos, et tandem sui" (l. 290), probably an allusion to the Augustan "pax Romana" after a time of civil wars (see, for example, Paul Petit, *La Paix romaine* (Paris: PUF, 1967));in addition to which the self-conquest about which Auriacus/Orange spoke in Act I will be in play. For such a (shorter) enumeration of names for the Roman people, cf. (for example) Verg. *Aen.* I, 282: "Romanos, rerum dominos, gentemque togatam".

For the Romans being born to trample the arrogance of the "reges Septi-montes" (l. 293) after the expulsion of Tarquinius Superbus by Brutus (cf. l. 60) see (for example) Cic. *Rep.* II, 30, 52: "Pulsoque Tarquinio [...] odium populum Romanum regalis nominis tenuit". These martial Romans now obey "Regum cinaedi". "Cinaedus" is a derogatory word, originally for a homosexual man, but also for others. To whom does the word "cinaedi" refer? The "reges" will be those in power in general (see the comm. *ad* l. 82; Sen. *Herc. f.* and the comm. of Fitch, *Seneca's Hercules Furens*, p. 174 *ad loc.*). Most likely it refers to the cardinals of the Vatican Curia, who, according to Inquisitio, do not act severely enough against heretics. Such derogatory names were not uncommon in pamphlets of the time. These Romans also obey a "monstro Deo", either ("deus" being used as a ruler) the Pope, which is likely because of the following 'to whom Jupiter left his lightning' (cf. ll. 275–282), or a 'monstrous conception of God'. This Jupiter, too, is not the famous supreme god, but the "obsoletus" one (i.e. the Greek Zeus) whose grave is on Crete, see (for example) Cic. *N.D.* III, 53: "Saturni filium, cuius in illa insula sepulcrum ostenditur"; cf. Pease's comm. *ad loc.*, pp. 1096–1097; Roscher 6, 578–591. The identification of popes and mythological gods is not unprecedented, cf. the sequel Julius II-Mars, Leo X-Minerva and Alexander VI-Venus.

282 *O quanta curas fata mortaleis agunt*   Cf. Persius 1, 1: "O curas hominum!"
283 *incumbens Deus*   Cf. Sen. *Pha.* 185–187: "premens [...] deus [= furor]".
288 *arx alta rerum*   Cf. (for example) Cic. *Cat.* IV, 11: "hanc urbem, lucem orbis terrarum atque arcem omnium gentium".
293 *Septimontium*   This form, gen. pl., is not attested in classical Latin. "Sep-timontium" (N. sg.) was used for the region of the seven hills, or the festival held here on 11 December (Stephanus, *Dictionarium*, p. 397v; *OLD* s.v.). Hein-sius may have thought of the adjective "septimons", see Vulcanius, *Thesaurus utriusque linguae* [...] (1600), in: 'Lexicon Graecolatinum Vetus', p. 473, where it is the translation of ἑπτάλοφος (seven-hilled, see Cic. *Att.* VI, 5, 2; *Ac. Post* XIV, 121; cf. Plut. *Aetia Romana et Graeca* 2, 280D). See also the comm. *ad Amico lec-tori* 17.
298 *arce ... Minoia*   A periphrasis for Crete, after its legendary king, cf. Verg. *Aen.* VI, 14: "Minoia regna".

L 286–287 These lines are abbreviated into: 'I have to confess that the world is turned upside down and that the changes are burdensome'.

L 287 The "cohortes" become grandsons, stressing the descent. In line with this "nati" become "pulli" (chickens).

L 290 The self-conquest of the Romans is made explicit: 'conquerors of themselves'.

L 291–292 A change of syntax from a participle ("vitans") into a subordinate clause ("quae [...] evasit").

L 295 To make "cinaedis" more explicit, "mollibus" is added, at the site of the interjection "pro pudor".

Praise of the Dutch

300–318 *At contumacis—domi* The Dutchmen have a "vis rebellatrix" (l. 300), understandably so for Inquisitio, just like "gens profana" (l. 303). This power arouses "acres impetus", cf. the comm. *ad.* l. 114. They have a fixed sense of liberty and love for their country. Just like in the chorus in Act I, this "patria" is probably first and foremost their own region, but perhaps also the joint regions (cf. the comm. *ad* l. 210). Inquisitio praises the Dutch, in a rhetorical *evidentia* through "vidi" (l. 305) and "vidi, ipsa vidi" (l. 310); cf. Sen., for example, *Tro.* 170: "vidi, ipse vidi"; *Herc. f.* 50; *Aga.* 656; *Herc. Oet.* 207; which at the same time emphasizes Inquisitio's involvement, cf. Fitch, *Seneca's Hercules Furens*, p. 135 *ad* Sen. *Herc. f.* 50; cf. also Benedicti, *De rebus gestis* II, 458: "vidi, vidi ipse". She praises their labour at sea, with their "picei vultus" (l. 306) and "atrae manus" (black hands, either from the sun, or from the tar of the ropes, l. 306). They defy "ruptae nubes" (cloudbursts, l. 307) and "procellosae Iovis magni ruinae" (308–309), cf. (for example) Verg. *Aen.* I, 129: "fluctibus oppressos Troas caelique ruina".

Furthermore, the Dutchmen, a seafaring people, dictate the sea and the winds, cf. Sen. *Med.* 319–320: "[Tiphys dared] legesque novas scribere ventis". "Legem dicere", a word from legal and mercantile language, also occurs in poets, for instance Hor. *Ep.* II, 2, 18: "dicta tibi est lex". The maritime entrepreneurship of the Hollanders (with their skills in orientation on the sea by means of a compass), resulted in such feats as an expedition to the Cape of Good Hope (1595) and the establishment of the VOC and its pre-companies, and the WIC, see (for example) *AGN* 7, pp. 174–254. On the image of the Dutch as a people of water, see Arie-Jan Gelderblom, 'Nederland waterland', in: Hans van Dijk a.o. (eds), *In de zevende hemel: Opstellen voor P.E.L. Verkuyl over literatuur en kosmos* (Groningen: Passage, 1993), pp. 124–128. and Grotius, *Parellelon rerumpublicarum*, ed. Meerman, 2, pp. 86–98: "De re maritima" Inquisitio saw them "insistere undae"

(l. 312) even when the Africus (cf. Verg. *Aen.* 1.85: "creberque procellis", see also *RE* 1, 716–717 s.v. Africus 2) raged in wintertime ("hybernum mare", l. 311). The metaphor of the feet is continued in "aerato pede" (l. 312), in which "pes" allows three interpretations: (1) the sheet of a sail (e.g. Cat. 4, 21 and Sen. *Med.* 321–322 "nunc prolato pede transversos captare notos"), pars pro toto for ship; (2) rowers ("navales pedes", Plaut. *Men.* 350), also a metonym for ship; (3) "pes" as the instrument with which one enters something, the ship. The adjective "aeratus" denotes a warship, cf. for this use of "aeratus" Nisbet-Hubbard 2, p. 264 *ad* Hor. *C.* II, 16, 21. The metaphor is concluded with "calcata tutam lympha praebebat viam" (l. 315), in classical Latin only used for walking on ice (Ov. *Tr.* III, 10, 39: "durum calcavimus aequor") or a dry riverbed (Stat. *Th.* I, 358: "calcataque flumina").

Inquisitio ends her praise of the Dutch with two dichotomies: on the one hand they are related to Aeolus, on the other to Nereus, and they are at home abroad and meanwhile strangers in their own home. For the Dutch as seafaring people and the voyages to the Indies, see the comm. *ad* ll. 219–230 and 1763.

308 *audax* For the construction, cf. Hor. *C.* I, 3, 25: "audax omnia perpeti".

L 305–306 The overall syntax was: 'I have seen that the fathers and the faces and the hands challenged the storms'. Perhaps because he deemed this metaphor too daring, Heinsius changes "vultus" into "patres", which almost alliterates with "piceos". For reasons of variation, he changed "patres" (l. 305) into "viros". The 'black hand on the ropes' became 'the sea that was impassable through [or for] the winds'.
L 308 The adjective "procellosus", paired with "ruinae" may have seemed too daring, therefore Heinsius inserts 'turbines' and, to contrast with the heavy storms, the 'light ship' ("levi carina").
L 314–315 Eventually Heinsius changed the syntax from concordant into subordinate. He kept "calcata", in spite of hesitations, witness 'submissive'.

Inquisitio has to go to the Low Countries

319–324 *Ilhuc remittor—relaxat* The drunkenness of Inquisitio now seems to reach its temporary climax. Once again she expresses her thirst for human blood and her desire to commit a crime that will outdo all previous ones. Before that she declares that she is 'sent' to that colony (remittor, l. 319), not so much indicating that she is 'sent back', as indicating that she is being sent to where she is supposed to be, see *OLD* s.v. refero 13a; here also a *compositum pro simplice* may have been used.

She should go to the "vetus colonia", in which "vetus" can indicate 'former' (but by 1584 already significantly freed), or 'since long', i.e. part of the Habsburg Empire since 1477. The word "mutanda" (l. 320) is also ambiguous, indicating 'to move' (*TLL* 8, 1726.34–50) or 'to convert'. The first possibility is the most likely, cf. l. 367 where her eyes are "flexaque in sedes novas". Cf. also Benedicti, *De rebus gestis* I, 56–72, where it is told that Allecto is sent to the Low Countries. Moreover, she states that 'every country, however small it may be, has paved the way for her *sacra*'. "Sacra" can be 'sacrifices', i.e. the victims of the inquisition, or (as 'holiness') it could refer to one of the terms for the Inquisition, viz. 'the Holy Office' (the Congregation for the Doctrine of Faith). For "sacra" in Seneca, see Fitch, *Seneca's Hercules Furens*, p. 139 *ad Herc. f.* 56 (also: *Herc. f.* 898).

321–322 *maximum explevi—parum est* If one is looking to associate this with a particular crime, it will be the Paris St Bartholomew's Day massacre of 23 August 1572. However, "semper" makes the statement more general, or it is used as a modality to express impatience. The greater crime obviously is the murder of Auriacus/Orange. In Sen. *Pho.* 269 and 273 "maius [...] scelus" and "crimen [...] maius" are used for patricide, in *Oed.* 17 and 629 "maius scelus" and "maximum [...] scelus" refer to incest.

Inquisitio's 'blood-thirst'

324–340 *Aridas—Cruor* It seems that Heinsius also exhibits his knowledge in this passage. Bacchus is addressed with his nickname Lyaeus, his function of leader of the Bacchantes is mentioned (l. 327), and he is further referred to as Liber (l. 332, cf. Sen. *Tranq. An.* 17, 8). The Bacchantes are also mentioned with other names, such as Thyades (l. 327).

Inquisitio gives an overview of all wines; no matter how excellent, they cannot help her. A list of excellent Italian wines is provided by Marquardt-Mau, *Privatleben* 2, pp. 449–453. For catalogues of wines see also Plin. *N.H.* III, 59–61 and XIV, 52–53, and Strabo V, 3.

(1) "Nyseïo qui colle distillat latex" (l. 328): there are several places called Nysa, but here one should probably think of the summit of Parnassus, devoted to Bacchus, Stephanus, *Dictionarium*, p. 321v s.v. Nysa: "unus ex verticibus Parnassi montis, Baccho consecratus"; cf. Verg. *Aen.* VI, 805: "celso Nysae de vertice".

(2) "Tuusque si quid [...] Maron [...] exhaurit" (ll. 229–230): this Maron is an educator of the young Bacchus (Lewis and Short s.v. 3), or a priest of Bacchus, who gave Ulysses the wine to make Polyphemus drunk (Hom. *Od.* IX, 197; also Roscher 2.2., 2382–2383). Scriverius remarks that this priest

has his own wine, called "vinum Mareoticum", which has associations with Cleopatra and Hor. *C.* I, 37, 14, and cf. the 'Mareonic wine', Plin. *N.H.* XIV, 53. Furthermore, this Maron is unsteady under the influence of wine, among "procaces [...] choros" (l. 330), in ll. 331–332 divided into "Panas", "Maenades" and drunken gods. The "Pans" are gods of woods and fields, looking like Pan, see (for example) Ov. *Met.* XIV, 638 and (for the plural) the comm. of Bömer's comm. *ad loc.* (7, pp. 203–204). For the Maenads, see supra. For Panas, cf. Nonnus, *Dionys.* XXVII, 25, 28 and 31.

(3) "Falerni quicquid vuarum est tui" (l. 333). Those who praise the wine from the Falernum area include Hor., e.g. *C.* I, 20, 10; cf. Cats, *Sinne- en min-nebeelden*, ed. Luijten 1, p. 116 and vol. 2, pp. 318–319, n. 4; Stephanus, *Dictionarium*, p. 207v.; *RE* 6, 1971–1972.

(4) "Quod Setia usquam, vel Velitrarum colunt Dumeta" (ll. 334–335). Setia is an old city in the mountains of Latium, now Sezzi, which was famous for its wines (e.g. Mart. XIII, 23, 1: "Chia seni similis Baccho, quem Setia misit"). Augustus made the wine popular (Plin. *N.H.* XIV, 61), cf. also Stat. *S.* II, 6, 90. For Velitrae, a Volscian city in Latium, as a producer of wine, cf. Plin. *N.H.* XIV, 6, 8, 65: "Veliternina vina". For the combination of Setia and Velitrae, see Sil. VIII, 376–377: "At, quos ipsius mensis seposta Lyaei Setia et e celebri miserunt valle Velitrae". See also Stephanus, *Dictiona-rium*, p. 399r s.v. Setia and *RE* 2.R. 2, 1924–1925.

(5) "vinorum parens Albana tellus, Caecubique honos cadi" (ll. 335–336). The wine from Alba Longa was famous (Stephanus, *Dictionarium*, p. 115r s.v. Caecubum; *RE* 3, 1243–1244), as was the one from the swampy region of Caecubum in the south of Latium, see (for example) Hor. *C.* I, 20, 9 and passim, and Mart. XIII, 115: "Caecuba Fundanis generosa cocuntur Amy-clis, vitis et in media nata palude viret" and see *RE* 3, 1243–1244.

This whole series of famous and excellent wines cannot quench Inquisitio's thirst; they are "paruum" (l. 338). She needs "merum" (l. 339): human blood, a theme recurrent in her speech, see the comm. *ad* ll. 340–347. Heinsius may have been inspired for this blood thirst by Benedicti, *De rebus gestis* I, 53–54: "Nocte dieque patent fauces, inhiantque cruori innocuo".

326 *pace hoc ... tua* Cf. Sen. *Tro.* 276–277: "pace dixisse hoc tua, Argiva tellus, liceat".

326–332 *Lyaee ... Deos* These lines contain reminiscences of Nonnus, *Dionysi-aca* XI, 121 (Maron), 123 (Lyaeus), 124 (Panes); Thyades (327), Bacchantes, is also a favourite word of Nonnus, although its plural can also be found in Cat. 64, 392; Hor. *C.* II, 19, 9; Ov. *Fast.* VI, 514; Stat. *Th.* XII, 791.

L 324–325 Heinsius changed the hendiadys in "sitis squallorque" into "squallidus sitis".

To quench the thirst

340–347 *Quid—vices* Emotions rise, which is expressed in the rhetorical question to the Spaniards who are not present. The horror of the murders is widely reported: by the various synonyms for blood ("merum", pure wine, as a metaphor for blood, l. 339); "cruor", blood outside the body, l. 340; "sanguis", blood in the body, a bloodbath, l. 341; "sanies", spoiled blood, l. 342; "tabum", clotted blood, pus, l. 344, through the hyperbole "recentes [...] cadaverum strues" (l. 343) and with salient details ("revulsis ossibus", 345). Finally, at the sound level, the high emotional movement is also made audible in the alliteration of "fluctuibus ferro et face" (l. 346).
   The exegesis of the phrase "rerum coactas vortere in sese vices" (l. 347) is not easy. Literally it means: '[Are you hesitating] to turn the forced change of things in themselves?' The "rerum [...] vices" evoke l. 3, hence: 'necessary course of events'. A paraphrase of the expression could be: 'Hurry up, Spaniard, perform what is inevitable with water and sword and fire'. For the vices and the implications of correctness and inevitability that the word has in Seneca, cf. Sen. *Tro.* 1145 and see Fantham, *Seneca's Troades*, pp. 379–380.

340–341 *cruor ... sanguine* "Cruor" is a poetic, "sanguis" a medical word for blood, see Hunink, *Lucanus Bellum Civile Book III*, p. 87; another difference is that "cruor" is blood outside the body, "sanguis" blood inside it (see above). The attention to blood is characteristic of silver Latinity.
340–341 *quid ... cessas* See, inter alia, Sen. *Aga.* 198. For more *loci*, see Tarrant, *Seneca Agamemnon*, p. 211 *ad loc.*
343 *recentes ... cadaverum strues* Cf. (for example) Benedicti, *De rebus gestis* I, 484: "caedum Cumulos".
346 *ferro et face* See the comm. *ad* 248.

L 343–344 In the Leiden copy, the construction in which the abstract 'mens' sees something becomes a variant in which the 'I' discerns something with her mind. Cadavers were 'slaughtered', expressing something of the activity the Romans should develop.

Inquisitio with a chalice on earth

348–365 Adsum—genus Inquisitio continues to insist on the shedding of human blood, with the assurance that she never came to the upper world without being drunk. Now she shows the chalice of human blood mentioned in the scene header, which must bring her to total ecstasy.

This passage has some ambiguous elements. The exact meaning of "pater" (l. 348) is not clear: is it a 'supervisor' (cf., for example, Hor. *Sat.* II, 8, 7: "cenae pater"), or inventor or performer of the sacrifices? In that case, Inquisitio would become less active herself. But then, who is the "scaeve sacrorum pater": the Spaniard in general, Philip II, or the Pope? By enforcing judgements, the Spaniards and Philip are the performers of Inquisition's "sacra"; the Pope as head of the Church can be said to "perform rituals".

She wonders whether she has left Tartarus for nothing and left the night for the 'welcoming daylight'. "Cruentum" (l. 349) may have to be interpreted here in a proleptic way: 'so that my foot could become bloodied there' from wading through the streams of blood.

Entering the earth is expressed in three ways: (1) she swapped the night for the day; (2) Inquisitio went to the "supernos [...] deos" (l. 351). This is of course a periphrasis of the upper world (in contrast to Tartarus, *OLD* s.v. supernus 1.b). It can be a description of "superi", which can indicate both non-subterranean gods and the world; or conceived as a metonym for the (human) world; or perhaps the "dei" are gods anyway. A third way of expressing her departure from the underworld is the 'halo of the sun' and the countries she saw. For the topical 'halo' of the sun see Roscher 1.1, 423.

In ll. 362–365 "Quid—genus?", Inquisitio addresses 'the black people from the earth', which may denote figures in the underworld, situated deep in the earth, and Megaera (see l. 254); the latter is no good daughter of her father (Hades, 'Crudelitas', the Spaniard or Philip II; cf. the "pater" of l. 348), since she does not act as expected by Inquisitio, i.e. does not ensure that someone will carry out the 'awful crime'.

348 Adsum Either 'Here I am' or 'I will help you'. Eur. *Hec.* in Erasmus' translation also begins with 'adsum', spoken by the shade of Polydorus looming from hell.

348 Quid hoc est In Seneca's drama this exclamation often indicates that the speaker has seen something surprising or unwelcome, see Tarrant, *Seneca Agamemnon*, p. 337 *ad* Sen. *Aga.* 68: "eheu, quid hoc est?" and Töchterle, *Seneca Oedipus*, p. 337 *ad* Sen. *Oed.* 353; also *Pha.* 105; *Herc. f.* 1042; cf. *Herc. f.* 939 "sed quid hoc?"; *Herc. Oet.* 1432, 1441 "quid hoc?" In this case Inquisitio sees something unpleasant, viz. *no* bodies. Seneca had adapted this expression from Greek tragedy, e.g. τί δ' ἐστὶ χρῆμα; (e.g. Aesch. *Aga.* 1307), τί δ' ἐστὶν; and τί τοῦτο; (Sophocles and Euripides, passim).

348 *scaeve sacrorum pater* For "scaevus" cf. Sen. *Tro.* 46: "scaeva manu"; Fantham, *Seneca's Troades*, p. 215, notes that "scaevus" is not found in tragedy or epic; its meaning is not 'left' but 'ominous', according to the Greek idea that left is a bad omen. For "sacra" cf. ll. 323 and 379.

354 *optatum* This should probably be taken as a substantive: 'which is desired', i.e. the murder.

359–360 *quicquid ... nobis relictum ... fuit* Cf. Sen. *Herc. f.* 96: "quidquid relictum est".

362 *fraena* For the metaphor of reins regarding mental processes, cf. Sen. *Aga.* 114: "da frena"; *Aur.* 142, Bömer, *Ovidius Metamorphosen* 1, p. 107 on Ov. *Met.* I, 280.

363 *germânum caput* Cf. Soph. *Ant.* 1: αὐτάδελφον Ἰσμήνης κάρα.

L 348 Heinsius changed the negative "scaeve" (perhaps being a *mot d'auteur*) through "saeve" into the positive "magne".

L 351 'To approach' became 'to penetrate' ("invasi").

L 354 The 'wished-for crime' became the 'commissioned crime'.

L 358–362 Eventually these lines changed into: 'let it flow through the depths of my ungodly heart and take away my mind and everything mild, pure, calm, and peaceful that has been hidden in my mind. That there will be a Bacchanal is certain. I wanted new powers. Let the cruel Dutchman tremble'. It is made explicit that the "animus" of Inquisition is at stake.

Full drunkenness

366–376 *At o—nefas* Since the rapture is complete—Inquisitio threatens to lose consciousness, but at the same time she is more resolute in her wish to carry out her plan—a trait of Seneca's drama is visible: the visualization of inner processes. Inquisitio makes it clear that she is losing consciousness by what she says: the darkness ("nubila", "atrum [...] diem", l. 366, "caliginosus [...] situs", l. 368 and "luce subducta", l. 369), but no less because of what she does, an implicit stage direction: she is staggering over the stage ("poplitum labat gradus", l. 370; "vestigiis [...] incertis", l. 371). For her faintness one can think of (for example) Sen. *Aga.* 726–727: "Fugit lux alma et obscurat genas nox alta et aether abditus tenebris latet", said by Cassandra.

Inquisitio also gives the cause of the fading of her consciousness: drinking blood. A "mysticus [...] furor" (l. 375) drives out her common sense. This rapture ("mysticus") is divine, as in ancient mysteries, whereas in "furor" the kinship with the Furies is expressed.

The rapture implies a problem in this passage: she is resolute in her wish to carry out the crime, yet the "furor" has affected her mind and her certainties, formulated in the etymological oxymoron "incerta certum (mens tamen volvit nefas)", l. 376.

371 vestigijsque ... incertis Cf. (for example) Sen. *Pha.* 374: "incerto pede"; also *Aur.* 801. For this metonym, in which the influence (uncertainty) is transposed to the influenced (the staggering foot), see Canter, *Rhetorical Elements*, p. 133.

L 368 Why Heinsius wished to change "obducit" into "involvit" is unclear; all the more so since "involvere" is also used in l. 366, whereas the author likes variation.

An important victim

377–386 Terra—queunt For the topicality of these three empires invoked by Inquisition, see (for example) Bömer's comm., pp. 291–292 *ad* Ov. *Fast.* V, 11; Nisbet-Hubbard's comm. *ad* Hor. *C.* I, 12, 15; Verg. *Aen.* VI, 124; in Seneca's drama, for instance in *Pha.* 1212: "regna tria"; *Herc. f.* 30–32: "tellus [...] pontus [...] aer". However, Heinsius adds 'palace of black night' to the word heaven. For Inquisitio heaven is where the night appears. This may also be a way of underlining the temporal structure of the play (see also pp. 362, 404, 409 and 426). These three empires have to open up their forces and ruses (for instance earthquakes, storms, inundations). Or perhaps one should think of heaven and earth as Jupiter's domain, the palace of the black night as the dominion of Pluto and the sea that is ruled by Neptune.

For the "sacra", cf. l. 348. The question is whether they here indicate sacrificial rituals, religion, holiness or temples. The interpretation 'religion' is supported by the fact that inquisition, as a bureau of investigation, safeguards the doctrinal orthodoxy in the Church, the interpretation of 'holiness' in a common name for the inquisition, the 'Holy Office'. However, the sacred rituals that Inquisitio carries out here (the wish to create a 'victim') suggests 'sacrifices'. For at the heart of her speech is "victima ingens [...] concidet" (ll. 380–381). The victim is, of course, Auriacus/Orange. The relationship between "hacce dextera" (l. 380, Inquisitio will make a fist, and threatens to carry out the slaughtering) and ll. 391–394 (in which she states that a madman should be found to do it) is not entirely clear. It may indicate the delight in the murder, but more likely Heinsius was guided by his literary model Seneca, *Tro.* 306: "Hac dextra Achilli victimam reddam suam" (see also below). It must also be remembered that a sixteenth- or seventeenth-century drama is often situational: what is important to the situation applies, regardless of what has been said or done in another scene, see intr., pp. 27–28.

The victim is compared to the sacrifice that Achilles' ghost demanded of the Greeks, Polyxena, since the Greeks want to sail away without paying tribute to his tomb. This story is told in Ov. *Met.* XIII, 439–488 (see also the comm. of Bömer, *Ovidius Metamorphosen ad loc.*, pp. 308–334, also Eur. *Hec.*). For this passage in *Auriacus*, however, the version of Sen. *Tro.* 181–202 applies (see Fantham, *Seneca's Troades*, pp. 236–240). In Ovid the fleet of the Greeks is anchored, whereas in Seneca's version it is about to set sail (*Tro.* 192–193: "Solvite ingratas rates per nostra ituri maria").

This passage in *Aur.* contains more elements from Seneca's version: "victor" (l. 382, *Tro.* 188); "emergens humo" (l. 382, cf. *Tro.* 181, cf. also Ov. *Met.* XIII, 442: "exit humo"), "soluebat" (l. 383, *Tro.* 192: "solvite"), "perfidas [...] rates" (l. 381, cf. *Tro.* 192: "ingratas rates"). For "Teucrum [...] victor [...] Ilia [...] humo", cf. *Tro.* 234: "Ilium vicit pater"; only in *Tro.* 911 Seneca uses "Teucri" for Trojans. "Pelasgum turba" (l. 383) is comparable to *Tro.* 409: "Phrygiae turba". In both versions Polyxena's death is discussed in religious terms: she becomes a "victima" by "mactare" (*t.t.* for sacrifices, see *Tro.* 196 and Ov. *Met.* XIII, 448), just like here Auriacus' death. Another similarity between the two sacrifices is their senselessness, the results of the whims of Achilles and Philip II or the Pope respectively. For the change of metre, see above, p. 389.

380–381 victima-concidet Cf. Muret, *Iul. Caes.* 124: "Mactatus hacce dextera tandem cadat".
385 *poscimur* Cf. 215 and the comm. *ad loc.*

L **381** Heinsius wishes to bring in logic, hence "concidet" has been changed to "quaeritur", in addition to which "ille" has becomes "olim".
L **382** It is not clear why "emergens" should become "surgens".
L **386** "Iberi" is made "illius" for metrical reasons, see the author's remark in *Amico lectori* 22–27.

A culprit should be found

387–405 *Magnae sorores—discat* The sisters (Furies) who have to find a murderer are periphrastically called 'the sacred race of Atthis' (Attica, cf. Eur. *Iph. Aul.* 247), here perhaps either pars pro toto Greece, or indicating the literature of Athens and surroundings in which the Erinyes were extant, for instance in Aesch. *Oresteia*. The latter interpretation is supported by the following indications, which are related to Athens and Attica, Erechtheus being a mythical king of Athens (Cic. *Tusc.* I, 48, 116; Stephanus, *Dictionarium*, p. 200v; Roscher 1, 1296–1300, esp. 1298); Cecrops the founder and first king of Athens (cf. Lucr. VI, 1139: "finibus in Cecropis"; see also Bömer's comm. 1, p. 377 *ad* Ov. *Met.* II, 555 and Roscher 2.1, 1014–1024). Perhaps Heinsius thought of these two figures because both had three daughters. However, such a periphrasis is topical. Heinsius refers to the equation of the Greek *Erinyes* with the Roman *Furiae*. Yet the Furies in *Auriacus* are the Roman goddesses who cause furor rather than the Greek goddesses of revenge and crime.

It is not only the Furies but also other magical powers that must help find a potential murderer. Inquisitio focuses on the stars and the moon, both connected with magic (Roscher 4, 1438 on the stars connected with *omina*; the moon is active in magic as Hecate, Roscher 1, 1885–1910) and all that belongs to the underworld: these too must look for someone who can inspire fear in the Dutch.

391 *ferox, vecors, furens* For "ferox" (wild), cf. the comm. *ad* l. 63; for "vecors" (mad), Sen. *Aga.* 734; *Med.* 123; *Pha.* 1155; *Oed.* 1005; "furens" will poignantly be 'maddened by the Furies'. This *tricolon* has its climax in "aut genere Iberus [...] aut mente" (ll. 392–393).

396 *ignei cives poli* Cf. Heinsius *De Deo* 10: "stellasque cives aurei vagos poli".

398 *invisa Phoebo luna, pars Phoebi tamen* Cf. for this topos inter alia *Aur.* 12–13; *ibid.* 1056; Sen. *Herc. f.* 905: "Phoebus et Phoebi soror"; see also Canter, *Rhetorical Elements*, p. 161 and Grotius *Ad. ex.* 77: "lucis non suae", Cat. 34, 15–16: "et notho's dicta lumine Luna", Verg. *Ge.* I, 396: "fratris radiis obnoxia [...] Luna", and Sen. *Med.* 97: "Phoebe lumine non suo".

402 *manu* In the first instance "manus" is the actual hand, in the second instance metonymically the deeds (cf. l. 64).

403 *mille* For "mille" as an instance of hyperbole and Seneca's predilection for determinate numbers over indeterminate, see Frank, *Seneca's Phoenissae*, p. 122 *ad* Sen. *Pho.* 153.

404 *ferrum et ignes* See l. 248.

405 *discat* Often 'learning' is the basis of a 'Senecan point', see Fitch, *Seneca's Hercules Furens*, p. 229 *ad* Sen. *Herc. f.* 398: "et disce regum imperia ab Alcide pari", and (for example) Sen. *Tro.* 730: "Discite mites Herculis iras", and Fantham, *Seneca's Troades*, p. 312.

L **389** The changing of "cognata" into "agnata" stresses the kinship through her father (Erechteus and Cecrops).

L **394** The idea is intensified: the murderer not only 'carries' the four Furies in his heart, but he 'accomodates' them.

L 397 A line is added: 'mother of the darkness, triple Hecate, surely the sky holds you', whereas l. 399 has been omitted.

L 400 In his own copy Heinsius struck out the 'band of servants' (the stars), probably because such an indication would be too positive, and changed this into the broadness of the sky: 'when you travel far away through the great sky, you take the orbit that was imposed upon you'.

L 403–405 These lines become: 'Let the Dutchman who is not shocked by the fear of Philip, nor his hard threats, nor by Rome with his lightning hand and by the Evening [Spain], get to know fear and die slowly'.

Inquisition's troops of evil powers

405–414 *Intereà—facem* A catalogue of abstractions of evil had been a literary topos since Homer (*Il.* IV, 440) and Hesiod (*Th.* 211–212), but see esp. Verg. *Aen.* VI, 273–281. For some other *loci* in Latin literature, see Austin *ad loc.*, to which Sen. *Herc.f.* 92–99 can be added; see also Töchterle, *Seneca Oedipus*, pp. 455–456; Jules Marouzeau, *Quelques aspects de la formation du latin litteraire* (Paris: Klincksieck, 1949), pp. 117–118 and Roscher 3.2, 2068–2169 s.v. Personificationen; Gessner, p. 89. Some of Heinsius' abstractions can be found in earlier catalogues: Furor in Stat. *Th.* (III, 424; V, 74; VII, 52), Livor in Sil. XIII, 584, and Fraus in Cic. *N.D.* III, 44. Nevertheless, the catalogue is Heinsius' own: Audacia, Vecordia and Crudelitas seem to be his inventions (cf. the list in Roscher 6, 76–78). The catalogue will have been inspired by ideas about the 'Black Legend' regarding the Inquisition, see above, p. 390 and Jan Bloemendal, 'Sancta Inquisitio et Libertas saucia: De Inquisitie in Daniel Heinsius, *Auriacus, sive Libertas saucia* (1602)', *Nieuwsbrief Neolatinistenverband* 5 (1993), pp. 7–17, esp. p. 7. The arrangement of the troops shows *enargeia* (or *evidentia*, see "isthaec", "haec", "illinc") which is heightened by the military *t.t.* "deducere" (l. 407, see *TLL* 6, 274–275) and "exercitus" (for this, cf. Sen. *Herc.f.* 101: "agmen"). The troops could well march on stage, finding a murderer. On the other hand, "subeat" (l. 408) and "claudat latus" (l. 411) may indicate the order in which the (imaginary) colon is seen, cf. Sen. *Herc. f.* 690–696 where "sequitur" (l. 694) has this function. For a similar procession of abstractions, see Grotius *Ad. ex.* 150–157, where Scelus, Superbia, Impietas, Error, Ambitio, Libido, falsi fides and Levitas appear.

413 *sic sic eundum est* Cf. Sen. *Herc. f.* 1218: "Sic sic agendum est"; *Herc. Oet.* 846; Grotius *Ad. ex.* 139: "Hoc, hoc videndum est".

L 406–407 The summoning of the troops is rephrased: 'Come as witnesses and accomplices of my crime, come, be present, hideous column, at the ritual'.

L 410   As in l. 270, death has become 'inactive' or 'rendering inactive'.

L 411   The Furies are added to the column, adding to the coherence of the scene.

L 412   Heinsius apparently wished to introduce Ruse in the procession, and changed "res bellicae" into the singular *metri causa*.

L 413   "fas sit" (divinely allowed) stresses the sacred aspect of the murder.

Act II, Scene 2 (415–610)

Summary

This scene consists of a dialogue between Loisa/Louise and an Old Man.

415–444   Loisa, with her baby (Frederick Henry) on her lap, calls the Daylight the giver of life. At first the child crawls around carefree, not struck by fate, and devotes his youth to games. In the following period he becomes familiar with sorrows.

445–486   Then Loisa turns to the baby, who is still capable of being carefree because he knows nothing. Later he will have to take on royal duties and be exposed to dangers. For now, however, he does not know any lust for power or greed, but can sleep peacefully. Loisa would almost wish to be as young as he was. She does fear, even things that are not there: a dream has frightened her.

487–522   A dialogue begins between her and an Old Man, who asks her why she is pale and crying. Eventually she tells him that she has had an ominous dream.

523–558   The Old Man tries to calm her, remarking that dreams are lies, and offering a theory that dreams bring about fear that torment during the day, and sorrows of the day impress the mind and torment at night. Dreams mingle lies and truth, which makes fears greater. When we awaken, the dream disappears, but not the fear.

559–574   Loisa, however, remains afraid, not in the least because of her experience, in spite of the many arguments of the Old Man: reason is obscured; if one cannot clearly distinguish lies, they hurt as if they were truth; her husband is protected by a fortress of cities, by water and by the love of his people.

574–610   At Loisa's objection that this love does not concern foreigners, the Old Man tells us that princes do not stick to borders and are at home on the whole earth. She knows that, but is still afraid. That aggravates her grief, but she cannot do otherwise: fear is strengthened when the cause is not clear.

The scene has the characteristics of a *domina-nutrix* scene: the main figure, Loisa, feels strong emotions, another figure, often the *nutrix*, here the *senex*, tries to calm him or her, see pp. 26–27 and 40. In the dramas by or attributed to Seneca, such a scene is typical of Act II, see C.J. Herington, 'Senecan Tragedy', in: Niall Rudd (ed.), *Essays on Classical Literature, Selected from Arion* (Cambridge, etc.: Cambridge University Press, 1972), pp. 170–219, esp. pp. 201–203 [= *Arion* 5 (1966), pp. 422–471, here pp. 453–455, and Tarrant, *Seneca Agamemnon*, p. 212 *ad* Sen. *Aga*. 203. Unlike in Seneca's plays, Loisa's emotion in itself does not bring about the catastrophe (cf. Herington, *loc. cit.*), but could have prevented it if it were to have been heeded. Dreams are common in Seneca's tragedies, and Calpurnia is said to have dreamt in the night before the Ides of March 44 BC that her husband Caesar would be killed (cf. Muret, *Iul. Caes.* III, 1, ll. 240–305). See also Hunink, *Lucanus Bellum Civile Book III*, pp. 34–35 on dreams in epic poetry, and Bloemendal, 'Mon Dieu, mon Dieu ...'.

Metre

The scene is written in iambic trimeters.

Commentary

Invoking the day

415–429 *O molientis—discit* The scene starts with an elaborated indication of the time, which constitutes a rest and indicates the temporal structure, see pp. 362, 404 and 426 since in this case the daylight is invoked as the origin of everything, these words are said in the morning, see (for example) Sen. *Herc. f.* 123–124: "Clarescit dies ortuque Titan lucidus croceo subit".

The passage has some ambiguities. It is not exactly clear what "molientis alta" (l. 415) means: (1) 'creating lofty things' (with in the background the derivation of "natura" from "nasci"; *OLD* s.v. natura); for a parallel *e contrario* see Heinsius, *In miseros mortem optantes* 2: "demolientis cuncta fortunae"; (2) 'setting heaven in motion' (for "alta" as heaven, see Verg. *Aen.* VII, 362: "alta petens" and I, 297: "Maia genitum demisit ab alto"), which is also compatible with other ideas in this passage, e.g. "rerum origo prima"; (3) 'plotting great plans' (cf. Luc. VI, 664: "quid moliretur rerum natura novarum"). In any case, it signifies the early time of the day. In all cases, Natura can be an allusion to the *Ratio* or *Logos*, the stoical ruling principle of physical reality, see the comm. on ll. 1–5.

What does the day being labelled "Naturae comes" mean? Perhaps it refers to the fact that the day, as giver of light and life helps Nature, so to speak.

"rerum origo prima" (l. 418) will refer to daybreak (cf. l. 416 and Lucr. v, 176: "donec diluxit rerum genitalis origo").

In order to make sense of "qui reconditas primus tueri syderum donas faces", the "syderum [...] faces" have to be interpreted as the light of the sun (*OLD* s.v. sidus 2c), or "tueri" should be taken as 'to protect', almost synonymous with "recondere". "Reconditas" is also ambiguous: proleptically used as 'stored', 'put back in its place'.

As a helper of Nature the day is the force that brings forth offspring, where the cradle is the grave: the child is "sepultus", "mortalis" and "mortuus". For this literary topos, see Von Moos, *Consolatio*, 3, p. 123, *sub* 598, citing as an example Sen. *Pol.* 11,3: "Quisquis ad vitam editur, ad mortem destinatur". For a Judeo-Christian parallel, cf. (for example) Ps. 103, 15–16: "As for man, his days are as grass: as a flower of the field, so he flourisheth. For the wind passeth over it, and it is gone; and the place thereof shall know it no more". (*KJV*) This "informe pondus impotensque, et haud suum" is put into light by the day. Yet the child is also part of the divine, a two-legged god, a spark of heaven (cf. the comm. on ll. 23–45), because he participates in the *Ratio* (see Sen. *Ep.* 41; Pohlenz, *Die Stoa*, passim), and because as a prince he is a god on earth, see (for example) Fokke Veenstra, 'Harmonieënleer in de renaissance', in: Ton Cram a.o. (eds), *Weerwerk: Opstellen aangeboden aan Professor dr. Garmt Stuiveling ter gelegenheid van zijn afscheid aan de Universiteit van Amsterdam* (Assen: Van Gorcum, 1973), pp. 187–200, and Veenstra, 'Dromen zonder Freud', p. 608 and n. 127. The child looks at the sky and gets to know heaven in two ways: breaking the dungeon of the womb and actually seeing the light, and from the dungeon of his body he sees the sky and understands nature (cf. de comm. on ll. 38–45).

The child (Frederick Henry) was born 29 January 1584, the murder taking place on 10 July of the same year.

In this passage the ways in which the child is described change from pessimism (mortality) to optimism (but divine). In ll. 429–434 (q.v.) the tone will become tender. This may be an attempt to lend Loisa's 'character' more depth. On the other hand these concepts fit in with the world view that was evoked in Act I.

415–418 *O molientis—prima* Cf. Heinsius, *De Deo* 7: "Oculum serenae lucis et vitae diem".

416–417 *sacrae—largitor* These circumlocutions do have a Lucretian colour, although they do not occur in this form in *De rerum natura*. However, cf. "vitae pater" with Lucr. II, 172 and 418: "dux vitae" and "rerumque Origo prima" with Lucr. I, 55: "rerum primordia". Furthermore, the passage vaguely recalls Lucr. I, 1–23 where Venus is worshipped as origin of life.

416 *tribune* A metaphorical use of the word (cf. "tribunus aerarius", a tax collector who paid the wages of solders; consider the derivation from 'tribuere'
and cf. l. 417 "largitor") is not classical, but also unusual for humanistic Latin.
Perhaps it is a neologism on the part of Heinsius. In medieval Latin a 'tribunus'
could be someone who speaks justice (Du Cange 8, 178). But an invocation with
all kinds of names and functions is very common, see (for example) Sen. *Herc.
f.* 592–594, esp. 592: "o lucis almae rector et caeli decus".
419 *primus* Either 'the first' or 'early in the morning'.
424 *imminentes* Cf. Ov. *Met.* II, 7: "caelumque quod imminet orbi" and the
comm. of Bömer, *Ovidius Metamorphosen* 1, p. 239 *ad loc.*
426 *bipes Deus* Probably a reaction to Cic. *N.D.* I, 95: "Quid [...] obstat quomi-
nus sit beatus si non sit bipes?"

L 415–419 These lines are changed such that day and breath of life are joined
and the day becomes the origin of light and time instead of the origin of the
world. Moreover, they are rendered less complex: 'Breath of life, and you, leader
of life, day, first origin of light, father of time'.
L 422–429 '[O you who] puts [the child] [...] who has not yet received the
light [...] in a tour under the high gates in the full possession of heaven. Then it
breaks out, brought out of his dungeon for the first time, the image of heaven,
care of the awesome God [...] and breathes the air.' These notions (which could
be Christian) are not absent in Seneca's works, cf. the comm. on 23–45, and
Sen. *Benef.* 29, 6. Finally Heinsius erased the passage and left only: 'O you,
who takes the mortal child, buried in his mother, although not yet born, yet
already deceased, a formless mass, not master of the light, into the height, in
the full possession of heaven. For then, for the first time taken out of his dungeon, an image of heaven, a concern for the awesome God, is crawling around
[...]'.

The carefreeness of youth

429–443 *parvulusque—petit* The child's lack of concern is emphasized by
many means: the diminutives "parvulus" and "primulum", the adjectives
"insons", "mitis" and "ignarus sui", the verbs that denote simple activities: "proserpit", "prosultat" (a non-classical combination of "pro" and "saltat") and
"exilit". The diminutives also express Loisa's tenderness.
   Yet here too an ominous undertone rings in "fluctuantis tyro fortunae", where
we see Heinsius' predilection for a substantive with complements, rather than
a relative subordinate clause. Later, the boy will get to know how fortune can
change; on the volatile fortune, see also the comm. on *Aur.* 1–5.

In this respect "ignarus sui" (l. 430) allows two interpretations, (1) 'not yet with the full knowledge of his own mind', or (2) 'not yet conscious of everything that will happen to him'. Cf. Sen. *Herc. f.* 184: "incerta sui" (i.e. uncertain of their nature and their true happiness, see Fitch, *Seneca's Hercules Furens*, pp. 177–178 *ad loc.*), *ibid.* 292: "oblitos sui" (cf. *ibid.* 808, *Med.* 560), and see *Aur.* 154, 180, 792 and 1024. Neither is the child "curae capax" (l. 432), an ambiguous combination: either he cannot be harmed yet, or the child cannot have cares himself. The latter is the connotation of "nescius" (l. 434).

Now the explanation for the carefreeness is given: the deity first sends a pleasant fate. I have not yet encountered parallels for such a notion of the carefree youth; usually youth was regarded as a time of education, preparation for better life, see (for example) J.B. Bedaux, 'Beelden van "leersucht" en tucht: Opvoedingsmetaforen in de Nederlandse schilderkunst van de zeventiende eeuw', *Nederlands Kunsthistorisch Jaarboek* 33 (1983), pp. 49–74. Youth is characterized by play. Here not the game of fortune (cf. l. 4), but children's games, two of which are mentioned: *tali* and *turbines*. "Tali" are a 'kootspel' or 'bikkelspel', see *WNT* 7.2, 5462–5463 s.v. koot and *ibid.* 2.2, 2686 s.v. bikkel; Spanoghe 3, p. 146, s.v. tales. The 'koot' game, a game of chance with bones or claws of oxen or pigs, was played by boys, the game with the smaller 'bikkels' (bones of sheep) by girls, see K. Kooiman, 'Koten, bikkels en misverstanden', *De nieuwe taalgids* 52 (1959), pp. 254–263. The first is intended, since Loisa speaks to the boy. For the toll ("turbo") as children's toys, see *WNT* 17.1, 932–934; Kilianus, *Etymologicum*, p. 676 s.v. tol; Spanoghe 3, p. 146, s.v. turbo 2. One might interpret the "turbines" figuratively as 'the turbulence of life', but the close relationship with "tali" makes that unlikely; although it finds support in classical Latin, in which 'turbo' is not used (the word 'trochus' is used, see *OLD* s.v. turbo and trochus), this meaning is known in Neo-Latin.

Through this game, life 'wasted' its bliss: it does not pay attention to the happiness it receives, or it makes use of it too abundantly so that nothing remains. In an oxymoron, Heinsius' formulation posits that playing is a hazard: "simul ludit luditurque" (l. 441): it plays itself and fortune plays with the child, because after the happy period comes the time of concerns, which 'settles down at the bottom like dregs', for which cf. Sen. *Ep.* 1, 8: "Non enim tantum minimum in imo, sed pessimum remanet" and 58, 33: "De hoc tamen quaeremus, pars summa vitae utrum faex sit an liquidissimum ac purissimum quiddam". See also Lucr. v, 497 and 1140 (in both cases 'faex' in combination with re- or subsido).

429 *parvulus* For the emotional overtones of "parvulus" in Seneca's drama and the use of this word by him, see Fitch, *Seneca's Hercules Furens*, p. 381.

Cf. also Verg. *Aen.* IV, 328: "Si quis mihi parvulus aula luderet Aeneas". Besides "parvulus" Seneca only uses the diminutive "quantulum", see Frank, *Seneca's Phoenissae*, p. 80. For "parvulus" see also *Aur.* 1129 and 1314.

L 431–432 These lines become: "May the child, unaware of his life, see [or "temnat", despise] the foolish destiny, and now that it has not yet come to know the normal fate, he lets himself go and jumps [...]".

L 436 "Favens" becomes slightly more passive: "parcens".

L 437–438 The 'preferable times' become 'better times'. Perhaps "potior" gave too much emphasis to the youth who, according to Heinsius, lived without interests, and in the midst of "minuta gaudia", as recorded in l. 438.

L 440 The "beatitas", blessedness, is for the gods, "felicitas", happiness, also for mortals.

The carefreeness for her baby

444–448 *O nate—nihil* The thought of the misery that awaits the child generates pathos. This is underlined by the *geminatio* in "O nate, nate" (l. 444, also 449, cf. Sen. *Tro.* 461 and *Aur.* 464: "Nate mi") and the *exclamatio* in l. 447: "O dulcis aetas!" See Konst, *De hartstochten in de tragedie*, pp. 74–124. "Dulce pignus" (l. 444) also indicates emotional involvement: the marriage of Louise and William of Orange is confirmed in the child. "Pignus" was used for the first time in this sense by Prop. IV, 11, 73, later also in Seneca's drama, including *Tro.* 766: "o dulce pignus". In *Tro.* 766–785 Andromache speaks to Astyanax. In spite of the identical situation (Andromache is heartbroken now that her husband Hector has died, and she speaks to her son gloomily), there are no more intrinsic or stylistic similarities between the two passages. See also Fantham, *Seneca's Troades*, p. 316. Cf. also the comm. *ad Aur.* III, 2, in particular 1234–1253.

447–448 *Scilicet primum—tamen, nihil* The train of thought is as follows: namely (scilicet), only knowing and not knowing exist. The primary thing is to know everything—which is only possible for God. The secondary thing is to know nothing. This is formulated so densely, that the grammatical position of "Deus" in the sentence becomes unclear, and can be (1) "Deus" = 'sicut Deus', i.e. such as God does, as is the case with God; (2) "Deus" must be placed between parentheses (and that is/does God); (3) "Deus" is a predicate noun, i.e. the primary is God/divine, knowing everything, but then there is nothing to know; (4) it is a kind of interjection. Cf. also Sen. *Herc. f.* 1098–1099: "Proxima puris sors est manibus nescire nefas".

The gods know everything, the most wise Socrates was aware that he knew nothing (Plato *Apol.* 23A–B). Here too, the *sententia* is highlighted by quotation marks. Perhaps Heinsius is once again referring to the idea that the prince as a ruler is divine, see above, the comm. *ad* ll. 178–185.

L 444–446 These lines are amplified into: "O sweet offspring of a famous family who look like your mother in your face, like your father in your behaviour, and surpass both of them by your sweet ignorance, now you spend your time, slow time, in your mother's womb with a sweet smile".
L 447 Because "est, Deus" is changed into 'it's the first good thing', the ambiguity of "Deus" is neutralized.

Very soon the baby will get acquainted with sorrows

449–464 *O nate—proximusque* Here, Loisa concentrates on the position that the child will later hold as a prince, and which will endanger him, and contrasts this with the child's current carefreeness. In an *amplificatio* she circles around the same thoughts, put into words in "imminentem purpurae [i.e. of kings] ferociam". The word 'ferocia' is related to 'ferox', so popular with the author, see the comm. *ad* l. 63. Furthermore, power causes *motus*, unrest and danger.

However, the child is carefree, since he does have a "regnum", but of "securitatis aureae", cf. the "aetas aurea" of (for example) Ov. *Met.* I, 89–112, and the combination "aurea Libertas", one of the figures that would be positioned on Orange's tomb in the Nieuwe Kerk of Delft. "Securitas" can indicate the ἀταρα-ξία of Epicureanism, see *OLD* s.v. securitas 1c, but a meaning of 'lack of danger' is more likely. He also has a servant, but this is innocence. For the notion that safety comes mainly through avoiding injustice, see Sen. *Ep.* 105, 7: "Securitatis magna portio est nil inique facere". There is also safety in not being aware of one's existence.

The baby does not have to fear anyone because nobody fears him (see below) and is also not affected by ambition, which causes deceit. He looks into the world open-mindedly and 'you consider everything you see to be yours, almost equal to that one god'. Here again the thought that the monarch is a resident of the world is probably playing a role, cf. the comm. *ad* 574–608.

456–457 *Nec potest—nullus timet* This could also mean 'It is not possible to fear someone whom no one fears'. For the opposite, cf. Publilius Syrus, *Sententiae* M 30: "Multos timere debet, quem multi timent"; Sen. *Prov.*, *Dialogi* IV, 11, 3: "necesse est multos timeat quem multi timent"; also Ps.-Sen. *De mor.* 61: "Homo qui a multis timetur, multos timet" (ed. Basel 1515, p. 633) and *Ep.* 105, 4:

"quod qui timetur, timet"; Ps. Ausonius, *Septem sapientium sententiae*, Periander 5: "Multis terribilis caveto multos" (see Cats, *Sinne- en minnebeelden*, ed. Luijten 1, p. 81 and vol. 2, p. 250, n. 13). For such a conviction in contemporary pamphlets, see Geurts, *Opstand in pamfletten*, p. 277, where the author refers to Cic. *Off*. II, 23: "Omnium autem rerum nec aptius est quicquam ad opes tuendas ac tenendas quam diligi, nec alienius quam timeri. Praeclare enim Ennius 'Quem metuunt oderunt; quem quisque odit perisse expetit'".

459–460 *ardor imperi—porrigo levis* Something similar is said in a pamphlet of the time, see Geurts, *Opstand in pamfletten*, p. 277: "de ambitie ende yver tot staet ende hoocheyt", translated from Cic. *Off*. I, 87: "Miserrima est omnino ambitio honorumque contentio". In classical Latin the word 'porrigo' is only used in a literal sense (*OLD* s.v. porrigo only mentions Fronto, *Ad Aurelium* for a metaphorical use: "scabies porrigo ex eiusmodi libris [i.e. of Seneca] concipitur"). In Dutch, however, 'schurft' (porrigo) can also indicate an inclination, see *WNT* 14, 1215; Spanoghe 2, p. 408 s.v. porrigo capitis offers 'furfures' among the meanings and on p. 54 s.v. furfures, under the derivation 'furfurosus': "metaph. pro scrupuloso etc., pro sordide avaro semel-knooper [i.e. a miser]".

461 *cuniculos que ... agit* This is a metaphor derived from sieges, see *OLD* s.v. 2b: 'to construct trenches'.

L 455 'No you do not debilitate any servant, except innocence.' "Tueri" becomes the more specific "fatigas" [i.e. to make tired with orders].
L 460–461 '[...] and the deceitful desire to possess whatever; ambition and greed have not spoiled your desires and hope.'
L 463 The somewhat ambiguous "ducis" (to consider or to lead) becomes "credis" (to think).

The child is to be envied

464–479 *Nate mi—minas* These lines focus on the quiet sleep of the baby, which is sleeping after drinking milk ("sopore lacteo", l. 466), breathes a honeyed sleep ("melleum", l. 469, cf. for the expression Prop. I, 3, 7: "mollem spirare quietem"). This sleep is given various names: "somnus" (ll. 465, 469), "sopor" (l. 466) and "quies" (l. 471). The variation is not just ornamental; she emphasizes the carefreeness of the baby, which is expressed in the fact that he is sleeping peacefully. For such combinations, cf. Sen. *Pha*. 100: "quies nocturna [...] altus sopor"; also *Pha*. 731; 1161–1163. Such a *variatio* is part of Seneca's mannerism, see Tarrant, *Seneca Agamemnon*, p. 306 *ad Aga*. 724. Such a series of words for sleep can also be found in Grotius *Ad. ex*. 661–665: "sopor [...] Somno [...] torpor [...] quies".

In addition to these are indications of the cradle: "thorus" (l. 472), "thalamus" (l. 473) and "cubile" (l. 474). "Torus" may have a double meaning: 'bed' and 'muscle', since it is Loisa's knees and lap that are the baby's bed. This intensifies her emotional involvement, which is enhanced through mention of the fact that she is almost jealous of the child and would like to be as young as he, to avoid the treacherous court. This aligns with the topos of the court's unreliability, see (for example) Sen. *Pha.* 982: "Fraus sublimi regnat in aula" and Luc. VIII, 493: "Exeat aula qui vult esse pius. Virtus et summa potestas non coeunt".

For sleep indicating someone's moral quality, see (for example) Hor. *C.* II, 16, 15–16: "Nec levis somnos timor aut cupido sordidus aufert", Nisbet-Hubbard 2, p. 261 *ad loc.*, and Sen. *Pha.* 520–521: "Certior somnus premit secura duro membra versantem toro". See also Bömer, *Ovidius Metamorphosen* 5, p. 405 *ad* Ov. *Met.* XI, 624. These cares are contrasted with sorrows he does not have: "motus", "ciuicum [...] metum" (l. 467; "civicus" meaning: 'of adults', or 'small-human', or 'civil', cf., for example, Hor. *C.* II, 1, 1: "motum [...] civicum" of civil wars). For the difference between "civicus" and "civilis" see *TLL* 3, 1213, quoting Isid. *Diff.* I, 133: "Civile est quod ad civem pertinet, civicum quod ipsi cives faciunt"; cf. also Sil. VIII, 21–22: "civica [...] invidia". Nor does the child have to fear the "tempestuosa casuum tonitrua" (l. 468, cf. Cic. *Tusc.* II, 66: "fulmina fortunae").

L 464   The change of "nate mi" into "tum levi" adds a temporal structure to the sentence.

L 467–468   The line becomes: 'and the thunders of the evil changes of fate'.

Sorrows from a dream

480–486 *Quin et—dies*   Only now does Loisa say that it was a dream that frightened her, referred to as "falsa" (deceitful images) and "noctis umbram", and somewhat more indirectly with "Sopor" and "ille curarum exactor acer dissipatorque omnium pater mearum". But the fear that arose at night continues to gnaw away at her during the day and the anxiety that caused daytime worries caused fearful dreams. The reader/viewer remains ignorant of the content of the dream.

Loisa knows what dreams owe their creation to. With this utterance (what one thinks about during the day is reproduced in the dream at night), Heinsius is dovetailing with the customary ideas of the 'somnium'; this absorbs the impressions and experiences of the individual when waking and reflects them in the dream. Such dreams are also distinguished by the physician Cardanus, see Veenstra, 'Dromen zonder Freud', pp. 602 and 605. The physician Johan van Beverwyck, who in his writings gives the state of the arts, deals with dreams

(among other things) in his *Schat der ongesontheyt* (1642). In the section of "na-
tuerlijcke Droomen" (natural dreams) he sums up the dreams that arise from
thoughts; he bases himself on Hippocrates "in sijn boeck van de Droomen"
('in his book of dreams'), Aristotle and Gerardus Vossius, *De theologia gentili
et physiologia Christiana* (1641) III, 35, see Van Beverwyck, *Wercken der Genees-
konste* [...] (Amsterdam: Schipper 1664), p. 66. Such a view found fertile soil in
Cicero's *Somnium Scipionis* 10: "Fit enim fere ut cogitationes sermonesque nostri pariant aliquid in somno".

Loisa knows the origin of dreams, and their deceit, yet she is afraid. For
the erroneous use of reason kindles fear in her. The dream as a literary phenomenon is widespread, cf. Verg. *Aen.* II, 791–794 (Aeneas stating that he saw
his wife Creusa in a dream); *ibid.* 700–702 (Aeneas telling his father that he
often dreamt of him); Sen. *Tro.* 438–460 (Andromacha seeing Hector in a
dream). See also Anton H.M. Kessels, *Studies on the Dream in Greek Literature*
(Utrecht: HES, 1974) Doctoral thesis Utrecht 1973; Veenstra, 'Dromen zonder
Freud', Bloemendal, 'Mon Dieu, mon Dieu ...'

482 *noctis umbram* Cf. (for example) Verg. *Ecl.* 8, 14: "frigida vix caelo noctis
decesserat umbra", and Stat. *Silv.* I, 6, 65: "noctis proprioribus sub umbris". Furthermore, the connotations of 'contours', 'visions' may be at play.
482–483 *curarum Sopor exactor* Cf. Sen. *Herc. f.* 1065–1067: "Tuque o domitor
Somne malorum, requies animi, pars humanae melior vitae" and *Aga.* 75–76:
"curarum somnus domitor pectora solvit".
484 *curaque haec illam premit* Either: 'one sorrow follows the other', or 'this
sorrow oppresses it [the mind]'.
485 *dubia ... fides* Cf. Luc. II, 461: "dubiamque fidem fortuna ferebat", Ov. *Her.*
19, 200: "non dubia [...] fide" and Liv. XXVIII, 6, 11: "fluxa fides". 'Dubious' can be
'wavering' or 'making uncertain'.
486 *diemque nox ... noctem dies* Cf. *Aur.* 789 "diesque nocte [...] nox [...] die"
(with the same chiasmus). Cf. Sen. *Herc. Oet.* 462: "Nox media solem vidit et
noctem dies".
486 *lacessit* See (for instance) *Aur.* 156, 716, 1100, 1531 and Sen. *Aga.* 980.

Cause and effect of sadness and fear

487–512 *Dignata—sopor* According to the conventions in the drama, the
senex has not heard Loisa's tirade to the baby and asks what is going on. Such a
representation of things—a protagonist who speaks her emotions in a monologue and is consoled by a supporting actor, while the latter has not heard the
words of the protagonist—also occurs in Seneca's theatre, e.g. the first act of

418 DANIEL HEINSIUS, AURIACUS: COMMENTARY

Pha. This other character elucidates the emotional state of the protagonist, just like in Seneca's drama, where a *nutrix* often tries to calm him or her. Heinsius is following the usual Senecan pattern: after an 'Affektrede' on the part of the protagonist this other character reacts to the protagonist's feelings, see Tarrant, *Seneca Agamemnon*, p. 192.

The *senex* sees external signs that betray Loisa's mood, as usual in Senecan drama. Here the most striking features are "pallor", caused by grief, as in (for example) Sen. *Herc. Oet.* 252: "Pallor ruborem pellit" and *Aga.* 762: "pallentes genae", and the tears, indicated with "guttae" and "lacrimosus [...] liquor".

Some elements from Sen. *Pha.* 1, 1 and this scene chime with one another: cf. *Pha.* 100–101: "non me quies nocturna, non altus sopor solvere curis" with *Aur.* 482–483; and for the ways in which the *nutrix* and the *senex* address the protagonist, cf. *Pha.* 129: "Thesea coniunx, clara progenies Iovis" with *Aur.* 487–489. The *senex* addresses the princess in a manner befitting his lower position, also indicating that she, a princess, should not cry. Thirdly Orange/Auriacus is ranked above de Coligny. In classical tragedies characters often address one another with periphrases, cf. Sen. *Aga.* 125: "Regina Danaum et inclutum Ledae genus", and *Herc. f.* 413: "es rege coniunx digna"; on this, see (for instance) Frank, *Seneca's Phoenissae*, pp. 75 and 78 and Sutton 1986, p. 57. For the combination "dignata [...] toro", cf. Molza, *Catharina Henrico VIII. Regi Angliae* 92: "Et Tecmessa toro principe digna fuit".

The *senex* asks Loisa in an *amplificatio* why she is aggrieved in several ways, emphasizing his question with: "mentis abdita exonera et aegrum pectus" (ll. 494–495). For the "mentis abdita", cf. Ov. *Met.* XI, 149: "praecordia mentis", and cf. Petr. 133, 3: "exonera mentem". Loisa answers the last question "Meroris ah quae causa?" with the oxymoron "Omnia et nihil", a stylistically, psychologically and dramaturgically strong answer, which makes the audience *attentus*. Then the *senex* asks: "An ipse sese nescit infelix dolor?", i.e. the cause or the character of your grief. Loisa's reaction limits itself to "nescit", which she resumes in a 'Stichworttechnik' (keyword technique, Bernd Seidensticker, *Die Gesprächsverdichtung in den Tragödien Senecas* (Heidelberg: C. Winter, [1969]), pp. 25–36) in "ambiguus" (the cause and character are unknown, see *OLD* s.v. ambiguus 1b). The antithesis of "omnia et nihil" returns in "ambiguus" and "certus", and in "milies" and "semel" (l. 497). The *senex* resumes (upon Loisa's "certus") the "nescit" (l. 496) in the metaphor of a whiplash: anyone fearing the strokes that fate inflicts, fears rightly, because he knows the origins of his "dolor" and his "cicatrix", and the wound itself. In another Senecan 'Stichworttechnik', Loisa responds to "dum scit" with "dum nescit" (l. 501). The implications of "plura" could be (1) a response to awareness of the wound: anyone unaware of the wound and having more things of which she is unaware, or (2) adverbially, a response to "merito pavet": he fears rightly, but more rightly he is afraid when he does not know the origin of the grief or the scar and the wound. However, such adverbial use of "plura" would be unparalleled.

Thus Loisa's answer goes into the measure of grief. Here, too, she resumes the uncertainty with "caecus" (l. 502). Remarkably, in all these *sententiae* with regard to grief and fear, knowledge is alluded to. For Seneca's treatment of feelings in terms of knowledge, cf. the comm. on l. 405.

Again in a 'Stichworttechnik' the *senex* resumes Loisa's "luget" and turns the conversation round: grief for future. His *sententiae* are typographically marked (cf. l. 58), and he proffers that whoever mourns what will happen, already mourns and appeals what he avoids. Indirectly he reproaches her revelling in sorrow (cf. Sen. *Marc.* 1, 7: "Fit infelicis animi prava voluptas dolor").

In the end Loisa gives the *senex* an explanation for her fear (cf. ll. 480–486 and the comm.): it was a dream that showed up. She does not give any of the *t.t.* for dreams, such as "somnium", "visio", "oraculum" or "insomnium" (see Veenstra, 'Dromen zonder Freud', p. 599), but calls her dream 'images of the night' and 'predicting sleep', attesting to Heinsius' predilection for periphrasis (see the comm. *ad* ll. 544–545).

The entire dialogue is sutured together by means of keywords and repetitions. It changes its subject (from cause and character of grief through its measure to grief for the future); the *senex* tries to give Loisa some insight into her grief and urges her to moderate her sadness, in vain.

488 *columen* Cf. Sen. *Tro.* 124: "columen patriae [Hector]" and *id. Oct.* 168: "columen augustae domus [Brittannicus]"; also *Pho.* 1–2: "fessi unicum patris levamen", see Frank, *Seneca's Phoenissae*, p. 77.

488 *magnanimi* In Sen. *Herc. f.* 310 "magnanimus" is used for Hercules. For its epic ring and the recollection of the Homeric μεγάθυμος, see Fitch, *Seneca's Hercules Furens*, p. 211 and Eduard Norden, *P. Vergilius Maro Aeneis Buch VI* (Leipzig, etc.: Teubner, 1926), p. 223 *ad* Verg. *Aen.* VI, 307; also *ibid.* VI, 649: "magnanimi heroes" and *Aur.* 1280, 1728 and 1730. See also Van Campen, *Lucanus Bellum Civile Liber II*, p. 195, Veenstra, *Ethiek en moraal*, pp. 45–49, and Heitmann, *Fortuna und Virtus*, p. 65 and n. 39.

497 *ambiguus ... semel* Do these words concern an unknown reason, or an undefined grief?

498 *Sortis flagello quisquis adversae stupet* Cf. Heinsius *In miseros mortem optantes* 6: "sortis flagello raptus adversae tremis".

504 *et modum sui [sc. nescit]* (1) grief does not know its size, or (2) is unmeasured.

508 *Gaudetque-fuit* For the thought, cf. Sen. *Thy.* 445: "Miser esse mavult qui felix potest?" and *Aga.* 664: "lacrimas lacrimis miscere iuva".

509 *succubuit animus* For such a description, cf. (for example) Sen. *Aga.* 5: "Horruit animus", *Med.* 670: "Pavet animus, horret", and *Aur.* 366, 1871–1874 and the comm.

L 489–491 These lines became: 'Tell me why a deep pallor and a sadness occupy your sad cheeks and make your bosom tepid by shedding tears'.
L 492 In the Leiden copy, Heinsius intensified the image by turning it into tears 'bursting' out the eyes.
L 493–494 The "rubor", contradicting "pallor" (l. 490) has been removed, and the explicit question as to the cause of grief has been changed into: 'and is your face damp in spite of itself?'
L 496 Lack of knowledge becomes consciously cheating ("sese fallit").

    Operation and origin of dreams

513–558 *At falsus—verè doles* The Old Man tries to calm Loisa with the argument that dreams are deceitful. He explains this with a dream theory, in which he (without knowing it) gives the same explanation as Loisa (see l. 486 and the comm.): Worries during the day appear at night in the mind's eye. On awakening the dream disappears, but the feeling of fear remains. This creates an interaction between day and night, between worries and dreams. The statement Heinsius assigned to Loisa in a few words is amplified in the *senex*.

He classifies Loisa's dream as a nightmare, cf. Macrobius in his comment on Cicero's *Somnium* 3, 4: "Est enim ἐνύπνιον quotiens cura oppressi animi corporisve sive fortunae, qualis vigilantem fatigaverat, talem se ingerit dormienti"; see also Veenstra, 'Dromen zonder Freud', p. 599. Such *insomnia* are by definition deceitful, cf. Verg. *Aen.* VI, 896: "falsa [...] insomnia". In this respect, the *senex* ignores the fact that Loisa, as a high person probably dreamed a true dream, cf. Veenstra, *op. cit.*, p. 608.

What is striking is the fierceness of the emotions that the *senex* describes: "acres [...] motus" (l. 521), "fervet et sese rapit" (l. 522), "metuque pallet gaudioque diffluit" (l. 523). The mind goes where it wants and holds the impressions. Thus things can be seen that do not exist (l. 530). The night binds the body, but leaves the mind free.

The question is whether "somnus" (ll. 517, 545) is sleep or, metonymically, the dream, cf. "somnia" (ll. 550, 555).

The passage is modelled after similar passages in Seneca's drama, cf. for "verisque falsa miscet" (l. 546) Sen. *Herc. f.* 1070: "veris miscens falsa" and the surrounding verses (which in turn imitate Ov. *Met.* XI, 623–628).

526 *huc illhuc* Cf. Sen. *Tro.* 458: "nunc huc, nunc" and *Aur.* 536: "Hinc inde".

527–528 *quidquid potest, simulque quidquid haud potest* The latter addition allows for two interpretations: (1) in the dream 'impossible' things are possible; or (2) this is an instance of polar oppositions with a reinforcing force (see J.D. Meerwaldt, 'Polaire tegenstellingen met eenzijdig versterkende kracht', in: *id.*, *Vormaspecten* (The Hague: A.A.M. Stols, 1958), pp. 71–88)—in other words, the mind really does think of everything.

539 *seminaque rerum* Events leave 'seeds' in the mind, so to speak, which are by definition images.

543 *in postscenio* Cf. Lucr. IV, 1186: "postscaenia vitae", in the background. The metaphor of the stage continues in the next line.

544 *Mimus diei, ludibundus histrio* In *De tragica constitutione* (1611), Heinsius criticizes these expressions from a stylistic point of view: "neque somnum mimum diei aut ludibundum histrionem [sc. dicam]" (*Trag. const.*, p. 216, cf. Heinsius, *On Plot in Tragedy*, pp. 121 and 141). In his own copy Heinsius underlined the words "postscenio" and "ludibundus", probably since they did not fulfil his ideas any more. See also the intr., p. 46.

545 *Proteusque* The prophesying sea god Proteus often changed his shape. On him, see Roscher 3, 3172–3178 and *RE* 23, 940–975. See (for instance) Ov. *Met.* II, 9: "Proteaque ambiguum" and Bömer's comm. 1, p. 240 *ad loc.*; also Stat. *Ach.* I, 32: "Agnosco monitus et Protea vera locutum", Grudius *Sylvae* I, 1, 24 (p. 152): "varius [...] Proteus"; Stephanus, *Dictionarium*, p. 368r; a prototype of cunning Hor. *Sat.* II, 3, 71: "effugiet tamen haec sceleratus vincula Proteus". Like Proteus, the dream changes everything, see also Bömer's comm. 4, pp. 238–239 *ad* Ov. *Met.* VIII, 731.

545 *vitae futilis Somnus pater* This is a position against the image of Sleep as giver of the better part of life (Sen. *Herc. f.* 1067, see above); it gives a 'dream life' that is 'futilis'.

547 *ceraeque adinstar* The image of the soul as a clog of wax is traced back to Plato *Theaet.* 191C–E, where Socrates compares the soul to a block of wax where the impressions form the recollection. Aristotle (*Anim.* 3.4.429b–430a) compares thoughts with writing on a tablet. Elaborating on this, Albertus Magnus (*De anima* III, 2, 17) and Thomas Aquinas (*Summa Theologiae* I, 79, 2) were able to speak of the soul as a "tabula rasa".

550 *laruataque ... somnia* The word "larvatus" here is not 'devilish', 'frenzied' (*OLD* s.v.). but 'spooky'. Perhaps the meaning is provided with a *larva*, a frightening mask, a continuation of the stage metaphor of ll. 543–544. This meaning is not attested for antiquity (not in *OLD* and *TLL*), but occurs in (for example) Macropedius *Aluta* (1535), Argumentum 9: "larvata reti luditur" and 456 "larvata faciem". Such *composita* with the suffix -tus mean 'provided with'. For

'larva' as mask, cf. (for example) Hor. *Sat.* 1, 5, 64: "nil illi larva aut tragicis opus esse cothurnis". The dreams as actors wear masks with which they frighten her.

L 526   Heinsius changed "adiudicatus" into "destinatus", more in keeping with Stoic Nature (see the comm. on ll. 1–4).
L 526   This line became: 'he breaks through the routes determined by the law of nature with his powerless wings and transcends them'.
L 533   Heinsius added: 'But when Phoebus has extinguished his radiant torch, the *aer* lights up, variegated with the golden sisters [the stars] of Phoebe, and light-heartedly the brothers pull the chariot of their father'.
L 536   In the Leiden copy, Heinsius added: 'and sleep occupies the heart when the light wanes. Then the soft god conquers the subdued mind and [...]'. Now in the following lines Morpheus is the subject, which is more logical.
L 543–544   For the underlined words, see above, the comm. on l. 544.
L 550   On second thoughts, Heinsius changes "incutere" into the more neutral "inducere".
L 556   Heinsius changed "at" into "hoc", probably because of the tautology of "at" and "tamen".

The attitude towards sadness

559–574 *Experta metuo—amore populi*   Now the conversation takes a slightly different turn: Loisa knew misery well, an allusion to St Bartholomew's Night in which her father and first husband died (see *ad* l. 1210). This is in response to the last remark of the *senex*: "quodque esse falsò reris" (l. 558): she has already experienced the murder of her husband, so she will probably be right.

Now the conversation continues in *sententiae* with regard to falsehood and its effect: error fills the fire of reason in darkness; it is pleasant in misery to deceive oneself (a reproach to the *senex* who tries to reassure Loisa); "falsa dum latent tamen ut vera laedunt", which one might paraphrase as 'whoever does not know that it is deception, thinks that it is real and because of this, it causes grief'. In short, Loisa's argument is reversed. The thought (and topos) that fate causes fear before it actually asserts its influence is repeated in an *amplificatio*.

559 *experta metuo*   Cf. *Thy.* 453: "expertus loquor".
563 *aetheris beate rex*   See the comm. *ad* l. 1. The lord of the ether Jupiter here is the god of weather, since tears are metonymically called 'rain', see Roscher 2, 618–672 s.v. Iuppiter; on Jupiter as god of weather, esp. 651–652.

566 saeva sors Cf. Sen. *Pha.* 991: "sors acerba et dura" and *Med.* 431: "O dura fata semper et sortem asperam".

L 563 "Aetheris beate rex" is changed into "Aetheris magni pater", maybe because "beatus" is more commonly used for deceased humans.

Everywhere at home

574–608 Haud tangit—quicumque princeps Against the Old Man's argument that her husband is safe through the love of his people, Loisa brings in Orange's foreign (German) descent. He was, after all, born at the Dillenburg and later a courtier from Brussels, no Dutchman.

For the idea that foreign rulers do not last long (l. 574) cf. Sen. *Herc. f.* 344–345: "Alieno in loco haud stabile regnum est"; cf. also Sen. *Tro.* 258: "Violenta nemo imperia continuit diu"; see also Otto, *Sprichwörter*, p. 296 s.v. regnum 3.

Then the *senex* states that princes, demigods, are at home everywhere, and compares them to the sun. For the idea that princes are almost gods, cf. Lipsius *Const.* I, 9 and Sen. *V.B.* 20, 5, and other places (Van de Bilt, *Lipsius en Seneca*, pp. 71–72 and 113–114). Lipsius mentions heaven as homeland in *Const.* I, 11.

The thought that a good, brave or high-minded man is at home everywhere is topical, esp. in the Stoa, see (for example) Sen. *Ep.* 28,4: "Non sum uni angulo natus, patria mea totus hic mundus est", but can also be read in, for instance, Ov. *Fast.* I, 493: "Omne solum forti patria est". For Greek examples and some Latin instances of this proverbial expression, see Bömer, *Ovidius Fasten*, p. 56 ad loc. Mieke B. Smits-Veldt, *Samuel Coster ethicus-didacticus: Een onderzoek naar dramatische opzet en morele instructie van lthys, Polyxena en Iphigenia* (Groningen: Wolters Noordhoff/Forsten, 1986) Neerlandica Traiectina, 29, Doctoral thesis Amsterdam, pp. 4–9, relates a similar thought, Samuel Coster's motto "OVER.AL.THUYS", to the printers' mark of the book trader and printer Blaublom: "Tecum habita". Cf. Socrates' words in Cic. *Tusc.* V, 37, 108: "Patria est, ubicumque est bene. Socrates quidem cum rogaretur cuiatem se esse diceret, 'mundanum' inquit; totius enim mundi se incolam et civem arbitrabatur".

594 Titana "Titan" is a fashionable metonym for the sun in poets of silver Latinity, and in Seneca is the most common indication for the sun (Tarrant, *Seneca Agamemnon*, pp. 334–335 *ad* Sen. *Aga.* 908 and Fantham, *Seneca's Troades*, p. 233 *ad Tro.* 170; an enumeration of places where Titan indicates the sun is given by Canter, *Rhetorical Elements*, pp. 132–133). Stephanus, *Dictiona-*

rium, p. 431v explains, s.v. Titan: "Ex Titanum numero fuit Hyperion, pater solis: quo factum est, ut poetae Titanem non raro pro ipso accipiant Sole".

604 *Thetyos* The use of the sea goddess Tethys to indicate the sea is a poetic metonym, having occurred since the Alexandrian poets and introduced in Roman poetry by Catullus (66, 70; 88, 5). It also occurs in Seneca and Lucan, see also Fitch on Sen. *Herc. f.* 887; also *Aur.* 1144, 1777, cf. Canter, *Rhetorical Elements*, p. 132. Yet metonymy and a personal presentation of Tethys are intertwined, cf. Ov. *Met.* 11, 68–69: "quae me subiectis excipit undis [...] Tethys" and Bömer, *Ovidius Metamorphosen* 1, p. 258 *ad loc.* Titan is a son of Tethys' brother Hyperion; "suae" will aim at this kinship. On the genealogy of the sun god, see Roscher 1, 1993–2026 s.v. Helios, esp. 2015–2016. Clearly this does not denote the mother of Achilles, Thetis, but rather the sea goddess Tethys. Hence in his own copy Heinsius corrected the spelling to "Tethyos". On both goddesses, see Stephanus, *Dictionarium*, p. 421r s.v. Tethys and 425r s.v. Thetis respectively.

L 589   "Generosus" became "sublimis", maybe because the original word was associated with 'genus'.

L 600   The *participium perfecti* "purpurato" gave way to the *participium praesentis* "purpurante", which made the construction an *ablativus absolutus*: "or when he is reborn at the moment the room is red, [...]".

L 604   See the comm. *ad loc.*

L 606   Maybe "fervor" (cf. l. 180) became "ardor" because of the derivation of 'cooking' and 'burning', the former indicating heat from outside, the latter a fire from inside.

Unreasonable sadness

608–610 *Omnia et scio—causa est metus* Loisa is now exactly the same as she was at the beginning of the scene: afraid of a dream that she rationally knows is deceit.

610 *Metusque causae nescius, causa est metus* The scene is ended with an artful *sententia* consisting of the double *polyptoton* (causae/causa and metus/metus—nom./gen.), and in a 'golden line' (metus—metus). For the thought, cf. l. 497 and Sen. *Herc. f.* 316: "prona est timoris semper in peius fides".

Act II, Chorus (611–737)

Summary

On the occasion of their imminent exile, the Flemish emigrants reflect about their stuffy position, set against a pastoral idyll.

611–627 The choir addresses the softly blowing, dewy westerly wind that floats over the water, or visits places where shepherds and shepherdesses feed their sheep and play their reed flute, people who are unfamiliar with misery.

627–633 Then the choir asks in despair where it will end up. In any case it will leave their beloved Flanders. One comfort remains: at the same time they will be leaving the Spaniards.

634–653 The unknown host country is being addressed, and the dawn. This dispels sleep, which makes worry forgotten, and so by dispelling sleep brings back the concerns.

654–661 Simplicity has now left human civilization and settled in distant regions, where each man runs its own house in a nomadic life.

662–710 There you can see animals living peacefully and hear the cricket. The chorus directs an apostrophe to this animal, which can chirp without worries, glistening with dew, and live in the shade of flowers. The war and the dangerous court are unknown to him. His realm consists of roses and grass, a flower or a reed hall is his palace, where he announces the dawn to the peasants. Not attacked by the Spaniards he does not have to protect himself with walls, living in complete peace, in the vicinity of the farmers for whom he makes the work more pleasant, and he does not know Alva and the Spaniards.

711–714 On the other hand, people are subject to the vagaries of fate.

715–728 However, low-ranking individuals have less to fear. But in general people are concerned. Emotionally, the chorus exclaims that rulers always want to possess more power. Tyrants and their courts must therefore disappear. High palaces have many worries.

728–735 The house of the chorus members should therefore be small: there may not be much room for the residents, but no space for cares. Their court will consist of their cottage, their people and their children.

735–737 The fall of him whose downfall entails the collapse of the world is too big.

This chorus song is built on the contrast between idyll and reality. The choir surrendered to musings about the idyllic landscape, using the cricket as a symbol of rest and the carefree life, by means of which it refers to Flanders in its former peaceful state. This idyll contrasts with the current miserable situation of Spanish rule and of imminent exile, as well as with court life.

The pastoral situation has a slightly erotic atmosphere, with the tamarisks and violets (ll. 613–615), which occur in pastoral poetry (for the tamarisk cf., for instance, Theocr, 1, 13; 5, 101 and Ecclesiastes 4, 2; 8, 54; 10, 13; for the violets cf. Secundus *Basia* 1, 2: "sopitum teneris imposuit violis"). The erotic atmosphere becomes somewhat more pronounced as the shepherdess Amaryllis makes a reed flute for the shepherd Thyrsis (ll. 623–625). This erotic framework is common in pastoral poetry, see Mieke B. Smits-Veldt and Hans Luijten, 'Nederlandse pastorale poëzie in de 17de eeuw: Verliefde en wijze herders', in: Peter van den Brink and Jos de Meyere (eds), *Het Gedroomde Land: Pastorale schilderkunst in de Gouden Eeuw*, Catalogue Utrecht (Zwolle: Waanders, [1993]), pp. 58–75, esp. pp. 58–62.

The idyll has characteristics of the *locus amoenus*: a shady, natural place, with trees, a meadow and a spring or brook (Curtius, *European Literature and Latin Middle Ages*, pp. 195–200, also Klaus Garber, *Der locus amoenus und der locus terribilis: Bild und Funktion der Natur in der deutschen Schäfer- und Landlebendichtung des 17. Jahrhunderts* (Köln etc.: Böhlau Verlag, 1974) Literatur und Leben, N.F., 16, pp. 86–111 and the literature mentioned there). Such a description of the simple life, combined with the topos 'live secretly', can be found in the first chorus song of Sen. *Herc. f.* 125–201. The contrast between the idealized country life and the rejected life at court, tracing back to Hor. *Epode* 2 ("Beatus ille [...]") is common in pastoral poetry, see Smits-Veldt and Luijten, *loc. cit.*, pp. 62–67.

The place of action is probably Flanders, since the chorus does not yet know where they will go. The chorus addresses dawn, so the song should probably be situated at daybreak, just like the previous scene; again the temporal structure is indicated. Furthermore, one is inclined to take the blowing of the west wind as another time indication denoting spring, due to its use in the literary tradition to indicate the coming of spring. In which case it would not only be the place but also the time of the year that would differ from the main action, i.e. Delft and summer. The first chorus of the Hollanders (ll. 1341–1405) is a spring song about the cosmic marriage between sun and moon, which makes everything blossom. The 'springtime' may also relate to Ovid's representation of the Golden Age as "ver aeternum" (*Met.* 1.107).

Metre

This song is written in anapaestic dimeters, interspersed with three monometers that can also be interpreted as *adonei* (-vv-x). The author, however, only had the indication "Anapaestici" printed above the song. Because of this, and because Grotius put above the first choral song in his *Adamus exul* (*Auriacus* is undoubtedly written in competition with this piece, see intr., p. 5) "Anapaestici Dimetri et Monometri", in which the 'monometri' could also in most cases be read as *adonei*, the three short lines in this song should be interpreted as anapaestic metres.

Anapaests are also common in the chorus songs in Seneca's drama, also in combination with *adonei*, see (for example) *Herc. f.* 125–203. In ancient Greek drama and in that of Seneca they are often associated with lamentations. See above, p. 381 and Crusius-Rubenbauer, *Römische Metrik*, pp. 122–123.

Commentary

The idyll of the west wind

611–627 *O qui—sortisque vagae* The chorus addresses Favonius, the mild west wind, blowing idyllically. In the first line the blowing is expressed in a metaphor derived from riding in a stringing wagon (*OLD* s.v. veho 3a and 5b; the "habenae" are metonyms for the wagon), cf. Sen. *Pha.* and see the comm. on l. 668. Favonius (or Zephyrus, l. 668) blew at the beginning of spring and advanced the growing of plants, cf. Plin. *N.H.* 11, 47,46 §119 and see *RE* 2.R. 10, 234–235 s.v. Zephyros. Serv. Verg. *Ge.* 1, 43 gives as the etymology τὸ ζῆν φέρων. One of its features is a slight moisture, see Bömer, *Ovidius Metamorphosen* 1, p. 37 *ad* Ov. *Met.* 1, 64; thus he also brings dew ("roris genitor", l. 612), cf. for instance Sen. *Pha.* 11: "rorifera mulcens aura Zephyrus".

The contrast between idyll and reality is already implicit in the first lines with the name Tityrus (l. 622), an allusion to Verg. *Ecl.* 1, where Tityrus is allowed to stay, whereas Meliboeus (here the Flemings) has to go into exile. Furthermore, the shepherdess of goats Amaryllis (l. 623) occurs in Verg. *Ecl.* (1, 5, also 8, 77), and in Ov. *Ars* 2, 267; *Tr.* 11, 537. The shepherd Thyrsis is one of the interlocutors in Verg. *Ecl.* 1, where Virgil adopted the three pastoral names from Theocr. *Id.* (e.g. in 3, 2 Tityrus appears; *Id.* 3 is devoted to Amaryllis and in *Id.* 1 Thyrsis plays a part).

624 *tibi* Either to "condit" or to "dulcem".
625 *felix* Either to Thyrsis, or to Amaryllis, or ἀπὸ κοινοῦ; in any case, it suits the bucolic atmosphere.

L 614 The tamarisks become 'always moist', adding to the unity of the song (cf. l. 612 "roris").

L 617 'To play' becomes 'to live', giving a closer relation to "pastus". The element of play is also somewhat removed, cf. l. 621.

L 619 Amplifying this, Heinsius added 'the dewy caves and the nests of birds'.

L 621 The simple sheep become 'carefree' instead of 'frisky', removing the element of play.

L 623 'Sweet Amaryllis' becomes 'the golden Phyllis'; perhaps this has to do with the sad ending of Theocr. *Id.* 3, where Amaryllis does not wish to hear the complaints of the I.

Exile

627–633 *Quam palantes—Iberus* The chorus sighs that, wherever they will end up, they will in any case be leaving their beloved Flanders, but fortunately everything that is called Spaniard as well.

627–628 *Quam ... prendimus oram* Cf. Verg. *Aen.* VI, 61: "iam tandem Italiae fugientis prendimus oras" and II, 322: "quam prendimus arcem?" These allusions associate the journey of the Flemings with Aeneas' journey from his destroyed city of Troy to the new homeland Italy.

629 *certe* For the meaning 'in any case', cf. Sen. *Pha.* 433; see *OLD* s.v. 26 and *TLL* 3, 937–938, s.v. B3b.

629–633 *Placitas—Iberus* The idea of leaving a fatherland and looking for another one is common, but a famous locus is Verg. *Ecl.* 1, 3–4: "Nos patriae fines et dulcia linquimus arva. Nos patriam fugimus". The fatherland is not the soil of birth, but the country where one is at home, as in (for example) Verg. *Ge.* II, 512: "Alio patriam quaerunt sub sole iacentem".

L 628 The coast is not 'taken' any more, but 'touched', both meaning 'to reach', but Heinsius may have considered "prendere" having too much an overtone of usurpation.

L 629 The pathetic element is sharpened by changing 'to leave' into 'to flee' (also in l. 631).

Dawn returns the cares

634–653 *Salvete tamen—curae* Although the dawn chases away the darkness (ll. 637–639), it also brings back the worries that one might have forgotten about during sleep, see already Verg. *Aen.* XI, 182–183: "Aurora interea miseris mortalibus almam extulerat lucem, referens opera atque labores"; see also *Aur.* 551–553 and 1552–1554: "Rex astrorum luce renata tremulos noctis clauserat ignes

Phosphorus". For greeting an (unknown) country, cf. Verg. *Aen.* VII, 120: "Salve fatis mihi debita tellus" and Sen. *Aga.* 783: "O cara salve terra". "Salvere" has a solemn, almost sacred ring.

638 *Aurora parens* "Parens" as adjective for Aurora may seem strange, but here she is returning light (cf. ll. 635–636 "lucis aurea mater" and see *OLD* s.v. parens 5); moreover, she is the mother of Phosphorus/Hesperus (ll. 640–645). Cf. also Sen. *Pha.* 959: "parens Natura" and *Aur.* 1, 38, 106, 131, 175, 233, 1895.

640–645 *Phosphorus ... Hesperus* For the planet Venus being both morning and evening star, see Roscher 3, 2519–2522. The change of name is topical, see (for example) Sen. *Aga.* 820–821: "Nomen alternis stella quae mutat seque mirata est Hesperum dici"; *id. Pha.* 750–752: "Lotus undis Hesperus, pulsis iterum tenebris Lucifer idem"; see also Cic. *N.D.* II, 20, 53, and cf. Grotius *Ad. ex.* 253–259: "Talis [...] fax Luciferi [...] fulget, quae mutato nomine surgens dux tenebrarum [...] exit Hesperus idem", and see the comm. *ad loc.* in Grotius, *Dichtwerken/Poetry* I, 1A/B, p. 35. This star is a daughter of Astraeus and Aurora. See also Stephanus, *Dictionarium*, p. 279r s.v. Lucifer: "Vna errantium stellarum, quam et Venerem appellamus, quae mane Solem praecedens unaque cum Aurora sese ostendens (unde et Aurorae filius fingitur) Lucifer dicitur: vesperi autem Solem subsequens, Hesperus nominatus".

Heinsius is using the Greek forms instead of the more common Latin Lucifer and Vesper. In Latin literature Phosphorus is rare, cf. inter alia Sen. *Herc. f.* 128: "Cogit nitidum Phosphoros agmen", see Fitch, *Seneca's Hercules Furens*, p. 164 *ad loc.* Also in *Aur.* 1552–1554.

649 *nos* One may add "fugimus" (we flee the gift of sleep) or "fugiunt" (the gifts of sleep flee us). The latter is associated with classical notions of emotions approaching people.

L 630 The adjective to Flanders morphed from 'beloved' through 'shady' to the pathetic "erepta" (stolen).

L 631 See l. 629 and the comm. *ad loc.*

L 642 The stars no longer flee 'unwillingly' but 'slowly' whereas the notion of pink remains, although Heinsius tried 'saffron'.

Simplicity leaving

654–661 *At Simplicitas—ferarum* A personification of Simplicitas in itself is new, although it is comparable to the goddess of justice Astraea or Iustitia, Ov. *Met.* I, 149–150: "Et virgo caede madentis ultima caelestum terras Astraea reliquit"; Verg. *Ge.* II, 473–474: "Extrema per illos Iustitia excedens terris vestigia fecit"; also in Sen. *Oct.* 423–425 Astraea leaves the earth; in Iuv. 6, 14–20 she does so together with Pudicitia, and in Sil. 11, 496 Fides leaves the earth. In Claud. *In Ruf.* 1, 354–387 it is Iustitia. For more parallels, see Grotius, *Dichtwerken/Poetry* 1, 2 3A/B, p. 97.

In these lines Simplicitas—in contrast to Astraea, Pudicitia and Fides—is not going to heaven, but to simple tribes: Taurians and Massagetes (as did Iustitia in Verg.). Simplicitas, the carefree life of shepherds and farmers, has left with the coming of the Spaniards.

655 *Taurosque* These inhabitants of the Chersonesus Taurica (now Crimea at the Bosporus) are symbolic for an 'uncivilized' (here: carefree) life and a remote country, cf. Sen. *Oct.* 980: "et Taurorum barbara tellus"; Cic. *Rep.* III, 15; Ov. *Pont.* III, 2, 45; Mela 2, 11 reports that they sacrifice strangers to Diana.

656 *Massagetas* This nomadic tribe in Scythia is living a remote (Hor. *C.* I, 35, 40: "Retusum in Massagetas Arabasque ferrum") and rough life (Sen. *Oed.* 470: "Lactea Massagetes qui pocula sanguine miscet"). Strictly speaking only the Massagetes live the nomadic life mentioned in ll. 658–660. See Stephanus, *Dictionarium*, p. 394r s.v. Scythia and *RE* 14, 2123.

L 654 Perhaps to obscure the personification, Heinsius deleted the capital in his own copy.

The carefree cricket

662–710 *Cernis—Iberque* The cricket (cicada, τέττιξ) is common in pastoral poetry, feeding itself with dew drops, e.g. Theocr. 4, 16 and Verg. *Ecl.* 5, 77: "dum [pascentur] rore cicadae"; *Aur.* 667. Aristot. *Hist. an.* V, 30 (556b) and Plin. *N.H.* XI, 32 (93–94) also mention this, see Cats, *Sinne- en minnebeelden*, ed. Luijten 2, pp. 305–306, D. 5.

Furthermore, cicadas in the pastoral are chirping pleasantly, as in Theocr. 7, 139, Verg. *Ecl.* 2, 13: "At me cum raucis [...] resonant arbusta cicadis" and *id. Ge.* III, 328: "Cantu querulae rumpent arbusta cicadae"; cf. *Aur.* 684–685: "lepido [...] ore"; 693: "garrula" and 702–703: "plena, plena [...] voce". For example, if the cricket indicates the working hours for the farmers, it may be an elaboration of Theocr. 5, 110–111: τοὶ τέττιγες, ὁρῆτε τὸν αἰπόλον ὡς ἐρεθίζω· οὕτω κύμμες θην ἐρεθίζετε τὼς καλαμευτάς ('See, crickets, see how vexed he be! See master Goatherd boiling! 'Tis even so you vex, I trow, the reapers at their toiling', trans. J.M. Edmonds). The time of the cricket chirp depends on the species, the climate and the temperature, but in the temperate climate of northern Europe crickets are silent in the morning and start to chirp at eleven o'clock at the earliest.

As Heinsius presents it, the apostrophe to the cricket is unparalleled. What is striking is the antithesis between what the cricket has and does not have: no fear for Spaniards, no court, but simplicity and carefreeness. Furthermore, the hymnic, almost sacred atmosphere is striking, evoked by the anaphoric repetition of "tu", cf. Sen. *Her. f.* 299–301. See also Eduard Norden, *Agnostos Theos: Untersuchungen zur Formengeschichte religiöser Rede* (Darmstadt: Wissenschaftliche Buchgesellschaft, 1956 [= Leipzig, etc.: Teubner, 1913]), pp. 149–163 and Nisbet-Hubbard 1, p. 131 *ad* Hor. *C.* I, 10, 9. The apostrophe in itself, frequently used in the chorus songs of Seneca's drama, adds to the liveliness and pathos (Fitch, *Seneca's Hercules Furens*, p. 178 on Sen. *Herc. f.* 186 f. and Konst, *De hartstochten in de tragedie*, e.g. p. 91).

662 *Cernis, cernis* Either used indefinitely ('one', 'people') or addressed to the cricket.

668 *Zephyri* Zephyrus (Ζέφυρος) is Greek name of Favonius, the mild west wind, associated with moisture and the coming of spring, see Bömer's comm. 1, p. 37 *ad* Ov. *Met.* I, 64; cf. Sen. *Pha.* 9–12: "Hac, hac [...] qua prata iacent quae rorifera mulcens aura Zephyrus vernas evocat herbas". Other loci in *OLD* s.v. Cf. also *Aur.* 616 (Favonius) and see the comm. *ad* ll. 616–627.

692–693 *mulgensque ... succos* The cricket feeds on dew, see the comm. on ll. 662–710.

698 *daedaleae* Lucretius uses "daedalus" in both an active (artistic) and a passive way (artfully made), e.g. I, 7–8: "Tibi suavis daedala tellus summittit flores". "Daedaleus", used by Heinsius, probably *metri causa*, is actually the adjective to "Daedalus", the Athenian architect.

700 *gramina campi* Cf. Hor. *C.* IV, 7, 1–2: "Redeunt iam gramina campis arboribusque coma".

701 *Felix, felix* For the ellipsis (of "es"), see Frank, *Seneca's Phoenissae*, p. 85 *ad* Sen. *Pho.* 25–26.

710 *Albae nomen, Iberque* "Iber" indicates a Spaniard in general, though here their soldiers will be meant (*totum pro parte*), or the King of Spain. For "Alba" as 'Iron Duke', see intr., p. 15.

L 702 The wandering ("vaga") and the view ("cernis") become admiration ("miraris").

L 709 'To comfort, console' ("solaris") became 'to accompany' ("comitaris").

L 709 Heinsius added a few lines mentioning the evening as the limit for the chirping, where the cricket accompanies the labour of the mowers 'with your lovely and your constant, industrious chirping, until the evening late covers the reddish lights, and the sea goddesses, the copper (one expects "caerula") people of the Ocean bring back Phoebus, wash him in the golden waves of the sea. You remain carefree in your homeland, resident everywhere'.

The position of man

711–714 *Nos—procellae* In these lines the chorus first refers to the infidelity of a 'you', probably the fate of perhaps the Spaniard. Just like the following lines, they refer to the topos of the miserable position of mankind, fate's plaything. Cf. l. 14 and the comm. *ad* ll. 1–5.

712–714 *Nos ludibrium—lususque sumus. Nos ... premit ... turbo procellae* Cf. Heinsius, *De fragilitate rerum* 6: "Lususque rerum, temporumque nascimur" and *ibid.* 9: "Seseque rerum turbidae premunt vices".

L **711–715** These lines become: 'We, sorrowful, are a plaything of unfaithfulness and cunning, of unfair destiny and fate. We always meet the gods with an indefinable wound'.

The miseries of a high position

715–728 *Leviora—curis* For this topos of the changeability of fortune, fate that saves the lower-class and attacks high-ranking people, see the comm. *ad* ll. 1–5, 84–96 and see Sonja F. Witstein, 'Hoofts "Achilles ende Polyxena"', in: *id. Een Wett-steen van de leught: Verzamelde artikelen: Bijeengebracht door Ton Harmsen en Ellen Krol: Met een inleiding van E.K. Grootes* (Groningen: Wolters Noordhoff, 1980) De Nieuwe Taalgids Cahiers, 7, pp. 127–138, esp. pp. 133–134 and Motto, *Seneca Sourcebook*, p. 45 s.v. chance 4 and p. 47 s.v. fortune 11. Examples of the volatility of the fortune that brought rulers to a low state in one go are given by Sen. *Ep.* 47, 10–11.

715–716 *Leviora levis—fata lacessunt* Cf. Sen. *Pha.* 1124–1125: "Minor in parvis Fortuna furit leviusque ferit leviora deus".
726 *aulaque fraudum perfida nutrix* For the topos of the court's fickleness, see (for example) Sen. *Pha.* 982: "Fraus sublimi regnat in aula", *Aga.* 79–81: "Iura pudorque et coniugii sacrata fides fugiunt aulas" and Luc. VIII, 493: "Exeat aula quisquis vult esse pius", and cf. *Aur.* 1217: "aulaeque latebras" and ll. 464–479 and the comm.
727–728 *immensa ... limina* Pars pro toto for palaces, see *OLD* s.v. 2c.

Live secretly

728–735 *Mea tecta—nati* The thought that it is better to live a simple life in a small cottage is topical, a variant on the famous λάθε βιώσας from Epicurus fr. 551 Usener and its Latin version, Ov. *Trist*. II, 4, 25: "Bene qui latuit, bene vixit"; see also Sen. *Aga*. 102–105: "Modicis rebus longius aevum est; felix mediae quisquis turbae sorte quietus aura strinxit litora tuta", *Pha*. 1126–1127: "obscura [...] casa", and 1138–1139: "Non capit umquam magnos motus humilis recti plebeia domus"; *Herc. f*. 196–201: "Me mea tellus lare secreta tutoque tegat. Venit ad pigros cana senectus, humilique loco sed cena sedet sordida parvae fortuna domus; alte virtus animosa cadit". For more *loci* in Seneca's drama, see Fitch, *Seneca's Hercules Furens*, pp. 180–181 *ad loc.*

For the implicit contrast 'alii [...] nos', cf. Tib. I, 1, and (for example) Secundus *Iulia Monobiblos Elegiarum* 1, 1 (Secundus, *Opera omnia*, ed. Bosscha, 1, p. 2).

The idea that in such a life one can see one's own children and grandchildren is also formulated in *Aur*. 2234–2236, q.v.

728–729 *tecta ... angusta* Cf. Iuv. 3, 165: "res angusta domi" and Prop. I, 8, 33: "angusto mecum requiescere lecto". For the meaning of "angustus" as 'poor', 'humble', see *OLD* s.v. 5a; *TLL* 2, 63.45–65 s.v. III (synonym: exiguus).

732 *domus exilis* Hor. *C*. I, 4, 17: "domus exilis Plutonia", and *id. Ep*. I, 6, 45: "exilis domus est".

The fall of a great man

735–737 *Nimium—ictu* For this thought, which indirectly refers to Auriacus/Orange, whose fall is a cosmic catastrophe, cf. ll. 1964–1965: "At cum ruina totius quisquis iacet gemendus illi est". It can also be found in Sen. *Herc. Oet*. 758–762, where Hyllus says to his mother Deianira, Hercules' wife: "Non sola maeres Herculem, toto iacet mundo gemendus. Fata nec, mater, tua privata credas: iam genus totum obstrepit. Hunc ecce luctu quem gemis cuncti gemunt, commune terris omnibus pateris malum". For the parallel between Auriacus/Orange and Hercules, see also the intr., pp. 38–39 and Bloemendal, 'Hercules'.

L 728–729 The roof of the humble house becomes "humilis" instead of "tenuis", because even a lower roof should ward off all fear.

L 733 The home becomes 'honourable', 'uncontested', instead of 'pleasant'.

Act III, Scene 1 (738–1048)

Summary

The assassin, who is very insecure, is being addressed by the commander of the guard. In the following conversation he tells the commander a story about his father who died for his faith.

738–765 The murderer is tossed about between fear and the desire to carry out his plan. He depicts this strong uncertainty in bright colours and compares his unrest with a volcanic eruption, which is first held in check by the earth, but then suddenly bursts upwards.

766–799 Apparently this outburst has come to him: he spurs himself on himself and states that the choice is between the death of Orange and his own. A dream has told him this. In it he had seen a big woman bending over his bed with a torch and shrieking. The murderer cries loudly, and he will follow this divine inspiration, although he does not know where that is leading to.

800–812 The commander asks himself whether the stranger he sees hanging around with signs of unrest, is afraid of a crime or is planning one. The murderer spurs himself on once again.

812–829 A conversation arises between the commander and the murderer. The latter says that he, unhappy as he is, wants to put himself in the service of Orange. He has fled his homeland and wants to go back there.

829–866 When the commander requires about his origin, the killer begs him not to open old wounds by telling all. After a short conversation, an exchange of *sententiae* with regard to expressing feelings, the killer tells his story.

867–947 His father died at the stake for the sake of faith and freedom, leaving his mother as a widow and himself as an orphan. He describes this execution, at which he himself was present, very vividly.

948–967 The commander still does not know why the stranger suddenly got so emotional. He offers freedom and faith as an explanation, as well as deceit of King and Pope, sorrow and bitter poverty, caused because the person who took his father's life also confiscated his property.

967–992 The soldier advises the man to avenge his father by (tragic irony) joining the Prince.

992–1044 The murderer agrees: he swore to avenge his father's fate. He will do so, even though poverty and the thought of the dead have wearied him. On the point of fatigue, he compares himself to an old warhorse, who once again regains his impetus when he hears the war trumpet. Like that horse, the murderer wants to go to war against the Spaniards, to avenge his father. The commander strengthens him in this thought.

1044–1048 The murderer gives assurance that he will return to his homeland in due course. But now he is looking for Orange, who is just arriving at that moment.

Apparently (though this is not shown in the play) the search of Inquisitio and the other Furies has been successful and a *sicarius* (stealthy murderer) has been found. He is significant to the drama as the future murderer of Auriacus/Orange. That is why he remains anonymous and is referred to as a murderer in prolepsis, even though he has not yet earned this designation.

Perhaps as significant as what the killer does say is what he does not talk about. Abstracting from specific current events, Heinsius does not let him specify his descent or the roles his father had, or *expressis verbis* the death of Anjou, who served as a pretext to come to the Prince, see (for example) Frederiks, *De moord van 1584*, pp. 66–67. The latter recurs in one of the preceding Orange plays, Salius, *Nassovius* (1589) 528–531: "Mors recens ducis Andium causas mei ad ventus probabiles feret. Simulabo ferre litteras ad Principem, et fata amici nuntiare tristia". A vague allusion is l. 819 "maximae interpres rei". According to *Een verhael vande moort* the murderer himself said that he wanted to join the Prince, especially after the death of his father (Frederiks, *loc. cit.*, p. 64). Heinsius makes the commander recommend that he do this. This presented additional opportunities for dialogue, to alternate between the monologues.

The third act in Seneca's drama is usually dedicated to a crucial confrontation showing the emotions of the protagonist at their peak (Tarrant, *Seneca Agamemnon*, p. 248). In the case of Auriacus that is, of course, impossible: he maintains his stoic calm. However, the murderer's emotions run high, and Loisa's will do so in the next scene. In this first scene of the third act, the action is dramatically advanced by showing how the killer gets the opportunity to approach the Prince, by dint of the advice of the commander of Auriacus' guards. Furthermore, Heinsius is able to show the man's cunning by making his unpalatable emotion acceptable with a story about his origin known from tradition. This narration of events of secondary importance (also common in Seneca's drama, see Tarrant, *Seneca Agamemnon*, p. 248) gives some relief to the figure of the *sicarius*. This story, albeit a lie, has the capacity to awaken pity on the part of the spectators because of the recognisability of the emotions (see Becker-Cantarino, *Daniel Heinsius*, p. 122). The emphasis he places on his father's old age (ll. 907–917) also increases the pathos of the scene.

The assassin can analyse his feelings fairly objectively, even in his intensely emotional state. This is also a characteristic of Seneca's drama, see Tarrant,

Seneca Agamemnon, pp. 199–200 *ad* Sen. *Aga.* 132 ff. and Fitch, *Seneca's Hercules Furens*, p. 131 *ad Herc. f.* 27–29.

The appearance of a Fury-like figure to the murderer gives Loisa's dream a counterpart, as a result of which both the pro-Orange side and his opponents get a dream scene, albeit that the Inquisitio's appearance to the killer is much less elaborated.

The killer describes the events in fairly explicit terms. With this, Heinsius connects with the 'cruelty' of the post-Augustan poets. Cf. Sen. *Tro.* 1110–1117 and 1156; see also Gordon Williams, *Change and Decline: Roman Literature in the Early Empire* (Berkeley: University of California Press, 1978), p. 73 on the *aemulatio* in descriptions of horrendous wounds.

Metre

The scene is written in iambic trimeters. Line 850 poses a metrical problem, which is solved when 'memoria' is read with synysis of -ia. The same synysis is necessary in ll. 871 and 873: "citius".

Commentary

The murderer's despair

738–752 *Quo? Quo?—nequit* Right at the beginning of his first appearance, the murderer is intensely emotional, wavering between the fervent desire to fulfil his act (which has not yet been specified, though the spectator or reader will know it to be the murder of Orange) and trepidation about carrying it out, despair typical of the drama of Seneca, e.g. *Med.* 123–124: "Incerta vecors mente vesana feror partes in omnes" and *Aga.* 131–144, where Clytemnestra is thrown to and fro between fear and jealousy on the one hand and love on the other (see also the comm. *ad* l. 786, and Regenbogen, 'Schmerz und Tod').

The *sicarius* describes his inner conflict in fierce terms: "feror" (l. 738), a "tempestas" (l. 739) plaguing the sea of his heart, his spirit "exaestuat" (l. 741). Such metaphors are already found in Seneca's drama, e.g. *Med.* 390: "aestuat", *Aga.* 63: "Vexatque animos nova tempestas". See also Canter, *Rhetorical Elements*, pp. 120–122.

Then the metaphor changes from the sea to battle: a "timor" (l. 742) 'hits' the "pectoris votum", which is on the one hand "ardens", and on the other "tremens" (l. 742). Finally, the image derails: the "sedes mentis" (l. 743) is pulled down by fear and fervent desire.

Moreover, the stylistic means—including the questions in l. 738, the *geminatio* and the *ellipsis* in "Quo? Quo?", the antithesis in "ardens tremensque" (l. 742) "metus [...] furor" (l. 744) and the antithetical chiasm in "ardet rursus et rursus nequit" (l. 752)—contribute to the emotionality; on the *elocutio* of the passions, see Konst, *De hartstochten in de tragedie*, pp. 74–124.

The underlying cause for the *sicarius* is the "tempestas dei" (l. 739), thus qualifying his emotions as being of divine origin, probably alluding to the Stoic deity, or fortuna. Cf. Sen. *Aga.* 63: "Vexatque animos nova tempestas". It should not be interpreted as God in the Christian sense, given the double effect that the "tempestas" has ("utroque certe"), unless the "deus" causes the fervent desire and the mind the fear, perhaps also the platonic "furor divinus" (the divine rapture, including the "furor poeticus", see e.g. Marsilio Ficino, *Opera omnia*, intr. Paul Oskar Kristeller, vol. 1 (Torino: Bottega d'Erasmo, 1962), pp. 612–615, and Heinsius, *De poetis et eorum interpretibus*, 1603, published in his *Poemata* (Leiden, Maire, 1610), pp. 481–493), but this seems less likely.

738 urges For "urgere" as an activity of the god, cf. Sen. *Herc. f.* 713–714: "Semel profecto premere felices deus cum coepit, urget".

738 Huccine anne illhuc Cf. (for example) Sen. *Med.* 938–939: "Variamque nunc huc ira, nunc illuc amor diducit?" and *Tro.* 616: "Sed et huc et illuc anxios gressus refert".

741 exaestuatque mens Cf., e.g., Verg. *Aen.* IX, 798: "mens exaestuat ira" and Sen. *Med.*390 (see above).

742 ardens tremensque These words can also be taken with "votum": 'an ambiguous impulse drives the desire of my heart to fervour and fear'.

742 pectoris votum "Votum" is ambiguous, meaning both 'wish' and 'vow'; the former meaning prevails here, since "pectus" is the seat of emotions (*OLD* s.v. 3a). For "votum" as a vow, see ll. 1638–1639.

743 sedemque mentis Cf. Ov. *Met.* XI, 149: "praecordia mentis" and Cic. *Parad.* I, 15: "Mentem e sua sede et statu dimovet".

745–746 cordisque ... vis For the construction in which a substantive takes the place of an adjective ('the power of my heart' for 'my powerful heart'), see the comm. on l. 1188.

750–751 ciet motum reluctans fervor For "ciere" cf. Sen. *Herc. f.* 901: "cuius in laeva ciet aegis feroces ore saxifico minas" and *id. Oed.* 352: "Infausta magnos sacra terrores cient".

L **742** The impulse ("tumor") becomes fear ("timor"). This also has consequences for "ardens tremensque", which instead of 'from desire and fear', becomes 'an uncertain anxiety, intense and vibrant [...]'.

L 743 The seat of the mind becomes the seat of the heart, centre of emotions.

Comparison with a volcanic eruption

753–765 *Sic cum—vapor* In order to characterize the state of mind of the murderer, Heinsius has him use a Homeric comparison. The restrained emotions
that eventually burst out all at once resemble a volcanic eruption: the earth
holds back the eruption for a long time, but eventually it yields. The comparison is intended more to intensify and to visualize in a vivid way than to clarify,
cf. the comm. *ad* ll. 131–168. A starting point for this comparison could have
been Sen. *Herc. f.* 105–106: "Acrior mentem excoquat quam qui caminis ignis
Aetnaeis furit", see also Fitch, *Seneca's Hercules Furens*, pp. 153–154 *ad loc.* and
Pha. 101–103: "Alitur et crescit malum et ardet intus qualis Aetnaeo vapor exundat antro". One could also think of the short didactic poem *Aetna* from the
Appendix Vergiliana, where an explanation is given for how volcanoes work
and come into being, rejecting mythological explanations and mentioning subterranean winds that fan the fire, compared to a smithy (*Aetna* 561–565). Its
example was Lucretius' *De rerum natura*, which also rejects mythological explanations.

The earth ('mother earth') is given human metaphors for intensificiation:
"praecordiis", "viscere" and "nutritur matris occulto in sinu". Such an analogy of
the earth as living being is common in Lucr. (e.g. II, 589–599; also *Aetna* 98–
101). For "praecordia" in a metaphorical sense, cf. Man. 1, 17: "Scire iuvat magni
penitus praecordia mundi"; for "viscere" Ov. *Met.* I, 138: "Itum est in viscera terrae" and Verg. *Aen.* III, 515: "viscera montis". The Notus and Africus (the south
and south-west wind) are the 'bellows' of Mt Etna. This presentation is not classical, although the smithy has bellows, cf. (for example) Verg. *Ge.* IV, 169–172:
"Fervet opus [...] ac veluti lentis Cyclopes fulmina massis cum properant, alii
taurinis follibus auras accipiunt redduntque". Heinsius may have found starting points in Lucr. VI, 680–702, imitated in *Aetna* 158–174. In these passages on
Etna, subterranean caves in which the winds blow are mentioned, see Vincent
J.C. Hunink, 'Ondergrondse stromen', *Lampas* 22 (1989), pp. 22–35.

754 *daedaloque* On this Lucretian word, see the comm. on l. 698. Probably a
first allusion to the smithy of the artist-smith Vulcanus.
756 *Noti ... Africique* Notus, the south wind, also Auster (cf. ll. 1142 and 1768),
is humid and nebulous (see Stephanus, *Dictionarium*, p. 320r and *RE* 17, 1116–
1120). For stormy Africus, the south-west wind, see l. 310 and the comm. *ad*
ll. 300–318.
757 *nutritur ardor* Cf. *Aetna* 281: "quid nutriat ignes".

The decision (1)

766–786 *Quo voluor—dedi ratem* These lines contain the first allusions to the murderer's dream ("portenta horrida", l. 772; "atra mentis omina", l. 773; "umbra", l. 774), the cause of his desperation. He gives two causes: his own mind ("atra mentis omina", l. 773), but mainly 'the deity' ("numen", l. 775). Here too the murderer presents a polarity: a good deity or the opposite, a devilish power. These may be polar oppositions with reinforcing power ('all possible deities', see J.D. Meerwaldt, 'Polaire tegenstellingen met eenzijdig versterkende kracht', in: *id., Vormaspecten* (The Hague: A.A.M. Stols, 1958), pp. 71–88 and see above, n.ll. 527–528), which also serve to intensify the atmosphere— even the murderer is not sure whether it is a good or bad power inciting him.

768–769 *mens ... pectus, masculique spiritus* Cf. Apul. *Met.* VI, 5: "Quin igitur masculum tandem sumis animum". On addressing one's own heart or mind, see Frank, *Seneca's Phoenissae*, p. 92; Williams, *Tradition and Originality*, pp. 461–463 and the comm. *ad* l. 264. For the use of "pectus" by Seneca, cf. Sen. *Tro.* 523 and Fantham, *Seneca's Troades*, pp. 290–291 *ad loc.*

772 *Quis? Quo? Quid? Vnde* This barrage of elliptical questions illustrates the murderer's emotionality. The questions should probably be supplemented as follows: 'Who causes me to act, to where is he driving me, what will he permit me to do, where is the dream that leads me to act?'

773 *obtestor* Cf., e.g., Sen. *Tro.* 28.

783 *rapit deus* The murderer is ἔνθεος, cf. Hor. *C.* III, 25, 1–2: "Quo me, Bacche, rapis tui plenum". In 1603 Heinsius would deliver a speech on poets' enthusiasm, *De poetis et eorum interpretibus.*

784 *nox* Either the night itself or metonym for a dream.

784 *seminatrix* Cf. Cic. *N.D.* III, 66: "Qui est versus omnium seminator malorum".

786 *ventisque ... dedi ratem* Cf. Sen. *Aga.* 143: "Fluctibus dedi ratem" and *ibid.* 443: "Credita est vento ratis". See also *Aur.* 1155.

L **783** In the original text god and night 'drag' the murderer; in the new one they 'guide' him, a less pregnant expression.

Vision of a dream

787–799 *Vidi, ipse vidi—nescit viâ* The dream the *sicarius* describes reminds one of the apparition of the Fury Allecto to Turnus, Aeneas' opponent in Verg.

Aen. There she is looming in the shape of an old woman, inciting him to fight the Trojans. If he mocks her, she shrieks and pushes a torch into his breast (Verg. *Aen.* VII, 406–457). As with many literary dreams, this occurs just before daybreak, which increases the level of truth, see intr., p. 39, n. 146.

787 *Vidi, ipse vidi*   Also *Aur.* 310; Sen. *Tro.* 170. These words anticipate the vision of the woman in ll. 793–794.

789 *diesque nocte ... nox ... die*   Cf. l. 486: "diemque nox [...] noctem dies" and the comm.

790 *impetus*   For "impetus", see l. 114 and the comm.; "impetus" also has an important role in the Stoic explanation of emotions, see Tarrant, *Seneca Agamemnon*, p. 198 *ad* Sen. *Aga.* 127: "feroces impetus", and John M. Rist, *Stoic Philosophy* (Cambridge, etc.: Cambridge University Press, 1969), pp. 22–36. Through Cicero it is the Latin equivalent of ὁρμή (*TLL* 7.1, 608; for ὁρμή, see Pohlenz, *Die Stoa* 1, e.g. p. 88). It regularly occurs in *domina-nutrix* scenes and here in this *sicarius-praefectus* scene.

792 *haud sui tamen*   Sc. *nescia* 'But not unfamiliar to itself.' The combination "haud nescius" also means 'premeditated', which will be one of the overtones. For this meaning, cf. Verg. *Aen.* IX, 552–553: "seseque haud nescia morti inicit", said of a wild boar.

795 *Ast*   This word, also used in Seneca's drama, e.g. *Herc. f.* 1006, is archaic and is only used before words starting with a vowel (pronouns and "ubi"), see Austin, p. 185 *ad* Verg. *Aen.* II, 467. In Sen. *Thy.* 721 it is used before "illi".

795 *gressu ... elato*   For "gressum efferre", cf. Verg. *Aen.* II, 753; Sen. *Oct.* 667; see also l. 116 and the comm. *ad* l. 800.

797 *ter*   By waving the torch three times the figure increases the (magical) action, but the number three also gives the action a religious connotation (see *OLD* s.v. "ter" 1a and *RAC* 4, 269–310 s.v. 'Drei').

L **791**   The 'broad' ways of the future become the 'first' ways.

Signs of emotionality

800–810 *Quo fluctuantes—paratve*   The commander sees the murderer and discerns all kinds of external signs that betray his mind, in this case fear and rage. On the Stoic background of such appearances see the comm. *ad* ll. 487–512. Initially, the commander draws the conclusion that the man is fearing or deliberating a crime. However, the man's story causes the soldier not to say a word about the second possibility.

800 *gressus refert* Cf. Sen. *Med.* 848: "referte gressus". Such a periphrasis stems from epic and tragedy, see Fantham, *Seneca's Troades*, pp. 289–290 *ad* Sen. *Tro.* 518: "Gressus nefandos [...] admovet [sc. Ulysses]"; also *Tro.* 616, see the comm. *ad* l. 738². For the doubt shown by the way of walking and the face, cf. Sen. *Tro.* 522–523: "dubio gradu vultuque".

801 *titubante passu* Cf. Phaedr. IV, 15(16), 10: "titubanti pede".

801 *incerto pede* The same expression occurs in Sen. *Pha.* 374. See also Canter, *Rhetorical Elements*, p. 133 *sub* 9: the adjective that relates to the person is transposed to what is influenced by it.

804 *supercilij* The brow betrays someone's emotion in Sen. *Pha.* 798–799, where the chorus says to Hippolytus: "Quam grata [...] pondus veteris triste supercili!"

805 *furore* This relates to the intense emotions of the *sicarius*, but also (indirectly) to his divine rapture, see also the comm. *ad* ll. 738–753 and 783, and *OLD* s.v. 1b.

805 *labentes genae* An ambiguous combination: the "genae" can indicate the cheeks (his sunken cheeks) or the eyes, see *OLD* s.v. 2 and Fantham, *Seneca's Troades*, p. 379. The latter possibility, combined with the meaning of "labi" ('fall', *OLD* s.v. labor 7b) may lead to the interpretation: 'his lowered eyes'.

809 *pectus* For 'breast' in the sense of 'young man', see *WNT* 3.1, 580–581, s.v. borst I, but cf. also Verg. *Aen.* v, 169: "fortissima [...] pectora". "Pectus" can be the seat of intellectual abilities (*OLD* s.v. 3b).

The decision (2)

810–812 *Quo feror?—cohibe* The murderer responds to the commander's remarks with an aside, to himself, that he must employ wiles and control his emotions. This is a signal to the viewer that the forthcoming story about the death of his father will be fabricated.

810–811 *dolos mens necte et astus* Cf. Sen. *Tro.* 523: "Nectit pectore astus callidos"; see also Fantham, *Seneca's Troades*, p. 291 on the new meaning Seneca attaches to "nectere" ('invent wiles') (e.g. *Tro.* 523 and 927–928; *Oed.* 92; *Ep.* 45,5). The same combination is also Benedicti *De rebus gestis* II, 44: "necte dolos". For the combination of "dolus" and "astu", see Sen *Tro.* 752: "dolis et astu".

811–812 *procellas pectoris fluctusque cohibe* Cf. Sen. *Herc. f.* 1092: "Pelle insanos fluctus animi".

L 811 In the Leiden copy, the 'plaiting' of wiles becomes the 'hiding' of them, more in line with the immediate continuation in which the murderer manages to keep his (external) calm and in line with the situation, since the commander has seen him and the murderer must present himself calmly and honestly. For the *sicarius* has forged his cunning plans.

In the service of Nassau

812–829 *Siste—relinquo* Now a conversation arises between the commander and the murderer. The commander will (with the exception of a longer clause in ll. 967–992) speak in the *imperatoria brevitas*. On this concision and the great influence of Lipsius on this form of brevity see Jeroen Jansen, *Brevitas: Beschouwingen over de beknoptheid van vorm en stijl in de renaissance* (Hilversum: Verloren, 1995), 2 vols, Doctoral thesis Amsterdam, pp. 424–429. This also raises the question of why Auriacus does speak extensively. However, his Stoic imperturbability is presented. He gives an exposé in the opening scene, he reassures his wife in extensive terms and reflects on the transience of life.

The murderer answers the questions of the *praefectus* to his homeland, himself and his origin (Cuias? Quis? Vnde?) only with the statement that he is suffering the most profound ailment. He shows rhetorical education by answering in a *tricolon*, as in ll. 820–821, the third colon having been broadened to the rules of art. Entirely in the Stoic tradition, the *sicarius* states that changing places will not result in success for either party, cf. Sen. *Ep.* 28.

814 *inclyti* This word is Ennian (Ann. 129, 146, 505 v.), epic and archaic. Cf. (for example) Verg. *Aen.* VI, 562: "dux inclute Teucrum [Deiphobos]"; Ov. *Met.* IX, 229: "Iovis incluta proles [Hercules]" and *ibid.* XIII, 178: "inclutus Hector". See also Bömer, *Ovidius Metamorphosen* 6, p. 346.

816–817 *cuius trophaea—ultimusque* This formula seems topical, but could not be found elsewhere.

818 *motusque* Although "motus" can be both emotions and actions, in the series of *proelia-bellum-minas* the latter meaning will prevail.

819 *maximae interpres rei* A vague allusion to the death of Anjou reported by the murderer to the Prince (*Een verhael vande moort*, Frederiks, *De moord van 1584*, pp. 66–67; see also above, p. 435).

820–821 *patre ... viduus* The murderer here alludes to a brief remark on 'Guyon's' father in *Een verhael vande moort* (Frederiks, *De moord van 1584*, pp. 63–64) "dat hy oock altijdts goede begheerte hadde ghehadt om hem dienst te doen, maer sonderlinghe zedert de doodt van sijnen vader [...] door quaet vermoeden ghevanghen hadde gheweest, midts dat by vande Religie was, ende ter doot ghebrocht wordt [...]" ('that he had always had the great desire to serve him, especially since the death of his father, who [...] had been imprisoned for a bad rumour, since he was of the (Protestant) Religion, and was brought to death [...]'). See also ll. 867–967.

822 *est animus tibi* Cf. Ov. *Met.* I, 1: "fert animus", a translation of θύμος.

823 *sors ... Deusque* This formulation raises the question of the relationship between fate and God. In Renaissance Stoic philosophy, which is a mixture of classical and Christian ideas, both institutions were almost synonymous, especially because in this philosophy the deity could bear different names, see the comm. *ad* ll. 1–5. The question of whether "Deus" is to be interpreted as God in a Christian sense or as the deity of Stoic philosophy cannot be solved just like that, but in this otherwise non-Christian play a classical-Stoic interpretation would seem more obvious. See also intr., p. 26.

824 *patriam rursus peto* This colon allows two interpretations: (1) The murderer wants to return to his homeland. This exegesis finds support in the historical sources. According to *Een verhael vande moort* 'Guyon' wants to return to France (Frederiks, *De moord van 1584*, p. 66). The beginning of the verse ("patriam reliqui"), where *patria* denotes his homeland France, supports this too. (2) He is looking for a fatherland to build a new life. For the latter interpretation of *patria* see the comm. *ad* ll. 632–633.

Remembering grief brings grief

829–850 *Quo parente?—dolor* Invoking the prosperity of the Dutch and the shedding of their yoke, his own tears and the future victories and praise of the Nassaus, the murderer implores the commander to be allowed to remain silent. The *locus classicus* for remembering and thus activating grief again is Verg. *Aen.* II, 3: "Infandum, regina, iubes renovare dolorem". See also (for example) Cic. *Brut.* 76, 266: "Praeteritorum recordatio est acerba". The clause is concluded with a summarizing *sententia*.

831–832 *secunda ... gentis Batavae fata ... nescia spei metusque corda* This presentation is a little too rosy—the revolt certainly was not always successful—but it contrasts with the murderer's own miserable situation as he himself outlines it. It is also a *captatio benevolentiae* for the commander.

833 *excussaque—iuga* An allusion to the "Placcaet van Verlatinghe", the abjuration of Philip II in July 1581, see intr., p. 17 and, inter alia, Ivo Schöffer a.o. (eds), *De Lage Landen van 1500–1780* (Amsterdam, etc.: Elsevier, 1978), pp. 142–143, and P.J. Rietbergen, *A Short History of the Netherlands: From Prehistory to the Present Day* (Amersfoort: Bekking and Blitz, [2015]), p. 80.

836 *Hesperuginis* For denominativa on -ugo see Manu Leumann, *Lateinische Laut- und Formenlehre*, vol. 1 of Leumann, Johann Baptist Hofmann, Anton

Szantyr, *Lateinische Grammatik* (Munich: C.H. Beck, 1977), p. 368. For instance, he gives 'vesperugo' (Evening star); *OLD* s.v. gives *loci* from Plautus, Varro, Vitruvius and Quintilian. Heinsius here applies the Latin suffix to the Greek form, with a pejorative nuance.

838 *tabentes genas* As in l. 805 the "genae" can refer to the cheeks or the eyes.

841 *solis corusci ... dies* Cf. Sen. *Pha.* 889: "coruscum lucis aetheriae iubar".

842 *genus Nereüum* Cf. l. 317: "Nereus pater".

849 *cicatrix* The scar is a very common image in works of consolation, see (for example) Erasmus, *De conscribendis epistolis* (*ASD* I, 2, pp. 443.13) "natura [...] sensim [...] cicatricem obducente". See Grotius, *Dichtwerken/Poetry* I, 2, 4A/B, p. 419 and Von Moos, *Consolatio*, 3, p. 232 *sub* 1069.

850 *Memoria doloris ipsamet saepe est dolor* Cf. Publilius Syrus P.48: "Post calamitatem memoria alia est calamitas" and Cic. *Fin.* 2.95; this *sententia* expresses a well-known thought, see above, the comm. on ll. 829–850, a variant on the *iucunda recordatio*-motif, see (for example) Von Moos, *Consolatio*, 1, p. 172.

Expression of feelings

851–866 *Tacito—potest* Both interlocutors participating in this dialogue reflect an opposite view of feelings. The murderer wants to keep quiet about his grief, not to revive the grief again through memory. He offers the following arguments for this: (1) grief knows only one remedy: forgetfulness; (2) if time can heal someone, he does not need help; (3) anyone mourning for a long time will, through experience, take the edge off his grief; (4) if speaking of one's grief does not prove beneficial, then it would be better to remain silent.

The commander expresses the opinion that talking about grief has a therapeutic effect. His arguments are: (1) if one is silent about one's sorrow, one will never get help, not even from the passing of time; (2) if one does not speak about it, one is partly responsible for the grief and may even be deriving some pleasure from it; (3) those who cannot build on their own strength can hope for help from others.

Although here the murderer is of course cunningly lying about not wanting to talk about his misery, his future story makes him more credible, and he is not solely portrayed as a villain. His arguments are reliable.

The 'Stichworttechnik' (keyword technique, Bernd Seidensticker, *Die Gesprächsverdichtung in den Tragödien Senecas* (Heidelberg: Winter, 1969) Doctoral thesis Hamburg, 1968) prevailed in the conversation. Hence the words "doloris", "nulla" and "succurrit" (l. 851) are resumed in "dolor", "sola" and "auxili" (l. 852) respectively. Even more clearly, this technique, often occurring in

Seneca, is seen in ll. 858–859, in which "dies", "mederi" and "solus" are reused in "dies", "mederi" and (in a paronomasia) "solet".

851 *tacito*   For such invisible emotions, which are called "tacitus" or "caecus", see *OLD* s.v. tacitus 8 and cf., for instance, Sen. *Pha.* 362: "aestu tacito".

852 *obliuione*   For the consolation in *oblivio*, see Von Moos, *Consolatio*, 3, pp. 231–232 *sub* 1068–1072. One of his examples is Publ. Syr. 250 (M): "Nam semper remedium doloris oblivio est".

853 *virtute maior*   This seems to be an objection to the current Stoic view that the wise man will overcome his fate and grief by his *virtus*, cf., e.g., Sen. *Ep.* 71, 30: "Sapiens vincit virtute fortunam" and Cic. *Lael.* 2, 7 "[...] humanosque casus virtute inferiores putes". For the idea that if the *ratio* cannot help, time can do, cf. Ps. Sen. *De mor.* 118: "Saepe ea, quae sanari ratione non poterant, sanata sunt tempore". See also the comm. *ad* ll. 1839–1846.

857 *Malisque—dolet*   For pleasure one can derive from grief, cf., e.g., Ov. *Tr.* IV, 3, 37: "Est quaedam flere voluptas" and Plin. *Ep.* 8, 16: "Est quaedam etiam dolendi voluptas", and see Von Moos, *Consolatio*, 3, pp. 55–57.

L **856**   The unity of this verse is enhanced by the change of 'he keeps sighing' into 'he grieves for his wound', and by putting "suum" at the end, and "vulnus" at the beginning of the verse, a stylistic 'golden line'.

The story of the murderer

867–947 *Age—dies*   In this long clause the murderer begins, using some *adynata*, to say that he will never tell of his unhappy life with dry eyes. The *adynaton*—a rhetorical expression in which the impossible is presented as being more likely than what is currently suggested (see, for example, Curtius, *European Literature and Latin Middle Ages*, pp. 94–98 and Canter, *Rhetorical Elements*, p. 60, n. 5; for examples from Seneca's drama see *ibid.* pp. 60–62)—relates to the sun and moon, who will sooner leave their orbits, and to the Dutch and the Spaniards who will sooner unleash their military turmoil and their wiles. The *praefectus* asks a question that the reader might also be pondering, namely: what exactly is the cause of his sadness? Then the murderer tells the story of his father's death at the stake as in a messenger speech. Heinsius thereby delivers a fact included in *Een verhael vande moort* (Frederiks, *De moord van 1584*, pp. 442–443, above), i.e. the story that his father would have died for his faith, with all details in mind. He follows the spirit of Seneca by expanding on the horrors. On this aspect of Seneca, see Regenbogen, 'Schmerz und Tod'; among the post-Augustan poets Seneca is not the only one who describes horrors with pleasure.

As said, the story has features of a messenger speech. Usually the messenger is initially afraid to speak, see Fantham, *Seneca's Troades*, p. 233. An indication of the time (also traditional) is left out here, though a relict of it is nevertheless seen in the adynata of sun and moon. The description of the place (descriptio, ἔκφρασις) is fully extant: a crowded square with a pyre. Exact dates that could have made the story—true or otherwise—more credible, are lacking. Thus the story is made more general. In addition, the murderer uses the formula typical of a messenger speech that he was there himself ("ipse spectator [...] aderam", ll. 892–893, cf. Sen. *Tro.* 170: "vidi, ipse vidi"). He also starts by giving a brief summary of the events (ll. 890–892), which occurs in Greek tragedy, early Roman drama and Seneca's plays (Fantham, *op. cit.*, p. 368 *ad* Sen. *Tro.* 1063–1067). Furthermore, the main story is told after another character asks for details (ll. 887–888, cf. Euripides, *Andromache*, ed. Philip T. Stevens (Oxford: Clarendon Press, 1971), p. 221 *ad* Eur. *Andr.* 1070–1165). Finally, the style, with its long-winded sentences (see the comm. *ad* 1002–1038) and the Homeric comparison with an old warhorse (ll. 1012–1029), is characterized by epic traits that often characterize a messenger speech as well.

In ll. 939–940 we find the literary topos of refusing to deliver the *coup de grâce*. Life can be worse than death, especially in the Stoic view, in which death is among the *indifferentia*, cf. Van Campen, *Lucanus Bellum Civile Liber II*, pp. 157–158 and 333.

Although the reader or spectator has been given an indication that the story is not true (see ll. 810–812 and comm.), this clause has the capacity to generate pathos, because there is a good chance that anyone from the early seventeenth century will have witnessed such an execution, perhaps even of relatives or friends.

868 *aerumnas* This is an elevated word, see Tarrant, *Seneca Agamemnon*, p. 230, and Sen. *Aga.* 305 and 491.

871–875 *Citius—Iber* For this first *adynaton* (the sun will sooner leave its orbit), see (for example) Sen. *Contr.* 1, 5, 2: "sol contrario cursu orbem ducat".

872 *Titan* See l. 594 and the comm.

876 *sicco lumine* Luc. IX, 1044.

877 *lucis* For "lux" as the light of life, see *OLD* s.v. 6a. For the thought that life was already full of sorrow at birth, cf. (for example) l. 717: "Homines curis gens nata sumus".

879 *fortunae manus* Cf. *Aur.* 17: "sortis infestae manus".

880–882 *aetatis ... vitae ... aeui* Heinsius seems to have used these three words for reasons of *variatio*, without exploiting differences in nuance or meaning.

883 *crescentibusque—malis* For the thought that grief gets worse with time, cf. (for example) Ov. *Rem.* 91–92: "Sero medicina paratur cum mala per longas invaluere moras".

887–888 *Quae—suos* Cf. Apul. *Mun.* 22: "imbres rumpuntur". No parallel has been found for "imbres" as an activity of Fortune, but cf. Vitr. 6 pr. 2: "fortunae tempestas iniqua", and the expression "fortunae turbo" (Apul. *Met.* VIII, 31; cf. Sen. *Thy.* 622; also Luc. II, 243: "fides, quam turbine nullo excutiet fortuna tibi") and "procella fortunae" (Apul. *Met.* X, 4); all these expressions are found mainly in authors from silver Latinity.

894 *quotacumque* Cf. Sen. *Aga.* 22: "pars quota" and Tarrant, *Seneca Agamemnon*, p. 171 *ad loc.*; Sen. *Herc. f.* 383 "quota" and Tib. II, 6, 54: "Moverit e votis pars quotacumque deos".

895 *sortis ignarus meae* Cf. Sen. *Herc. f.* 295: "ignara nostrae sortis".

896 *reciso stipite* Foliage and side branches have been removed, but here too a staggered beam could be considered.

897 *pyram* The same word in (for example) Verg. *Aen.* IV, 504, a transliteration of the Greek πυρά, whereas Sen. uses the Latin equivalent "rogus" (e.g. *Herc. Oet.* 1484). There are more parallels between Verg. *Aen.* IV and this scene: the foliage ("coma", l. 896, and "fronde", *Aen.* IV, 506; "roborum", l. 987, and "ilice", *Aen.* IV, 505; "strui sub auras", l. 898 and "sub auras erecta", *Aen.* IV, 504–505). For "ingentem pyram" (l. 897), cf. Sil. II, 422: "pyram ingentem" and for "roborum" cf. also Luc. VI, 824–825: "Robore multo exstruxit illa rogum".

898 *nemoris immensi luem* This combination, an apposition to "pyram" is not entirely unequivocal. The word "lues" can indicate the forest that has been affected ('the rotting remains') by the decay it will bring ('the devastating force made of parts of an immense forest'). One would expect the acc. "luem".

899–903 *Dum iactor—perdit error* The passive role of the speaker is striking: he is driven ("iactor", l. 899), the mob pushes him ("voluit", l. 900) in an indeterminate direction ("error", l. 903) which makes him lose his way ("perdit", l. 903). The mob is like a storm at sea, cf. "confluentis" (l. 899), "procellas" (l. 901) and "undantis" (l. 902). It causes him to lose his way, but paradoxically also to find his father ("inveni patrem", l. 903).

904–906 *teque-parens* The *apostrophe* to the father arouses pathos, see Konst, *De hartstochten in de tragedie*, e.g. p. 91. For the metaphorical meaning of "fulcrum" in classical Latin, see *TLL* 6.1, 1507.35–43. Heinsius could derive this use from the verb "fulcire", which could also indicate mental support, see *OLD* s.v. fulcio 4. The 'languorous soul' helped is that of the murderer, cf. "opes meae".

913 *nix* For "nix" in the sense of snow-white hair, cf. Hor. *C.* IV, 13, 12: "capitis nives".

914 *messis* A metaphorical use of "messis" is mentioned in *TLL* 8, 859–860, but not for beard growth.

919–923 *Et—vitavit suam* Heinsius expressly states here that the man almost died of fear before his torture was fully implemented. "Sibi" (l. 922) can refer to the mind ('had stolen himself for the sake of himself', i.e. had succumbed to save himself even more pain, according to the translation) or to the enemy ('had taken away from him', had escaped the enemy due to a premature death).

924 *bis—manus* Hercules also lifted his hands to confirm his prayers to Jupiter, see Sen. *Herc. Oet.* 1695: "Tum manus tendens ait". The murderer's father does it twice, which increases the power of expression. For "is" cf. (for instance) Sen. *Oed.* 176–177; *id. Herc. f.* 322; Verg. *Aen.* VI, 32–33.

928–931 *Tu—inquit* The father may address God, but does so in expressions suited to Phoebus Apollo, the all-encompassing sun, or the ruler of heaven Jupiter. This is supported by formulations in Seneca's drama, e.g. *Pha.* 960: "igniferi rector Olympi", *Herc. Oet.* 1275: "summe pro rector poli". Also *Herc. f.* 205; 592; *Pha.* 671: "magne regnator deûm"; *Thy.* 1077–1078: "summe caeli rector, aetheriae potens dominator aulae".

933 *aeternùm vale* Verg. *Aen.* XI, 97.

935–936 *Tortor—sonum* The executioner can no longer hear the man's moaning.

937 *eminus tamen* The executioner pushes his victim into the flames, so to speak.

938 *paena* Cf. Sen. *Herc. f.* 604–606: "In poenas meas atque in labores non satis terrae patent Iunonis odio", where "poena" can be both 'punishment' and 'suffering'. For the latter meaning, cf. Sen. *Tro.* 300 and *Ep.* 5, 5.

943–947 *unaque—dies* The father was happy (unaware of the forthcoming events), imprisoned and deceased in a single day ("una luce", l. 943; "idem [...] dies", l. 947).

L 893–895 In l. 893 the 'neutral' "inscius" changed to the more subjective "ignarus". For *varietas* "ignarus" in l. 895 had to be deleted, without Heinsius having a good alternative.

L 899–903 After several attempts, Heinsius made these lines: "While I was being pushed back and forth innocently, and only going back and forth, I followed the masses as much as my wish, and the procession of the crowd in motion". Heinsius changed the story such that the assassin now states more explicitly that he was looking for his father ("in votum"), whereas in the original version it was almost a coincidence ("error"). The author also modifies the metaphorical "undantis", rendering it the neutral "euntis".

L 904–905 In these lines Heinsius changed a *part. fut. act.* into a gerund construction, which in later Latin has the function of the *part. fut. pass.* The expression becomes more powerful: not only will the son never see his father again. The gerund also stresses the inevitability of the fact.

L 930 Heinsius creates a parallel in the twofold "si".

L 932 The "gens pusilla" is changed into "parvi greges".

L 934 Here too the thought is rendered more logical: the word does not stop in the father's throat, because he still speaks it, but it 'wandered around', and was only recently spoken.

L 936 The dative "voci" (for the voice he broke the sound), becomes a more logical genitive "vocis" (he broke the sound of the voice).

L 937 Retaining the meaning, Heinsius changes "tamen" (its use at one word is very unusual and not found in *OLD*) into the ordinary "licet" (*OLD* s.v. 4c).

L 939 The slightly superfluous exegetical sentence 'he could not die' becomes an apposition to "lethi" (death which long threatened him), which makes the statement more pathetic.

L 941 The neutral "prorumpit" becomes more specific in "colla circundat", again generating the pathos.

Causes of emotionality

948–967 *Et quae—nullos* Now the perspective changes slightly from the former grief to a sudden outburst on the part of the murderer, finding its cause in freedom and faith, to which he (cunningly) adds that the commander and his peer must also suffer for it. He also mentions the unhappy condition of his mother and poverty.

952 *tyranni* The tyrant may refer to Philip, but perhaps Alva is meant here, who is often portrayed as a tyrant, for example in *Een liedeken van Ducdalba* (1573), ll. 35–36 "Maar God heeft door den prins zeer goed den tiran zeer beladen" ('But by the very good prince God did well corner the tyrant', W.J.C. Buitendijk, *Nederlandse strijdzangen 1525–1648* (Culemborg: Tjeenk Willink/Noorduijn, 1977² [= Zwolle 1954¹]), p. 110). Cf. also the *Gents Vader Onze* (Ghent Paternoster, 1572, Buitendijk, *op. cit.*, p. 92) in which Alva is described as "helse duuvel" ('hellish devil'). If the "tyrannus" denotes Alva, it also creates a *tricolon*: Alva, Philip and the Pope. The genitive "tyranni" can be both subjective and objective.

952–953 *rituumque adulteri regis sacrorum* If Heinsius is referring to something specific in "adulter", this may be Philip's reputed affair with the Countess of Eboli, but it could well be general opprobrium. The "rituum [...] sacrorum" allude to Philip's religious fanaticism to be the defender of the Catholic faith, see (for example) Parker, *Philip II*, pp. 96–116. For "sacra" see also the comm. *ad* ll. 319–324 and 348–365.

953 *frausque Romani patris*   The deceit of the Pope in Rome was topical around 1600 among Protestants.

960–961 *tumor ... furor*   Both words are almost synonymous with strong emotion, though "tumor" is mainly connected to "ira", and "furor" rather to frenzy. The adjectives used "pervicax" at "tumor" and "legisque certae ignarus" also seems to refer to this distinction.

960 *peruicax mentis tumor*   The adjective "pervicax" in connection with words of emotion only occurs in post-classical authors, for instance Curt. VIII, 6, 1: "Pervicacioris irae fuit".

L **960**   The "mentis tumor" becomes somewhat more neutral in "mentis calor". *L* **961**   Just like in ll. 893–895, the author changes between "nescius" (or "inscius") and "ignarus".

Enter into the service of the Prince

967–992 *Surge—Marti*   The soldier invites the murderer to serve the Prince. As a righteous soldier, he pleads for the battle without tricks. The shadow of his father calls him to this, who is a 'creditor'.

967–968 *aduerso ... corde*   Cf. Tac. *Ann.* III, 29: "adversis animis" and perhaps Quint. II, 15, 7: "pectore adverso", cf. also l. 1323: "pectore adverso".

970 *campoque aperto*   The 'open field' is almost topical in epic, cf. (for example) Verg. *Aen.* XI, 493: "campoque potitus aperto" and see infra the comm. *ad* 992–1044 as well as Sil. XI, 415–416: "Non acer aperto desudat campo sonipes".

984 *ciet*   See *Aur.* 750 and the comm.

986–990 *Feruet ... feruidas*   On the metaphor of the choppy sea of the mind, see Van Dam, *Statius Silvae, Book II*, p. 274. Here it is expressed in a *figura etymologicum*.

991 *effunde habenas*   For the metaphor of the bridles in Seneca's drama, see (for example) *Tro.* 279; *Med.* 591–592 and 866–867.

Revenge—comparison with a warhorse

992–1044 *Scilicet—exposcit ille*   The murderer emphasizes in his story that the misery fatigues him. Yet he is seeking revenge. He compares his condition with an old warhorse that pricks up his ears when the trumpet sounds. This Homeric comparison with a warhorse that once again becomes his former self is a novelty. However, the warhorse ("bellator equus") is extant in Latin literature, e.g. Verg. *Ge.* ii, 145: "Hinc bellator equus campo sese arduus infert" and *Aen.* xi, 89; also Sil. vii, 67–68: "ilia [...] bellatoris equi". The comparison resembles that of Hector with a horse that has stood in a stable and gallops onto open ground after a good feed (Hom. *Il.* xv, 263–268, also in Scal. *Poet.* v, 3, p. 242bB; Scaliger, *Poetica/Dichtkunst* 4, p. 282.7–13), cf. Hom. *Il.* vi, 506–511 and Verg. *Aen.* xi, 492–497, where Turnus is compared to such a stable horse, also in Scal. *Poet.* v, 3, pp. 242bD–243aA; Scaliger, *Poetica/Dichtkunst*, p. 284.11–16. Heinsius found another point of reference in Ov. *Met.* iii, 704–705: "Vt fremit acer equus, cum bellicus aero canoro signa dedit tibicen pugnaeque adsumit amore", or in Verg. *Ge.* iii, 83–88, where a thoroughbred horse is described which pricks up his ears in a warlike manner: "Tum, si qua sonum procul arma dedere, stare loco nescit, micat auribus et tremit artus" (83–84). Cf. also Apoll. Rhod. iii, 1259–1270.

993 *Ergo* With *ergo* the *sicarius* resumes the story that had been interrupted by the *praefectus*.

994 *lanuginis* For "lanugo" cf. Pac. *Trag.* 362: "Nunc primum opacat flora lanugo genas"; Lucr. v, 889: "Molli vestit lanugine malas"; Verg. *Aen.* x, 324: "flaventem prima lanugine malas".

994–995 *lanuginis—genas* For this expression cf. the Dedication to Scaliger 47: πρὶν τὴν ὑπήνην ἀνέρπειν, περὶ τὸ στόμα τοὺς κροτάφους τε and the comm. *ad loc.*

995 *autumnus* This word could be referring to 'autumn' (the beard appears in this season), but could also be construed as having the connotation 'harvest time': now that he has reached the age of the first downy beard, it is time to avenge his father.

1000–1001 *fata—genitor* Just as in ll. 904–906 (and see the comm.), the murderer uses the apostrophe to underline his story and enhance the pathos.

1002–1038 *Nunc quoque—copiamque* In these lines the epic style is underlined by syntax. It begins with a concessional clause ("licet—virtutibus", ll. 1002–1009), after which the main clause starts ("tamen", l. 1010) in which a temporal clause is embedded ("quoties [...] cumque [...] fodit calcaribus", ll. 1010–1011). This clause is interrupted by the comparison with an old warhorse ("ceu—restituit sibi", ll. 1012–1029), after which the main clause is resumed ("sic", l. 1030) and continued with "sic quoque" (l. 1036). In this clause another concessional clause is embedded ("colla quamvis—dextram", ll. 1030–1036).

1002 *futurus ultor* Sen. *Tro.* 660; see also Fantham, *Seneca's Troades*, p. 304 *ad loc.* The recurrence of the expression in l. 1235 adds to the cohesion of the drama.

1009 *aedilis*   One of the tasks of the "aedilis" was to check the prices of corn, see *TLL* 1, 928–933 and *RE* 1, 448–464, esp. 454–458. Perhaps this role is being echoed in this line, in which case the metaphor could be explained thus: grief is the *aedilis* who monitors heroic deeds and curbs them.

1011 *sensus*   For "sensus" as consciousness, cf. Sen. *Tro.* 659, and see Fantham, *Seneca's Troades*, p. 304 *ad loc.*

1011 *calcaribus*   The spurs introduce the comparison to the warhorse.

1012 *ille*   This word refers to the 'well-known' warhorse as it occurs in epic scenes.

1013 *cornipes*   Such compounds belong to the lofty style of the epic genre, and also occur in Seneca's drama, e.g. *Aga.* 630 "sonipes" (see also Tarrant, *Seneca Agamemnon*, p. 291 *ad loc.*); *Pha.* 1081 "corniger". "Cornipes" occurs as adjective, but also as substantive, e.g. Verg. *Aen.* VI, 591; Sen. *Pha.* 809; Luc. VIII, 3; Stat. *Th.* VII, 137; VIII, 539; Sil. II, 72; IV, 231.

1015 *glomerare gressus*   Verg. *Ge.* III, 117: "[the Lapiths] equitem docuere sub armis insultare solo et gressus glomerare superbos". One might consider 'prancing' in this regard.

1017 *ferri*   Usually the metonym refers to swords, but here iron bullets could also be intended.

1018 *toruus*   Cf. Sen. *Tro.* 1000: "vultuque torvo" and *Pha.* 117. It can be almost synonymous with "ferox", see Manu Leumann, 'Literaturbericht für das Jahr 1930', *Glotta* 21 (1933), pp. 198–199.

1024–1025 *litui ... tubaeque*   These two instruments are topical in descriptions of a battlefield, see Franz E. Erbig, *Topoi in den Schlachtberichten römischer Dichter* (Gdansk: O. Lauter, Jr, 1931) Dissertation Würzburg, whose list could be supplemented with Hor. *C.* I, 1, 23–24: "lituo tubae permixtus sonitus", Sil. IX, 554: "lituique tubaeque" and Stat. *Th.* VII, 622–623: "tubaeque [...] et litui".

1040 *cassam*   Sen. *Tro.* 570. For parallels, see Fantham, *Seneca's Troades*, p. 295. "Cassam laude" is somewhat unclear: either the praise the speaker will gain, or the praise that the sun will give to everyone who overcomes the Spaniards.

1040 *sol praesens*   (1) this day; (2) the sun that is my witness.

1042 *sitientes*   I.e. calling for revenge.

L 1004   The predicative "saeva", a metaphor for poverty, becomes the more neutral adverb "male". The author deleted ll. 1004–1006, thereby somewhat abbreviating the long-winded sentence that starts at 1002 and can be taken to end at 1036.

L 1009   The "aedilis", taking care of the market, becoming a tyrant.

L 1025   The metaphorical 'to drink' becomes the more neutral 'to receive'.

L 1033–1035   These lines become: '[...] and the hard-hearted need. Likewise, the sick mind is heated by an invisible movement and enters into the devious heart pregnant with unusual efforts'.

Transition to the next scene

1044–1048 *Patriam—pedem* To conclude the scene, the arrival of a character is announced. For such announcements in Seneca's drama, cf. (for example) *Tro.* 522–523, where the arrival of Odysseus is signalled, and *Aga.* 408–411, where the chorus notices the arrival of a soldier and Eurybates. See also *Aur.* 1815–1818 and the comm. This is a segue, a way to connect scenes.

1047 *splendidae culmen domus* This can be explained in two ways: (1) 'the ridge of a beautiful house', i.e. the most important descendant of a splendid family, or (2) 'the ridge of my beautiful house', the one who will (by his death) ensure that my mission succeeds and I will get a great reward.

1048 *refert pedem* Cf. l. 800: "gressus refert" and Sen. *Tro.* 516: "referamus hinc alio pedem".

***L* 1045** The somewhat far-fetched metaphor of the road that 'dissolves' becomes "decedet" (will leave).

Act III, Scene 2 (1049–1340)

Summary

In this dialogue Auriacus tries to calm his frightened wife Loisa.

1049–1063 Auriacus sees signs of sadness in his wife, including paleness, and anxiously asks the cause.

1063–1094 Only recently was there cause for concern, when only the narrow Rhine lay between him and the enemy, because a separation by land was never sufficient for his safety. Now, however, the sea—the Holland Water Line—has intervened.

1095–1122 Auriacus was the first to resist Philip when the latter attacked the Netherlands, and Auriacus called upon the sea to rescue him. That was necessary, because princes want to own more and more. Particularly in this case: the Spaniards even fought a civil war.

1123–1166 Once again Auriacus beseeches Loisa to have no fear, but she cannot do otherwise. She compares her fear with a storm at sea: the swell announces the approaching storm even before it really comes. Similarly, she too is already afraid of what is yet to come.

1166–1222 To a remark from Auriacus that her fear is unfounded because the hostile armies are far away, Loisa replies that sometimes peacetime makes people carefree and she refers to the St Bartholomew's Night massacre, in which both her father and her husband died, without foreign enemies being around.

1222–1233 Loisa sighs that she would like to believe his words, but is still afraid. Then she asks to get the baby (Frederick Henry), which makes her sad: if something happens to Auriacus, the child will also suffer the consequences.

1234–1312 Auriacus then speaks to the baby, who must take revenge should anything happen to him. The Spaniards are already shivering for this boy. He must protect his mother and the fatherland and show himself worthy of the Nassau family. The child is almost obliged to do this, because the whole world is watching him. He will have to fight both on land and at sea, in battles initiated by the Dutch, Zeelanders, Gelderlanders and Frisians. The homeland will still experience much violence and the power of the water—enemy and ally—because the sailors also take loot from everywhere.

1312–1338 Then Auriacus turns back to Loisa: she has to tell the baby about the glorious actions of his father and spur him on, to prevent him from weakening. He recently showed signs of courage: when a soldier threw his lance and the trumpet sounded, he visibly took pleasure in it. To the child he says that he has every confidence in his martial character.

1339–1340 Auriacus turns to Loisa again: it is dinner time.

This scene shows Auriacus and Loisa each in their own mood: Loisa full of woe and anxiety, Auriacus self-assured on the basis of his constancy. The third act is an appropriate place for this; in Seneca's drama it is usually also devoted to a crucial confrontation that highlights the affects of the protagonist(s), see intr., pp. 26 and 37 and Tarrant, *Seneca Agamemnon*, p. 248. In the previous act, Loisa's emotion was rendered visible through the reactions of and her reactions to a secondary figure, whereas here the contrast between the two protagonists intensifies the representation of their emotional state.

Loisa's fear is underlined by the elocution. In particular, the apostrophe to her dead husband (l. 1197), the *geminatio* of "his" and "in hoc" (l. 1199), the anaphora of "inter" (ll. 1205–1206), the rhetorical question (l. 1211) and the anaphora of "quis" in the rhetorical question (1215–1217), as well as the chiasmus in ll. 1207 and 1217–1218 (in the latter case involving the repetition of "nemo") and the contrast in ll. 1188–1189 (q.v.) contribute to the rhetoric of "movere". On the portrayal of the passions in the tragedy see Konst, *De hartstochten in de tragedie*.

Metre

This scene consists of iambic trimeters.

Commentary

Visible emotions

1049–1063 *Quid immerentes—statione ruptâ* In his wife Auriacus discovers external characteristics and behaviour (tears, paleness and avoidance) that betray her inner state of mind. For the Stoic character of such a description, see the comm. *ad* ll. 487–512. Loisa's paleness is compared with the pallor of the moon, who derives light from her brother Phoebus, the sun. For this, cf. l. 398. When the moon hides itself in dark clouds, the stars leave their place in the sky; one is inclined to add that this is unsurprising, since the stars are obscured by the same dark nebulae. The motif returns in ll. 1341–1342. I have not found parallels.

1049 *immerentes rori commendas genas* Cf. Ov. *Trist.* I, 3, 18: "Imbre per indignas usque cadente genas", and Ov. *Met.* x, 360: "Tepido suffundit lumina rore"; Sen. *Pha.* 381–382: "Lacrimae cadunt per ora et assiduo genae rore irrigantur". The reading of the edition 1602 (the abl. "rore") does not make sense.

1051–1054 *nec suave—rubor* Cf., e.g., Sen. *Aga.* 710–711: "Silet repente Phoebas et pallor genas creberque totum possidet corpus tremor".

1055 *luctu* This reading has been chosen from *L*. The original edition had "luctuis" (gen. sg., see Neue-Wagener 1, 536–537). *TLL* does not give any examples of this form.

1056–1057 *Phoebi ... Phoebe* Cf. Sen. *Herc. f.* 136: "Phoebi [...] soror". See also l. 12 and the comm.

1056 *spoliatrix* For the use of "spoliare" with respect to light, cf. Lucr. IV, 377: "Spoliatur lumine terra". For the thought, cf. l. 398 "pars Phoebi". In *spoliatrix* Heinsius shows his predilection for *agens*-words on -tor and -trix, see the comm. *ad* l. 68.

1057 *caecum* This word should probably be taken to be proleptic, 'that it becomes invisible'.

1060–1063 *trepidique-ruptâ* The stars (planets and "stellae fixae") are situated according to the Ptolemaic vision of the cosmos in the aether (cf. "aetheris magni chori"), which Heinsius also (inaccurately) calls "caelum" (l. 1062). "Caelum" usually indicates the "caelum empyreum", the space where the gods are dwelling. On the ancient cosmology, see John L.E. Dreyer, *A History of Astron-*

omy from Thales to Kepler, rev. foreword by W.H. Stahl (New York: Dover, 1953²).
On the Ptolemaic world view and its effect, see Lewis, *The Discarded Image*,
pp. 96–97. The stars are afraid of the dark.

L 1049 "Commendas" gives way to "tingis"; *metri causa* "rori" became "imbri-
bus": 'Why do you wet your innocent cheeks with a torrent of tears?'
L 1051 "Visus" ('to see') is rendered more specific: "vultus" ('seeing' and 'face').
L 1052 Probably due to the tautology with "laetae", "hilarum" became "purum".
L 1054 Having second thoughts, the writer used the adverbial "circum" to indi-
cate that the blush is all over the face. Cf. also l. 1055 where "luctu(is)" became
"vultu".
L 1055 A line is added: 'You look at the ground, your face is twisted with grief'.
Then Heinsius underlines it, apparently searching for another formulation, or
perhaps intending to eventually delete it.

Land versus sea as a separation

1063–1094 *Non ita pridem—vetat* Auriacus points out here that in the past he
had to be cautious of the tyrant, because only the Rhine formed a separation,
and even if the whole mainland were between him and the Spanish King, he
would still have feared the enemy's wiles. Only the sea offers sufficient protection against the enemy. The sea calls to mind the Holland Water Line and other
inundations, which played a major role during sieges, including the Siege of Leiden. On this, see Hans Brand and Jan Brand, *De Hollandse Waterlinie* (Utrecht,
etc.: Veen, 1986) and the comm. *ad* ll. 110–126.

1064 *consors thori* Cf. Sen. *Aga.* 256: "thalami consortem tui" and its example,
Ov. *Met.* I, 319: "cum consorte tori". Such circumscriptions are regularly used in
silver Latinity, belonging to an elevated style, see Bömer, *Ovidius Metamorphosen* 1, p. 115 *ad* Ov. *Met.* I, 319 and *ibid.*, p. 194 *ad* I, 620.
1066 *perduelles* It concerns residents of hostile powers, in other words "ini-
mici", personal enemies (*OLD* s.v. perduellis). A "hostis" is also a state enemy,
but in that case an individual who commits hostile activities.
1067 *Rhenus* Heinsius' mentioning of this river is obvious, as it was important for the inundation and Relief of Leiden. The "parvus alveus" is a slight
exaggeration, inspired by the contrast with the 'broad current' of the inundation.
1074 *Pyrenes ... iuga* Cf. Sen. *Pha.* 69: "ferocis iuga Pyrenes".
1075 *Celtas* Strictly speaking, the "Celtae" are a people in southern France, as
usual used pars pro toto for all Frenchmen, cf. Grotius Εἶδος 71: Κελτάς.

1076 *discriminata que Alpium cacumina* "Discriminata" may designate the 'separate' summits, or the danger they represent. In l. 1080 it is said that the summits are surrounded by clouds, cf. (for example) Luc. I, 188–189: "Alpis nubiferae colles".

1079 *aestivo gelu* An oxymoron.

1081–1082 *terraeque quicquid ... succumbit* Cf. Luc. VI, 274: "succubuit siqua tellus" and Sen. *Herc. f.* 332–333: "omne quidquid uberi cingit solo obliqua Phocis". For a similar enumeration, cf. Sen. *Med.* 211–215. Fitch, *Seneca's Hercules Furens*, p. 214 *ad* Sen. *Herc. f.* 332–335 gives some *loci* from Greek drama.

1082 *arcu flammeo* For the "arcus" as a designation for one of the five zones in the sky, cf. Ov. *Met.* I, 129 and Bömer's comm. 1, p. 274 *ad loc.* Because of the adjective "flammeum", the "arcus" should perhaps be interpreted as "caelum Empyreum", the outer heaven, the space without time or matter, but more likely it denotes the "stellae fixae" in the *aether*, immediately under the "caelum Empyreum".

1083–1084 *inhorruique—manum* These lines are structured around the oppositions *eminus-comminus* and *fraudes-manum*: the deception is to be feared, even if it is far away; Orange does not fear the army, even if it is close. The lines 1085–1086 constitute an elaboration of the 'distant deceit' to be feared. Somewhat unclear is whether "timui" is already part of the sentence or whether it only starts with "solo". "Eminus" is not used here in the proper sense 'at a distance' (as in l. 937); the enemy is further away, whether it is Philip or Alva. "Comminus" can be regarded as 'even if it had been close', but also, more firmly: 'never before his army power in vicinity...' The question is whether Orange is thinking of a hostile army that has or has not been in the vicinity.

1087 *profanus* This word should probably be understood here as: unsuitable for a nobleman. Monarchs, as well as their peers, the other nobles, are in theory also the most excellent beings on earth, morally speaking, of whom fear is unbecoming; see, e.g., Veenstra, *Ethiek en moraal*, p. 29.

1088 *testor ... deos* For a parallel in Seneca's drama, see (for instance) *Oed.* 14: "Caelum deosque testor". Cf. also *Aur.* 117 and 264.

1090–1094 *At nunc—vetat* In these lines Auriacus speaks about the inundations (see above). The sea is "sequester" and "arbiter". "Sequester" is a legal term indicating a third party with whom disputed property is deposited. Here, however, it is a third party who intervenes. The "arbiter" is also a term from the legal sphere: an arbitrator who does not make legal pronouncements on the grounds of laws (such as the "iudex") but according to his own judgement (the meaning 'ruler' plays no part here, as is the case in ll. 89 and 265). This term also refers to the separation formed by the sea.

Auriacus opposing Philip using the water

1095–1114 Primus Philippum—repressi manum Orange stood against Philip partly with the help of the Holland Water Line, see the comm. *ad* ll. 110–126 and the literature mentioned there. The pierced dikes and the open locks had particularly rendered their service in the Relief of Leiden (Motley, *Dutch Republic*, pp. 569–570). Here, one might also consider the opposition between the Sea Beggars and the Spaniards: the former were superior at sea, the latter had the upper hand on land.

The monarchs who must be rejoicing because Orange is putting his life at risk will probably include Queen Elizabeth of England and Francis II and Charles IX of France, if reference is being made to specific monarchs.

1095 patriam vrgentem viam Philip is going the way of his father, namely being lord of the Netherlands and ruling the world. This is in accordance with *orbisque habenas* [...] *volventem*, see infra, and the sequel, in which Heinsius makes Philip say (alluding to the motto of his father) that he wants to own the world (see the next annotation). The interpretation of "tuli" remains difficult: 'I have tolerated it', or 'I stopped it'.

1096 Orbisque—suâ This is an allusion to Charles V's motto "Plus ultra", which in itself is a reversal of the ancient conviction that beyond the Pillars of Hercules (the Strait of Gibraltar) there is no more inhabited area, cf. also Pind. *Nem.* 3, 21–22, pointing out that the sea beyond Gibraltar cannot easily be sailed. On "Plus ultra", see Earl Rosenthal, 'Plus ultra, non plus ultra, and the Columnar Device of Emperor Charles V', *Journal of the Warburg and Courtauld Institutes* 34 (1971), pp. 204–228, and Klaus Bartels, *Geflügelte Worte aus dem Griechischen und Lateinischen* (Darmstadt: Wissenschaftliche Buchgesellschaft, 1992), p. 118. Cf. also ll. 1103 "universi candidatus" and 1111 "venturus ultra".

1097 hoc voui latus The word "latus" can be interpreted as (1) pars pro toto: Orange has made himself servant of the war against Philip; for this use of "latus", see Frank, *Seneca's Phoenissae*, p. 77 *ad* Sen. *Pho.* 2, and cf. *Aur.* 166 and 911; or (2) "latus" may indicate a military wing (*OLD* s.v. 5), in which case the meaning would be: 'I have been the first to deploy my wing [or: army]', cf. l. 411. In l. 1596 "latus" is used in the strict meaning of 'flank, part of the trunk of a body'.

1103 vniuersi candidatus est Iber In *Trag. const.* Heinsius rejects this line on stylistic grounds (Heinsius 1611, p. 216; Heinsius, *On Plot in Tragedy*, p. 121, cf. *ibid.* p. 141 n. 55).

1104–1106 reges, proximum—divûm propago For the conviction that princes are of divine descent and almost identical to gods, see comm. *ad* ll. 415–419; cf. also Scaliger 1615, p. 29.13: "Principes, Iovis semen".

1110 *soli patentem ... viam*   This expression is probably related to what was told about the Habsburg Empire, viz. that the sun never set on it (e.g. Parker, *Philip II*, p. 159). In which case "soli" is the dat. of "sol" (unpunished, he went the way that is open for the sun), but it could also be the gen. of "solum" (unhindered, he took possession of the whole world), which would result in an opposition of "solum" and "mare".

1111 *venturus vltra*   Another allusion to Charles' motto "Plus ultra", see the comm. on l. 1096.

1112–1114 *Terra-manum*   These lines, too, deal with the opposition of land and sea, although whether their subject is the piercing of dykes and the Holland Water Line or the Sea Beggars and their successes at sea is a moot point.

1114 *saeuam ... repressi manum*   This can be interpreted as: (1) I have stopped his cruel hand; (2) I have reduced his cruel army (*manus* as a group); (3) I have thwarted his cruel actions (*manus* as a metonym of cause for consequence).

L 1098   Heinsius changed "prurientes" into "insolentes" (overconfident), which he underlined, apparently not satisfied with it.

Hunger for power

1115–1120 *Namque—crescit ruinas*   These verses, marked as *sententiae*, revolve around the idea that princes' hunger for power increases the more they possess. For the topos, consider such expressions as: many have too much, nobody has enough.

L 1116   "Gliscendo" becomes a direction 'up high'; cf. 1280.

War of Spaniards against their own citizens

1120–1122 *quodque supremum—armauit suos*   "Albanus" can be the adjectival form of the name Alba (Alva). Which would make this the 'fury of Alva', who had committed all possible crimes, according to the Dutch. With his hard line he fought a fierce civil war against people who were in fact citizens of the Spanish Empire. In their eyes, the Dutch were certainly not "hostes"; enemies of the state, they remained loyal to the King as long as possible and opposed Alva in particular. Consider in this regard the Spanish-speaking cities of Amsterdam and Utrecht which hosted Spaniards, cf. Benedicti *De rebus gestis* I, 439–450, esp. 439–440: "Vrbs Amstela moenibus hostem excipit, exceptaque propinquas armat in urbes" and 443–444: "Quis furor, o cives, latronibus urbe receptis in proprios saevire lares?" However, the verses may also be referring to the Spanish Fury in Antwerp, 4 November 1576, when Alva had already been away for three years. In which case, "Albanus" would refer to the Spanish commander at the time of this savagery, Don Sancho d'Avila.

1120 *quodque supremum reor* Cf. 1285 and Benedicti *De rebus gestis* I, 439: "Maius adhuc superest", i.e. that Amsterdam and Utrecht were on the side of Alva and received Spanish troops.

'Cheer up'

1123–1133 *At tu—lenibusque gaudijs* Now Auriacus makes an immediate appeal to his wife to cast off her sorrows and its outward signs. Again, outer appearance and inner feelings are closely connected, see also the comm. *ad* ll. 487–512. He himself also wants to relax and be free from his cares for his country by embracing his youngest child, Frederick Henry, who remained anonymous in the play.

1125 *supercili* Cf. l. 804. The brow shows someone's mood, see *OLD* s.v. 2a, and cf. Hor. *Ep.* I, 18, 94: "Deme supercilia nubem"; for "frontis [...] nubem", cf. Sil. VIII, 611: "nec nubem frontis amabat".
1126–1127 *cultus ... habitusque* These words have been interpreted as hendiadys, referring to expression instead of clothing.
1128 *commune pignus* See the comm. *ad* ll. 444–448 (444 "dulce pignus") for children as a pledge of love and marriage. For an instance in Neo-Latin poetry, see Secundus *Odae* 5, 12: "socii pignora lectuli".
1128–1129 *collum premat breuibus lacertis* Cf. Ov. *Met.* I, 485: "in [...] patris blandis haerens cervice lacertis"; *Fast.* VI, 497: "insanis natum complexa lacertis".
1129 *paruulum germen domus* Cf. Sen. *Tro.* 456: "parvulam stirpem domus". The use of "germen" for child in Latin is post-classical (*TLL* 6.2, 1923–1924).
1131 *Belgiaeque pondere* Cf. ll. 51–52: "Belgia his cervicibus inclinat, incubatque".
1132–1133 *turbidam ... mentem* Because of the burden that his care for his country puts on him, Auriacus has emotions, albeit moderate ones.

Fear of the future

1134–1166 *Metuo marite—metuo marite* The essence of this passage is Loisa's anxious premonition, before the disasters that she fears actually occur. In a Homeric simile she likens this premonition to a storm at sea. Before the real storm comes, there is already a harbinger, the hollow sea. A storm description has become commonplace since Hom. *Od.* V, 291–312 and Verg. *Aen.* I, 81–123 and is almost standard in epics, see Bömer, *Ovidius Metamorphosen* 5, pp. 345–347. For the mixing of sea and air see Tarrant, *Seneca Agamemnon*, p. 268 *ad* Sen. *Aga.* 490 and *ibid.* p. 263 *ad Aga.* 471. The winds often blow against each other, cf. Sen. *Aga.* 476 and Tarrant, *Seneca Agamemnon*, p. 265; also Hor. *C.* I, 3, 13 and Nisbet-Hubbard 1, p. 50 *ad loc.*

1134 *plura non queo tamen*   The replacement of "queo" with "possum" (in *L*) reveals the meaning, see *OLD* s.v. possum 8a.

1139–1142 *ferox ... Corus ... insanus Auster*   For Corus or Caurus, the north-west storm, cf. Verg. *Ge.* III, 356: "Semper hiems, semper spirantes frigora cori" and see Stephanus, *Dictionarium*, p. 165v. Corus is also mentioned in Luc. I, 406 and II, 617. Cf. also Iuv. 14, 268: "coro semper tollendus et austro" and see *RE* 3, 1808–1809. For the Auster, the warm, tepid south wind, also Notus, see Stephanus, *Dictionarium*, p. 88r. The adjective "insanus" induces us to interpret Auster *in malam partem*, as in l. 1768 (and Notus in l. 756). On Auster see also Bömer, *Ovidius Metamorphosen* 3, p. 336 *ad* Ov. *Met.* VII, 532.

1139 *nec ante tanto*   sc. "timore". Another interpretation is that in the past it was not tossed about by such a great fear.

1143 *dei*   This form is probably a *collectivum* for the two gods of the wind, or it is referring to the one last mentioned, the Auster.

1144 *Thetys*   It seems as though Heinsius here, as in l. 604, is confusing the goddesses Thetis and Tethys, see the comm. *ad loc.*; here, too, he changes the spelling in his own copy.

1149 *dubia*   This adjective should be taken as 'wavering', i.e. it is sloshing calmly against the rocks, but not yet in full intensity, and as 'dangerous', 'treacherous' (*OLD* s.v. 9).

1149 *vix credens sibi*   Cf. Sen. *Aga.* 393: "vix credens mihi" and Ov. *Met.* V, 213: "credensque parum sibi"; XI, 108: "vixque sibi credens".

1158 *Lyaei dona ... mitis Ceres*   In his predilection for metonymy Heinsius uses Bacchus and Ceres for wine and bread, as in the well-know dictum "sine Cerere et Bacchus Venus friget". For the use of the Greek name in this combination, see (for example) Verg. *Aen.* IV, 58: "legiferae Cereri Phoeboque patrique Lyaeo" and *id. Ge.* I, 343–344. For "Lyaei dona", cf. Sil. XIII, 416: "dona Lyaei", a variant of "Bacchi munera" which occurs more often, e.g. Sil. XI, 285, Ov. *A.A.* I, 565 and Mart. VIII, 68, 4. Cf. also Sil. VII, 748–749: "Nec prius aut epulas aut munera grata Lyaei fas cuiquam tetigisse fuit".

1162–1163 *luminum ... orbes*   For the combination, see *OLD* s.v. orbis 8 and Bömer, *Ovidius Metamorphosen* 1, p. 415 *ad* Ov. *Met.* II, 752: "luminis orbem".

1163–1164 *lapsu graui noctis profundae* "Lapsus" can indicate the course of
the stars, in this case of night, but the adjective "gravis" gives "lapsus" the connotation of sliding downwards, which suggests that "nox" is a metonym for sleep.
The adjective "profundus" can refer to both the darkness of night (cf. Verg. *Aen.*
IV, 26: "noctemque profundam") and the depth of sleep (*OLD* s.v. 7a).

L 1129–1131 These lines become: '[...] the sprout of the old house and of our
tribe; this is how I want to relax my heart that is heavy and worried by effort
[...]'.
L 1135 Apparently because Heinsius wanted to delete "graves" he replaced it
with a possessive "suos".
L 1144 The spelling of the name Tethys was corrected (see above).

War in times of peace: St Bartholomew's Night

1166–1222 *Scilicet pacem tremis—Fuere et omnes* Loisa is afraid in peacetime,
when people are no longer on their guard and can be attacked using the element of surprise. Orange could indeed refer to the years before 1584 as being
relatively quiet, despite some attempts on his life, of which the one made by
Jean de Jaureguy on 18 March 1582 is the best known. Cf. for the contradiction:
'in the past there was danger, now the situation is safe', as well as l. 1063: "Non
ita pridem" versus l. 1090: "At nunc".

   However, Louise's experience is that an ostensibly peaceful situation can
turn into a bloody battle, as was the case with St Bartholomew's Night or the
Parisian Blood Wedding of 24 August 1572. At the wedding, after the marriage
ceremony of Henry de Navarre and Margaret de Valois—17 August—thousands
of Huguenots were murdered. The massacre shocked the whole of Europe and
was also a significant event for Orange, as it put an end to the much hoped-
for support for the Revolt from the French Huguenots, see also intr., pp. 15–
16. For the role of this event in pamphlets, see Duits, *Van Bartholomeusnacht
tot Bataafse opstand*, pp. 43–50. Louise's father, de Coligny was the main victim. On this admiral see (for example) *DBF* 9, 222–226 s.v. 3 Coligny, Junko
Chimizu, *Conflict of Loyalties: Politics and Religion in the Career of Gaspard
de Coligny, Admiral of France, 1519–1572* (Geneva: Librairie Droz, 1970) Travaux
d'Humanisme et Renaissance, 114, and *Actes du colloque "L'Amiral de Coligny
et son temps" (Paris, 24–28 octobre 1972)* (Paris: Société de l'histoire du protes-
tantisme Français, 1974). Tomasso Sassetti wrote a report about his death, ed.
John Tedeschi, 'Tomasso Sassetti's Account of the St. Bartholomew's Day Massacre', in: Alfred Soman (ed.), *The Massacre of St. Bartholomew: Reappraisals
and Documents* (The Hague: Martinus Nijhoff, 1974), pp. 112–152, esp. 135–140;

in addition, there is an anonymous *Discorso* of which fragments are included in Soman, *op. cit.*, pp. 164–178. Her husband Charles de Téligny (marriage on 24 March 1571) was also killed. See Philippe Erlanger, *Le massacre de la Saint-Barthélemy, 24 août 1572* (Paris: Gallimard, 1960) on this slaughter, and pp. 156–159 and 166 on the killing of Coligny and Téligny; also the comm. *ad* l. 1190.

A leading role on St Bartholomew's Night was played by the Guises, a branch of the House of Lorraine. The family, esp. Henry de Guise, conducted a vendetta against de Coligny, because they thought he had a hand in the murder of Henry's father Francis. It was therefore a squadron under the leadership of Henry de Guise that murdered de Coligny (Erlanger, *op. cit.*, pp. 156–159). Through the marriage of Charles III of Lorraine (the ruling Duke in 1572) to a daughter of Catherine de Medici, the family was allied with the royal family. Even then, mass bloodshed was considered impossible.

For the idea that cautiousness is needed when people are not alert, cf. Sen. *Aga.* 791: "Festus et Troiae fuit" and *ibid.* 798–799: "Nullum est periculum tibimet. At tibi magnum. Victor timere quid potest? Quod non timet".

1167 *non arma quondam* The word "quondam" can be taken as an adjective to "arma", or as an adverb: 'but in the past you did not do that for war'.

1167–1174 *Pace—suae* It is not clear who is meant. Initially one thinks of her father and husband (see above), but they are actually killed by the "Celtae furor" (l. 1170). Perhaps Loisa is speaking in general, but this is contradicted by the perf. from "vidit" (l. 1174).

1170 *Celtae* Cf. l. 1075 and the comm. This probably refers to the massacre of St Bartholomew's Night, or perhaps to the French Fury in Antwerp, 17 January 1583 or other troubles with regard to Anjou. Heinsius may have chosen the loaded word "Celta" instead of the usual "Gallus" for the connotation of violence.

1171 *factionum saeua ... manus* We may not need to have a special occasion in mind. Incidentally, the passage is somewhat illogical. Loisa speaks of peacetime, in which people who have not been killed by partisanship can perish, and she refers to the peacetime on St Bartholomew's Eve. But on that occasion, the party's struggles were intense.

1175 *secura metuis* Cf. Verg. *Aen.* IV, 298: "omnia tuta times".

1188 *sacra vis Colignij* Cf. Hom. *Od.* II, 409: ἱερὴ ἲς Τηλεμάχοιο (the holy power of Telemachus). See also Kühner-Stegmann 2.1, pp. 242–243 and Pease's comm (Cambridge, MA: Harvard University Press, 1935), pp. 182–183 *ad* Verg. *Aen.* IV, 132: "odora canum vis". For contemporary instances, cf. Grotius *Silva ad* [...] *Cuchlinum* 41: "vis incluta Iuni" (and see Grotius, *Dichtwerken/Poetry* I, 2, 1B, p. 37); Grotius *Docte flos* [...] 7: "Heurnii vim" and *Ad. ex.* 762.

This 'hanging between heaven and earth' (see also infra) is a counterpart to the passage in the story of the murderer, when he describes how his father hangs at the stake, between heaven and earth, and hovers between life and death (inter alia ll. 896–898 and 938–940). In this way the author creates inner coherence in the piece.

1188–1189 *potensque—neci* In these lines "potens" contrasts with "emancipatus".

1190 *interque—tenet* The fact that de Coligny floats between heaven and earth is based on events as related: he was stabbed in a room on the upper floor, but was still alive. He was defenestrated. He held himself for a moment, then collapsed. His head was cut off and shown in the Louvre, see Philippe Erlanger, *Le massacre de la Saint-Barthélemy, 24 août 1572* (Paris: Gallimard, 1960), pp. 158–159.

1192 *sydera* Because in Stoic terminology the "sidera" originate in the "aether" and are made of fire, they can be called "ignes" in l. 1993. See also Van Campen, *Lucanus Bellum Civile Liber II*, p. 209 and n. 67.

1194 *vicem* "Vicem" here has the function of "invicem".

1197–1198 *Quis—necem* In these lines, Loisa addresses (in an apostrophe, as well as a rhetorical question) de Téligny. This contributes to the emotionality, see pp. 383 and 392. The idea that her husband died on her lap is poetic fiction. He was stabbed and his body was thrown into the street, see Philippe Erlanger, *Le massacre de la Saint-Barthélemy, 24 août 1572* (Paris: Gallimard, 1960), p. 166.

1201 *oculosque morte iam natantes* Cf. Ov. *Met.* V, 71–72: "Iam moriens oculis sub nocte natantibus atra circumspicit Athin" (see also Bömer, *Ovidius Metamorphosen 2*, p. 246) and Stat. *Th.* XI, 558: "gravis oculos atque ora natantia leto".

1202 *exangues genas* Cf. Cic. *Tusc.* III, 12, 26: "exanguis genas".

1204 *auras* Cf. l. 218 and the comm. *ad* ll. 212–218.

1208 *pondus graue* Sen. *Tro.* 491.

1209 *vel sic* Vgl. Sen. *Pho.* 2–3: "nata, quam tanti est mihi genuisse vel sic"; see also *OLD* s.v. vel 5a and b.

1217 *aulaeque latebras* For the topos of the unreliability of court, see the comm. on l. 726.

1218–1220 *Desine ... metus ... vanis ... curis* For such a call to stop to fear, cf. (inter alia) Sen. *Oed.* 801–802: "Timere vana desine er turpes metus depone".

1220 *firmus ... locus* Possibly this is a fortified place, a fortress, or specifically Delft. It can also be a collective singular: the fortified cities.

1221–1222 *Nullus hic hostis fuit ... Fuere et omnes* Cf. Sen. *Aga.* 798–799, quoted above, *ad* ll. 1166–1222.

L 1195 Heinsius replaces the redundant "ille" with the adverb "una" (at the same moment).

L 1196 The somewhat strange "tutus" becomes "rectus", which makes more sense.

L 1219–1220 Heinsius changed this into: 'and do not with pleasure succumb to fruitless cares'.

Cares for the child

1222–1233 *Vocibus certè tuis—caput* Loisa yields to the request of Auriacus (1127–1133) and asks her servants to get Frederick Henry. The sight of the child exacerbates her concern, which she expresses to her husband. Lines 1224–1225 are an indirect stage direction.

1222–1224 *Vocibus—marite* For the thought that despite knowing the truth of the words someone can remain emotional, cf. Sen. *Pha.* 177–179: "Quae memoras scio vera esse, nutrix; sed furor cogit sequi peiora".

1224 *famularis manus* For the mannerist form "famularis" (also l. 1859) for "servilis", see Fantham, *Seneca's Troades*, p. 313 *ad Tro.* 747.

1226 *dulcis effigies tui* The likeness of baby and parent is generally a human one and needs no parallels, but for a case from Seneca's drama, cf. *Tro.* 464, where Andromacha says in an apostrophe to her baby Astyanax: "nimiumque patri similis"; see also 1545–1575 and the comm. *ad loc.*

1127 *pars mei, pars et tui* In classical Latin the expression "pars mei" does occur (e.g. Hor. *C.* III, 30, 3–7: "Magnaque pars mei vitabit Libitinam"), though not with regard to children (*OLD* s.v. pars; *TLL* 10, 448–488).

1230 *luminis ... notas* Cf. Curt. VIII, 3, 13: "oris notas".

The child as a consolation

1234–1253 *Accedat agedum—patriae virum* For Auriacus/Orange, seeing his child is not a cause for concern, but rather a cause for comfort and hope. It must grow up quickly so that it can take action and avenge him. It is striking that it is not Maurice who is the avenger, for he, the eldest son, would be the first in line, but rather the baby (Frederick Henry). See intr., p. 41.

The passage has traces of the sensitive words of Andromacha to her son Astyanax (and about him and her husband Hector, with whom she compares her child) in Sen. *Tro.* 461–474. In both speeches "nate" is used (*Aur.* 1234, 1235, etc., *Tro.* 461, 469); cf. also "vultus meos" (l. 1241) with *Tro.* 464: "vultus meus", "dissipata [...] comae" (ll. 1244–1245) with *Tro.* 468: "dissipans [...] comam", and "certam manum" (l. 1246) with *Tro.* 466: "fortes manus".

1235 *futurus ultor*　Cf. l. 1002 and the comm.

1235 *surge, age*　A combination with an epic ring, e.g. Verg. *Aen.* III, 169.

1239–1240 *moestae … matres*　Cf. Verg. *Aen.* VIII, 556: "Vota metu duplicant matres", and in *ibid.* 592–593 the mothers are present in the background, full of fear. It is not only the mothers that fear; Philip does too, for the Low Countries.

1242 *decusque latae frontis*　For the combination, cf. V. Fl. IV, 241: "frontis decus" and Sen. *Pha.* 281: "Non habet latam data plaga frontem". In the Renaissance a broad forehead was a sign of nobility. Cf. also l. 1452 "frontisque augustae decus" and see *TLL* 5.1, 236.4–65. The description of the forehead was also a topos in *epithalamia*, see Grotius, *Dichtwerken/Poetry* I, 2, 3A/B, p. 321.

1242 *toruas*　See l. 1018 and the comm.

1244–1247 *dissipata nobilis … aususque magnos*　This phrase is ambiguous: (1) 'ramified branch of noble tribe' (*OLD* s.v. 1e), 'your violent scream guarantees […]'; (2) 'the wide aristocratic hair and your heavy screams guarantee […]'. The hair apparently betrayed someone's descent. The second possibility seems the most probable, given the context: the broad forehead (l. 1242) and the screeching. Moreover, "dissipata […] comae" is reminiscent of Sen. *Tro.* 468: "cervice fusam dissipans iacta comam".

1248 *caeptam parenti … viam*　Cf. 1095 "patriam […] viam".

1249 *rerum … exordia*　Cf. Lucr. I, 827: "rerum […] primordia". Heinsius' change in his own copy made the expression closer to Lucr.

1251 *solamen*　Cf. (inter alia) Sen. *Pha.* 267: "Solamen annis unicum fessis" and *Aur.* 1313. See also Tarrant, *Seneca Agamemnon*, p. 268 *ad* Sen. *Aga.* 491: "levamen […] aerumnis".

1251–1252 *patri vultu—laudibus tibi*　This phrase can be paraphrased thus: when Auriacus/Orange will die, the child must make him live on in his features, and in his own glorious deeds.

L 1249　For the change of "exordia" to "primordia" (an echo of l. 84) see also supra, the comm. on l. 1249.

L 1251　Apparently Heinsius thought "maestae" more suitable to "solamen" than the proleptic "viduae".

The child will be an avenger

1254–1275 *At cum iuventae—Europae salus* For the thought, cf. the story of the murderer, ll. 993–1002. Both passages have similarities, namely the opportunity to pursue vengeance once one's youth is over. Equally, however, they contrast the misery and poverty of the murderer, whose father has already been murdered, and the happiness and wealth of the baby, whose father is still alive, but who may yet experience disaster.

1257–1258 *metum sibi ... subdat* The boy will also have to suppress his emotions. Cf. for the self-conquest the comm. on ll. 110–126.

1260 *Adolphi* Orange's brother Adolph died in the Battle of Heiligerlee (cf. *Wilhelmus* 29–30: "Graef Adolff is ghebleven, in Vrieslandt in den Slach", i.e. 'Count Adolph died in battle in Friesland'). This is a more likely candidate than an ancestor, the Count and King Adolph who died on the battlefield at Gollheim in 1298 (Petrus J. Blok, *Willem de Eerse, Prins van Orange* (Amsterdam: J.M. Meulenhoff, 1919–1920) 2 vols, vol. 1, p. 2 and Nicolaas Japikse, *De Geschiedenis van het Huis van Oranje-Nassau* (The Hague: Zuid-Hollandsche Uitgevers Maatschappij, 1937–1938) 2 vols, vol. 1, p. 28), which does not, however, have to be completely left out of consideration. In his adaptation of Heinsius' drama, *Het Moordadich Stvck* 842, Duym has Orange say to Frederick Henry: "I want you always to think of your great-grandfather Adolph". Serrarens and Wijngaards (Duym, *Het Moordadich Stvck*, p. 107) explain "oud-vader" as uncle, but this meaning is not found in *WNT* 11, 1568–1569 s.v. Duym here means the 'old' Count and King.

1262 *dium Renatus nomen* René of Châlon was an uncle of William of Nassau, from whom William inherited the principality and the title of Orange; he died on the battlefield at the Siege of St-Dizier. On him, see, for instance, *ADB* s.v. Renatus (Friedrich Otto); F. Hamant, 'René van Châlon, Prins van Oranje 1518–1544', in: F.L.J. Krämer a.o. (eds), *Je maintiendrai: Een boek over Nassau en Oranje* (Leiden: A.W. Sijthoff, 1905), pp. 103–125; D.C.J. Mijnssen, 'René van Chalon', *Jaarboek 'De Oranjeboom'* 4 (1951), pp. 75–94; also Grotius, *Dichtwerken/Poetry* I, 2, 4A/B, pp. 247 and 257–258.

1262 *sanguis* For 'blood' in the sense of offspring, see *OLD* s.v. 10. As a word for son, also vocative, it is in Verg. *Aen.* VI, 835: "Proice tela manu, sanguis meus".

1263 *lux haec* This day, i.e. the moment Auriacus/Orange mentioned in ll. 1254–1255.

1265–1266 *aerata ... carina* For examples of copper-clad ships, see *OLD* s.v. aeratus lb. Cf. also Sil. XI, 586: "aeratas [...] carinas".

1265–1266 *spumeum ... secans sulcum* Cf. Sen. *Tro.* 1027: "secans fluctum rate singulari"; also *id. Pha.* 88 and Hor. *C.* I, 1, 13–14: "trabe Cypria Myrtoum pavidus nauta secet mare". The expression is Homeric, e.g. *Od.* III, 174–175.

1265–1266 *spumeum ... sulcum* The *sulcus* is the wake (*OLD* s.v. 3b). The colon is a contamination of Man. I, 708: "sulcum ducente carina" and expressions such as "fluctum secare" (see supra).

1268 *lares* Here the word "Lares" (tutelary deities in antiquity) probably indicates saints' statues. Since the "Lares" could be metonym for houses, this line can also be interpreted as the conquered and looted houses.

1270 *Batauum, Belgiaeque* Here the seafaring Hollanders (cf. "e puppe") are probably meant, as opposed to the Flemings, cf. the opposition of both choruses: indigenous Hollanders ("Batavi") and Flemish immigrants; in l. 1288 Heinsius uses the term "Cattus" for Hollander (q.v.). Nevertheless, he may have considered "Batavus" and "Belgia" to be synonymous here.

1271 *togae* For "toga" as a metonym for authority, cf. Luc. V, 382: "iam doctam servire togae".

1272–1273 *Patresque magnos ... et Ichnaeae decus sanctum senatum* The words "senatus" and "patres" indicate the States of Holland (and Zeeland), or perhaps the States General and its members, dependent on the issue of who possessed sovereignty, which was not a foregone conclusion, see G. de Bruin, *Geheimhouding en verraad: De geheimhouding van staatszaken ten tijde van de Republiek (1600–1750)* (The Hague, 1191) Doctoral thesis Utrecht, p. 120. The expression "Ichnaeae decus" is not easy to explain in this respect: Ἰχναῖος, of Ichnae in Thessaly, i.e. of Themis (LSJ s.v.), goddess of justice, see Stephanus, *Dictionarium*, p. 246r s.v. Ichnae and *id.* p. 424r s.v. Themis; Roscher 5, 570–606; *RE* 2.R. 5, 1626–1630. In *Hom. hymn. Apollo* 94 Themis is called Ἰχναίη. Strabo (IX, 5, 14) recounts the fact that Themis is worshipped there. The provincial States and the States General were no juridical courts. Heinsius probably means that these *gremia* made light decisions, or the words refer to the Court of Holland. "Sanctus" is an *epitheton ornans* of "senatus", also called "sanctum concilium patrum". Cf. Verg. *Aen.* I, 426: "sanctumque senatum" and Ov. *P.* IV, 9, 17: "sancti [...] turba senatus".

L 1259 The 'great' becomes the 'holy' family, more fitting in the context of "Divos" (l. 1259) and "dium" (l. 1262); cf. also l. 119 "sanctiora nomina".

L 1260 The change puts "altus" to "indoles", which makes more sense than the possibly ambiguous 'high heart'.

L 1263 The relative "qua" becomes the (temporal) conjunction "cum".

L 1265 The metaphorically used "secans" (to cut a furrow) becomes the more neutral "trahens" (to draw a furrow); see also supra.

The world awaits its ruler

1276–1280 *O nate—gliscentis aeui* This passage begins with something resembling a commonplace: for famous people it is impossible not to stand out, in contrast to living secretly (see the comm. *ad* ll. 728–735).

L 1280 Heinsius has an aversion, or so it seems from "gliscere". Both in l. 1116 and here he removes the word, replacing it here with "surgentis" (your rising age).

Fighting on land and at sea

1280–1285 *Nate—Natura nate* For the topos that the "Batavus" (Dutchman or Hollander) is at home at sea, cf. ll. 305–318. Here he fights on two fronts: on land and at sea; for "terraque angusta est nimis", cf. Huygens' *Scheeps-praet* 13: "Mouring, die de Zee te naw hiel" ('Maurice, who considered the sea too small'). It is *Natura* that draws Frederick Henry into the light ("in lucem trahit"). One might consider in this regard Frederick Henry's own character, which revealed itself at a young age (see ll. 1328–1338), or perhaps Nature as a deity is intended, cf. the comm. *ad* ll. 1–5.

1280 *magnanimus* See the comm. *ad* l. 488.
1283 *angusta est nimis* The same combination can be read in ll. 1762 and 1982.

L 1280 In the second half of the line Heinsius removes "magnanimus", perhaps since this word is used for nobility par excellence (see Veenstra, *Ethiek en moraal*, pp. 45–47). Now the sentence translates: 'Child, the Dutchman shows your courage [...]'.
L 1283 The metaphor of travelling ("semita", l. 1282) is continued since "modus" is replaced with "iter". Juxtaposition becomes subordination, indicating the relationship between the statements ("si", 'since').
L 1285 Heinsius probably wanted to make it clearer, through the addition of "rerum", that nature as cosmic order is intended.

Called upon to fight

1285–1294 *quodque supremum—stravit labor* Just like Auriacus himself (see comm. *ad* ll. 51–58), the baby will not fight of his own accord but because his country calls upon him to do so. This is specified by residents of the various provinces: Hollanders, Zeelanders, Gelderlanders and Frisians, inhabitants of the northern Netherlands. The southern Netherlanders (including the inhabitants of the Generality provinces) are left out. This is unremarkable in a period in which the southern Netherlands were almost considered hostile, although it must be borne in mind that Heinsius, as a Fleming, would have thought otherwise. For the relationship between the northern and southern Netherlands around 1600, see, e.g. Ivo Schöffer a.o. (eds), *De Lage Landen van 1500–1780* (Amsterdam, etc.: Elsevier, 1978), pp. 152–155.

1285–1286 *quodque supremum ... arbitror* Cf. l. 1120: "quodque supremum reor".

1287 *poscerisque* 'Your help is wished for.' The passive "posci", from epic style, connotes the call of fate. Cf. Verg. *Aen.* VIII, 533: "Ego poscor Olympo", and one of the variants in Hor. *C.* I, 32, 1: "poscimur"; Ov. *Met.* II, 144. See also Bömer's comm. 1, p. 278 *ad loc.* and Sil. II, 44. The form "posceris" is found in Stat. *Th.* II, 400.

1288 *Cattus* On the 'Catti', see Stephanus, *Dictionarium*, p. 137v and cf. Hooft's *Baeto*, in which the eponymous hero is ruler of the *Catten*. The Catti (Chatti) were a Germanic tribe, here representing the Hollanders (alongside the Gelderlanders, Zeelanders and Frisians); cf. furthermore the name "Cattorum vicus" (Katwijk); also Benedicti *De rebus gestis* I, 349–350: "Est regio, imperii quondam pars magna Quirini Cattorum populis habitata, Batavia nomen tunc fuit, hinc prisci Batavos dixere colonos".

1289 *Walachri* See Stephanus, *Dictionarium*, p. 447v s.v. Walachria: "Zelandiae primaria insula"; here used pars pro toto for Zeeland.

1290 *Geldrus, et Friso* See Stephanus, *Dictionarium*, pp. 218r and 211v–212v respectively. The addition of "aetatis suae profusor" to "Geldrus" will be a reference to the fact that he is putting his life at stake for his country, cf. Cic. *Phil.* 14, 11, 30: "qui pro patria vitam profuderunt". In these lines the use of *nomina agentia* on -(t)or (regnator, profusor, victor, ultor) is remarkable.

L 1287 Whatever prevailed, in order to delete the tautological "posceris" (cf. "coactus"), indicating the storms at sea, or to qualify the Hollanders as courageous, Heinsius changed this line into: 'Hence the controller of the stormy sea, the brave Dutchman [...]'.

The future of the Netherlands

1295–1312 *Quae o nate—late verrit* In these lines Auriacus suggests that Frederick Henry 'reads' the future of the Netherlands. For this, cf. Verg. *Ecl.* 4, 26–27: "At simul heroum laudes et facta parentis iam legere et quae sit poteris cognoscere virtus". Through this allusion Frederick Henry is, as it were, compared with the child of salvation from this fourth *Eclogue*. For the epic one can think of Verg. *Aen.* VIII, 626–728 (the description of Aeneas' shield); cf. further *ibid.* I, 466–493 (scenes on the door of the temple of Juno) and VI, 20–33 (the door of the Apollo temple). On the doors of the underworld Aeneas *cum suis* 'read' ("perlegerunt", Verg. *Aen.* VI, 34) various scenes. For such ἔκφρασεις see also ll. 1792–1814 and the comm.

1296 *aestus—fluxas vices*   Here, implicitly, the ancient metaphor of the ship of state is used (already in Plato *Rep.* VI, 488 and Demosthenes *Corona* 194; further in Cic. *Sest.* 46, *Pis.* 20; see also *OLD* s.v. navis le; Hermann Wankel, *Demosthenes: Rede für Ktesiphon über den Kranz* (Heidelberg: Winter, 1976), 2 vols, 2, pp. 914–915; *WNT* 14, 699), which is in the surf of the sea ("aestus"). The "fluxas vices" will mean the tides or wave action.

1297 *ruptumque regi foedus*   On 23 August 1566 Margaret of Parma made an agreement with the nobles: Protestant preaching was allowed where it already existed, provided the Catholics were left unharmed. The Inquisition would also be abrogated. All this on the condition that the Covenant of the Nobles would be dissolved and the nobles would help to restore order. Margaret guaranteed to protect the nobles as far as her power was concerned. The agreement was, however, dependent on Philip's approval. Later Margaret had to revoke her concessions on his orders. After the capture of Valenciennes (24 March 1567) and the crushing defeat of the army of Brederode at Oosterweel (13 March), Margaret was in control again. Cf. Benedicti, *De rebus gestis* I, 62: "violato foedere". It might also refer to the violation of privileges, for example by executing the counts of Egmond and Horne, in violation of the Order of the Golden Fleece, or by the institution of the tenth and twentieth penny tax.

1297 *dapes*   This could refer to a special event, or the slaughter of people in general, prey for the Spaniards.

1299 *atro Mosa spumauit vado*   The Spaniards regularly drowned enemies in a local river, such as in the city of Zutphen, see Motley, *Dutch Republic*, p. 497. It is not known if the Meuse also witnessed such a scene, but this is surely being referred to, cf. Benedicti *De rebus gestis* I, 437–438: "Mosam civibus undantem et congesta mole tumentem". In 1572 the city of Rotterdam fell victim to a murderous onslaught (Motley, *Dutch Republic*, pp. 467). "[A]tro [...] vado" probably refers to dirty water or a black bed in general. "Stagno [...] turbido" could refer to muddy water, or to intense turbulence, caused by the bodies thrown into the water. In which case "turbidus" would be synonymous with "turbatus".

1301 *Honta*   The Honte or Westerschelde (Western Scheldt) is the western arm of the Scheldt, flowing between South Beveland and the district of Hulst (Van der Aa, *Aardrijkskundig woordenboek* 5, p. 747). As a river god, the Honte has *cor-*

nua (horns), unless this means the river arms (*OLD* s.v. cornu 6c). In the case of the Scheldt, too, poetical exaggeration is in play, rather than actual events, unless the Spanish or French Furies are meant (see above, ll. 1120–1122 and 1170).

1303 *cadauerumque mole* Cf. Benedicti, *De rebus gestis* I, 437–438: "congesta mole" (see l. 1299).

1303–1304 *praeclusus sibi quaesiuit in se sese* The river, Heinsius suggests, was so littered with corpses, that it stagnated ("praeclusus sibi") and the bed was no longer visible ("quaesiuit in se sese"). As a result of all this, it burst its banks (ll. 1304–1305 ingentem viam–fuit). Incidentally, these lines are written in a far-reaching form of *obscuritas*. For the blocking of a river by corpses, cf. Luc. II, 212–214.

1306–1312 *Qua—verrit* In 1572, the city of Vlissingen expelled the Spanish occupants on the very day that Spanish reinforcement troops arrived by sea. These were driven away with a few shots. Vlissingen received help from the Sea Beggars and for some time the fighter Willem Bloys of Treslong (ca. 1529–1594) (cf. "nauita", l. 1311; see Motley, *Dutch Republic*, pp. 467–470; *NNBW* 6, 121–123) ruled the city. The adjective "fraenatrix Sali" is usually employed for Zeelanders, here for the people of Vlissingen, cf. Grotius, *Dichtwerken/Poetry* I, 2, 3 A/B, p. 301.

1306 *Qua primus Albae terror* The word "primus" here means 'before', just like the adverb 'primum' (*OLD* s.v. primum 2 5). Vlissingen was not the first city to experience Alva's terror, but it was actually the first city to expel the Spaniards after the conquest of Brill (Den Briel, Brielle). Heinsius knew Vlissingen from his youth; he attended the Latin school there, see Ter Horst, *Daniel Heinsius*, pp. 13–14.

1310 *curru marino vectus* A similar metaphor can be seen in *Pro Auriaco suo* 30: "veliferum [...] currum", and in *In Hispanum et Batavum* 17–18.

1311 *nauita* This probably refers to Willem Bloys of Treslong (see supra), though the Sea Beggars of the Hollanders in general may also be meant.

L 1295–1298 Heinsius modifies these lines so that the *nomina*, the breach of contract on the part of the Spanish King and the meals disappeared. They became: 'Child, what kind of wars will you read, what a great turmoil and sudden changes of fortune in the falling fatherland and what kind of wiles of the Spaniards?'

Education to courage

1312–1326 *At tu—lateat vigor* Auriacus asks his wife to raise the child in such a way that it will later perform brave acts. He portrays the military art in epic terms. For example, "tubae" (l. 1316), "hastae" and "pulvis" (l. 1317) are characteristics of the ancient battlefield. On the mention of whirling dust at the beginning of the battle, see Franz E. Erbig, *Topoi in den Schlachtenberichten römischer Dichter* (Gdansk: O. Lauter, Jr, 1931), Inaugural dissertation Würzburg, p. 8. See also infra, the comm. on the various lines.

1313 *solamen* Cf. l. 1251.

1314–1315 *memento ... ducere* Heinsius uses a metaphor of 'guiding past' for 'telling about'.

1318 *equi ... spumantis* Cf. *Pro Auriaco sua* 10: "spumantem [...] equum". For "lupatis", cf. Verg. *Ge.* III, 207–208: "negabunt [...] duris parere lupatis". A "lupatum" is a bit with metal points, used for uncooperative horses, see Nisbet-Hubbard 1, pp. 112–113 *ad* Hor. *C.* I, 8, 6.

1320 *aperto vertice* (1) on an open summit; (2) bareheaded. For the second interpretation, cf. "aperto capite" (*OLD* s.v. apertus 6).

1323 *pectore aduerso* Cf. ll. 967–968 "aduerso ... corde" and the comm.

Signs of courage

1327–1338 *Virtutis—genus* At a young age the baby already shows signs of his later calling and courage. The motif may be topical, as an expression of proud parents, but examples from classical literature have not been found. Earlier, Auriacus mentioned promising signs: the hair and the screeching (ll. 1244–1245).

1330 *arma vibrabat manu* Cf. Sen. *Tro.* 775: "arma [...] tractabis manu".

Time for a meal

1339–1340 *At nos—inuadit polum* A temporal closing of a scene is not lacking in Seneca's drama, e.g. *Herc. f.* 827–829. It is also a means of structuring the play in time (see the comm. *ad* ll. 6–12). Incidentally, Heinsius combines this with historical fact: the murder took place after lunch; see also intr. pp. 19–20.

L **1339** On second thoughts Heinsius was not satisfied with "suetae" without having a proper alternative.

L **1340** Heinsius realized that the wagon of the sun god does not 'enter' the sky, but (more logically) 'ascends' into it.

Act III, Chorus (1341–1405)

Summary

The choir (consisting of indigenous Hollanders) have seen nebulae around the moon and fear an omen. But from the marriage of the moon and the sun, spring comes into being. They also saw a comet, a bad omen for princes.

1341–1347 Is the moon enveloping itself without reason, or does it announce wars? But those who believe in the stars will be disappointed.

1348–1392 From the cosmic marriage of the moon and the sun, flowers, young cattle and children arise. The birds sing bridal music, the west wind is a bridal gunner and the wine grapes grow luxuriantly.

1393–1399 The chorus saw a comet near the Great Bear and Little Bear, an ominous sign.

1400–1405 Such bad signs strike kings. Insignificant people have nothing to fear. Prosperity will automatically fall.

This chorus of indigenous Hollanders is the counterpart to that of the Flemish exiles. That chorus also raised a hymn to nature and contrasted rich (threatened by Fortuna) with poor (but safe).

The chorus connects two cosmic marriages: that of the moon goddess and the sun god (ll. 1348–1361) and that of Heaven and Earth (ll. 1362–1392). From these connections full of love, new life arises (see the comm. *ad loc.*). This idyllic representation of things is a stark contrast to the opening lines and the final ones, in which the choir mentions frightening signs: the moon behind clouds and a comet in the sky. On the *locus amoenus*, see (for example) Curtius, *European Literature and Latin Middle Ages*, pp. 183–202, esp. 195–200.

Metre

As the heading suggests, this chorus song consists of choriambs, iambic dimeters, dactylic tetrameters and pentameters, and Sapphic hexameters. Lines 1341–1363 consist of choriambs, which are in fact Asclepiadeans (---vv--vv-vx) (such as Hor. *C.* I, 1 "Maecenas atavis, edite regibus"). The verses 1364–1372 are written in iambic (catalectic) dimeters (i.e. the last foot is not full: v-v-v-x), ll. 1373–1384 in dactylic tetrameters (-vv-vv-vv-vv). This metre also occurs in Seneca's drama, in *Oed.* 449–465 and *Herc. Oet.* 1947–1962, see also Crusius-Rubenbauer, *Römische Metrik*, pp. 60–61. The passage from *Oedipus* in particular is important for this passage, because it also includes the flourishing of nature. In ll. 1385–1392 the usual dactylic pentameters are used and in ll. 1393–

1399 dactylic hexameters. The chorus song ends with hendecasyllables (-v ---vv-v-x) and an adonius (-vv-x).

Commentary

Portents

1341–1347 *Frustran'—sideribus fidem* The chorus sees that the moon is hidden behind clouds and interprets this as a sign of impending doom. In classical literature, especially in the *vitae* of Suetonius and Plutarch (though see also Ov. *Met.* xv, 746–851), the violent death of princes was often preceded by signs (Henk Duits, 'Onheilspellende voortekenen in Hoofts "Henrik de Gróte"', in: Hans van Dijk a.o. (eds), *In de zevende hemel: Opstellen voor P.E.L. Verkuyl over literatuur en kosmos* (Groningen: Passage, 1993), p. 75). But there is more to this. Stoic cosmology encompasses the principle of *sympatheia*. Everything is interrelated, as a condition (bond, kinship) and as a process (influencing), as in a 'chain of being'. "Elke'oorsaeck heeft haer moederoorsaeck weder" (every cause in turn has its own cause), wrote Hooft (*Noodlot*); cf. Epictetus *Diss.* I, 14, 2: the earthly experiences the influence of heaven; Cic. *Div.* II, 34 gives the definition of συμπάθεια: "coniunctio naturae and quasi concentus et consensus", see also Cicero, *De divinatione libri duo*, ed. A.S. Pease (Darmstadt: Wissenschaftliche Buchgesellschaft, 1963), pp. 411–412 *ad loc.* and Rosenmeyer, *Senecan Drama and Stoic Cosmology*, pp. 109–112.

The chorus contrasts this with an Epicurean idea that one should not attach too much faith to astrology, cf. Sen. *Ep.* 88, 14–18, where the idea is expressed that knowledge of astrology does not contribute anything to practising virtue.

1341–1342 *Frustran'—nubibus* Cf. Ov. *Her.* 17, 74: "si dubitas, caecum, Cynthia, lumen habes"; Sen. *Aga.* 470: "luna conditur"; also Hor. *C.* II, 16, 2–4: "simul atra nubes condidit lunam neque certa fulgent sidera nautis".
1341 *sollicitis condita vultibus* The 'faces' could be the sight of the people, but also aim at the appearance of the moon, its phases. In which case the translation would be 'hidden with a worried face', possibly with enallage and medial use of the participle: 'anxiously concealing her phases'.
1342 *Cynthia* Diana, the goddess who was born on the mountain Cynthus, was identified with the moon, see Stephanus, *Dictionarium*, p. 174v; Roscher 2.1, 1707 s.v. Kynthia and *RE* 12,41. In Hor. *C.* III, 28, 12 'Cynthia' is another name for Artemis.
1344–1345 *belli dubios ... impetus et Mauortis opus* In an *amplificatio* Heinsius says the same thing twice in different words, see also intr., e.g. p. 139.

Cosmic marriage

1348–1392 *Namque illa—in scatebras* From the cosmic marriage between the moon goddess and the sun god—she receives light and thus energy ("ignibus", l. 1350) from him—the new life is created, Heinsius suggests. This cosmic marriage has a long tradition; for its origins, see Roscher 2.2, 3157–3163 s.v. Mondgöttin, where such texts as Hes. *Th.* 371–374 and Nonnos X, 214 are quoted. Within the compass of this tradition, the proemium of Lucr. I, 1–43 particularly stands out, i.e. the prayer to Venus: the love that causes everything to come into being.

This love also affects the *Aether* and the earth (ll. 1362–1392). According to (for example) Verg. *Ge.* II, 323–345, the *Aether* fecundates 'mother' earth with its rain during spring. This view returns in Grotius *Ad. ex.* 518–519: "Coeloque nudum Terra monstraret sinum, fructus sequenti iussa produxit". Cf. also Lucr. I, 250–253 and Sen. *Oct.* 404–405. In Verg. *Aen.* IV, 166–168 cosmic phenomena, lightning and rain, accompany the gathering of Aeneas and Dido. A spring song is also found in Secundus *El.* III, 6 (Secundus, *Opera Omnia*, ed. Bosscha, 1, pp. 173–181).

Heinsius combines this with elements from wedding hymns (*epithalamia*): the "Hymen Hymenaee" is sung, and the bride is accompanied to the chamber of the bridegroom, for an *amplexus* (i.e. sexual embracing, see *OLD* 1a). On the epithalamic genre, see Scal. *Poet.* III, 100, pp. 150b–155a, esp. p. 151a; Scaliger, *Poetica/Dichtkunst* 3, pp. 62–98, esp. pp. 66–68, and see also Th.M. Greene, 'Spenser and the Epithalamic Convention', *Comparative Literature* 9 (1957), pp. 215–218; Forster, *Janus Gruter's English Years*, pp. 104–115; Virginia Tufte, *The Poetry of Marriage: The Epithalamium in Europe and Its Development in England* (Los Angeles: Tinnon-Brown, 1970); and M.A. Schenkeveld-van der Dussen, 'Theorie en poëzie: Een epithalamium van Six van Chandelier', *De nieuwe taalgids* 72 (1979), pp. 391–396 and *id.*, 'Poëzie als gebruiksartikel: Gelegenheidsgedichten in de zeventiende eeuw', in: Marijke Spies (ed.), *Historische letterkunde: Facetten van een vakbeoefening* (Groningen: Wolters Noordhoff, 1984), pp. 75–92.

1348 *emeritis ... cornibus* I.e. the new moon.
1352 *dulcis humus parturit* Cf. Verg. *Ecl.* 3, 56: "Nunc omnis ager [...] parturit"; *Ge.* II, 330: "Parturit almus ager Zephyrique tepentibus auris laxant arva sinus".
1353 *Favonij* For Favonius or Zephyrus, the humid, sweet west wind announcing the beginning of spring, see the comm. *ad* l. 1352 and Stephanus, *Dictionarium*, p. 451r. See also the comm. *ad* ll. 611–627 and 668.
1354 *daedalei ... soli* Cf. l. 698 and Lucr. I, 7: "daedala tellus" (= *ibid.* I, 228).

1355–1357 *violae ... Rosa* These flowers are no symbols, but specimens that make the earth "daedalus".

1359 *Lucinam patitur* Cf. Verg. *Ge.* III, 60: "Lucinam [...] pati", i.e. to give birth. Lucina or Juno Lucina is the goddess of birth giving, sometimes identified with Diana (Cynthia, see l. 1361). Stephanus, *Dictionarium*, p. 184r s.v. Diana: "Hanc parturientes Iunonis Lucinae nomine invocabant". For the meaning of the name Lucina ('who brings to light') see loc. cit.: "Lucinam [...] quod partum in lucem proferre putaretur". See also Stephanus, *Dictionarium*, p. 279r and Roscher 2.1, 579 s.v. Iuno.

1362 *Caelum—solum* Cf. Grot. *Soph.* 1119–1124 and Grotius, *Dichtwerken/Poetry* I, 4, p. 316 *ad loc.* The motif of love nourishing everything is known from *epithalamia*, see above.

1363 *faederibus* For these treatises, cf. Luc. I, 79–80 (see the comm. *ad* ll. 1644–1668).

1374 *hymen hymenaee* Cf. Catullus 61 passim.

1380 *regales ... sinus* Cf. Ov. *Her.* 1, 3: "indue regales, Laudamia, sinus".

1382 *Illinc* This accomplishes the triad of "illinc" (ll. 1352 and 1354). This is also followed by a corollary of the cosmic marriage between sun and moon.

1383–1384 *Ceres ... Bacchi* For the combination of Ceres and Bacchus, see l. 1158 and the comm.

1384 *Foemineus Bacchi ... liquor* For "Bacchi liquor", see Sen. *Thy.* 687. The addition of "foemineus" may refer to (1) the Maenads, or (2) the effemination caused by drinking wine.

1385 *tremulis* The branches are moved by the wind or bend due to the abundance of grapes.

1387 *pectoribus* For "pectus" as a seat of intelligence and feeling, see (for example) Sen. *Tro.* 523: "Nectit pectore astus callidos" and see Fantham, *Seneca's Troades*, p. 290 *ad loc.* See also *OLD* s.v. 3a.

A comet

1393–1399 *Vidimus—ab ausu* For comets that accompany the death of princes, see the comm. *ad* ll. 1341–1347. A specific case of a comet as a sign is given by Cic. *N.D.* II, 14, see Pease, pp. 584–585; see further Cic. *Div.* I, 18 and Pease's comm., pp. 105–107. A comet also appeared upon the death of Caesar, according to Plut. *Caes.* 69 and Verg. *Ge.* I, 488. Grotius, *Ad. ex.* 495–497 mentions the comets as a harbinger of impending doom ("index cladis"); see also Grotius, *Dichtwerken/Poetry* I, 1B, p. 48. The comet may also be a reference to the apotheoses of Romulus and Caesar, cf. Ov. *Met.* XV, 746–851, esp. 849–850: "flammiferumque trahens spatioso limite crinem stella micat". The appearance of a comet here is a purely literary phenomenon, which is not based on actual events at the time of Orange's death (see Bloemendal, 'Mon Dieu, mon Dieu ...').

1394–1398 *auriga ... maioris ... Vrsae ... Orion*   The constellation Auriga ('Charioteer') is near Ursa Maior, see Pease, pp. 819–820 *ad* Cic. *N.D.* II, 110; pp. 805–807 *ad* II, 105 and p. 32 *ad* II, 113. for Ursa Maior see also Stephanus, *Dictionarium*, p. 447v and for Orion *id.*, p. 328r–v. The rise and fall of Orion was associated with stormy weather; it is a small step from this to interpreting Orion as a bad omen. On Orion, see *RE* 18.1, 1065–1082, esp. 1075–1078.

1398 *ensis*   Poets prefer "ensis" to the ordinary word "gladius". See also ll. 1017 and 1686. "Gladius" is not used in *Aur.*

         Stars threaten high-ranking people

1400–1405 *Regiae ... dehiscit*   For the theme of the high-ranking who fall quickly, see the comm. *ad* ll. 715–728. For the collapse of the high and mighty cf. Luc. I, 81: "in se magna ruunt".

1404 *sors ... secunda*   "Secunda" may refer to prosperity in general, though more probably to the fate of the high-ranking and prosperous.

1404–1405 *propriâ—dehiscit*   Cf. Sen. *Aga.* 88–89: "cedit [...] oneri suo".

         Act IV, Scene 1 (1406–1502)

Summary

This scene is divided into two parts. In the first part the murderer hesitates, briefly interrupted by Alecto, in the second part Inquisitio urges her sisters the Furies to prepare a magic potion to fuel his bloodlust.

1406–1422   The murderer strongly hesitates over his plan, which he has been considering for so long. Yet he must carry it out to prevent shame.

1422–1441   A bad omen stops him: he stubbed his toe three times against the threshold. Nevertheless, he will commit the murder, however great the opposition is or however bad the consequences are, otherwise shame will be his lot.

1442–1449   Philip II may be happy: this day will end the war and he will overcome himself without having done anything himself.

1450–1459   Then he is paralysed by fear again.

1460–1462   Alecto summons Megaera to incite the man with a torch dripping with blood and with poison from hell.

1463–1472 The murderer sees in his madness the sun returning in the middle of the day and disappearing behind a cloud, but asks him to wait: the murderer will leave the earth and stones will shatter his head if he does not fulfill his plan.

1473–1496 Inquisitio urges the Furies to prepare a magic potion consisting of mythological substances (ll. 1475–1480 Medea and Cerberus; ll. 1481–1484 Ino and Athamas), the moisture of half-mythological animals (ll. 1484–1485 raging mares), 'ordinary' ingredients (ll. 1486–1496 animal parts, including bones, livers, entrails) and abstract evils (ll. 1490–1493 blindness, crime, murder, tears and blood). They must dunk the head of the man in it; the rage of Echidna must permeate him as well.

1497–1501 The snakes that accompany the Furies should announce the demise of the Dutch to them by hissing, since the day of doom has arrived.

1501–1502 Unsuspecting, the family goes to lunch.

The murderer still hesitates seriously, shaken, and again torn between longing and fear. He is capable of analysing himself objectively, despite his intense emotion; this combination ils characteristic for Seneca's drama. Eventually the actions of the Furies tip the balance in favour of his desire to commit the murder. For their appearance, not lacking in Seneca's drama, see the comm. *ad* ll. 1460–1462 and 1473–1493. Heinsius made their appearance plausible by having the murderer describe a dream (see below) featuring a woman with traits of Inquisitio (ll. 787–796). The passage is reminiscent of the scene after the first chorus song in Sen. *Aga.*, in which Clytemnestra expresses her hesitations when she is about to commit a murder (i.e. of her husband).

Metre

The ll. 1406–1472 consist of iambic trimeters, ll. 1473–1502 of trochaic catalectic tetrameters, like Sen. *Med.* 740–751, *Pha.* 1201–1212 and *Oed.* 223–232.

Commentary

Hesitation and fearing shame

1406–1422 *Ignosce—perge hac* Heinsius opens the scene with an elliptical sentence. "Victus" refers to the fear that has overwhelmed the murderer. "Roma" is a concise expression for the Roman Catholic Church along with its institutions, and in particular the Pope and the Curia, who form their administration (see also *WNT* 13, 993–994). They are also mentioned separately, the Pope as "sacerrimi [...] patris" (the Holy Father, 1407–1408, for this indication *WNT* 18, 166), the cardinals of the Curia as "fibulati patres".

The word "fibulati" may refer to the signet ring of the Pope, cardinals and bishops—just as soldiers in the Roman Empire received a "fibula" as a sign of distinction, with the stone determining the value of the ring, ecclesiastical dignitaries received a ring too. This symbolized their power and their loyalty to the Church (see *WNT* 13, 493). Heinsius will have avoided the more usual "anulatus" for the ambiguity of this word. Perhaps he wished to vary on "causiati patres" (after the "causia" the hat with wide brim, or "purpurati patres" dressed in red), circumlocutions for cardinals, see Kilianus, *Etymologicum*, p. 289 s.v. kardinael. However, "fibulati" may also hint at the habiliments of prelates, which could be held together by a precious pin (Du Cange 3, 482 s.v. fibulatorium, a cloak that is held together by a buckle; J. Braun S.J., *Die liturgische Gewandung im Occident und Orient nach Ursprung und Entwicklung, Verwendung und Symbolik* (Freiburg im Breisgau: Herder, 1907), pp. 321–326, the "fibula" as clasp of the "pluviale"). Furthermore, the glove of bishops was adorned with "fibulae" (Braun, *op. cit.*, pp. 375–378). "Fibulati" (connected with a pin) can also be used metaphorically just like "patres conscripti" (the 'enrolled' fathers, the senators), as a metaphor for the administrators of the Church. Being bound can hint at the cardinals' silence or the prohibition for cardinals of the Curia to leave Rome without explicit permission from the Pope (thanks to R.C. Engelberts).

The murderer is afraid and describes the fear in terms of warfare—"victus", "fuga", "superatus", "cedere", the fear "invicta mentis moenia obsedit meae"— and he holds a "triumphus". He is taken prisoner ("trahor", or perhaps: carried away by his emotions), albeit before the actual "pugna" already.

1408 *votaque, et fides mea*   Initially one is inclined to view these words as an apposition with "sacerrimi tutela patris", the Pope on whom he has established his hope and to whom he has given his word of faith. The murderer uses "votum" elsewhere (l. 1417) for his vow to kill the Prince, which could also be the point here. In which case he would be calling on the Pope and the Cardinals of the Curia, and evoking (as slightly alien elements in the series) his vow and word of allegiance, indirectly given to the same Pope and Curia.

1411 *mihique cessi*   Cf. ll. 1721–1722: "Deseror rursus [...] et me reliqui".

1416 *lustrator*   Here the *aether* takes the position of the sun as the one who sees and irradiates everything, cf. (for example) Ov. *Met.* II, 32: "oculis [...] quibus adspicit omnia", and see Bömer, *Ovidius Metamorphosen* 1, pp. 230–231 *ad* Ov. *Met.* I, 769.

1417 *bis senis* Indeed, the murderer had sworn to kill the Prince in 1578, six years before the actual murder. This period is given literary form in "bis senis", cf., e.g., Sen. *Aga.* 812: "bis seno"; also Tarrant, *Seneca Agamemnon*, p. 323 *ad loc.*

1419 *Dubitamus, anime* It is not uncommon in tragedy and other elevated poetry to address one's own heart; it also occurs frequently in Seneca's drama, e.g. *Aga.* 108–109: "Quid anime [...] fluctuaris." It is an imitation of the Greek use of θυμός, καρδία and ψυχή, see Tarrant, *Seneca Agamemnon*, pp. 194–195 *ad loc.* and Williams, *Tradition and Originality*, pp. 461–463. The plural seems strange, but could be *pluralis modestiae* or intended to make a connection between the I and his or her mind; the murderer continues in the second person sg.

1419 *caeca consilia aduocas* Here "caecus" has the meaning 'doubtful' (cf. "dubitamus") 'fruitless', 'insecure'. The words "advocare" and "arguere" (l. 1418) stem from juridical language, see *TLL* 1, 892–895. For "caeca consilia", cf. Stat. *Th.* 11, 489–490: "O caeca nocentum consilia", but cf. Sen. *Aga.* 108: "Quid, segnis anime, tuta consilia expetis?" Also Sen. *Pha.* 180: "sana consilia appetens".

1420 *Hac hac eundum est* Cf. Sen. *Herc. f.* 1218: "Sic sic agendum est" and *Aur.* 413 and 1596. In his own opinion, the murderer must carry out his plan.

1420–1421 *Cernis—via* In these lines the murderer addresses his "animus". In this respect it is not quite clear whether "fores" should be taken literally, as the door through which Auriacus/Orange will come out, or figuratively, as an image for the journey the killer has to make ("eundum est" and "via"), i.e. to commit the murder, with all the consequences this will entail for him. Line 1421 is also ambiguous: (1) to commit the murder 'will make you, or nobody happy', or (2) 'will make you happy or a nobody'.

L **1406** The vivid "salit" becomes the clearer "fugit", where Heinsius accepts the tautology with "fugam versat".

A bad omen

1422–1430 *Omen—paupertas iugo* The *offensio pedis*, the stubbing of the toe against the door or threshold, especially at the beginning of something, is a traditional bad omen, cf. Tib. 1, 3, 19–20: "O quotiens ingressus iter mihi tristia dixi offensum in porta signa dedisse pedem!"; and see Smith 1964, p. 240 *ad loc.* Stubbing it three times is even worse, cf. Ov. *Met.* x, 452: "ter pedis offensi signo est revocata"; see also Bömer, *Ovidius Metamorphosen* 5, p. 155 *ad loc.*; Ov. *Trist.* 1, 355 and see *RAC* 4, 296–310 s.v. "Drei".

1424–1425 *haud capit periculum angustior mens* This is a sententia-like expression ('He who is afraid does not take risks'), in the original edition highlighted with quotation marks. The interpretation of "capit" is uncertain: 'has no room for', 'is not capable of' (*OLD* s.v. 29) or 'controls' (*OLD* s.v. 27).

1425–1427 Cede—refer   Characters in Seneca's drama regularly urge their souls to action or accuse them of inactivity, see (for example) Sen. *Pha.* 592: "aude anime", and Sen. *Aga.* 108: "segnis anime". See also the comm. on l. 1419.

1425 Cede prohibenti deo   This does not refer to the Judeo-Christian God, nor to a specific classical deity, but rather implies: 'Give in to the deity, whichever, who tries to stop you with these omens'.

1427 gressum refer   Cf. Sen. *Tro.* 616: "gressus refert". For the epic ring of this expression, see the comm. *ad* l. 116.

1428 dedecus comes tibi est   For this figurative use of "comes", cf. Sen. *Herc. Oet.* 613: "comes invidia est".

Carrying out the plan in spite of possible consequences

1431–1441 Quid agimus?—diuellant rotae   The *sicarius* ensures that he will carry out his plan. The form in which he does this, with the wording 'even if [...]', is reminiscent of the *adynaton*. The possibilities he suggests are, however, very real. The 'whole army' with drawn swords refers to the Prince's guards. This army can threaten him with water or with fire. This can be intended generally, but it is more likely that two specific penalties are being referred to, namely drowning (see *WNT* 24, 1520–1521) or death at the stake. He could also imagine that he will be stabbed and then strangled. The final punishment that the murderer mentions is "radbraken" or "rabraken" (l. 1441). This was a punishment in which the limbs of a criminal were first broken and then his body was put on a wheel. Thus he was slowly tortured to death; see *WNT* 12 (3), 144–146.

1431 Quid agimus   This expressses confusion, see *OLD* s.v. ago 19b.
1432 mucronibusque ... destrictis   Cf. Caes. *B.G.* I, 25, 2: "gladiis destrictis".
1435 impetu caeco   Cic. *Fin.* I, 44, 3: "in alios caeco impetu incurrunt".
1441 non si—rotae   This line elaborates the *adynaton* ('nor even if [...]') which mainly occurs in relation to poetry ('even if I had hundred tongues [...]'), e.g. Verg. *Aen.* VI, 625; *Ge.* II, 43; Ov. *Met.* VII, 533. Cf. also Hor. *C.* II, 14, 5–7: "Non, si trecenis, quotquot eunt dies, amice, places inlacrimabilem Plutona tauris".

Victory for Philip II

1442–1449 Gaude Philippe!—claudit dies   As an expression of his excitement, now that he has given himself courage, the villain is turning to Philip II and the winds in apostrophes. Philip will overcome, although unarmed and even absent. The winds must convey the murderer's message to Philip. For the apostrophe as a means of expressing emotions see (for example) Konst, *De hartstochten in de tragedie*, p. 91. Now it is the end of the war. That end is expressed in a pleonasm of "belli supremum terminum haec claudit dies". As is often the case, Heinsius makes a character say the same thing twice in different terms ("proelii [...] finis" and "belli supremum terminum").

1443 *trophaeis* Metonym for victories, see Lewis and Short *s.v.* tropaeum II A.
1444 *hostem ... tuum* Heinsius seems to ignore the difference between "hostis" and "inimicus" here, as in ll. 70 and 1136–1137; the enemy of a prince is automatically an enemy of the state he embodies.

Fear

1450–1459 *Quo voluor ... accedo tibi* This passage is not entirely unambiguous. The murderer is highly emotional. For "furor" as a term for emotion, cf. Hor. *Ep.* I, 2, 62: "Ira furor brevis est". In a shipping metaphor, the murderer urges his mind to assuage his passion: 'take your sails and keep your helm straight'. In other words, control your emotions and use them to carry out your plans. He subsequently fails to master his passions yet again, a fact that is reflected in his rhetorical question (on this see, for example, Konst, *De hartstochten in de tragedie*, p. 91) to himself: how can you walk around with head held high whilst knowing what a terrible act ("fraudis") you are planning to commit (ll. 1452–1453), immediately continuing with the (no longer rhetorical) questions of whether he will not go ahead with the murder out of fear ("victus", l. 1454), or his voice will now refuse service because his fear of execution is stronger ("potentiori [...] metu", l. 1455), and if his hands will shake ("horrebunt", l. 1456, shiver). He notes that he is sweating heavily. Eventually the fear prompts him to exclaim that the Netherlands will have to include him in their victory signs now that he (overcome by fear) will come to them; by getting cold feet he is contributing to the glory of the Netherlands.

1450–1451 *vela ... lege* For the expression "vela legere" (to roll up or fold up the sails), cf. Verg. *Ge.* I, 373: "Omnis navita ponto umida vela legit" and *id. Aen.* III, 532: "Vela legunt socii".
1450 *mens impos* Also *Aur.* 180 and 290. Here, as is often the case, "sui" to "impos" is omitted, see *TLL* 7.1, 666.23–25.
1451 *clauum* "Clavus" continues the shipping metaphor. For "clavus" as the helm see (inter alia) Serv. Verg. *Aen.* V, 277; X, 218. The ship of state also has

a helm, see Cic. *Sest.* 9, 20: "clavum tanti imperii tenere et gubernacula rei publi-
cae tractare".

1452 *decus* Cf. l. 1242.

1454–1458 *Linguaque—artus* The murderer fears the same phenomena as the
lover fears in Cat. 51, 8–9: "Nihil est super mi vocis in ore, lingua sed torpet";
however, "vocis in ore" is a conjecture and in the edition by Joseph Scaliger
from 1582, for instance, this line is not filled in, whereas in the comm. of Marc-
Antoine Muret the conjecture "quod loquar amens" in this poem (an imitation
of Sappho 31) is rejected. Cf. also Lucr. III, 155: "Infringi linguam vocemque
aboriri". Sweat is one of the phenomena mentioned by Lucr. (III, 154), but can
also be observed empirically in violent emotions.

1459 *titulis* The honorary titles of ancestors, cf. Sen. *Herc. f.* 339: "altis inclutum titulis genus" and the comm. of Fitch, *Seneca's Hercules Furens*, p. 215 *ad
loc.*; also Prop. IV, 11,32: "Et domus est titulis utraque fulta suis".

The Furies' torch and poison

1460–1462 *Cessas—toxico* Alecto urges her sister Megaera to hold a torch near
the face of the murderer and to sprinkle him with the poison of the Acheron.
The torch is a customary attribute of the Furies, and Alecto throws one on Turnus to wake him, cf. Verg. *Aen.* VII, 456: "Facem iuveni coniecit". Just like the first
time Inquisitio appeared, this passage can also be interpreted as the murderer's
dream. This can be taken as being all the better because Alecto also appears
asleep in the aforementioned *Aeneid* passage. But perhaps the appearance of
Alecto here should be understood as a thought principle—in daylight—of the
murderer, also in view of the designation in the list of characters as τὰ νοητά;
see also Jan Bloemendal, 'Sancta Inquisitio et Libertas saucia: De Inquisitie in
Daniel Heinsius, *Auriacus, sive Libertas saucia* (1602)', *Nieuwsbrief Neolatinistenverband* 5 (1993), pp. 7–17, esp. pp. 10–11.

1460 *Megaera* In Seneca's plays this is the most common Fury, see the comm.
on l. 254.

1460–1461 *sanguine—taedam* Cf. Ov. *Met.* IV, 481–482: "madefactam sanguine
[...] facem".

Shame for the sun

1463–1472 *Pudet—collident caput* The fear still prevails in the murderer, now
brought to shame. He no longer dares to see the sunlight and states that either
the sun or he himself should disappear. In his imagination, the sun is already

obscured by clouds. When that happens and the killer thinks the sun is going east again, he implores him. He will leave the earth, go to the sea, and stones will crush his head. The flight from the sun is already mentioned in Sen. *Herc. Oet.* 891: "Ipse me Titan fugit" and before that in Ov. *Met.* IV, 488: "Solque locum fugit".

1466 *cernitis* The murderer is either addressing the audience, which would be the only place in *Aur.* where this occurs, or addressing his mind again (cf. l. 1419).

1467 *Titan* For this designation of the sun, often in Seneca's drama, borrowed from Ov. *Met.*, see the comm. on l. 594.

1471 *Pontus* An ambiguous word, which may refer to the sea in general (as opposed to the land), but the capital suggests that the Black Sea is intended, the place of Ovid's exile (regardless of whether this exile was historical or literary), which may therefore suggest exile. The Black Sea and the adjacent area had a negative ring, cf. Phaedr. IV, 7, 10: "inhospitalis [...] Ponti sinus". This announced voluntary exile also serves to clarify that the murderer's act cannot bear the sun (or vice versa).

1472 *hoc scelestum ... caput* The head of the murderer himself, who perhaps wishes to kill himself, since he is well aware of the fact that he will be committing a crime (cf. ll. 1453 "fraudis" and 1456 "facinus"). For the expression, cf. Sen. *Oed.* 871: "congerite, cives, saxa in infandum caput", and Soph. *Oed. Col.* 435 where Oedipus considers being chased off by stoning. Such stoning can be a purification, see *RE* 3A, 2295 s.v. "Steinigung" and Robert Parker, *Miasma: Pollution and Purification in Early Greek Religion* (Oxford: Clarendon Press, 1983), pp. 194–195, n. 20.

A poisonous drink

1473–1493 *Noctis ignauae—aere versentur cauo* This clause from Inquisitio is metrically accentuated by the use of trochaic metre. She summons her three sisters, the Furies, to prepare a poisonous drink. This preparation corresponds to a passage in Ov. *Met.* IV, 500–505: "Attulerat secum liquidi quoque monstra veneni, oris Cerberei spumas et virus Echidnae erroresque vagos caecaeque oblivia mentis et scelus et lacrimas rabies and caedis amorem, omnia trita simul, quae sanguine mixta recenti coxerat a cavo viridi versata cicuta". The ingredients of Inquisitio's poison are a mixture of Ovidian and Horatian elements (i.e. *Ep.* 5, 15–28, where the sorceress Canidia prepares a drink). For detailed similarities between the three passages see the comm. on the individual lines. A discussion of the passage from Horace can be found in Tupet,

La magie, pp. 309–329. For the passage from Ovid, see *ibid.*, pp. 82–83. Incidentally, the preparation of a poisonous drink also occurs in Seneca's drama (*Med.*
731–738).

The ingredients are presented in a *distributio*, the various parts of which are
grouped together with "siquid" (l. 1475) and "quicquid" (ll. 1477, 1481, 1484 and
1486). The enumeration begins with mythological figures (Medea, Cerberus,
and Ino and Athamas). The half-mythological mares mentioned then form a
transition to the next group, those (parts of) animals that are traditional elements collected by a *saga* (sorceress), namely bones of an owl, intestines of a
bitch, the liver of a night owl, the pubic parts of a toad, blood and toad ashes.
The final group consists of abstractions (blindness, crime, murder and such-
like).

Cf. also Sen. *Med.* 690–738 and Ov. *Met.* VII, 192–237, where Medea enu-
merates all kinds of evil powers. Both passages are also instances of the Stoic
attempt to catalogue nature (Rosenmeyer, *Senecan Drama and Stoic Cosmology*, pp. 160–203, Ch. 7 'The Rage to Embrace Nature').

1473–1474 *Noctis—serpentibus* An appeal to the Furies is topical in epic and
drama, cf. (for example) Sen. *Herc. f.* 86–88, Ov. *Met.* IV, 447–454 and Verg. *Aen.*
VII, 331–340, where it is always Juno who incites a Fury to cause fury. The Furies
are more often daughters of the night (e.g. Verg. *Aen*, VII, 331: "virgo sata Nocte",
and Ov. *Met.* IV, 452: "Nocte [...] genitas") or servants in the underworld (Sen.
Herc. f. 100: "famulae Ditis"). In l. 1473 the adjectives can be applied to both
substantives, but cf. the change that Heinsius made in his copy in l. 244, where
"ignavus" is also used as an adjective at "nox".

The winding snakes are also topical for the Furies, e.g. Ov. *Met.* IV, 454:
"Deque suis atros pectebant crinibus angues". See also the comm. *ad* ll. 243–
253.

1475–1477 *Et veneni—audax* The first ingredient of the drink is the poison
of Medea, referred to (in an antonomasia) as "Phasias" (after the River Phasis
in Cholchis, cf. Ov. *Met.* IV, 298; *id. A.A.* II, 382 and Sen *Herc. Oet.* 950: "Phasi-
aca coniunx"); see also Tarrant, *Seneca Agamemnon*, p. 197 *ad* Sen. *Aga.* 120
for Seneca's and Ovid's predilection for forms such as "Phasiacus", "Phasis" and
"Phasias". "Colchos" is the Greek nom. sg., used as *collectivum*. It is not only
the inhabitants of Colchis but also those of adjacent regions ("Pontus") who
fear the poison. For Medea as poisoner, see (for example) Roscher 2.2, 2482–
2515, esp. 2483–2486; for her role in texts regarding magic, see Tupet, *La magie*
passim; she is the eponymous heroine of Sen. *Med.* For an explanation, see
Stephanus, *Dictionarium*, p. 159r: "Est autem haec regio venenorum feracissima:
quae res videtur locum fecisse fabulae, quam de Medaeae veneficiis comminis-

cuntur poetae", referring to Hor. *C.* II, 13, 8–10: "Ille et venena Colchica, et quic-quid usquam concipitur nefas, tractavit". Medea is "victa", either overwhelmed by emotions, or overcome by Jason who took her to Corinth, far from her country.

1477–1480 *quicquid—diem* An amplification of the Ovidian "oris Cerberei spumas" (*Met.* IV, 501) in combination with Sen. *Herc. Oet.* 23–24: "Sed trepidus atrum Cerberum vidit dies et ille solem". Heinsius also refers to the commission that Hercules (Alcides, see for this periphrase, the comm. *ad* l. 93) had to perform, namely getting Cerberus out of hell, cf. Sen. *Herc. f.* 888: "Alcidae [...] labor". His three heads are topical, cf. (for example) Verg. *Aen.* VI, 417: "latratu trifauci" and Sen. *Herc. f.* 783–784: "Stygius canis qui terna vasto capita con-cutiens sono regnum tuetur". He guards the "umbrosa domus", see also the comm. *ad* l. 256. On Cerberus see (inter alia) Van Dam, *Statius Silvae, Book II*, pp. 162–163.

1481–1484 *Quicquid—vagijsset* Cf. Ov. *Met.* IV, 416–542 where Tisiphone mad-dens Ino and her husband Athamas using snakes and poisons instigated by Ino's stepmother Juno because she adopted Jupiter's illegitimate son Bacchus. Calling Juno "Herculis noverca" heightens the horror; for stepmothers were proverbially cruel, see (inter alia) Otto, *Sprichwörter*, pp. 245–246 and cf. Sen. *Pha.* 356–357: "saevas [...] novercas". This implicitly adds to the identification of Auriacus/Orange with Hercules (cf. *Aur.* 95; Bloemendal, 'Hercules').

The question is whether the addition "Dactylos inter furentes et Cabirorum choros" should be taken with "furtum" (hidden between the raging Fingers and the Cabires' reefs) or with "vagijsset" (had screeched between [...]). The "Dactyli" are the "Dactyli Idaei", mythical creatures associated with Mt Ida on Crete (Plin., *N.H.* VII, 197 and XXXVII, 170). They are, according to Stephanus, *Dictionarium*, p. 176v, equated with Curetes and Corybantes and by making noise would have saved the child Jupiter from the hands of his father Satur-nus. Heinsius refers to this story with "furentes" and "vagijsset". On these, see also *RE* 4. 2018–2020.

In some versions of his birth myth Bacchus is considered to be the son of Cabirus, or is himself called one of the Cabires, see Pease's comm., p. 1122, *ad* Cic. *N.D.* III, 58: "tertium Cabiro patre", whereas it should be noted that Cabiro is an emulation of Betuleius in his commentary from 1550 for the transmit-ted "caprio" (son of a goat). See also Roscher 2.2, 2522–2541 s.v. Megaloi Theoi and *RE* 10, 1399–1450 s.v. Kabeiros und Kabeiroi. In addition, the Cabiri can also be used for Demeter, Persephone and Hades, so that they are possibly— but not likely—a metaphor for the underworld. Incidentally, "furtum" is also slightly ambiguous. It can refer to the story that Dionysus is hidden in the hip of Jupiter (before his birth) or hidden among other gods (thereafter), or to the aforementioned story about the birth and upbringing of Jupiter. For the tiger as Dionysus' mount, see the comm. on *Pro Auriaeo sua* 48. Euan is one of Bacchus' names.

1481 *mente deieetus sua* Cf. Sen. *Herc. f.* 110: "mente deiectam mea".

1484–1485 *quicquid—equae* This is the *hippomanes* (poison of mares) from Tib. II, 4, 58 quod: "hippomanes cupidae stillat ab inguine equae"; Prop. IV, 5, 18. It fits in with such a poisonous drink, cf. Verg. *Ge.* III, 280–283 "[...] hippomanes [...] quod saepe malae legere novercae miscueruntque herbas et non innoxia verba". The origin of this sense of *hippomanes* stems from Arist. *H.A.* VI, 18 (572a). See also Tupet, *La magie*, pp. 79–81. For Noctiluca as moon goddess, cf. (inter alia) Hor. *C.* IV, 6, 38. The moon is in the shape of Hecate, the goddess of sorcery, see (for example) Bömer, *Ovidius Fasten ad* Ov. *Fast.* I, 141. The night still counts as the domain of the sorceress; see Tupet, *op. cit.*, p. 13.

1486–1489 *Saeua—cinis* In these lines it is (parts of) animals that are collected. The example for this passage is esp. Hor. *Ep.* 5. Cf. for "sepulcris [...] legit" Hor. *Ep.* 5, 17: "sepulcris caprificos erutas". What this is in *Aur.* is not clear: everything related to digging has magical power (see Horatius, *Oden und Epoden*, ed. Adolf Kiessling, Richard Heinze and Erich Burck (Berlin: Weidmann, 1964¹¹), p. 506 *ad loc.* and Tupet, *La magie*, pp. 87–88). The "bubo", the horned or eagle owl (a night owl), is in particular a bird of bad omens (*TLL* 2, 2221–2222). The "strix" is also a night owl, though also a vampire, cf. Hor. *Ep.* 5, 20: "plumamque nocturnae strigis". Here, as with Prometheus, the liver of the animal is torn out. The birds come together as harbingers of bad times in Sen. *Herc. f.* 686–687. They are more often an ingredient of magic potions, see Tupet, *op. cit.*, pp. 68–69.

Unlike the aforementioned fifth *Epode* of Horace, here it is not the food of a bitch that is taken (i.e. 23: "ossa ab ore rapta ieiunae cani") but the entrails of the beast. For (parts of) dogs in magical potions, see Tupet, *La magie*, p. 72. Horace makes Canidia use "uncta turpis ova ranae sanguine" (loc. cit. 19). Heinsius' Inquisitio seasoned the "inguen" of a toad with fresh pus ("pus novum"). He could have come to know of this toad ("bufo") from Verg. *Ge.* I, 184 "inventusque cavis bufo". Inquisitio also uses the ashes of "rubetae" (toads), which were also considered poisonous (e.g. I, 69–70: "quae molle Calenum porrectura viro miscet sitiente rubeta"). It seems that Heinsius is using "bufo" and "rubeta" as synonyms, as part of his tendency to engage in variation. For the use of these animals in magical potions, see Tupet, *op. cit.*, pp. 66–67.

1490–1493 *Inter—cauo* With the final group, consisting of abstractions that are rather poetic phrases than based on reality, Heinsius returns to the passage from Ov. *Met.* IV, showing the "errores [...] mentis" (l. 502), the "scelus" (l. 503), the "caedis amorem" (l. 503), the "lacrimas" (l. 503), the mix with fresh blood ("sanguine mixta recenti", l. 504, and "sanguine immistas recenti", l. 1492). The closing of "aere versentur cavo" (l. 1493) is an echo of "coxerat aere cavo [...] versata" (*Met.* IV, 505).

> Immerse the killer in the poison

1494–1496 *Perfidum caput—profunda pectoris* The Furies mostly influence the breast or heart of their victim, the seat of senses and feeling; similarly in Ov. *Met.* IV, 504–505: "Vergit furiale venenum pectus in amborum praecordiaque intima movit". Here, the head must be brought to fury (*furens, furor*), an etymologization. For the Furies as allegories for fury and passion, see intr., p. 42 and n. 158. The poison of the Echidna—which Ovid connects with the Hydra of Lerna, a dangerous water monster and one of the tasks of Hercules (*Met.* IX, 69)—must enrage him. Cf. for this *ibid.* IV, 501: "virus Echidnae" and the comm. of Bömer, *Ovidius Metamorphosen* 2, p. 168 *ad loc.*

> Hissing snakes

1497–1501 *Densioribus—intentat ictum* For the snakes, see also Ov. *Met.* 491–494: "nexaque vipereis distendens bracchia nodis caesariem excussit: motae sonuere colubrae, parsque iacent umeris, pars circum pectora lapsae sibila dant". They are topical for Furies, see the comm. *ad* ll. 243–253. Here their hissing should tell the Low Countries that soon ("prorumpens") someone will die, and that the 'final blow' (death) is near. For the role of snakes in magic, see Tupet, *La magie*, inter alia pp. 64–65.

L 1500 The changes enhance the contrast: 'the secretly nearing death strikes the blissful home of the hero [...]'.

> Transition

1501–1502 *Nescium sortis—funus operitur suum* The family is still carefree ("nescium sortis", cf. Grotius *Ad. ex.* 1486: "nescius sortis"). She is "inter dapes", cf. ll. 1339–1340 and the comm. These lines are a conclusion, a time indication and a transition to the next scene. The fact that Loisa is unhappy is not a problem: these emotions are situational and need not be consistent.

Act IV, Scene 2 (1503–1595)

Summary

In a dialogue, Loisa speaks very emotionally with her nurse, who tries unsuccessfully to calm her down. Now she recounts the contents of her dream.

1503–1521 Loisa would prefer to go far away and cry, saddened by something undefined.

1522–1539 The nurse urges her mistress to cease her lamentation, so as not to weaken the courage of her husband. She compares this with forging steel: normally very hard, it is softened by a small flame. In this way, the heart of a courageous man remains fearless, but is quickly wiped by female cranes.

1539–1544 Tears and inexplicable anxiety arouse tears in such a man, for often fear provokes fear.

1545–1575 Loisa tells her what she dreamt: she saw her husband die in her arms, after he had told her to arrange his funeral. This dream caused concern, which also remained after the dream had disappeared.

1–25 In this insert, added after the actual text, Loisa exclaims that her husband was killed near the Scheldt, and she wondered why she is sad again. She wanted a simple life, so as to deceive fate.

1576–1590 The nurse tries to calm Loisa with the argument that dreams are deceitful: They are seen at night and frighten, but during the day it turns out that they were untrue. The cause of the dream is, according to the nurse, the great love Loisa has for her husband; it is this that causes her worries.

1591–1595 The Princess asks her nurse who the unknown man is with his unsavory appearance. She will have to go in.

As in II, 2, in this *domina-nutrix* scene the emotional state of the protagonist is apparent from the reaction to a secondary figure who tries to calm her down, in this case the nurse, Loisa's confidante. This scene is the pinnacle of Loisa's performance, explaining the content of her dream. The fact that a nurse plays the role of confidante, fulfilling the functions of both mirror and sounding board and elucidating the feelings of the protagonist, is customary in classical drama, especially that of Seneca, see intr., pp. 26 and 36; also (inter alia) Tarrant, *Seneca Agamemnon*, pp. 192–193 and Konst, *De hartstochten in de tragedie*, pp. 79–80. This scene differs from the normal pattern in Seneca—where the secondary figure often responds to a monologue from the protagonist—in that Loisa's clauses remain relatively short.

Metre

Lines 1503–1521 are written in anapaestic dimeters and monometers, ll. 1522–1544 in iambic trimeters. Lines 1545–1575 and the insert again consist of ana-paestic dimeters and monometers, ll. 1576–1590 of iambic trimeters, whereas ll. 1591–1595 are written in anapaestic tetrameters.

Written in anapaestic metres, Loisa's clauses make a more hasty impres-sion than the calm and calming clauses of the *nutrix* who speaks in iambic metres. The difference in emotionality manifests itself metrically. Something similar can also be found in (for example) Sen. *Tro.* 705–735, where Andro-macha addresses an emotional speech to Ulyxes in anapaestic dimeters and a monometer, who in turn answers in iambic trimeters.

Commentary

Seclusion

1503–1521 *Quis me—cernere curas* Loisa would prefer to avoid contact with people. To this end, she does not choose the obvious way of death—the way of Dido, for example—but that of voluntary exile to rough (unspoilt) nature, where she can let her tears run freely. Cf. Sen. *Herc. Oet.* 185–206, where Iole longs in her grief to go to inhospitable regions. In *id. Pha.* 777–787 the chorus tells Hippolytus that it makes no sense to hide in "deserta" and "avii loci". For *loci* on going to deserted areas, see *TLL* 5.1, 688.76–689.10 s.v. desero (deser-tum).

The clause is structured around the opposition *cognitus-ignotus*, which was previously mentioned in the conversation between Loisa and the *senex*, ll. 498–504. He who knows why he is sad, has limited pain, but he who mourns for something unknown and immeasurable is very worried. Also fitting in with this opposition is the "mens caeca" (the mind that is blinded by all misery), cf. Ov. *Met.* IV, 502: "caecaeque oblivia mentis". In Sen. *Ep.* 119, 8 and 120, 18, the 'spiritual blindness' refers to a philosophical misunderstanding of the truth.

1506–1507 *querulos volucrum luctus* The chorus in Sen. *Aga.* sings a θρῆνος giving examples of birds who sing a lamentation (ll. 664–690 and Tarrant, *Seneca Agamemnon*, pp. 297–300). The starting point may be the song of the swan, cf. Plato, *Phaedo* 84E–85B, where Socrates denied the conviction that swans sing a sad farewell song before their death. Cf. also Aesch. *Aga.* 1444–1446 (Clytemnestra states that Cassandra sang like a swan at the hour of her death), and the description in Arist. *H.A.* 615b2. See also Tarrant, *Seneca Agamemnon*, p. 299 *ad* Sen. *Aga.* 680 and D'Arcy W. Thompson, *A Glossary of Greek Birds* (Hildesheim: Olms, 1966 [= London, etc.: Oxford University Press, 1936]), pp. 180–183. The kingfisher was also thought to sing a threnody, see Tarrant, *Seneca Agamemnon*, p. 300 and Thompson, *op. cit.*, p. 47. And cf. *Sen. Pha.* 508: "Hinc aves querulae fremunt".

1508 *lachrymis ... pascere* Cf. Sen. *Herc. Oet.* 448: "quicquid dolorem pascit".

1510 *fraena* For this widespread metaphor, see Sen. *Aga.* 114: "da frena" and Tarrant, *Seneca Agamemnon*, p. 196 *ad loc.* Further Ov. *Met.* I, 280: "totas immittite habenas" and Bömer, *Ovidius Metamorphosen* 1, p. 107 *ad loc.* Also Verg. *Aen.* XII, 499: "Irarumque omnis effundit habenas" and Sen. *Herc. Oet.* 277: "frena dolorem".

1512–1513 *Felix—ignotus* This *sententia* seems to be a quotation or allusion, which could not be traced.

***L* 1514** Towards the end of the play, the changes in the Leiden copy are of an increasingly provisional character. Here the author changes "mens" into "sponte", so that "caeca" no longer has a congruent noun.

Women's tears relax courage—comparison with smithy

1522–1539 *Alumna ... sexus impotentis* The nurse bids Loisa to no longer bother her husband with her grief, arguing that a heroic man is weakened by women's tears, which is strictly speaking not restraining emotions but hiding them. Through this indirect mode of expression, Heinsius departs from the concepts that can be found in Seneca's drama. There, the secondary character constantly insists on restraining emotions, e.g. Sen. *Pha.* 256: "animos coerce" (Tarrant, *Seneca Agamemnon*, p. 212). Virgil alludes to it in *Aen.* IV, 437–449, esp. 438–439: "Sed nullis ille movetur fletibus" and 449: "Mens immota manet, lacrimae volvuntur inanes".

   The nurse enlivens her argument (see the comm. *ad* ll. 131–168) with a Homeric comparison with the smithy. For such a comparison, cf. (inter alia) Ov. *Met.* XII, 276–279 and IX, 170; see Hom. *Od.* IX, 391–394; on this, S.G. Owen, 'Ovid's Use of the Simile', *Classical Review* 45 (1931), pp. 97–106, esp. p. 101 and J. Richardson, 'The Function of Formal Imagery in Ovid's *Metamorphoses*', *Classical Journal* 59 (1963–1964), pp. 161–169, esp. p. 164.

1529 *lacertorum* Heinsius is probably using this term—which specifically indicates the upper arm—for its connotation of muscular strength (see *OLD* s.v. 2).

1534 *labascit* Cf. Acc. *Trag.* 684: "Nullum est cor [...] tam ferum, quod non labascat" and Gell. xv, 2, 7: "Neque mentem animumque eius consistere, sed vi quadam nova ictum labascere"; see also *TLL* 7.2, 1529.

1534–1535 *improbrae sortis* More than one meaning of "improbus" seems to be in play here: (1) 'malicious', 'base'; (2) 'greedy'; (3) 'unrelentingly'; see *OLD* s.v. 2 and 5, resp., and cf. Verg. *Ge.* I, 145–146: "Labor omnia vicit improbus".

1535 *loco cedit suo* For this combination as a military *t.t.* see *OLD* s.v. cedo 3b and cf. Sen. *Aga.* 88–89: "cedit oneri suo". It may be a variant on Erasmus' motto "cedo nulli"; see Niek van der Blom, 'Erasmus en Terminus', *Hermeneus* 28 (1957), pp. 153–158.

1538 *unus ... dolor* The word "unus" has two connotations: (1) only grief; (2) one single grief.

1538 *invictaque ... pectora* Either in general, or (in a poetical plural) applied to Auriacus.

L **1524** The tautological "animum" (cf. l. 1523 "mentem") is replaced with "pectus" as the seat of emotions.

Grief causes grief

1539–1544 *Lacrimae gemitusque—fomes sibi est* In these lines the nurse uses *sententiae* to qualify Loisa's sorrow as excessive and unreasonable (see also pp. 106–108). These *sententiae* are set in quotation marks (see the comm. *ad* l. 58). She closes her clause with them, as happens in Seneca's drama, see the comm. *ad* ll. 219–230.

1541 *rationis expers* Cf. Sen. *Tro.* 903–904: "ratione [...] careat [...] magnus dolor".

1542 *obsonium* This metaphorical use of *obsonium* ('catering', from the Greek ὀψώνιον) is unusual in Latin, but may have been used because it opened up the possibility of figuratively using the Dutch words for 'food' and 'feed' for emotions (*WNT* 22.1, 125 and *ibid.* 81–82). It is not attested in *TLL* 9.2, 235–236. In addition, the metaphorical use of "fomes" (l. 1544) may have inspired Heinsius.

1544 *fomes* For "fomes" in a metaphorical sense, see *TLL* 6.1, 1020–1022.

L **1542–1544** Heinsius removed "obsonium" and changed the sentence to: 'and tears are the cause of tears, so that [...] [i]n this way it becomes its own fuel'. Eventually he deleted it.

The dream

1545–1575 *Somnia—longior ipso est* Loisa relates the contents of her dream, which she had just before dawn: she saw her man bathing in blood dying in her arms. This dream is part of a tradition including, for example, Calpurnia, who saw her husband Caesar die in her arms, in the night before the Ides of March 44 (Plut. *Caes.* 63), see Bloemendal, 'Mon Dieu, mon Dieu ...'. There is also a long tradition of dreaming in dramas, cf. Sen. *Tro.* 438–488, where Andromacha sees Hector's ghost rise and tells this to a secondary figure—an old man (see also Fantham, *Seneca's Troades*, pp. 279–284 *ad loc.*)—and in epic: a famous specimen is the dream in which Aeneas sees Hector, Verg. *Aen.* II, 268–297. The fact that Loisa is getting her dream just before the morning adds to its truthfulness. This is reinforced because Auriacus ensures that it is a true dream. For such a dream, cf. Muret, *Iul.* Caes. IV, 1 (ll. 334–437), where Calpuntia tells her dream to Caesar.

In the dream Auriacus asks his wife to fulfil the "ultima munera". This is a variant of "munera suprema" or "extrema", the last duty in relation to the dead, the burial. Cf. (for example) Verg. *Aen.* XI, 24–26: "egregias animas [...] decorate supremis muneribus"; see *TLL* 8,1666.70–1667.10. It is not entirely clear whether Heinsius had in mind a Roman (or in any case antique) or a contemporary funeral like Orange had received. For Roman funeral rites, see Marquardt-Mau, *Privatleben*, pp. 346–385, J.M.C. Toynbee, *Death and Burial in the Roman World* (London, etc.: Thames and Hudson, 1971), esp. pp. 43–61 and Fantham, *Seneca's Troades*, p. 264 *ad Tro.* 371–376 and *ibid.* p. 253 *ad Tro.* 298–300, about the annual memorial offerings to the dead; the ceremonies in the Netherlands are discussed in Henk L. Kok, *De geschiedenis van de laatste eer in Nederland* (Lochem: De Tijdstroom, 1970), the funeral of Orange in (inter alia) P.J. Blok, *Willem de Eerste, Prins van Oranje* (Amsterdam: Meulenhoff, 1919–1920) 2 vols, 2, pp. 217–220. Perhaps it is also necessary to think of bewailing the loss of the deceased, e.g. Ov. *Met.* XI, 669–670, where Morpheus, in the shape of (the drowned) Ceyx, calls on Alcyone to weep for him. Hor. *C.* II, 1, 38 uses "munera" in combination with "neniae" (chant for the corpse), see Nisbet-Hubbard 2, pp. 30–31 *ad loc.*

When Auriacus is ready, he disappears "procul aetherias [...] in auras". Heinsius seems to more or less oppose the idea of Hom. *Il.* XXIII, 62–101 (in particular 100–101), where the shade of Patroclus appears to Achilles and then disappears under the earth, or Verg. *Aen.* IV, 570: "sic fatus nocti se immiscuit atrae". Incidentally, it is topical in these kinds of scenes for the dead (or dying) individual to disappear when addressed, with the dreamer waking up at the same time. The ghost of Auriacus enters the aether, which reinforces Platonic and Stoic views, see the comm. *ad* ll. 23–45.

1548 *sensibus* The vision of the dream plays 'deep in the senses' (the mental and physical ability to discern, *OLD* s.v. 4a). Perhaps the meaning 'consciousness' is also in play, cf. Sen *Tro.* 659 and Fantham, *Seneca's Troades*, p. 304 *ad loc.* See also ll. 1579 and 1590.

1551 *maiora metu* Cf. Sen. *Tro.* 168: "maiora veris monstra"; either 'worse than reality' or 'too bad to fear'.

1552 *rex astrorum* Cf. Sen. *Thy.* 836: "dux astrorum".

1553 *tremulos* Two intertwined interpretations are possible: the 'fires' of the stars disappear from fear, but they also twinkle; consider in this regard flickering flames.

1554 *Phosphorus* The Greek name is uncommon in Latin, see l. 640 and the comm. *ad loc.* It is an allusion to Sen. *Herc. f.* 125–128 "Iam rara micam sidera prono languida mundo; nox victa vagos contrahit ignes luce renata, cogit nitidum Phosphoros agmen". For "luce renata", cf. also Grot. *Ad. ex.* 483: "redeunte [...] luce".

1554 *domitor curae* Cf. Sen. *Aga.* 75: "curarum somnus domitor", and *Herc. f.* 1066: "domitor, Somne, malorum". The metaphor is used more often, see Tarrant, *Seneca Agamemnon*, p. 187 *ad* Sen. *Aga.* 75.

1556–1557 *oculosque ... vinxerat* Cf. Ov. *Met.* XI, 238: "ut somno vincta iacebas" and see Bömer, *Ovidius Metamorphosen* 5, p. 302 *ad loc.*; further Ov. *R.A.* 500: "somno lumina victa dedi" and see *TLL* 9.2, 386.29–53 s.v. occupo. Verg. *Ge.* IV, 190: "Sopor occupat artus", and *id. Aen.* VIII, 26–27: "Terras animalia fessa per omnis [...] sopor altus habebat".

1560 *sanguinis imbres* Cf. Sen. *Oed.* 348–349: "Huius exiguo graves maculantur ictus imbre" and Soph. *O.R.* 1278–1279: ὁμοῦ [...] ὄμβρος (a shower of blood).

1560 *attonitos* For the emotional values of this word ('struck by lightning') in Seneca, from frenzy to fear, see Fantham, *Seneca's Troades*, p. 280. Here it is something like staggering mortal fear.

1561 *vicinae necis* Cf. Sen. *Ep.* 30, 7: "morte vicina".

1571–1572 *aetherias ... in auras* Cf. Ov. *Ars.* II, 59: "aetherias [...] per auras ibimus". The conviction that the soul escapes the body after death can be found in literature from Homer onwards, also in Lucretius and Virgil, and in Seneca's drama, e.g. *Tro.* 379–381 and see Fantham, *Seneca's Troades*, pp. 265–266 *ad loc.* For "fluere" with respect to 'breath [of life]', cf. Sen. *Ep.* 54, 6: "nec [...] ex natura fluit spiritus".

Insert: a simple life deceives fate

1–25 *Talis ad undas ... tutus in ipso* Here Loisa is thinking of the topos that who lives a simple life and observes the *aurea mediocritas* is happy. The *locus classicus* is Hor. *Ep.* 2 ("Beatus ille [...]"). See also the comm. *ad* ll. 715–716 and 728–735. She implicitly contrasts carefree shepherds' dreams with her own nightmare. Lines 15–16 indicate what shepherds dream about: the loss of a few sheep or their flute, a minor loss when compared to the death of a husband.

1 *Scaldi*   The vocative of "Scaldis". For this word (next to Honta, l. 1301), cf. Secundus *Iulia* I, 9, 30 (Secundus, *Opera Omnia*, ed. Bosscha, 1, p. 65).

7 *nubila*   For this metaphorical use of "nubilum" (gloomy thoughts), cf. Plin. *N.H.* II, 13: "Humani nubila animi serenat" and Sen. *Thy.* 934: "Saevi nubila fati pelle".

8–9 *modicos ... pectore motus*   Loisa is longing for μετριοπάθεια, measure in emotions, originally part of the doctrine of Peripatetics, but annexed by the Stoa, see Konst, *De hartstochten in de tragedie*, pp. 9–14, who ascribes *metriopatheia* only to Aristotle.

9–10 *Felix placidi rector aratri*   This is a distant allusion to Hor. *Ep.* 2, 1–3: "Beatus ille qui [...] paterna rura bobus exercet suis".

18 *res*   This word is ambiguous, referring to the possessions, and more or less synonymous with house, or with cares, i.e. everything that happens to him.

19–25 *Felix—in ipso*   These *sententiae*, set in quotation marks, circle around the theme of the life in secret, cf. ll. 715–723 and the comm. Here Loisa indirectly contrasts this with her husband's life, who as the Prince rises above the mob and will be a target for fate.

L 10   The 'tender', 'fragile' flock (which can be sizeable) become the 'small', 'insignificant' one.

   Consolation: dreams deceive

1576–1590 *Fidem—iacent*   The nurse gives the same explanation for the origin and effect of dreams as the old man did in ll. 515–558: what the mind deals with during the day, appears at night in the dream. However, the nurse adds hope to the fear mentioned by the *senex* (and joy, l. 523) and thus arrives at the combination of 'hope and fear'. With this proto-psychological explanation of dreams, Heinsius is in accordance with the Stoa, the system of Posidonius that explains the origin of predictive dreams from the activity of the soul itself (see Veenstra, 'Dromen zonder Freud', pp. 600–601). Such ideas also existed in the medical world. In his *Synesiorum Somniorum*, the seventeenth-century physician Hieronymus Cardanus distinguishes (inter alia) dreams that are generated by emotional movements (see Veenstra, *op. cit.*, pp. 604–605 and Cardanus, *Opera omnia* 1966, 5, pp. 597–599).

1577 *noctisque fucum* For this meaning of "fucus" (lie, pretext), see *TLL* 6.1, 1462.39–77 and *OLD* s.v. 4.

1577 *aemulos* Either 'be at odds with', or 'lies in dreams resemble truth'.

1581 *venator imbrem* (*sc. exhorret*) A starting point for this simile is probably Sen. *Pha.* 1053–1054: "Omnis frigido exsanguis metu venator horret".

1581 *conditus* Either 'withdrawing' or (with "nocte") 'safe in the night'.

1583 *traducit* Here "traducere" is used in the sense of to show, to ridicule (*OLD* s.v. 4).

1589–1590 *sopor ... somno* Here Heinsius does not distinguish between "sopor" (deep sleep) and "somnus" (sleep).

1590 *sensusque ... iacent* The "sensus" can be the senses, pars pro toto the body—in which case ll. 1589 and 1590 are more or less synonymous—or 'consciousness' could be intended. The "sensus" are "liquefacti", i.e. (1) 'melted', 'effeminated', e.g. Song of Songs 5, 6: "Anima mea liquefacta est ut locutus est", or (2) 'cleared up', 'without clouds', cf. "liquidus" (*OLD* s.v. liquidus 1; see also supra, the comm. *ad* l. 1011 and *TLL* 7.2, 1477.15–61).

A unsavory stranger

1591–1594 *Quis nouus ille—suspecta fides* This scene, too, ends with remarks about daily life. Loisa asks here who is the unsavory type she sees. Here, Heinsius is borrowing a comment from *Een verhael vande moort* (Frederiks, *De moord van 1584*, p. 68): Louise asked "mijnen Heere den Prince [...], wie dat hy was, ende dat hy een seer quaet ghelaet hadde [...]" (my lord the Prince [...], who he was, and that he had a wicked face [...]). In addition, this comment tallies with the Stoic perspective: the face reveals the character, see the comm. *ad* ll. 487–512. "Missus" can be regarded as *simplex pro composito* "admissus", or as 'sent': Gerards was sent to Holland to bring the news of Anjou's death.

L 1588 In the end, Heinsius refrained from keeping the additional lines: 'when the colourful sky brightens, variegated with the fiery sisters of Phoebe [cf. the change in l. 533 in *L*], and the golden choruses in the sky are shining [...]'.

L 1589 The subordinating "cum" becomes in *L* the juxtaposing "tunc".

Transition

1595 *Nos domus intro pignusque vocant* Loisa goes in, which is mentioned in an implicit stage direction. Whether she was present at the murder is not clear from *Een verhael vande moort* (Frederiks, *De moord van 1584*, pp. 68–69). Heinsius makes her absent, probably for theatrical-technical reasons: after the murder, he can still make Loisa briefly doubt whether her husband is still alive or not, thereby enhancing the pathos. Furthermore, he may have questioned what her presence in the crucial third (murder) scene could add in terms of content or drama.

1591–1592 *vel quibus ... vectus ab oris* Cf., e.g., Verg. *Aen.* III, 369: "Quibus aut venistis ab oris?"
1595 *domus* Either (1) 'house', 'family', or (2) 'household'.
1595 *pignusque* For "pignus", see l. 444 and the comm.

Act IV, Scene 3 (1596–1751)

Summary

This is the crucial scene in which the deadly shot will be fired. Before this happens, the murderer remains hesitant until the last moment, and Auriacus persists in reflecting upon the inevitability of death. After the shot, the murderer is chased.
1596–1643 The murderer tells how he has hidden his pistol and relishes (in gruesome detail) the idea that he will be prolonging his victim's agony. Yet some trepidation returns, though he realizes that the gods are supporting him. Then he sees Auriacus coming.
1644–1668 Auriacus reflects that everything in the world has its steady course, everything is in perpetual flux. One year succeeds another, one generation follows another and the cosmos will return to chaos.
1668–1719 In the midst of all these changes of fate, man is the only one on earth who knows this. But he has added more causes of death to all the existing ones, and in the course of time what used to be murder has now become a victory. He gives as historical examples the Romans and the Persians, who both conquered much territory with only limited means. The current generation has extended the arsenal of killing tools with the addition of firearms. In particular, Auriacus refers to the Dutch as forerunners in this arms race.

1720–1734 The murderer still does not dare to carry out his deed, yet he spurs himself on. He addresses the Prince and requests a passport. He shoots. The Prince falls and the murderer tries to get away.

1735–1738 Auriacus stammers his supposed last words: 'Mon dieu ayez pitie de mon ame [...] Mon Dieu ayez pitie de ce pauvre peuple' ('God, have pity on my soul, [...] God have pity on this poor people').

1738–1751 The commander urges the guards to pursue the murderer, which they do. He himself takes care of the Prince.

This passage accords with what was known about the murder. Heinsius has the murderer request a passport and almost simultaneously shoot the Prince. He also renders the traditional last words of the Prince. Implicit stage directions are not lacking here. At the beginning of the scene the murderer describes aspects of his appearance: he wears a cloak over a shoulder, which also hides the pistol, his other side is not covered by the cloak (see below, the comm. *ad* ll. 1596–1603).

In this scene the storylines pro and contra Orange come together: the dream comes true, the murderer meets the Prince. Cf. intr., pp. 36–38.

Metre

The lines in these scenes consist of iambic trimeters. The *hiatus* in l. 1619 ("o, o, dies") and 1620 ("O una") are striking. Lines 1739–1742, which use hanging indentation, are written in trochaic tetrameters.

Commentary

The pistol hidden

1596–1603 *Sic sic eundum est—meos* The murderer imagines what preparations he has made to commit the murder and presents these to the audience. He has a cloak over his shoulder. One should not be thinking of the "pallium collectum" from the comedy, the cloak that slaves slap over their shoulder in order to move faster (G.E. Duckworth, *The Nature of Roman Comedy: A Study in Popular Entertainment* (Princeton: Princeton University Press, 1971), p. 91). The word "chlamys" used suggests that it is the soldier's coat (*ibid.*, p. 89). For images of contemporary combat garb, see Ger Luijten (ed.), *Dawn of the Golden Age: Northern Netherlandish Art 1580–1620* (Zwolle: Waanders; Amsterdam: Rijksmuseum, 1993) Exhibition catalogue, cat. No. 16.1–12, pp. 350–351. The murderer, who pretended to have a diplomatic mission, probably wore civilian clothes. P.C. Hooft gives this description in his *Neederlandsche His-toorien* (1642): "met den mantel op de slinke schouder, de zinkroers aan den riem" ('with the cloak on his left shoulder, and a gun on his belt', Martinus Nijhoff, *P.C. Hooft's Nederlandse historien in het kort* (Amsterdam and Brussels: Elsevier, 1947), p. 346). Cf. also Benedicti *De rebus gestis* II, 312–314: "Attritam gestans chlamydem, quae pendeat uno nixa humero, nudumque simul latus arguat armis armatumque tegat, ne sit simulatio fraudi". For clothing with the cloak hanging over a shoulder, see Eva Nienholdt, *Kostüme des 16. und 17. Jahrhunderts: Ein Brevier* (Braunschweig: Klinckhardt and Biermann, 1962), fig. 10.

Just like Benedicti, with this description of the murderer Heinsius deviates from official descriptions, which tell that the murderer actually showed the guns, see Frederiks, *De moord van 1584*, p. 38 and Peter P. de Baar, Els Kloek and Tom van der Meer, *Balthasar G.: Het relaas van een katholieke jongen die Willem van Oranje vermoordde en bijna heilig verklaard werd* (Amsterdam: Syndikaat, 1984), p. 45.

1596 *Sic sic eundum est* Cf. ll. 413 and 1420, and Sen. *Herc. f.* 1218: "sic sic agen-dum est".

1597 *sclopumque* One of the translations of "sclopus" is "sinckroer", used by the murderer, see Frederiks, *De moord van 1584*, p. 68. This was a short musket, a pistol or gun (Kilianus, *Etymologicum*, p. 584 s.v. "sengh-roer"). Benedicti (*De rebus gestis* II, 311) also uses this word.

1598 *fidemque facto praestat* Heinsius uses the expression "fidem praestare" in an unusual sense: (my cloak) offers a situation of trust in which I can com-mit the crime; the combination is almost synonymous with "dolos tegit nihil tegendo". The normal meaning 'adhere to a promise' does not make real sense here.

1600 *pectoris ... vias* The 'ways of the breast' are probably the veins and arter-ies in the breast, which are clogged. The same image for corridors in the chest is to be found in l. 461 "cuniculos".

1602–1603 *ferri ... sica* "Ferrum" can be a metonym for the gun or the bullets, or already for the dagger, which apparently falls out of the "sinus". He can use the knife to cut open the body. In that regard, a "sica" is an obvious instrument for a "sicarius". *Een verhael vande moort* also mentions a dagger (Frederiks, *De moord van 1584*, p. 67): the murderer, who calls himself 'François Guion' entered the Prince's bedroom while he was in bed a few days before the day of the mur-der: "ende heeft de selfde Guion naerderhandt bekent, ghevanghen zijnde, hoe dat hy als doen soude de Prince op sijn bedde vermoort hebben, waert dat hy sijn dagge by hem ghehadt hadde" ('and the same Guion afterwards confessed, after he was captured, how he then would have killed the Prince on his bed had he had his dagger with him').

Prolonging the death

1604–1635 *Vtinam reuulsis ... inuadet genas* The murderer would like to kill Auriacus cruelly, show him his guts while he is still alive. Even in Seneca's drama horrors of this magnitude do not occur, but this is perhaps redolent of (for example) *Med.* 1009–1013, where Medea wants revenge. It should be remembered that atrocities in the sixteenth and seventeenth centuries were less unusual than they supposedly are now, cf. (for example) the execution of the murderer, described in *Historie vanden neerslach* [...], see Nanne Bosma, *Balthazar Gerards: Moordenaar en martelaar* (Amsterdam: Rodopi, 1983), pp. 110–111. For such atrocities, cf. also 2 Maccabees 7.

1610–1612 *cani ... volucribus* To be devoured by birds and dogs has both an antique tradition, e.g. Verg. *Aen.* IX, 485–486: "heu, terra ignota canibus data praeda Latinis alitibusque iaces!" and a Judeo-Christian one, e.g. 1 Kings. 14, 11 "Him that dieth of Jeroboam in the city shall the dogs eat; and him that dieth in the field shall the fowls of the air eat" (*KJV*), and the baker who is torn by the birds (Gen. 40).

1610 *extaue obscenae cani* This is an echo of l. 1487: "exta ieiunae canis", although the meaning of both expressions differs. Cf. also Ov. *Fast.* IV, 936: "Turpiaque obscenae vidimus exta canis". "Obscenus" allows more interpretations, aiming at the ugly appearance of the animal, and at the bad omen it represents for Orange. See also Bömer, *Ovidius Fasten*, p. 289 *ad* Ov. Fast. IV, 936 and Franz Bömer, 'Die römischen Ernteopfer und die Füchse im Philisterlande (Interpretationen zu Ovid, Fasti IV 679 ff. 901 ff.)', *Wiener Studien* 69 (1956), pp. 372–384, esp. pp. 381–383.

1616 *ter* The sacred number of three, adding extra weight to the deed (see *RAC* 4, 296–310 s.v. "Drei"), is, as it were, portrayed in the *tricolon* "funesta, horrida, novaque semper".

1618 *Vna mors poenae parum est* Cf. Sen. *Herc. Oet.* 866: "Levis una mors est. Levis? At extendi potest" and Hor. *C.* III, 27, 37.

1619 *nec digna nobis* It is not fully clear whether the murderer considers himself too weighty to make Auriacus die only one death, or whether in his view Orange is not worthy of only one death. In other words: "nobis" can be abl. with "digna" ('worthy of me') or dat. ethicus ('in my eyes').

1622 *Belgarum caput* This is ambiguous: (1) object to "mactamus" (in which case it refers to Orange); or (2) apposition to Alba (Alva), the Governor of the

Netherlands. Although his reign lasted only until 1573, for a long time his name remained the prototype of the cruel Spaniard.

1623 *mactamus* By using the word "mactare" the murderer is lending his deed a sacred overtone, cf. Sen. *Aga.* 219: "Hunc domi reducem paras mactare" and Tarrant, *Seneca Agamemnon*, p. 214 *ad loc.* Cf. also ll. 380–381, where Inquisitio speaks about Orange as a ritual victim, and the comm. *ad loc.* For "mactare" as killing with sacred connotations, see *TLL* 8, 21–23, esp. 22.70–23.9. In which case it concerns (inter alia) the sacrifice of Iphigenia (e.g. Prop. III, 7, 24; Ov. *Met.* XIII, 185) and of Polyxena (inter alia Ov. *Met.* XIII, 448; Sen. *Tro.* 196 and passim).

1627–1628 *extendam ... maiusque reddam* As often, Heinsius formulates the same thought twice in an amplification, see above, n.ll. 1442–1449.

1628–1629 *Pectore ingenti exigam scelus futurum* Is "pectore ingenti" a variant of "toto pectore" (with heart and soul, *OLD* s.v. pectus 4b) or does it mean 'with great courage'? The word "exigam" is also ambiguous, and could mean (1) 'to concoct' (*OLD* s.v. exigo 10b) or (2) 'to carry out' the crime (*OLD* s.v. 5a). The former interpretation is most plausible, because the murderer visualizes with a five times repeated "sic" (ll. 1629–1634) how the Prince will face his death anxiously, how he will collapse and he himself will escape. Incidentally, the killer tells the story *hysteron proteron.*

1633 *multa caede* These words (lit. 'by much death') can mean (1) many shots, or (2) the fact that Orange is completely dead ("caede" used as a synonym of "nece", l. 1634), or (3) that he looks "triste" because of the loss of much blood (*OLD* s.v. 4). Cf. also Hor. *C.* III, 23, 14: "multa caede bidentium" and Ov. *R.A.* 28: "Et victor multa caede cruentus eat".

1635 *toruusque totas pallor inuadet genas* In Seneca's drama pale cheeks are also a common phenomenon with fear and other emotions, cf. (for example) *Aga.* 237: "sed quid trementes circuit pallor genas"; also *Aga.* 710–711; *Pha.* 832 and *Herc. Oet.* 1722. For "torvus" cf. l. 1018 and the comm.

Assent of the gods

1636–1639 *Adhuc moramur?—caelum meis* The murderer urges himself not to hesitate. That is not necessary either, his heart pounds and has given the familiar *tessera*: the gods (God?) agree with his plans.

1637 *notamque ... tesseram* Convulsions, for example of the heart, could be a consequence, in the παλμός or *salitatio*, see Auguste Bouché-Leclercq, *Histoire de la divination dans l'antiquité* (Paris: Ernest Leroux, 1879–1882) 4 vols, 1, pp. 160–165 ("divination palmique"). This was also known in the early seventeenth century. In *L. et M. Annaei Senecae Tragoediae cum notis Thom. Farnabii* (Amsterdam: Blaeu, 1632), p. 298, Farnaby annotates at *Herc. Oet.* 708 ("cor attonitus salit"): "καρδίης παλμός, qui inter divinationes salitorias".

1638 vocamur In this way Aeneas (Verg. *Aen.* III, 494), in this way Auriacus were called (ll. 171–172). Cf. also l. 1287 "posceris" and the comm.

1638 cura Diuorum Cf. Verg. *Aen.* III, 476: "cura deûm".

Transition

1640–1643 En, ipse ... occurrit suo As happens regularly, one character announces the arrival of the other. Usually this occurs at the end of a scene, as an announcement of the next. If one regards a scene technically as a part that starts with the emergence of a character, a new scene would start at 1644. The *sicarius* announces Auriacus' departure from court and arrival in the court-yard. Heinsius however sees the whole thing as one scene.

These lines contain some implicit stage directions regarding the entrance of the Prince: the path he takes (see above), how he does so and in which company.

1640 rara ... manu The composition of this small group is shown by the speaker headings in ll. 1738 and 1743, *Armiger* and *Chorus satellitum* respectively. Loisa is probably not part of this, witness her reaction in 1835–1836, when she wants to see if her husband shows a sign of life.

1641–1642 turbido ... ore The causes of the 'confusion' of the face are not clear: perhaps they are cares, fear or grief, which would not suit the Stoic represen-tation of Auriacus, or it could be concentration or his care for his country (cf. Act I).

Fixed changes in nature—ἐκπύρωσις

1644–1668 Dies diei cedit—suetumque fusum volvit Auriacus here proclaims the insight that days, years and centuries (a climactic *tricolon*) alternate, in which the world returns to chaos. With this insight, he seems to be referring to the Stoic conception of the ἐκπύρωσις, the purifying destruction of the cosmos by fire (Pohlenz, *Die Stoa* 1, pp. 75–81 on the ages of the world, on the ἐκπύρω-σις esp. pp. 79–81). Seneca, too, uses this view for his visual power, although he rejects it as such, see Fantham, *Seneca's Troades*, pp. 266–267. As a transition from the interweaving days, years and centuries to the purification of the cos-mos, Heinsius mentions the concept of the mutual struggle between water and land, devouring each other.

The great example of such exercises about the changeability of time and the incorruption of nature is the conversation between the Greek scholar Pythagoras and King Numa, or the philosopher's speech to the monarch, as described in Ov. *Met.* XV, 60–478, esp. 165–478. In the speech of Auriacus, no verbal similarities with the passage from the *Metamorphoses* can be discerned, but the basic ideas agree: the idea that time is passing in the cosmos; that land and sea are at war; that nature always makes new forms and—in Pythagoras' speech indirectly—that man can oversee all these things. See also the comm. infra. Heinsius adds the aforementioned ἐκπύρωσις to it, as well as the notion that man devised violent causes of death in addition to the existing ones. For such a notion, see Hor. *C.* I, 2, 5 and Nisbet-Hubbard 1, p. 22 *ad loc.*

The concept of the ages of the world can also be found in the philosophical work of Seneca, e.g. *Ep.* 71, 12–14. The Judaeo-Christian notion of a perishing of heaven and earth, the emergence of a new heaven and a new earth where righteousness resides, as shown in (for example) 2 Petr. 3, is not relevant in this passage, although it must be borne in mind that Stoic and Christian notions are considered to be interrelated (e.g. Jason L. Saunders, *Justus Lipsius: The Philosophy of Renaissance Stoicism* (New York: Liberal Arts Press, 1955), p. 208). Some Jews also believed in a flood at the end of the world. Cf. further (inter alia) Luc. I, 79–80: "Totaque discors machina divulsi turbabit foedera mundi".

1644 *dies diei cedit*   A similar formulation of the passage of time is given in Hor. *C.* II, 18, 15: "Truditur dies die"; see also Otto, *Sprichwörter*, pp. 112–113 s.v. dies 1, and the comm. *ad* ll. 14–22. The concept is also found in (for example) Ov. *Met.* XV, 183–184: "Tempora sic fugiunt pariter pariterque sequuntur et nova sunt semper" and Secundus *Silvae* 3, 80–81: "Cuncta recurrunt ordine certo". For the concept in Seneca, see (for instance) *Herc. f.* 178–180: "Properat cursu vita citato volucrique die rota praecipitis vertitur anni". In the context of "annus" and "saeculum", 'day' was chosen as the interpretation of "dies" rather than 'time' in general. In that regard, the author is playing with the meaning of "cedit". The expression "dies cedit" is used as a juridical term for the day in which an agreement will be reached, legislation will be passed, etc. (*OLD* s.v. cedo 6b). But at the same time "cedere" is used for the passage of time (*OLD* s.v. 5a).

1645–1646 *vltimus ... finis*   This pleonasm refers to 'the final chord'. Cf. also (for example) Sen. *Oed.* 980–994, esp. 987–988: "Omnia secto tramite vadunt primusque dies dedit extremum". For the formulation, cf. Sen. *Herc. f.* 209–210: "Finis alterius mali gradus est futuri". For the "gradus" of the ages, cf. Sen. *Herc. f.* 291: "tot per annorum gradus"; on the peculiarity of the expression, see Fitch, *Seneca's Hercules Furens*, p. 207 *ad loc.*

1648 *helluo*   In a metaphorical sense this word also occurs in Cic. *Sest.* 26: "helluo, patriae!" For the idea that sea and land devour each other, cf. (for example) Ov. *Met.* xv, 262–263: "Vidi ego, quod fuerat quondam solidissima tellus, esse fretum, vidi factas ex aequore terras". People experience the power of water in, for instance, the St Elizabeth's Floods of 1404, 1421 and 1424. In his *De tragica constitutione* (1611) Heinsius criticizes the expression "continentis helluo" as far-fetched (*Trag. const.* 1611, C. 16, p. 216; Heinsius, *On Plot in Tragedy*, p. 121 and p. 142, n. 55).

1650–1652 *destinatas fluminum—caeruli potum senis*   These lines refer to the fact that rivers sometimes dry out. The earth gathers, as it were, the water of these rivers—the water that should flow to the sea. In other words: the water from the riverbeds ("vias fluminum"), which is destined for the sea ("cano parenti"), is swallowed by the land before it reaches the sea ("praevia"); the land takes possession in advance ("praeoccupat") of the water that the sea would have received. The sea is indicated periphrastically by means of "caerulus senex". It is apparently not important for the author to indicate whether a special god is or is not intended—the sea god par excellence, Neptune, or the one in *Aur.* most frequently referred to as Nereus.

1652 *caeruli*   This is a word cherished by the author, and it occurs eleven times in the play with regard to the sea, and once in connection with the sky. In antiquity the adjective is found associated with both Neptune (e.g. Prop. iii, 7, 62) and Nereus (e.g. Ov. *Her.* 9, 14), and other sea and river gods and goddesses, see *OLD* s.v. 3. It is redolent of a formulation by Dousa in a letter to Victor Giselinus of April 1569, travelling: "equo ligneo per vias caeruleas", and therefore reminiscent of Plaut. *Rud.* 268–269, also used by Dousa in his *Nova poemata* 1576, p. Q6r, see Chris L. Heesakkers, *Praecidanea Dousana: Materials for a Biography of Janus Dousa Pater (1545–1604): His Youth* (Amsterdam: Holland Universiteitspers, 1976) Doctoral thesis Leiden, pp. 56 and 58 n. 23.

1653–1657 *Sic cuncta—veteresque soluit*   For this concept of changes in nature, where nothing is lost, cf. Ov. *Met.* xv, 165: "Omnia mutantur, nihil interit" of which l. 1655 is almost a paraphrase. For ll. 1653–1654 "lege nascendi [...] pereuntque rursus, ut resurgant denuo", cf. Ov. *Met.* xv, 255–258: "Nascique vocatur incipere esse aliud, quam quod fuit ante, morique desinere illud idem. Cum sint huc forsitan illa, haec translata illuc, summa tamen omnia constant". For the ever new forms, cf. *ibid.* 170: "nec manet ut fuerat nec formam servat eandem", and *ibid.* 252–253: "Rerumque novatrix ex aliis alias reparat natura figuras".

1653–1668 *Sic cuncta—fusum voluit*   The earth saves everything, only to eventually return to original chaos. This is a representation of the Stoic doctrine of world eras, where the cosmos passes through the fire to return to order, the ἐκπύρωσις (see supra). Heinsius, however, does not mention the fire.

For a contemporary text reflecting this view, one can turn to Lipsius *Const.* I, 16: "Abeunt omnia in hunc nascendi pereundique fatalem gyrum [...] eat hic rerum in se remeantium orbis, quamdiu erit ipse Orbis"; see also Jason L. Saunders, *Justus Lipsius: The Philosophy of Renaissance Stoicism* (New York: Liberal Arts Press, 1955), pp. 202–210. As said, this part of the Stoic doctrine does not occur in the passage from Ov. *Met.* xv.

1660 *machina* Cf. Grotius *Ad. ex.* 60: "caeli machina" and the comm. *ad loc.*, Grotius, *Dichtwerken/Poetry*, p. 26, explaining: "opus fabricatum", which sits well in this context of decay and being rebuilt. Cf. also Lipsius, *Const.* I, 16: "Longaevum aliquid in hac machina, nihil aeternum"; Luc. I, 79–80 (see above) and Cats, *Sinne- en minnebeelden*, ed. Luijten, vol. 1, p. 178 (24.C.5) as well as vol. 2, p. 436, n. 13. See also the Dedication to the States 46.

1661 *Magni—poli* For the concept of the world resting in the arms of heaven, see the comm. *ad* ll. 1348–1392.

1663–1664 *Eritque rursum—cum nullus esset* This colon explains chaos: the cosmos will be what it was when no cosmos yet existed, i.e. chaos.

1665 *natura ... retexit vias* Cf. Ov. *Met.* xv, 249: "Retro redeunt idemque retexitur ordo".

1668 *fusum voluit* Here it is remarkable that Natura uses a shuttle or spindle. Heinsius apparently equates nature as a physical whole with Nature as a deity (see comm. *ad* ll. 1–5). Divine Nature can be synonymous with fate, of which the Parcae are possibly the accomplices. These Parcae handle the "fusus", cf., e.g., Cat. 64, 310–314. Also the "pensum" (l. 1667), the weighed amount of wool that spinners had to spin, is associated with the activity of the Fate goddesses, e.g. Sen. *Herc. f.* 181: "Durae peragint pensa sorores"; see also Fitch, *Seneca's Hercules Furens*, p. 176 *ad loc.* It may be that the "fusus" is a metaphor for the world axis.

L 1656 In his copy, the author introduces the subject "artifex", and deletes "interim".

L 1659 'Slipping' becomes 'falling apart' ("cadens").

Man learns his destiny

1668–1672 *Has inter vices—nescit suam* In the midst of these "vices", man, a small part of the whole, sees "vota sua", and is the only one on the earth who gets to know his fate, but does not knows it. The exact meaning of these lines is obscure. What are the "vota sua"? What does the paradox "sortemque solus discit, et nescit suam" mean? Perhaps it indicates that man does get to know his fate, but does not fully understand it. Should "cum" (l. 1671) be taken concessively or causally? For the notion that man is capable of contemplating the whole, see the comm. *ad* ll. 23–45. Man distinguishes himself from animals by reason, which gives him insight, as the Stoa taught, see (for example) Cic. *Leg.* I, 7, 22. Thus enabling him to contemplate his destiny and try to know it. According to Auriacus or Heinsius, real insight is apparently impossible.

1668 *Has inter vices*   These are the alternations of the seasons and other time periods, containing the notion of inevitability, and hence, secondarily, changes of fate. Hence Heinsius is using "vices" in the same way as Seneca, see Fantham, *Seneca's Troades*, pp. 379–380.

1669 *quotacunque*   Cf. l. 894 and the comm.

1672 *discit, et nescit*   Again, a cognitive process takes primacy, cf. l. 405 and the comm. *ad loc.*

Man increases the number of causes of death

1673–1719 *Idemque vitae—fudit viros*   A catalogue of causes of death is a topos; for its popularity in literature, rhetoric and philosophy, see Van Dam, *Statius Silvae, Book II*, p. 176 *ad* Stat. *Silv.* II, 1, 213–218; also Frank, *Seneca's Phoenissae*, p. 121 *ad* Sen. *Pho.* 151–153: "Vbique mors est. Optime hoc cavit deus: eripere vitam nemo non homini potest, at nemo mortem; mille ad hanc aditus patent", and (for example) Sen. *Pha.* 551: "mille formas mortis" and Luc. III, 689: "mille modos leti". Such a list fits in with the Stoic 'Rage to Embrace Nature' (Rosenmeyer, *Senecan Drama and Stoic Cosmology*, pp. 160–203).

For such a pessimistic world view, cf. (for example) Verg. *Ge.* I, 505–508: "Quippe ubi fas versum atque nefas; tot bella per orbem, tam multae scelerum facies, non ullus aratro dignus honos, squalent abductis arva colonis, et curvae rigidum falces conflantur in ensem". A thread of positivity has been woven into these pessimistic lines: the Dutch have achieved military successes through the use of firearms. This seems slightly ill-considered by Heinsius, but it is undoubtedly motivated by his positive view of Holland.

1670 *excelsa mente*   Cf. l. 23: "igneae lux alta mentis"; here, too, it is the "mens" feeling at home in the *aether*, see also the comm. *ad* ll. 23–45.

1671 *cernat*   The "mens", locked up in the body as though it were a prison, is still capable of contacting the world through the senses; see Veenstra, *Ethiek en moraal*, pp. 130–132.

1676 *mille*   For "mille" as an instance of hyperbole and Seneca's predilection for specific numbers over non-specific numbers, see Frank, *Seneca's Phoenissae*, p. 122 *ad* Sen. *Pho.* 153. Cf. also l. 1683.

1679 *arte* As is often the case, here "ars" is opposed to "natura", already mentioned in ll. 1677–1678 (sea, earth and sky) and later expanded upon with wild animals and monsters (ll. 1687–1688).

1679 *creuit* Either a *perf. gnomicum* or a 'real' perf.

1691–1692 *Factumque ... nobis triumphus—scelus* Cf. ll. 1703–1704: "fortis quilibet semper fuit ut saevus esset".

1693 *Hac lege* The 'law' (also in l. 1703) refers to the revaluation of crime as a triumph.

1696 *altum ... extulit terris caput* This colon may mean (1) raised (his head) high above the lands (*OLD* s.v. effero 9b; Verg. *Ge.* IV, 352: "Arethusa [...] summa [...] caput extulit unda"); (2) has gone to distant countries (a variation of signa efferre; *OLD* s.v. 1b).

1696 *Quirinus* This god is often identified with the deified Romulus (*OLD* s.v., Stephanus, *Dictionarium*, p. 374v; Roscher 4, 15–17), standing here for the Roman people who considered cruelties a triumph.

1697 *Persenque* A "Perses" can be an inhabitant of Persia or of Parthia (*OLD* s.v. Perses (1) 1b).

1697 *Hydaspen* The Hydaspes is a tributary stream of the Indus; also used as a typical eastern river, e.g. Verg. *Ge.* IV, 211: "Medus Hydaspes", see also Stephanus, *Dictionarium*, p. 241r; *RE* 9, 34–37 s.v. Hydaspes 1.

1697 *Bactraque* Bactria was part of the Parthian Empire, now Turkistan—metonym for the east, e.g. Verg. *Aen.* VIII, 687–688: "Vltima secum Bactra vehit". Stephanus, *Dictionarium*, p. 91v calls it a province of Scythia; see also *RE* 2, 2804–2805 and *TLL* 2, 1669.

1697 *Schyten* The nomadic Scythes lived north and north-east of the Black Sea; for their cruelty, see Stephanus, *Dictionarium*, p. 394r: "Ad bella magis, quam ad ullum studium humanitatis appositae"; see also *RE* 2.R 2, 923–942 (s.v. Scythae) and 942–946 (s.v. Scythia).

1698 *rupemque falsi pendulam Promethei* This rock lies at the Black Sea. "Falsus" refers to two events: Prometheus cheated Zeus in the distribution of a sacrificial animal, and he stole fire to give it to mankind. See Roscher 3.2, 3032–3110 (on the myth in poetry, esp. 3054–3076).

1699 *Caspiumque ... mare* The Romans thought of the Caspian Sea (in Russia) as the residence of the Scythes—distant, uncivilized and stormy. On the sea, see Stephanus, *Dictionarium*, p. 134r–v and *RE* 10, 2275–2290.

1700–1701 *fabulosis—rupes* The Pillars of Hercules or Strait of Gibraltar. For "Tirynthius" for Hercules, see *OLD* s.v. b and Stephanus, *Dictionarium*, p. 431v: "[...] Tiryns generis foem. nomen patriae Herculis in Peloponneso, quae proxima Argis, a Plinio Tyrintha vocatur. Vnde et Hercules Tirynthius appellatus est: quamvis Thebanus quoque dicatur". Bacchus' role in this combination is unclear. Perhaps it refers to rocks in the east, where Bacchus would have been, see the comm. on Pro *Auriaco sua* 37. The word "fabulosus" (on which or on whom stories are told) has appeared in Latin literature since Horace, see Nisbet-Hubbard 1, p. 267 *ad* Hor. *C.* I, 22, 7. The syntactic function of "fabulosis Tirynthio Bacchoque" is not fully clear. It may be dat. to "asperas" or perhaps abl. loci.

1701 *Hesperumque limitem* For Hesperus as the west, see the comm. *ad* l. 10.

1702 *parciorem ... diem* This can mean: (1) the country where daylight is scarcer since the sun sets there, cf. Sil. XIV, 8: "extremumve diem [i.e. Spain]" and Grotius, *Inauguratio regis Britanniarum* 378: "longior ipsa dies" (Grotius, *Dichtwerken/Poetry* I, 2, 3A/B, pp. 78 and 107–108); or (2) a shorter time.

1703 *Hac lege* See the comm. *ad* 1693.

1706–1707 *liberos morti sinus et vela ... pandimus Belgae* The "sinus" and the "vela" are almost synonyms. The shipping metaphor is suitable for the Dutch. For "sinus pandere", cf. (inter alia) Sen. *Pha.* 1190: "[death] pande placatos sinus"; for "vela pandere", see (for example) Ov. *A.A.* III, 500: "plenaque curvato pandere vela sinu".

1707 *tota* Either to "manu", a metaphor for 'all out', or to "vela", meaning 'the whole sails'.

1708–1716 *Prius—agmen* These lines describe warfare with gunpowder and guns. Cf. the comm. on *Pro Auriaco sua* 1–19. The Dutch imitate the "Dei [...] ignes", Jupiter's lightning. Their 'pressed glow', the bullets fired with high pressure, frighten the sky by flying through it.

1712 *globo* This may indicate a dense vapour (e.g. Verg. *Aen.* IX, 36: "Quis globus, o cives, caligine volvitur atra?"), reviving the "vapor" of l. 1711, or a spherical mass, a bullet.

1716–1718 *Parua quin etiam loquor, necantur vrbes* Cf. Benedicti *De rebus gestis* I, 531: "Parva loquor: totae veniunt in vincula classes", and Ov. *Met.* II, 214: "Parva queror: magnae pereunt cum moenibus urbes", followed by a description of all mountains burnt by Phaeton's failure (216–226).

1717 *saxaque et moles deûm* This probably does not refer to any particular rocks or mountains, but if it does, one might consider the enumeration in Ov. *Met.* II, 216–226 (see above), esp. Mt Olympus and the rock where Prometheus was bound (225 and 224 resp.).

The decisive moment

1720–1734 *Pudet fateri ... pedibus hoc restat meis* The murderer is still not entirely self-assured, is still shaking with tension, his tongue refusing service and his knees knocking. Again the mood of a character apparent from external characteristics, see l. 1454 and the comm. Heinsius thus links up with the literary (and Stoic) tradition, but also with the data he could derive from the reports of the murder: "d'welcke hy was eysschende [...] met een bevende stemme en verbaest zijnde" ('[a passport], which he demanded [...] with a tremulous voice and afraid', *Een verhael vande moort*, Frederiks, *De moord van 1584*, p. 68).

1721 *Deseror rursus* Sc. "a me" (I am left behind by myself, I do not control myself), synonymous of l. 1722 "me reliqui".

1724 *dicta modo constent tua* These words may apply to the vow (cf. ll. 742 "votum" and 767) that he must keep, or to the words he should speak to Orange with a steady voice.

1727–1730 *Longa nos tandem dies ... patriam versus trahit* The long waiting time is also attested to in *Een verhael vande moort*: the murderer was delayed in Luxembourg; here it is used to increase the pathos.

1728 ... 1730 *magnanime* See the comm. *ad* l. 488.

1731–1732 *fauoris obsides ... tui ... tabellas* The murderer's request for a passport is known from the reports: "ende commende by den selven Prince, heeft hem een passepoort gheeyscht [...]" ('coming to the Prince, he [the murderer] asked of him a passport', *Een verhael vande moort*, Frederiks, *De moord van 1584*, pp. 67–68). In his *Neederlandsche Histoorien* (1642), P.C. Hooft will call this a "vrijereyzbrief" (letter of free travel, Martinus Nijhoff, *P.C. Hooft's Nederlandse historien in het kort* (Amsterdam and Brussels: Elsevier, 1947), p. 346). For "obsides", see also *TLL* 9.2, 219.8–29. With "liceat" something like 'ire' should be supplied. The murderer stammers ("rursus in medio sonus defecit ore"), as illustrated by the repeated "longa [...] princeps" and by the anacoluthon.

1734 *satellitum vis* "Vis" may be the 'group' of soldiers or their 'power'. For "vis" see also the comm. on l. 1188, and cf. Verg. *Aen.* IV, 132: "odora canum vis".

Auriacus'/Orange's last words

1735–1738 *O magne rerum genitor ... populi meique* This passage renders Orange's traditional last words: "Mon Dieu aie pitié de mon âme, je suis fort blessé; mon Dieu aie pitié de mon âme et de ce pauvre peuple" ('My God, have mercy on my soul, I am seriously hurt; my God, have mercy on my soul and this poor people'; in the translation of *Een verhael vande moort*, Frederiks, *De moord van 1584*, p. 68: "Heere Godt weest mijn siele ghenadich, ick ben seer gequetst, Heere Godt weest mijn siele, ende dit arme volck ghenadich", 'Lord, have mercy upon my sould, I am seriously hurt. Lord, have mercy upon my soul and this poor people'). The question of whether these last words are actually spoken or not (on this issue, see C. Vergeer, 'De laatste woorden van prins Willem', *Maatstaf* 28 (1980), pp. 67–100 and the reactions of J.A.L. Lancée, 'Oranjes beeld in later ogen', *Maatstaf* 29 (1981), pp. 38–51, esp. pp. 50–51 n. 2 and L.J. van der Klooster, 'Drie gelijktijdige berichten over de moord op Prins Willem van Oranje', *Jaarboek 'Oranje-Nassau Museum'* 1984), pp. 37–83) is not relevant in this respect. Heinsius uses words that befit the Stoic character of the tragedy: "magne rerum genitor" and "maxime pater" (cf. l. 1 "rerum beate rector") can indicate the Stoic *Logos* or *Ratio*, see the comm. on ll. 1–5. He also fits in with the humanistic use of classical Latin words for Christian notions, see also Bloemendal, 'Mon Dieu, mon Dieu ...'.

1735–1736 *praeceps ... fluo* Lit. 'I feel life flowing out of me'.

The murderer pursued

1738–1751 *Pergite—manus* Heinsius illustrates the confusion after the attack with stylistic means: in the appeal of the "armiger" (trochees instead of iambs, see supra); by the repetition of "pergite", combined with "ah ah"; in the reaction of the "satellites" with the *distributio*, indicated by the repetition of "pars" nine times; by the Gorgian figure (also paronomasia) in ll. 1746–1747: "parsque ne lateat dolus [...] parsque ne pareat via"; and by the accumulation of the substantively used adjectives and the substantives in ll. 1748–1749.

The excitement is also known from stories about the murder, e.g. *Copie ut Delft van het claghelijck feyt, te Delft gheschiet*: "[...] de schutters waren terstond inde wapen, alle hoecken ende straten beset, de gantsche vestenen ende poorten gesloten zijnde, worden bewaert" ('the militia were immediately in arms, all corners and streets were occupied, the whole fortress and the closed gates were guarded'; Frederiks, *De moord van 1584*, p. 50).

1745–1746 *iuratos duces proceresque* Indeed, the opinion was that it was a conspiracy. Which was not incorrect, as in the end Balthasar Gerards had discussed his plans in advance with the nobleman and diplomat from the Southern Netherlands Christoffel d'Assonleville (ca. 1528–1607) and responded to the ban that Philip II had imposed on Orange. In this connection, "iurati" may be regarded as a *simplex pro composito* ("coniurati"). It could be objected that "proceres" is only used *in bonam partem*, and "iurati" is often related to magistrates. Meeting these arguments one could conceive of "sistere" as 'to detain and inform'; then the lines could be paraphrased: a part must come to the mayors, bailiffs and aldermen and inform them of the events.

1751 *prementes* "Premere" can denote the pursuit or the hands that grip him.

Act IV, Chorus (1752–1818)

Summary

As with the previous one, this chorus consists of indigenous Hollanders. Their praise of their own people is interrupted by commotion in town.

1752–1791 The Hollanders defy the waves—they would even endure a deluge—and the Spanish enemies, and trade everywhere. They are at home all over the world, both on land and at sea.

1792–1814 The stars show them the way, laugh at the weak Spaniards and tell about the victory of General Worst, the foundation of Leiden University and the role of the pigeons in the Relief of Leiden.

1815–1818 Then the chorus hears whimpering in town, which frightens them.

The triumphant tone of this chorus song is a case of tragic irony. They do not know that Orange was murdered. The praises of the Hollanders who, as it were, put the Spaniards in awe, either in general (e.g. ll. 1790–1791 and 1797) or on special occasions (victories of Admiral Worst, ll. 1801–1803, and the Relief of Leiden, ll. 1805–1811) and the certainty that the gods are favourable to the Dutch (ll. 1812–1814) are belied by the events.

Stylistically this chorus song stands out for the frequency of expressions with substantives (part. on -tor) where an adjective subordinate clause could be expected: "magni domitor tyranni" (l. 1752); "vasti dominus profundi" (l. 1753); "Nerei rector" (l. 1754); "victor amborum" (l. 1760); "fati contemptor" (ll. 1760–1761); "publicus mundi pavor" (l. 1764); "caeruli fluctus equitator" (l. 1766); "aemulus Glauci" (l. 1779); "magni inquies mundi peragrator ille" (ll. 1782–1783).

Metre

This chorus song is written in Sapphic metres: hendecasyllables alternating with adonei. The last four lines (1815–1818), strictly speaking not part of the song but a response to the action, consist of iambic trimeters, the measure fitting in with the action. In l. 1754 the second "a" of Batavus (mostly metrically long) is shortened. Cf. *In Hispanum et Batavum* 14 Βατάβῳ (and *ibid.* 11 Βαταύου).

Commentary

Praise of the Dutch—everywhere at home

1752–1791 *Hactenus—tutus ab illos est* The chorus praises the Dutch or Hollanders as sailors. Moreover, travelling land and sea they reach the Indies (see below, and *AGN* 7, pp. 174–254). They are, as it were, at home everywhere. For such a praise of the Dutch, see also ll. 300–318 and the comm. *ad loc.* Heinsius used the notion of being at home everywhere in ll. 574–608 as well. However, this was more about the idea that princes and high-minded people are at home everywhere, whereas here what is intended is that the Dutch go all over the world for their trade, and thus, as it were, feel at home everywhere, in the east and west.

They would not even fear a flood (ll. 1769–1773). They call it "undae" (the waves) and "trepidum castae saeculum Pyrrhae". The latter refers to the ancient Flood story, as told in (for example) Ov. *Met.* I, 244–415 (Deucalion and Pyrrha survive the flood; see also Stephanus, *Dictionarium*, p. 183r s.v. Deucalion, *RE* 24,77–78 and Roscher 1.1, 994–998). The description of the rivers and fountains flooding (ll. 1770–1772) and the heavy showers (1772–1773) resemble Ov. *Met.* 1.260–261, on Jove: "Poena placet diversa, genus mortale sub undis perdere et ex omni nimbos demittere caelo"; in the biblical story of the Flood (Gen. 6–7) it is also rain showers and a flood that destroy the earth. In many countries such stories existed (see, for example, *RAC* 2, 788; also Nisbet-Hubbard 1, p. 22 *ad* Hor. *C.* I, 2, 6). The words "saeculum Pyrrhae" (see also infra) indicate that the Greco-Roman version prevails here. Even amidst this violence, the Dutch seafarer is safe.

1752 *tyranni* For "tyrannus" as sea god or the sea, cf., e.g., Hor. *C.* II, 17,19: "tyrannus Hesperiae Capricornus undae". As often, Heinsius repeats the same thought in different words ("vasti dominus profundi", l. 1753; "Nerei rector", l. 1754). But perhaps Philip II is meant. This interpretation is supported in ll. 1758–1759, where Spaniards and storms are mentioned together. Which would make this an instance of tragic irony: the chorus does not yet know that Philip achieved an indirect victory through the murder of Orange.

1756–1757 *Aquilonis ... Boreae* Aquilo, the north (or north-north-east or north-east) wind is called Βορέας in Greek. For the frightening aspect of this storm, see Bömer, *Ovidius Metamorphosen* 1, pp. 37–38 *ad* Ov. *Met.* I, 65; Aquilo also occurs in Ov. *Met.* I, 262. Heinsius apparently distinguished between both winds. See also Stephanus, *Dictionarium*, p. 60v s.v. Aquilo: "Ventus dictus a vehementissimo volatu instar aquilae: Graecis Βορέας, siccus et frigidus" and *ibid.* p. 107r s.v. Boreas and *RE* 3, 720–721 s.v. Boreas 1.

1760–1761 *per vtramque ... Arcton* For the Great Bear and Little Bear, see the comm. *ad* l. 1792. Stephanus, *Dictionarium*, p. 64v s.v. Arcton also distinguished two Bears, called Cynosura and Helice. Here the North-East Passage is meant; on this, see Marijke Spies, *Bij Noorden om: Olivier Brunel en de doorvaart naar China en Cathay in de zestiende eeuw* (Amsterdam: Amsterdam University Press, 1994).

1763 *Indum* For the passage to the 'Indies', see the comm. on ll. 219–230, esp. 227 "incoctum solibus Indum", echoed by "sole torrentem [...] Indum".

1768 *Austrum* Auster (Gr. Νότος) is one of the main winds, the raining south or south-west wind, see (for example) Ov. *Met.* I, 66 and *ibid.* 264–269; Stephanus, *Dictionarium*, p. 88r: "Ventus meridionalis calidus et humidus exitialis et morbosus, ab haurendis aquis dictus: unde etiam Graece eadem ratione νότος appellatur: quoniam νότος Latine humor dicitur". See also the comm. *ad* l. 756.

1769–1770 *trepidumque ... saeculum Pyrrhae* Cf. Hor. *C.* I, 2, 6: "grave [...] saeculum Pyrrhae".

1775 *Protei pecus* Cf. Hor. *C.* I, 2, 7: "Proteus pecus egit" (see also the comm. *ad* ll. 1769–1770). If a particular kind of 'cattle' is meant, these will be seals (l. 1776: "phocae"), since Proteus was the shepherd of Jupiter's seals, see Hom. *Od.* IV, 411–413 and Verg. *Ge.* IV, 387–395. In which case "-que" in "horridasque" is explicative. For "horridasque [...] Phocas", cf. Verg. *Ge.* IV, 395: "turpis [...] phocas".

1776 *auara Cete* The "cetus" (nom. and acc. pl. N. "cete") is a big sea creature— a whale, a porpoise or a dolphin. Cf. Verg. *Aen.* V, 822: "Tum variae comitum facies, immania cete, et senior Glauci chorus".

1777 *blandas Thetidis sorores* For Thetis, the mother of Achilles and one of the fifty daughters of Nereus (Nereids), see (for example) Stephanus, *Dictionarium*, p. 315v s.v. Nereus: "[...] ex Doride uxore, eademque sorore, maximam Nympharum turbam suscepit, quae a nomine patris Nereides appellantur", and Roscher 3.1, 207–237.

1778 *nabit* Often "nare" is a synonym for 'to sail'. Here the two possibilities combine: the Dutch sail at sea, but are "aemuli Glauci", as sea gods going through the water, and "incolae ponti", they live in the sea. The Hollanders or Dutch were so familiar with the sea that they even swim in it, which was unusual for sailors.

1779 *aemulus Glauci* In Greek mythology, Glaucus was a fisherman becoming a god (Ov. *Met.* XIII, 904–XIV, 39, esp. XIII, 904–906); he has the gift of prophecy (on him, see Bömer, *Ovidius Metamorphosen* 6, pp. 453–455; Stephanus, *Dictionarium*, p. 221r; Roscher 1.2, 1678–1686 s.v. Glaukos 7).

1779–1780 *patrijque ... ponti*   Since Nereus is the father of the Dutch (l. 317), the sea is "patrius".

1784 *terminos rerum*   In contrast to ll. 30–31 here the corners of the earth are intended. Cf. Sen. *Herc. f.* 290: "rerum terminos".

1787–1790 *Vesperumque—merces*   These lines refer to the demise of the Armada, the Invincible Fleet, lost in a storm in 1588, chased by Dutch and English ships; see also the comm. on *In Hispanum et Batavum* 18.

L 1754   The gulfs are turned from 'sparkling' to 'proud', for an unclear reason.

   Victories

1792–1814 *Pleiadum ... dissilit aether*   The Pleiades (the Seven Sisters, see below) talk about the achievements of the Dutch. This catalogue is epic and is reminiscent of ἔκφρασεις; as in Verg. *Aen.* VIII, 626–728 (Aeneas' shield); cf. also *ibid.* I, 466–493 (scenes on the door of the temple of Juno) and VI, 20–33 (the door of Apollo's temple). See also ll. 1295–1312 and the comm.

1792 *Pleiadum ... choreae*   The Pleiades are the seven daughters of Atlas and Pleione, who become seven stars. They announce the time when sailing was possible (cf. Hes. *Erga* 383–384). Even as far back as antiquity their name is explained as 'the flight of doves', and they are mention in Hom. *Il.* XVIII, 486 (on the shield of Achilles). See also Stephanus, *Dictionarium*, p. 357v and Roscher 3.2, 2549–2560. "Choreae" are chorus dances, but it is also used for the circular movements of the stars (Var. *Men.* 269: "cum pictus aer fervidis late ignibus caeli chorean astricen ostenderet"; Man. I, 671: "Exercent varias naturae lege choreas"; Varr. ap. Non. p. 451.11: "choreae astricae").

1803 *Worstus*   Native of Vlissingen Ewoud Pietersz. Worst († 1573) was a Zeeland admiral, who had his greatest successes in 1572–1573. See Frederik Nagtglas, *Levensberichten van Zeeuwen: Zijnde een vervolg op P. de la Rue, geletterd, staatkundig en heldhaftig Zeeland* (Middelburg: J.C. and W. Altorffer, 1890–1893). 2 vols, 2, pp. 1003–1005; Johan E. Elias, *Schetsen uit de geschiedenis van ons zeewezen* (The Hague: Martinus Nijhoff, 1916–1930) 6 vols, vol. 1, p. 66. He is also mentioned in Benedicti *De rebus gestis* I, 551–552: "Worstum Mattiacae classis ductorem".

1805 *Patareia*   This name may refer to the 'woman connected to Apollo', the Muse. It refers to Apollo's sanctuary in Patara.

   The foundation of the University made the Muses move to Leiden (Penates here used metonymically for settling, cf. Sen. *Oed.* 23 and Töchterle, *Seneca Oedipus*, p. 157 *ad loc.*). The lines refer to the opening of the University on

1 February 1575, when Apollo and the nine Muses sailed through the Rapenburg (R. van Luttervelt, 'De optocht ter gelegenheid van de inwijding der Leidse Universiteit', *Leids Jaarboekje* 50 (1958), pp. 87–104, esp. pp. 88–89). Dousa may also be alluding to this in his *Heinsiades Musae* 59: "Per caussam Delphis Leidam dum mutat Apollo"; Benedicti, too, refers to it in his *De rebus gestis* I, 681–682: "Quid? quod et auspiciis tanti Ducis inclita Leidae moenia Parnasso Musae petiere relicto?"

Patareia could also indicate the City Virgin; consider in this regard the pseudonyms used by Orange and the cities of Holland in their secret correspondence (Enkhuizen—Triton; Amsterdam—Saturn; Muiden—Phoebus; Delft—Apollo; see Hooft, *Neederlandsche Histoorien* [...] (Amsterdam: Elzevier, 1642), pp. 198–199). It is unclear whether "iterum" should be taken with "flexos" (cf. "Musae reduces") or with "ire".

1805–1811 *quales—miserat olim*   At the Relief of Leiden in 1574 Dousa and the leader of the Sea Beggars, Boisot, used pigeons. Dousa wrote some poems, which were the "precium" of the Muses. The Camaenae are called "doctae", since Dousa presented himself as a "poeta doctus".

In a mythological periphrasis the pigeons are called "aureas blandae volucres Diones"; doves were associated with Dione's daughter Venus, see (for example) Prop. III, 3, 31: "Veneris dominae volucres, mea turba, columbae"; Stat. *Silv.* III, 5, 80: "Dionaea [...] columba"; cf. also Ov. *Met.* XV, 386: "Cythereiadasque columbas" and Verg. *Aen.* VI, 190–192. The doves are "consciae rerum": they are knowledgeable and aware of the situation.

Transition—lamentation

1815–1818 *Sed quid—nondum dolor*   The chorus breaks off its lyrical hymn and wonders what noise it hears. Such a closing to a choral song, in line with the immediate action, is also found in Seneca's drama, for example, *Herc. Oet.* 1128–1130: "Sed quis non modicus fragor aures attonitas movet? Est et Herculeus sonus"; ('But what kind of uncontrollable screaming hits my bewildered ears? It is, indeed, the sound of Hercules'); *Aga.* 408–411 (the chorus announces the arrival of a soldier), *Pha.* 828–834 (the chorus sees Theseus approaching) and *ibid.* 989–990 (a sad messenger arrives). The change from lyrical metres to iambs, the metre of action is appropriate.

The commotion described by the chorus is in a literary tradition, but is also based on the testimonies concerning the murder of Orange. On the clamour after the murder, see *Copie wt Delft van het claghelijck feyt, te Delft gheschiet*: "Dat gantsche hof waer vol truerens ende clagens ende schreyde al watter waer [...] de gantsche stadt van Delft terstont vol remoers" ('The entire court was full of mourning and complaining and everyone cried [...] the entire city of Delft was immediately full of clamour', Frederiks, *De moord van 1584*, p. 50); or, in the words of P.C. Hooft: "'T gerucht van dit helsche bedryf vloogh ter yl de gansche stadt oover, en baarde grouwzaame ontsteltenis. Men sloot'er de poorten: yghelyk sprak vuur en vlam, en donderde met afgryzelyke vloeken op den verraader" ('The rumour of the hellish act ran quickly though the entire city, and caused great consternation. The gates were closed; everybody spoke fire and fury, and vehemently cursed the traitor', Hooft, *Neederlandsche Histoorien* [...] (Amsterdam: Elzevier, 1642), p. 894).

1817 *magnum* Either adverbial, or substantive.

Act v, Scene 1 (1819–1911)

Summary

This scene depicts the reaction to the murder. Loisa wails, her nurse tries unsuccessfully to calm her down, a chorus shares in her grief.

1819–1838 Fate has unleashed all its forces on Loisa, so that tyrants and other high-ranking people no longer have to fear. For the second time she is a widow. She is stopped by the nurse under protest—she wants to go to her husband to see if he is still alive.

1839–1846 The nurse tries to calm Loisa with the argument that time will heal the wounds.

1847–1856 Loisa is now extremely emotional. This disaster has also revived her grief about her previous losses, the deaths of her father and her first husband. The nurse should not try to comfort her any more, or return her husband.

1856–1858 Faith is only attached to her dream, now it is too late.

1859–1875 She orders courtiers to see if Auriacus is still alive, but then she sees his sad sister and she knows that all hope is lost. She faints; the nurse tries to revive her.

1876–1911 The chorus is of the opinion that Loisa should not mourn, a task it reserves for itself. Every day women lose their husbands, but rarely does a people lose their sovereign. The chorus has lost its prince and wail for him. Then it recalls that fate brings down the high and saves the low, using ruses to this end; how many wiles see the sun every day! That is why every evening the shame of which colours his cheeks at sunset.

Loisa's violent reaction fits in with the pathos of Senecan drama. The protagonist holds an "Affektrede" (passionate monologue), to which the antagonist,
often the nurse, responds with sobbing remarks (see, for example, Tarrant,
Seneca Agamemnon, p. 192; also p. 409, the comm. *ad* II, 2). Her eruption is
also attested to in the descriptions of the murder of Orange, cf. *Copie wt Delft
van het claghelijck feyt, te Delft gheschiet*: "bovenal sach men groot hartenleet
aen de nieuwe Princerse, de welcke [...] hem niet wilde verlaten" ('above all,
great suffering was seen in the new Princess, who [...] did not want to leave
him', Frederiks, *De moord van 1584*, p. 50).

Metre

The scene consists of iambic trimeters, with eleven lines (1889–1899) in anapaestic dimeters and monometers (see also pp. 426–427, the comm. *ad* II, 3).
The change of metre underlines the other (sententious) content.

Commentary

Fate has consumed all its forces

1819–1829 *Fortes tyranni—vel in me* Fortuna or fate has a force that can also
be self-destructive. Heinsius found this idea, depicted both in l. 1824 and in
ll. 1828–1829, in Sen. *Aga.* 691: "Fortuna vires ipsa consumpsit suas"; a similar
idea is given in Ov. *Pont.* II, 7, 41–42: "Sic ego continuo Fortunae vulneror ictu,
vixque habet in nobis iam nova plaga locum". The idea is discussed by Rosenmeyer, *Senecan Drama and Stoic Cosmology*, p. 74.
    Loisa lost a father once, a husband twice (ll. 1825–1827), referring to St
Bartholomew's Night, when her father and her first husband were killed, see
also the com. *ad* l. 1211.

1820 *euectus* This is the *vox propria* for going high; cf. Sen. *Herc. f.* 132; Fitch,
Seneca's Hercules Furens, p. 166 *ad loc.*; *Aur.* 49.
1820 *arce* The word "arx" is used here in a double figurative sense: (1) the high
position of fate (*OLD* s.v. 3b); and (2) indicating the lofty position of tyrants
(*OLD* s.v. 1c).
1822 *felicitati proximum quicquid mali est* Fortune can change happiness to
its opposite in no time, see (for example) Otto, *Sprichwörter*, pp. 142–143 s.v.
fortuna 5. Perhaps one could think of "arx" as heaven, see (for example) Claud.
Cons. Hon. III 167–168: "Stetit arce suprema, algenti qua zona riget Saturnia
tractu".

1827 *vidua nunc rursus feror* Cf. Sen. *Herc. Oet.* 757: "nunc vidua [...] ferar". Perhaps here the meaning of 'calling' (*OLD* s.v. 34) is in play.

1828 *si possem et orba* These words can be interpreted in two ways: (1) if it had been possible, then malicious Fortuna would have orphaned Loisa once again (but that is impossible, because she only has one father); or (2) Loisa also lost a father in William, as it were.

No consolation

1829–1838 *Quid meos—ah, nutrix, eo* The nurse tries to calm Loisa, not only with words but also with gestures: she embraces her bosom and holds her hands. Loisa will therefore have beaten her chest with her hands in the style of the antique lamentation and possibly have pulled her hair out.

1829 *Quid meos cohibes sinus* Cf. Sen. *Tro.* 792: "Quid meos retines sinus". An implicit stage direction.

1833 *qui incipere nescit* This refers to the beginning of grief or its expression.

1835 *Ibo, ibo* Sen. *Pho.* 12–13 and 407, cf. *ibid.* 40: "sequor, sequor"; Grotius *Ad. ex.* 1688: "Ibo, ibo solus". The *geminatio* expresses impatience, a reassurance (I will go, certainly) and an inner impulse (I have to go). On this, see Frank, *Seneca's Phoenissae*, p. 75; Canter, *Rhetorical Elements*, pp. 156–157.

***L* 1837** In the Leiden copy the ambiguous subordinate sentences become equivocal: 'if something is left, I will go and see'.

Reason and time as consolations

1839–1846 *Alumna—reddis tibi* For the advice of the *nutrix* to her foster child Loisa, cf. Sen. *Dial.* VI, 8, 3 (to his mother Marcia upon the death of her son, after he said that time will heal grief): "Quanto magis hoc morum tuorum elegantiae convenit, finem luctus potius facere quam exspectare nec illum opperire diem, quo te invita dolor desinat! Ipsa illi renuntia"; see also C.E. Manning, *On Seneca's 'Ad Marciam'* (Leiden: E.J. Brill, 1981) Mnemosyne. Bibliotheca Classica Batava, Supplementum 69, pp. 58–59, Von Moos, *Consolatio*, 3, pp. 228–233 (reason and time) and pp. 17–19 (the intractability of the first emotion), and Motto, *Seneca Sourcebook*, p. 210 s.v. time 8a; p. 199 s.v. sorrow 20d. For this topos in Seneca's drama, see *Aga.* 130 (the nurse to mourning Clytaemnestra): "Quod ratio non quit saepe sanavit mora", and see Tarrant, *Seneca Agamemnon*, p. 198 *ad loc.* Grotius used it in *Ad. ex.* 1615–1618: "Comprimere primos impetus si non potes, novusque mentis raptus ignorat modum, recolligendo tempus indulge tibi, rationis usu spiritum indomitum exue", cf. Grotius, *Dichtwerken/Poetry* I, 1A, pp. 152–153. See also Grudius, *Funera* I, 2, 71–72: "Et genitrix, quae nunc subito exanimata dolore est, sensisset medicam temporis esse moram" (*Poemata et effigies* 1612, p. 122). See also Cats, *Sinne- en minnebeelden*, ed. Luijten 1, p. 68 and vol. 2, pp. 220–221 and p. 228, n. 9; Rudolf Kassel, *Untersuchungen zur griechischen und römischen Konsolationsliteratur* (Munich: Beck, 1958) Zetemata, 18, Habil.schr. Würzburg 1955, pp. 17–32 about the psychotherapeutic goal that Stoics and Epicureans were pursuing with the practice of *consolationes*.

1840–1841 *surdus—amens* For the first grief being uncontrollable, see Von Moos, *Consolatio*, 3, p. 17 *sub* 14.
1844 *eluendos* In Neo-Latin the gerund may function as a part. fut. pass.

Hope for life?

1847–1856 *Desiste—peractum est* In these lines Heinsius depicts the human reactions of disbelief and hope.

1853–1854 *Reddas—patrem* Cf. Sen. *Aga*. 967–968 [Clytaemnestra and Electra]: "Redde nunc natum mihi.—Et tu parentem redde". Heinsius artfully elaborates the *antimetabole* with *variatio*.

Finally belief in the dream

1856–1858 *Languor hoc—fides mihi est* In contrast to what is common in drama, Loisa returns to her dream. They should have believed her; even though the old man, Auriacus and the nurse were right in their doubt about the predictive value of dreams, her nightmare has come true.

1856 *languor* In classical Latin it does not mean 'sleep', but "languidus" and "languens" can be attributes of sleep (see, for example, Kilianus, *Etymologicum*, p. 592 s.v. slaep and *OLD* s.v. languidus 1c). Perhaps "languor" and "visa" should be taken as *hendiadys* (the sickening visions), or "languor" is being stressed: 'for this reason I was languishing'.
1858 *nempe* For the irony in this word, see *OLD* s.v. 1b.

No hope any more

1859–1875 *Properate famuli—extollas tuam* Loisa sees Orange's *germana* coming with sad face. Indeed, his sister, the Countess of Schwarzburg, was present at the time of the murder. She caught his last word: "waer dat hy niet meer en sprack, dan soo mijn Vrouwe de Gravinne van Swertzenborch sijn suster in Hoochduyts vraechde, Oft by sijn siele niet en stelde inde handen Christi Jesu, soo antwoorde by inde selve tale, Jae, ende en heeft noyt meer ghesproken" ('since he [Orange] did not speak any more, only after my Mistress, the Countess of Schwarzburg, his sister, asked in upper German, if he did not put his soul in the hands of Jesus Christ, he answered in the same language: Yes, and did not speak ever more', *Een verhael vande moort*, Frederiks, *De moord van 1584*, p. 68). It is Orange's younger sister Catharina, who married on 17 November 1560 with Count Günther von Schwarzburg. On her, see Eduard Jacobs, *Juliana von Stolberg, Ahnfrau des Hauses Nassau-Oranien: Nach ihrem Leben und ihrer geschichtlichen Bedeutung quellenmässig dargestellt* (Wernigerode and Halle a/S: Hendel, 1889), pp. 195–211 and L.J. van der Klooster, 'Drie gelijktijdige berichten over de moord op Prins Willem van Oranje', *Jaarboek 'Oranje-Nassau Museum'* 1984, pp. 37–83 (her portrait on p. 53). Heinsius introduces her as a mute character (not mentioned in the list of characters), but apparently did not wish to include her asking him to put his soul in Christ's hand in his Stoic play, in contrast to Benedicti, *De rebus gestis*, where she speaks a lamentation (II, 357–406).

1861 *Lapsa relliquias legam* Or: 'I will assemble my last fleeting forces'.

1863 *pectoris latebras* Cf. Verg. *Aen.* X, 601: "latebras animae pectus mucrone recludit".

1867 *Agnosco vultus* This probably means: 'she has the same expression of grief as I have', or 'I recognize her', i.e. William's sister Catharina.

1870 *dehiscit* Probably because upon fainting Loisa's soul or mind leaves her body.

1874 *quid praeceps abis* Loisa apparently really does try to go to her companion, as she had announced. However, the nurse's statement, an implicit stage direction, seems to contradict l. 1872 "concidit" (she collapsed, i.e. fainted). Unless one understands "praeceps abis" as: 'your mind goes away quickly', 'you fall silent'.

1875 *Alumna—tuam* More literally rendered: 'My child, resume your power and regain it'.

L **1870–1871** Heinsius removes "tenebris aeviternis", provisionally replacing it with "perenni", thus leaving a lacuna.

Mourning becomes the chorus

1876–1889 *Quid maesta—Ah, ah, ah, ah* The chorus meditates on the common death of husbands related to the particularity of the passing of a monarch. The exemplary passage is Sen. *Herc. Oet.* 758–764, where Hyllus addresses his mother Deianira on the influence of her husband's death: "Non sola maeres Herculem, toto iacet mundo gemendus. Fata nec, mater, tua privata credas: iam genus totum obstrepit. Hunc ecce luctu quem gemis cuncti gemunt, commune terris omnibus pateris malum. Luctum occupasti: prima, non sola Herculem, miseranda, maeres". See also *Aur.* 735–737, 1963–1965 and the comm.

The people of which this chorus consists remains implicit, as it could be the sentinels, the Flemish exiles, the indigenous Dutchmen, or a combination of these. Since this scene plays out at court, the first possibility seems most plausible, see also E.M.P. van Gemert, *Tussen de bedrijven door? De functie van de rei in Nederlandstalig toneel 1556–1625* (Deventer: Sub Rosa, 1990) Deventer Studiën, 11; Doctoral thesis Utrecht, p. 180.

1886 *at inter omnes* Dependent on the punctuation, these words can be taken to apply either to the previous ones ('but that applied to everybody') or to the following ones ('but among all ordinary deaths, my prince is deceased').

Fate's fickleness

1890–1898 *O quam vario—nulla est* These *sententiae*, indicated with quotation marks, express thoughts about the transience of the fate of persons of high station. They maintain their high position with trickery and deceit. Fortuna does not enter the cottage of a simple person. For these motifs, see *Aur.* 715–735, 1400–1415 and the comm. For the idea, see also Sen. *Pha.* 1123–1148, esp. 1138–1140: "Non capit umquam magnos motus humilis tecti plebeia domus. Circa regna tonat".

The first words of this passage are somewhat problematic: do they refer to Orange specifically, or to 'what is highly placed' in general?

Apparently Heinsius—in Stoic tradition, see the comm. on ll. 1–5—identified Fortuna, Natura and Parcae, for "parens" would is more likely to be used in the case of Natura than in the case of Fortuna; turning the shuttle (l. 1896) is something the Parcae do (on them, see Roscher 2.2, 3089 s.v. Moira).

The sun is ashamed of the many wiles

1899–1911 *Hei mihi—è terris abit* In these lines Heinsius combines the evening red (which he could see himself, but also had a literary tradition, e.g. Sen. *Herc. Oet.* 488–489: "cum ferens Titan diem lassum rubenti mergit Oceano iugum" and Ov. *Met.* XV, 192–193: "Ipse dei clipeus, terra cum tollitur ima, mane rubet, terraque rubet cum conditur ima") with the sun's shame at injustice (e.g. Sen. *Herc. Oet.* 891: "Ipse me Titan fugit", and *id. Pha.* 678–679: "Radiate Titan, tu nefas stirpis tuae speculare? Lucem merge et in tenebras fuge") See also Stat. *Th.* V, 296: "exoritur pudibunda dies".

1904–1905 *solem—sub vndas* Cf. Verg. *Ge.* I, 438: "cum [sol] se condet in undas".

1908–1909 *mergens ... rubore ... nouo* This 'new red colour' is sooner expected at sunrise than at sunset. "Mergens" could be interpreted as *simplex pro composito*, although this is not a real solution, cf. ll. 1903 "seram [...] facem" and 1911 "e terris abit". 'Again and again' would seem to be the better interpretation of "novo".

Act V, Scene 2 (1912–2105)—Libertas saucia

Summary

Liberty, injured by Auriacus' death and intent on leaving the earth, mourns beside his body.

1912–1936 Liberty's sorrow is too great for herself alone: the cosmos must rage with river water, rain and darkness, because the death of the Prince concerns all.

1937–1962 This brave man has now died; even his death makes it clear that he was invincible, because a ruse was required to commit the murder, as was the case with Achilles and Agamemnon.

1963–1978 Private losses can be wept by individuals, but the death of this man concerns all, and the universe must also mourn his death with earthquakes and thunder.

1979–1997 The Dutch must shroud the city in mourning colours and dig a grave for the Father of the Fatherland and his country that has gone down with him.

1998–2051 Auriacus must be buried and the universe must form part of the procession: nature must feel aggrieved, and the stars and constellations must join in the mourning procession. The constellation of Leo must defend the interests of the Low Countries, Boötes (near the Little Bear) must leave its orbit to raise the Prince's corpse and to show the Spaniards their wiles, while the constellation of the Swan must sing an elegy.

2052–2067 Liberty asks—the corpse is present on stage—who will be able to put his shoulders underneath this: even Hercules is not, only Atlas is capable of carrying the bier.

2068–2105 She leaves her freedom hat and her locks with the body and even sacrifices herself: she will leave the civilized world and live with wild tribes. She is tired of people, because in the midst of all animals man is an utter monster. She leaves, now the Prince has died.

Libertas is standing next to the laid-out corpse of Auriacus, cf. (for example) ll. 2068–2069: "Pileum hic linquo meum iuxta cadauer illud". Heinsius could consult reports about the death of Orange, see (for example) *Copie wt Delft van het claghelijck feyt, te Delft gheschiet*: "alsoo den Prince geleyt worde op de tafel" ('the Prince was laid on the table', Frederiks, *De moord van 1584*, p. 50).

The lamentation of Libertas is an elegy, a lament containing 'refrains': "Adeste cives", "concidit, iacet, iacet" and "Ah, ah, ah, ah" and "Heu, heu, heu heu". Libertas undoubtedly made the usual oriental mourning gestures. It is still debatable whether the elegy starts at l. 1912 or no sooner than l. 1937, see the comm. *ad* l. 1937. The elegy is sung next to the "rogus", the bier, and is therefore a *nenia*, cf. Scal. *Poet.* I, 50, p. 52a B; Scaliger, *Poetica/Dichtkunst* 1, p. 414.21–22: "Quae ad rogum dicerentur, erant naeniae".

Such formal elegies are also extant in Seneca's drama. In *Herc. Oet.* 1863–1939, Alcmena mourns the death of her son Hercules. There are no verbal correspondences with the Libertas scene, but the repetitive character of the song is similar, in Alcmena's song expressed in the repetition of "flete" and "fleat". Another similarity is the mourning of the cosmos, in the case of Hercules motivated by the fact that he has taken over the heavenly vault from Atlas' shoulders. Cf. also ll. 1964–1965 with Sen. *Herc. Oet.* 758–759. The notion of the cosmos also mourning is part of the *iacturae demonstratio*, which motivates the *luctus*. This *luctus* works mainly on *pathos*, the *affectus*, see (for example) Witstein, *Funeraire poëzie*, pp. 113–115.

For the departure of Liberty, see also Benedicti, *De rebus gestis* I, 155–156: "Libertas aurea quondam vix iam tuta fuga est", and *ibid.* I, 228: "Libertas finibus exsul". In this epic, the Hollanders also gather around Orange's corpse: II, 506: "stant Batavi circum".

Libertas calls on a few constellations to mourn for the Prince; one of them, Boötes, is to lead him into heaven. Presumably Heinsius opens the part just before dawn, and now ends after sunset: the apostrophe suggests that Freedom can actually see the constellations.

Metre

This scene consists of iambic trimeters, alternated with extra-metrical exclamations ("ah ah ah ah" and "heu heu heu heu"), shouts known from Greek drama, e.g. ἰὴ ἰὴ, ἰὼ ἰὼ, and αἰαῖ αἰαῖ. Such exclamations do not feature in Seneca's drama, but the expression "heu me" is found.

Commentary

The world should also lament

1912–1936 *Tellus et aequor—funus iacet. Ah, ah, ah, ah* For the cosmos joining in the general mourning, cf. Sen. *Herc. f.* 1104–1109: "Gemitus vastos audiat aether, audiat atri regina poli [...] resonet maesto clamore chaos [...]" and *id. Tro.* 108–116: "Rhoetea sonent litora planctu, habitansque cavis montibus Echo [...] totos reddat Troiae gemitus". The cosmos itself being in mourning is found in Sen. *Herc. Oet.* 1863–1939 and in *id. Herc. f.* 1054–1060. See also ll. 735–737, 1933–1934, 1963–1965 and the comm.

The emphasis is on the seas and rivers, and on the air insofar as rain stems from it. This emphasis is primarily inspired by the association with tears, but no less by the relationship the Dutch have with the water. See, for example, ll. 300–318 and the comm.

In the first part of this passage, the emphasis was on the cosmic implications of Auriacus' death, whereas in ll. 1928–1935 it is mainly the impossibility of showing sufficient mourning and the fact that his death concerns all people.

1920 *incumbe terris* The clouds must form a pressing burden, either by raining or by obscuring the light.
1921–1922 *occidunt soles duo ... longa nox* Cf. Cat. 5, 4–6: "Soles occidere et redire possunt [...] nox est perpetua una dormienda".
1922–1923 *longa nox—dies* For the wish for darkness, cf. Sen. *Thy.* 51: "Nox alia fiat, excidat caelo dies" [i.e. lose the light of stars and moon]; cf. *ibid.* 891–892: "Ne quid obstaret pudor, dies recessit".
1935 *publicum funus* See Marquardt-Mau, *Privatleben*, p. 350, for the Roman "funus publicum" (a funeral on the basis of a *senatus consultum*). Orange's death also concerns the state and the States.

L 1928   The logic is enhanced by changing "dolor" into "malum": the disaster is too bad to be lamented. The underlining of "dolor" in ll. 1926, 1928 and 1930 suggests that the substitution also has to do with variation.

Invincibility

1937–1962 *Spectate ciues—proh, proh dolor. Ah, ah, ah, ah*   Auriacus' death is compared with that of Achilles and Agamemnon. The *tertium comparationis* is the treacherous murder after military successes. The parallel with Agamemnon is more striking in that the Greek leader and Auriacus were both murdered in their own homes.

1939 *dictumque Marti pectus*   Cf. Stat. *Th.* IV, 305: "iurataque pectora Marti".
1942 *Grudij feroces*   Sc. tremuere. This refers to the year 1572, which was relatively successful for Orange. Cf. Benedicti, *De rebus gestis* I, 341–342: "Captisque repente Mechilinia Grudiisque ferocem tendit in hostem". On 23 May 1572, a turning point for Orange, his brother Louis took Bergen in Hainaut. Alva besieged the city. On 14 August, Orange took Roermond and held a campaign that was dependent on the help of Gaspard de Coligny. However, the Frenchman died on 24 August (St Bartholomew's Night). Orange continued the campaign, conquered some cities, while other ones sided with him. On 9 September, he reached Bergen. Alva avoided a battle and Orange had to stop the fight; on 19 September, Louis had to give up the city. On 30 August Orange had taken Mechlin. On this, see (for example) Motley, *Dutch Republic*, pp. 470–494. Benedicti (I, 337–348) attributed the actual defeat (Bergen was given up) to the loss of the help of the French; thus Orange is still the (moral) victor. In this way, Heinsius can write that the "Grudii" (southern Netherlanders) trembled. The Grudii (mentioned by Caesar, *B.G.* V, 39 as a people living in Gallia Belgica) lived in Groede or Gronde, near Oudenaerde.
1943, 1989 and 2052 *adeste cives*   Cf. Sen. *Thy.* 1002–1003: "Adeste, nati, genitor infelix vocat, adeste", and *Pha.* 725: "Adeste, Athenae, fida famulorum manus fer opem". "Adeste" not only implies presence, but also help, here in the lamentation.
1944 *transmissum latus*   I.e. of Liberty. Cf. Grotius, *Iambi* 125–127: "Sed pectus, eheu, saucium vulnus gerit quod ante Princeps". "Illud" suggests that she is referring to her wound. This does not exclude the possibility that the wound is also that of Auriacus/Orange.
1946–1947 *ipsumque lethum—nequisse vinci*   Does Heinsius mean that the murder should be surpassed by wiles, i.e. that 'honest' violence is not enough? Or does the fact that the murder required a ruse mean that Orange himself was in fact invincible? Then "lethum" is a metonym for 'dead'.

1947–1952 *Talis—infelix iacet* Achilles—of whom the Phrygians in Ilium, i.e. the Trojans, were afraid—will marry the daughter of the Trojan King Priam, Polyxena ("ultimus Priami gener", l. 1949). She consents to marriage but causes Achilles to be treacherously murdered ("fraude", 1946), either by Deiphobos, who took possession of Helen after Paris' death, or by Paris, who as her extra-marital friend is Helen's 'near-spouse'. See also Roscher 3.2, 2720–2723 s.v. Polyxena; on Achilles' death, see Roscher 1.1, 11–66, esp. 47–48. P.C. Hooft had produced a drama on this story (before 1598?), *Achilles ende Polyxena*. On this work and its sources Dares Phrygius and Dictys Cretensis, see Th.H. d'Angremond in his edition of Hooft, *Achilles en Polyxena* (Assen: Van Gorcum, 1943) and L.M. Gilbert, 'What is New in Hooft's *Achilles en Polyxena*?', *Dutch Crossing* 36 (1988), pp. 3–38.

1953–1958 *Talisque—superstes* Agamemnon returned victorious from the Trojan War, but was cunningly killed at home by his wife Clytemnestra and her lover Aegisthus ("fraude", l. 1956). Through his love for Cassandra, the daughter of Priam, Agamemnon is his son-in-law, cf. Sen. *Aga.* 188–191: "Nunc novum vulnus gerens amore Phrygiae vatis incensus furit, et post tropaea Troica ac versum Ilium captae maritus remeat et Priami gener". See also Stephanus, *Dictionarium*, p. 23v: "Cassandra Priami filia ei in sortem cessit". For "spoliator Asiae", cf. Sen. *Aga.* 204–205: "victor [...] Asiae". See also Roscher 1.1, 90–97 and 2.1, 1235–1240, and the comm. ad *Illustrissimis* [...] *Ordinibus* 39–54.

1959 *fateor* Libertas acknowledges that Philip succeeded in getting Orange to be killed, but he needed the help of a *scurra*. This pejorative word indicates how unworthy Philip's victory was. See Spanoghe 3, p. 67 s.v. scurra. While in ancient times a *scurra* was always a jester, a parasite, Kilianus has translated more than twenty scam words with *scurra*.

1960 *vincendo male* The words refer to the victory by means of an assassin.

L **1937** In the edition of 1602 there is an 'L.' to indicate a clause. Perhaps the elegy *stricto sensu* begins here, with the expression "Spectate ciues", occurring here for the first time.

L **1959** Perhaps "scurrae" became "tali" to make it more general.

The universe has to mourn too

1963–1978 *Priuata—quod fecit nefas. Ah, ah, ah, ah* Just as the chorus did in the first scene of this Act, Libertas speaks of the opposition of the death of private individuals and of princes and other special men (cf. ll. 1876–1889 and the comm. *ad loc.*). The death of the latter has implications for the entire world.

Cf. "ruina totius" (l. 1964) with Sen. *Herc. Oet.* 1149–1150 (Hercules): "Conde me tota, pater, mundi ruina". Hyllus expressed the thought earlier in the play (*Herc. Oet.* 758–764, see the comm. on 1876–1889; also ll. 735–737: "[...] cum mundi totius alto corruit ictu" and the comm.). The thought, part of the *iacturae demonstratio*, was also expressed by Grotius upon the death of the Leiden professor of theology Franciscus Iunius (1545–1602), who died 23 Oct., *Epitaphium Francisci Iunii* 19–20: "Privati non sunt in tanto funere questus: humani generis publica cura perit", see Grotius, *Dichtwerken/Poetry* I, 2, 3A/B, pp. 29 and 351.

Here the allusions to the Prince's funeral start. Jupiter's lightning should sing the *nenia* (elegy, l. 1972) with its thunder, and serve as a "tuba", the instrument used in Roman funeral rites (see Marquardt-Mau, *Privatleben*, p. 351 and *OLD* s.v. 1c). See also p. 524 on the *nenia*.

The special feature of the lightning is its destructive effect on Otus (one of the Gigantes *Culex* 234) and the Titans. The giants Otus and Ephialtes stormed the sky and Olympus, and were thrown back by Jupiter's lightning (see Stephanus, *Dictionarium*, p. 330r, Roscher 3.1, 1231–1232 and 1.1, 253–255). The same happened to the Titans (Hes. *Th.* 689–699, Roscher 1.2, 1639–1673, esp. 1643–1651). The addition of "flammarum patres" suggests that Heinsius, like others, was confusing the Titans and the Giants, who used fiery tree trunks as spears, especially since he had just mentioned Otus. According to Ovid, Jupiter used the lightning as a weapon for the first time at the Gigantomachia (*Fast.* III, 439–440, *Met.* I, 253). For the confusion of Giants and Titans, partly inspired by the fact that the Giants are considered sons of Titan and Gaia, see Stephanus, *Dictionarium*, p. 220r s.v. Gigantes and 432r s.v. Titan, and Roscher 5, 987–1019, esp. 1000.

1973 *sepulto* The person who will be buried, cf. l. 2074.
1975 *suae* The Titans are thrown back on earth 'where they belong'; for this meaning of "suus", see *OLD* s.v. 12. Mostly "suus" refers to the subject of the clause, but not always, see Kühner-Stegmann 2.1, pp. 603–604.
1976 *Vesper* Cf. l. 2014 "Hesperus".
1977 *ruptoque ... orbe* Either earthquakes or volcanic eruptions.

Mourning cloths and funeral

1979–1997 *At vos Batavûm corda ... patriae est pater. Heu, heu, heu heu* It is not only the people who must mourn, but also the animals. The horses must also wear mourning blankets. On a print by Goltzius, representing the procession at Orange's funeral, this is actually shown. The words "alter [...] dolor"

(l. 1987) also refer to this phenomenon. In this respect "natura" (l. 1982) will indicate a 'biological' nature rather than a Stoic one (as in, for example, l. 2).

The loss of Auriacus, the Father of his country, is also a great loss for the country and its freedom. For such a connection, cf. Sen. *Tro.* 124–129, where Hector's death and the fall of Troy are connected, e.g. "Tecum cecidit summusque dies Hectoris idem patriaeque fuit" (ll. 128–129). Libertas expresses an almost Epicurean view that nothing will be left but dust, cf. Sen. *Ep.* 54 and *Tro.* 378–379: "An toti morimur nullaque pars manet nostri?"

1984 *ostro superbum cornipes tollit caput* Cf. Verg. *Aen.* IV, 134: "Ostroque insignis et auro stat sonipes"; Sil. VII, 641: "Ostro ipse ac sonipes ostro"; Stat. *Th.* XI, 398: "Instratusque ostro sonipes". For "cornipes", cf. l. 1013 and the comm.

1989 *patriae fulcrum* Cf. Sen. *Tro.* 124: "columen patriae" (Hector). Hector and Orange are also connected in Hooft's *Achilles ende Polyxena*, see L.M. Gilbert, 'What is New in Hooft's *Achilles en Polyxena?*', *Dutch Crossing* 37 (1989), pp. 3–52, esp. pp. 31–33.

1990 *sopore* The topos of death as eternal sleep has a long tradition, starting with Homer, e.g. *Il.* XVI, 671–672. See also Cat. 5, 6: "Nox est perpetua una dormienda". For Senecan drama, see *Herc. f.* 1069: "frater durae languide Mortis" (see also Fitch, *Seneca's Hercules Furens*, p. 397).

1996 *patriae … pater* Here Auriacus/Orange is given the honorary title "Pater Patriae", in antiquity reserved for men who had saved their country, including Marius, Pompeius and Caesar (*OLD* s.v. pater 5c; cf., for example, Ov. *Fast.* II, 637: "bene te, patriae pater, optime Caesar"), see also Bloemendal, 'Mon Dieu, mon Dieu …'; already in Benedicti *De rebus gestis* I, 664–665: "Nec enim laudem Deus invidet illi quem Patriae Patrem voluit" and *ibid.* II, 186: "patriaeque parentem". Cf. further *Illustrissimis* […] *Ordinibus* 375 "Patriae parentis".

L 1979 This line becomes: 'But you, famous race of father Nereus […]', perhaps because the combination "gens Neptunia" already occurs in l. 845.

The starry sky joins in the mourning

1998–2033 *Efferte funus—consueuit fides. Heu, heu, heu heu* Some constellations are also required to mourn. Heinsius lists them, in a manner akin to Seneca's predilection for creating catalogues (see Canter, *Rhetorical Elements*, pp. 74–76; by Rosenmeyer, *Senecan Drama and Stoic Cosmology*, pp. 160–203, associated with the Stoic desire to encompass nature, see also the comm. *ad* ll. 1473–1493). A list of constellations can be found in (for example) *Herc. f.* 6–18, see also Fitch, *Seneca's Hercules Furens*, p. 119 *ad loc.*

The constellation of the zodiac Leo opens the line (for a discussion of the individual constellations, see infra). This is undoubtedly inspired by the concept of the *leo Belgicus*, the Dutch lion (cf. l. 2023 "leo Batavus"). In his vicinity are the Scorpion and the Hydra. Second comes Callisto, the Great Bear, who has to take her son Areas with her. She is the precursor for Boötes (Herdsman), who is equated with Arctophylax (namely keeping the Great Bear and the Little Bear) (see below).

1998 *Praefica* On these women hired in the Roman world to lament the dead at the beginning of the procession and singing the *nenia*, see Marquardt-Mau, *Privatleben*, p. 352 and *TLL* 10.2, 619.

2002–2003 *Sequitur et retro venit ... redundans* The words "retro" and "redundans" are slightly ambiguous. They can refer to the ebb and flow of tides; but "retro" can also mean 'after it' and "redundans" can mean 'overflowing'.

2003 *flebile* For this form, which seldom occurs as an adverb, see *OLD*. s.v. 3b.

2005–2007 *Sydera ... stellae minores* The "sydera" are the constellations, next to the 'smaller stars'; or the difference is between the "stellae vagae" and the "astra" (or "stellae fixae"), the planets and the stars (e.g. Luc. IX, 12–13). See also Lewis, *The Discarded Image*, i.a. p. 96. For "stellae minores", cf. Luc. I, 535.

2006 *comitetur* "Comitare" can indicate participation in a funeral, *OLD* s.v. 1b; Ov. *Pont.* I, 9, 47: "Funera non potui comitare".

2007–2012 *Tuque qui—hodie vacabis* These lines allude to the Milky Way. Its 'citizens' are the stars, who should joint in the procession, except for the evening star (see the comm. *ad* ll. 640–645), since it is not fitting for this symbol for Spain (cf. l. 1976 Vesper, and comm.) to mourn for the Prince.

The Milky Way is also called "heroum domus". This alludes to ideas expressed by Cic. in the end of *Rep.* (*Somnium Scipionis*) VI, 16: "[...] ea vita via est in caelum et in hunc coetum eorum, qui iam vixerunt et corpore laxati illum incolunt locum, quem vides. Erat autem is splendidissimo candore inter flammas circus elucens, quem vos [...] orbem lacteum nuncupatis". See also the comm. on ll. 23–45. The stars are the citizens, but probably also the souls of the deceased who return to the starry sky; according to catasterism they even become stars. Cf. also Grotius, *Pontifex Romanus* 107: "inclita vos virtus promissis inserat astris" and Grotius, *Dichtwerken/Poetry* I, 2, 1B, p. 62 *ad* Grotius, *Pontifex Romanus* 90. The Milky Way is associated with to the myth of Hercules, originating in spoilt breast milk, see *RE* 7, 560–571, esp. 566–567 s.v. γαλαξίας. On the Milky Way and views on it, see H.L. Spiegel, *Hert-spiegel*, ed. Fokke Veenstra (Hilversum: Verloren, 1992), p. 235.

2010 *Genijsque* The *genii* are tutelary deities of persons, cf. Tib. III, 11, 8; Hor. *Ep.* I, 7, 94.

2016–2022 *Tuque—vultus* In the case of Leo it is the Nemean lion, killed by Hercules and put into the sky by Juno. Cf. Pease, p. 819 *ad* Cic. *N.D.* II, 110. On the constellation in general, see Roscher 6, 954–956; *RE* 12, 1973–1992. Again an allusion to Hercules; see also intr., pp. 38–39. The choice of the lion is partly inspired by the Dutch lion (l. 2023), which developed as a cartographical idea, see Bram Kempers, 'Assemblage van de Nederlandse leeuw: Politieke symboliek in heraldiek en verhalende prenten uit de zestiende eeuw', in: *id.* (ed), *Openbaring en bedrog. De afbeelding als historische bron in de Lage Landen* (Amsterdam: Amsterdam University Press, 1995), pp. 60–100, esp. pp. 80–81, and above. The words "igneorum magne signorum […] regnator" may refer to the fact that in the hottest period of the year the sun is in Leo (*RE* 12, 1981–1982).

2018 *Chelas rapaces* If Hydra is identified with the constellation Snake (often considered part of the Ophiuchus), this will be a connection with the "Chelae" (Scorpions) because Ophiuchus touches it with his feet, see Pease, p. 815 and Roscher 6, 966–967. The "chelae" are the pedipalps or scissors of the Scorpion, which was commissioned by Artemis to kill Orion. See (for example) Hom. *Il.* XVIII, 486; Aratus 634 ff.; Ps.-Eratosth. *Katast.* 32. Sen. *Thy.* 859 (Scorpio) Arat. 88–90. They can also indicate Libra, see Van Campen, *Lucanus Bellum Civile Liber II*, p. 402.

2019 *horrentis Hydrae* The Hydra, or Anguis (Snake, Cic. *Arat.* 214), is considered to be part of the constellation Ophiuchus, see Cic. *N.D.* II, 109, Pease, pp. 814–815; Roscher 6, 1008–1009; *RE* 9.44–50, esp. 48; 11, 1614–1615 s.v. Krater; 18, 650–651. s.v. Ophis. The name of Hydra is another allusion to Hercules (cf. the comm. on ll. 2016–2022). For the combination of Hydra and snake, and for "caede vivacis sua", cf. Sen. *Med.* 701–702: "Et Hydra et omnis redeat Herculea manu succisa serpens caede se reparans sua".

2025–2030 *Tuque a Tonante—vel cum sagittis* Lycaon's daughter Callisto, hunting with Diana, was raped by Jupiter. The son who was born, Areas, became Arctophylax (Boötes; see Bömer, *Ovidius Fasten*, p. 93). To punish her, Juno changed her into a she-bear, after which Jupiter put her in the sky as a constellation (Ov. *Met.* II, 409–530; Stephanus, *Dictionarium*, p. 122r s.v.), also ἄμαξα or Plaustrum, see Roscher 2.1, 931–935 s.v. Kallisto 1 and *RE* 10, 1726–1729 s.v. Kallisto.

2025 *at faemina* The indication of being a woman can stress the opposition with Auriacus, or the god Jupiter.

2026 *Lycaone prognata* Cf. Ov. *Met.* II, 496: "Lycaoniae […] parentis"; Grudius *Sylvae* I, 1, 82: "Lycaone nata" (*Trium fratrum*, p. 154). *Ibid.* 81–84: "Et chara ante alias nostrae comes una Dianae, saltibus Arcadiis, defessa, Lycaone nata, deposito curvoque arcu, gravidaque pharetra, captabat molles fruticum sub tegmine somnos".

Apotheosis of Auriacus

2034-2051 *At tu, Boote ... magna Belgarum salus. Heu, heu, heu, heu* After
Boötes, Lyra and Cygnus close the procession. They can play mourning music
at the funeral, where the Lyre has to tow the constellation Dolphin.

The constellation Boötes (see infra) must bring Auriacus into heaven in his
chariot. Consider in this regard the notion of catasterism (see above), though
the notion of a 'non-catasteristic' apotheosis makes more sense. Heinsius has
Auriacus/Orange be received in heaven, just as Benedicti had done by having him carried to heaven in a beautiful chariot by Religio (*De rebus gestis* II,
407–443: "Occiderat Princeps, media cum constitit aula Religio, nulli cernenda,
animamque recentem Auraici nitido devexit in ardua curru", 407–409; "Iamque
polo vicina regentem plaustra Booten attigerat", 423–424). However, one significant difference between Benedicti's representation and Heinsius' is that in
the former Orange, carried along by Religio, comes near God and His angels,
whereas in the latter he comes near the stars, in a non-Christian environment,
brought there by Boötes: the carrier also lacks any Christian element.

The apotheosis has a long tradition, beginning with eastern rulers who were
gods during or after their lives, and running through to Hellenistic rulers, Caesar and the Roman emperors, who were deified after their death (see *RE* suppl.
4, 806–853 s.v. Kaiserkult; *RAC* 3, 269–294 s.v. Consecratio I and II). In the
Renaissance, too, rulers were glorified, esp. Maximilian I and Henry IV. Others
also received an apotheosis, such as Count Maximilian of Egmond by Grudius
(Nicolaus Nicolai Grudius, *Apotheosis illustris ac vere magnanimi herois, domini
Maximiliani ab Aegmonda* [...] (Leuven: Servatius Sassenus, 1549)), or learned
humanists: Reuchlin by Erasmus ('Apotheosis Capnionis'), Erasmus by Sapidus
and Macropedius by Vladeraccus (Erasmus *ASD* I, 3, pp. 267–273 [= LB p. 689];
LB 1, p. *** *** *** 3v-*** *** *** *; and Christophorus Vladeraccus, *Apotheosis
Georgii Macropedii extemporali carmine per Christophorum Vladeraccum Sil-
viducum lusa* [...] (Antwerp: Guilielmus Silvius, 1565)).

Platonism also assumed the soul's 'flight into heaven', formulated by Cic. in
his *Somnium Scipionis*, but also by Lucan in *Pharsalia* IX, where the high ascent
of Pompey's soul is described, cf. Lewis, *The Discarded Image*, pp. 32–33.

The apotheosis is also depicted in the visual arts. Images of apotheoses
from antiquity are also known, see (for example) Hans P. L'Orange, *Apotheosis in Ancient Portraiture* (Oslo: H. Aschehoug, 1947) and *id., Likeness and Icon:
Selected Studies in Classical and Early Mediaeval Art* (Odense: Odense University Press, 1973). Consider in this regard also the painting of the Assumption,
the apotheosis of Eliah, and the way princes were taken into heaven, sometimes depicted as Hercules. On this, see Otto G. von Simson, *Zur Genealogie*

der weltlichen Apotheose im Barock, besonders der Medicigalerie des P.P. Rubens (Leipzig, etc.: Heitz, 1936), Arthur E.R. Boak, 'The Theoretical Basis of the Deification of Rulers in Antiquity', *CJ* 11 (1916), pp. 293–297; further references on the identification of rulers with Hercules in Bloemendal, 'Hercules', p. 166, n. 29.

2034 *Boote* For the constellation Boötes, already occurring in Homer (*Od.* V, 272–273), see Cic. *N.D.* II, 109: "Arctophylax, vulgo qui dicitur esse Bootes", and Pease, pp. 816–817; also *RE* 3, 717–718; Roscher 6, 886–892 and Stephanus, *Dictionarium*, p. 197r. Cf. also. Sen. *Aga.* 70: "Lucida versat plaustra Bootes" and *id. Med.* 314–315: "Flectitque senex Attica tardus plaustra Bootes".

2037 *diuisque* These are (1) the stars, deified souls; consider the aforementioned constellations, all human beings; (2) the gods; in which case the Spanish wiles should be made known to the gods.

2038 *Lyra* The lyre made from the shield of a tortoise by Hermes also became a constellation, see (for example) Varro, *R.R.* II, 5, 12: "quod Graeci vocant Lyran, fidem nostri". For the synchronism of Lyra and Leo, see, (inter alia) Ov. *Fast.* I, 653–656: "Septimus hinc oriens cum se demiserit undis, fulgebit toto iam Lyra nulla polo. Sidere ab hoc ignis venienti nocte, Leonis qui micat in medio pectore, mersus erit" (see also Bömer, *Ovidius Fasten*, p. 73). On the constellation, see Stephanus, *Dictionarium*, p. 280r; Roscher 6, 904–906 and *RE* 13, 2489–2498. Cf. Ov. *Met.* XI, 52: "flebile nescio quid queritur lyra".

2041 *Delphina* For the constellation Dolphin, brought back by Amphitrite to Poseidon, but also associated with the dolphin who saved the singer Arion, see Roscher 6, 926–928; *RE* 4, 2509–2510; Arat. 315–318; cf. *Phaenom.* 91–101; see also Pease, p. 832 *ad* Cic. *N.D.* II, 113.

2042 *Neptunios ... choros* This may refer to Amphitrite's journey on the back of the Dolphin, which would make the 'choruses of Neptune' sea gods. They can also indicate fish.

2043 *in iusta nostra* The "iusta" are ceremonies, a funeral ritual (*OLD* s.v. iustus 3). "Nostra" indicates 'the ceremonies I am concerned with now'. Cf. Ov. *Fast.* III, 560: "germanae iusta dat" (Anna giving the usual sacrificial gifts to her sister Dido).

2044 *Cygne* Jupiter gave the swan a place among the stars because he came to Leda in the shape of this bird. It is also called Avis (Roscher 6, 906–908; *RE* 11.2442–2451 s.v. Kyknos 9). Perhaps the story of the change of Cycnus into a swan after he was killed by Achilles (Ov. *Met.* 2.367–380) is also at play here.

2044 *praetentas iter* Cf. Tib. II, 1, 77: "pedibus praetemptas iter".

2046 *Fatale—melos* After the Leiden copy, "triste" has been replaced with "tristi": the sadness is now connected with the voice, and the verse became a 'golden line' (fatale (tristi voce) melos).

2047–2048 *Caystrijs ... in vndis*　The Cayster, a river in Lydia, was well known for its swans, cf. Verg. *Ge.* I, 384; Ov. *Met.* II, 253; Mela I, 88. See also Stephanus, *Dictionarium*, p. 138v; *RE* II, 100–101 s.v. Kaystros l. The "Caystrius [ales]" is the swan (Ov. *Tr.* V, 1, 11), see Thompson 1966, pp. 179–186.

2049 *lateque canta*　(1) sing everywhere; (2) sing a comprehensive elegy.

2050 *cor illud orbis*　Cf. Sen. *Herc. Oet.* 749: "decus illud orbis", to be bewailed by the entire world (*ibid.* 758–759).

L 1998　By changing "est" into "it", Heinsius is emphasizing the fact that Libertas is describing a funeral procession.

L 2010　The tutelary deities become the shades.

L 2025　This line becomes: 'You too, unhappy crime of the Thunderer, come [...]'.

Atlas as bearer

2052–2067 *Adeste, ciues—o fatum, o Dei. Heu, heu, heu, heu*　Auriacus on the bier cannot even be carried by the stars. Hercules is better equipped, since he had carried the heavenly vault for Atlas. Then he feigned fatigue, but now it is really too much for him. Atlas should come and carry the bier for his grandson Mercury (see infra). See Stephanus, *Dictionarium*, p. 82v.

2052 *graues*　Either (1) heavy with worries; (2) encumbered under the burden of the bier (proleptic); (3) the shoulders of the significant.

2056 *Alcides*　See also *Aur.* 93, 1479. Seneca regularly uses this name for Hercules, e.g. *Pha.* 844. Here Heinsius uses the Latin form instead of the Greek one as in l. 93.

2057 *occumbet*　Hercules will fall down, either to be able to lift the bier, or to be overwhelmed by grief for Auriacus, or because the bier is too heavy.

2058 *Pleiones nepos*　Mercury, son of Maia, the daughter of Pleione. Mercury is keen to go and get Atlas, because he is his grandson and the messenger of the gods (Stephanus, *Dictionarium*, p. 299v–300r; Roscher 2.2, 2802–2831). Cf. Ov. *Her.* 16, 62: "Atlantis magni Pleionesque nepos" and Ov. *Fast.* IV 169 ff. For the Scorpio, *ibid.* 163 f.

2059 *Tegeatice ales*　E.g. Stat. *S.* V, 1, 102: "ales Tegeaticus". Mercury (or Areas) is here named after the city of Tegea in Arcadia.

2059–2060 *inter errantes—inferosque*　These words can be taken with "sistas", but perhaps fit better with "subis totidem labores", all works Mercury has done. "Totidem" will refer to the many messages he has brought, as many as there are gods in heaven and the underworld. "Huc" is 'here at the bier'; "divos" will indicate only gods, in contrast to l. 2037.

2064 *ruptis postibus*   Atlas will probably have to force the gates of heaven to get to the bier or to give Auriacus the possibility to enter heaven; for the expression cf. Verg. *Aen.* VII, 622: "Belli ferratos rumpit Saturnia postis".

2063 *licet*   Cf. l. 2026.

Libertas is leaving—the hat of freedom and locks

2068–2105 *Spectate, ciues—Sancta Libertas abit. Heu, heu, heu, heu*   As a sign of the loss of freedom and mourning, Libertas leaves her *pileum* and she brings a sacrifice of hair. The *pileum* or *pileus* was the hat of freedom of released slaves, which was buried with them at their funeral (Marquardt-Mau, *Privatleben*, p. 355). The presence of the *pileum* at a funeral is therefore logical. Its function is, of course, completely different in this ritual: it is a symbol of the freedom that is buried with Orange. Libertas would be portrayed with such a freedom hat on her head on the monument of Orange in the New Church in Delft too.

The hair sacrifice has both a Greco-Roman and a Christian tradition, see Alexiou, *Lament*, pp. 7 and 27 respectively: with the Greeks, those mourning devoted a lock of hair with χοαί, a libation of wine (she cites as examples Aesch. *Ch.* 6–7 and Sop. *El.* 51–53 and 448–458); in the Christian tradition the mourners covered the body with their shaved hair. For this use in Latin literature, cf. Ov. *Met.* XIII, 427–428: "Hectoris in tumulo canum de vertice crinem, inferias inopes crinem lacrimasque reliquit". This sacrifice also occurs in Seneca's drama, cf. *Tro.* 799–806 and Fantham, *Seneca's Troades*, pp. 321–322, and 810–811, and *Pha.* 1181–1182, where Phaedra speaks to Hippolytus' corpse: "Placemus umbras. Capitis exuvias cape, laceraeque frontis accipe abscissam comam". For further literature on this subject, see Bömer, *Ovidius Fasten*, pp. 184–185; Bömer, *Ovidius Metamorphosen* 6, pp. 307–308 *ad* Ov. *Met.* XIII, 427–428; *RAC* XIII, 181–185 and *RE* 7, 2105–2109.

Libertas leaves the earth, as Simplicitas (l. 654) and Astraea or Iustitia (see the comm. *ad* ll. 654–661).

2074 *sepulto*   Cf. l. 1973.

2077 *fauoris munus*   Perhaps these are the duties Libertas fulfils for Auriacus, a result of her affection for him.

2084 *gressumue referam*   Cf. l. 800 and the comm. *ad loc.*

2084 *Sarmatarum vltra niues*   The Sarmates were a people living between the Vistula and the Don (see, for example, Stephanus, *Dictionarium*, pp. 387v–388r), serving to represent cold, inhospitable regions, cf. (for example) Sen. *Herc. f.* 539: "intonsis [...] Sarmatis" (see also Fitch, *Seneca's Hercules Furens*, p. 261 for "intonsus" as a characteristic of untendedness). Ovid regularly mentions them, esp. in *Tristia* and *Epistulae ex Ponto*, the poetry of his exile, e.g. *Tr.* V, 1, 13: "Sarmaticas longe proiectus in oras" and (for the cold) *Pont.* II, 7, 72: "Frigore perpetuo Sarmatis ora riget".

2085 *Tanaimque et Istrum* The Tanais (Don, in Sarmatia) and the Ister (Danube) are symbols of the cold north-east ends of the Roman Empire in (for example) Prop. II, 30, 2: "tu licet usque ad Tanain fugias"; Verg. *Ge.* IV, 517: "Tanaimque nivalem"; Hor. *C.* III, 10, 1: "Extremum Tanain si biberes". See Stephanus, *Dictionarium*, pp. 415v and 256r, resp.

2086 *Boreae* For the Boreas, the cold north wind, see ll. 1756–1757 and the comm. It may be a metonym for the north, e.g. in Hor. *C.* III, 24, 38.

2086 *Schyticus ... rigor* Scythia is a region between the Don and the Danube (cf. l. 2085). It is proverbially cold; see (for example) Stephanus, *Dictionarium*, p. 394r. Cf. l. 1697 and the comm. on their rudeness.

2094–2100 *Tot truces—tegit* These *sententia* centre around the idea of "homo homini lupus", Plaut. *As.* 495.

2102 *quem videtis hic tamen* The audience sees Auriacus, either actually on the bier or because he was shown on stage. Cf. for this *Illustrissimis* [...] *Ordinibus* 137–139.

L 2068–2070 After provisional corrections these lines become: 'The earth has my hat of freedom and our dead. With this, I leave everything that has been of him to the shades and to you, cruel death'.

Act V, Maurice Scene

In this (added) scene, Maurice, returning from Leiden, where he had studied mathematics, promises to avenge his father if his age permits.

1–8 Maurice addresses the Netherlands. They have lost hope, he has to mourn for his father. He cannot, however, mourn, because someone with a heroic nature who can avenge cannot weep.

9–18 He calls upon the Dutch to mourn. His youthful age unfortunately prevents him from taking action. Children of princes, who are already godly at birth, become men too slowly.

19–29 Goddess Libertas may not leave and thus despise him: though he is still young, the divine fire already burns in him and does not count his years.

30–41 The shade of Orange must, when he is in heaven, report to the ancestor of the Nassau that his descendant Maurice will attack Spain and satiate his father's shade with Spanish blood.

Maurice places responsibility on a Deus several times. It seems that he means the Stoic God—obviously Christianity and Stoa can be mixed together. In l. 27 in particular the deity, the "virtutis autor igneae", can be identified with the Stoic *Logos*, cf. (for example) l. 25: "tardi spiritus dux".

Metre

The scene consists of iambic trimeters.

Commentary

Revenge excludes weeping

1–8 Batava tellus—potest Maurice cannot express his grief, because he will be able to take revenge with his heroic vigour. The *sententiae* in ll. 6–8 are, as often in the play, set in quotation marks in the margin.

1 Batava tellus For the periphrasis of the country with "tellus", cf. l. 213 and the comm. *ad* ll. 212–218. In this line the "tellus" of the Low Countries is the substantiation of the "sedes".
1 coeruli sedes Dei Because of the richness of the water, the Low Countries are a dwelling for the sea god Nereus. For "coerulus Deus" cf. l. 75: "caerulus […] pater".
2 in hoc vocamur Maurice is called from Leiden to Delft for this 'miserable situation', the death of his father.
6 Herois This form can be adjective with "vigor", derived from the substantive "herois", or dat. pl. of the adjective "herous", used as a substantive: 'the power in the case of heroes'.

Maurice rues his youth

9–18 Lugete, cives—viri sumus The Dutch citizens are called upon to weep for Orange, as Libertas called for mourning in her speech. They too are orphaned like Maurice: after all, it should be added, the Father of the Fatherland has died. Just as the citizens are indignant at the murder committed, Maurice is annoyed about his youth: born in 1567, he was seventeen at the time of the murder.

17–18 O Deus—viri sumus This *sententia* formulates a paradox: princes who are born gods are too late men, i.e. capable of acting like men. For the idea that rulers are divine, cf. ll. 415–419 and the comm. *ad loc.*, and cf. ll. 1104–1106. In that regard, all humans are "divi" according to the Stoa, since they all possess a spark of the *Ratio/Logos*.

Goddess Libertas cannot leave

19–29 *At tu—saeculumque despicit* In the scene that originally closed the play, Libertas left the Netherlands. The underlying idea is that with the death of Orange freedom is gone. Maurice asks her not to reject his youthful age and his hands. In him lives a "Deus", a fiery spirit spurring him on to courageous deeds. He cannot yet perform these acts because he is still too young. In this respect the "deus" can be identified with the Stoic *logos* or *ratio*, consisting of fire, see the comm. *ad Aur.* 1–5 and 23–45.

Liberty, called "sancta" in the play, is even "diva" here. In later Latin, "divus" was reserved for people who were deified after their death, such as the emperors. This does not fit well in this context. "Diva" (two short syllables) seems to be a metrical variant of "sancta" here.

The fact that Heinsius states in this scene that Liberty has not fully gone may have been inspired by the ten successful years of Maurice, who secured important victories in the years 1588–1598, see above, p. 344.

21 *numen meum* Maurice is referring either to himself or to his father Orange. **22–24 *quam—dies*** This subordinate clause (to "fraudem") allows two interpretations: (1) the murderer will always be plagued by the fraud; or (2) Maurice will never forget the ruse. The use of "illo" (l. 23) favours the first possibility.

Maurice will take revenge

30–41 *At vos—satiabo tuos* Maurice asks the shade of his father, who flies to the upper reaches of the sky, to ask his ancestors to forgive his (i.e. Maurice's) youth. He will avenge him later. The shade of Orange goes to the "aureas Deum vias", i.e. the *aether*, the 'space' where the gods reside and where the souls of the deceased, especially those who have made themselves worthy of the State, can fly, see the comm. *ad Aur.* 32. There are already more Nassaus there. Examples are the ancestors of William of Nassau, Prince of Orange, and his brothers, including Count Adolph (1540–1568), who gave their lives for the struggle of the Dutch for their freedom.

In the last lines (e.g. l. 38 "Tuque") Maurice addresses the dead who have to wait in peace for the time being until his son will have avenged him.

It is striking that in this passage there is no reference to Maurice's motto, "Tandem fit surculus arbor", which does feature in the play by Caspar Ens (l. 367: "E surculo arbor factus").

L 23 The fraud is transposed from 'that breast' (i.e. of the Spaniards) to 'my heart', i.e. of Maurice, who will never forget the Spanish wiles.

L 24 In the second instance, Heinsius takes "dies" as feminine. "Dies" in the sense of 'day' is mostly masculine, whereas in the sense of 'time' it is feminine. For that reason, and because it fits in with the metre more easily, Heinsius uses the word 'mater'.

Appendix 1: Paratexts to *Auriacus* and Texts from the *Iambi* Added to the Play, and From Heinsius' Seneca Edition (1601) Relevant for *Auriacus*

[1]   IN COLUMBAS LVGDVNI VLTRO CITROQUE MISSAS IN OBSIDIONE, quarum in Tragoediâ nostrâ fit mentio.[1]

PERFIDVS ingentem vesano milite Leydam
  Cinxerat, et vasto robore miles Iber.
Terra, salumque, inquit, mea sunt: via nulla salutis:
  Nulla patet puppi semita, nulla viro.
5 DOVSA meus medio, spe libertatis, in hoste
  Liber, et inuicto pectore tutus erat.
Ille, Polus (dixit) domini est immunis Iberi,
  Et tua sola mihi, Iupiter, aula vacat.
Hinc quoque fas nobis patriae sperare salutem:
10 Ille mihi Minos hàc fugiendus erit.
Quò patriae non tendit amor? Mandata referre
  Postquam hominem nequiit mittere, misit auem.

Ipsas autem literas pennis columbarum inclusas, ad Nobilissimum et Amplissimum IANVM DOVSAM, patronum nostrum vnicè colendum datas, domi ipsius vidimus, cùm apud eum aliquandò diverteremus.

[2]   ΔΙΟΝΥΣΩΙ ΤΩΙ ἈΡΙΣΤΩΙ ΚΑΙ ΜΑΡΩΝΙ ΤΩΙ ΦΙΛΟΠΟΤΗΙ ΤΟΙΝ ΤΗΣ ἘΝΑΓΩ-
ΝΙΟΥ ΤΡΑΓΩΙΔΙΑΣ ἘΠΙΣΤΑΤΑΙΝ.[2]

Λῦτο δ' ἀγὼν Διόνυσε· Μάρων φίλε σοι δὲ μελήσει
  Σῶμα περ ἀργαλέῳ γήραι τειρομένῳ
Στήσασθαι κρητῆρα βεβυσμένον ἡδέος οἴνου
  Βακχιάδος γλυκερῆς ἔγκυον εὐφροσύνης·

---

1   Printed in Daniel Heinsius, *Auriacus, sive Libertas saucia* (Leiden: Cloucquius, 1602), in the same quire as the addition of Maurice, between pp. 84 and 85.
2   Daniel Heinsius, *Auriacus, sive Libertas saucia: Accedunt eiusdem iambi, partim morales, partim ad amios, partim amicorum causa scripta* (Leiden: Andreas Cloucquius, 1602) [hence Heinsius, *Auriacus*], p. 85.

© KONINKLIJKE BRILL NV, LEIDEN, 2020 | DOI:10.1163/9789004425361_006

5   Νοννιακῆς οἷον πάλαι ἐν σελίδεσσι πέπωκας
       Ἀμφὶ τάφον φίλου χευομένος Σταφύλου.
      Οὐ τράγου εὐπώγωνος ἐμοὶ μέλει, οὐ μὰ δι' οὐδέν,
       Λάτρις ἐγὼ Μουσῶν· τὶ τράγε σοι καὶ ἐμοί;
      Μοι τραγικοῦ περ ἀγῶνος ἀέθλια πινέμεν εἴη,
10   Ἐκ δὲ πίοντ' ἱεραῖς μαρνάμεναι λατάγαις.³
      Γυμνασίῳ Βρομίοιο τάδε πρεπε· σὺν γὰρ ἀέθλῳ,
       Λυσαμένῳ πᾶσαν φροντίδα λυσάμεθα.
      Τ' ἄλλα σοι οὖν ἀφίημι πάτερ· διψῶν γὰρ ἐγώ τοι⁴
       Οὐ τράγον, ἀλλὰ μόνους φίλ' ἄγαμαι⁵ βατράχους.

ΔΑΝΙΕΛ ῞ΕΙΝΣΙΟΣ.

[3a] Nobilissimo, Amplissimo, Clarissimoqve Viro Iano Dovsae Domino
in Noortwyck.⁶

Nvperrime cum apud Heroa nostrum coenarem, Nobilissime Domine, ille vt semper
de communibus Musis agit, schedam mihi quandam tradit de Batauiae vestrae Mirandis, in quâ obiter eadem commemorata erant, eodemque ordine quo hic vides. Petiit
autem vt ipse Latino carmine ea complecterer; se quoque argumentum idem tractatu-
rum. Ego, cum cogitarem quanto cum fructu meo semper ab eo victus fuerim, parui
imperatori meo, vt gregarium militem aequum est. Ille quoque idem praestitit, seu
potius praeivit, et vt hunc veternum meum excuteret, vtraque linguâ a se conscripta
mihi tradidit. Volui autem, quòd de Batauiâ vestra in Tragoediâ meâ multa occurrant,
hic potissimum legi, tibique illa mittere: quoniam et ipse magnus ille vir sermonem ad
te direxit, Dousa Nobilissime.

    Ego autem cum omnia in divino illo literarum Monarcha mirari soleam, tum maxi-
me tam promptam hac senectâ aetate venam, praecipueque in poesi Graecâ, in quâ
fateor nullum ne inter veteres quidem esse, qui palmam prae illo ferre possit. Ille,
quotiescunque me videt (quod fit quotidie) 'Lacessam te,' inquit, 'mi Heinsi', ac cum
dicto Martialem arripit ac epigramma aliquod in Graecum sermonem conuertendum
proponit mihi, idemque agit ipse: ita fit vt et sua tradat mihi, et pro eis recipiat mea,
reuera χρύσεα χαλκείων. Noui autem ego quanto cum fructu meo illi cedam: vt magis
e re victi id fit, quam vincentis. Interim te ac quicumque haec lecturus est obtestor,

---

3 10 Ἐκ ... λατάγαις} A: del. L.
4 13 σοι οὖν A: δὲ σοι L. ἐγώ τοι} A: ἐγώ γε L.
5 14 φίλ' ἄγαμαι A: del. L.
6 Heinsius, Auriacus, p. 86.

Dousa Nobilissime, te per domesticam, tibique propriam Deam Humanitatem, quae cum eruditione coniuncta, virum magnum ac generosum perficit, per Musas omnes et sacra nostra: ne ostendandi, aut gloriolae captandae gratiâ, mea cum ipsius me iunxisse existimes, sed exercitii tantum. Scio enim ne ipsis quidem gigantibus τὸ θεομαχεῖν bene successisse.

Vale nobilissime Domine, et Hesiodum nostrum, cum quinque Graecis interpretibus sub nomine tuo breui (vt spero) edendum, expecta.

[3b.1]   De mirandis Batauiae.[7]

Ignorata tuae referam miracula terrae
    Dousa, peregrinis non habitura fidem.
Omnia lanitium hic lassat textrina Mineruae.
    Lanigeros tamen hinc scimus abesse greges.
5   Non capiunt operas fabriles oppida vestra.
    Nulla fabris tamen haec ligna ministrat humus.
Horrea triticeae rumpunt hic frugis acerui.
    Pascuus hic tamen est, non Cerealis ager.
Hic numerosa meri stipantur dolia cellis.
10   Quae vineta colat nulla putator habet.
Hic nulla, aut certè seges est rarissima lini.
    Linifici tamen est copia maior vbi?
Hic mediis habitamus aquis. Quis credere possit?
    Et tamen hic nullae Dousa bibuntur aquae.

[3b.2]   Idem Graece.[8]

Ὑμετέρης ἐρέω νηπευθέα θαύματα γαίης,
    Δουσιάδη, δύσπιστ᾽ ἀλλοδαποῖς ἀΐειν.
Ἐνταῦθ᾽ οὐκ ἀρκοῦσ᾽ ἐρίοις ἱστῶνες Ἀθήνης·
    Πῶϋ δὲ φροῦδον ἅπαν εἰροπόκων οἴων.

---

7 Heinsius, *Auriacus*, p. 87.
8 Heinsius, *Auriacus*, p. 87. Also published with the title: Iosephi Scaligeri Carmen de mirandis Bataviae. See Collegium Classicum c.n. M.F., *Bataafs Athene: Een bloemlezing van klassiek
   Griekse poëzie van de hand van Leidse humanisten van de zestende tot en met de twintigste eeuw:
   Kritische teksteditie met inleidingen, vertaling en noten* (Leiden: Collegium Classicum c.n. M.F.,
   1993), p. 2. On p. 3 Scaliger's Latin translation is given.

5   Ἄστεα χειροβίους οὐ χωρεῖ τέκτονας ἄνδρας·
       Ἐργασίμης δ' ὕλης ἔστ' ἀγόρηγον ἔδος.
       Σιτοδόκους πυροῦ σωροὶ ῥηγνῦσι καλιάς·
       Βούβοτος ἡ γαίη δ' οὐ φιλόπυρος ἔφυ.
       Ἄπλετοι ὧδ' οἴνοιο νενασμέναι εἰσὶ πιθάχναι·
10   Οὐδενὸς οἰνοπέδου δ' ἐστὶ φυτηκομίη.
       Οὐδαμὸς ἢ σπάνιος τῇδε σπόρος ἐστὶ λίνοιο·
       Ποῦ ποτὲ δ' εἰσὶ λίνου πλείονες ἐργασίαι;
       Οἰκίαι εἰσὶ μέσοισιν ἐν ὕδασιν. τίς κε πίθοιτο;
       Ὑδροποτεῖ δ' οὐεις ἐνθάδε, Δουσιάδη.

IOSEPHVS SCALIGER, IVLII CAESARIS F.

[3b.3]   De iisdem.[9]

       Dousa faue: in vestris quaedam mihi visa Batauis
           Pauca quidem mens est dicere, vera tamen.
       Omnia Palladiae complerunt oppida lanae
           Laniferas hic quis pectere discit oues?
5   Plurima cum fabris fabrilis copia ligni est;
           Ligna tamen vobis omnia, terra negat.
       Plus Cereris nusquam est: nusquam paene educat illam
           Terra parens bubus officiosa suis.
       Dolia sunt hic, Bacche, tui plena omnia, suntque
10   Plurima, cum desit vinea, vina tamen.
       Nullaque gignendis lassantur pascua linis,
           Linificas lassant hic tamen illa manus.
       Tantalidae nos Dousa sumus: circumdamur vnda,
           Et tamen hanc tantas quis bibit inter aquas?

[3b.4]   Idem Graece.[10]

       Ἴλαθι Δουσιάδη, τὰ τεῶν μεμάθηκα Βαταύων
           Παῦρα, λίην δὲ φέρω θαύμασιν εἰδόμενα.

---

9   Heinsius, *Auriacus*, p. 88.
10   Heinsius, *Auriacus*, p. 88. Also included in Collegium Classicum c.n. M.F., *Bataafs Athene: Een bloemlezing van klassiek Griekse poëzie van de hand van Leidse humanisten van de zestiende tot en met de twintigste Eeuw: Kritische teksteditie met inleidingen, vertaling en noten* (Lediden: Collegium Classicum c.n. M.F., 1993), p. 58. There also a Latin translation

Εἴρεα μὲν πάσας σφίσιν ἐπλήρωσε πόληας·
Εἰροπόκους δ' ὑμῶν τὶς κομέει ὅιας;
5   Ξυλόπονοι πέλον ἄνδρες ἀπειρέσιοι, ξύλαθ' ὧδε.
Ἄξυλον αὐτὰρ ὅλον σφιν γέγονεν πεδίον.
Οὐδαμόθι πλεῖον Δημήτερος. Οὐδὲ μιν ὑμῶν
Ἔτρεφε γῆ, βουσὶν πλεῖσται, χαριζομένη.
Πας δὲ πῖθος Διόνυσε σέθεν γέμε· πολλοὶ ἔασιν
10 Ἀμπελινοὶ καρποὶ, ἄμπελος οὐδεμίη.
Οὐδὲ λίνοις ἁπαλοῖσι καταβρίθουσιν ἄρουραι·
Τὰς δὲ λίνα πλήθει χειροβίων παλάμας.
Ταντάλιον γένος ἐσμὲν, ἐπεὶ ποταμοῖς στεφόμεθα.
Τὶς δὲ τόσων γεύει Δουσιάδη ποταμῶν;

DANIEL HEINSIVS.

[4]   IN ANNALES NOBILISSIMI ET AMPLISSIMI HEROIS Iani Dousae.[11]

[...]
Namque ille rerum machinator spiritus
Auriga tardi dux herusque corporis,
Vanaeque molis imperator strennuus,
115 Suique semper, eminus licet, poli
Ciuisque verus municepsque, patriâ
Proscriptus olim sede, quam cernit tamen
Telluris huius inquilinus, erroque,
Extorris, exul, carcete impactus suo
120 Ineptientis dexterâ Promethei
Illa, illa nostri pars superba, ventus est
Flamenque siccis excreandum faucibus
Fatalis horae cùm ciet necessitas,

---

is published, made by Heinsius himself: "Pauca tibi referam, sed quae mihi mira videntur | in Batavis; at tu, maxime Dousa, fave. | omnia Palladiae complerunt oppida lanae; | lani-feras hic quis pectere discit oves? | plurima cum fabris fabrilis copia ligni est; | ligna tamen vobis omnia terra negat. | plus Cereris nusquam est; vix hanc tamen educat usquam | terra parens, bubus officiosa suis. | dolia sunt hic, Bacche, tui plena omnia: suntque | plurima, cum non sit vinea, vina tamen. | nullaque gignendis lassantur pascua linis; | linificas las-sant hic tamen illa manus. | Tantalidae nos, Dousa, sumus: circundamur unda, | et tamen hanc ipsas quis bibit inter aquas?" It is a reaction to Scaliger's poem.

11 Heinsius, *Auriacus*, pp. 98–105, esp. pp. 102–104, ll. 112–153. In l. 139 ainmque is corrected into animumque.

Ingensque rerum vellit aurem terminus
125   Diesque sunma. Nec minus, tamen tamen
In alta pergere ardet, igneaque vi
Sursum reluctans tendit, et caelum suum
Procul fatigat prouocatque, et inquies
Aeternitati mente praeludit suâ,
130   Dignumque caelo spirat in terris opus,
Mortalitatis ferre leges insolens,
Seseque versat, erigitque; dùm leuis
Ruptisque mentis igneae repagulis,
Et his profanis corporis faedi notis
135   Pars aetheris sit vndecumque, et portio
Magno vniverso huic imputatus, et sibi.
Illic coactus ille, tot pressus graui
Annos ruinâ; vasa colligit sua,
Colo animumque mutat, exilitque ouans
140   Rudemque sentit, pileumque, mancupum
Exlex laboris compedumque; denuò
Praetore nempe redditus liber Deo.
At nos caducae saeculi propagines
Puluis misellus, halitusque, quem dies
145   Caelique lumen visque nobilis movet;
Queis fomes imo pectore infusus sedet,
Ingensque in altum promouet vires calor,
Extraque vulgi semitas ordo vocat
Munusque rerum, flammeumque pectus, et
150   Occulta magnae aeternitatis semina,
Originisque conscius suae vigor;
Factis ab alto destinata gens sumus
Dictisque: […]

[5]   In livorem.[12]

Liuoris atri noxiâ abreptus gemis
Spirans profanam, pectoris foedi luem,

---

12   Heinsius, *Auriacus*, pp. 110–111, also in *L. Annaei Senecae philosophi divini libelli quinque,*
       quorum seriem versa pagella indicabit: Accesserunt iambi morales aliquot ex Catone: Da-
       nielis Heinsii, Gandensis (Leiden: ex officina Plantiniana, apud Christophorum Raphe-
       lengium, 1601) [hence *Senecae libelli quinque*], p. H3v. Variants: title In livorem *A*: In

Tuique vindex, ne sit impunis caues
Furor tuarum pestilens Erynnidum
5   Noxasque fundis, vindicas idem tamen,
Iudex reusque, punienda qui geris
Punisque solus, sceleris infandi pater
Idemque vindex, dum scelesta mens suae
Correpta labis lurida afflatu gemit
10   Ridesque nunquam in bono elatus tuo
Maloque nostro, gaudiique fons tui
Dolor tuorum est, nec beata lux tibi
Nisi immerentes obrui cernas viros
Lues nefanda, criminum infelix pater
15   Beata cernas cuncta, te praeter tamen,
Bonoque nostro perfruaris, vt tuo
Carere possis, vsque et vsque qui nisi
Aduersa cernas, haud secunda noueris.

[6]   De fragilitate rerum.[13]

Quacunque vastus luminis magni parens
Censorque rerum, flammeum per aëra
Sol candicantes igne temperat rotas,
Coelumque habenis peruagatur aureis
5   Rotamur omnes orbe vago,
Lususque rerum, temporumque nascimur.
Nihilque firmum magnus annorum pater
Dies tuetur, turbinum potentia
Seseque rerum turbidae premunt vices,
10   Cunctisque ab annis mensibusque, ad vltimum
Provoluimurque ducimurque. Se tamen
Perire nemo sed perisse conspicit.

Invidum S: 1 noxiâ A: turbine S; 3 impunis A: innocens S; 5 vindicas A: vindicasque S;
9 lurida A: nescia S; 10 in S: ni A; 13 immerentes A: beatos S. Copy used: Bibliothèque
Nationale de France, Paris, shelfnr. R 17898]. This edition of philosophical works by Seneca
is contains: pp. 5–18: Liber de providentia seu cur bonis viris mala accidant; pp. 18–49:
Liber de vita beata; pp. 49–70 Liber de tranquillitate animi; pp. 70–91: Liber de brevitate
vitae; pp. 91–109: An in sapientem cadat iniuria [= De constantia sapientis].

13   Heinsius, *Auriacus* (*A*), p. 111; also in *Senecae libelli quinque* (*S*), p. Hr. Variants: l. 5: voluimur
A: tollimur *S*; l. 8 potentia *A*: potentiae *S*; l. 10 ad vltimus *A*: et huc et huc *S*.

[7]   In naturae prodigia (si sunt tamen) qui ἄθεοὶ dicuntur.[14]

Quicunque vastas aetheris magni domos
Sublimibusque regna luminum globis,
Gemmata late caeruloque fornice
Suspensa mundi moenia immensi vides
5   Polumque pictis nocte flammantem ignibus
Phoebumque purâ semper ardentem comâ
Oculum serenae lucis, et vitae diem
Phoebenque ciues inter audentem suas.
Surrepta fratri mutuare lumina,
10   Stellasque gentem caeruli vagam poli
Coelo coruscis subsilire vultibus,
Fluctusque vastos, impetusque caerulos,
Reciprocique turgidas sali vices
Rursusque viuam vere tellurem novo
15   Miti serenos imbre pandentem sinus.
Sublimius vagare celsius sub his
Imperuiumque luminum obtutu latet,
Mens illa rerum, terminusque vitaque
Mundique origo, spiritusque, surrigens.
20   Fouensque cuncta, Mentis vtendum hic ope est,
Mens illa mente conspici nuda potest.
Mens alta perge, remige alarum procul
Trans claustra mundi, atque Herculis magni domos
Finesque summos, transque flagrantem aëra
25   Tremulumque semper lumine ardenti polum
Euecta tende, quicquid hic latet tuum est.
Surge illa nostri purior pars, aspicis
Sublimiores aeris sacri fores
Fons inde nostri est, condita aspectu patent

---

14   Heinsius, *Auriacus*, pp. 111–113; also in *Senecae libelli quinque*, pp. H1r–H2v. Variants: title
In naturae—dicuntur *A*: De Deo *S*; 2 luminum *A*: syderum *S*; 3 flammeoque cardine *A*:
caeruloque fornice *S*; 6 purâ *A*: celsa *S*; 8: Phoebenque ciues *A*: Phaebena fratres *S*; suas
A: suos *S*; 9 fratri *A*: Phoebo *S*; 10 gentem caeruli vagam *A*: cives aurei vagos *S*; between 10
and 11 *S* has: Choreasque dulces syderum micantium; between 11 and 12 *S* has: Lususque
molles nectere, et leves choros; 12 caerulos *A*: et horridam *S*; between 12 and 13 *S* has: In
se residentem aequoris magni viam; between 13 and 14 *S* has: Spumantibusque Neraea
undantem vadis; 18 vitaque *A*: vitaeque *S*; 26 tende *A*: tendes *S*; 29 nostri *A*: nostri est *S*;
patent *A*: patens *S*; 39 ducit *A*: mulget *S*.

30   Aeterna menti, mens poli, polo latet,
      Humo ossibusque nostra vinculis suis
      Obstructa semper impotensque, deuia
      Erransque palpitansque, cassa lumine
      Dei suoque pondus exantlans graue.
35   Suppressa semper baiulansque, nec sibi
      Spectanda, tantum mole compacta latens
      Infusa terra. Mentis aeternae tamen
      Scintilla nostra est, fomitem hinc vitae trahit
      Viresque mulget, elicitque, debiles
40   Et hac et illa luminum obtutus fugit.
      Miraris ergo vana gens, quod haud queas
      Animam vniuersi cernere, haud cernis tuam.

[8]   In miseros, mortem tamen optantes.[15]

      Pressus cruentae viribus potentiae
      Demolientis cuncta fortunae, paves
      Leges nouercae, quae procacibus rotis
      Victrix superbas digerit rerum vices,
5   Et insolentis turbo mobilis deae
      Sortis flagello quassus aduersae tremis
      Saeuis labascens verberum vibicibus
      Mortemque poscis, suêtus optatae prius
      Gremio fauentis agere fortunae dies
10   Morique votum est. ah miser, miser queas,
      Mortemne ferre, ferre qui vitam nequis!

[9]   Ad impium.[16]

      Quacunque vultus feruidique duplices
      Vagantur orbes luminis caelum tenet

---

15   Heinsius, *Auriacus*, p. 113; also in *Senecae libelli quinque*, p. H2v, with the title In mis-
      eros mortem optantes. Variants: l. 1 superbae ... licentiae *A*: cruentae ... potentiae *S*; 5
      Et insolentis—deae *A*: Ludibriosaeque impotens turben Die *S*; 6: quassus *A*: raptus *S*; 9
      fauentis *A*: fauenteis *S*.
16   Heinsius, *Auriacus*, pp. 113–114; also in *Senecae libelli quinque*, pp. H2v–H3r. Variants: 5–6
      Suspendit ... magnus pater | Aduersa nostris *A*: Obiecit ... nostris deus | Spectanda sem-
      per *S*; 11 Inuitat *A*: erexit *S*; 12 ducit *A*: fixit *S*; 13 Iubet *A*: Iussit *S*; 16 Ardensque semper *A*:
      Semperque flagrans *S*; lati *A*: vasti *S*.

Haec cuncta circum, penduloque ab aëre
Ambimur omnes et tenemur undique:
5 Suspendit illa vultibus magnus pater
Aduersa nostris, aureisque luminum
Signata templa, siderumque motibus.
Quocunque celsa dirigas acumina,
Radiosque verses luminis, polum vides
10 Vrbemque nostram patriamque, inertia
Inuitat ora gentis humanae pater
Vultusque in alta ducit, et tuerier
Iubet micantem lumine aeterno domum
Nolis velisue gens profana, conspicis
15 Regis superba fulgurantis atria
Ardensque semper aetheris lati decus,
Inclusaque imminentibus coeli plagis
Et hinc et inde es, pallidoque vertici
Arx altae machinantis incumbit Dei,
20 Ceruicibusque caerula impendet via
Reumque cingit. Quo vagare? Fulgido
Teneris orbe, nec fugae patet locus,
Ergo o profane, mortuus Deum queas
Fugisse, viuus fugere qui coelum nequis?

[10] De conscientia.[17]

Veneris nefando coecus impetu ruis
Scelerisque terra pondere, atque aer tui
Gemit pavetque, nec sat vna nox tegat
Virus scelesta depluens contagia
5 Latere cunctos ista dum speras, tui
Oblitus ipse, teste nam carere vis
Te nesciente quod tamen fieri nequit,
Testisque eorum quae latere vis, tibi
Inuitus ipse es, nec sine arbitro licet
10 Solus vagare, iam tibi tergum premit

---

17 Heinsius, *Auriacus*, pp. 114–115; *Senecae libelli quinque*, p. H4r. Variants: 1 instinctu *A*:
impetu *S*; 3 pavetque *A*: tremitque *S*; 6 Oblitus *A*: Ignarus *S*; 9 ipse *A*: ultro *S*; 12 Alium
A: Alios *S*.

Celeratque. Quo vagaris? Ipse ades tibi
Alium velis latere, te ipse non potes.

[11]   In Scortationem.[18]

Lascivientis improbâ tentigine
Scorti vagaris impeditus unguibus
Manceps proteruae destinatus accubae,
Lubensque foedo colla summissus iugo,
5   Omnem tremiscis abnuentis impetum
Iocosque mille, mille ineptias iacis
Suauiori deditus tyrannidi,
Miles pusille tune viribus potis
Martis tot alta dissipare moenia
10   Victis superbis insolenter hostibus?
Domasque ferro, sed domaris osculo.

[12]   In paupertatem.[19]

Magistra rerum, disciplinarum parens
Sublimioris dura naturae comes,
Regina egestas, sola quae semper minus
Habendo, nunquam maior esse desinis.

[13]   De miseris mortem metuentibus.[20]

Fastidientis sorte Fortunae miser
Gemitusque ab imo pectore infelix trahis
Mortesque mille, mille dum viuis neces
Geris, perisque. Nec minus necis tamen
5   Gelidae flagellum mente percussus tremis.
Ergon' quater miselle, dulce sit tibi
Toties perire, triste sit semel mori?

---

18   Heinsius, *Auriacus*, p. 115; also in *Senecae libelli quinque*, pp. H3r–H3v. Variants: 1 improbâ
      A: improbae *S*; 4 summissus *A*: subditus *S*; 8 potis *A*: potens *S*.
19   Heinsius, *Auriacus*, p. 115.
20   Heinsius, *Auriacus*, pp. 115–116.

[14]   Quae videntur perire omnia.[21]

    Obtusa quicquid luminum vagantibus
    Acies pererrat motibus, minax sibi
    Mors poscit, immortalia aspectum latent
    Sublimiora vultibus nostris, neque
5   Dum viuis ipse cerneris tibi, leuis
    Quod cernis vmbra est, puluis et compes tui,
    Animique vestis haud decora, pallidae
    Imago mortis et focus caliginum
    Tumulusque vivus, mortuae vitae domus
10   Te cernere ipsum non sinens tibi, neque
    Lustrare mentis igneae templum tuae.
    Vago hoc solutus ergo carcere, id vide
    Videre possis quod videre non potes.

[15]   In tyrannum.[22]

    Ciues superbae viribus potentiae
    Nixus cruenti moderamine imperi
    Saevisque habenis, oris improbi minas
    Et intonantis alta linguae verbera,
5   Et quicquid amens pectoris saeui tumor
    Vel atra bilis, vel superbus ingerit
    Insanientis vanae naturae rigor
    Horrere cogis, cunctaque exhorres prius
    Terrens tremensque, namque iustus arbiter
10   Aliena terrens crimina, tremis tua
    Metuque subdis, subderisque, nec prius
    Timere cessas quam timeri desinis.

---

21   Heinsius, *Auriacus*, p. 116; *Senecae libelli quinque*, p. H4r. Variants: 1 Obtusa quicquid *A*:
    Quodcunque caeca *S*; 7 pallidae *A*: luridae *S*; 8 focus caliginum *A*: caliginum focus *S*; after
    l. 13, *S* has: Finis.
22   Heinsius, *Auriacus*, p. 116; also in *Senecae philosophi divini libelli quinque*, p. H3r. Variants:
    title: In tyrannum *A*: In Tyrannidem *S*; 1–2: Ciues—Nixus *A*: Auctor superbi legibus poten-
    tis iugi | Cives; 7 vanae *S*: vana *A*; 8 prius *A*: prior *S*.

[16] Ad Hugonem Grotium iuuenem sine exemplo, elegantissima ab eo donatus Tragaedia ADAMO EXVLE.[23]

> Ingens cothurni splendor, o dium caput,
> Qui syrma voce regia sacrum trahis,
> Soccoque magnum tundis exultans solum,
> Tandem renatae maxime Orchestrae pater,
> 5   Ignosce fasso: cogitur retrò tuus
> Pedem referre cultor, et suauibus
> Sacri prioris exulare lusibus:
> Exulque, quamdiu exulem spectat tuum,
> Magnae videtur urbis, et Quiritium.
> 10   At tu profane faecis antiquae parens
> Imbellis Euan, matre prognate e Deo,
> Vnquamne leges Bacche transilui tuas
> Nonnumue laesi? Dum tuli praesens opem,
> Phoebeiamque vulneri admoui manum?
> 15   Baccharis Heinsi: Bacchus haud vsquam tuus
> Sublime thyrso parcius pectus ferit.
> At illa rerum magna culpanda est tibi
> Natura nutrix, obstetrixque, quae prius
> Nouerca cunctis, Grotio mater fuit.
> 20   Senex ephaebus ille, quem Batauia
> Miratur omnis, optat Hetruscus sibi,
> Omnisque Gallus, ille dum puer fuit
> Vir esse cepit. Namque relliqui, viri
> Tandem fuere: Grotius vir natus est.

[17] Danieli Heinsio suo Hugo Grotius, cum Adamum Exulem suam offerret. CHOLIAMBI.[24]

> Heinsi vetustae restitutor Orchestrae,
> Ornas cothurno qui pedes Sophoclaeo,
> Primusque syrma vincis Euripidaeum,
> Et Aeschylaeos, et Lycophronis faeces,
> 5   Et quicquid vsquam perditum Tragoedorum

---

23   Heinsius, *Auriacus*, pp. 118–119; Grotius, *Dichtwerken/Poetry* I, 1A, p. 313.

24   Heinsius, *Auriacus*, pp. 119–120; Grotius, *Dichtwerken/Poetry* I, 1A, p. 311.

Desideratumque hactenus, repensasti,
Sume hoc amici (nomen hoc inaequales
Si non recusat) sin minus, tui saltem
Poema, in arrham quod sacrae clientelae
10   Postremus offert principi poetarum:
Lecturus illud ut beatus exultes,
Cum nos videbis velle, posse te solum.

[18]   IN AVRIACVM, DANIELIS HEINSII Poëtae incomparabilis Tragoediam, IANI
DOVSAE NORDOVICIS ELEGIA.[25]

HEINSIADES MVSAE (neque enim iam nomine Pimplae
Dicendae posthac, aut Heliconiadum:)
HEINSIADES inquam, mea cura potissima, Musae:
Dicite, sed vestrâ (Numina sancta) Fide;
5   Fors quaenam, aut Ratio nostris vos appulit oris,
Huc Aganippaeo tam procul à nemore?
Numina quisue deus Batauae dare nomina Leidae
Compulit, extremi littus ad Oceani?
Sic ego, sic nobis DVLCES ANTE OMNIA MVSAE
10   Haud imprudenti haec Quaestio mota tibi.
Scilicet exsilii tibi sors incognita nostri est,
Aut sola cur toties versa Cytheriasin?
Barbaries, doctas quae desolavit Athenas,
Deserere Argolicam prima coëgit humum.
15   Protenus in Latium hinc faelix nos expulit error
Hetrusco acceptas comiter hospitio.
Nec tamen Hesperias intra fuga constitit Alpes,
Sed Rhenum et Boios ivimus Vlterius.
Nos Theuto, et Gallus, nos excepêre Britanni,
20   Astur, et Illyricus, Sarmata, Pannonius,
Certatim insinuans se quisque; nec hospita nobis
Vel rigidos inter tecta negata Getas.
Et Scotus hos nobis habuit, hos Danus honores:
Omnia Nassovius sed superavit amor.
25   Cattorum qui nos voluit considere regnis,
Et stabilem Hollando figere in orbe pedem.

_____

25   Heinsius, *Auriacus*, pp. 132–135. In l. 69 Principere is corrected into Principe.

Fiximus, atque loci dulcedine delinitis
    Suave fuit placitâ conditione frui:
Iusta quòd hic nostris decreta stipendia Mystis,
30   Nutrit honos artes, ingeniumque facit,
Percontere licet; non inficiabitur istud
    Lipsius, et magni stemmata Scaligeri.
In medios Romam qui traduxere Batauos,
    Et Graios nobis restituêre choros.
35 Et bene, nî tantos Patriae inuidisset honores
    Dux pecoris suilli, pro sale queis anima est,
Hinc Verres, Tragus inde, nimis bene compositum par;
    Corrupto Veri palmite vterque nocens.
Digni ambo, Thuscus Bromio quos mactet Aruspex:
40   Ille vti Maialis fiat, at ille Caper.
Parte aliâ nobis extrema minantur Iberi.
    Abstineas crudas gens (precor) atra manus,
Abstineas gens atra precor; spes nulla rapinae
    Hic tibi; vbi vindex praesidet AURIACVS.
45 Sit satis indigna Sicarî fraude peremptum
    Nassovium terris praeripuisse Patrem.
Ah nullâ (ah) mage caede nocens Hispania; saltem
    Debuit hoc sceleri non licuisse tuo.
Sin fuit in Fatis, tali vt nece victor obiret,
50   Nunc saltem Furiis contrahe fraena tuis.
Viderit ista Deus; at si quid possumus ipsae,
    Tollet nulla dies hanc tibi, Maure, notam.
Heinsiadi sed enim laus haec et gratia nostro
    Scaligeri ipsius debita iudicio.
55 Heinsiadi, cuius inter tot lumina Vatum
    Enthea mens nostrae non eget artis ope.
Ipsius potius Genii est opus alite nobis,
    Alternis soliti verba praeire choris.
Per caussam Delphis Leidam dum mutat Apollo,
60   HEINSIADIque suas mandat obire vices.
Quò, nisi vt interea GROTIANAE ORACLA SIBILLAE
    Consulat; haud spernens discere, quae docuit.
At laudando aliàs dabitur locus Hugeiano;
    Nunc satis HEINSIADI reddere posse vicem.
65 HEINSIADI, tantum cui nos debere fatemur,
    Quantum alicui nostrum soluere difficile est.

Debet et Auriacus, quod non velut ante vagatur,
   Vmbraque trans Stygios errat inulta lacus.
Fallimur, hoc siquidem de Principe credere, vanum est,
70   In Coelum Pietas cui sua struxit iter.
Divini hinc meritus Vatis praeconia Diuus,
   Otia qui nobis vindiciasque dedit.
Et bene, quod tanto Heroi par contigit haeres,
   Maranos natus vincere MAVRITIVS,
75   Imperii dignus Dominas qui tractet habenas,
   Sospite quo Belgis nil metuendus Iber.
Plaude tuo vati Princeps; redit alter Homerus,
   Heroô exaequet qui tua facta sono,
Materiae ingenium cui par industria felix,
80   Materiam ingenio Fata dedere parem,
Sicari facinus Tragico dum plangit hiatu,
   Dumque novum Caelo consecrat Indigetem,
Syrmate conspicuus picturatoque Cothurno:
   Ipse quibus Magnus plaudit, et ore favet.
85   I nunc, grandiloqui Iephtem obiice Buchanani,
   Caesara Mureti, Luciferum Aemerii.
Francia si Flandris, Gandae Levinia praestat;
   Huius et illorum fac monimenta legas:
Illa quidem magnis iurabis scripta Poetis,
90   Haec Nisae et Cyrrhae composuisse Deos.

[19]   IN EVNDEM.[26]

Sol, ocule caeli, temporis seni pater,
Orbem citato flammeum cursu vehens
Inane vastum per micantis aetheris:
Necdumne abhorrens tot videre tristia
5   Stas irretortus, os et aduersum tenes?
Non aureum te, at ferreum mortalibus
Putare fas: miserrimis mortalibus.
Natura mollia dedit auro pectora,
Non vim proteruiamve sustinentia
10   Vllius vnquam. Vim pati, aut proteruiam,

---

26   Heinsius, *Auriacus*, pp. 135–138. In l. 9 sustinetia is corrected into sustinentia.

Et non moueri, conuenit ferro truci,
Quod Mulciber, quod triste Cyclopum genus
In officinis mulcet vsque Lemniis.
Ergo ille mundi rector et specimen sui,
15   Proles Tonantis atque imago maximi,
Cui cuncta prono seruiunt fastigio,
Et vsque et vsque pressus aerummâ gravi,
Acerba semper experitur munia
Insontis aeui? Phoebe fers haec, et vides?
20   Ah, dure Phoebe, Phoebe dure, quamdiu?
Auerte vultus, nubibus densis caput
Atratus infer, et dolori lacrymas
Testes doloris funde perpetes tuo.
Et tu, triformis Luna, fraternos age
25   Imitare luctus, regna noctis abijce.
Peritura semper quid resumis cornua,
Et damna toties te fatigas in noua?
Quin pone curas, et quiesce: taedeat
Aliquandò tandem viuere mori vt debeas.
30   Ducem requirat orba stellarum cohors
Errans tenebris inuiis, et semitâ
Caecâ viarum non suum tenens iter.
Obductus aether igneas condens faces,
Quarum benigno suevit orbem lumine
35   Lustrare laetus, seculorum millia
Fleat, pluatque; tristis ipse gurgite
Dominator alti ab infimo Nereus feret
Opem, suoque humore flentem nutriet,
Ne sit dolore luctus improbo minor.
40   Confundat et se quicquid uspiam latet,
Hominisque doleat fata, fata tristia,
Indigna fata sorte tanti Principis,
Quem Parca magnae destinârat arbitrum
Telluris huius, quem profundi, et mox poli.
45   Deiectus ergo sede regiâ iacet
Ille ille princeps, iura rebus anteà
Dictare natus omnibus; miser iacet.
Tenent habenas, quae tenere nesciae,
Curae, labores, lacrymae, aerumnae, doli,
50   Ambitio, visque, iniuriae, periuria,

Vindicta trux, invidia, et irae plumbeae,
Scelus, nefasque, et quicquid atram trans Styga
Peperére Furiae, prolis infestae, malae.
Moderamine isto, talibusque legibus
55 Regnatur orbis, hisce dominis subditus
Suspirat altè, et optat antiquum chaos:
Gestit perire, fataque incusat suis
Ignava votis; seculum momenta sunt.
  Ad prima tantae machinae incunabula
60 Imperia reges gentibus dabant suis
Honesta, mitia: nulla vis, iniuria,
Non ambientum fastus, aut superbia,
Populos premebat, et sacrum cunctis erat
Nomen tyranni nescijs tyrannidis.
65 Non legibus quisquam teneri, principum
Arbitria leges promptius parentibus:
Rex pro parente, subditi pro liberis,
Regnum familia, regium in regno nihil.
Augusta ligno sceptra fiebant rudi,
70 Armenta queîs nunc terreat pastor sua.
Corona non auro gravis, non iaspide,
Sed lana mollis nubiebat verticem.
Integritas ô sancta, et ô simplex fides!
O terror iste qui timendus nemini,
75 Et fastus in quo cerneres fastûs nihil.
Suum cuique erat satis: non patrios
Proferre cura, non cupido terminos.
Quod quis tenebat hoc putare amplissimum:
Non quaerere ultrà quidpiam, nec sanguine
80 Contaminare iusta patrimonia.
Speciem vniversi cuncta complexu suo
Habere, et omnem parua mundum patria.
Beata secla ter, quater! Secla aurea!
  Sed haec fuêre! Ah, ah, fuêre! Nunc miser
85 Rotatur orbis, sistiturque in verticem,
Pendetque praeceps, atque in ima Tartara
Metuit ruinam, molis haud vltrà potens.
Et ille pressis caelifer vestigiis
Excussus Atlas, dente terrarum sola
90 Iam provolutus mordet, ac casum gemit:

Caelumque quamuis fornice astrictum suo,
Vix sustinens se, mox premet tibicinem.
    Hoc ergo rerum, Heynsi, atque temporum statu
Aptè cothurnum pedibus imponis tuis,
95 Belgîque turbas ore sublimi canis.
Quin latiore Musa ducat tramite
Posthac euntem, sume quidquid obvium.
Habebis isto ubique dignum Carmine.
Tragoedia aetas omnis, omnis orbis est.

IOANNES MEVRSIVS.

[20] Apostrophe ad Belgium.[27]

Illa dies magnum quae funere mersit acerbo
    AVRIACVM, quot tunc tristia damna dedit!
BELGIA quae fueras hoc tanto Principe foelix,
    Illo interfecto nil nisi funus eras.
5   Et tibi prae luctu ingenti vox faucibus haesit,
    Cum domini cuperes plangere fata tui.
MAVRITIO regnante iterum nunc ora resoluis,
    (Aurea qui nobis saecula restituit,)
AVRIACI indignam mortem dum carmine plangis
10   HEYNSIADAE, quo quis doctior, aut melior?
Cui puero dixit (cum quondam quaereret) Echo,
    MAEONIDEM AVRIACO me fore reris? Eris.
O foelix Princeps, cui vates obtigit ille,
    Qui poterit factis scribere digna tuis.
15 O foelix HEYNSI, cui tantus dicitur Heros,
    Qualem vix vnquam postera saecla ferent.
Manibus AVRIACI reddis nunc BELGIA grates,
    HEYNSIVS vt possis reddere digna, facit.
Ergo suo debet nunc quantum BELGIA vati?
20   AVRIACO, HEYNSIADES: HEINSIADAE, AVRIACVS?

Balthazar Lydius M.L.F. [= M. Lydíi Filius] Palatinus

---

27   Heinsius, *Auriacus*, pp. 138–139.

[21]   Ad eundem.[28]

Principis AVRIACI superatam vulnere vitam
    HEYNSIVS in numeros cogit abire suos.
Dumque parat memori solemnia soluere versu,
    AVRIACVM vitae reddidit et patriae.
5 Parce, parentalis quisquis feralia busto,
    Et tumulis reddis ultima dona suis:
Vivit adhuc Famae AVRIACVS, consorsque futuri:
    Inter mortales non moriturus agit.
HEYNSIVS hunc morti subduxit: et exuit atro
10   Sacratum tenebris nomen inane rogo.
Est aliquid morti memoratâ morte mederi,
    Et tumulo tantos eripuisse viros.
Scilicet huic frustra mortem meditatus IBERVS,
    HEINSIADE medicâ si medeare manu.

Amico non è multis posui D. HEREMYTIVS. Antuerp.

[22a]   Eruditione et Pietate conspicuo viro D. Nicolao Olivario Praeceptori suo aeternum observando Daniel Heynsius S.D.[29]

Tacui aliquamdiu, Praeceptor Observande, invitus tamen, nec tam vitio meo, quam mearum: Musarum inquam quas ut amas tu, sic et illas silentium interdum amare nosti. Ecce autem dum cessant opera, dum reliqua quae praelo commisi mea, per chartarum inopiam (quae hodie ubique magna) aut omnino non progrediuntur, aut tarde aliud ago, et ut reliquorum ferculorum desiderium lenius feras, promulsi dena praemitto.

Senecae Philosophi libellos aliquot publico dare visum est, et simul tibi. Qui a forma commendari poterunt et ab animo; ab illa quod parva, ab hoc quod magnus in te et tua, addo et ab auctore qui primus Romanorum philosophus et solus, cuius profecto rerum gravitas, sententiarum praegnans acumen et pondus ut Graecorum supercilium minus moleste feramus suo iure sibi postulat. Sicut apes minus diu pungunt, diu afficiunt tamen, sic ille parum cum dixit, multum efficit, vitiorum censor in Republica Stoicorum acerrumus et acuta brevitate quadam aures subito praetervolat, animum sibi vindicat. Sicut fulgura diu esse non videmus, fuisse tamen, diu cogitamus, sic inexpectata illa et fatalis brevitas, plus in mente relinquit quam dedit, ac ut pes in via

---

28   Heinsius, *Auriacus*, pp. 139–140.
29   *Senecae libelli quinque*, pp. A1r–A1v.

vestigium suum non se, sic ille in pectore et aciem cogitationum inter legendum perstringit tantum, post lectionem afficit et rapit. Qui tantum de animae immortalitate, de
futuro beatorum consortio, de providentia alibi, de Deo ubique novisse videtur solus,
quantum ignorarunt omnes, Christianae scientiae cum Epicteto suo conterminus vere
et vicinus. Horreo saepe et obstupesco, cum hominem profanum a ratione accepisse
video, quae nos a Deo, et natura duce investigasse, quae cum ea pugnant.

Habes igitur ab HEYNSIO tuo magni Philosophi munusculum parvum, sed ut in
exigua puerorum statura, grata est praecox sapientia, sic in parvo libello utilitas non
parva, qui domi tibi convitia futurus est, foris comes.

Vale Praeceptor observande, et hac hyeme qua frigent omnia ne mirere si mens mea
et ingenium.

Lugd. Bat. e Typographia nostra, AN. M.D.CI.

[22b]   D. Eliae Putschio.[30]

Amice Putschi. Iambos aliquot meos, ne vacent pagellae hae, ad finem libelli huius adi-
ungendos curavi, Iambos inquam quos ante annos aliquot pueri scripsimus, excepto
uno et altero recens nato, qui id ut spero per se indicabunt. Alias vero cum ex professo
morales meos versus publico dabo, id agam ut te, mi Putschi, expleam, nunc vero ut
chartam.

---

30   *Senecae libelli quinque*, p. Hr.

Appendix 11: Texts Regarding the Reception of *Auriacus*

[1] *Auriacus* inspired Grotius to write three poems: the long *Quis ille tanto* ..., included in the preliminary poems (here pp. 102–111), and two shorter ones. *Gordunis lux* ... was published in the *Poemata collecta* of 1617, the Greek verse and Grotius' own Latin translation are preserved in Ms. *Pap.* 10 (University Library Leiden).[1]

[1a]   Ad Heinsium.

> Gordunis lux magna tuis, o carmine posthac,
>   Te quoque cum superes, non habiture parem,
> Heinsiade, quem syrma decet, quem iuncta cothurno
>   Sceptra poetarum principe sumpta manu:
> 5 Legimus Auriacum Libertatemque Batavam,
>   Hic ubi Mauritiam saucia poscit opem.
> Legimus et Mores et emicum munus Iambos,
>   Hic ubi nulla mea pagina laude vacat.
> Gratia magna tibi est. Alienae munere famae
> 10   Lectorisque tui credulitate fruar.
> Scilicet esse aliquid Grotium peregrina putabit
>   Turba nec ignoto iam licet esse mihi.
> Sed qui tanta meae leget hic praeconia Musae,
>   Quam vereor, Musem ne legat ille meam.

[1b–1]

> Αἰδόμενος, καὶ ἀοιδὸς ἅμ' εἰκέλω· ἔξοχος ἀρχῶν
>   Αὐρίακος, τραγικῶν δ'ἔξοχος Εἰνσιάδης.
> Ἥσσονε δ' ἀμφοτέρω τοῖν Βελγίδος ἀμφοτέροιιν,
>   τοῦ μὲν Ἴβηρ Σενέκας, τοῦ δὲ Φίλιππος Ἴβηρ.

---

1 Here quoted after Grotius, *Dichtwerken/Poetry* I, 2, 3 A, pp. 344, 348 and 350.

[1b–2]

> Qui canitur hic et qui canit
> Sunt alter alteri pares,
> Uterque primas obtinet:
> Auriacus inter Principes,
> Inter Tragoedos Heynsius.
> Et hoc et illo quos duo
> Superba iactat Belgica,
> Philippus Hispanus minor,
> Annaeus Hispanus minor.

[2]   Josephus Justus Scaliger to Isaac Casaubon, 8 December, 1601.

(...) Propediem uberius tibi scribam, quum mittam Tragoediam Heinsii. Lugd. Batavorum VI Eid. Decembris Iuliani MDCI.[2]

[3]   Casaubon

[3a]   Isaac Casaubon to Josephus Justus Scaliger, 12 June, 1602.[3]

Plures a te paucis diebus, praestantissime Scaliger, literas accepi: sed omnes brevissimas, et quae ad nullam trium epistolarum, quas ad te mensibus Martio et Aprili misimus, responderent. (...)
Deus Opt. Max. te servet, o salus literarum unica.
Vale. Lut. Pat. prid. Eid. Jun. MDCII.

---

2 J.J. Scaliger, *Epistolae omnes* (Leiden: Bonaventura and Abraham Elzevier, 1627), p. 198, epist. LXIII; Paul Botley and Dirk van Miert (eds), *The Correspondence of Joseph Justus Scaliger* 4 (Geneva: Droz, 2012), p. 150.

3 I. Casaubon, *Epistolae quotquot reperiri potuerunt, nunc primum iunctim editae: Adiecta est epistola de morbi eius mortisque causa; deque iisdem narratio Raphaelis Thorii* (The Hague: Theodorus Maire, 1638), pp. 536–537, Epist. CCCCXLVII; Paul Botley and Dirk van Miert (eds), *The Correspondence of Joseph Justus Scaliger* 4 (Geneva: Droz, 2012), pp. 310 and 312–313. Part of this letter has been copied in the copy of *Auriacus* (from the library of Ioannes Forcadus Vasco), now in the National Art Library of the Victoria & Albert Museum London (shelfnr. Dyce D 5 E 8 [4587 M 4to]). On the bract at the end of the book first the 'P.S.' is written (*Accepi nuper—illum Grotium*, ended by *etc.*), then a fragment of the letter itself is recorded, cf. this Appendix no. [10].

Accepi nuper Heinsii tui Tragoediam. Miratus sum molitionem tuam, qui αὐτὴν τὴν ἑπτάλοφον non quae nunc est, sed quae olim, isthuc transtuleris. O elegantem gravitatem! O dignum tanto doctore discipulum! Parabam ad illum literas et nescio quae in Nonnum et Hesychium (sic enim vult ipse), item ad eximium illum Grotium item tuum, et Meursius quoque. Sed impediit maturior quam putabam tabellarii profectio. Velim illis me excuses, si grave non est, et magis apud amplissimum legatum Busenvallium.

[3b]   Josephus Justus Scaliger to Isaac Casaubon, 23 June, 1602.[4]

Non possum satis mirari infelix fatum literarum mearum, quae nunquam, aut vix tandem, perferuntur. Equidem, carissime, ad omnes tuas me puto respondisse, quae quidem in manus meas pervenerunt. [...]

De Heynsio magis mirareris, si et adolescentem nosses, et eius Poematia, quae aliquando edet in publicum, legisses. Itali nihil habent, quod Transalpinis obiiciant. Noli putare illum iuvari ope nostra. Ego potius eo utor magistro. Non excessit xx. annum, ideoque si de eius meritis praedicavero, amori potius, quam vero id concedere videbor. Quare malo aliquando ipse scriptis suis virtutis suae fidem facias, quam ego praedicatione mea.

Vale. Lugd. Batavorum x Kalend. Quintilis Iuliani MDCII.

[3c]   Isaac Casaubon to Daniel Heinsius, 10 July, 1602.[5]

Auriacum tuam, eruditissime Heinsi, ex literis magni Scaligeri primum mihi notam, vidi, legi. Quaeris quid sentiam? Ignosce mihi, dicere non possum. Ἔτι γὰρ ἡμᾶς ἐκ τοῦ θάμβος κατέχει ἀφασίη. Plane quod iis solet qui lupum priores viderunt, id mihi accidit cum tragoediam illam tuam ἐς πόδας ἐκ κεφαλῆς percurrerem: tanta enim admiratione defixus obstupui, ut haereret vox faucibus. Tum demum cognovi haud temere ab illo semone scriptum, eam esse compositam a te Tragoediam, cui scribendae unus tu ex omnibus qui literas nunc colunt, par esses. Mirabar adeo ἀπότομον tanti viri ἀπόφασιν, et (fatebor enim) aegre accedebam. Diffidebam enim non ingenio tuo, sed aetati ad quaevis alia, ut rebar, aptiori quam ad tragicas ὑποθέσεις et gravissimos cothurnos. At tu, doctissime Heinsi, non aequales solum tuos, sed omnes omnino, si quid iudico, longe a tergo reliquisti, qui a multis seculis in hanc arenam descenderunt. Omnia in tuo dra-

---

4   J.J. Scaliger, *Epistolae omnes* (Leiden: Bonaventura and Abraham Elzevier, 1627), pp. 217–222. Epist. LXXII; Paul Botley and Dirk van Miert (eds), *The Correspondence of Joseph Justus Scaliger* 4 (Geneva: Droz, 2012), pp. 315 and 319.
5   Isaac Casaubon, *Epistolae quotquot reperiri potuerunt, nunc primum iunctim editae: Adiecta est epistola de morbi eius mortisque causa; deque iisdem narratio Raphaelis Thorii* (The Hague: Theodorus Maire, 1638), pp. 43–44. Epist. XLVIII.

mate ἄξια θαυμασμοῦ. Argumentum magno iudicio electum, et iis, quae nunc geruntur, accomodatissimum, inventio totius διασκευῆς ingeniosissima, ἡ λέξις πάνυ μελισταγὴς καὶ ὡς ἀκριβέστατα ῥωμαΐζουσα· τῶν παθῶν ἡ δεινότης μεγίστη· καὶ ἵνα μὴ μακρολογῶ, δοκεῖς μοὶ ὠτὰν καὶ τὰ νοήματα καὶ τὰς λεκτικὰς ἀρετὰς κατορθωκέναι.

Deus tibi, γονιμώτατε ποιητά, has dotes. Illi igitur honos, illi gloria. Ille te novis subinde benedictionum suarum incrementis augeat, ille servet, fortunet, et in omnibus quae institues, quae molieris, δοίη σοὶ εὐοδουμένῳ ἐκτὸς πημάτων ἔχειν πόδα. Si quis est qui gloriae tuae faveat, is ego sum: quod serio persuadeas tibi velim. [...]

Vale, amicissime Heinsi, et vive quam diutissime, αἰὲν ἀριστεύων καὶ ὑπείροχος ἥλικος ἥβης. Lutetiae Parisiorum VI. Eid. Jul. MDCII. [...]

[4]   Janus Dousa to Johan van Oldenbarnevelt, 21 January, [1603].[6]

Salve Vir Nobilissime.

Venit ad te aliquando Auriacus Heinsii nostri: qui quum ipsemet Amplitudinem tuam adire; tibique succidaneum hunc ingenii sui foetum praesens praesenti commendare et vellet et (quae tua est humanitas) iure suo et quidem meritissimo posset; tamen nescio quâ iuvenili verecundia praepeditus, ad hanc rem Dousa potius intercessore uti maluit; cum bona spe, fore, ut (quod absque molestiâ tuâ fiat) Cothurni ipsius gravitati, publico Amplissimorum Ordinum nomini inscripti, maximum herculi ac gravissimum commendationis tuae pondus accedat.

Haud denegabis, scio, patrocinium nobello Clienti tuo, Candidato huic nostro, benevolentiae tuae gratiâ (si quis alius) dignissimo, iuveni ad summa aliquando evasuro, si (id quod voveo ac spero) per istud adolescentiae tam floridae tamque literis perpolitae ad Autumnitatem porro suam pervenire contigerit.

Qua de re quum plura apud te, et quidem haud paulo speciosiora, cum Adolescentis ipsius industria tum supra aetatem doctrina praedicare nos hortentur, prohibet Heinsianae modestiae indoles: et potius ipsius animo mos geretur, adeo ingenue verecundantis; ideoque sane non indigni, cuius modestissimis cupiditatibus Fortuna praestet fidem. Atque haec ipsa me non nimia erga communis studii cultorem Faventia, sed certo asseverare indicio scies, simulatque tantum tlbi a republica otii superfuerit, ut, si non aliud, saltem argumenti ipsius dignitatem rerumque pondus ac sententiarum acumen in re presenti consideres: paria omnia veterum Tragicorum maiestati, vel

---

6   Den Bosch, Rijksarchief Noord-Brabant, Collection Cuypers-van Velthoven (inventarisreeks, no. 22, p. 263), no. 2240 'Letter from Janus Dousa to Joannes van Oldenbarnevelt about the Auriacus by Daniel Heinsius (1603?)'. Probably no autograph, but a "copie transfiguée". In the name of Heinsius Dousa asks for a recommendation for Auriacus. He will have done this at the time of the publication of the play, so the letter will stem from 1601 or 1602. Thanks to Marten Jan Bok who pointed out the existence of this letter.

certe praeferenda. Deus Optimus Maximus te quam diutissime Reipublicae ac nobis sospitem superstitemque conservet.

Vale Vir Nobilissime et Literarum impolitiae ac lituris nostris ignoscas velim.

IIX Idus Februarias.

Tibi tuaeque Amplitudini meritorum tuorum virtuti multo devotissimus DOVSA.

[Address:

Nobilissimo Amplissimoque viro Domino Ioanni ab Oldenbamevelt Iuris Consulto Domino de Tempel et Hollandiae, West Frisiaeque Ordinum advocato, Principis Consiliario, Magnique sigilli Custodis Domino ac fautori suo optime merito.]

[5]   J. van der Burch to Constantijn Huygens.[7]

Parum abfuit, quin a lectione Limburgi mei vir amplissimus van den Broeck erupit in illud hodie morere, quod Scaligerum Heinsio, ubi Auriacam suum exhiberet, dixisse ferunt. [...] Hagae-Comitis, ex aedibus Hackii, tabellionis publici, vico vulgo dicto de Poten. 26 Novemb. 1633.

[6]   Pieter Cornelisz. Hooft, *Reden vande Waerdicheit der Poesie*.[8]

[...] De philosophen hebben aen dese konste tijdt en vlijdt welbesteedt geacht. Aristoteles heeft geen ander stoffe soo nauw ondersocht, soo sinnelijck, soo tentich gehandelt. Plutarchus en andere proncken doorgaens haer schriften met de bloemen der Poeten. Seneca, de wijsheit der Romajnen, heeft selve in haer gildt willen rilesen, en de toverijen en helsche wraeckgiericheit van Medea in dat treffelijck Treurspel vervaet.

Maar soo verre niet te loopen; op dat ick al de anderen, deses Eeuws, geleerden voorbij gae, 't nieuw en is noch niet van 't Treurspel, waer in de Hoochgeleerde Daniel Heins de schaedelijcke doodt en hoochgedachte deuchden onses Prinçen en verlossers Wilhelms van Nassau, wtbromt. [...]

[7a]   Pieter Cornelisz. Hooft to Daniel Heinsius.[9]

Aen mijn Heere, Mijn Heere Daniel Heins Professor inde vermaerde Universiteit, tot Leiden.

---

7   Constantijn Huygens, *De briefwisseling (1605–1687). Eerste deel 1608–1614*, ed. J.A. Worp (The Hague: Martinus Nijhoff), pp. 430–431.

8   P.C. Hooft, *Sonnetten: Reden vande waerdicheit der Poesie*, ed. Pierre Tuynman (Amsterdam: Athenaeum, Polak and Van Gennep, 1971), p. 69 [1610–1615].

9   H.W. van Tricht a.o. (eds.), *De briefwisseling van Pieter Corneliszoon Hooft*, 3 vols (Culemborg: Tjeenk Willink/Noorduijn, 1976–1979), no. 18, vol. 1, pp. 124–125.

Ick en ben geen schrijver: al heb ick somtijts ijet om de geneuchte gedicht, dat tot mijn becommering onder de gemeente geraeckt is. ick ken mijn onvolmaecktheit soo wel, dat ick haer noch bij vroomen jonst, noch bij spotters vajlicheidt kan versekeren. Doch van onberispte schriften sal misschien UE^s treffelijck Treurspel 't eerste wesen. 'T is troostelijck voor de swacken dat selfs den lof der dapperen niet suiver is. Jae ick twijffel of den aldervolmaecksten, door sijn schriften, oijt van billijcke Rechters soo veel eeren bejegende, als wederwaerdicheits van de nijt en d'onwetentheit, die soo geweldighen aenhang hebben. Over al dit, corts met herlesen van U E^s Prins van Oragnien, eenich vermaen van anderden druck gewaer geworden, can ick mij niet houden van daer 't mijne toe te seggen. Vindt U E geraeden mij onder sijne loovers openbaere plaets te geven, ick sal goedt sijn om d'ander te doen wtsteken. Haest, dat de goede wil voor 't werck genomen, mij den toegang van U E^s vriendschap opene; dat ick over lange gewenscht hebbe: waer mij 't Geluck niet inde weghe geweest. Maer heb ick jonste bij U E soo verclaert mij de gebreecken van mijn gedicht; of wijst mij de fraejicheden aen; om 't corste werck. Wie weet? of ick wat leeren mochte? ick hoop wat tijdts te hebben. Maer bidde om Latijnsch antwoordt dat ick beter meen te verstaen als Duitsch weet te schrijven; indien ick waert ben ijet te verwerven van de waerde handt, dewelcke ick eerbiedelijck kusse mij gebiedende van harten aen UE, die Godt genaedelijck besorge,

U E^s Toegedaene Dienstwillighe P C Hóóft.

In Amsterdam xix April. xvj^{c}x.

[7b]   Pieter Cornelisz. Hooft, Gedicht Op de prins van Oragnien of de gewonde vrijheit.
       Treurspel van D. Heins.[10]

      Het leelijcke gedrocht der alnaespeelende aepen
      'T welck van Natuir, te spot, ons schijnt gelijck geschaepen,
         Hangt over sijn geslacht (soo 't waer is dat men zeit)
         Het moederlijck gemoedt met sulcke' onwetenheidt,
5   Dat zij gesint om met haer armen te bestricken
      Haer jongen troetelwijs, de selve wel versticken.
         Recht eveneens soo gaet (indien m' er wel op acht)
         Het met haer eigenliefd der menschen broos geslacht.
      Gelijckm' er veele vindt in alle 's werelds deelen,
10   Die om de sinnen met een vliende vreucht te strelen,
         Door 't schittrich branden van haer hete lust, verblindt
         Al eer de naedruck van de weelde wert versint,
      Haer lichaem, aen een schaer van sieckten en van quaeden
      Te machtich Tijdt en Raedt, wel raedeloos verraeden:
15   Soo sijnder meer, die Macht altoos onvast gesticht,
         Verwaende rijckdoom, Roems becoorlijck flickerlicht,
      Waerderen boven waerde', en metse nae te speuren,
      'T geduirich goedt van haer gewetens vreuchd verbeuren.
         Degene die Juppijn heeft voor sijn eighen lust
20   Sich wtgelesen, en in haer gemoedt gesust
      De tochten weigertoomsch, en d' innerlijcke plecken
      Voor billickheit geschickt met haylighe vertrecken
         Betimmert, en de borst in 't eerlijck opgesoôn,
         Soo dat sij deuchd wt liefd inhaelen metter woon,
25   Sijn deerlijck dun gesaejt. Men vinter naulijck seven
      Die Brutus of sijn oom gelijcken in haer leven;
         Of hem, die eighen ban, tot 's plompen nijders hulp,
         Daer onrecht recht sijn moest, ging schrijven in een schulp.
      Dit maeckt de nóót van 't quaet te straffen 't goedt te lóónen,
30   Om ijder tot sijn plicht te drijven en te tróónen.
         Tot leidtsliên des gemeents met dus een toom beknelt
         Van straf en lóón, sijn op verheven trap gestelt
      De vorsten van het volck, en haylighe' overheden;

---

10   P.C. Hooft, *Gedichten*, ed. P. Leendertz Wz. en F.A. Stoett, 2 vols (Amsterdam: P.N. van Kam-
      pen & Zoon, 1899), vol. 1, pp. 103–105.

De vingeren Juppijns; die waerdelijck becleden
35   Des Godtheits naeste plaets; in billijcke geboôn,
       In macht, in voorsicht, Gods Stadthouders; Aerdsche Goôn.
Dees hoocheidt is 't bestier der redelijckste dieren
Van hooger handt verleent; maer wie sal haer bestieren?
       Haer: voor de welcke niet te vinden ander stóf
40   Van straf en loon en is, als laster en als lóf.
Den spitschen Aretijn won, bij sijn tijdtgenóóten,
De princengeessels naem, omdat hij in de gróóten
       De schrick brocht met sijn pen; mits hij sich onderwond
       Met sulcken bitschen tael en vinnicheit van mondt
45 Haer af te maelen, en haer schand te voorschijn brochte,
Dat self den grooten Turck sijn gunst door gaven cochte,
       En dat aen hem Franchois den franschen Coninck sandt
       Van tongen t' saemgevoecht een gouden halsebandt,
Ten tijde', als Caisar, Paus, Spaensch Coning oock, van haeren
50 Beide' afcoomst en geboort, twee Nederlanders waeren.
       Maer even als het loon den vorsten dierder staet,
       Dan wel de straf, die vaeck gevordert wort om baet',
Soo gaet, in waerdicheidt, het heerelijcke loven
De schrandre schamperheit van 't lasteren te boven.
55   Dit onderstaet nu Heins, die brammende trompet
       Verwart in laurenblaên, aen heilghe lippen set,
En gaet in 't blaesen tróts een dappren adem tóónen,
Om met sijn Treurspel braef, ons gouden Prins te lóónen.
       Het luistert al wat leeft; d' hel wtgeborsten clanck
60   Slaet van de claere Son den op en onderganck;
En van den geest geschudt der teeckenrijcke wóórden,
Den rancken hemel dreunt in 't Zuiden en in 't Nóórden.
       Wel was 't een gouwden Prins wiens moed verstandt en vlijt
       De gouwden vrijheidt ons en schanck den gouden tijdt;
65 Voor d' ijsselijcke tijdt, daer 't ijser hardt bij haelen
Op veel nae niet en mach; welck onder de metaelen
       Verlooren moeite doet met soecken naeme wreedt;
       Dewijl natuir geen stof soo streng te scheppen weet;
Den Moyses, die ons, van veel droever slavernijen
70 Als oyt Israel leed, quam tegen hoop bevrijen.
       Want was 'er boose tijdt, die dees gelijcken mach,
       Op Aerden sint de nacht geschift is van den dach?
Den wrev'len Marius, en sijnen vyandt woedich

Ontvolckten Rome, met bannissementen bloedich,

75   De driemans speelden 't nae; sij waeren hen gelijck,
En scheurden, elck sijn gaîng van het gebuite rijck.

Den derden Caisar loos, deurtrapt, geveinst van zeden,
Verbolghen, wrockigh, wreedt, vol nijdt en bitterheden,
Brocht in sijn tijdt door lust of vrees een groote som

80   Van 't volck, en ridderschap, en van de besten om.

Den vierden was verwoedt; doe sachmen tijden lóópen,
Al had Juppijn ontsint den hemel laeten slóópen
En schieten nederwaerts met onbesuisde val,
Te plettren 't Roomsche rijck; soo craeckte' en borst het al.

85 Den vijfden was een dwaes, en als een tol te drijven
Van vlaeijers onbeschaemt en onbetemde wijven.
Maer dees noch Nero self, ruim waerdich diemen stack
Met dubble sim, en slang in dubble leêren sack,
En hebben soo veel quaets, als Neerlandts smart gebrouwen,

90 Noch al wie Rome sint van Prinslijcke rabouwen,
Van schudden fielen guits, bij 's wereldts ongeluck
In heerschappij geraeckt, bereden met het juck.

Ach! 't harte tziddert, en 't gemoedt terug wil deisen
Door schrick en afkeer, van de droevighe gepeisen,

95   Wanneer de Tyrannij vernieuwt wort in 't gedacht,
Die landt en steden groot hield leggen in onmacht
Met droefheit overstelpt. Doe braeden, branden, schróócken
En varsch vergoten bloedt het aerdrijck staech deed roocken.
Verdrencken, delven naer, onthalsen, wurgen bang

100   Ging, of het had geweest onvliebre pest, in swang.
En dat van menschen die op niemandts hinder dochten,
Maer slechs om dat sij God met beter meening sochten.
Jonckheit, noch ouderdoom, noch swackheit van geslacht
Ymandt verschoonen mocht; maer wierden omgebracht

105 Dorre' ouden, jongers kintsch, ontwaepende vertsaechden,
Weerloose vrouwen, en niet wel huwbaere maechden.
Geen huis was buiten anxt. Soo vaeck de Son verrees
Aen elck hij nieuwe rouw, nieuwe benautheit wees:

[8]   Constantijn Huygens

Ethopoeia Illustriss.mae principis Louisae interfecto marito.[11]

    Proh dolor infelix! venit lacrymabilis hora,
    Venit quod semper tempus miseranda timebam!
    Ah facinus! tantumne ducem, quo maior in armis
    Numquam miles erat, scurrae succumbere dextra?
5   Huc huc, o cives, lachrymas effundite mecum,
    Huc Coelum, huc tellus, fluvyque, huc aequor, et amnes,
    Et qui per Batavos leni fluis agmine Rhene,
    Huc inquam et lachrymis vestras adiungite nostris.
    Nam iacet a scurra victus numquam antea victus.
10 At nunc desistat, si quis temeraria dicit
    Somnia, namque meo didici verissima casu.
    Ah quoties coniux, coniux charissime, dixi,
    Sis cautus, struit insidias tibi saevus Iberus;
    Ah quoties nostros terrebant somnia visus!
15 Nox erat et terris animalia somnus habebat,
    In somnis ecce ante oculos mihi visus adesse
    Territus, et subiti distillans sanguinis imbres,
    Et quater ingenti moestus clamore vocare,
    Ah coniux, coniux, coniux, solve ultima, coniux,
20 Munera, nam retro trahor atras noctis ad umbras.
    Talia saepe quidem narravi tristis, at ille, ut
    Militis est animus, quid tandem nescia somno
    Credis? ait, sunt, crede mihi, sunt somnia vana.

---

11   Constantijn Huygens, *Gedichten*, ed. J.A. Worp, vol. 1: *1607–1623* (Groningen: J.B. Wolters, 1892), pp. 15–16. Written in the beginning of April 1609. The poem is mentioned in a letter by Constantijn to his father (Library of the Royal Netherlands Academy, *ms.* No. XLIV) of IV Id. (10) Aprilis; by then it was almost ready.
       Resemblances between this *Ethopoeia* and *Auriacus*: 1 Pro dolor infelix *Aur.* p. 107, a poem for Scaliger, beginning with the same words; cf. also *Aur.* 1961; 4 scurrae [...] dextra *Aur.* 1959; 6–7 huc tellus ... Rhene *Aur.* 1912–1915; 8 lachrymis ... nostris *Aur.* 1918–1919; 10 desistat *Aur.* 1847; 14 nostros ... visus *Aur.* 1545; 17–20 et subiti ... umbra *Aur.* 1558–1569; 22–23 Quid tandem ... credis *Aur.* 1576; 24 Hei mihi *Aur.* 1899; 24–25 nunc credor ... quam mihi sera fides! *Aur.* 1858–1859; 25–26 Ah quantos ... spectas *Aur.* 1899–1902; 27–28 Bis ... viduor *Aur.* 1825–1828; 28–29 Quid demens ... flete *Aur.* 1855–1856; 29–30 Sed istos ... dolores? cf. *Aur.* 1931–1932; 34–35 nunc scurrae ... Philippe *Aur.* 1958–1961. Huygens primarily adopts expressions from the second part of *Auriacus*.

Hei mihi nunc credor, sed quid iam proderit? eheu!
25 Quam mihi sera fides! Ah quantos aethere vecte
Phoebe dolos coelo, scelerum quot nomina spectas!
Bis miseranda virum amisi, semel orba parentem,
Nunc rursus viduor. Quid demens prisca recordor?
Sufficit hoc quod nunc factum est nunc flere, sed istos
30 Quis possit lacrymis tantos aequare dolores?
Ah iacet egregium patriae caput, et decus aevi:
Ardua cui toties tribuit Victoria palmam,
Qui numquam victus toties superaverat hostes,
Nunc scurrae est victus, et eum quia vincere bello
35 Numquam quivisti, superasti fraude, Philippe.
Ast ego quid frustra lacrymor? quid nocte dieque
Luctibus indulgere iuvat? quid pectora pugnis
Foedare? et vanos iactare ad sydera fletus?
Scilicet ista semel, semel omnibus ista petenda
40 Est via. Quin hos ergo etiam tot passa labores
Pepetior miseranda? Dabit Deus his quoque finem.

[9a] Jacob Duym, 'Tot den Leser'.[12]

Hier sal u goetwillighe Leser voor ghestelt worden het leelijck ende moordadich stuk
van Balthasar Gerards begaen aen den persoon van den Prince van Oraignen, het welck
over sommighe jaeren is in den Latine ghesteld gheweest, by den Hoogh Vermaerden
Professoor ende Poët Daniel Hensio, in sijnen Auriaco: Die het selfde seer fray ghevonden ende met veel schoone Poetische spreuken verciert heeft, des en begheeren wy die
sonderlinghe eer die hem toecomt gheensins te verminderen, maer alsoo onse Nederduytsche sprake soo veel wijdloopighe spreucken niet verdraghen en mach, ende dat
die selvighe niet bequamelijck en konnen van woorde tot woorde over gheset wotden,
soo hebben wy hem ter eeren nochtans den selven Auriacum ghevolgt, ende sommighe
Personagien ghevoechelick naer onsen sin verandert. [...]

---

12 Jacob Duym, *Een Ghedenck-boeck, het welck ons leert aen al het quaet en den grooten
moetwil van de Spaignaerden en haren aenhanck ons aen-ghedaen te ghedencken. Ende de
groote Iiefde ende trou vande Príncen uyt den huyse van Nassau, aen ons betoont, eeuwelick
te onthouden* (Leiden: Haestens, 1606), fol. A iij v. Jacob Duym, *Het Moordadich Stvck*, ed.
Serrarens and Wijngaards (inntr., n. 186), p. 62.

[9b] *In Balthasaris Gerardi execrandum facinus, a Nobili viro Iacobo Duymio vernacula lingua conscriptum.*[13]

Iberi scelus improbum, dolusque,
Victori miserabilis Batavo,
Cum princeps populique patriaeque,
Uno concidit impetitus ictu,

5   Nostro cum steterat prius cothurno,
Favit maxima Leida, favit ipsa
Totis plausibus annuens imago:
Favit Douza sui pater Lycei,
Favit maxima Caesaris propago,

10   Et Graiae columen Faber Camenae,
Et Groti pia cura, Scriverique,
Et Graias Latiasque qui Camenas
Et Graias Latiasque amaret artes.
Muto caetera gens stetit theatro

15   Solis nescia gestibus doceri.
Vetat Duymius: et vetans latere,
Belga protenus induit cothurno.
Belgae Belgia plaudit: et, quid, inquit,
Rem decet populique patriaeque,

20   Et patrem populique patriaque
Quis Belgis periit, loqui Latinis?

Stans pede in uno
Daniel Heynsius.

[10] Tragoediae argumentum.[14]

VÍNDEX BATAVI magnus ille nominis
NASSOVIORVM Ductor, AVRANSI VIGOR
Fati beatum nescius movet Pedem,
Coeloque vultum monstrat et genti suae:

---

13   Jacob Duym, *Een Ghedenck-boeck* [...], fol. ** ij v. Jacob Duym, *Het Moordadich Stvck*, ed. Serrarens and Wijngaards, pp. 52–53.

14   This poem is written on the bract in the beginning of the the copy of Daniel Heinsius, *Auriacus* (1602), now at the Victoria and Albert Museum—National Art Library—Dyce collection D 5 E 8 [4587 M 4to]. The same copy contains a part of a letter of Casaubon (here no. 3a), in the same hand.

5   At quarta Erynnis, HESPERI proles nova
       Stipata sacris proruit Sororibus,
       Multaque caede, turbidoque sanguine
       Haustuque tabis, ipsa praeludit sibi,
       PARENS pudica gestat HENRICVM manu,
10   Primaeque dulces optat aetatis dies
       Moestaque scaeva mente versat omina.
       Hic ille nostrae parricida Patriae
       Tetro scelestos pectore evolvit dolos,
       Aulamque Magni callidus subit Ducis.
15   At perfidorum Dux Iberorum Pavor
       Tristem benigna coniugem mulcet manu
       Natumque poscit: Natus in complexibus
       Blandisque in ulnis fraude perituri patris
       Recumbit insons innocensque. Squallidum
20   Mox cogit agmen NATA Romani Patris
       Armata taedis PERFIDVMque mobili
       Adhuc labantem corde per scenas agit.
       LOISA moestae noctis admonitu stupet,
       Et ipsa casus mente cognoscit suos.
25   Horrete terrae: sulphure et flammantibus
       Instructus aulam glandibus praedo petit
       HEROSque fato Noster occurrit suo.
       At moesta CONIUNX et BATAVORVM manus
       Atrasque rasa SANCTA LIBERTAS genas
30   Fatale FVNVS plangit, et nostris parat
       Abire terris. NATVS hanc magni DVCIS
       Ultorque sacra sistit abeuntem manu.

Pronunciavit Ioann. Forcadus Vasco.

Index